RETHINKING CANADA

FIFTH EDITION

The Promise of Women's History

Edited by Mona Gleason and Adele Perry

OXFORD
UNIVERSITY PRESS
70 Wynford Drive, Don Mills, Ontario M3C 1J9
www.oup.com/ca

Oxford University Press is a department of the University of Oxford.
It furthers the University's objective of excellence in research, scholarship,
and education by publishing worldwide in

Oxford New York
Auckland Cape Town Dar es Salaam Hong Kong Karachi
Kuala Lumpur Madrid Melbourne Mexico City Nairobi
New Delhi Shanghai Taipei Toronto

With offices in
Argentina Austria Brazil Chile Czech Republic France Greece
Guatemala Hungary Italy Japan Poland Portugal Singapore
South Korea Switzerland Thailand Turkey Ukraine Vietnam

Published in Canada
by Oxford University Press

First published 2006

Library and Archives Canada Cataloguing in Publication Data
Rethinking Canada : the promise of women's history /
edited by Mona Gleason and Adele Perry. — 5th ed.

Includes bibliographical references.
ISBN-13: 978-0-19-542350-1
ISBN-10: 0-19-542350-X

1. Women—Canada—History. 2. Women—Canada—Social conditions.
I. Gleason, Mona, 1964– II. Pery, Adele

HQ1453.R48 2006 305.4'0971 C2005-907439-6

Cover Design: Sonya Thursby/Opus House

Cover Image: City of Vancouver Archives, CVA 677-351

3 4 - 09 08 07
This book is printed on permanent (acid-free) paper ∞.

Printed in Canada

Table of Contents

Acknowledgements vi

Introduction 1

Kateri Tekakwitha's Tortuous Path to Sainthood 10
Nancy Shoemaker

Gender, Family, and Mutual Assistance in New France:
Widows, Widowers, and Orphans in Eighteenth-Century Quebec 26
Josette Brun

Slavery in Early Canada: Making Black Women Subject 45
Maureen Elgersman Lee

Women and the Escheat Movement: The Politics of Everyday
Life on Prince Edward Island 61
Rusty Bitterman

Women at the Hustings: Gender, Citizenship, and the Montreal
By-Elections of 1832 73
Bettina Bradbury

'The Law Should Be Her Protector': The Criminal
Prosecution of Rape in Upper Canada, 1791–1850 95
Patrick J. Connor

From 'Marrying-In' to 'Marrying-Out': Changing Patterns
of Aboriginal/Non-Aboriginal Marriage in Colonial Canada 115
Sylvia Van Kirk

'A Fragment of Heaven on Earth'? Religion, Gender, and
Family in Turn-of-the-Century Canadian Church Periodicals 124
Lynne Marks

Rediscovering our Foremothers Again: Racial Ideas of Canada's
Early Feminists, 1885–1945 144
Janice Fiamengo

Claiming a Unique Place: The Introduction of Mothers' Pensions
in British Columbia 163
Margaret Hillyard Little

Indispensable But Not a Citizen: The Housewife in the Great Depression 179
Denyse Baillargeon

From 'Mothers of the Nation' to Migrant Workers:
Immigration Policies and Domestic Workers in Canadian History 195
Sedef Arat-Koç

Carrier Women and the Politics of Mothering 210
Jo-Anne Fiske

A Platform for Gender Tensions: Women Working and Riding
on Canadian Urban Public Transit in the 1940s 224
Donald F. Davis and Barbara Lorenzkowski

Passing Time, Moving Memories: Interpreting Wartime Narratives
of Japanese Canadian Women 242
Pamela Sugiman

Recipes for Democracy? Gender, Family, and Making Female Citizens in
Cold War Canada 264
Franca Iacovetta

The Heterosexualization of the Ontario Woman Teacher in the Postwar Period 278
Sheila L. Cavanagh

Victims of the Times, Heroes of Their Lives: Five Mennonite Refugee Women 287
Marlene Epp

Rethinking Class in Lesbian Bar Culture: Living 'The Gay Life' in Toronto,
1955–1965 301
Elise Chenier

Race, Culture, and the Colonization of Childbirth in Northern Canada 323
Patricia Jasen

Violence and Poverty on the 'Rock': Can Feminists Make a Difference? 336
Glynis George

Against the Current: Child Care and Family Policy in Quebec 344
Jane Jenson

On the Same Wavelength? Feminist Attitudes Across Generations of
Canadian Women 365
Brenda O'Neill

Who is Canadian Now?: Feminism and the Politics of Nation after
September 11 381
Mary-Jo Nadeau

Contributors 394

Index 396

To honour Veronica Strong-Boag's unparalleled commitment to honouring the lives of Canadian women, past and present, we dedicate this book to the lives of Michelle Lynn Rosa and Daphne Strong-Boag.

Acknowledgements

We would like to thank Veronica Strong-Boag for her continuing involvement in this project, Krista Walters for her excellent research assistance, and Tamara Myers for her expertise and willingness to share it. Jarett Henderson also helped us out with suggestions and feedback. We are blessed with contributing authors who are a pleasure to work with: Bettina Bradbury and Patrick J. Connor deserve special thanks for joining in on the editing process. Laura Macleod, Rachael Cayley, Daleara Hirjikaka and Jessica Coffey at Oxford University Press Toronto were critical in putting the book together. Adele Perry gratefully acknowledges the Canada Research Chairs Programme.

PERMISSIONS

SEDEF ARAT-KOÇ. 'From "Mothers of the Nation" to Migrant Workers: Immigration Policies and Domestic Workers in Canadian History' from *Not One of the Family: Foreign Domestic Workers in Canada*, Abigail Bakan and Daiva Stasiulis, eds. © University of Toronto Press 1997. Reprinted by permission of the University of Toronto Press.

DENYSE BAILLARGEON, translated by Yvonne M. Klein. 'Indispensable But Not a Citizen: The Housewife in the Great Depression', copyright © 2002 by Denyse Baillargeon, translated by Yvonne M. Klein, reprinted from *Contesting Canadian Citizenship: Historical Readings*, ed. By Robert Adamoski, Dorothy E. Chunn, and Robert Menzies, Peterborough, ON: Broadview Press, 2000, pp. 179–98. Reprinted by permission of Broadview Press.

RUSTY BITTERMAN. 'Women and the Escheat Movement: The Politics of Everyday Life on Prince Edward Island', from *Separate Spheres: Women's Worlds in the 19th Century Maritimes*, Janet Guildford and Suzanne Morton, eds. (Fredericton: Acadiensis, 1994). Reprinted by permission of Acadiensis.

BETTINA BRADBURY. 'Women at the Hustings: Gender, Citizenship, and the Montreal By-Elections of 1832'. A version of this essay will appear in the forthcoming *Women on their Own: Interdisciplinary Approaches*, Rudolph M. Bell and Virginia Yans-McLaughlin, eds. (New Jersey, NJ: Rutgers University Press, 2006). Reprinted by permission of the author.

JOSETTE BRUN. 'Gender, Family, and Mutual Assistance in New France: Widows, Widowers, and Orphans in Eighteenth-Century Quebec' (abridged) from *Mapping the Margins: The Family and Social Discipline in Canada, 1700–1975)* (Montreal and Kingston: McGill-Queen's University Press, 2004). Reprinted by permission of the publisher.

SHEILA L. CAVANAGH. 'The Heterosexualization of the Ontario Woman Teacher in the Postwar Period'. This article first appeared in *Canadian Woman Studies/Les cahiers de la femme*, Spring 1998, 'Women and Work' (Vol. 18, No. 1). Reprinted by permission of the author.

ELISE CHENIER. 'Rethinking Class in Lesbian Bar Culture: Living "The Gay Life" in Toronto, 1955–1965' (abridged), *Left History* 9.2 (Spring/Summer 2004): 85–117. Reprinted by permission of *Left History*.

PATRICK J. CONNOR. '"The Law Should Be Her Protector": The Criminal Prosecution of Rape in

Upper Canada, 1791–1850' (abridged) from *Sex Without Consent: Rape and Sexual Coercion in America*, Merril D. Smith, ed. (New York: NYU Press, 2001). Reprinted by permission of NYU Press.

Donald F. Davis and Barbara Lorenzkowski. 'A Platform for Gender Tensions: Women Working and Riding on Canadian Urban Public Transit in the 1940s' (abridged), *Canadian Historical Review* 79 (September 1988): 431–65. © University of Toronto Press Incorporated. Reprinted by permission of University of Toronto Press Incorporated (www.utpjournals.com).

Maureen Elgersman Lee. 'Slavery in Early Canada: Making Black Women Subject'. Copyright © 1999, from *Unyielding Spirits: Black Women and Slavery in Early Canada and Jamaica* by Maureen G. Elgersman. Reproduced by permission of Routledge/Taylor & Francis Group, LLC.

Marlene Epp. 'Victims of the Times, Heroes of Their Lives: Five Mennonite Refugee Women', from *Great Dames,* Elspeth Cameron and Janice Dickin, eds. © University of Toronto Press 1997. Reprinted by permission of the University of Toronto Press.

Janice Fiamengo. 'Rediscovering our Foremothers Again: Racial Ideas of Canada's Early Feminists, 1885–1945' (abridged), *Essays on Canadian Writing* 75 (Winter 2002): 85–117.

Jo-Ann Fiske. 'Carrier Women and the Politics of Mothering', from *British Columbia Reconsidered: Essays on Women,* Gillian Creese and Veronica Strong-Boag, eds. (Vancouver: Press Gang Publishers, 1992). Reprinted by permission of the author.

Glynis George. 'Violence and Poverty on the "Rock": Can Feminists Make a Difference?', *Canadian Women Studies* 20.1 (Winter 2000), 181–5. Reprinted by permission of the author.

Margaret Hillyard Little. 'Claiming a Unique Place: The Introduction of Mothers' Pensions in British Columbia', *BC Studies* 105/106 (Spring/Summer 1995): 80–102. Reprinted by permission of BC Studies.

Franca Iacovetta. 'Recipes for Democracy? Gender, Family, and Making Female Citizens in Cold War Canada', *Canadian Woman Studies/Les cahiers de la femme* 20.2 (Summer 2000), 12–21. Reprinted by permission of the author.

Patricia Jasen. 'Race, Culture, and the Colonization of Childbirth in Northern Canada' (revised), *Social History of Medicine* 10.3 (1997): 383–400. Reprinted by permission of the author.

Jane Jenson. 'Against the Current: Child Care and Family Policy in Quebec', Copyright © 2002, from *Child Care Policy at the Crossroads: Gender and Welfare State Restructuring*, edited by Sonya Michel and Rianne Mahon. Reproduced by permission of Routledge/Taylor & Francis Group, LLC.

Lynne Marks. '"A Fragment of Heaven on Earth"? Religion, Gender, and Family in Turn of the Century Canadian Church Periodicals', *Journal of Family History* 26.2 (April 2001): 251–71. Reprinted by permission of Sage Publications, Inc.

Mary-Jo Nadeau. 'Who is Canadian Now?: Feminism and the Politics of Nation After September 11'. This article was originally published in *Atlantis: A Women's Studies Journal* 27.1 (Fall 2002), www.msvu.ca/atlantis.

Brenda O'Neill. 'On the Same Wavelength? Feminist Attitudes Across Generations of Canadian Women', from Manon Tremblay and Linda Trimble, eds., *Women and Electoral Politics in Canada*. © 2002 Oxford University Press. Reprinted by permission of the publisher.

Nancy Shoemaker. 'Kateri Tekakwitha's Torturous Path to Sainthood'. Copyright © 1995, from *Negotiators of Change: Historical Perspectives on Native American Women* by Nancy Shoemaker. Reproduced by permission of Routledge/Taylor & Francis Group, LLC.

Pamela Sugiman. 'Passing Time, Moving Memories: Interpreting Wartime Narratives of Japanese Canadian Women' (abridged), *Histoire Sociale/Social History* 73 (May 2004): 51–80. Reprinted by permission of *Histoire Sociale/Social History.*

Sylvia Van Kirk. 'From "Marrying-In" to "Marrying-Out": Changing Patterns of Aboriginal/Non-aboriginal Marriage in Colonial Canada', *Frontiers* 23.3 (2002): 1–11. Reprinted by permission of the author.

Introduction

Rethinking Canada: The Promise of Women's History is premised on the assumption that women are a distinct group of people with a particular story to be told and analyzed. It also rests on the more implicit belief that Canadian society has valued and treated women differently, and usually more unequally, than men. Do these contentions hold up today? If we consider Canadian women's history through the filter of formal indicators of progress towards equality we see both continuity and change between past and present. Women live longer, get married later, and have fewer children than they once did. By 1999, females made up the majority of the country's population (50.4 per cent) and represented 70 per cent of the population over the age of 85. Between 1971 and 1997, a woman's average age at first marriage rose from 22 to 28 years. The recent legalization of same-sex marriage will, no doubt, shift the profile further as lesbian couples find their way into the national marriage statistics. While the average family had two children in 1971, this statistic has declined more recently to an average of one child per family.[1]

It is in the worlds of paid work and education where we see the clearest indicators of potential equality between men and women. In 2001, 60.2 per cent of Bachelor and first Professional degrees went to women. At both the university undergraduate and master's degree level, women made up the majority of students enrolled, at 51.8 per cent and 57.8 per cent, respectively.[2] Statistics Canada reported in 2003 that the entry of a large number of women into the paid labour force was 'one of the dominant social trends in Canada over the last half century'. In that year, 57 per cent of all women over the age of 15, compared with 42 per cent in 1976, had paid jobs. Moreover, and contrary to notions that mothers should be full-time child care providers, a sharp increase in the employment rate of women with children has taken place in the past quarter century. In 2003, 63 per cent of women with children under three years of age were employed. This is double the number of working mothers with young children recorded in 1976 when only 28 per cent of these women were employed outside the home.[3] While women continue to dominate employment areas labeled 'traditional female work', such as nursing and health-related fields, service work, and teaching, they have increased their representation in several professional fields related to business, finance, and various managerial roles once deemed solely the domain of men. In 2003 women made up more than half (52 per cent) of all doctors and dentists in Canada.[4]

Where do women fit in Canada's government? The 2004 election returned a federal House of Commons that was overwhelmingly male, as are all current provincial legislatures. Despite this result, Paul Martin's minority Liberal government congratulated itself with what it considered a clear record of achievement in women's interests and promised to commit more money and resources to achieving it. After the 2005 budget's release, Liza Fruella, then Minister of Canadian Heritage and Minister responsible for the Status of Women, praised the Liberal government's budget commitment to improving gender equity. According to Fruella, 'The . . . federal Budget reflects that strategy, with its commitments to significant advances that respond to the specific concerns of women, including the national child care program, and builds on initiatives of previous Budgets, such as compassionate care leave.'[5] The Martin government was only the latest in a decade of successive governments that have promised national budgets responsive to the inequalities between women and men and expressed their formal support for women's equity by signing various United Nations human rights treaties, most notably the 'Beijing Declaration' of September 1995. Only time will tell how the traditionally more right-wing policies of the minority Conservative government—elected in January 2006 under the leadership of Stephen Harper—will effect Canada's developing gender equality.

Significant changes in women's roles in marriage and the family, growing equality in key areas of education and paid work, and optimistic words and promises of equity flowing from Ottawa are belied by a more complicated reality. One need only consider the 1989 House of Commons unanimous all party resolution to 'achieve the goal of eliminating poverty among Canadian children by the year 2000'. In 2004 it was estimated that 1,065,000 children, many in lone mother families, continue to live below poverty lines.[6] Data such as this suggests that women have a distinct and unequal status in Canada, and the resources of the state have yet to be sufficiently committed to addressing women's very real needs. A Statistics Canada 2003 update on women and work, for instance, prefaces the gains women have made in their paid employment rates by pointing out that 'regardless of their level of educational attainment, women are still less likely than their male counterparts to be employed.' Lone female parents, representing 19 per cent of all families with children in 1996 (up from 10 per cent in 1971), are less likely to find employment than mothers in two-parent households.[7] Reflecting the racialized dimensions of poverty and under-employment, these women are more likely to identify themselves as First Nations. In 1996, 43 per cent of Aboriginal women 15 years of age and over had incomes below Statistics Canada's Low Income Cut-offs (LICO) as compared to 20 per cent of non-Aboriginal women and 35 per cent of Aboriginal men.[8] Despite the fact that recent immigrant women tend to have higher levels of education than Canadian-born women (in 1996, for women aged 24–44, 39 per cent of recent immigrants had as least some university education compared with 28 per cent of Canadian-born women), their rates of unemployment remain 10 per cent higher than Canadian-born women.[9] Additionally, regional disparities are often most keenly felt by women. In the Atlantic Provinces, for example, minimum wage hovers around $6.00 per hour. This is well below the $8.00 minimum 'training' wage in British Columbia and $0.60 below the national average. In the city of Halifax, 63 per cent of workers making minimum wage are women over 19 years of age employed in part-time jobs.[10] Clearly, coming to terms with female oppression based on gender alone is not, and as historians of women have demonstrated, has never been, enough.

Clearly, women have not found much relief in the world of provincial politics. Lest we are left with the impression that British Columbia is a haven for women's equality, it is important to remember that in 2003, the province was singled out by the United Nations as 'not meeting is obligations to women under international human rights law'. In its review of Canada's compliance with the United Nations Convention on the Elimination of All Forms of Discrimination Against Women (CEDAW), the UN commission made clear its concern over budget cuts made by the provincial Liberals under the leadership of Gordon Campbell. These included devastating cuts to legal aid and many forms of welfare assistance: rules for welfare eligibility were narrowed, the freestanding Ministry of Women's Equality and the independent Human Rights Commission eliminated, and deep cuts to support programs for victims of domestic violence were made.[11]

Wage gaps remain a striking indication of gender's power to shape social expectations and experience. In 2000, the average wage for full-year, full-time female workers was $34,892 compared with $42,224 for similarly employed men. Race further complicates gender, and therefore has an impact on average wages. Racialized, visible minority women have average incomes significantly lower than non-minority women and visible minority men.[12] Similarly single Aboriginal mothers struggling with poverty continue to be over-represented in the statistics surrounding family poverty. While 24 per cent of lone-parent families headed by men are poor, rates for lone female-headed families reach as high as 56 per cent. The experience of poor lone mothers signals how less visible, but no less real, social responsibilities and expectations continue to be borne unequally by women. Care-giving duties for elders, for example, continue to fall disproportionately on the shoulders of women. In 2002 Statistics Canada found that one-quarter of female care-givers (24 per cent) had to change their work patterns compared with 14 per cent of men in the same category.[13]

Recent studies also show that women remain vulnerable to violence, particularly in their homes by someone they know. Spousal violence against women in Canada continues to temper any claims of equality between women and men. In 1998 700,000 women, approximately 8 per cent of all women either married or in common-law relationships, had experienced some kind of violence at the hands of their partners over the previous five years. If we turn our gaze to the global community of women we are confronted with United Nations reports that state approximately 5,000 women worldwide are killed each year by their husbands over dowry disputes.[14] While women are most often the victims of violent crimes (51 per cent in 1998), female children in Canada suffer most from sexual offences. Over half of the female victims of sexual assault in 1998 were under the age of 18 years, 32 per cent were aged 12–17, and 21 per cent were under the age of 12.[15] Recent reports suggest that the numbers of reported cases of sexual assault against children are declining in Canada but front line workers tell another story. Audrey Rastin of the Toronto Child Abuse Centre cautions that '(i)t's still a very serious problem and in our agency, requests for services have not gone down, it fact they have increased.'[16]

Even a cursory review of the mainstream press in Canada over the last five years reveals that harm to female children makes very good press copy. The frenzied media attention to the tragic cases of Tamra Keepness of Regina, Saskatchewan, and of Holly Jones and Alicia Ross, both of Toronto, Ontario, belies the inattention to structural inequalities that position women and girls as possible (and indeed probable) victims. It is equally telling that other kinds of violence against girls and women slip under the public radar. The Native Women's Association of Canada estimates that approximately 500 Aboriginal women have gone missing in the last two decades, many of them are presumed dead.[17] In 2004 Amnesty International brought international attention to the story of what is becoming called Canada's 'missing women'. The number of Aboriginal women found dead, simply not found, or not even looked for, it argued, indicated the profound failure of the Canadian justice system to protect Indigenous women.[18] Violence haunts girls and women, and the way that Canadian society has coped—or failed to cope—with that fact tells us much about how gender operates in contemporary Canada.

Fed by a popular culture that portrays women and girls as either saints or whores, conniving 'desperate housewives' or cultural dupes who shop to fight off feelings of self-loathing, it is not difficult to conceive of the 'equity glass' as less than half empty.[19] The depressing dance of such negative and positive indicators of change for Canadian women, and indeed women around the world, promises to be interrupted by the passionate commitment of a whole new generation of young feminists critiquing women's spot in contemporary society and agitating for change. In a special edition of *Canadian Woman Studies/Les cahiers de la femme* dedicated to 'young women, feminists, activists, grrrls', university student Lauren Anderson called herself a feminist because '(o)ffically women [and men] are equal in the eyes of the law. . .and yet, women are oppressed, and there is no denying it.'[20] As Brenda O'Neill's essay in this volume points out, comments about the slow death of feminism are challenged by a new generation of Canadians more firmly committed to sexual and racial diversity and the feminist ideal of reproductive freedom than their baby-boomer mothers.

Women's uneven, and at times contradictory, place in contemporary Canadian society is mirrored by women's contested role in historical knowledge and scholarship. If the surfeit of popular books and television programmes are any indication, Canadian history has a new popularity. Thirty years of scholarship into Canadian women's history, however, seems to have had little, if any, impact on the popular treatments of Canadian history that grace our television screens and our bookstore shelves. The top ten selection for the 2004 'Greatest Canadian' contest did not include any women. Singer Shania Twain was the only woman to make it into the top twenty.[21] Women continue to be underrepresented in academic history departments as well.[22] Donald Wright's careful study of the development of the Canadian historical profession makes clear that gendered patterns of professional life were not accidental, and that the exclusion of women was in fact a central way that historians defined themselves and their work.[23] It was not that women did not think, talk, or write about history; they simply did so as authors, teachers, journalists, and members of historical societies that operated at some distance from academic scholarship.[24]

Yet it would be pessimistic and simply incorrect to conclude that women remain huddled at the margins of historical scholarship as either authors or subjects. Women's history has made enormous strides in Canada, and the field is steadily increasing the range and the variety of its challenges to traditional accounts.[25] As in the American context discussed by Joan Scott, the last few decades have seen Canadian feminists 'change the discipline fundamentally by writing women into history and by taking our rightful place as historians'.[26] The increasingly secure role of women's history in the academy produces a set of new challenges associated with the crises of faith that invariably accompany a shift in social positioning and the pressing need to make feminism relevant to a future seemingly dominated by war, violence, and dispossession. A clear sign of the growing maturity of the field and the continuing challenges before it was the celebration of the Canadian Committee on Women's History's (CCWH) 30th Anniversary, an event marked by numerous sessions and celebrations at the Canadian Historical Association meetings in London, Ontario, in 2005. The previous year, a subcommittee of the CCWH was struck to investigate ways to attract both new scholars and scholars working in areas that continue to struggle for recognition, such as those highlighting women of colour, disabled women, and First Nations women.[27]

The enormous growth, changing intellectual role, and shifting priorities of women's history in Canada are all mapped, in microcosm, in the pages of successive editions of *Rethinking Canada: The Promise of Women's History*. The first edition, published in 1986, was co-edited by Simon Fraser University historians Veronica Strong-Boag and Anita Clair Fellman. That book won recognition from the Canadian Institute for the Advancement of Women as the best feminist book by Canadian authors. Three more editions appeared between 1991 and 2002. The fourth edition, published in 2002, represented a generational shift as Mona Gleason from the University of British Columbia and Adele Perry from the University of Manitoba joined Strong-Boag, then at UBC as well, as editors. Each respective edition offered a new vision of the Canadian past, one that reflected the changing demands of the present. Careful revisions to these successive editions signaled that feminist historians were not only rethinking the country's history, but also that they were rethinking the supposedly unitary category of 'woman'. From this perspective, we believe that *Rethinking Canada* remains a bellwether of important new work in feminist approaches to the multilayered facets of Canadian women's histories. The various editions of this book help chart answers to enduring questions: Where have we come from and how has the field evolved? What holes still distort our view of women's role in shaping the past and what has been uncovered by innovative analyses? How might a fuller appreciation of women's past experiences give us more purchase on solutions to enduring problems of inequality in our midst?

Greater attention to the diversity amongst women is the clearest indicator of change. *Rethinking Canada* had always acknowledged the importance of Aboriginal women to Canadian women's history, but only four of the seventeen articles in the first edition of the book dealt, in whole or part, with issues of immigrant and Native women.[28] When the second edition appeared in 1991, this total increased to seven articles out of 24 in total. As in the previous edition, all of these articles dealt with Aboriginal women or European migrants, and none with migrant women of colour with roots in Africa, Asia, or Latin America.[29] This shifted again with the arrival of the third edition in 1997. Essays placing the experience of non-majority women at the centre of their analysis rose to about one-third of the book; about ten of the total number of 27 articles. Contributing what have become classic works regarding the experiences of racialized and immigrant women to the history of Canada, Midge Ayukawa's 'Good Wives and Wise Mothers: Japanese Picture Brides in Early Twentieth-Century British Columbia', Franca Iacovetta's 'From Contadina to Worker: Southern Italian Immigrant Working Women in Toronto, 1947–1962', and Sedef Arat-Koç's 'Immigration Policies, Migrant Domestic Workers, and the Definition of Citizenship in Canada', all included in the fourth edition of *Rethinking Canada*, were indicative of a new generation of scholars eager to include heretofore neglected experiences into women's history in Canada and to remake the field in the process. The history of Native women in Canada was likewise taken to new levels of complexity with the contributions of Carol Devens and Diane P. Payment. Their work revised staples of Canadian history—the Prairie revolts of the late 1800s and the impact of European colonization on Native peoples around the Great Lakes—by placing *both* gender and race in centre of the interpretive table.

In this latest version of *Rethinking Canada* we continue to revise our understanding of Canadian women's history along racial, religious, national, and ethnic lines. By continuing a commitment to rethinking women, this volume is also rethinking the entity we know as 'Canada'. We begin with Nancy Shoemaker's insightful analysis of how Kateri Tekakwitha, a Mohawk woman, was able to put European and Roman Catholic institutions to her own purposes in the seventeenth-century. Maureen Elgersman Lee's chapter on women and slavery in Canada explores another way that womanhood was racialized, and in doing so, not only adds women to the history of slavery, but challenges versions of Canadian history that script non-white peoples as recent arrivals. Sedef Arat-Koç's treatment of women and domestic work shows us not only the importance of race for explaining women's experience, but reminds us how it has shifted over time. Janice Fiamengo's treatment of race in first-wave feminist writing shows us how we must use the category of race to understand even those women racialized as 'white'. Pamela Sugiman's article draws on oral interviews and personal experiences to tease out how Japanese Canadian women have narrated and remembered their wartime experience, thereby interrupting racialized and racist notions of their natural 'acquiescence' to the demands of Whites. Marlene Epp discusses the life histories of German-speaking Mennonite women who came to Canada as refugees at the end of the Second World War, while Franca Iacovetta shows us the connections between the ideas of gender, nation, and democracy in Cold War discussions of women and food. The final essay presented in this new edition, Mary-Jo Nadeau's analysis of the controversy that greeted Sunera Thobani's 2001 speech critiquing the American response to the terrorist attacks of September 11, provides us not only with an example of anti-racist feminist activism, but reminds us that this work remains very much contested.

To some extent, the analytic category of class and concern for labour and work has shifted away from the centre of analysis at the same time that race and ethnicity have shifted in. Early versions of *Rethinking Canada* reflect the close relationship between labour history and women's history and, more generally, between socialism and feminism in late twentieth-century Canada and second-wave feminism's concern for workplace equity. In the first edition, essays by Susan Mann Trofimenkoff on industrial women and work, Graham S. Lowe on women, work, and the office, and Julie White on part-time work all dealt with questions of women, work, and protest, as did the personal narrative from labour activist Anne B. Woywitka. In the second edition, essays by Bettina

Bradbury, Lynne Marks, Joan Sangster, and Franca Iacovetta all used class and labour as central tools of analysis. Class and labour were less central in the third edition, published in 1997, which featured four of 27 articles grappling with economic class and its subsequent questions. The complex history surrounding women and work was explored in the fourth edition in five out of 26 articles. Essays by Kathryn A. Young, Bettina Bradbury, Jeff Keshen, Sedef Arat-Koç, Barbara Neis, and Susan Williams expanded our appreciation of the breadth of working women's history from New France, through industrialization, the war and postwar years, and into contemporary Canada. Sedef Arat-Koç's essay on migrant domestic servants focused much needed attention on the politics of race and racism in this history. While the current edition deals with the experience of slave women, housewives, domestic servants, and teachers, as a whole it does not emphasize class and labour as much as it once did. Some will associate this with a general shift away from materialist explanations of historical change and toward the realm of culture and cultural explanations for change. More optimistically, we might argue that an awareness of class is deeply imbedded within the analyses of marriage, politics, and citizenship offered in these pages.

The record on sexuality is less clear. The history of sexuality, and more particularly gay and lesbian experiences, in Canada has developed alongside women's history, but at a different pace. It was not until the 1997 edition of *Rethinking Canada* that an essay focusing on lesbian experience—Line Chamberlain's insightful article on lesbian bar-culture in Montreal—was included. In the fourth edition Valerie Korinek offered an analysis of lesbian content within, and lesbian readings of, a very mainstream Canadian women's magazine, *Chatelaine*. In the current volume readers are provided with a window into lesbian life in working-class Toronto through Elise Chenier's careful study. The volume also includes Sheila L. Cavanagh's essay on teachers and heterosexualization, which demonstrates how historians are paying increasing attention to the process whereby normative identities are constructed alongside alternative ones.

Successive editions of *Rethinking Canada* suggest that region is another shifting historiographical terrain for historians of women. Ontario has always received significant attention, and that attention reflects its status as the population centre of English-Canada and the seat of much English-language historical production. The first edition of *Rethinking Canada* gave a prominent role to Quebec, with about one-quarter of the articles dealing specifically with that society. In that edition, another three essays grappled with prairie Canada, and none with British Columbia. The generations of *Rethinking Canada* that would follow held the emphasis on Quebec relatively constant, reflecting both the quality of historical work on women in Quebec and the editorial commitment to exposing students in English Canada to it. British Columbia and Atlantic Canada have remained on the map and the North, with Patricia Jasen's article on colonization and childbirth, was first introduced in the 2002 edition. But it is worth noting that the prairies, as a region of study, have almost entirely disappeared from the most current edition. Van Kirk, Fiamengo, and Epp seriously undertake prairie women and issues, but no essay shines its spotlight on that part of Canada alone. This reflects, to some extent, shifts in emphasis in historical work more generally.[30] It also suggests that historians are using wider national, and sometimes transnational, frames to help us think of gender and women beyond the local. The costs of this shift are felt more strongly in some areas of historical scholarship literatures than others.

Another barometer of change is an increasing engagement with explicitly theoretical material and perspectives. Early editions of *Rethinking Canada* included one essay that grappled with questions of method and theory: in 1986 and 1992, Margaret Conrad's treatment of time and place in Canadian women's history, in 1997 and 2002 Joan Sangster's discussion of women's history and oral history. In this most current edition, we find that theory and method are discussed throughout the text, as authors discuss how we might come to understand widows, church periodicals, feminist writing, the gendering of space, popular culture, or the memories of women who were interned during the Second World War. Such work showcases the interpretive and methodological impact of increasingly sophisticated theoretical developments in feminist and poststructural analysis and in the fields of gender studies, queer studies, subaltern, and postcolonial studies on archivally based historical research. At the same time, the successive versions of *Rethinking Canada* have witnessed a gradual, though by no means total or uncontested, shift away from 'women's history' conceived as a self-explanatory and essentially contained topic towards a treatment of women's history as an important aspect of a gendered history constituted by both men's and women's experiences.

This increasing complexity and diversity takes the field well past initial efforts to, in a somewhat compensatory way, include women in the historical record. Perspectives central to the development of Canadian women's history first published in the late 1970s and 1980s—most notably Jan Noel's argument about women in New France, Sylvia Van Kirk's analysis of women's centrality to the Western Canadian fur trade, Veronica Strong-Boag's analysis of Nellie McClung's first-wave feminism, and Ruth Roach Pierson's reconsideration of the Second World War's promises of female equality—were included in the first, second, and third editions. Gradually, *Rethinking Canada* increased the number of newly published articles alongside these 'classics'. The ratio shifted further with the fourth edition, published in 2002. With Canadian history textbooks and edited collections increasingly giving reasonable air-space to some key ideas in women's history, it no longer seemed necessary to provide readers with what had become the 'classics' in the field. For the first time, the central contrapuntal works of Canadian women's history were re-positioned as influential and valued predecessors to new work.

Not everything has changed about *Rethinking Canada*. From its first incarnation in 1986 to this fifth edition, *Rethinking Canada* is a deeply interdisciplinary work that shows how feminist scholarship has worked across disciplinary boundaries. In these pages readers learn about the past, but from the perspectives of anthropologists, literary critics, sociologists, and political scientists as well as from historians. It has also been marked by a deep commitment to seeing women's history not as an end in itself, but as a tool to rethink Canadian history writ large. In the first three volumes of this book, Sylvia Van Kirk re-wrote the Canadian fur trade, as she does again in this volume, though here with new interpretative lenses developed in the 1990s and 2000s. Rusty Bitterman takes women's participation as the starting-off point for a rethinking of the escheat movement of Prince Edward Island, while Pamela Sugiman, in some respects, does the same to shift the perspective on Japanese Canadian internment. Bettina Bradbury sheds new light on women's roles as voters in early nineteenth-century Montreal, and in doing so, fundamentally revises some central contentions of Québécois historiography. In their treatment of women working and riding on Canadian public transit in the 1940s, Donald F. Davis and Barbara Lorenzkowski offer a significant rethinking not only of the Second World War but also of Canadian urban development.

Some of the enduring topics of Canadian women's history—marriage, politics, poverty, protest, social roles, and violence—remain very much with us, albeit defined and mobilized in different and new ways. Josette Brun shows us how women managed widowhood and motherhood in New France, articulating a set of concerns about women, family, and daily survival that is taken up later by Denyse Baillargeon's analysis of housewives and citizenship in depression era Quebec and by Jo-Anne Fiske in her treatment of Carrier women and the politics of mothering. Margaret Hillyard Little's discussion of mother's allowance in British Columbia and Jane Jenson's treatment of child care policy in Quebec both raise questions about women's relationship to the state. Patrick J. Connor's analysis of women who were raped in Upper Canada raises a theme of violence that is explored further in Glynis George's analysis of feminist work on violence and poverty in contemporary Newfoundland. Lynne Marks delves into the available social roles offered to women by mainstream religion in the *fin de siècle*, echoing a concern for the parameters of women's experiences that undergrids much of the work presented here and in previous editions of *Rethinking Canada*.

However much it has changed, *Rethinking Canada: The Promise of Women's History* still aims to provide Canadian women with a history and, in doing so, to offer a challenge to understandings of the Canadian past that leave women out most, and sometimes all, of the time. A quick survey of the contemporary scene and an equally speedy examination of current mainstream historical writing both show that these goals remain valid if not unchanged. Over the years, how we have seen and thought of the history of Canadian women in these pages have changed in revealing ways. No doubt this process of change will continue in the future as well: as Joy Parr has noted, one of the greatest contributions of feminist historical scholarship has been the acknowledgement that our knowledge of the past is never total or conclusive, and the more radical contention that this is a positive thing, one that scholars should enthusiastically embrace rather than grudgingly bear.[31] Future editions of *Rethinking Canada* will look different than this one, and so they should. It is the only way that a book like *Rethinking Canada* can adequately address the lives of living Canadian women, expand our changing knowledge of what women's lives were like in the past, and embody our hopes and demands for what women's lives might be like in the future.

Mona Gleason and Adele Perry
2 November 2005

Notes

1. Statistics Canada, *Women in Canada 2000: A Gender-Based Statistical Report* (Ottawa: Minister of Industry, 2000), 17, 30, 36.
2. Wendy Robbins, Michèle Olliver, John Hollingsworth, and Rosemary Morgan, compilers, *Ivory Tower: Feminist and Equity Audits, 2005* (Canadian Federation for the Humanities and Social Sciences, 2005), http://www.fedcan.ca/english/issues/ivoryaudit.
3. Statistics Canada, *Women in Canada: Work Chapter Updates, 2003* (Ottawa: Ministry of Industry, 2004), 6.
4. Ibid., 19. In 1976, 8.6 per cent of women and 14.3 per cent of men (expressed as a percentage of total employed) were self-employed. In 2003, 11.3 per cent of women and 18.9 per cent of men were self-employed.
5. Status of Women Canada New Release, 'Canada Celebrates International Women's Day', 8 March 2005, http://www.swc-cfc.gc.ca/newsroom/news2005/0308_e.html.
6. Campaign 2000, 'One Million Too Many: Implementing Solutions to Child Poverty in Canada' (Campaign 2000, 2004 Report Card on Child Poverty in Canada), http://www.campaign2000.ca/rc/rc04/04NationalReportCard.pdf.
7. Statistics Canada, *Women in Canada 2000*, 32; Statistics Canada, *Women in Canada: Work Chapter Updates*, 2003, 7–8.
8. Statistics Canada, *Women in Canada 2000*, 259.
9. Ibid, 199.
10. John Jacobs and Stephanie Hunter, 'Low Income Earners in Nova Scotia Need a Raise', Editorial, 1 March 2003 (Ottawa: Centre for Policy Alternatives, 2005), http://www.policyalternatives.ca.
11. Shelagh Day and Margot Young, 'UN Singles out BC Government on Women's Rights', Editorial, 1 March 2003 (Ottawa: Canadian Centre for Policy Alternatives, 2005), http://www.policyalternatives.ca.
12. Statistics Canada, *Women in Canada 2000*, 231.
13. Isabellla Bakker, 'Gender Budget Initiatives: Why They Matter in Canada', *Alternative Federal Budget 2006* (Ottawa: Canadian Centre for Policy Alternatives, 2005), 2–4, http://www.policyalternatives.ca.
14. Ann Duffy, 'The Feminist Challenge: Knowing and Ending the Violence', in *Feminist Issues: Race, Class, and Sexuality*, 2nd ed., Nancy Mandell, ed. (Toronto: Prentice Hall, 1998).
15. Statistics Canada, *Women in Canada 2000*, 166–7.
16. Gloria Galloway, 'Study shows fewer cases of sex assault on children', *The Globe and Mail* (5 October

2005), A5. Excluding Quebec, where statistics are gathered differently, the study shows that between 1998 and 2003, the number of sexual abuse investigations involving victims under 16 in Canada fell from 4,322 to 2,935. All other types of child abuse were shown to have doubled in the same time period. It is not known whether the decline in child sexual abuse rates is due to amelioration of the problem, or a drop in reporting to authorities.

17. http://www.sistersinspirit.ca/engmissing.htm.
18. 'Stolen Sisters: A Human Rights Response to Discrimination and Violence against Indigenous Women in Canada', http://web.amnesty.org/library/Index/ENGAMR200012004.
19. A number of feminist sociologists have challenged the misogynist caricatures that dominate much of the commercialized culture aimed at girls, in particular. Their work attempts, as Shauna Pomerantz recently writes, to 'challenge of the authority of an essentialized girlhood'. Shauna Pomerantz, 'Dressing the Part: Girls, Style, and School Identities', PhD Dissertation, University of British Columbia, 2005. Other works include Catherine Driscoll, *Girls: Feminine Adolescence in Popular Culture and Cultural Theory* (New York: Columbia University Press, 2002); Julie Bettie, *Women without Class: Girls, Race, and Identity* (Berkeley: University of California Press, 2003); Marnina Gonick, *Between Femininities: Ambivalence, Identity, and the Education of Girls* (Albany: State University of New York Press, 2003).
20. Lauren Anderson, 'Why I'm a Feminist', *Canadian Woman Studies/Les cahiers de la femme* 20.4 and 21.1 (Spring/Summer, 2001), 33.
21. In his introduction to the 1998 list of 100 important Canadians in history, Jack Granatstein explained that 'We know the present list gives too much weight to "dead white males" from central Canada who held power and had the greatest opportunities thought key periods in history...'. J.L. Granatstein, '100 Canadians', *Maclean's*, 111, 26 (1 July 1998): 14.
22. Ruby Heap, 'The Status of Women in the Historical Profession in Canada: Results of 1998 Survey', *Canadian Historical Review* 81.3 (September 2000): 436–51; Dianne Dodd and Geneviéve Postolec, 'Report on the Survey on Women in Public History', ibid., 452–66.
23. Donald Wright, 'Gender and the Professionalization of History in English Canada before 1960', *Canadian Historical Review* 81.1 (March 2000): 29–66.
24. See Beverly Boutilier and Alison Prentice, eds., *Creating Historical Memory: English-Canadian Women and the Work of History* (Vancouver: UBC Press, 1997); Cecilia Morgan, 'History, Nation, and Empire: Gender and Southern Ontario Historical Societies, 1890–1920s', *Canadian Historical Review* 82: 3 (September 2001): 491–528.
25. See Diana Pedersen, *Changing Women, Changing History: A Bibliography of the History of Women in Canada* (Ottawa: Carleton University Press, 1996); Margaret Fulford, *The Canadian Women's Movement, 1960–1990: A Guide to Archival Sources/le mouvement Canadien des femmes, 1960–1990: guide de resources archivistiques* (Toronto: ECW Press, 1993); Klay Dyer, Lucy Sussex, and Sue Martin, compilers, *Canadian Women's History Bibliography: Catalogue/ Bibliographie de l'histoire des femmes canadiennes: catalogue* (Ottawa: Canadian Institute for Historical Microreproductions, 1997).
26. Joan W. Scott, 'Feminism's History', *Journal of Women's History* 16.2 (2004): 10.
27. http://www.cha-shc.ca/ccwh-cchf/english/ccwh-frame.html
28. These include essays by Anne Woywitka, Jan Noel, Eleanor Leacock, and Sylvia Van Kirk. We are indebted for this thematic breakdown of previous editions to Veronica Strong-Boag's unpublished conference paper entitled 'Rethinking Canada: The Promise of Women's History, 1886–2002', presented to 'Transculturalisms: Cultures, Generations, Gender', Canadian Studies Association in German Speaking Countries, Gruneau, Germany, February, 2004.
29. Essays by Joy Parr and Franca Iacovetta highlighted issues of immigration—two more by Noel and Potter did so tangentially. Three essayists, Leacock, Sylvia Van Kirk, and Jean Barman, focused on Native women.
30. On recent work on the prairies, see Kathryn McPherson, 'Was the "Frontier" Good for Women?: Historical Approaches to Women and Agricultural Settlement in the Prairie West, 1870–1925', *Atlantis* 25.1 (Fall 2000).
31. Joy Parr, 'Gender History and Historical Practice', *Canadian Historical Review* 76.3 (September 1995): 354–76.

Kateri Tekakwitha's Tortuous Path to Sainthood

Nancy Shoemaker

EDITORS' INTRODUCTION

History challenges sweeping generalizations about women's lot. It shows us that the roles, responsibilities, and powers accorded to women have varied enormously in different cultures and at different points in time. What it meant to be a woman in seventeenth-century Iroquoian society was profoundly different than what it meant to be a woman at the same time in France. France, like other European societies, was patriarchal. Women might find avenues for authority and influence, but they did so in a framework that structurally and symbolically institutionalized men's authority within the family, state, and church. The Huron and Iroquois people who lived around the Gulf of St Lawrence possessed a gendered division of labour, but afforded women considerable scope for political authority and personal autonomy. Women were central to the economic activities of foraging, agriculture, and food distribution. They could choose their sexual partners and instigate divorce. Like the North Coast societies of the Pacific, the Huron and Iroquois reckoned descent matrilineally, which suggests the strength of women's influence within the family, the lineage, the clan, and the nation.[1]

When Europeans began arriving around the Gulf of St Lawrence in meaningful numbers these differing conceptions of womanhood were brought into contact and perhaps conflict. The Jesuit mission to New France began in 1611 and by the end of the century this Roman Catholic order had established a presence from Labrador to Lake Winnipeg. They worked to convert Aboriginal peoples to Christianity, a sedentary life-style, and European notions of gender and the family. Historians have debated the extent to which they succeeded in re-aligning the status of First Nations women. Karen Anderson and Carol Devens have both argued that undermining female authority was central to the Jesuits's conversion efforts, although Anderson emphasizes Jesuit victory while Devens stresses female resistance.[2] This debate is essentially mirrored by one about the effect of the fur-trade and colonialism on Tsimshian women in the nineteenth-century.[3] Beyond this a rich scholarship on the connections between gender and early contact and colonialism is developing in Canada, represented most clearly by the articles in Katie Pickles and Myra Rutherdale's edited collection, *Contact Zones*.[4]

In this article, Nancy Shoemaker tries to get away from the binaries that sometimes haunt discussions of women and colonialism. She examines the still-revered 'Mohawk Saint', Kateri Tekakwitha, and suggests that Catholicism could empower as well as repress First Nations women. Tekakwitha, not unlike a select handful of prominent settler women in New France, continues to attract historical attention and debate. Allan

Greer has recently published *Mohawk Saint: Catherine Tekakwitha and the Jesuits*, a full-length biography and exploration of the relationship between Tekakwitha, her Jesuit biographers, and the politics of colonialism. In a footnote, he critiques Shoemaker for relying heavily on an imperfect translation.[5] Yet Shoemaker nonetheless offers a useful analysis of the relationship between Christianity, contact, and Aboriginal women. Women like Tekakwitha, she argues, were able to turn Christianity to their own advantage, incorporating the rituals of baptism, Christian societies, virginity, and penance as a means to shore up their role in a rapidly changing Iroquois society. Carol J. Williams's recent treatment of Tsimshian Methodist converts certainly confirms the real satisfaction and authority Aboriginal women could reap from their roles within missionary projects.[6] As Greer points out, the fact that Tekakwitha is so celebrated and revered in Aboriginal communities across North America suggests her continuing power as a symbol of Indigenous survival against enormous odds. Her example suggests the countless numbers of other Indigenous women who, like the twentieth-century Carrier women discussed by Jo-Anne Fiske in this volume, found creative, ingenious, and sustaining ways to work within the changing opportunities available to them.

Notes

1. See Natalie Zemon Davis, 'Iroquois Women, European Women', in *Women, 'Race', and Writing in the Early Modern Period,* Margo Hendricks and Patricia Parker, eds. (London and New York: Routledge, 1994).
2. See Karen Anderson, *Chain Her by One Foot: The Subjugation of Native Women in Seventeenth-Century New France* (London: Routledge, 1991); Carol Devens, *Countering Colonization: Native American Women and Great Lakes Missions, 1630–1900* (Berkeley: University of California Press, 1992).
3. Jo-Anne Fiske, 'Colonization and the Decline of Women's Status: The Tsimshian Case', *Feminist Studies* 17.3 (Fall 1991): 509–3; Carol Cooper, 'Native Women of the Northern Pacific Coast: An Historical Perspective, 1830–1900', *Journal of Canadian Studies* 27.4 (Winter 1992–3): 44–75.
4. Katie Pickles and Myra Rutherdale, *Contact Zones: Aboriginal and Settler Women in Canada's Colonial Past* (Vancouver, UBC Press, 2005).
5. Allan Greer, *Mohawk Saint: Catherine Tekakwitha and the Jesuits* (New York: Oxford University Press, 2005)
6. Carol J. Williams, *Framing the West: Race, Gender, and the Photographic Frontier in the Pacific Northwest* (New York: Oxford University Press, 2003), Chapter 3.

Questions for Critical Reading

1. Anthropologists contend that some North American Aboriginal societies, including the Iroquois and Huron, offered men and women different roles but accorded them roughly similar levels of social power. Is that possible? Can women ever really be 'different but equal'? Why or why not?
2. What sources does Shoemaker use for her study? Who has written them? What are the limitations to analyzing First Nations women by studying the writings of European men?
3. Compare European and Aboriginal ideas about women and gender. Where were they similar and where were they different? On what issues did these different ideas of women and gender meet? On what issues did they come into conflict?
4. What did organized religion offer women? Why might some women, like Kateri Tekakwitha, have wanted to become nuns? What does that tell us about women's position in society in general?

Kateri Tekakwitha died at Kahnawake in 1680 in the odour of sanctity (a sweet odour filled the room). Pilgrims from all over New France journeyed to her tomb to ask her to intercede with God on their behalf. In 1683, Tekakwitha's divine intervention saved several Jesuits from certain death when a windstorm caused the mission church at Kahnawake to collapse around them.[1] Ten years later, André Merlot's 'inflammation of the eyes' healed after he made a novena to Tekakwitha, rubbing his eyes with a solution of water, earth from Tekakwitha's grave, and ashes from her clothing.[2] Colombière, canon of the Cathedral of Quebec, testified in 1696 that his appeal to Tekakwitha relieved him of 'a slow fever, against which all remedies had been tried in vain, and of a diarrhea, which even ipecacuana could not cure'.[3] The Roman Catholic Church acknowledged Tekakwitha's holiness by declaring her venerable in 1943. In 1980, Tekakwitha was beatified. Perhaps soon, Tekakwitha will pass the next and final step of canonization and be recognized as a saint. She is the only Native American to rise so far in the saintly canon of the Catholic Church.[4]

Kateri Tekakwitha appears in most historical accounts of missionization in New France except, oddly enough, those that deal explicitly with women and missionization.[5] The now classic research of Eleanor Leacock and two recent books on women and missionization, one written by Karen Anderson and the other by Carol Devens, do not mention Tekakwitha.[6] More surprising is that the historical literature on Native women and religion in New France ignores the Iroquois, even though there is a voluminous literature debating the power of Iroquois women before and after European contact.[7] Leacock and Devens confined their studies to the Montagnais (an Algonquian-speaking tribe), while Anderson's research focused on the Montagnais and Huron, who were culturally and linguistically related to the Iroquois but often at war with them.

Tekakwitha's experience does contradict the usual argument that missionaries forced Native people to adopt patriarchy along with Christianity and that missionization helped to devalue women's role in Native societies. The usual narrative of missionization's impact on Native women in New France describes how epidemic disease and progressively deeper involvement in the fur trade created an economic imbalance and a crisis of faith within Native communities; the Jesuits' persistent vilifying of Native customs, especially marriage customs, eventually led missionized Indians to abandon the old ways and accept the basic tenets of Christianity and Western culture.

The choicest pieces of evidence used to support the argument that Native people in New France ultimately conformed to missionary preachings and Western patriarchy come from a 1640 Jesuit account of the Montagnais mission at Sillery, which was recovering from a severe smallpox epidemic. One particular incident figures prominently in the arguments of Leacock, Anderson, and Devens. Several Montagnais women complained to the Jesuits that the men had brought them to a council to reprimand them:

> 'It is you women', they [the men] said to us [the women], 'who are the cause of all our misfortunes—it is you who keep the demons among us. You do not urge to be baptized; you must not be satisfied to ask this favor only once from the Fathers, you must importune them. You are lazy about going to prayers; when you pass before the cross, you never salute it; you wish to be independent. Now know that you will obey your husbands.'[8]

Leacock and Anderson gave this as evidence of missionized Indian men dominating women. Devens used this example to show that Native women resisted Christianity, partly because of its patriarchal implications. However, Devens' argument is weakened by her own discussion of how some women eagerly embraced Christianity.

These arguments presume a linear, assimilationist model of change and seem to come from a

Western narrative tradition that depicts people as one thing, and after a crisis of some sort, they become another thing. However, it seems more likely that historical change is constantly in motion, perhaps moving in many different directions at once. Crisis may not lead automatically to permanent change but instead may simply be the moment in time when competing interests clash in a visible and tangible way. Smallpox made 1640 an especially stressful year in this Montagnais village, and men and women may have become embattled as they sought to reassert some control over their lives. Montagnais men were probably not successfully dominating women, but they may have been trying to and may have tried using the symbols of Christianity to do so. Some women may have in similar moments called upon the symbols of Christianity to assert their own identity and authority within the Native community.

This narrative of a decline into patriarchy appeals to those of us with historical hindsight; however, even though we may view Christianity as part of a patriarchal, Western tradition that assisted in the conquest of America, Native people may have interpreted it differently. First, Roman Catholicism, especially in the way the Jesuit missionaries presented it, paralleled Iroquois religious beliefs, allowing certain aspects of Christianity to be easily incorporated. Second, Roman Catholicism, perhaps more than any other Christian religion, employs feminine imagery, such as the Virgin Mary and women saints, which could be co-opted by women as symbols of power. And third, while scholars of missionization in New France have emphasized Jesuit efforts to enforce monogamous, life-long marriages on Native converts as crucial to women's disempowerment, they have ignored the Jesuits' even more profound admiration of women who refused to marry, a novel idea when introduced to the Iroquois and one that some women may have appreciated as an alternative to their prescribed role within Iroquois society. The Jesuits preached patriarchy, but also brought to the Iroquois a toolkit of symbols, stories, and rituals that portrayed women as powerful or that gave women access to power. Just as Native people transformed Europeans' material toolkit of guns, blankets, and glass beads to suit their own needs, Iroquois women and men may have sometimes adopted, sometimes rejected, but continually worked to transform the spiritual and symbolic toolkit of Christianity to meet the needs of the moment.

The Jesuit compulsion to missionize in the Americas was partly the product of a religious revival that swept through elite circles in France in the early 1600s.[9] Jesuits first arrived at the French colonial settlement of Quebec in 1625. After briefly losing the colony to an alliance of English colonists and the disaffected French Protestants known as Huguenots, France re-established Quebec in 1632, and within the year the Jesuits arrived again, this time to set up permanent missions. At first, the Jesuits concentrated their missions among the Hurons, Montagnais, and Algonquins. They made several attempts to missionize the Iroquois but did not survive long in any of the Iroquois villages. However, some Iroquois, many of them Huron or Algonquin war captives who had been adopted into Iroquois families, left their villages to form Christian communities. One of the largest and most successful of these 'praying towns' was Kahnawake.

Kahnawake (or Caughnawaga) originated at La Prairie de la Madeleine near Montreal in the late 1660s. La Prairie consisted of three distinct, but interacting, communities: the Jesuit Mission of St Francis Xavier, a village of French colonists, and a growing Native village of Algonquins, Hurons, and Iroquois. The first Native settlers at La Prairie were Catherine Gandeacteua, an Erie women, and her Huron husband, François Xavier Tonsahoten. Both of them had previously learned about Christianity at Jesuit missions but had been taken captive and adopted into the Oneida tribe, one of the five Iroquois nations. By the early 1670s, Gandeacteua, Tonsahoten, and other members of their family had left their Oneida village and permanently settled near Montreal. For a variety of reasons, the Native village and the mission moved a few miles up the St Lawrence River to Sault St Louis in 1677. Although the French usually called this Indian settlement 'the

Sault', the Native inhabitants named their village Kahnawake, meaning 'at the sault' or falls in Mohawk, a reflection of the growing number of Mohawks who had joined the community. As the easternmost of the Iroquois tribes, the Mohawks were the first to feel most intensely the disruptive consequences of European contact, and many Mohawks came to see Kahnawake, with its strict prohibitions against alcohol, as a haven from the alcohol-induced violence plaguing Iroquois villages in the late 1600s.[10]

According to Tekakwitha's two hagiographers, the Jesuits Pierre Cholenec and Claude Chauchetière, Tekakwitha was one of the many Mohawks who sought refuge at Kahnawake.[11] She was born in 1656 at Gandaouague (now Auriesville, New York) near present-day Albany. Her mother was an Algonquin who had been missionized by the Jesuits at Trois-Rivières, and her father was Mohawk and a 'heathen'. When Tekakwitha was about four years old, a smallpox epidemic killed her immediate family and left Tekakwitha disfigured and with weak eyes that could not bear bright light. She was raised by her aunts and by an uncle who was considered one of the most powerful men in the village as well as a vehement opponent of Christianity.

As a young girl, Tekakwitha did what all Iroquois girls did. (However, she was also 'gentle, patient, chaste, innocent, and behaved like a well-bred French child'.[12]) She helped gather firewood, worked in the cornfields, and became skilled at various decorative crafts. And although she later 'looked back upon it as a great sin' requiring 'a severe penance', she arrayed herself in typical Iroquois finery and engaged in other vanities.[13] When Tekakwitha reached marriageable age, her relatives began pressuring her to marry. At one point, they even arranged a marriage, but when the intended bridegroom came into the longhouse and seated himself next to Tekakwitha, by which custom the arranged marriage was revealed to her, she 'left the lodge and hid in the fields'.[14]

Tekakwitha first encountered the Jesuits as a young girl when Fathers Frémin, Bruyas, and Pierron stayed in her uncle's lodge while arranging to establish missions among the five Iroquois Nations. It was not until several years later, however, that Tekakwitha received her first instruction in Christianity. Jacques de Lamberville, then Jesuit missionary to the Mohawk, visited Tekakwitha's lodge and found her eager to hear more, or at least she was one of the few Iroquois he could get to listen. (Her eye problems and other ailments often kept her confined to the longhouse while other women went to work in the cornfields.) He baptized her in 1676 and gave her the Christian name of Catherine.[15] Harassed by the non-Christian majority, Tekakwitha fled to Kahnawake about a year and a half later, arriving shortly after the village had relocated from La Prairie to Sault St Louis.

While at Kahnawake, Tekakwitha's enthusiasm for Christianity became more intense. She moved in with her adopted sister and faithfully learned Christian prayers and the lives of the saints from Anastasia, 'one of the most fervent Christians in the place' and the matrilineal head of the family in that longhouse.[16] Her first year there, she went on the winter hunt as was the custom for residents of Kahnawake, but could not bear being deprived of Mass, the Eucharist, and daily prayer. She built her own shrine, a cross, in the woods and prayed to it, but would have preferred to be back in the village. The next winter, she refused to go on the hunt, which meant that she also chose to go without meat for the entire winter.

Once again, Tekakwitha's relatives, including Anastasia, pressured her to marry. They even solicited Cholenec's assistance in convincing Tekakwitha of the importance of marriage. At first Cholenec took the side of the relatives, for he knew that in Iroquois society women were dependent on men for clothing (provided through the hunt and later through the fur trade), and that, without a husband to contribute meat and hides to the longhouse, Tekakwitha was not helping herself or her longhouse family. But Tekakwitha insisted that she could 'have no other spouse but Jesus Christ'. Finally persuaded that she was 'inspired by the Holy Spirit', Cholenec changed sides in the family dispute and began to defend Tekakwitha's decision to remain unmarried.[17]

Meanwhile, Tekakwitha had formed a close friendship with another young woman, Marie Therese. They dedicated themselves to each other, to Christianity, and to leading lives modelled after that of the nuns in Quebec and Montreal. Cholenec ascribed their knowledge of the nuns to Tekakwitha, and said that she had for herself seen how the hospital nuns in Montreal lived and had learned of their vows of chastity and penitential practices.[18] However, Chauchetière credited a third young woman, Marie Skarichions, with suggesting to Tekakwitha and Marie Therese that they model themselves after the nuns.[19] Skarichions was from Lorette, a community similar to Kahnawake but located near Quebec, and she had once been cared for there by the Sisters de la Hospitalière.

These three women determined to form their own association, in which they dedicated themselves to virginity and helped each other in their self-mortifications. Tekakwitha's penances were many and varied. She walked barefoot in ice and snow, burned her feet 'with a hot brand, very much in the same way that the Indians mark their slaves [war captives]', put coals and burning cinders between her toes, whipped her friends and was whipped by them in secret meetings in the woods, fasted, mixed ashes in her food, and slept for three nights on a bed of thorns after hearing the life story of Saint Louis de Gozague.[20] Tekakwitha's self-mortifications eventually took their toll, and she became ill—so ill that Cholenec, making an exception for her, had to bring all his ritual equipment to her lodge to perform the last rites. She died at age 24 on 17 April 1680.

This narrative of Tekakwitha's life needs to be interpreted from two different perspectives. First, there is the issue of Tekakwitha as a Jesuit construction. Why did they think she might be a saint? How did their own culture shape the narrative of Tekakwitha's life story? Second, what was she really doing? Was she forsaking traditional Iroquois beliefs to become Christian or did her actions make sense within an Iroquois cultural framework?

Undeniably, Tekakwitha was to some extent a Jesuit construction.[21] If you were to strip this narrative of its occasional Iroquois element—the longhouse, women in the cornfields, the winter hunt—it could have taken place in fourteenth-century bourgeois Siena. Her life story follows the hackneyed plot line typical of women's hagiographies, especially that of Saint Catherine of Siena, except that Tekakwitha did not live long enough to become an adviser to popes and kings.[22] First, there are the unrelenting relatives who try to force Tekakwitha into marriage, purportedly for her own sake but primarily for the economic advantage of the family as a whole. Then, there is her complete devotion to Christian ritual: persistent prayers, a particular emotional intensity expressed for the Holy Eucharist, and her feelings of desperation and longing when deprived of the ritual experience. And finally, like other women who by the seventeenth century had been recognized as saints or likely saints, Tekakwitha's reputation for holiness was based entirely on her dedication to virginity and her proclivity for abusing her own body. Because Tekakwitha's life story follows an established hagiographical model, it could be that Cholenec and Chauchetière fictionalized their narratives to make her life fit the model. However, it is more likely that they thought she might be a saint because her life fit the model so well.

There were other potential saints among the Indians at Kahnawake. There was, for instance, Catherine Gandeacteua, the founder of the Native village at La Prairie. The Jesuits praised her effusively, but according to the other model typical for women saints. Instead of being a self-mortifying virgin, Gandeacteua, 'like Saint Anne', impoverished herself through her charity to others. She died before the village moved to the Sault, and so her body was buried at La Prairie. When the Native village moved, the Indians and the French colonists at La Prairie vied for who should possess her corpse.[23] The Indians probably planned to rebury Gandeacteua's body near the new village. The French at La Prairie, however, must have thought Gandeacteua had virtues worthy of a saint, for they wanted the body, 'the relics', presumably so they could have access to her intercessory powers with God. It was the custom in Europe to pray for a saint's intercession at the tomb or to the more portable relics (the saint's bones, clothes, dirt from near the tomb, whatever had physically been the saint or been touched by the saint).[24] French colonists were probably suffering from saint-deprivation, for there were as yet no saints' tombs in New France and most of the more easily transported relics were still in Europe. In this unusual colonial struggle, the French won and Gandeacteua's body remained at La Prairie.

There were even more saintly possibilities among Tekakwitha's peers at Kahnawake. She was merely one of many to join a penitential fervour that raged through the village in the late 1670s and early 1680s. According to Chauchetière,

> The first who began made her first attempt about Christmas in The year 1676 [the year before Tekakwitha arrived at Kahnawake], when she divested herself of her clothing, and exposed herself to The air at the foot of a large Cross that stands beside our Cemetery. She did so at a time when the snow was falling, although she was pregnant; and the snow that fell upon her back caused her so much suffering that she nearly died from it—as well as her child, whom the cold chilled in its mother's womb. It was her own idea to do this—to do penance for her sins, she said.[25]

Chauchetière then described how four of her friends, all women, followed her example but invented other, more elaborate forms of penance. Tekakwitha learned about penance from other Indians at Kahnawake and did not initiate the practice.[26]

Moreover, penitential practices seem to have reached their peak after Tekakwitha's death. Chauchetière gave the clearest account of this development in his short history of the Mission at the Sault. After referring to how, in 1680, the 'mission gave to paradise a treasure which had been sent to it two years before, to wit, the blessed soul of Catherine Tegakwita, who died on the 17th of april', Chauchetière recounted the events that transpired later that year:

> The demon [the devil], who saw the glorious success of this mission, used another kind of battery. Transfiguring himself as an angel of light, he urged on the devotion of some persons who wished to imitate Catherine, or to do severe penance for their sins. He drove them even into excess,—in order, no doubt, to render christianity hateful even at the start; or in order to impose upon the girls and women of this mission, whose discretion has never equaled that of Catherine, whom they tried to imitate. There were Savage women who threw themselves under the ice, in the midst of winter. One had her daughter dipped into it, who was only six years old,—for the purpose, she said, of teaching her penance in good season. The mother stood there on account of her past sins; she kept her innocent daughter there on account of her sins to come, which this child would perhaps commit when grown up. Savages, both men and women, covered themselves with blood by disciplinary stripes with iron, with rods, with thorns, with nettles; they fasted rigorously, passing the entire day without eating,—and what the savages eat during half the year is not sufficient to keep a man alive. These fasting women toiled strenuously all day—in summer, working in the fields; in winter, cutting wood. These austerities were almost continual. They mingled ashes in their portion of Sagamité; they put glowing coals between their toes, where the fire burned a hole in the flesh; they went bare-legged to make a long procession in the snows; they all disfigured themselves by cutting off their hair, in order not to be sought in marriage. . . . But the Holy Ghost soon intervened in this matter, enlightening all these person, and regulated their conduct without diminishing their fervor.[27]

For the Jesuits, who knew that one saint was rare and ten or twenty completely implausible, the only way to explain this was to distinguish Tekakwitha's self-mortifications as inspired by God and everyone else's as inspired by the devil.

Despite their attempts to isolate Tekakwitha as especially holy, the Jesuit accounts show that the entire village of Kahnawake—both men and women, but especially the women—were taking Christianity to an extreme. The Jesuits frequently mentioned having to intervene to 'regulate' penitential practices, and as Chauchetière admitted, 'The Savage women sometimes propound to us doubts in spiritual matters, as difficult as those that might be advanced by the most cultured persons in France.'[28] The Christian Indians at Kahnawake were inventive and self-motivated, exhibiting an independence and intensity which frightened the Jesuits because they risked being unable to control it. But still, from the Jesuits' perspective, Tekakwitha and the other Indians at Kahnawake were behaving in ways that were comprehensible as Christian.

However, the historical literature on missionization in New France has shown how Christian Indians created a syncretic religion, a new religion that melded traditional Native beliefs and Christian rituals.[29] The Jesuits assisted the syncretic process in their accommodationist approach to Native cultures. Similarities between Christianity and Iroquois religious beliefs, which the Jesuits rarely admitted to, also made syncretism possible.

The Jesuits' previous missionizing experiences and their scholarly emphasis led them to develop a somewhat sly missionary philosophy. They learned the native language and worldview in order to package Christianity in a conceptual framework that was familiar to the people they were attempting to missionize. In China, the Jesuits had first tried to ease into Chinese society by looking and acting like Buddhist monks. They then switched to the more comfortable role of scholar and began to dress and act like the Chinese literati.[30] In New France, the Jesuits retained their usual style of dress (which is why the Indians called them 'Black Robes') but slid into the only social category that approximated what they were: shamans. And even though the Jesuits saw themselves as superior to the Native 'conjurors', they did act just like shamans. They performed wondrous miracles by foretelling eclipses.[31] They interpreted 'visions', while railing against Native shamans who interpreted 'dreams'.[32] To cure people, they had their own set of mysterious and powerful rituals, such as bleeding, songs, and prayers, and strange ritual implements.[33] Since they feared backsliders and usually only baptized adults who were on the verge of death, they were often perceived as either incompetent shamans or shamans who used their powers for evil purposes.[34] But in any case, the Indians were able to view them as people who had access to special powers.

These special powers were most observable in the new rituals which the Jesuits introduced to the Indians. Tangible manifestations of Christianity proved to be more important than theology in assisting the missionizing effort. Visual images and stories about people, either Bible stories or saints' lives, were the most efficacious missionary tools. Chauchetière was especially proud of his collection of religious paintings and drawings, some of which he drew himself or copied from other works. His depiction of 'the pains of hell' was 'very effective among the savages'. The mission church at Kahnawake also had on display 'paintings of the four ends of man, along with the moral paintings of M. le Nobletz', and eventually, after Tekakwitha's death, a series of paintings by Chauchetière depicting events in her life.[35]

Although the Jesuits shied away from attempting to explain the abstract principles of Christianity, which could not easily be translated into Native languages anyhow, there were conceptual similarities between Iroquois religious beliefs and seventeenth-century Catholicism which also furthered missionization. Christian stories, from Adam and Eve to the birth of Jesus Christ, are similar to the Iroquois origin story, which even has an Immaculate Conception.[36] The Holy Family—the somewhat distant and unimportant Joseph; the powerful and virtuous Virgin Mary; her mother, Saint Anne; and the son, Jesus Christ—was structurally more like the matrilineal Iroquois family than the patriarchal nuclear family of Western culture.[37] And the rosary, a string of beads with spiritual significance, resembled

Iroquois wampum—belts and necklaces made of shell beads, which had spiritual and political meaning.[38] Indeed, many of the actions of Christianized Indians, which the Jesuits proudly recorded and took credit for, conformed to the cultural norms of traditional Iroquois society. Gandeacteua's Christian virtues—her generosity, especially in giving food and clothing to the poor, and her complete disavowal of all her personal possessions when she heard, mistakenly, that her husband had died—were more than virtues among the Iroquois: they were established customs.[39]

In emphasizing the syncretism of Christianity at Kahnawake, however, I do not want to belittle the significance of becoming Christian as people at the time perceived it. Christian Indians did see themselves as different, and non-Christian Indians ascribed a distinct identity to Christian Indians, even if they lived within the same village and spoke the same language. Also, even though the Indians at Kahnawake maintained many of their traditional beliefs and customs, they agreed to conform to some Jesuit demands, such as their prohibition of divorce.[40] For an Iroquois in the seventeenth century, becoming Christian and choosing to live near the Jesuits would have been a difficult decision, for the Iroquois rightly associated Christian missions with the French, who were, except for brief interludes, their enemies. The tensions arising from such a decision reached their peak in the early 1680s, when the Iroquois at Kahnawake reluctantly joined the French in a war against the main body of Iroquois to their south.[41]

Also, despite the conceptual similarities between Iroquois beliefs and Christianity, those who converted to Christianity do seem to have been already marginal within their communities. As Daniel Richter has observed, many of the residents at Kahnawake were former war captives who had been adopted into Iroquois families.[42] This might also explain the prominence of women in the mission accounts of Kahnawake. Since female war captives were more likely than men to be adopted permanently into the tribe, many Iroquois women had a dual ethnic identity. Tekakwitha's marginality came from two directions: her mother and her disfigurement from smallpox. The Mohawks in Tekakwitha's original village thought of her as an Algonquin, suggesting that her mother, although presumably formally adopted as Iroquois, still strongly identified as Algonquin or was strongly identified by others as Algonquin.[43] According to her hagiographers, Tekakwitha was also self-conscious about her weak eyes and her smallpox scars. Unlike other Iroquois women, she always tried to keep her face covered with her blanket. Supposedly, some of her fellow villagers ridiculed her and said, after she died, 'that God had taken her because men did not want her'.[44]

The marginality of Tekakwitha and adopted Iroquois women might explain why they, and not others, chose Christianity, but it does not explain what they saw in Christianity. In Tekakwitha's case, there seem to have been three conceptual similarities between Iroquois beliefs and seventeenth-century Catholicism which make her actions comprehensible from both the Iroquois and Jesuit cultural perspectives. First, the Iroquois Requickening ceremony and the Christian ceremony of baptism, though conducted through different kinds of rituals, achieved the same end of renewal through imitation. Second, the Iroquois and the Jesuits employed voluntary societies as an additional level of social organization beyond the family and the political council. Voluntary societies served as an avenue by which individual women and men could acquire prestige, authority, and kin-like bonds within the larger community. And third, Iroquois and Jesuit beliefs about the body, the soul, and power were similar enough to allow for a syncretic adoption of self-denial and self-mortification as spiritually and physically empowering acts.

Undeniably, the Jesuits favoured men in their daily administration of the mission. If given the choice, the Jesuits would have preferred to have more male converts, especially men of influence, than female converts. The Jesuits also granted men more authority and prestige by giving them roles as assistants in church services and by making them 'dogiques' (Native catechists). However, women turned Christianity to their advantage and incorporated the ritual of baptism, Christian societies, virginity, and penance as means to establishing a firmer place for themselves in a changing Iroquois society.

First, the Christian ritual of baptism resembled an Iroquois Requickening ceremony. In both ceremonies, someone assumed the name and the metaphorical identity of an important person who had died. In both ceremonies, water played a purifying role. The Jesuits sprinkled holy water to mark the baptismal moment, whereas the Iroquois drank 'water of pity' to signify the transition to a new identity. Among the Iroquois, names of important people were passed on within clans. Individuals from later generations assumed these names and were expected to live up to them by imitating the person who had died and by fulfilling the obligations that went along with the name. For instance, when the Jesuit Lafitau arrived as a missionary at Kahnawake in 1712, the Iroquois requickened him in the place of Father Bruyas.[45] Although men and women could be renamed and 'requickened', the ceremony was also held as part of the Condolence ceremony, the raising up of a new chief, and therefore was in its most prestigious manifestation held as a ceremony for men.[46]

The Jesuits introduced the Iroquois to new images of women in their stories of the Virgin Mary and women saints, and then provided the ritual, baptism, which encouraged imitation of these seemingly powerful women. When Tekakwitha was baptized, 'The spirit of Saint Katherine of Sienna and of other saints of this name, was revived in her.'[47] She was at the same time requickened as Saint Catherine of Siena, a woman whom the Jesuits featured prominently in their stories and devotions. Tekakwitha probably was deliberately modelling herself after her namesake. She would have heard the story of Saint Catherine's life many times—the fasting and penitential practices, her refusal to marry and her marriage to Jesus Christ in a vision, and her later role as an adviser to male political leaders. Tekakwitha and the other women at Kahnawake may have sensed the underlying patriarchy of the Jesuit mission, but also heard the Jesuits talk of powerful women, like Saint Catherine of Siena, and were urged to imitate them.

Second, the women at Kahnawake used the model of the Christian society to enhance their collective role as the women of the village. One such Christian association was the Confraternity of the Holy Family, an organization of men and women which the Jesuits established at Kahnawake to bind the most devoted Christians together.[48] Women appear to have been among the most active participants in this organization. Perhaps the Jesuits' use of the Holy Family as the model for this society's devotions inspired its members to assume a matrilineal organization for determining members' relationships, mutual obligations, and decision-making powers.

The Jesuits viewed the Confraternity of the Holy Family as a successful operation but expressed some doubts about the indigenous Christian organizations sprouting at Kahnawake. For example, Tekakwitha and her two friends attempted to form a nunnery. They planned to leave the village and set up a separate community of Christian women on Heron Island, until Father Frémin talked them out of it.[49] Chauchetière described another women's organization in connection with the penitential practices adopted at Kahnawake:

> The use of these [instruments of penance] Daily becomes more general. And, as The men have found that the women use them, they will not Let themselves be outdone, and ask us to permit them to use these every Day; but we will not allow it. The women, to the number of 8 or 10, Began The practice; and The wife of the dogique—that is to say, of him who Leads the Singing and says The prayers—is among the number. She it is who, in her husband's absence, also causes The prayers to be said aloud, and Leads The Singing; and in this capacity she assembles the devout women of whom we have spoken, who call themselves sisters. They tell One another their faults, and deliberate together upon what must be done

> for The relief of the poor in the Village—whose number is so great that there are almost as many poor as there are Savages. The sort of monastery that they maintain here has its rules. They have promised God never to put on their gala-dress. . . . They assist One another in the fields; They meet together to incite one another to virtue; and one of them has been received as a nun in The hospital of monreal.[50]

Chauchetière's account suggests that women deliberately formed these societies as an alternative to the gender-mixed Confraternity of the Holy Family and that the men at Kahnawake viewed women's societies as a challenge to their own authority and status.

However, 'confraternities' were fundamental, well-established components of Iroquois village life. Iroquois women used similar 'confraternities' to organize their work and acknowledge women's achievements.[51] The Iroquois also had healing societies, like the False-Faces, which possessed a specialized knowledge and their own healing rituals.[52] The women at Kahnawake added to this familiar kind of social institution the newly introduced Christian example of the nunnery, of which several existed in New France. In Quebec in 1639, the Ursulines arrived to start a mission school for Indian girls, and the Sisters de la Hospitalière opened a hospital. Later, Montreal also had some hospital sisters.[53] Although the Catholic Church restricted the authority of women's religious orders by making them ultimately subject to a male director, the women at Kahnawake were more likely to be aware of how these women, because of their unusual lifestyle and their healing activities, appeared to be powerful and respected members of French colonial society. As their husbands became the Jesuits' 'dogiques', women may have refashioned their work-oriented organization after the Christian model to reassert a traditional balance of power, which the Jesuits were disrupting by appointing men to positions of power and high status. The women's dedication to penance, and the envy among the men which this inspired, further suggests that both men and women at Kahnawake came to view penance as an empowering ritual.

Iroquois and Jesuit philosophies about the relationship between the body, the soul, and power illuminate why Tekakwitha and the other residents of Kahnawake accepted the Christian ideals of virginity and penance. In Catholic and Iroquois religious traditions, there was an ambivalence about the connection between the body and the soul. Both belief systems characterized the soul as a separate entity from the body, but elaborate funerary rites and the homage paid to soulless corpses show that they were reluctant to disavow all connections between the soul and the body. In Catholic theology, the soul left the body upon death and, in the case of saints and other holy people, resided in heaven. The Iroquois believed the soul left the body at death and lived an afterlife that would be like life on earth, but better.[54] The Iroquois also believed that the soul left living bodies while they were asleep. Dreamers made trips to this other world and brought back important messages needing interpretation. Shamans' skills included diagnosing these dreams so that they could be acted upon for the good of the individual and the community.[55] Although Iroquois dream interpretation was from the Jesuit point of view one of the most despicable and pagan aspects of Iroquois culture, in the Catholic tradition, holy people also bridged these two worlds. In their lifetime, they might have visions which connected them to the Virgin Mary or Jesus Christ, and after their death, they became the intercessors for others.

Saints functioned like guardian spirits, which in Iroquois culture were not people who had died but instead were animals or some other being that was part of the natural world.[56] In Iroquois tradition, a token (which might be a feather, a pebble, or a piece of oddly shaped wood) was the physical key to the spiritual world, just as Catholics prayed to the saint's physical remains, to a relic, or at the tomb to reach guardian angels and saints.[57] Since the Iroquois believed everything in nature had a soul (unlike Christians, who believed only people did), their range of possible guardian spirits was broader.

However, the idea of appealing to a guardian spirit for miraculous cures, for success in hunting and warfare, for love and happiness, or for special powers was part of both religions. Among the Iroquois, everyone and everything had some power, or 'orenda', but some had more than others.[58] This power could be called upon by appeals to guardian spirits, and could be used for either good or bad. The Jesuits believed that only a few were graced with divine power. And even though they had earthly authority as administrators of Christianity, few Jesuits were also graced with divine authority, as martyrs or as people who exhibited such extreme devotion to Christian ideals that they had to be saints.

Within the Christian tradition, it was difficult for women to acquire authority on earth, but mystical experiences and Christian virtue carried to extremes produced saints. Self-mortification, virginity, and especially fasting appear in most hagiographies but especially dominate in the stories of women saints' lives. Refuting other scholars' claims that bodily abuse was an expression of women's hatred of their bodies, Rudolph Bell in Holy Anorexia and Caroline Walker Bynum in Holy Feast and Holy Famine argued that women seeking a sense of identity and self-assertion tried to control their world through the only means available, by controlling their own bodies and by controlling the symbols of women's domestic authority, such as food distribution. By fasting, making a vow of chastity, and engaging in penitential self-abuse, Catherine of Siena and other women saints revealed that they were among the select few graced with divine authority. As in the case of Catherine of Siena, a woman saint's divine authority could bring her some earthly authority as well, authority over her own life as well as over the lives of others. Saint Catherine of Siena's marriage to Jesus Christ in a vision partly explained why she could not marry on earth and also gave her the authority to tell kings and popes what to do.

In Iroquois society, one could similarly acquire power by controlling one's own body through fasting and sexual abstinence. Although lifelong celibacy struck the Iroquois as odd, virginity and sexual abstinence were conceived of as sources of power.[59] Virgins had certain ceremonial roles, and Iroquois legends told of there having once been a society of virgins.[60] The Iroquois viewed sexual abstinence as an avenue to physical and spiritual strength and as essential to men's preparations for war and the hunt. Fasting and tests of physical endurance also could be used as a means to acquire power. The Iroquois coming-of-age ritual for young men and women was a vision quest.[61] They went into the woods by themselves, fasted, and hoped to receive a vision or token from a guardian spirit. Those with especially powerful visions might become shamans (professional healers and visionaries).[62] Since some Indian residents at Kahnawake accused Tekakwitha of being a 'sorceress', apparently the same acts that inspired the Jesuits to think of her as holy also gave her access to 'orenda'.[63]

Bell and Bynum revealed how virginity and fasting had a special meaning for women saints in medieval Europe. In contrast, among the Iroquois, virginity and fasting seem to have been equally available to men and women as sources of individual empowerment. Still, Bell's and Bynum's analyses of the relationship between food and control can shed light on why the Iroquois had a more democratic understanding of who could acquire 'orenda' and how. Although Iroquois women controlled the distribution of food, both men and women made important complementary contributions to food production. Women grew corn, and men hunted meat. Moreover, both men and women equally shared in their fear of starvation during winter. Iroquois rituals—many of which involved fasting, feasting, or cannibalism—all show an obsession with food, which may have been a cultural expression of daily anxieties about an uncertain supply of food in the future.

Virginity and fasting resonated with Iroquois traditions. Penance was an entirely new ritual, but one that paralleled Iroquois ritual torture of war captives. The Iroquois adopted all war captives into the place of deceased clan members, and clans then chose whether the adoptee would live or die in the spirit of their namesake. Those consigned to die in the place of a mourned relative were put through a lengthy and painful series of tortures, after which parts of their bodies might be eaten. If the captive had died an especially brave death, he (usually it was a he) was more likely to be eaten because his body parts were seen as possessing that strength and courage. Through ritual torture, war captives became the repositories for violent emotions; by directing anxiety, stress, and grief for dead relatives outward, the Iroquois kept peace among themselves.[64]

Although the Jesuits condemned Iroquois torture, they recognized awkward similarities between Iroquois cannibalism and the Eucharist. The Eucharist is a metaphoric ritual in which participants eat the body of Christ and drink his blood, a reference to the theological notion that Christ sacrificed himself so that others might live. Fearing that the Iroquois might think they condoned cannibalism, the Jesuits translated the Eucharist to mean a feast and did not tell the Iroquois about its sacrificial connotations.[65] If it had not been so uncomfortably reminiscent of Iroquois ritual cannibalism, the Eucharist might have been a useful missionizing tool with which the Jesuits could have offered the Iroquois a ritual to replace the torture of war captives.

However, David Blanchard has argued that the Indians at Kahnawake replaced the ritual torture of war captives with ritual self-torture. They called their penitential practices 'hotouongannandi', which Chauchetière translated to mean 'public penance'.[66] According to Blanchard, a better translation of the term would be 'they are making magic', suggesting that the Iroquois saw penitential practices as a ritual source of power. Blanchard emphasizes the importance of this ritual in helping the Iroquois, as in their dreams, to leave the world on earth and visit 'the sky world'.[67] It is also important to emphasize, however, that they used visits to 'the sky world' to control and improve life on earth.

The Indians at Kahnawake probably saw penance as a powerful healing and prophylactic ritual. Since the penitential practices at Kahnawake began at about the same time as a 1678 smallpox epidemic, which ebbed quickly and caused little damage, penitents at Kahnawake may even have viewed penance as an especially effective ritual to counter new diseases like smallpox.[68] The rise of penitential practices in Europe, evident in such movements as the Flagellants, which emerged after the Bubonic Plague, suggests that Christians in fourteenth-century Europe also thought that self-induced abuse of the body was a means to control the uncontrollable.[69] Also, the Iroquois at Kahnawake may have viewed penance as a prophylactic ritual to prevent torture and death at the hands of one's enemies. The Jesuits deliberately drew analogies between Christian hell and the torture of war captives practised by northeastern Indians, and promised that Christian devotion would save one from an eternity in hell.[70]

In conclusion, the Iroquois who adopted Christianity did so for reasons that made sense within an Iroquois cultural framework. Certain Christian rituals fit easily into traditional Iroquois beliefs, while the new ritual practices, like penance, offered a special power lacking in traditional Iroquois rituals. Whereas the Jesuits emphasized the importance of Christian ritual in determining one's place in the afterlife, Tekakwitha and other Christian Iroquois had new and pressing needs for empowering rituals to control the increasingly uncertain, earthly present. Smallpox, increased warfare, alcohol, and the economic and political assaults on traditional gender roles did create a growing sense of crisis in Iroquois communities. To deal with that crisis and control their changing world, many Iroquois women and men turned to Christianity. However, they did not become Christian in the way the Jesuits intended; instead, they transformed Christianity into an Iroquois religion.

During one particular moment of crisis, at Kahnawake in the 1670s and 1680s, Iroquois women and men struggled to reshape the Jesuits' preaching into something meaningful to them. Part of the struggle had to do with the patriarchal structure of Christianity. The Jesuits supported male authority in the village by promoting men as administers of Christianity and church activities. Women responded by using Christian symbols to assert their authority and identity within the community. Through a syncretic transformation of the ritual of baptism, the Christian society, virginity, and self-mortification, Tekakwitha appeared holy and Christian to the Jesuits while pursuing status and a firmer sense of her own identity within Iroquois society. The Jesuits tried to implement patriarchy at their missions, but they also brought the symbols, imagery, and rituals women needed to subvert patriarchy.

Notes

The author thanks Deborah Sommer and Louis Dupont for their help with this article.

1. Claude Chauchetière, 'Annual Narrative of the Mission of the Sault, From its Foundation Until the Year 1686', in *The Jesuit Relations and Allied Documents: Travels and Explorations of the Jesuit Missionaries in New France, 1610–1791 (JR)*, Reuben Gold Thwaites, ed. (NY: Pageant, 1959), 63, 229; Pierre Cholenec more elaborately tells how Tekakwitha appeared to Chauchetière in a vision and prophesied the destruction of the church in 'The Life of Katharine Tegakoüita, First Iroquois Virgin' (1696), Document X, in *The Positio of the Historical Section of the Sacred Congregation of Rites on the Introduction of the Cause for Beatification and Canonization and on the Virtues of the Servant of God Katharine Tekakwitha, the Lily of the Mohawks*, Robert E. Holland, ed. (NY: Fordham University Press, 1940), 312.
2. Peter Rémy to Father Cholenec, 12 March 1696, Document IX, in *The Positio*, 227.
3. Colombière is quoted in 'Letter from Father Cholenec, Missionary of the Society of Jesus, to Father Augustin Le Blanc of the Same Society, Procurator of Missions in Canada', in *The Early Jesuit Missions in North America: Compiled and Translated From the Letters of the French Jesuits, with Notes*, William Ingraham Kip, ed. (Albany: Joel Munsell, 1873), 115.
4. '"Lily of the Mohawks"', *Newsweek* 12 (1 August 1938), 27–8; 'The Long Road To Sainthood', *Time* 116 (7 July 1980), 42–3. At about the time of Tekakwitha's beatification, the Catholic Church undertook a major reform of the saint-making process and reduced the number of miracles required for beatification and canonization. Under the old rules, Tekakwitha needed two documented miracles to be beatified or declared 'blessed'. Under the new rules, she only needed one. However, even though Tekakwitha is credited with many miracles, not one was able to meet the documentation standards required by the Catholic Church. Pope John Paul II waived this requirement for her, perhaps to give American Indians a saint of their own. To be canonized and thereby declared a 'saint', she would need two miracles according to the new rules, but since the documentation standards have already been waived for her, it is not clear whether there are any remaining obstacles to her canonization. Kenneth L. Woodward, *Making Saints: How the Catholic Church Determines Who Becomes a Saint, Who Doesn't, and Why* (NY: Simon and Schuster, 1990), 99, 117–88, 208, 217.
5. James Axtell, *The Invasion Within: The Contest of Cultures in Colonial North America* (NY: Oxford University Press, 1985), 23–127; Cornelius J. Jaenen, *Friend and Foe: Aspects of French–Amerindian Cultural Contact in the Sixteenth and Seventeenth Centuries* (NY: Columbia University Press, 1976); Daniel K. Richter, *The Ordeal of the Longhouse: The Peoples of the Iroquois League in the Era of European Colonization* (Chapel Hill: University of North Carolina Press, 1992), 105–32.
6. Eleanor Burke Leacock, 'Montagnais Women and the Jesuit Program for Colonization', *Myths of Male Dominance: Collected Articles on Women Cross-Culturally* (NY: Monthly Review Press, 1981), 43–62; Karen Anderson, *Chain Her By One Foot: The Subjugation of Women in Seventeenth-Century New France* (NY: Routledge, 1991); Carol Devens, *Countering Colonization: Native American Women and Great Lakes Missions, 1630–1900* (Berkeley: University of California Press, 1992), 7–30. An exception is Natalie Zemon Davis' article 'Iroquois Women, European Women', which argues that Christianity may have given Indian women in New France access to a public voice denied them in traditional Iroquois oratory. This article is in *Women, 'Race', and Writing in the Early Modern Period*, Margo Hendricks and Patricia Parker, eds. (NY: Routledge, 1994), 243–58, 350–61.
7. W.G. Spittal, *Iroquois Women: An Anthology* (Ohsweken, Ontario: Iroqrafts, 1990).
8. *JR* 18 (1640), 105–7; Leacock, 52; Anderson, 219; Devens, 7.
9. W.J. Eccles, *France in America* (NY: Harper and Row, 1972); Cornelius J. Jaenen, *The Role of the Church in New France* (Toronto: McGraw-Hill Ryerson, 1976); J.H. Kennedy, *Jesuit and Savage in New France* (New Haven: Yale University Press, 1950).
10. Chauchetière, *JR* 63 (1686), 141–245; *JR* 61 (1679),

239–41; Henri Béchard, *The Original Caughnawaga Indians* (Montreal: International Publishers, 1976); E.J. Devine, *Historic Caughnawaga* (Montreal: Messenger Press, 1922); Gretchen Lynn Green, 'A New People in an Age of War: The Kahnawake Iroquois, 1667–1760' (Ph.D. diss., College of William and Mary, 1991).

11. The historical documents on Tekakwitha are conveniently available in *The Positio*, the compendium of materials used by the Vatican to determine whether she was worthy of Veneration. Cholenec, who headed the mission at Caughnawaga during Tekakwitha's stay there, wrote at least four versions of her life, which are usually but not entirely consistent. The 1696 'Life' (Document X in *The Positio*) is the most elaborate in describing Tekakwitha's virtues, trials, and posthumous miracles. Document XII, which also appears in Kip, is Cholenec's 1715 letter to Augustin Le Blanc and is a more straightforward account. Chauchetière's 'The Life of the Good Katharine Tegakoüita, Now Known as the Holy Savage', probably first drafted in 1685 and revised or amended in 1695, is Document VIII in *The Positio*. Cholenec, Chauchetière, and Frémin (who apparently chose not to write a life of Tekakwitha) were the Jesuits stationed at Kahnawake during the time Tekakwitha lived there.
12. Chauchetière, *The Positio*, 121.
13. Cholenec, in Kip, 83.
14. Chauchetière, *The Positio*, 125.
15. Catharine, Katharine, Katherine, Catherine, Kateri ('gadeli' as it is pronounced among the Mohawks), and Katerei all appear in the records; Kateri seems to be the more accepted contemporary term.
16. Cholenec, in Kip, 95.
17. Cholenec, in Kip, 105.
18. Cholenec, in Kip, 108.
19. Chauchetière, *The Positio*, 175.
20. Cholenec, in Kip, 111; Cholenec, *The Positio*, 295.
21. K.I. Koppedrayer, 'The Making of the First Iroquois Virgin: Early Jesuit Biographies of the Blessed Kateri Tekakwitha', *Ethnohistory* 40 (1993): 277–306.
22. Rudolph M. Bell, *Holy Anorexia* (Chicago: University of Chicago Press, 1985); Caroline Walker Bynum, *Holy Feast and Holy Fast: The Religious Significance of Food to Medieval Women* (Berkeley: University of California Press, 1987); Donald Weinstein and Rudolph M. Bell, *Saints and Society: The Two Worlds of Western Christendom, 1000–1700* (Chicago: University of Chicago Press, 1982).
23. Chauchetière, *The Positio*, 161, 165.
24. Peter Brown, *The Cult of the Saints: Its Rise and Function in Latin Christianity* (Chicago: University of Chicago Press, 1981).
25. Chauchetière, *JR* 62 (1682), 175.
26. Cholenec, in Kip, 98–9.
27. Chauchetière, *JR* 63 (1686), 215–19; also see Cholenec, in Kip, 106–8.
28. Chauchetière, *JR* 62 (1682), 187.
29. See Axtell; Jaenen, *Friend and Foe*; David Blanchard, '. . . To the Other Side of the Sky: Catholicism at Kahnawake, 1667–1700', *Anthropologica* XXIV (1982), 77–102. Also see Henry Warner Bowden's discussion of the Hurons and the Jesuits in *American Indians and Christian Missions: Studies in Cultural Conflict* (Chicago: University of Chicago Press, 1981), 59–95; James P. Ronda and James Axtell, *Indian Missions: A Critical Bibliography* (Bloomington: Indiana University Press, 1978).
30. Jacques Gernet, *China and the Christian Impact: A Conflict of Cultures* (NY: Cambridge University Press, 1985); Charles E. Ronan and Bonnie B.C. Oh, *East Meets West: The Jesuits in China, 1582–1773* (Chicago: Loyola University Press, 1988).
31. *JR* 58 (1673–74), 181–3; *JR* 62 (1683), 199.
32. *JR* 60 (1675), 61–3.
33. Le Jeune's 1634 *Relation* of his mission among the Montagnais, in *JR* 7, shows in great detail how Jesuits deliberately competed with shamans to prove their superior access to supernatural authority.
34. *JR* 6 (1634), 139; *JR* 58 (1673–74), 191, 219–21; *JR* 61 (1679), 229.
35. Chauchetière, *The Positio*, 115–16, 146. See also *JR* 5 (1633), 257–9. François-Marc Gagnon, *La Conversion Par L'Image: Un Aspect de la Mission des Jésuites Auprès des Indiéns du Canada au XVIIe Siècle* (Montréal: Les Éditions Bellarmin, 1975).
36. Hazel W. Hertzberg, *The Great Tree and the Longhouse: The Culture of the Iroquois* (NY: Macmillan, 1966); J.N.B. Hewitt, 'Iroquoian Crosmology', Part Two, *Annual Report*, Bureau of American Ethnology, 1925–1926 (Washington, DC: 1928), 465.
37. For example, see Pamela Sheingorn, 'The Holy Kinship: The Ascendency of Matriliny in Sacred Genealogy of the Fifteenth Century', *Thought* 64 (1989), 268–86. Also, for a fascinating discussion of how the Jesuits responded to Iroquoian matrilineality and their own need for a patriarchal authority structure to justify their role as 'fathers', see John Steckley, 'The Warrior and the Lineage: Jesuit Use of Iroquoian Images to Communicate Christianity', *Ethnohistory* 39 (1992), 478–509.
38. *JR* 58 (1673–74), 185–9; Blanchard's '. . . To the Other Side of the Sky' discusses the rosary-wampum syncretism at length.
39. Chauchetière, *The Positio*, 162.
40. *JR* 58 (1672–73), 77.
41. Daniel K. Richter, 'Iroquois versus Iroquois: Jesuit

Missions and Christianity in Village Politics, 1642–1686', *Ethnohistory* 32 (1985), 1–16.
42. Richter, *The Ordeal of the Longhouse*, 124–8.
43. Cholenec, in Kip, 87.
44. Chauchetière, *The Positio*, 123.
45. Lafitau, Volume II, 240; Volume I, xxxi; J.N.B. Hewitt, 'The Requickening Address of the Condolence Council', William N. Fenton, ed., *Journal of the Washington Academy of Sciences* 34 (1944), 65–85.
46. Lafitau, Volume I, 71; *JR* 60 (1675), 37.
47. Chauchetière, *The Positio*, 169, 137.
48. *JR* 58 (1672–73), 77; Cholenec, *JR* 60 (1677), 281.
49. Chauchetière, *The Positio*, 176.
50. Chauchetière, *JR* (1681–83), 179. See also Chauchetière, *JR* 63 (1686), 203–5.
51. Arthur C. Parker, 'Secret Medicine Societies of the Seneca', *American Anthropologist*, n.s., vol. 11 (1909), 161–85; Lafitau, Volume II, 54–5.
52. William N. Fenton, *The False Faces of the Iroquois* (Norman: University of Oklahoma Press, 1987).
53. Joyce Marshall, ed., *Word From New France: The Selected Letters of Marie De L'Incarnation* (Toronto: Oxford University Press, 1967).
54. Lafitau, Volume II, 230–1, 237–8; for a comparison of Huron (Iroquoian) and Christian conceptions of the soul, see *JR* 7 (1635), 293; *JR* 10 (1636), 287. Also see John Steckley's linguistic analysis of these concepts in Huron in 'Brébeuf's Presentation of Catholicism in the Huron Language: A Descriptive Overview', *Revue de l'Université d'Ottawa / University of Ottawa Quarterly* 48 (1978), 93–115. Much of my perspective on Christian beliefs about the soul and body is based on Caroline Walker Bynum's work, especially the articles collected in *Fragmentation and Redemption: Essays on Gender and the Human Body in Medieval Religion* (NY: Zone Books, 1991). Although her discussion refers to medieval Europe, she could just as easily have been describing the beliefs of seventeenth-century Jesuits, as revealed by their self-reflexive remarks on Iroquois differences in the Jesuit Relations.
55. Lafitau, Volume I, 231–4; *JR* 54 (1669–70), 65–73; Anthony F.C. Wallace, 'Dreams and the Wishes of the Soul: A Type of Psychoanalytic Theory among the Seventeenth Century Iroquois', *American Anthropologist* 60 (1958), 234–48.
56. Lafitau, Volume I, 230.
57. Lafitau, Volume I, 236, 243; 'Narrative of a Journey into the Mohawk and Oneida Country, 1634–1635', in *Narratives of New Netherland, 1609–1664*, J. Franklin Jameson, ed. (NY: Charles Scribner's Sons, 1909), 137–62.
58. J.N.B. Hewitt, 'Orenda and a Definition of Religion', American Anthropologist, n.s., 4 (1902), 33–46; Hope L. Isaacs, 'Orenda and the Concept of Power among the Tonawanda Senecas', in *The Anthropology of Power: Ethnographic Studies from Asia, Oceania, and the New World*, Raymond D. Fogelson and Richard N. Adams, eds. (NY: Academic Press, 1977), 167–84.
59. Lafitau, Volume I, 218. Also see Marina Warner, *Alone of All Her Sex: The Myth and Cult of the Virgin Mary* (NY: Alfred A. Knopf, 1976), 48–9, for a discussion of how the Christian ideal of virginity has roots in classical beliefs about virginity as a magic source of power.
60. Lafitau, Volume I, 129–30.
61. Lafitau, Volume I, 217.
62. Lafitau, Volume I, 230–40.
63. Chauchetière, *The Positio*, 208.
64. Lafitau, Volume II, 148–72; *JR* 54 (1669–70), 25–35; Daniel K. Richter, 'War and Culture: The Iroquois Experience', *William and Mary Quarterly* 40 (1983), 528–59; Thomas S. Abler and Michael H. Logan, 'The Florescence and Demise of Iroquoian Cannibalism: Human Sacrifice and Malinowski's Hypothesis', *Man in the Northeast* 35 (1988), 1–26.
65. See Jaenen, *Friend and Foe*, 145; Steckley, 'Brébeuf's Presentation of Catholicism in the Huron Language', 113.
66. Chauchetière, *JR* 64 (1695), 125.
67. Blanchard, 97.
68. Chauchetière, *JR* 63 (1686), 205.
69. Philip Ziegler, *The Black Death* (NY: John Day Company, 1969), 86–98; also see Andrew E. Barnes, 'Religious Anxiety and Devotional Change in the Sixteenth Century French Penitential Confraternities', *Sixteenth Century Journal* 19 (1988), 389–406, which is about a resurgence of penance during the crisis of the Protestant Reformation and simultaneous with Catholic-Huguenot violence.
70. See Axtell's discussion of the Jesuits' conflating hell and torture as a way to attract converts, in *The Invasion Within*, 114–15; Steckley, in 'The Warrior and the Lineage', shows how the Jesuits described hell as worse than the ritual torture practised by northeastern tribes.

Gender, Family, and Mutual Assistance in New France: Widows, Widowers, and Orphans in Eighteenth-Century Quebec

Josette Brun

EDITORS' INTRODUCTION

The nature of women's status and authority in seventeenth- and eighteenth-century New France was one of the first questions about women and the Canadian past to generate sustained and serious scholarly attention. This reflected, in part, the significant spot held by women like Madeleine de Verchères—claimed to have saved her family from Iroquois attack in 1692, at the young age of fourteen—in modern Québécois popular culture. In a recent study, Colin Coates has shown how this 'warrior woman of New France' was largely forgotten after her death in 1747. But in the late nineteenth-century de Verchères was rediscovered and recuperated not only as a historical figure, but also as a nationalist icon and a symbol of the 'golden age' of French Canada before England's victory at the Plains of Abraham.[1]

Historians have also found the women of New France inspiring and intriguing, if for different reasons. In 1981, Jan Noel made a provocative argument that women in the French territories of northern North America had unusual latitude for power, self-expression, and authority. They were, to borrow directly from her title, 'les femmes favorisées'.[2] Noel explained this unusual situation as a result of the flexibility of *ancien régime* practice, if not thinking, on sex roles, the logic of colonial demography, the prevailing practices of the Catholic church, and the pressure of economic necessity. Women of New France were favoured because the prevailing social conditions and culture of their time and place made them so. Noel's relatively short article did three things that women's history does best: encouraged us to think in new ways about the past, and reminded us of the enormous variations that have characterized women's roles over time and space, and generated controversy. 'Les femmes favorisées' did not find unanimous favour with feminist historians writing in French. Most notably Micheline Dumont criticized Noel for drawing attention to exceptional examples of female authority and misconstruing the conditions of the vast majority of women's lives in New France.[3]

Josette Brun's article provides a new and more nuanced perspective on the question of female authority and independence in New France. It is based on painstaking research in the notarial archives that provide such an unusually vivid window into how people were born, married, and died in colonial North America. Brun uses these records to show how people in eighteenth-century Quebec City coped with the death of a spouse—a common enough occurrence in a pre-industrial society where disease, mishap, and accident took the lives of young people with distressing regularity. While acknowledging that a minority of women used widowhood as a springboard to new careers, she finds that most women continued to live within the confines of the dominant expectations of women's roles. Her findings are echoed by

Molly G. Richter's study of widows in eighteenth-century Montreal, that stresses that widows had few options to support themselves and their families and were compelled by circumstances to quickly remarry.[4] Studies of single mothers and marital separations tell us that the oppressive mix of pity, shame, and censure dealt out to women who lived outside the boundaries of expected female norms elsewhere were also present in New France.[5] In different ways, the articles by Maureen Elgersman Lee and Sylvia Van Kirk in this volume remind us that racialized structures of inequality also ensured that Aboriginal and enslaved women, whether Black or Native, were offered few liberties in New France.

Seen from this vantage point, the shrewd entrepreneurs studied by Kathryn Young,[6] the powerful religious women like Ursuline nun Marie de L'Incarnation, and celebrated saints like Kateri Takakwitha were exceptions rather than the rule. Yet however unusual, the existence of these powerful female figures in New France continues to remind us how different social, legal, political, and religious conditions can open up spaces for different visions of womanhood and occasional opportunities for genuine autonomy and authority, however fleeting and unusual they may be.

Notes

1. Colin M. Coates and Cecilia Morgan, *Heroines and History: Representations of Madeleine de Verchères and Laura Secord* (Toronto: University of Toronto Press, 2002).
2. Jan Noel, 'New France: Les femmes favorisees', *Atlantis* 6.2 (Spring 1981): 80–98.
3. Micheline Dumont, 'Les femmes de la Nouvelle-France étaient-elles favorisées', *Atlantis* 8.1 (1982): 118–24.
4. Molly G. Ritcher, 'Widowhood in New France: Consequences and Coping Strategies', *French Colonial History* 4 (2003): 49–61.
5. See Marie-Aimée Cliché, 'Unwed Mothers, Families, and Society during the French Regime', *Social History/ Histoire sociale* 21.4 (May 1988): 39–69 and Sylvie Savoie, 'Women's Marital Difficulties: Requests of Separation in New France', *History of the Family* 3: 4 (1998): 473–85.
6. Kathryn A. Young, '". . . sauf les perils et fortunes de la mer": Merchant Women in New France and the French Transatlantic Trade, 1713–46', *Canadian Historical Review* 77 (1996): 388–407.

Questions for Critical Reading

1. Why might English Canadian and French Canadian scholars have different views of women's position in New France?
2. Did the pre-industrial family offer women more opportunities and latitude than the post-industrial family? Why?
3. In contemporary society we generally associate widowhood with old age. How were things different in the eighteenth-century?
4. Is it important to women generally if a few are visibly successful? Why?

New France, like other Western pre-industrial societies, was characterized by high mortality rates in the adult population. Death occasioned frequent ruptures of the marital community, thus causing serious fissures in the structure and organization of the family, which was founded upon the union of the couple, the husband's authority within the marriage, and the gendered division of labour.[1] In such circumstances, widows and widowers found themselves outside the framework of the 'normal' family and had to face an uncertain social and economic situation created by the loss of their spouse. A number of questions arise from an examination of these contexts of rupture[2] especially surrounding the relationship maintained by the surviving parent with his or her family. What type of mutual assistance was established between widowed persons and their children as a function of the sex and age of each during widowhood or widowerhood? What family strategies or sources of assistance were most often resorted to? What role does 'gender'[3]—that is, the way in which male and female roles were conceptualized—play in this process?

This type of historical discussion, anchored in demographic evidence and notarial documents,[4] is necessary in order to shed new light on family dynamics[5] and social relations between the sexes in French colonial society in North America. Like a number of recent studies that have questioned an older and still influential interpretation, which presents the colonial period as a golden age of women's status and condition,[6] this essay aims to offer a more nuanced assessment of the experience of women in New France.

The first half of the eighteenth century was a period of relative peace in New France. Even though death rates in the colony compared favourably with those prevailing in the home country,[7] death frequently struck the adult population in the town of Quebec. Consequently, in this important colonial capital, which had been established at the beginning of the seventeenth century in the St Lawrence valley, widows and widowers formed a numerous social group.[8] Between 1710 and 1744, 192 women and 169 men[9] experienced the end of their first marriage through the death of their spouse, and these individuals swelled the ranks of those who were already widows or widowers.[10] They thus constituted a highly visible group within a town comprising only a few thousand people. Of these, 137 widows and 147 widowers were permanent residents of Quebec, most having spent the greater part of their married life in the town.[11] These people were predominantly of artisanal families—especially in the building trades—and merchant families, a circumstance that was not surprising in a seaport where most people depended upon trades and commercial activities (see Table 1.1). At the upper and lower ends of the scale, families of officers and unskilled labourers were far less numerous, the latter clearly under-represented.[12]

The death of a husband or wife marked a real rupture in family organization in New France, as male authority within the marriage and the gendered division of labour were firmly entrenched among couples of all occupational groups. Husbands, as legally designated heads of the conjugal household, managed both its property and its economic affairs and rarely delegated these powers to their wives, who were deemed minors under the law.[13] However, the participation of women sometimes took on a greater importance, particularly in merchant families and often in daily experience.[14] Domestic tasks remained, in all social settings, an exclusively female domain. In losing her husband, a woman found herself outside the 'normal' framework of womanhood—marriage and subordination to male authority—and she received full legal capacity and even the status of head of the family. On the other hand, the loss of a wife did not affect a man's social status. Moreover, the death of one partner created a disequilibrium in the family economy that affected both sexes but placed them in very different situations: the loss of a husband deprived the family of its principal source of income, while the death of a wife meant that it lost its purveyor of domestic services, as well as an indispensable helpmate.[15]

In addition to encountering different problems, widows and widowers could not expect to resolve these in the same way—that is, to simply take upon themselves the duties attributed to the other sex. Women, whether married or not, were expected to undertake certain 'male' activities without aspiring to the same status enjoyed by men in colonial society. When widowed, they acquired new rights over the management of family property and work which, in principle, allowed them to support both themselves and their children without becoming a burden upon society.[16] Although widowers remained the economic mainstays of their family, they found themselves in

Table 1.1: Number of Persons who Became Widows or Widowers at Quebec in the Eighteenth Century, According to the Sex and Occupational Category of the Surviving Spouse

	Widows		Widowers	
Occupational category	*No.*	*Percentage*	*No.*	*Percentage*
ARTISAN	54	39.4	77	52.4
Building trade	24	17.5	48	32.7
Food	15	10.9	15	10.2
Clothing/leather	11	8.0	11	7.5
Luxury	4	2.9	—	—
Other	0	0.0	3	2.0
MERCHANT	35	25.6	28	19.0
UNSKILLED	18	13.1	5	3.4
OFFICER	14	10.2	16	10.9
Civil	7	5.1	10	6.8
Military	7	5.1	6	4.1
OHER NOTABLE	4	2.9	3	2.0
UNKNOWN	12	8.8	18	12.2
Total	**137**	**100**	**147**	**100**

an unprecedented situation because they had to devote themselves to their occupation, and it would work to their disadvantage if they assumed 'female' tasks, since these were accorded an inferior status by society.

Men as well as women would have been able to rely upon the assistance of their families in the event of need. Mutual assistance and economic support, even among members of the extended family, were effectively imposed by the state. Equally, the church clearly established the responsibility incumbent upon children to care for their parents.

As colonial society became more stable during the course of the eighteenth century, and as 'social practices began to correspond more exactly with the policy of sensitization pursued by civil and religious authorities which exhorted children to come to the aid of their parents',[17] widows and widowers came to rely more and more upon the assistance of their families. Indeed, the colonial government did not hesitate to intervene in the 'rare instances' where children failed to do their duty and left their parents indigent, a situation that occurred primarily when they were geographically separated from them. However, reality was usually more complex because in some cases, widows and widowers did not have children, and for a single parent, one's progeny could be a source of worry as well as of support. The problems encountered by men and women varied according to age and sex of children, factors that also determined the types of support upon which men and women could in theory rely.[18] The vast majority of widows and widowers—four out of five—had at least one child living at the time of their spouse's death;[19] while the others did not have to worry about the fate of their progeny, they also did not have access to the help that children could give at this critical juncture. On average, widows and widowers had between three and four children, with ten offspring as the upper limit.

Widows and widowers with young children were far more numerous than those with adult sons and daughters, who were more capable of supporting them. The majority had children under twelve, requiring at least a modicum of care and attention,[20] but widowers (67 per cent) were faced with this responsibility more frequently than widows (52 per cent), and it was one that hitherto had not fallen within the scope of their competence. Nearly half the widowers (48 per cent) had to provide an attentive presence for children who had not yet attained the age of reason (age seven); most of these (40 per cent) had urgently to avail themselves of the assistance of a wet nurse,[21] a fact that illustrates the sad fact of maternal mortality. About one in four widows was faced with the task of supervising children at each age level.

Raising children of the opposite sex presented a challenge for a minority of widows and widowers, but twice as frequently for men as for women. Between the ages of twelve and twenty, children were regarded as young adults undergoing apprenticeship and preparation for their life's duties under the supervision of the parent of their sex.[22] One in five widowers (21 per cent) had at least one girl who had to be taught the role of mother and housekeeper, but the rigidity of male roles did not permit him to undertake this task, for which he himself had no training. Thirteen per cent of widows benefited from a certain level of experience, new rights, and a more open attitude of the community that allowed them, at least in principle, to watch over the training of their sons. Twice as many widows as widowers could call upon adult children—those aged twenty or over—to assist them,[23] especially to carry out tasks that would normally have devolved upon their dead spouse. One in four widows (27 per cent) was eventually supported by a son, and one in three (35 per cent) by a son or son-in-law, while fewer than one widow in five could call upon an adult daughter (18 per cent) or daughter-in-law (20 per cent). These widows, far more than their widowed male counterparts (22 per cent versus 8 per cent), who were economically better situated to establish their children in life, now had the added burden of finding eligible partners and providing dowries for their daughters once they reached marriageable age.[24]

How did widows adapt to their new status as head of the family and to the economic and occupational responsibilities that went with it? How did widowers resolve the impasse they faced in taking care of household tasks, the care of young children, and the training of future mothers and homemakers? The preferred method, especially for men of all ages (see Table 1.2) was remarriage in order to simply replace the deceased spouse, a course taken by 68 per cent of all widowers. However, women evinced a far less frequent tendency towards remarriage (42 per cent), particularly after age forty, as age then became a handicap to finding a spouse.[25] Significantly, eight out of ten widows in their twenties remarried, a rate comparable to widowers under fifty. Women tended to take a new husband fairly frequently during their thirties (59 per cent), but the proportion declined during their forties (42 per cent), and widows almost never remarried after age fifty.[26] On the other hand, nearly one in four widowers fifty or older was able to contract a second marriage. If women's behaviour was fairly consistent across occupational groups,[27] this variable tended to have a greater effect on male strategies. Remarriage was far less frequent among merchants (50 per cent) than among artisans (75 per cent) and was highest among widowers employed in the building trades (79 per cent), a category that in the town of Quebec included over two-thirds of tradesmen. Because men engaged in commercial activities were usually more economically secure, they were often able to replace their wife by hiring a domestic servant.

Widows and widowers who were parents did not remarry more frequently than others, unless they happened to have young children. Thus the majority of women who had children under age twelve (59 per cent) preferred to abdicate their status as family head to a new husband, compared to only 23 per cent of those who did not have children to raise. Eighty per cent of widowers with young children, as opposed to only 45 per cent without, contracted a second marriage.[28] However, the determining factor appears to have been the presence in the family of children aged twenty or older, no matter what their sex or

Table 1.2: Proportion of Remarriages as a Function of the Sex and Age of Surviving Spouse at Widowhood or Widowerhood at Quebec

	Women		Men	
Age at widowhood or widowerhood	*No. / total**	*%*	*No. / total**	*%*
Under 30	28 / 35	80.0	17 / 19	89.5
30–39	16 / 27	59.3	49 / 55	89.1
40–49	13 / 31	41.9	24 / 30	80.0
50 and older	0 / 44	0	10 / 42	23.8
Not known	0 / 1	0	0 / 1	0
Total	**57 / 137**	**41.6**	**100 / 147**	**68.0**

* Includes the number of remarriages out of the total of widows and widowers in each age cohort.

marriage status, or the existence of younger siblings. In this situation, their parents, especially in the case of women, tended to remarry far less frequently (7 and 63 per cent respectively), but this pattern also held true for men (29 and 78 per cent respectively). These young men and women were in a position to demand their portion of the family property, and this may well have had the effect of giving suitors pause. In addition, these older children could offset the loss of a spouse either through their work contribution or by marriage, in which case daughters-in-law or sons-in-law would be added to the network of family assistance. However, among women, age remained the key factor governing remarriage.

Those who remained widows or widowers for a longer period before either remarrying or dying[29] were forced to adopt rather ingenious expedients in order to ensure their own survival or, in some cases, that of their children. Their strategies of assistance were a function of gender, were based upon the sex of their children and the presence of other kin and neighbours, and followed a notion of male and female roles. Because widows were far less likely than widowers to remarry after age thirty, large numbers of them engaged in occupations in order to replace the male head of the household. This was a necessity that was recognized both by the people of the colony and by the government, which frequently intervened to ease women's access to various occupations. Thus Intendant Raudot commissioned one widow to be the doorkeeper of prisons in Quebec, 'as a replacement for her husband', on condition that her son, 'who would remain with her in said prisons', would stand security for her.[30] Bégon, his successor, decided that in reference to the company which held the rights to porpoise fishing near Rivière-Ouelle, 'the widows of Noel Pelletier and Jean Dechene will be received in the stead of their husbands by having them each furnish a man able to work in this fishery like the other associates.'[31] In a similar vein, Intendant Hocquart averred that Canadian women possessed a certain 'business acumen' (*disposition pour les affaires*).[32]

Many other widows in Quebec left evidence of very diverse occupational activities.[33] Even though they were barred from holding public or military office, nothing prevented them from engaging in trade, owning an inn or tavern, or supervising the activities of a workshop or artisan's stall, even a blacksmith's shop or tannery.[34] However, one should not attribute too much social importance to this phenomenon.[35] Widows were often ill-prepared to step into their husband's vacated economic function,[36] and because they had to fulfill other gender-specific tasks, they were often unable, by simply relying upon their own labour, to replace the male head of the family. In fact, their economic activities can best be regarded as an ad hoc response, over time, to changing needs and circumstances. Frequently, they turned to another male in their kinship network to compensate for the loss of their husband. In such cases, male kin would either fully or partially take over the family's trade or business, support the widow economically, and in some cases, especially if they were elderly, make full provision for their care. Sons, sons-in-law, and nephews formed the front line of this male support network, and they also derived benefits from this type of collaboration.[37]

Many widows were supported by their sons at the occupational level. However, although the latter thus actively collaborated in maintaining the family trade or business after the death of their father, they constituted only a part of the male workforce available to the widow. Madeleine Roberge, widow of the merchant Charles Perthuis, was able to benefit from the support of her eldest son, who followed in his father's footsteps. When the younger Charles married two years after his father's death, he brought 4,000 livres to the family, money that 'he had earned and amassed by his cares, pains and work. This is to be considered beyond the services he has already rendered to the aforementioned Widow Perthuis in her business after the death of the late Mr Perthuis.'[38] This widow, aged forty-one, could rely upon more than her son for male support. Two months after the death of her husband, Claude Hurel, a tanner and leather worker, engaged himself to act as overseer of a tannery and 'all the works and business that the aforementioned Mrs Perthuis shall consider appropriate', and 'to watch over the business like a good husband and father'.[39] When the contract with Hurel expired, she hired another tanner,[40] an agreement signed shortly before her son Charles was married. The latter continued to support his mother for many years, notably by undertaking certain business dealings on her behalf,[41] a practice that was fairly common in New France. Madeleine Roberge would also have been able to count on the assistance of her daughters [42] or domestic servants[43] to care for her two younger boys, thus enabling her to attend to her business dealings, especially with her brothers, one a sea captain and the other a merchant.[44] Ironically, in twenty-five years of married life, Widow Perthuis had only gone once to see a notary, and that to sign a pew rental agreement with her husband!

Madeleine Delauney was in her fifties and had a number of grown children when her husband died. However, she stated fifteen years later that she could only rely upon her son Joseph Enouille, who stood by her during her widowhood and had supported her since he was twenty. This young man 'was the only one of the children who had supported her and had usefully sustained her through his work and his steadiness at her side in all tasks to support the household and the tobacco manufacture that was her business'.[45] In order to secure Joseph's commitment to 'continue his services to her for as long as he is able', she agreed to assign him half the conjugal community's property 'which always subsists and continues' as a deed of gift, although she reserved the personal use of this property until she died.[46]

Joseph Vergeat was apprenticed to a maker of edge tools six years before the death of his father, Jean Vergeat, a soldier in the Canadian militia.[47] Joseph always contributed his earnings to the support of his family, which included five adult daughters. His mother, the widow Jeanne Boisselle, found herself unable to repay 'the sum of 4,200 livres that her son gave to her before and after the death of his father, and she offers to charge this amount to all her property when she dies, on condition that he takes care of her until then'.[48] Three years later, when she made a deed of gift under the same conditions of half the house in which they lived, the widow likewise sought to protect herself from the legal complications that might arise if her son took a wife and at the same time to assure herself of another source of assistance. The contract stipulated, in effect, 'in case he marries and has children that nothing will change or diminish the said obligations, and in case that he is assured of property either by his marriage contract or other sources, he will commit his aforementioned wife to the same obligations.'[49] However, Jeanne Boisselle could not foresee that her son would predecease her, without having married, only three months later.[50] She then was able to benefit from another widespread form of family assistance by relying upon her eldest daughter, Charlotte, and her son-in-law.[51]

This was an expedient that many widows resorted to when their sons failed to answer the call, and they assured themselves of the assistance of sons-in-law either by inheritance or by outright gift. Thus the 'son by marriage' (*fils par alliance*) replaced the husband's earning power.[52] Jacqueline Marandeau, widow of carpenter Guillaume Nicolas, was able to rely upon the assistance of her young daughter following the death of her husband,[53] and she conferred upon her daughter and her husband, in exchange for maintenance, a deed of gift of a building lot, a house, and furniture upon them that had belonged to the community: 'In light of her advanced years and the continued poor health that has long afflicted her, and wishing to recognize the kindness and friendship that Mr Etienne Parent her son in law and his wife Marie Joseph Nicolas have shown towards her, and that she hopes they will continue for the remainder of her days.' [54] The couple undertook to lodge with her, to feed her, and to 'provide all the necessaries for her required by her station' and to provide care for her if she is ill, this obligation to continue until the hour of her death.[55]

Even those widows who conferred unconditional deeds of gift upon or committed themselves to housing and feeding their daughters and new sons-in-law without asking for maintenance or work obligations from them undoubtedly expected a helping hand if they were in need.[56] This was the wish expressed by Madeleine Lemire, the widow of an unskilled worker, who asked for nothing in return for the deed of gift of a building lot and a house she bestowed upon her daughter and son-in-law. The action of this widow, which aimed at one level to reward her daughter for 'the good and useful services and kindnesses that she always displayed' towards her father and mother, left her 'hopeful that she and her aforementioned husband will continue to do so in the future'.[57] However, daughters frequently stepped forward even to offer monetary assistance without waiting to get married. Many elderly widows who had never remarried pointed out, either in their wills or other notarial acts, 'the kind services' rendered by their daughters. One woman in her sixties, Catherine Nolan *dit* Lamarque, widow of the merchant Mathieu Martin Delino, commended her daughter Marie-Anne for having remained with her since her father's death, which had occurred fifteen years earlier, and stated that she 'was very satisfied and content with this assistance, effort, and care that she had received from her'.[58] This spinster, who was aged thirty-five when her father died, had allowed her mother to sell jewellery, furniture, clothing, and lace that had belonged to her, and to put the money 'towards her subsistence and upkeep'.[59]

Daughters also assisted their mothers by taking upon themselves the assembly of their trousseau 'through their own effort, care, and industry' and their own personal savings.[60] The spinsters Therese and Madeleine Robitaille collaborated with their mother, Marguerite Blute, in running a tavern that the widow had managed with her husband. Shortly after the latter's death, the widow, then in her sixties, 'in consideration of the fact that the advanced age that she has reached does not allow her to work or earn her living', made a deed of gift to her daughters of 'the little property that she had inherited from her late husband, [which] is not sufficient to feed or sustain her in the necessaries of life.'[61] On the same day, her son Charles made over to his sisters his portion of the inheritance from his father and what he might expect to inherit from his mother 'on the condition that they [his sisters] will take good care of their mother, that they will feed her, maintain her, and launder for her for the rest of her days.'[62]

When widows had neither sons nor sons-in-law upon whom to rely, they sometimes looked to other kinsmen, especially to nephews, who were often well placed to help their aunts because they would receive a portion of the inheritance. This was the course adopted by Jeanne Elisabeth

Cartier, who was aged fifty-two when her husband, the butcher Charles Larche, died. This economically secure widow had, for some time, taken care of her husband's business, a period during which she would have relied upon her in-laws, who lived close by; upon her only daughter, who lived with her; upon a nephew, who was old enough to help out with the daily chores; and finally, upon two sons-in-law—a navigator and a merchant—who successively entered the family circle. The second son-in-law, who before his marriage was already helping mother and daughter—by this point both widows—subsequently took charge of administering the community of property that still existed between the two women.[63] As a last resort after her daughter's death, the widow, now in her eighties, finding herself 'unable to realize the little property remaining, and this so little to suffice for her food and upkeep', conferred upon her nephew as a deed of gift her rights to her old community of property, thus recognizing 'the kind care and services' he had already rendered to her, and made him promise 'to continue these for the remainder of her days.'[64]

Marie-Françoise Huppe, widow of blacksmith Pierre Payment, was only thirty years old when her husband died. Although she never remarried and lost her only child, she nonetheless benefited for many years from the assistance of her brother André, who lived nearby. Two years after her husband's death, she gave her brother half a building lot in Quebec,[65] and he undertook a number of financial dealings on her behalf.[66] When she was quite elderly (age sixty-six) 'and unable to survive with so little property and to realize it, but knowing the affection her nephew Augustin Brousseau has for her, as he has for many years fed and cared for her without monetary reward', the widow bestowed all her property upon him, on condition that he provide her with lodgings, food, fuel, and maintenance until her death.[67]

Married nieces could also serve as substitutes for daughters in bringing their husbands' labour power to the assistance of their aunts. In this case, a common practice was to use property given to them by the widow to procure her subsistence. As with daughters, it was not necessary for them to be married in order to assist their aunts in a number of ways. When the wholesale merchant Jean Lestage died, his widow, Marie-Anne Vermette, was taken in by her niece and her husband, as her own adult son and daughter were absent from Quebec.[68] Indeed, 'she lived with them for many years and even died in the room that was their common abode in a house belonging to Widow Maufait.'[69] Widow Vermette, then in her fifties and crippled[70] willed them furniture and household utensils 'to reward them for the kindly services that they rendered her since she has lived with them and which they continue to render to her and also to reward them for the kind services she has especially received from the aforementioned Dame Magdelaine Bureau, her niece, before her marriage'.[71]

Anne Mossion, a childless widow, had depended upon her niece during an illness that, in 1733, had lain her low before carrying off her husband, Paul Laferriere, a military officer. Her will made special reference to 'the special love she has for me', and willed the niece 200 livres in recognition of 'the pains and cares she took with me during my illness and at other times'.[72] Marie-Anne Begas, herself a widow, was living with Anne Mossion when the latter died in her fifties after nine years of widowhood. The two women did not live in comfortable circumstances, for 'the indigence in which she found herself' during her widowhood had not allowed Anne Mossion to respect one of the last wishes of her husband, which was to distribute 600 livres to the poor, 'which she has not been entirely able to fulfill'.[73]

Widowers, by contrast, always had full financial responsibility for the family and were less economically vulnerable than their female counterparts. However, household chores, the oversight of young children, and the training of female children represented conundrums for them, as the status of widower did not open new and wider definitions of male roles that would have allowed them to adapt more easily to their new situation of single man or single parent. For most widowers, a new wife was a lifesaver. This is what happened in the case of Nicolas Rousset, a carpenter, who declared in his will 'that it was only the . . . efforts and care of his . . . second wife that enabled him to subsist until now',[74] and he especially enjoined recognition of this by his children. The difficulty for fathers to balance work and child care was clearly expressed by Joseph Racine, a joiner who, after the death of Marguerite Pilotte, his wife, 'was left with the care of seven young children and found himself considerably embarrassed in trying to provide them with the necessary instruction, and finding himself alone and frequently obliged to leave his house to work at his trade or where his masters wanted to employ him, his earnings were not nearly adequate to feed and maintain himself, let alone his family'.[75] This thirty-eight-year old widower, who did not remarry for ten years, was an exception to the general pattern, because his poverty was relieved by the priests of the Seminary of Quebec, to whom he had 'exposed his hardship and wants', and who 'wanting to be sympathetic, charitably took into their care four of the aforementioned children, whom they instructed, fed, and maintained.'[76]

However, widowers were usually assisted in their difficulties in raising young children by their older daughters, kinswomen (either their own or in-laws), and occasionally, domestic servants or friends. This was a reciprocal arrangement, as these women, who were often spinsters, widowed, or deserted, found in it a means of mutual assistance. Thus, when his wife died in childbirth, the merchant Pierre Normandin was able to call upon his eldest daughter Angelique, aged nineteen and also on a female servant[77] to care for five children who ranged in age from a few days to eight years. Shortly after the death of his eldest daughter, this widower hired a young girl aged nine 'to be a servant and to obey him and the daughters who manage his household',[78] notably Marie-Catherine, then aged seventeen. Other men had to rely upon close relatives to compensate for the loss of the mother and homemaker. Merchant Louis Gosselin, who waited twenty-one years before remarrying, placed his children and his estate in the hands of his widowed mother when he was absent on business,[79] because his only daughter was married and attending to her own family responsibilities.[80] An unskilled labourer and father of six young children, Claude Vivier turned to his mother-in-law, who was obliged to 'keep and take care of his family as she had already been doing',[81] on condition that her son-in-law pay her rent for the next two years and provide her with sufficient food. In this case, the mother-in-law benefited from the arrangement because her own husband was absent. Finally, Michel Cotton put his daughters, aged between five and ten, in the care of his sister and neighbour 'because, being a widower with five children, two boys and three girls, whom he can barely keep alive and maintain, and having no source of income other than his trade, and because he presently has little work, this is barely sufficient for his own food and upkeep. He has proposed this arrangement to his aforementioned sister who is aware of his situation, and who is anxious to attend to his needs and undertakes to raise, feed, maintain, and instruct his three young daughters in her own trade of seamstress.'[82] These young girls were required to live with their spinster aunt until age twenty and 'during this time they will each be obliged to stay with her and to work at her trade, carrying out all her instructions in a seemly and orderly way . . . She wishes to be a good mother to them and has no other aim than to rescue her aforementioned nieces from an extreme poverty and to furnish them with a Christian education and a station appropriate to their birth and sex.'[83]

Such adversity could also create bonds of mutual assistance between unrelated men and women who had lost their spouses and who found themselves in similar situations. Thus widowers occasionally benefited from the work of widows, generally as servants or domestics.[84] Jacques Larcher, a wholesale merchant, found himself at age forty with five children to raise, and he remained a widower until his death thirty years later. When he drew up his will, eight years after his wife's death and with at least one very young daughter, he gave part of his property to the widows, one being a servant and the other a friend who lived in the same house with him, making special mention of their good deeds.[85] The merchant made arrangements so that 'little Cornette', the daughter of one of the widows, was placed for six months with the nuns of the Hôpital-Général of Quebec or with the Ursulines, proof of the regard he had for her mother's 'kind services', which may have been directed to caring for his own children. Elderly widowers who wanted to wind down their trades or businesses or who found themselves unable to provide for themselves were also forced, like widows too poor or otherwise unable to face their new responsibilities, to find ways of compensating for their inability to work.

Sometimes the death of a spouse led to role reversal in which widows took complete charge of men unable to provide for themselves especially those too old or too poor to do so. Catherine Gautier, widow of the merchant Jean-Baptiste Lecoudray, did this for her sixty-three-year-old brother, who owned a house near Quebec. He placed himself in her hands by investing her with all his property, because 'of advanced age which no longer allows him to work to earn his living and because the paucity of revenue from his property is not enough to feed and provide for his necessary upkeep.'[86] The widow promised to 'lodge, provide fuel, and maintain the aforementioned donor and give him all that is necessary to his condition whether in health or sickness until the day and hour of his death.'[87] In turn, fifteen years later she herself, was 'obliged by the infirmities of advancing age' to resign herself into the complete care of her son-in-law and daughter.[88]

Of all the children of the elderly Mathurin Palin Debonville (aged eighty-one), a former merchant or seafarer,[89] only his daughter Angélique, a widow who lived near him,[90] 'wanted to take care of him, which she has done for three years with very little contribution from him'.[91] He deeded a gift of 620 livres to his daughter to cover his food and upkeep in sickness or health, 'and so she will give him, as she has done before, all the care and attention she owes him.' However, she was not allowed to dispose of this sum 'except with the permission of her aforementioned father, who will remain in full charge of it'.[92] Ten years later, a more common expedient was reached to care for the elderly widower, now aged ninety-three, by which his son and daughter-in-law agreed to support him.[93] Finally, Francoise Douville a young widow in her twenties, contributed financially and managed the shop of her uncle, a merchant with whom she lived, for nearly a quarter-century after the death of her aunt. Charles Boucherville, aged forty when he brought his niece into his household in 1743, acknowledged thirty years later that he had personally profited from the 400 livres that belonged to her as a minor following her husband's death but also of 'more still from her savings and work, for she managed and administered his business affairs after the death of his wife'.[94] Prevented 'by the miseries occasioned by the late war' from repaying her, he deeded all his movable property, including his silverware, to her, in exchange for which she would 'continue without payment to run his shop as she has done for more than twenty-five years'.[95]

Conclusion

During the first half of the eighteenth century, very few widows and widowers in the town of Quebec found themselves alone, most sharing their mourning with one or more orphaned children. At times, the presence of these children served as a support network for the surviving spouse, but frequently they posed a problem, as caring and raising them had been a task that had devolved upon the now-departed spouse. Widowers generally found themselves saddled with young children who required a wet nurse or at least a minimum of care and attention, and frequently they had young daughters who needed to be instructed in their duties as future mothers and housekeepers. For them, the situation constituted an impasse, because these were tasks explicitly assigned to women. Widows were somewhat better situated to look after the toddlers that nearly half of them had, even though they had to take on the economic and occupational responsibilities attendant upon their new status as head of the family. By contrast with widowers, they were often able to turn to a daughter who was old enough to assist them with household tasks, although daughters of marriageable age posed an added burden because widows had to ensure that they were properly established in life.

In facing these challenges, men generally replaced their dead spouse with a new wife, who would take both the household in hand and the young orphans under her wing. Young widows in their twenties, favoured by age and less experienced at an occupational level than older women who were assisted by adult children, also tended to remarry quickly. Widows in their thirties and forties appear to have had greater access to work, although some met this challenge with greater difficulty than others, affected by variables of occupational, family, and personal situation. Because this was a phenomenon whose existence has been observed for other societies and other chronological periods, nothing in it would allow us to state that the colonial context of New France especially 'favoured' women. As well, the formation of support networks seems to have followed a fairly narrow notion of male and female social roles. Thus it was the sons of widows who most frequently stepped into their father's shoes, without necessarily displacing the new female head of the family, who took an active role in the transition. When widows were more isolated and more vulnerable, sons-in-law and nephews came to their aid over time. Daughters and nieces also constituted a recognized support structure, assisting their mothers and aunts during their spinsterhood and gaining additional male support for them through marriage.

Fathers who were left single relied as far as possible on their daughters or hired female servants, spinsters, or widows, to attend to household chores or care for younger children. In the absence of these, they turned to other single kinswomen—sisters, mothers, and mothers-in-law—who found in exchange for these domestic services a source of financial support for themselves. At a more advanced age, the destinies of men and women tended to converge, with widowers abdicating—if necessary to a woman—their power to support themselves, a responsibility that had hitherto devolved upon them as men, husbands, and fathers. At times, there was a clear role reversal, revealing the extent to which the gender of women is at all stages of life—as is that of men at the end of their lives—a set of shifting boundaries.

Notes

This essay was translated by Michael Gauvreau.

Notarial Registers in the Archives Nationales du Québec cited in the Notes

Quebec

Barc-qc	Barolet, C. (1728–61)
Barj-qc	Barbel, J. (1703–40)
Boin-qc	Boisseau, N. (1730–44)
Boug-qc	Boucault de Godefus, G. (1736–56)
Decjb-qc	Decharnay, J. B. (1755–9)
Dubje-qc	Dubreuil, J.E. (1708–34)
Dulch-qc	Dulaurent, C.H. (1734–59)
Dupn-qc	Duprac, N. (1723–48)
Hich-qc	Hiche, H. (1725–36)
Lacf-qc	Lacetiere, F. (1702–28)
Lanpaf-qc	Lanouillier *dit* Desgranges, P.A.F. (1749–60)
Louc-qc	Louet, C. (1739–67)
Loujc-qc	Louet, J.C. (1718–37)
Panjc-qc	Panet, J.C. (1744–75)
Pinjn-qc	Pinguet de Vaucour, J.N. (1726–48)
Ragf-qc	Rageot de Beaurivage, F. (1709–53)
Saija-qc	Salilant de Collegien, J.A. (1750–76)
Sans-qc	Sanguinet, S. (1748–71)

Trois-Rivieres

Ducn-tr	Duclos, N. (1751–69)
Petp-tr	Petit, P. (1706–35)
Pill-tr	Pillard, L. (1736–67)

1. This study is based on the fifth chapter of my doctoral dissertation, 'Le veuvage en Nouvelle-France: Genre, dynamique familiale et strategies de survie dans deux villes coloniales du XVIIIe siecle: Québec et Louisbourg' (Université de Montréal, 2000).
2. For a more general discussion of this theme, see Josette Brun, 'Le veuvage dans les sociétés occidentales préindustrielles: Réflexions autour du concept de

genre', *Cahiers d'histoire* (Université de Montréal) 18 (automne 1998): 19–38; Bettina Bradbury, 'Widowhood and Canadian Family History', in *Intimate Relations: Family and Community in Planter Nova Scotia, 1759–1800*, Margaret Conrad, ed. (Acadia University: Planter Studies Centre, 1995).

3. See Joan Scott, 'Gender: A Useful Category of Historical Analysis', in *Gender and the Politics of History* (New York: Columbia University Press, 1988), 1–53.
4. The family record files taken from the 'Registre de population du Québec ancien' of the Université de Montréal's Programme de démographie historique present a portrait of the family situation of widows and widowers: number of living children, sex and age of the surviving parent and orphans, and length of widowhood or widowerhood (ended by death or remarriage). Notarial documents offer insight into how networks of family interdependency were formed, especially since they contain evidence of sources of support available from outside the nuclear family. I have been able to identify those legal documents pertaining to widows and widowers thanks to the PARCHEMIN finding aid, which contains an analytical inventory of the notarial archives of the colony. See Helene Lafortune and Normand Robert, *La banque PARCHEMIN: Un accès illimité et instantané au patrimoine notarial du Québec ancien (1635–1775)* (CD-ROM) (Montréal: Archiv-Histo, 1998). The marriage contracts of those persons orphaned of either a father or a mother (128 acts) and all the wills, deeds of gift, division of property, and other declarations and agreements involving widows and widowers (155 acts in total, of which 36 deal with widowers) form the basis of the present analysis. The codes used henceforth in the notes identify each notary and are fully referenced above under their full name as well as the chronological period covered. I have also examined transcripts of the censuses of 1716 and 1744 in Quebec in order to understand the life course of widows and widowers.
5. Our understanding of the colonial family draws upon demography and studies of property transmission and social reproduction. See Geneviève Ribordy, 'La famille en Nouvelle-France: Bilan historiographique', *Cahiers d'histoire* 12 (été 1992): 24–50. The history of affectional and sentimental life within the family has remained hitherto marginal to historians. See, however, Lorraine Gadoury, *La famille dans son intimite: Echanges épistolaires au sein de l'élite canadienne du XVIIIe siècle* (Montréal: HMH, 1998).
6. The pioneering article by Jan Noel; 'New France: Les femmes favorisées', first published in *Atlantis* in 1981, has been republished in many collections of essays between the 1980s and the end of the 1990s, most notably in *Rethinking Canada: The Promise of Women's History*, 2nd edition, Veronica Strong-Boag and Anita Clair Fellman, eds. (Toronto: Copp Clark Pitman, 1991), 28–50. This interpretation is found in other guises in the articles of Catherine Rubinger, 'The Influence of Women in Eighteenth Century New France', in *Femmes savantes et femmes d'esprit: Women Intellectuals of the French Eighteenth Century*, Roland Bonnel and Catherine Rubinger, eds. (New York and Paris: Peter Lang, 1994), 419–44; and Terence Crowley, 'Women, Religion, and Freedom in New France', in *Race and Gender in the Northern Colonies*, Jan Noel, ed. (Toronto: Canadian Scholars' Press, 2000), 101–10. The main arguments that sustain this hypothesis are, however, contested. The lack of women varied according to chronological period and region; wars took men away from their families in societies other than New France; the fur trade only rarely drew its labour force from married men; the law, as in other societies, restricted the rights of wives; and the important role of religious congregations did not modify the status of lay women. For the debate, see Micheline Dumont, 'Les femmes de la Nouvelle-France étaient-elles favorisées?' *Atlantis* 8 (1982): 118–24; response by Jan Noel, ibid., 125–30; Allan Greer, 'Les femmes de la Nouvelle-France', in *Brève histoire des peuples de la Nouvelle France* (Montréal: Boreal, 1998), 79–96; and Ribordy, 'La famille en Nouvelle-France'.
7. Danielle Gauvreau, *Québec: Une ville et sa population au temps de la Nouvelle-France* (Sillery: Presses de l'Université du Québec, 1991).
8. In fact, their number was three times greater in the town of Quebec in the mid-eighteenth century than it had been at the beginning of the century—86 in 1716 and 223 in 1744. See Serge Lambert, 'Les pauvres et la société de 1681 à 1744' (doctoral dissertation, Université Laval, 1990), 225, table 24.
9. In Quebec, as elsewhere in New France, the largest proportion of marriages was ended by the death of the husband, 57 per cent as opposed to 43 per cent, primarily because the age gap between spouses at marriage was heavily tilted towards men. See Gauvreau, *Québec,* 115. Consequently, the death of a spouse particularly affected women, especially as they remained widows more frequently and for a longer time than did widowers, a reflection of the lesser chance—or greater lack of will—to remarry. From 1716 the capital of New France numbered three times more widows than widowers. See Lambert, 'Les pauvres et la société', 225, table 24.
10. The present analysis considers only those couples in their first marriage so as to study the most widespread

experience of marriage through a homogeneous and representative cohort.

11. All of them had lived in Quebec for at least five years before the death of their spouse. This methodological choice has enabled me to examine what these families had in common: urban life in the capital of New France before experiencing the death of a spouse.
12. Gauvreau, *Québec*, 88. For lack of a better description, the categorization of families follows the husband's occupation, a determining factor in the family economy for both widows and widowers.
13. Unlike single women of at least twenty-five years of age, married women suffered from legal incapacity. They rarely represented the conjugal society before the notary, but regularly accompanied their husbands in dealing with questions relating to their own property or, less frequently, to the common property of the family. See Brun, 'Le veuvage en Nouvelle-France', chapter 3. These results call into question the argument advanced by Jan Noel that women in New France were 'favoured' and adds a key qualification to the question of the relative flexibility of women's social roles at this time. See Noel, 'New France: Les femmes favorisées', 28–50.
14. The experience of women at administrative and professional levels is evident from examination of certain notarial acts (power of attorney given to wives) and, more indirectly from other documents and activities that a number of women engaged in during the period of their widowhood. See on this point, Brun, 'Le veuvage en Nouvelle-France'. The statement by one member of the Superior Council of Quebec that 'most of the members of council have their business affairs taken care of by their wives or their children [la majeure partie des membres du conseil font faire leur commerce pars leurs femmes ou leurs enfants]' effectively illustrates a certain reality. See Archives nationals du Canada (ANC), MG1, Archives des colonies, CIIA, Correspondence generale, Canada, 1575–1774 (henceforth cited as série CIIA), VOL. 2-2, C-2375, 602–4, after 1710, observations made by Martin de Lino, member of the Superior Council, on the difficulties encountered in the execution of certain articles of ordinances of 1667, 1669, and 1681.
15. It goes without saying that the loss of a spouse would also have had an impact at the emotional level, a subject that I do not treat in the present study. See, however, Nathalie Pilon, 'Le destin de veuves et de veufs de la région de Montréal au milieu du XVIIIe siecle: Pour mieux comprendre la monoparentalité dans le Québec préindustriel' (MA research paper, history, Université de Montréal, 2000), 44–7.
16. Parent and Postolec, 'Quand Themis rencontre Clio'.
17. Lambert, 'Les pauvres et la société', 229: 'les pratiques sociales en viennent à mieux correspondre à la politique de sensibilisation des autorités civiles et religieuses exhortant les enfants à porter assistance aux parents.'
18. The data that follow appear in the tables or are drawn from my bank of demographic data, which has been reconstituted with the EXCEL software program.
19. I have not treated as living those children whose year of death could not be determined. However, this total does not perfectly take account of the real presence of children, as some could have been absent—in religious communities, as apprentices, as domestic servants, or living with other families—or have moved away, a situation especially apparent among adult children. As well, some may have survived but cannot be confirmed from data contained in parish registers. Qualitative analysis enables us to fill a number of gaps by alerting us to a number of key dynamics affecting family life.
20. According to canon law, girls were reckoned to have reached the age of puberty at twelve and were thus able to marry. Boys were deemed to be young men a little later, at about fourteen or fifteen—censuses habitually placed them in a separate category—but like girls, they could be apprenticed at age twelve. See Peter Moogk, 'Les petits sauvages: The Children of Eighteenth-Century New France', in *Childhood and Family in Canadian History*, Joy Parr, ed. (Toronto: McClelland and Stewart, 1983), 19, 26–31.
21. Children under age two were considered infants.
22. Moogk, 'Les petits sauvages'.
23. The age of twenty marked the coming of age, as boys could demand their emancipation (five years before attaining full adulthood), and in Quebec, the average age of marriage for women was in the very early twenties. See Gauvreau, *Québec,* 99–101.
24. This involved single girls aged twenty or more.
25. Age forty marked the end of female fertility. Since the main objective of a Catholic marriage was procreation, an older woman's second marriage was less justifiable in the eyes of the church. These results illustrate the international phenomenon of greater social problems faced by older women. See Ida Blom, 'The History of Widowhood: A Bibliographic Overview', *Journal of Family History* 16 (1991): 191–210. The average age of widows in Quebec was comparable to that of men and generally fell m the early forties (42 years versus 43.7 years respectively).
26. While it was possible for women to remarry after this age, it was rare.
27. The proportions among widows of artisans (40.7 per cent), merchants (42.8 per cent), and unskilled workers (38.9 per cent) show little variation. Interestingly, widows of merchants were not sought in

marriage or drawn to it in greater numbers than other groups. See Gauvreau, *Québec,* 133.

28. Similarly, for the region of Montreal, Pilon notes that the propensity to remarry was inversely proportional to the age of children. See 'Le destin de veuves et de veufs', 67–71.
29. Persons who had lost their spouses generally remarried after two or three years. This was more rapid among men (2.4 years for widowers, versus 3.2 years for widows), who were twice as likely to remarry before the end of the first year of mourning. This was a choice made by one-third of men (33 per cent) but only 14 per cent of women. Widowers who did not remarry generally died after ten (10.6) years, whereas women lived through a much longer period of widowhood (17.2 years).
30. *Chronica 3: Inventaire des ordonnances des intendants de la NouvelleFrance (1665–1760)* (CD-ROM), 4 vols, vol. 1, Raudot, cahier 4, 26 jan. 1710.
31. Ibid., Michel Bégon, cahier 6, 16 mai 1715: 'Les veuves de Noël Pelletier et Jean Dechêne y seront reçues au lieu et place de leurs maris en fournissant chacune un homme capable de travailler à la dite pêche comme les autres associés'.
32. ANQ, série CIIA, vol. 67, C-2392, 40–62, 1737, detailed survey of the entire colony by Intendant Hocquart.
33. Liliane Plamondon, 'Une femme d'affaires en Nouvelle-France: Marie-Anne Barbel, veuve Fornel', *Revue d'histoire de l'Amerique française* 31 (sept. 1977): 165–86; Kathryn Young, '" . . . sauf les perils et fortunes de la mer": Merchant Women in New France and the French Transatlantic Trade, 1713–46', *Canadian Historical Review* 77 (Sept. 1996): 388–407; Josette Brun, 'Les femmes d'affaires en Nouvelle-France au 18e siècle: Le cas de l'Île Royale', *Acadiensis* 27 (autumn 1997): 44–66.
34. Guilds were never introduced into the colony, and thus they could not, as in France, limit the access of widows to certain trades. See Peter Moogk, 'In the Darkness of a Basement: Craftsmen's Associations in Early French Canada', *Canadian Historical Review* 57 (Dec. 1976): 399–439.
35. Noel's argument that women's economic activities outside the home were particularly important in New France is interesting, but it is difficult to prove in the absence of further quantitative and comparative studies. See 'New France: Les femmes favorisées'.
36. Many widows emphasized that they were ignorant of the business transactions engaged in by their husbands on behalf of the family. This was the obvious consequence of a well-entrenched gender division of power and work. See Brun, 'Le veuvage en Nouvelle-France', 209–11.
37. Widows and widowers were not more likely than married couples to prepare for their retirement by placing their property in their children's hands in exchange for a provision of support, when the latter signed a marriage contract. This conclusion is drawn from my analysis of 268 marriage contracts made by children of couples. Eighty-five of these occurred with women, and forty-three with men. In the case of those contracts made with both parents living, I have examined only those made by children of couples whose marriages ended by the death of the husband at Quebec.
38. Barj-qc, 18 déc. 1724: 'contrat de mariage entre Charles Perthuis et Louise Brousse': 'quil a gaigné et amassé par ses peines soigns et travaux indepadament des services quil a rendus a lad. Veuve Perthuis dans son commerce depuis le deces dudit feu sieur Perthuis.'
39. Lacf-qc, 2 mai 1722, 'marche pour la conduite des travaux sur une tannerie entre Marie-Madeleine Roberge, veuve de Charles Perthuys, et Claude Hurel, maître tanneur, corroyeur et braconier.' In addition to being housed, fed, and kept warm at the widow's, he was entitled to a salary of 500 livres a year and a jar of good brandy a month.
40. Lacf-qc, 23 avril 1724, 'engagement de Jean-Elie Gautier, maître tanneur, corroyeur et braconnier, à Marie-Madeleine Roberge, veuve de Charles Perthuis.'
41. See especially Lacf-qc, 21 mai 1722, 'obligation de Jean Gatin, marchand, à Charles Perthuys, au nom de sa mère Marie-Madeleine Roberge, veuve de Charles Perthuys'; Barj-qc, 13 juin 1730: 'quittance de François Parent, habitant, à Charles Perthuis, au nom de Marie-Madeleine Roberge, sa mère'; Boin-qc, 30 mars 1732, 'vente d'une goélette par Charles Perthuys, négociant, au nom de Marie-Madeleine Roberge, veuve de Charles Perthuis, sa mère, et son frère Denis Roberge, à Louis Boche dit Lajoye, marchand.'
42. Two of her daughters died and one married in the two years following the death of their father. The three others appear not to have married and undoubtedly lived with their mother, unless they followed the example of their elder sister and entered a religious order. See Pept-tr, 11 sept. 1732, 'convention entre les Ursulines des Trois-Rivières et Marie-Madeleine Roberge, veuve de Charles Perthuis, au nom et comme tutrice de Marie-Anne Perthuis, sa fille.'
43. In 1716, six years before the death of her husband, two domestic servants were listed as members of the household. In her will, nearly twenty years after the death of her husband, Madeleine Roberge alluded to the wages paid to the 'fille qui la servira au jour de son decez.' See Pinjn-qc, 20 Jan. 1741, 'testament

de Marie-Madeleine Roberge, veuve de Charles Perthuis'.

44. Barjc-qc, 24 oct. 1729, 'convention entre Denis Roberge, capitaine de navire de La Rocheile, et Jacques Roberge, de la ville de Québec, frères; et Marie-Madeleine Roberge, veuve de Charles Perthuis.'
45. Dulch-qc, 15 mars 1759, 'donation de biens mobiliers et immobiliers par Marie-Madeleine Delaunay, veuve de Louis Enouille dit Lanoix, cabaretier, à Joseph Enouil, son fils': 'le seul de tous ses enfants qui l'aye secondé et aussi utileman a soutenu par ses travaux et son assiduité au pres d'elle dans tous services pour le soutien de sa maison, et de la fabrication de tabac en poudre dont principalement elle fait profession.'
46. Ibid. See also Sans-qc, le 9 juillet 1767: 'cession de droits successifs mobiliers et immobiliers par Jean-Baptiste Enouil dit Lanoix, forgeron, de la région de Montréal, du consentement de sa mère, Marie-Madeleine, Del'aunay, veuve de Louis Enouil dit Lanoix, aubergiste, à Joseph enouil dit Lanoix, marchand de tabac, son frère.'
47. I have not observed any marked tendency for families headed by a widow or widower to place their children out as apprentices. It is possible that such agreements were never officially recorded before a notary, but it is more likely that children of an age to be apprenticed out were instead required to help support their own families.
48. Dubjo qc, 29 juillet 1726, 'obligation de Marie-Jeanne Boisset, veuve de Jean Vergeat dit Prenoveau, a Joseph Vergeat, son fils': 'la somme de 4200 livres que son fils lui a fourni avant et depuis le décès de son pere, lui offre de prendre ce montant sur tous ses biens a son décès, à condition qu'il prenne soin d'elle jusque-là.'
49. He had to 'nourir, blanchir, entretenir, loger [et] chauffer la dite donnatrisse la soigner tant saine que malade, et en ce dernier cas la faire penser et medicameter et la faire inhumer': Hich-qc, 9 juillet 1729, 'donation de la moitié d'une maison par Jeanne Boissel, veuve de Jean Vergeat dit Prénouveau, à Joseph Vergeat, son fils': 'au cas qu'il se marie et ait des enfants qu'il n'y aura rien de changé n'y de diminué aux dites charges, et en cas qu'il engage a le bien alluy donné soit par son contrat de mariage ou aturement qu'il fera obliger sadite femme aux memes charges.'
50. I have also found many instances of mutual aid among widows, notably among mothers and daughters who faced the difficulties occasioned by their new status together. Young widows in their twenties, especially if they had been recently married, frequently returned to their family household, often headed by a widow, while awaiting remarriage. However, this type of collaboration was never formalized before a notary.
51. Pinjn-qc, 3 september 1731, 'donation de la moitié d'un emplacement par Jeanne Boisselle, veuve de Jean Vergeat dit Prénouveau, à Louis Evé et Charlotte Vergeat, son épouse, son gendre; 20 déc. 1731, 'cession et abandon d'un emplacement par Jeanne Boisselle à Louis Evé et Charlotte Vergeat, son épouse. In this latter act, 'a la priere de ses enfans qui lui auroient exposés leurs besoins et declarez le plaisir qu'elle leur feroit en leurs abandonnant des a present le bien qu'elle leurs auroit voulu conserver pour leur legitime et dont elle se seroit reserve lusufruit pendant sa vie,' she gave them 715 livres.
52. See in addition to the case cited below, Hich-qc, 3 oct. 1735, 'donation d'un emplacement par Madeleine Lemire, veuve de Pierre Moreau, à Jacques Tessier et Angélique Moreau, son épouse; Dubjc-qc, 5 nov. 1731, 'testament de Louise Froc, veuve de Julien Meusnier.'
53. The census of 1744 revealed that a young daughter aged seventeen lived alone with her mother three years after the death of her father and four years before her marriage.
54. Barc-qc, 2 oct. 1758, 'donation d'une emplacment par Marie-Jacqueline Marandeau, veuve de Guillaume Nicolas, ô Etienne Parent, son gendre, et Marie-Josephe Parent, son épouse'; 'attendu son age avance et les indispositions continuelles dont elle se trouve affligée depuis longtemps et voulant reconnaistre la bienveillance et lamitié qui luy temoignent depuis plusieurs années le S Etienne Parent son gendre et Marie Joseph Nicolas sa femme, et quelle esperi qu'ils luy continueront le reste de ses jours.'
55. Ibid.: 'l'entretenir de toutte choses necessaires a l'entretien selon son etat.' See also Louc-qc, 15 oct. 1741, 'contrat de mariage entre Michel Rouillard et Marie-Anne Languedoc'; Pinjn-qc, 17 nov. 1735, 'contrat de mariage entre François Cousigny et Marie-Louise Ducharme'; Loujc-qc, 2 juin 1726, 'testament de Marguerite Niel, veuve de Jean Coutard'.
56. Lou-qc, 25 juin 1729, 'contrat de mariage entre Pierre Langlois et Marie-Catherine Boucher'; Pinjc-qc, 1 jan. 1744, 'contrat de mariage entre Yves Ezequel et Francois Enouille, dit Lanoix'. In the marriage contract between Simon Soupiran and Marie-Anne Gauthier, the widow Madeleine Guyon promised to 'loger et nourir dans sa maison a sa table et a ses depends les dits furuurs espoux un an et demy', without prejudice to their rights to inherit their parents' property and 'sans quils soient obligez a payer de pention ni a aucun traveaux'. See Lacf-qc, 16 mai 1727.
57. Hich-qc, 3 oct. 1735, 'donation d'un emplacement par Madeleine Lemire, veuve de Pierre Moreau, à Jacques Tessier et Angélique Moreau son épouse': 'des bons et utils services et amitiés quelle a toujours portés . . . lesperance quelle et sondit mary luy continurons a lavenir.'

58. Dulch-qc, 25 juillet 1746, 'donation d'une rente par Catherine Nolan veuve de Mathieu Martin de Lino, à Marie-Anne de Lino, sa fille': 'est tres satisfaite et contente des secours, peines et soins qu'elle a reçus d'elle.'
59. Dulch-qc, 25 juillet 1746, 'obligation de Catherine Nolan, veuve de Mathieu Martin de Lino, à Marie-Anne de Lino, sa fille.'
60. Barj-qc, 21 sept. 1728, 'contrat de mariage entre Pierre-Simon Chanazart et Marie-Jeanne Reiche'; Dulch-qc, 18 mai 1747, 'contrat de mariage entre Jean-Claude Louet et Marie-Anne Lacoudraye'. The former brought 500 livres to the communal marriage property; the latter, 990 livres. Marie-Anne Languedoc's marriage contract, cited above, specified that the fiancee would bring to the marriage 'six chaises de pins venant de ses ouvrages'. See Louc-qc, 15 oct. 1741.
61. Ragf-qc, 2 avril 1715, 'donation de biens meubles par Marguerite Blute, veuve de Jean Robitaille, à Marie-Madeleine Robitaille et Marie-Thérèse Robitaille, ses filles': 'considerant le grand age dans laquelle elle est avancé quil ne lui permet plus de travailler et de gagner sa vie . . . peu de bien quelle a herite de son dit feu mary [qui] n'est pas suffisant de la faire subsister ny de lentretenir de ce qui luy est necessaire.'
62. Ragf-qc, 2 avril 1715, 'renonciation à la succession de ses parents par Charles Robitaille, en faveur de ses soeurs Marie-Madeleine Robitaille et Marie-Thérèse Robitaille'; 'a conditions quils auront bien soins de leur mere quils la nouriront entretiendront et la blanchiront le reste de ses jours.'
63. François-Philippe Poncy loaned them 76 livres to purchase provisions in 1762, two years before marrying the widow's only daughter. See Louc-qc, 22 oct. 1764.
64. Panjc-qc, 22 oct. 1771, 'donation de droits successifs mobiliers et immobiliers par Jeanne-Elisabeth Carrier, veuve de Charles L'archevesque, à Louis Normandin, son neveu'; 'hors d'etat de faire valoir le peu de biens qui luy revient iceluy ne pouvant point suffire a ses nourrture et entretien.'
65. Dupn-qc, 10 mai 1728, 'transport de la moitié d'un emplacement par Marie-Francoise Huppé, veuve de Pierre Payment, maître forgeron, à André Huppé dit Lagroix, son frère; Dubje-qc, 1 jan. 1729, 'bail à loyer d'une maison par André Huppé, au nom et comme charge de pouvoir de Françoise Huppé, veuve de Pierre Payment, sa soeur, à Jean-Baptiste Marandas.'
66. Dubje-qc, 1 jan. 1729, 'bail à loyer d'une maison par André Huppe, au nom et comme chargé de pouvoir de Françoise Huppé, veuve de Pierre Payment, sa soeur, à Jean-Baptiste Marandas.'
67. Saija-qc, 9 août 1762, 'donation de biens mobiliers et immobiliers par Marie-Françoise Huppé dit Lagroix, veuve de Pierre Payment, forgeron, de la ville de Québec et demeurant à Charlesbourg, à Augustin Brousseau, navigateur, de la Rivière Ouelle, son neveu': 'hors d'etât de vivre avec le peu de bien quelle a faute de pouvoir le faire valoir connoissant d'ailleurs l'affection d'Augustin Brousseau son neveu qui depuis plusieurs années la nourrit et la soigne sans aucun lucre.' Other nephews came forward to assist their aunts. See Ducn-tr, 17 avril 1758, 'donation de biens meubles et immeubles par Elisabeth Duchesne, veuve de Jean-Baptiste Lecot, sergent, de Batiscan, à Joseph-Alexandre Reneaux et Marie-Louise Bergevin, son épouse, son neveu et sa nièce; Barc-qc, 18 oct. 1735, 'convention portant définition de compte entre Louis Lambert, pour la veuve de feu Jean-Baptiste Demeulle et Denis Goyette, négociant de La Rochelle stipulant pour les frères Pascaut, banquiers de La Rochelle'; Barc-qc, 15 mai 1736, 'testament de Marie Durand veuve de Jean Coignet.'
68. Jean-François and Marie-Anne, who died at Quebec long after their mother, were of legal age when she became a widow, but they never married. It seems that they may have entered religious communities. The widow's will mentions the absence of her two children without entering into further detail. See Pinjc-qc, 4 mars 1732, 'testament de Marie-Anne Vermet, veuve de Jean Lestage.'
69. Pinjn-qc, 7 mars 1732, 'inventaire des biens de la communaute des defunts Marie-Anne Vermet et Jean de Lestage': 'avec lesquels elle a demeuré pendant plusieurs années et meme est decedée dans la chambre qui fesoit leur demeure commune dans une maison appartenant à la veuve Maufait.'
70. She declared herself 'ne pouvoir escrire ni signer et ce depuis un grand nombre d'annees.' See Pinjn-qc, 7 mars 1732, 'inventaire des biens de la communauté des défunts Marie-Anne Vermet et Jean de Lestage.'
71. Pinjn-qc, 4 mars 1732, 'testament de Marie-Anne Vermet, veuve de Jean Lestage': 'pour les récompenser des bons services qu'il luy ont rendus depuis qu'elle demeure avec eux et qu'ils continuent de luy rendre actuellement et encore pour recompense des bons services qu'elle a receu en particulier de la dite demoiselle Magdelaine Bureau sa niece avant son mariage.' The other property had to be shared between her two absent children.
72. Pinjn-qc, 22 déc. 1732, 'testament de Anne Mossion, veuve de Paul Ferrier, officier dans les troupes': 'les peines et soins qu'elle aprise aupres d'elle pendant sa maladie et en d'autres tems'.
73. Pinjn-qc, 13 déc. 1741, 'inventaire des biens de la communauté des défunts Anne Mossion, veuve de Paul Ferrière.' Another widow, Jeanne Pluchon,

who died seven months after her husband, benefited from the attentions of her niece during her brief widowhood, as well as those provided by several long-time employees and domestic servants. See Ragf-qc, 3 mai, 1729, 'déclaration de Jeanne Pluchon, veuve de Florent de la Cettière, notaire'.

74. Dulch-qc, 23 nov. 1757, 'testament de Nicolas Rousset, charpentier de navire'; 'Quil n'y a eu que les . . . peines et soins de sa . . . seconde femme qui l'ont aidé et fait subsister jusqu'a present.'
75. Pinjn-qc, 12 juillet 1733, 'déclaration par Joseph Racine dit Beauchesne, veuf de Marguerite Pilotte, tuteur de ses enfants mineurs': 'serait demeuré chargé de sept enfants en bas age et tres embarassé pour leurs donner l'education qui leurs etoit necessaire se trouvant seul et souvent obligé de laisser sa maison pour travailler de son metier ou les bourgeois le vouloient employer, ses revenus n'etat pas a beaucoup suffisants pour le nourier et entretenir avec sa famille.'
76. 'Voulant bien compatir auroient charitablement pris a leurs charges quatre desdits enfants qu'ils auroient faits instruire, nourir et entretenir.' Joseph Racine gave to the seminary his claim to the sum of 1,100 livres from the property of the community 'for the subsistence and maintenance' of the children, affirming that he 'could do no more'; see ibid. See also Pinjn-qc, 1 août 1733, 'cession d'un emplacement par Joseph Racine dit Bauchesne, veuf de Marguerite Pilotte, à ses enfants mineurs, Clément Racine, leur tuteur, acceptant pour eux et du consentement de Jean-Baptiste Brassard, subrogé-tuteur.' Bettina Bradbury has also alluded to this type of strategy in her article 'The Fragmented Family: Family Strategies in the Face of Death, Illness, and Poverty, Montreal, 1860–1885', in Parr, *Childhood and Family in Canadian History*, 109–28.
77. Geneviève Fagot, aged twenty, was recorded in the 1716 census as in the couple's service, three years before the death of Pierre Normandin's wife.
78. 'Pour le servir en qualité de servante et luy obeir et aux filles quy gouvernent son menage.' Marie-Catherine was only eight years old when her mother died. The household undoubtedly had another servant, because the two other daughters were still young.
79. Loujc-qc, 2 juin 1736, 'quittance de Louise Guillot, veuve de Pierre Haymard, chargée du soin des enfants et des biens de Louis Gosselin (marchand), son fils absent, à Jacques Fleury, négociant.'
80. The data on this family only records the existence of one other child, a young boy, but others appear to have been still living.
81. Dubje-qc, 1 mai 1718, 'bail à loyer d'un logement en une maison par Marie Pivin et Jean de Louvoy, son époux, à Claude Vivier'; 7 juillet 1718, 'quittance de Claude Vivier, veuf de Marie-Anne Glinel, à Marie Pivin, veuve de Jacques Glinel, sa belle-mère, qui lui a remis les vêtements à l'usage de ses enfants mineurs'; 22 avril 1719, 'transport d'une maison par Marie Pivin et Jean de Louvoy, son époux, présentement absent, à Claude Vivier, son gendre:' 'avoir et prendre soing de sa famillie ainsy comme elle a cy devant fait.' In the latter document she left her son-in-law her house for one year at a rent of 120 livres.
82. Pinjn-qc, 7 mars 1744, 'convention entre Michel Cotton orfèvre et Marie-Marguerite Cotton (majeure), maîtresse couturière, sa soeur:' 'etant resté veuf avec cinq enfants, deux garcons et trois filles qu'il a peine a faire vivre et entretenir n'ayant aucune faculté que ce que luy procure la profession qui peut a peine luy suffire pour sa seule nouriture et son entretient travaillant peu, il auroit propose a sa ditte soeur qui connoist sa situation et qui veut bien se prester a ses besoins pour pouvoir eslever, nourir, entretenir et instruire de sa proffession de couturiere les trois filles toutes en bas ages.'
83. Ibid.: 'pendant lequel tems elles seront tenues de rester avec elle l'une apres l'autre et de travailler de sa profession en tout ce qu'elle leur commandera d'honeste et licitte . . . leur voulant servir lieu d'une bonne mere n'ayant d'autre vue que de retirer sesdittes nieces d'une extreme misere et de leur procurer une education chretienne et un etat honneste a leur naissance et a leur sexe.'
84. See, for example, the will of Louis Guinière, in which he gave a legacy 'to the Widow Gregoire, who up until now has been the servant of the aforementioned Testator, and has now remarried [a la veuve du nomme Gregoire, qui a este cy devant domestique du dit Sieur testateur elle a present remariee].' See Barc-qc, 22 juillet 1754, 'testament de Louis Guinière'.
85. Barc-jc, 8 nov. 1751, 'testament de Jacques Larcher, marchand.' This concerned what appears to have been a mother and a daughter, Widow Brodière and Marie-Anne Brodière, widow of Cornette. Marie-Anne Brodière, daughter of Joseph and Marie-Angélique Dubreuil, married Pierre Cornette on 30 Oct. 1741. He was listed in the 1744 census, but left no subsequent record.
86. Pinjn-qc, 2 sept. 1732, 'donation de biens meubles et immeubles de la paroisse Saint-Laurent par Jean Gaultier à Catherine Gaultier, veuve de Jean-Baptiste Lagoudrais': 'le grand age dans lequel il seroit avancé qui ne luy permest plus de travailler pour gagner sa vie d'ailleurs que le peu de biens qu'il a n'est point suffisant par ses revenus pour le nourir et entretenir de tout ce qui luy est nécessaire.'

87. Ibid.: 'loger, chaufer, nourir et entretenir ledit donateur et luy fournir de tout ce qui luy sera necessaire selon sa condiition tant en sante qu'en maladie jusques au jour et heure de son décès.'
88. Lanpaf-qc, 19 mars 1756, 'convention entre Catherine Gaultier, veuve de Jean-Baptiste Lacoudray, et Jean-Claude Louet et Marie-Anne Lacoudray, son épouse, son gendre et sa fille.' She acknowledged that she had gone to live with the couple eight years earlier.
89. He had several adult children: three unmarried sons and one son and four daughters who were married.
90. At the census of 1744, he seemed to be living alone or with his daughter, the widow of an unskilled labourer, who herself had three children to support.
91. Panjc-qc, 14 mars 1747, 'donation par Mathurin Palin Dabonville à Angélique Palin, veuve de Jean Demitte, sa fille'; 'qui veuile se charger de luy, ce qu'elle a fait depuis trois ans sans qu'il luy aye fourni que tres peu de chose.' One year later, he gave a payment of 20 livres per year to his son; see Ragf-qc, 3 juin 1748, 'obligation de Antoine Palin *dit* Dabonville à Mathurin Palin.'
92. Ibid.: 'avoir pour lui ainsy qu'elle a fait cy devant tous les egards et attentions qu'elle luy doit . . . que de l'agrement de son dit pere qui en demeurera le maître.'
93. Decjb-qc, 14 jan. 1756, 'bail de nourriture par Antoine Palin Dabonville et Barbe Brulot, son épouse, à Mathurin dit Dabonville, son père.'
94. Panjc-qc, 28 mai 1773, 'obligation et vente de meubles par Charles Boucher, sieur de Boucherville, à Françoise Jeremie Douville, veuve Belan': 'surplus en ses epargnes, travaux, ayant geré et administré des affaires de commerce depuis le deces de son epouse.'
95. Ibid.; 'continuer sans aucune recompense a faire valoir son magasin comme elle l'a toujours fait depuis plus de vingt cinq ans.'

Slavery in Early Canada: Making Black Women Subject

Maureen Elgersman Lee

EDITORS' INTRODUCTION

Contemporary Canadians often proudly proclaim our country's history to be untouched by the sharp hierarchies of race, class, ethnicity, and religion that have divided other societies. That Canada does not share the United States's history of slavery is especially central to what feminist sociologist Sherene Razack calls an everyday national mythology of Canada as a 'kinder, gender, nation' rooted in a 'history without racism'.[1] Yet Canada does have a history of slavery, albeit a different and shorter one. In this chapter Maureen Elgersman Lee brings the female side of this history to light. She reminds us how powerful it is for historians to 'name' the women whose roles and lives have been obscured and denied by the combined work of sexism and racism.

Forms of human unfreedom were part of Aboriginal North America, and a codified system of legal enslavement arrived in Canada along with French law and settlement. From 1681 to 1818 there were approximately 4,100 slaves in French Canada. In mainland Canada, about 65 per cent were Aboriginal 'Panis', while in Île Royale, present day Cape Breton, over 90 per cent were black.[2] Most female slaves performed domestic labour. That they were enslaved did not mean they were without ingenuity, ambition, or agency. Marie Marguerite Rose, a native of Guinea born in the early 1700s, spent her adult life raising the twelve children of her owners. In the 1750s she obtained her freedom and married, and together she and her husband established a tavern. When she died prematurely in 1757, she left an estate valued at 274 livres.[3] Slave women could resist the conditions of their lives, sometimes violently. In Montreal an African slave named Marie-Joseph Angélique was informed that she would be sold to a West Indian plantation in 1734. She responded by setting her mistress's house on fire, and destroyed forty-six houses in the process. Two months later, Angélique was put to death.[4] Slavery persisted in Canada after Britain's victory at the Plains of Abraham.[5] Slave women, likewise, continued to resist. As Elgersman Lee points out, it was Chloe Cooley's determination to resist her sale and removal that prompted Upper Canada Lieutenant-Governor John Graves Simcoe to mandate slavery's eventual extinction in 1793.

While slavery was abolished from the British empire in 1833, the racism that underpinned it persisted, and continued to work in gendered patterns that effected women and men differently. School segregation based on race was common by the 1840s, and recognized by the Canadian government in the Separate Schools Act of 1850.[6] Even though no laws prevented marriage across racial lines, few African Canadian women wed outside their own community in nineteenth-century Vancouver Island.[7] Occupational segregation persisted even when formal barriers and restrictions were absent. African Canadian women were concentrated in domestic service throughout the nineteenth and twentieth centuries. It was in part the demand for cheap domestic labour that pushed the Canadian government to increase the number of immigrants from the British Caribbean into Canada through its Caribbean Domestic Scheme in 1955,[8] the implications of which form part of the discussion in Sedef Arat-Koç's article in this volume. 'Really and truly, we weren't allowed to go into factory work until Hitler started the war,' explained Marjorie Lewsey to historian Dionne Brandt.[9] It is because of such patterns that the Caribbean nurses studied by Karen Flynn have 'developed forms of resistance that enabled them to work and live in environments not always hospitable to their presence'.[10]

Evidence of such survival strategies are illustrated throughout the growing scholarship on African Canadian women's history. Shirley Yee has shown that black women were central community-builders in nineteenth-century Ontario.[11] Abolitionist and journalist Mary Ann Shadd Cary established *The Provincial Freeman* newspaper in 1853, and in doing so, 'broke the editorial ice' for black women across North America.[12] In 1946, businesswoman Viola Desmond was charged for sitting in the 'white' section of a New Glasgow, Nova Scotia movie theatre, and used her conviction to attempt a legal challenge of practices of racial segregation across the province.[13] In the 1950s and 60s, African Canadian women worked with civil rights organizations like the Nova Scotia Association for the Advancement of Coloured People and the community development movement to improve and expand opportunities and services available to Black people.[14] The Congress of black Women, formed in 1973 in Toronto, continues to provide a national voice for the concerns of black women. Rosemary Brown, the first black woman to be elected to provincial public office in Canada, ran for leadership of the New Democratic Party in 1975 and spent much of her life in public service on behalf of women.[15] While historians know that we should never equate the prominence of a few with the equality of many, it will be interesting to see if the appointment of journalist Michaëlle Jean Governor General in 2005 will shift the real opportunities available to black women in Canada. Jean, the descendent of Haitian slaves, is the first black woman to be Governor General, and the first woman to balance parenting a young child with that position. By carefully reading colonial newspapers and legislation, Elgersman Lee uncovers new information about the history of enslaved women in Canada, and in the process, reminds us Jean can lay claim to a long history of black womanhood in Canada.

Notes

1. Sherene H. Razack, *Dark Threats and White Knights: The Somalia Affair, Peacekeeping, and the New Imperialism* (Toronto: University of Toronto Press, 2004), 4, 13.
2. Brett Rushford, '"A Little Flesh We Offer You": The Origins of Indian Slavery in New France', *William and Mary Quarterly* 60.4 (October 2003): 777–808.
3. Kenneth Donovan, 'Slaves and their Owners in Île Royale, 1713–1760', *Acadiensis* 25.1 (Autumn 1995): 29.
4. Allan Greer, *The People of New France* (Toronto: University of Toronto Press, 1997): 85–9.
5. Gretchen Green, 'Molly Brant, Catharine Brant, and Their Daughters: A Study in Colonial Acculturation', *Ontario History* LXXXI.3 (September 1989): 235–50.
6. Peggy Bristow, '"Whatever You Raise in the Ground You Can Sell in Chatham": Black Women in Buxton and Chatham, 1850–1865', in *'We're Rooted Here and They Can't Pull Us Up': Essays in African Canadian Women's History*, Peggy Bristow, et al, eds. (Toronto: University of Toronto Press, 1994).
7. Sherry Edmunds-Flett, '"Abundant Faith": Nineteenth-Century African-Canadian Women on Vancouver Island', in *Telling Tales: Essays in Western Women's History*, Catherine A. Cavanaugh and Randi R. Warne, eds. (Vancouver: UBC Press, 2000), 274.
8. Agnes Calliste, 'Canada's Immigration Policy and Domestics from the Caribbean: The Second Domestic Scheme', in *Race, Class and Gender: Bonds and Barriers*, Jessie Vorst, et al, eds. (Toronto: Between the Lines, 1989).

9. Dionne Brand, '"We Weren't Allowed to Go into Factory Work Until Hitler Started the War": The 1920s to the 1940s', in *'We're Rooted Here and They Can't Pull Us Up': Essays in African Canadian Women's History*, Peggy Bristow, et al, eds. (Toronto: University of Toronto Press, 1994).
10. Karen Flynn, 'Experience and Identity: Black Immigrant Nurses to Canada, 1950–1980', in *Sisters or Strangers? Immigrant, Ethnic, and Racialized Women in Canadian History*, Marlene Epp, Franca Iacovetta, and Frances Swyripa, eds. (Toronto: University of Toronto Press, 2004), 396.
11. Shirley J. Yee, 'Gender Ideology and Black Women as Community-Builders in Ontario, 1850–1870', *Canadian Historical Review* 75.1 (March 1994). Also see Nina Reid-Maroney, 'African Canadian Women and New World Diaspora, circa 1865', *Canadian Woman Studies* 23: 2 (Winter 2004): 92–7.
12. Jane Rhodes, *Mary Ann Shadd Cary: The Black Press and Protest in the Nineteenth-Century* (Bloomington: Indiana University Press, 1998); Rinaldo Walcott, '"Who is she and what is she to you?" Mary Ann Shadd Cary and the (Im)possibility of Black/Canadian Studies', in *Rude: Contemporary Black Canadian Cultural Criticism*, Rinaldo Walcott, ed. (Toronto: Insomniac Press, 2000).
13. Constance Backhouse, 'Bitterly Disappointed at the Spread of "Colour-Bar Tactics": Viola Desmond's Challenge to Racial Segregation, Nova Scotia, 1946', in *Colour-Coded: A Legal History of Racism in Canada, 1900–1950* (Toronto: Osgoode Society for Canadian Legal History, 1999), 174–225.
14. Wanda Thomas Bernard and Judith Fingard, 'Black Women at Work: Race, Family, and Community in Greater Halifax', in *Mothers of The Municipality: Women, Work, and Social Policy in Post-1945 Halifax*, Judith Fingard and Janet Guilford, eds. (Toronto: University of Toronto Press, 2005).
15. Rosemary Brown, *Being Brown: A Very Public Life* (Toronto: Random House, 1989).

Questions for Critical Reading

1. Why have historians only recently broached the questions of African Canadian women's history? What does this tell us about Canada and its historians?
2. Elgersman Lee's essay outlines some of the things historians can learn about enslaved women in Canada's past. The article also suggests some of the barriers to reconstructing the world of enslaved women. What challenges do historians face when trying to learn about the history of women and slavery in Canada?
3. Both men and women were enslaved, but slavery meant different things for men and women. Why and how might this be the case?

In her article, 'Naming Names, Naming Ourselves: A Survey of Early Black Women in Nova Scotia', Sylvia Hamilton references the presence of a 'continuum of Black women's struggle for equality and dignity' that began in the slave era and proceeds into the twentieth century. She also chronicles Black women's struggle for survival, battling 'slavery, servitude, sexual and racial discrimination, and ridicule' in a society that prescribed their position according to the intersection of race and gender.[1] This double jeopardy of being Black in a society that privileged whiteness and of being female in a society that empowered males would inform the history of Black women in Canada, just as it informs the history of Black women throughout much of the diaspora.[2]

This chapter will explore the experience and place of Black women in slavery within a historical outline of the institution during Canada's British regime. In making Black women subject, instead of seeing them solely as object, a vantage point is developed that allows for new insight into the institution of slavery under the British. Not only is this a manifestation of the political resistance of loving Blackness, as bell hooks writes, but it also supports the idea that these women were 'more than the collective pain black females have historically experienced'.[3]

More fundamental than Hamilton's idea of the continuum of struggle, is—for this chapter—the importance of naming Black women and naming their experiences within slavery in early Canada. This approach addresses the need to bring the personhood of Black women out of the obscurity of early Canadian history and out of the traditional way of reporting the history of slavery in Canada that seems to have 'assumed that their status and experience were the same as that of males within the community'.[4] It also helps restore the dignity of the human experience in an institution that was, even in its most basic form, dehumanizing.

In assigning names, that is, identifying Black women by name despite their imposed slave status, the objectification inherent in chattel slavery is directly challenged. Having said that, it is important to understand that many of the names assigned to Black women in slavery were not theirs originally, or of their own choosing. These names then are markers or signs that identify individual Black women, distinguish them from each other, and recognize parallel experiences between them. These markers are somewhat artificial in that they may be products of convenience for the slaveholding class and do not necessary reflect how the women referenced themselves or each other.[5] And while we recognize that many names, like slavery itself, were imposed, it is obvious that many historical sources failed to identify women by their names, as is clearly evident in newspapers that advertised the sale of Black women. This failure not only reflects, but also encourages, maintenance of a mindset that sees Black experiences as generic and indiscriminate. When and where Black women are seen but not named, the historian has an obligation not to allow the absence of a personal title to dismiss the humanity of the situation, for the ability to alter, deny, or omit names is just one aspect of the privilege that slavery assigned to slaveholders and denied to the enslaved.[6]

The British Transition

Britain's 1763 victory in the Seven Years' War permanently ended French control of Canada, and with the arrival of British administrators, settlers, and legal codes, the enslavement of Blacks was transformed in both theory and practice. The British showed a clear preference for Black slaves over Panis slaves, and increased the Black slave population.[7] An important question remains, however, concerning the extent to which the general complacency toward the reproduction of Black slave women seemingly present during the French regime would persist under the British, and what the implications of these conditions would be in this new era.

British occupation of New France actually began before the end of the Seven Years' War. The years 1760 to 1763 represent the transition period from French colonial rule to British colonial rule and, thus, from French colonial slavery to British colonial slavery. The terms of the capitulation of Montreal ensured that slavery would not be disrupted and that it would easily survive the transfer of colonial power, as Blacks and Panis would retain their chattel status and remain the property of their owners. Owners would continue to have the right to keep or sell them as they saw fit.[8] One example of the British willingness to buttress slavery in Canada is the case of James Murray, newly appointed Governor of Quebec, and his immediate appeal to individuals in nearby New York for assistance in procuring slaves. In 1763, Murray wrote:

> Black Slaves are certainly the only people to be depended upon, but it is necessary, I imagine they should be born in one or other of our Northern Colonies, the Winters here will not agree with a Native of the torrid zone, pray therefore if possible procure for me two Stout Young Fellows, who have been accustomed to Country Business, and as I shall wish to see them happy, I am of the opinion there is little felicity without a Communication with the Ladys, you may buy for each a clean young wife, who can

wash and do the female offices about a farm. I shall begrudge no price, so hope we may, by your goodness succeed.[9]

Murray's appeal replicates the 1689 directive of Louis XIV concerning slavery in New France on two levels. First, it sanctions the enslavement of Africans and their place in the institution as 'the only people to be depended upon'. Second, Murray's appeal for Blacks from the northern colonies continued to support popular beliefs concerning Blacks' inability to adapt to a cold climate. The desperate need for labourers that Murray alleged to exist in British Canada, however, is not reflected in his appeal. Murray 'earnestly entreated' the assistance of New York colleagues to help fill a significant labour void, but only requested four slaves. If the labour shortage was as significant as suggested and Murray would not 'begrudge any price', one might ask why he did not try to purchase more than four slaves. It is reasonable to conclude that what Murray identified as a labour need was actually a labour preference informed by a firmly entrenched, racial hierarchy.[10]

Murray's appeal is revealing in a way that the 1689 directive by Louis XIV was not, in that it introduces the reader to attitudes about Black women in slavery. Numerous scholars have made reference to Murray's appeal, but have failed to explore how it might reflect the place of Black women in the slave system of British Canada. Scholars have also failed to recognize and critically examine the patriarchal overtones clearly present in his request and the fraternity of consciousness implied between Murray and his correspondent.[11] The request for two female slaves is clearly predicated upon their instrumentality in the happiness of the two male slaves requested, the primary focus of Murray's appeal. This apparent preference for male slaves over female slaves is reminiscent of other slave societies in the Americas.[12]

The 'Communication' to which Murray makes reference is surely sexual in nature, and suggests a highly utilitarian model of the role Black women were to play in this slave regime. Not simply were they to be workers, but Black women seem to be constructed as objects of pleasure for Black men. Murray's interest in the sexual 'felicity' of his future slaves seems an anomaly in an age that feared and often attempted to subvert Black male sexuality.[13] However, if this sexuality could have been channeled or controlled by providing a wife for each man, it might have reduced the likelihood of escape or the possibility of interracial relationships between these men and Quebec's general female population.[14] In that sense, Murray's request takes on a strategic characteristic that suggests that while slavery in Canada was practiced on a smaller scale than in Jamaica, for example, it was still a complex institution.

Murray's request also offers a possible model of the place of the Black family in the construction of slavery in early Canada and may reflect some degree of respect for the marriage of Blacks. Marriages between slaves were legal, but the request indicates that these unseen women and men would have no choice in deciding to whom or when they would marry.[15] If Murray intended to create a familial base on which to increase his slave population and his investment in slave ownership, a 1769 issue of the *Quebec Gazette* suggests that he failed, at least in part. The newspaper advertised the sale of a young Black woman and her infant and described them as the former property of General Murray.[16]

Paradoxically, while James Murray urgently petitioned for the importation of Black slaves, local newspapers advertised the sale of Black slaves already residing in Canada because there was no work for them. In 1770 the *Quebec Gazette* advertised the sale of a 'Negro fellow' only 'because of no employ for him' and through no fault of his own.[17] Some years later, in 1783, the newspaper advertised the sale of a Black woman for the same reason. The *Quebec Gazette* read:

> To Be Sold.
> A Negro Wench about 18 years of age, who came lately from New York with the Loyalists. She has had the Small Pox.— The Wench has a good character and is exposed to sale only from the owner having no use for her at present.

Likewise will be disposed of a handsome Bay Mare. For particulars enquire of the Printer.[18]

The exact meaning of the description 'good character' is unknown, but there are at least two possible readings of the phrase. The woman for sale may simply have been esteemed by her owner as personable, pleasant, or compliant. Additionally, and closely related to the first argument, is the premise that the owner stressed the woman's good character to assure potential buyers that she was not being sold because she was unruly, unmanageable, or rebellious. Her good character might also be read as a signifier that she was sexually modest. There remains an intertextuality in the sale advertisement in that the Black woman is aligned, both in text and in image, with the bay mare. Both female, both of property status, and both seemingly of good disposition, the woman and the horse could be sold and disposed of. Their reproductive ability could also be exploited according to the needs of present or prospective owners, since any offspring would belong to them.[19]

Loyalists did bring slave women and men into Canada during and after the years of the American Revolution, but they often found it necessary to sell them. Economists describe early Canada as a colony whose economy was focused on the import and export of raw materials and many of whose colonists lived in poverty.[20] In 1790, a year before the official division of Canada into Upper Canada (Ontario) and Lower Canada (Quebec), the British Parliament, upon the agitation of colonists, passed a law allowing Loyalists and other potential Canadian residents to bring their slave property with them as long as they had the permission of the Lieutenant-Governor.[21] This seems more of a ploy to attract residents than to extend slavery, since the aforementioned advertisement in the *Quebec Gazette* shows that Loyalists had already been bringing their slaves to British Canada during the previous decade. This legislation succeeded in increasing the presence and voice of slaveholders in Canada, a collective voice that would remain vigilant when, before the end of the decade, they would fight abolitionists to maintain the institution.

While British Canada was hospitable to arriving slave owners, it was also cordial to the slaveholders of the French regime. In the transition from the French regime to the British regime in 1763, Canadian law allowed slaveholders to keep their property. The Quebec Act of 1774, passed to retain the loyalty of French colonists who had come under British rule, reintroduced French civil and property law in French-populated areas.[22] Under French civil and property law, slavery was protected because it had been legally instituted in 1689 by Louis XIV. In 1792, however, British civil law was reintroduced and wiped out slavery's legal foundation in French civil law. These transitions between French and British law contributed significantly to confusion about the rights of Canadians to hold slaves as their legal, personal property.[23] To find the answer, Canadians looked to the content of British civil law for a decision on slavery.

Technically, slavery was illegal in Britain and, as a result, many British citizens could boast that the air of England was 'too pure' for such an institution. However, whether it was illegal or not, numerous British citizens did indeed have slave property; it seems that custom simply preceded law and de facto slavery ruled where de jure slavery did not.[24] This de facto slavery seems to have been predicated on the belief in the fitness of Blacks for enslavement and an inherent right of white men to participate in the institution if they could afford to. Because of the illegality of slavery in Britain, many residents of British Canada erroneously believed that the reintroduction of British civil law abolished slavery in the colony.[25]

In 1793, the position and future of slavery in Canada shifted significantly when the Statute of 1793 was passed, largely through the power and influence of Lord John Graves Simcoe, Lieutenant-Governor of Upper Canada (Ontario). Known in Britain for his personal campaigns against slavery, Simcoe continued his abolitionist agitation when he assumed his political post in Upper Canada. Simcoe pushed for absolute, sweeping legislation that would wipe out slavery, both present and future, but he had to settle for a compromise as many Canadian slaveholders argued for their right to have slave property, even though it had already proven unnecessary and expendable for many of their fellow citizens.[26]

The 1793 statute, 'An Act to prevent the further introduction of Slaves and to limit the terms of contracts for servitude within this Province', had four basic tenets. First, and most dramatically, it provided that any Blacks entering the colony after the law's passage would be free. At the same time, none of the Blacks who were enslaved at the time were freed by this legislation. Any persons born into slavery after the passage of the statute would be freed at the age of twenty-five, and, finally, if any of these same persons gave birth before reaching their twenty-fifth birthday, their children were to be considered free at birth.[27] Given the comparatively small Black slave population in early Canada, the generation of slaves to be freed at age twenty-five was probably small. In fact, many scholars believe that by 1834, the date of the comprehensive prohibition of slavery in British Canada, there were few, if any, slaves remaining there.[28]

The enactment of the 1793 statute came in the same year that the United States passed its first federal fugitive slave law, which would change the relationship between the two regions until slavery was abolished in the United States in 1865. Canada no longer held the promise of security for slave owners, but it would soon become a haven that Blacks, free and enslaved, would risk their lives to reach. Slavery, while still legal for those Blacks who were enslaved in Canada, could not be applied to other Blacks who fled to Canada or who were taken there by their owners, thereby creating a legal and moral dichotomy in terms of the status of Blacks inside and outside of Canada. While not a fatal blow, the Statute of 1793 helped ensure that slavery would eventually become extinct. Additionally, the new colonial legislation also required that slave owners provide for the physical needs of slaves until they were manumitted, which put the burden of responsibility on the slave owners.[29]

Prominent Black Women

The immediate, local catalyst for Simcoe's decision to push for the complete abolition of slavery is an incident that involved Chloe Cooley, a Black woman who was being bound for transport and sale to the United States. Resisting her treatment and her impending sale, Cooley fought considerably and required more than one man to restrain her.[30] The ferocity with which Cooley resisted her treatment suggests that she experienced slavery in Canada as an invasive and inhumane institution.

Rather than being sympathetic to the dehumanizing treatment of Cooley, Simcoe reportedly commented on the nuisance that such scenes brought to the Canadian public. His agenda, then, was to rid the public of similar future disturbances.[31] Simcoe was more concerned with the alleged inconvenience experienced by citizens who observed such incidents than with the brutal nature of Cooley's treatment. Another reading of this historical moment might suggest that Simcoe used the issue of public nuisance to gain the popular support he would need to abolish slavery in Upper Canada. Simcoe may have needed to convince Canadians that abolition was in their best interests. Even the most generous interpretation of Simcoe's response to the exercise of Cooley's imposed chattel status suggests that Simcoe did not read Cooley's treatment as an insult to her womanhood or recognize her resistance to reclaim an agency that was rightfully hers.[32]

Simcoe's unique brand of abolitionist zeal was not shared by all Upper Canadians, and when he left the colony three years after the passage of the statute, the provincial legislature proposed a bill to repeal the Statute of 1793. The bill was not passed, and was never reintroduced for debate.[33] Simcoe's legislation helped undermine slavery directly, just as the Act of 1790 had helped to undermine slavery indirectly. Subsequently, owners who failed to see an adequate return on their investments, or who anticipated a decline in the need for slave labour, simply sold their slaves to buyers in other Canadian colonies or in the parts of the United States that still maintained the institution.[34]

The manner in which Chloe Cooley was taken out of Upper Canada resembles the way in which Sophia Pooley, a Black slave woman, was introduced to Upper Canada (Ontario) earlier in that eighteenth century. Pooley's notoriety is rooted in the fact that she belonged to Joseph Brant, a British Loyalist and celebrated leader of the Mohawk Indians.[35] Born in New York to Oliver and Dinah Burthen and into the condition of slavery, Pooley and her sister were kidnapped as children, transported to Canada, and sold to 'old Indian Brant'.[36] Pooley relates this about her capture:

> My parents were slaves in New York State. My master's sons-in-law, Daniel Outwaters and Simon Knox, came into the garden where my sister and I were playing among the currant bushes, tied their handkerchiefs over our mouths, carried us to a vessel, put us in the hold, and sailed up the river. I know not how far nor how long—it was dark there all the time. Then we came by land.[37]

Despite obvious differences in the dimensions of time and place, Pooley's account of her transport to Canada bears striking similarity to Africans' account of the Middle Passage, the transport of Africans from Africa to the Caribbean basin or the United States. Pooley's description mirrors the Passage in that much of her journey was spent in darkness in the vessel's hold; successfully disorienting her perception of time and distance. Being a young child, Pooley was probably fearful of what might happen to her when she arrived at the unknown destination, and certainly would have grieved the loss of her parents.[38]

Pooley's narrative of her life in Canada, which was recorded in the mid-1850s, provides a rare opportunity to understand slavery in Canada from the perspective of an enslaved person. Even more rare is the opportunity to understand it from the perspective of a Black woman.[39] By her own account, Pooley lived twelve or thirteen years with the Brants before being sold to an Englishman when she was approximately twenty. It was soon after this sale that Pooley was told she was free, and her owner released her from enslavement. She remained in Upper Canada into old age, and was given aid by local residents. Pooley did not indicate that she had given birth to any children. Pooley makes no further reference to the plight of her sister; it is likely, therefore, that she never saw her again.[40]

Although Pooley did not give the specific date of her arrival in Canada her narrative offers some clues about it. Pooley says that she arrived well before the American Revolution and that she was an adult when Lord Simcoe arrived in Canada in 1793. By her own account, Pooley was 'the first colored girl brought into Canada', and when she was interviewed in the mid-1850s, stated that she was more than ninety years old.[41] Based on these clues, Pooley may have arrived in Canada in the early 1760s.

Pooley's statement that she was the first Black girl in Canada was probably made in error, although it does help support the theory that she did not enter Canada with her sister. The 1767 census report for Nova Scotia, for example, listed a total of 101 Black residents—35 men, 18 boys, 30 women, and 17 girls. Slaves were also active in the building of Halifax in 1749, and Marie Joseph Angélique, a slave resister and martyr in Montreal, had two children in 1732 before her act of arson and subsequent execution in 1734.[42] While Pooley may not have been correct about being the first Black girl in Canada, there remains within her narrative an implied experience of physical isolation from other Black women that probably fed her sense of being the 'only' and the 'first' Black woman. Pooley recounts having had close contact with Mohawk Indians, a white woman, and a Black man, but nowhere in her narrative does she mention having had any contact with Black women. She married a Black man named Robert Pooley, and was enslaved with two Black men, Simon Ganseville and the father of a man named John Patten.[43] Significant slave populations could be found in Lower Canada, but because Pooley resided in the larger Grand River region of Upper Canada

(Ontario)—an area that she states 'hardly had any white people'—and within the Mohawk community, she may not have been afforded sustained contact with other Black women.[44]

It appears very probable, therefore, that some Black women enslaved during the British regime lacked significant opportunity to create social bonds with other Black women based on shared gender, race, and legal status. Such isolation would have made it impossible for many Black women to go to other Black women for respite from the degradation of physical or sexual abuse, for assistance in raising children, or for celebrating religious or labour holidays.[45] It is highly possible that where Black women lacked such support systems, they may have found the slave experience even more trying than it was for women who had such support. These conditions also may have encouraged more slave resistance and flight.[46] Black women may have also forged relationships with women outside of their race which could be positive or negative.

Sophia Pooley's early experience in Canada allowed her to construct her experience as the first, but the last decades of the eighteenth century witnessed significant increase in the visibility of Black slave women, if only in printed advertisements offering their sale or soliciting opportunities for their purchase. The *Upper Canada Gazette* advertised the following notice in July of 1795:

> For Sale, for three years from the 29th of this present month of July, a Negro Wench, Named Chloe, 23 years old, understands washing, cooking &c. Any gentleman willing to purchase, or employ her by the year or month, is requested to apply to ROBERT FRANKLIN, at the receiver general's.[47]

The demand for Black females remained visible as the same newspaper advertised a generous price for securing a 'Negro girl about 12 years old' on 18 January 1792. The notice appeared in the next edition of the newspaper a week later.[48] The following advertisement ran for four consecutive weeks in the *Upper Canada Gazette* during October 1792.

> Wanted to purchase,
> A NEGRO GIRL, from 7 to 12 years of age, of good disposition.—For further particulars apply to the subscribers.
> W. & J. Crooks[49]

The Crooks family seems to have been quite wealthy. James Crooks, merchant son of William Crooks, Sr, and Margaret Ramsay, lived in the town of Niagara. Married in 1808, James Crooks moved to West Flamborough around 1813, and within ten years had established 'an industrial empire' in Crook's Hollow.[50]

The object of less successful attempts at abolition than in Upper Canada (Ontario), slavery in Lower Canada (Quebec) was more resilient. Lower Canada had been the slave center of New France, with the district of Montreal leading in the slave population. The census of 1784 listed a slave population of 212 for Montreal and 88 for Quebec. There was no breakdown according to race or gender.[51] Although subject to the act that banned the further importation of slaves, the provincial government of Lower Canada did not manage to pass is own act against slavery in 1793 as had been done by its western neighbor. In that year, the House of Assembly in Lower Canada proposed a bill that supported the complete abolition of slavery, but it was tabled and never revived. While Greaves notes that there seemed little popular interest in continuing slavery, absolute abolition was equally contested as slaveholders 'guarded their property jealously'.[52] It seems that Canadians with interests in the institution objected more to losing their right to be slaveholders than to forfeiting any financial investment with abolition. In reality, however, investments in human property were still relatively secure, and since slavery was still thriving in the United States, Canadian slaveholders could have sold their slaves and regained all or part of their investment. Agents were often secured by slave owners to sell slaves on their behalf and reimburse them for the sale price.[53] Perhaps, there were more localized class interests fueling the drive to preserve slavery, in that the absence of slavery and of slaves as signs of wealth threatened to make the distance between the elite and others less discernible.

In spite of the institution's earlier resiliency, the last few years of the eighteenth century, from 1797 to 1799, witnessed a genuine decline in slavery in Lower Canada. This decline has been attributed to three distinct developments: judicial liberalism, Parliamentary repeal, and manumission. Provincial judges, whether interpreting colonial or imperial law, increasingly ruled in favor of enslaved Blacks and effectively reduced the power of slave owners. As Blacks recognized that the law was on their side, they pushed the boundaries of their status and created even more freedom for themselves. First, some of the province's judges, in a series of cases brought before their courts, adopted the policy that unless an individual could prove ownership of his alleged slave in a court of law, said slave was considered a free person. Ownership had to be established upon the presentation of a written title.[54] While this requirement did not always translate into freedom for Blacks, it did begin to erode the foundation of slavery and helped chip away at the basic assumption of slave societies that negritude was synonymous with slave status. This is also a very specific reversal of United States policy where Blacks accused of being fugitive slaves had to produce papers to prove their liberty; indeed, slave owners' claims to Blacks as property were rarely questioned.[55] The racial order dominant in most slave societies was being challenged and upset by the courts in Lower Canada.

In one case brought before Montreal's Court of King's Bench, a magistrate released two Black women, Charlotte and Jude, from service. The decision for Jude's freedom was based on the basis that her admission to jail for punishment violated a sixteenth-century English legal code. People could be committed to a house of correction for punishment, but not to jail. The magistrate ruled that since there were no houses of correction in Lower Canada, Jude was free.[56]

In 1799, the Court of King's Bench argued that the Imperial Act of 1797 did in fact abolish slavery and that slaves were under no obligation to continue to perform their services as slaves.[57] This began a steady wave of rebellion as Blacks left their houses of enslavement or negotiated wages and other conditions for their continued service. Though still essentially legal until it was abolished in 1834, the institution of slavery was 'virtually inoperative in Lower Canada by 1800'.[58] By the turn of the century, judicial interpretation of slavery proved more important than the actual legality of slavery. Legal precedent and judicial liberalism conspired to further weaken slavery and to give slaves the legal protection they needed to contest successfully their status or abandon the system completely. Ironically, some Blacks in Canada fled to the United States for refuge.[59]

Officers and advertisements for the sale of Black women remain visible in the newspapers of Lower Canada. The following advertisement was featured in the *Montreal Gazette*, 4 April 1793:

> To Be Sold
> A very stout Negro wench of about 25 years of age. She can wash, Iron, Cook, and do any kind of House work. For further particulars, apply to Mr. McMurray.[60]

This advertisement seems to appeal to the myth of the superwoman that cast Black women as hardy figures capable of performing any task or carrying any burden required of them. This investment in the idea of the superwoman was the necessary antithesis of white women, particularly those of wealth, who personified the true image of womanhood. The use of the term 'stout', while likely meant to be a physical descriptor, serves to feed the idea of the propriety of Black women as chattel and the necessary distinction between Black women and white women on which their chattel condition was, to a significant degree, based and defended.[61]

The *Montreal Gazette* advertised in three consecutive editions in August of 1791, the following announcement:

> For Sale
> Ten years service of a Negro Girl aged about seventeen years—Enquire of the Printer.[62]

Nova Scotia, the site of Canada's first permanent non-Aboriginal settlement, based a significant Black population of both freed and enslaved persons. Greaves reports that at the end of the American Revolution, 3,000 free Blacks migrated there and no less than 1,300 slaves were brought to this eastern region by their owners. This influx of Black and white settlers made Nova Scotia the province with the largest Loyalist concentration in the entire Canadian possessions. Halifax, the province's central city, was built in 1749 with the labour of slaves, and Blacks were soon common fixtures there.[63]

Despite the presence of thousands of Blacks, the exact legal foundation of slavery in Nova Scotia was still tenuous. A colonial act of 1762, revised in 1783, made reference to 'Negro slaves' even though the actual ordinance was designed to deal with the regulation of liquor sales. An obscure piece of legislation, the law allowed that any persons, soldiers, sailors, enslaved Blacks, or others, who gave a liquor vendor a deposit toward the payment of a debt of more than five shillings, could go before the Justice of the Peace and have the deposit returned. The vendor would be fined twenty shillings for taking advantage of the poor. The mention and recognition of enslaved Blacks were claimed by slave owners as evidence of the legality of the institution itself. In 1797, the Colonial Assembly rejected the claim that the mention of 'Negro slaves' was official recognition of the legality of slavery. For slavery to be legal, there had to be a document that clearly allowed slavery, and mention of the objects of slavery did not make the institution actual or legal.[64] Riddell explains the ambiguity of the situation:

> It was recognized that slavery might exist in Nova Scotia, but it was made as difficult as possible for the master to succeed on the facts. Except the act already mentioned there was no stature recognizing slavery and an attempt in 1787 to incorporate such a recognition in the statute law failed of success by a large majority.[65]

As in Upper Canada and Lower Canada, de facto slavery existed in Nova Scotia even if de jure slavery did not. In 1808 Nova Scotian slave owners sought legal protection for slavery from the provincial legislature. A bill to regulate Negro servants was introduced; it passed its second reading but never became law.[66] The tenuous status of slavery in Nova Scotia, neither permitted nor forbidden, did not translate into a quality of life for Blacks that was superior to that experienced in other parts of Canada. In the same year, the Atlantic slave trade was abolished and the external supply of Africans was greatly diminished.[67]

Provincial judges wrestled with the legality of slavery in the Maritimes, and often arrived at an impasse during deliberations. One such case, *Delancy v. Wooden*, came before the courts of Nova Scotia. James Delancy's slave, Jack, ran one hundred miles away from his residence in Annapolis to Halifax where a man identified only as Mr Wooden hired him for wages. Wooden refused to return Jack to Delancy on the basis that Jack's humanity kept him from being the property of Delancy or anyone else. The court's decision was to award Delancy seventy pounds for damages, but a motion for appeal was filed based on the premise that Jack was not property, and, therefore, Delancy was not entitled to property damages. Several lawyers submitted editorials that indicated their opinions of the case, and they all supported Delancy's right to claim property damages. The case was dismissed in 1803, even though Delancy could document his ownership of Jack. Delancy's death in 1804 terminated attempts to retrieve Jack from Wooden.[68]

Blacks in Nova Scotia had a history of discriminatory treatment and social marginalization. Free Blacks were ostracized from major cities and towns, and settled in enclaves that would later become popular Black settlements. Birchtown, Africville, Tracadie, and Shelburne were some of the most prominent centers of Black settlement. In addition to social marginalization, Blacks who desired to be independent farmers received land grants of smaller size and inferior quality than acreage promised to them and awarded to whites. Ultimately, Blacks in the Maritime Provinces did not fare as well as those in Upper and Lower Canada; many Blacks from Nova Scotia and New Brunswick would migrate to the West African colony of Sierra Leone in the 1790s.[69]

Slavery in Prince Edward Island (PEI) was more clearly established than in other parts of Canada. In 1781, the Legislature of Prince Edward Island passed an act legally recognizing slavery. This act had two important components. The first clause indicated that all Black servants residing on the island as well as those who would be brought in as slaves would not be freed by baptism or conversion to Christianity. The second clause indicated that all children born to enslaved women would be considered the property of the woman's owner. In this perspective, Prince Edward Island confirmed early Canada's adherence to the basic tenet of perpetual slavery found in other slave societies wherein the condition of the slave child in Canada followed that of the mother.[70] While this legislation emulated the standard formula regarding slave baptism and the ownership of children, it was repealed in 1825. The Act of 1825 initiated the following change in the configuration of slavery:

> Be it therefore enacted by the Lieutenant Governor, Council and Assembly, That from and after the passing hereof the said Act, intitled, 'An Act declaring that Baptism of Slaves shall not exempt them from Bondage', and every Clause, matter and thing therein contained be, and the same is hereby, repealed.[71]

Scholars are careful to point out that the specific conditions of slavery were repealed, but the institution itself was not. The act was repealed in order for abolitionism to gain momentum; it succeeded in creating confusion about the nature of slavery in the province, but did not abolish the institution itself.[72]

Slavery in New Brunswick was intrinsically tied to slavery in Nova Scotia because both were part of the same province until 1784. In that year many of the recently arrived Loyalists rejected the Halifax government and desired their own community. William Spray's study *The Blacks in New Brunswick* explores the course of slavery in the province and emphasizes that because Nova Scotia and New Brunswick were initially united as Acadia, it is difficult to estimate the number of slaves who resided there. Early census reports can only offer vague guidelines. The 1686 census lists 101 'Negroes'—54 males and 47 females—without regard to class or legal status.[73] Of the approximately 1,200 to 1,300 slaves who were taken to the eastern province after the American Revolution, it has been estimated that at least 500 resided in the St John area. Slaves were a common sight in New Brunswick, as they were in Nova Scotia, but scholars have noted the presence of at least one community, Beaver County where no slave owners or slave traders were allowed to live.[74]

The legality of slavery in New Brunswick appears tenuous. Spray concludes that no law was ever passed that specifically legalized slavery in New Brunswick, but notes that settlers were routinely permitted entrance into the province with their slave property. Two separate bills allowing for the legal institution of slavery as well as for the physical protection of old and infirm slaves were introduced in the House of Assembly in 1801, but opposition kept them from being passed.[75] Slavery was neither legal nor illegal in New Brunswick; it simply existed. Where the law neither explicitly legalized slavery nor rendered it illegal, custom dictated that it would be a feature of New Brunswick's economic and social order.

As ambiguous and inconsistent as the legal foundation for slavery was, the treatment of Blacks was certainly that of chattel. Spray offers some of the most graphic and inhumane accounts of slavery in the entire Canadian colony. He details two accounts as follows:

> [A] slave master was a former loyalist officer, who rode up to the local tavern every day for a glass of liquor. He was followed by his slave on foot who had to get his glass and then return it after it was empty. In the process the slave was made to perform 'lively movements worthy of an acrobat', in order to avoid the blow from his master's whip which invariably accompanied the return of the glass. Another slave owner in Maugerville is reported to have had the habit of tying his slaves up in the barn and whipping them on the slightest pretext. There are also a number of stories of slave quarters in old loyalist homes where chains were used to lock up slaves who might attempt to run away.[76]

A study of slavery in Canada reveals much about the history of Blacks in that country. In New France, slaves were legally recognized by royal decree in 1689. Under the British regime, the presence of French or British civil law was said to determine the legality of slavery in the colony; in those provinces where the question of slavery's legality went unanswered, however, slaves were simply bought, sold, and exploited on the assumption that slavery was entirely legal. Each province in British Canada that supported significant slave populations—Upper Canada, Lower Canada, Nova Scotia, and New Brunswick—had its own distinct history of undermining and reducing the potency of slavery in its jurisdiction. What is common to all provinces is the fact that they failed to create an environment that was conducive to the foundation and maintenance of a significant, cohesive Black slave population. Because there was little uniform de facto or de jure slave policy, it became unlikely that slavery would be anything other than a very disjointed institution.

Even though Canadian slave populations were small and fragmented, Black women had a more significant presence in the history of slavery in colonial Canada than has been previously suggested. Advertisements in the *Royal Gazette, Montreal Gazette, Quebec Gazette*, and *Upper Canada Gazette* are public markers that confirm the presence of Black women and inform that position that most Black women enslaved in early Canada laboured in domestic capacities. More difficult to fully decipher are early census reports, and more obscure to the average reader are the legal judgments concerning the legal development of slavery after the French regime. Although evidence of the identity of some women is limited to a brief advertisement or an obscure historical document, other women are less anonymous. Sophia Pooley's narrative gives her a historical *voice* and offers reflection on slavery, and the actions of Chloe Cooley and Marie Joseph Angelique offer profiles in resistance. Far from being silent fringe characters in history, Black Canadian women were wives, mothers, workers, and resistors who left indelible marks on the institution of slavery in their respective times and places.

Notes

1. Sylvia Hamilton, 'Naming Names, Naming Ourselves: A Survey of Early Black Women in Nova Scotia', in *'We're Rooted Here and They Can't Pull Us Up': Essays in African Canadian Women's History*, coordinator Peggy Bristow (Toronto: University of Toronto Press, 1994), 13.
2. Frances M. Beal, 'Double Jeopardy; To Be Black and Female', in *AfroAmerican History: Primary Sources*, 2nd ed., Thomas R. Frazier, ed. (Belmont, CA: Wadsworth Publishing Co., 1988), 428–32.
3. bell hooks, *Black Looks: Race and Representation* (Boston: South End Press, 1992), 9, 45.
4. Sylvia Hamilton, 'Naming Names', 13.
5. Wilma King, *Stolen Childhood: Slave Youth in Nineteenth-Century America* (Bloomington and Indianapolis: Indiana University Press, 1995), 6–8.
6. King shows how 'naming' and 'calling' could create conflict as slave children and youth had to choose between loyalty to a parent or to an owner, with neither choice having positive consequences; Wilma King, *Stolen Childhood: Slave Youth in Nineteenth-Century America* (Bloomington and Indianapolis: Indiana University Press, 1995), 68.

7. Robin W. Winks, *The Blacks in Canada: A History* (New Haven: Yale University Press; Montreal: Montreal Queen's University Press, 1971), 23.
8. James W. St G. Walker, *'Race', Rights and the Law in the Supreme Court of Canada: Historical Case Studies* (Waterloo: Wilfrid Laurier University Press and Osgoode Society for Canadian Legal History, 1997), 137.
9. William Renwick Riddell, 'Documents; Notes on Slavery in Canada', *The Journal of Negro History* 4 (October 1919): 396.
10. Kenneth M. Stampp, *The Peculiar Institution: Slavery in the Ante-Bellum South*, 2nd edition (New York: Random House, 1984), 5. Stampp writes that 'the use of slaves in southern agriculture was a deliberate choice (among several alternatives)' and that the rise of the institution 'was inevitable only in the sense that every event in history seems inevitable after it has occurred'.
11. I borrow this idea from Darlene Clark Hine, who used the parallel term 'sorority of consciousness' in a discussion about the relationship between enslaved Black women and white women in the US South (Multicultural Women's Studies Institute: UMO, May 1998).
12. Herbert S. Klein argues that this preference for male slaves was due, in part, to the general absence of women in the Atlantic slave trade caused by a significant African continental trade in African women. See Klein, 'African Women'. Peggy Bristow comments on Murray's request; she implies the instrumentality of Black women to Black men, but does not develop the idea further. See Bristow, '"Whatever you raise in the ground you can sell it in Chatham": Black Women in Buxton and Chatham, 1850–65', in *'We're Rooted Here and They Can't Pull Us Up': Essays in African Canadian Women's History*, coordinator Peggy Bristow (Toronto: University of Toronto Press, 1994), 71.
13. Winthrop Jordan, *White Over Black* (Chapel Hill and London: University of North Carolina Press, 1968), 150–78.
14. Winks notes the presence of interracial relationships in New France; Winks, *Blacks,* 11–13.
15. Kenneth Stampp relates that although many American states allowed slaves to marry, these unions could be dissolved if it was in the planter's interest to sell one or both of the spouses; Stampp, *Peculiar,* 198.
16. Winks claims that most interracial relationships involved Black men and white women; see Winks, *Blacks,* 11. Coincidentally, Sophia Pooley, a Black slave woman, said her husband left her for a white woman, as reported in Benjamin Drew's *A North-Side View of Slavery. The Refugee; or the Narratives of Fugitive Slaves in Canada, Related by Themselves* (New York: Negro Universities Press, 1968), 195.
17. William Renwick Riddell, 'Le Code Noir', *The Journal of Negro History* 10 (July 1925): 303.
18. *Quebec Gazette,* 6 November 1783.
19. The hardiness with which Black women were believed to be able to bear children and endure physical labour is also present in this configuration.
20. W.T. Easterbrook and Hugh G.J. Aitken, *Canadian Economic History* (Toronto: Macmillan Company of Canada, Ltd., 1970), 94–8.
21. Société Historique de Montréal, *Mémoires et documents relatifs à l'histoire du Canada* (Montreal: Duvernay, Frères, 1859), 24.
22. Ibid., 377–80.
23. Ibid., 375–6.
24. Campbell, *Lives of the Chief Justices,* Vol. 2,419; quoted in William Renwick Riddell, 'The Slave in Canada', *The Journal of Negro History* 5 (July 1920): 273–6.
25. Ibid.
26. Leo W. Bertley, *Canada and Its People of African Descent* (Pierrefonds, QC: Bilongo Publishers, 1977), 32.
27. Société Historique, *Mémoires,* 25–7; William Renwick Riddell, 'The Slave in Upper Canada', *The Journal of Negro History* 4 (October 1919): 373–7. Simcoe's legislation stressed that the statute did not free slaves. It stated 'Provided always—that nothing herein contained shall extend, or be construed to extend to liberate any Negro.' The statute is also referenced in the *Upper Canada Gazette,* 11 July 1793; *Upper Canada Gazette; or, American Oracle,* 18 April 1793 to 26 December 1801, microfilm, LAC.
28. Winks, *Blacks,* 110. The 1827 census returns for Upper Canada, Lower Canada, and Nova Scotia make no reference to slave populations; Canada, Dominion Bureau of Statistics, *Censuses of Canada, 1665 to 1871* (Ottawa: I.B. Taylor, 1876), 93–8.
29. Riddell, 'The Slave in Upper Canada', 382–3.
30. Ibid., 377–8.
31. Ibid., 377–80.
32. Riddell argues that the reintroduction of English civil law in Upper Canada strengthened the property status of slaves, and deprived slaves of all rights 'marital, parental, proprietary, even the right to live'; Riddell, 'The Slave in Upper Canada', 376. Despite Simcoe's resolve to get rid of slavery, he does not seem to have had a deeper appreciation for the rightful agency of Blacks.
33. Ida C. Greaves, *The Negro in Canada* (Orilla, ON: Packet Times Press Ltd, 1930), 14.
34. Winks, *Blacks,* 12.
35. For more information about Joseph Brant, see Daniel G. Hill, *The Freedom Seekers: Blacks in Early Canada*

(Agincourt, ON: Book Society of Canada Ltd, 1981), 191–3.

36. Benjamin Drew, *A North-Side View of Slavery; The Refugee; or the Narratives of Fugitive Slaves in Canada, Related by Themselves* (New York: Negro University Press, 1968), 192.
37. Ibid.
38. Although certainly more graphic and detailed than Pooley's account, Olaudah Equiano, kidnapped from Africa in the 1750s and enslaved in the Americas, shared the horrors of the Middle Passage experience with the public when his narrative was published in the 1780s. Equiano described the stench of the ship's hold, the shrieks and moans of the other captives, and overall emotional intensity of the passage. See Robert J. Allison, ed., *The Interesting Narrative of the Life of Olaudah Equiano Written by Himself* (Boston: St. Martin's Press, 1995), 1, 56.
39. The narrative of Sophia Pooley is found in its entirety in Drew, *North-Side*, 192–4. It is one of the many narratives of Black Canadians recorded and compiled by Benjamin Drew in the 1850s. Most of the persons represented in the text were fugitive slaves from the United States. The Pooley narrative covers less than four full pages and is a rare primary account of slavery in Canada.
40. Drew, *North-Side,* 192–5. There is disagreement about the reliability of Pooley's narrative. Hill argues that she probably confused the chronology of events and exaggerated some points; Hill, *Freedom,* 191. Linda Brown-Kubisch suggests that Pooley remained with Brant for twelve or thirteen years and that she was not freed until 1834; Linda Brown-Kubisch, 'The Black Experience in the Queen's Bush Settlement', *Ontario History* 88 (June 1996): 107.
41. Drew, *North-Side,* 192–4.
42. Census of 1767, Nova Scotia. *Censuses of Canada*, 71. For the birth of Marie Joseph Angelique's children, see Notre-Dame-de-Montreal, Parish registers, entry dated 26 May 1732, NAQM.
43. Drew, *North-Side*, 194.
44. Ibid., 192.
45. Barbara Bush, *Slave Women in Caribbean Society 1650–1838* (Bloomington and Indianapolis: Indiana University Press, 1990), 106, 107.
46. In her chapter 'The Female Slave Network', Deborah Gray White notes how important the community of Black women was in slavery. Women depended on each other for child care and rearing, as well as for carrying out the daily demands of survival in the position of slave. See White, *Ar'n't I a Woman?: Female Slaves in the Plantation South* (New York: W.W. Norton and Company, 1985), 119–41.
47. *Upper Canada Gazette; or American Oracle*, 19 August 1795. Microfilm, 18 April 1793 to 26 December 1801, LAC.
48. *Upper Canada Gazette; or American Oracle*, 18 January 1797 and 25 January 1797. Microfilm, 18 April 1793 to 26 December 1801, LAC.
49. *Upper Canada Gazette; or American Oracle,* 4, 11, 21, 28 October 1797. Microfilm, 18 April 1793 to 26 December 1801, LAC.
50. 'James Crooks', *Flamborough Marriage Records, 1794–1829* (Waterdown: Waterdown-East Flamborough Heritage Society, 1988), 3.
51. Census of 1784, *Censuses of Canada,* 74.
52. Greaves, *Negro*, 10.
53. *Mallard v. McKowan*, 1788, New Brunswick; *Mullen v. Lovitt*, 1785; New Brunswick; *Hall v. Bennison*, 1792, Nova Scotia. PANB.
54. W.A. Spray, *The Blacks in New Brunswick* (Fredericton: Brunswick Press, 1972), 26.
55. Greaves, *Negro,* 16; a similar case is *King v. Jones,* 1799, New Brunswick. PANB.
56. Winks, *Blacks,* 100.
57. Ibid., 61.
58. Riddell, 'Slave in Canada', 359; the decline of slavery in Lower Canada is discussed extensively in Société Historique, *Mémoires*, 34–43. The study is in French.
59. William Renwick Riddell, 'Additional Notes on Slavery; Reciprocity of Slaves Between Michigan and Upper Canada', *The Journal of Negro History* 17 (July 1932): 368–77.
60. *Montreal Gazette,* 4 April 1793. Microfilm, 7 July 1791 to 30 December 1790, LAC.
61. Michele Wallace, *Black Macho and the Myth of the Superwoman* (New York: Dial Press, 1978), 106–7; White, *Ar'n't I a Woman*, 38–9, 44–5;
62. *Montreal Gazette*, 7, 14, and 28 August 1797. Microfilm, 7 July 1791 to 30 December 1799, NLC.
63. Greaves, *Negro*, 61.
64. Riddell, 'Slave in Canada', 368.
65. Ibid., 361.
66. Greaves, *Negro,* 16.
67. John H. Franklin and Alfred A. Moss, *From Slavery to Freedom: A History of African Americans* (New York: Knopf, 1994), 120–1.
68. *Opinions of Several Gentlemen of the Law, on the Subject of Negro Servitude in the Province of Nova Scotia* (St John: John Ryan Printers, 1802), 4–5,23–5, PANS; Winks, *Blacks*, 106.
69. W.A. Spray, *The Blacks in New Brunswick* (Fredericton, NB: Brunswick Press, 1972), 29–70 passim. Spray explains that Blacks suffered from discrimination and marginalization by Canadian citizens. Although the law was on their side, Blacks were disenfranchised,

were refused entry into predominately white schools, and were denied merchants' licences. Spray, *Blacks,* 29–41; Winks, *Blacks,* 34–45: For a full treatment of the emigration of Blacks from Nova Scotia and New Brunswick to Sierra Leone, see Mavis C. Campbell, *The Maroons of Jamaica, 1655–1796: A History of Resistance, Collaboration, and Betrayal* (Granby, Mass.: Bergin and Garvey, 1988); Mavis C. Campbell, *Back to Africa: George Ross and the Maroons from Nova Scotia to Sierra Leone* (Trenton, NJ: Africa World Press, Inc., 1993).

70. Spray, *Blacks,* 70; William Renwick Riddell, 'The Baptism of Slaves in Prince Edward Island', *The Journal of Negro History* 6 (July 1921): 308–9.
71. William Renwick Riddell, 'The Baptism of Slaves in Prince Edward Island', *The Journal of Negro History* 6 (July 1921): 309.
72. Spray, *Blacks,* 70; Riddell, 'Baptism', 309.
73. Census of 1686, Acadia; Census of 1767, Nova Scotia; *Censuses of Canada*, 20, 71.
74. Spray, *Blacks,* 16, 17.
75. Regardless of the failure to pass these laws, affidavits of court cases in the late 1700s indicate that Black slaves were present in New Brunswick and that their ownership was contested. See *Mallard v. McKowan,* 1788; *Charles v. Urion,* 1786; *Richards v. Tyrill,* 1785; *Mullen v. Lovitt,* 1785; *King v. Jones,* 1799. PANB.
76. Spray, *Blacks,* 27.

Women and the Escheat Movement: The Politics of Everyday Life on Prince Edward Island

Rusty Bitterman

EDITORS' INTRODUCTION

When and why are politics a woman's affair? Such questions lie at the heart of a number of articles in this collection, including those by Bradbury, Little, and Fiamengo, and vitally inform the questions asked by George, O'Neill, and Jenson. While political history used to be, and in some quarters still is, history with women left out, new political history seeks to understand the different forms that politics take among groups that at first glance seem to lack opportunities for action or consciousness. Whether as grass-roots activists or through direct involvement in the public political sphere, women have consistently struggled to control circumstances often imposed upon their lives.

Bitterman's award-winning article investigates a familiar staple of Canadian history, the Prince Edward Island escheat protests. In this grass-roots movement, rural tenants challenged landlords' claims to large parts of the colony. Growing opposition to an Old World proprietorial system, with its more than a hint of feudal obligations, was the necessary precursor to the achievement of Responsible Government in 1851. It was also a spur to Confederation, making good its promise in 1873 to settle the longstanding land question.

This conventional sequencing of events implies a rather inevitable extension of manhood democracy in the New World frontier. The characters are unrelentingly male and the result is unambiguously progressive. This article enlightens readers on both accounts. Prince Edward Island's women were, we learn from Bitterman, following in the tradition of Europe and Great Britain's labouring poor in defending themselves and their families against the claims of the powerful. Their common experience as rural tenants united both sexes in their resistance to authority, whether male, as is the case with the law officers mentioned here, or female as was the landlord, Flora Townshend.

The escheat movement had special relevance for women, particularly since it had a direct impact on their ability to care for their families. The participation of women like Isabella MacDonald springs from, Bitterman demonstrates, the character of life for the rural majority of the population. For the average smaller farm household there were no distinctive and inflexible female and male spheres of activity. Womanhood for the majority of British North Americans was very far from protected, secluded, or inactive. When it came time for a demonstration of 'common people's politics', women had no reason to stand aside. Common protest was a logical extension of the day-to-day reality they lived. That sentimentalized notions of women's moral authority might protect them from some of the harsher punishments meted out to men who challenged the status quo only encouraged them to protest.

Female combativeness was a longstanding feature of European experience, both for elite settlers such as New France's Madeleine de Verchères and for poorer folk like those in Prince Edward Island. Victorian notions of propriety, however, increasingly contested such traditions. In this volume, Marks's analysis of church periodicals illustrates a Canadian example of this idealized image of a middle-class household, in which women served as the 'angel of the home' while men took charge of all public matters, provided the measure by which all else was judged inadequate. The demand for 'respectable' behaviour from women, based on the ideology of 'separate spheres', came increasingly from governments, in the person of the legal officials and others, and from allied institutions such as churches and schools. Before we knew as much as we do now about the variety of female experience, historians of women like American scholar Barbara Welter accepted this ideology at face value.[1] Even today it is sometimes favoured as an explanation but we need to remind ourselves to look beyond prescription to see how women actually behaved. As historian Willeen Keough's perceptive investigation into the regulation of Irish women's sexuality in Newfoundland's South Avalon region has revealed, other imperatives held greater sway in early settler societies.[2]

The ideology of separate spheres was prescriptive rather than descriptive, but, as Bitterman's analysis suggests, it was not irrelevant to the lives of women in British North America. The construction of politics as male weakened the position of women and undermined the moral authority, and the real capacity of the labouring poor in general, to make their wishes known to authority. This loss in Prince Edward Island, capped with women's legal disenfranchisement in 1838, matched the situation around the same time in Lower Canada described by Allan Greer and in the Upper Canadian context analyzed by historian Cecilia Morgan.[3] The fragmentary opportunities for political decision-making exorcized by women in Montreal would be decisively closed, not to be opened for almost a decade. Bitterman's observation that 'one of the many prices popular forces paid for entrance into the formal political arena in the nineteenth century was the relegation of women to a sphere outside direct participation in political life' reminds us that the extension of 'manhood' suffrage in the Great Reform Bills of Great Britain or throughout the nineteenth century in the United States was just that. Women were, as many women's rights activists understood, the losers.

Historian Ian McKay has recently argued that historians need to rethink nineteenth and twentieth-century Canadian history through a revisioning of what he calls the 'liberal order', defined as a society 'that encourages and seeks to extend across time and space a belief in the epistemological and ontological primary of the category of "individual"', almost invariably defined as male. Where might women's history fit in this? Ruth Sandwell points out that unless we pay greater attention to how family has complicated the 'liberal order', women and children 'will simply occupy a larger, more homogeneous, but equally opaque position at the margins of the liberal gaze'.[4] To begin to understand women's place in the nineteenth-century world discussed by Bitterman, Bradbury, Connor, Elgersman Lee, Van Kirk, Marks, and others, we need to acknowledge how that world simultaneously excluded women from formal power, depended on them all the same, and provided occasional opportunities for them to voice their grievance.

Notes

1. Barbara Welter, 'The Cult of True Womanhood, 1820–1860', *American Quarterly* 18 (1966): 151–74.
2. Wileen Keough, 'The Riddle of Peggy Mountain: Regulation of Irish Women's Sexuality on the Southern Avalon, 1750–1860', *Acadiensis* 31.2 (Spring 2002): 38–70.
3. Allan Greer, *The Patriots and the People: The Rebellion of 1837 in Rural Lower Canada* (Toronto: The University of Toronto Press, 1993); Cecilia Morgan, '"When Bad Men Conspire, Good Men Must Unite!": Gender and Political Discourses in Upper Canada, 1820s–1830s',

in *Gendered Pasts: Historical Essays in Femininity and Masculinity in Canada*, Kathryn McPherson, Cecilia Morgan, and Nancy M. Forestell, eds. (Toronto: Oxford University Press, 1999).

4. Ian McKay, 'The Liberal Order Framework: A Prospectus for a Reconnaissance of Canadian History', *Canadian Historical Review* 81.4 (December 2000): 617–45; R.W. Sandwell, 'The Limits of Liberalism: The Liberal Reconnasiance and the History of the Family in Canada', *Canadian Historical Review* 84: 3 (September 2003).450.

Questions for Critical Reading

1. How and why do the actions of women in the escheat movement challenge the image of the ideal nineteenth-century woman? Why might the authorities and the community at large have viewed women's public protest differently than men's?
2. Compare the strategies of resistance used by women in the escheat movement with those of the first-wave feminists discussed by Fiamengo and the contemporary activists portrayed by George and Nadeau. Why do women opt for particular kinds of protest at particular times?
3. Some historians argue that rural, pre-industrial societies like nineteenth-century Prince Edward Island offered women more opportunities for agency and expression than did industrializing, urban societies. Does Bitterman's study confirm or challenge this argument?

In September of 1833, Constable Donald McVarish, acting on behalf of Flora Townshend, the resident owner of an estate in eastern Prince Edward Island, made his way to her property with a bundle of papers in hand. These were warrants of distress, legal documents which permitted Townshend to seize the goods of her tenants for back rents which she claimed were due. It was not to be a pleasant day for McVarish. Rents were going unpaid, as always, because tenants found it difficult to meet these costs, but growing military resistance to the entire structure of landlordism made rent resistance a political act, too. In the wake of political initiatives begun earlier in the decade, the dream of an escheat was the talk of the countryside. Members of the House of Assembly and the rural population alike were discussing the legitimacy of proprietorial claims to the colony's land and arguing that because landlords had never fulfilled the settlement obligations of the original grants of 1767 they did not in fact have valid deeds; their grants had reverted to the Crown by default. Establishment of a court of escheat, it was contended, would expose the fraudulence of landlords' claims on the Island's tenantry and permit them to gain title to the farms they had made productive. McVarish, acting for the landlords, could no longer count on deference to law officers in the rural regions in the fall of 1833. Believing that the existing land system was fundamentally flawed because the titles that supported it were invalid, rural residents balked at complying with the laws pertaining to rents.

McVarish's mission to the Naufrage region of northern Kings County took him into a region that was known for the strength of its anti-landlord sentiments—arguably, the heartland of agrarian radicalism on the Island. William Cooper, the leading advocate of the idea of an escheat, had propounded his ideas on the flaws of proprietorial title and the rights of tenants in Kings County during the general election of 1830 and then again in a by-election in 1831. The support he received ultimately permitted him to promote these ideas from the House of Assembly. The enthusiastic response from country people in Kings County and elsewhere, expressed in public meetings, petitions, and rent resistance, marked the beginning of what came to be known as the Escheat movement. The loaded pistol that McVarish had tucked in his pocket before leaving home probably reflected his understanding of rural sentiments in the region, as did his attempts to hide his mission from those he met and his decision to sometimes travel through fields rather than on the road. McVarish's precautions notwithstanding, he was seen and confronted by a cluster of the tenants for whom his warrants were intended. Hard words were spoken and McVarish drew his pistol. He was, nonetheless, knocked to the ground, disarmed, and conveyed to the main road. Having promised he would never return, he was released and helped on his way with a blow from a board.[1]

The person wielding the board was Isabella MacDonald, then well advanced in a pregnancy. Judging from testimony from a subsequent trial, Isabella was the most vociferous party in the altercation. McVarish claimed that the three male and two female tenants who confronted him 'were all alike active and threatening', but when he pulled his pistol he aimed it at Isabella. It would seem that he perceived her as the most violent of the group. This move allowed men who were not receiving McVarish's primary attention to pull him down from behind and disarm him, in turn exposing him to Isabella's wrath. Her blow with the board was the only gratuitous violence McVarish received. Perhaps she was settling scores for his aiming his pistol at her, perhaps fulfilling the promise of violence which had prompted McVarish's move in the first place.

McVarish's discomfiture at the hands of Isabella and her companions was not an isolated incident. It cannot be explained simply as the act of a particularly forceful female tenant, a matter of personality. Again and again over the course of the Escheat movement, women assumed prominent roles in physically resisting the enforcement of landlords' claims in the countryside. This paper examines these women's behaviour and argues that the modes of resistance they employed had roots in, and were extensions of, the conditions of their daily lives. To discern this, however, it is necessary to move away from the image of rural women most commonly found in North American literature on the pre-industrial countryside. The conception of the rural woman's sphere that dominates this literature draws too heavily from middle-class experiences and sentiments and does not provide an appropriate starting place for understanding the actions of women such as Isabella MacDonald. Attentiveness to the early-nineteenth-century perceptions that gave birth to these pervasive images may, however, help us to better understand the roles rural women assumed in violent confrontations. Upper-class beliefs concerning women's sphere shaped the context in which Escheat activism unfolded. Being perceived as the weaker sex and the guardians of domesticity may have permitted women more latitude than men in their use of violence.

While it is important to recognize the significant part that women played in direct action, their participation in this form of popular politics needs to be set in the broader context of the Escheat struggle in the 1830s and early 1840s and the political changes which were occurring during this period. Direct action was not Escheat's main focus. The Escheat challenge was primarily grounded in the development of a new mass politics in the formal political arena. Formal politics, unlike community-level direct action, excluded women. To examine the role of women in the Escheat movement is to be reminded that the changes associated with the rise of bourgeois democracy included the decline of an older popular politics which once afforded women a substantial place.

Direct resistance to the claims of landlords, the area of Escheat activism in which women were most prominent, occurred in two forms. There were household-level defences, such as that Isabella MacDonald engaged in, and there was larger community-organized resistance. Women were active at both levels. In the first, the members of a single household, or perhaps adjoining households, responded defensively to the arrival of law officers. When officials attempted to serve legal papers, remove possessions, or arrest members of the household, those directly involved resisted. Women took part in such protective actions on their own and in the company of men. Catherine Renahau and her husband, John, acted together to resist the enforcement of their landlord's claims against their premises in southern Kings County in the spring of 1834. In this case, the wife and the husband were both indicted and found guilty of assaulting and wounding the constable who had arrived at their door.[2] The actions of Mrs MacLeod and her husband, Hugh, fit the same pattern. When a constable and a sheriff's bailiff came to seize their cattle in the summer of 1839, Mrs MacLeod took up a pike and Hugh an axe. Together they rebuffed the law officers. When a posse was subsequently sent to arrest the two, the entire family took a hand in attempting to prevent the high sheriff and his deputies from invading their house.[3] Charges laid against Mary and Margaret Campbell for assaulting constable William Duncan in 1834 provide some evidence that women also acted without men in farm-level defences.[4]

In addition to these sorts of spontaneous farm-level defences, tenants were involved in more broadly organized actions aimed at securing entire communities or regions from the enforcement of landlords' claims. Women figured prominently in many of these actions. Attempts to arrest the five tenants charged with repelling McVarish provoked two major community-level confrontations. In the spring of 1834, a posse was dispatched from Charlottetown to Naufrage to arrest the miscreants. They were turned back at the Naufrage bridge by a crowd, said to include 'a large number of women', which had assembled in anticipation of their arrival.[5] Armed with muskets, pikes, and pitchforks, the assembly informed the deputy sheriff that they were prepared to fight and die before they would permit him to arrest the five tenants he sought. When yet another posse led by the sheriff himself attempted a similar mission the following year, women were said to make up more than one-third of the armed crowd that waited for the posse in the pre-dawn darkness and again blocked the sheriff.[6]

Women were active as well in a series of major community-level confrontations in the fall and winter of 1837–8 that, with the mass meetings being held in support of Escheat, prompted some observers to believe that the Island, like the Canadas, was on the verge of civil war. The first of these confrontations concerning land title was on Thomas Sorell's estate in northern Kings County. In September 1837, when the sheriff and his deputies attempted to enforce court orders Sorell had obtained against John Robertson, a long-time resident on the estate, they were repulsed by a crowd wielding sticks and throwing stones. As well, one ear was removed from each of the law officers' horses, which had been left at a distance from the farm.[7] Women were part of the crowd that blocked the sheriff, and they were reputed to be the primary actors in the violence.[8] Later that winter, women made up part of an armed party which assembled near Wood Islands to repel people whom they believed to be law officers initiating rent actions in that district. In a case of mistaken identity, shots were fired over the head of the rector of Charlottetown and his elite friends, who were on a baptismal mission on behalf of a spiritual lord rather than a rental mission on behalf of a secular one.[9] While the actions of the tenant group were misdirected, they nonetheless served notice that those who might attempt to enforce rent collection in the region were not welcome. On the Selkirk estate the following month, women again were active in coordinated crowd actions which blocked the enforcement of rental claims. In several locales, bailiffs attempting to seize farm goods were confronted by tenants armed with pitchforks and sticks. Men and women alike took a hand in resisting the seizure of goods and driving law officers from the communities they had attempted to enter.[10] The cumulative effect of these actions was, for a time, to bring the enforcement of rental payments to a halt across much of the Island and to force the government to consider whether it was willing to hazard deploying troops—then in short supply due to the demands made by the risings in the Canadas—in order to uphold the claims of the Island's landlords.

That rural women would be active in household defences and collective action of this sort would come as no surprise to the student of Old World popular protest. In locations on the eastern side of the Atlantic, a rich array of research has pointed to the importance of women in protest actions and has suggested ways of understanding this activity in terms of their everyday lives.[11] The evidence of female involvement in the popular resistance associated with the Escheat movement fits less easily within North American historiography and its portrayal of rural women. To be sure, the literature is broad and varied, and blanket descriptions are misleading. Nonetheless, what emerges again and again in North American descriptions of women in northern pre-industrial rural settings is the image of the farm woman as nurturing caretaker of the domestic sphere. Though her work was tiring and she was often incessantly busy, hers was an existence bounded by walls and sheltered from the coarser aspects of life. Women looked after the household and, perhaps, the adjacent garden and barns, while the men tended to rough work and public affairs.

In his late-nineteenth-century reminiscences on rural life in Ontario in the first half of the century, Canniff Haight drew the common distinctions: 'The farmer was a strong, hardy man, the wife a ruddy cheerful body, careful of the comforts of her household.'[12] Male muscularity was applied to the exterior world, female gentleness and diligence to the interior: 'While the work was being pushed outside with vigour, it did not stand still inside. The thrifty housewife was always busy.'[13] 'The work' was of course male. The division is clear as well in Robert Leslie Jones's characterization of farm life on the Upper Canadian frontier. While the man of the house 'split rails, built worm fences, and erected his log cabin', his wife attended to 'various household industries, ranging from spinning and sometimes weaving, to the preservation of fruits by drying, and the making of butter and cheese'.[14] Or, in a recent version of the theme as played out in Lower Canada: Féllicité tended to 'feeding, washing, and cleaning the family, its clothes, and its house' as well as 'milking the cows, making butter, and feeding the fowls'. Théophile ploughed, 'erected fences around the fields', and saw to 'repairs to house, barn and equipment'.[15] 'Women's work', Christopher Clark has argued in the case of pre-industrial rural New England, 'remained separate, functionally distinct from men's': 'In addition to cooking, cleaning, and looking after children, women undertook the myriad tasks associated with preserving food, making and mending clothing, and keeping up their houses.'[16] Or, as a classic textbook of Canadian women's history has it, farm women 'scrubbed clothes on scrub boards (if they were lucky enough to have one), hauled water from the creek or the well, cooked on wood stoves, and made most of the family clothes. In addition they grew vegetables, gathered fruit, preserved and baked, and looked after their children.'[17]

No doubt many 'ruddy' farm women did spend their days tending to berries, butter, bread, and babies in eighteenth- and nineteenth-century North America and, no doubt, there were many households where prosperity and culture blended to create the domestic feminine sphere that is described in so much of the literature.[18] The scholarship that has given rise to this image is not incorrect. But in the absence of more nuanced studies of the experiences of women in rural settings, it has sustained misleading impressions. A vision of country life rooted in the experiences of relatively prosperous, well-established households and heavily grounded in mid-nineteenth-century circumstances has, often enough, come to stand as a general portrait of the pre-industrial rural world. Thus, our view of the rural past tends to be too uniform and too rosy.[19] One might profitably explore the reasons for the dominance of this image and its significance to broader myths concerning rural life and North American exceptionalism. For comprehending the actions of women within the Escheat movement, the immediate problem is finding a more appropriate starting place for explaining how Mrs MacLeod came to pick up a pike and Isabella MacDonald a board, and how other country women came to join in the armed groups organized to repulse law officers in Naufrage, Wood Islands, and elsewhere about Prince Edward Island in the 1830s. While some of these women no doubt tended to the domestic duties that have been assigned to the feminine sphere of rural life, there is much that these sorts of descriptions leave out, matters that go a long way toward helping us to understand how women came to participate as they did in the Escheat movement.

For most country women in Prince Edward Island in the early nineteenth century, life was much rougher and the bounds of work much broader than the prevailing images suggest. Indeed, for the rural poor, of whom there were many, the notion of a distinct feminine sphere could not have had much meaning. While there was work that was exclusively female, even in poorer households—having babies, early childcare, and so on—it is less clear that there was much work about the farm that women could avoid because it was securely outside their domain. In many rural households, particularly the poorer ones, the men were away for extensive periods earning wages in the woods, shipyards, and other sites where farm income might be supplemented.[20] Of necessity, then, women's work expanded beyond the women's sphere that is described in much of the literature. In such households, women often assumed the dominant role in maintaining the farm.[21] In farm households where life was lived on the margin, even when men were present, women often participated in heavy tasks such as clearing, planting, and harvesting. In his early-nineteenth-century observations on life in Prince Edward Island, Walter Johnstone spoke disparagingly of rural women from comfortable backgrounds who were 'unable and unwilling to take the hoe, and assist their husbands in planting the seed, and raising the crop'.[22] To make a go of it in the New World, immigrant women needed to apply themselves to the hard outdoor tasks of farm-making. Land-clearing work, which Johnstone described as being 'the most dirty and disagreeable' and 'tiresome as any I have seen in America', was shared by the entire family, women and men alike.[23] Similar observations of women's roles in the hard task of farm-making are found in the works of John MacGregor and George Patterson, who commented as well on women's part in the subsequent tasks of planting and harvesting.[24] Women, MacGregor observed, 'assist in the labours of the farm during seed-time, hay-making, and harvest'.[25] Getting the crops in, Johnstone noted, was the work of the entire household—'man, wife, children, and all that can handle a hoe, must work, as the season is short'—and disaster loomed for the poor if the crops were not successful.[26] It is not surprising then that Island evidence from the 1832 murder trial of Martin Doyle indicates that Martin and his wife were working side by side among the charred stumps of their field on the day that Martin was said to have shot his brother.[27] From the scattered evidence that is available concerning women's work, such was a common pattern of rural life.

The dominant image of the daily lives of rural women is inadequate not only because women's work could be much broader than it depicts, but also because the domestic sphere of work was often much narrower, too. Again and again the existing literature emphasizes the long hours that women spent cleaning house, washing clothes, preparing meals, and spinning and weaving. No doubt long hours were spent in this work by those who possessed frame houses and ample wardrobes, ate a varied diet, kept sheep, and had spinning wheels and looms. We need to recognize, though, that many did not. In the Maritimes of the early nineteenth century, this picture of the woman's sphere pertains to the rural middle class and does not reflect the circumstances of the whole of the rural population. Indeed, for many, the physical requirements for the woman's separate sphere—multi-roomed house, kitchen and pantry, area for textile manufacture, adjoining dairy, and poultry shelters—quite simply did not exist. It did not take long to clean a one-room dwelling, assuming that this was even an objective, nor did cooking and washing absorb a day's labour when household members ate boiled potatoes and oatmeal and possessed little clothing beyond what they were wearing. We need not paint the picture this starkly, however, no matter how real it was for many, to point out that much of the existing view of the rural women's sphere assumes material circumstances that were far more comfortable than those of much of the rural population.

As well, we must re-examine the notions of domesticity and of lives sheltered from the rough and tumble of the public world, which are commonly associated with characterizations of the pre-industrial North American farm woman, if we are to understand the behaviour of the women who were involved in direct action during the Escheat movement. In part because many Island women did engage in outdoor farm labour, they, like men, became involved in physical disputes over resources and household relations. Margaret Taylor and Jane Maclachlan fought it out with fence pickets and fists in the spring of 1830 when they differed over ownership of a piece of ground.[28] A similar physical dispute over land and fencing brought Catherine McCormack and Alexander Macdonald before a court later that year.[29] The same court session that heard the Taylor/Maclachlan case also heard the case of Elizabeth Cahill and Margaret Shea, whose personal differences had moved to the level of heaving stones.[30] As with women's work, evidence bearing on women's use of violence, or the threat of violence, in the public realm is fugitive.[31]

Certainly what emerges in the court record is but a fraction of a broader phenomenon. What percentage of the disputes where women picked up a stick or a stone or brandished their fists ultimately ended up before a judge or a justice of the peace? And what percentage of these disputes is preserved in the incomplete legal record?

In addition to engaging in direct violence, Island women were also repeatedly cited for resorting to maiming animals.[32] In this traditional form of rural retribution, livestock received the violence directed toward their owners. Vengeance was taken, or a threat communicated, by hamstringing, slashing, or otherwise mutilating the animals of an enemy.[33] There was nothing unusual in the methods used against the horses of law officers who came to Robertson's farm in the fall of 1837; they were employed against the mounts of law officers on many other occasions. Animal-maiming, by women and men, was not uncommon in intra-household disputes.

Women's participation in violent actions was not an unusual feature of the Escheat movement, nor was the targeting of law officers. Consider, for instance, the 1836 rescue of Rose Hughes from a constable's custody. Arrested near Fort Augustus in the late fall of 1836 for obtaining goods under false pretenses, she was forcibly released when the arresting constable, Angus MacPhee, was attacked by a group who had pursued him beyond the community. Though there were four men present in the rescue party, they remained in the background. The assault itself was said to be the work of nine women.[34]

We need, then, to broaden our notion of female lives and experiences if we are to make sense of women's participation in direct action during the Escheat movement. Isabella, used to hard physical labour, is unlikely to have thought it peculiar, or inappropriate, for women to use physical means to uphold their interests. When we examine the role of women in the Escheat movement, we see in part an extension of the normal patterns of work and life to meet the challenges thrown up by the land war of the 1830s. Women familiar with the rough and tumble of outdoor rural life dealt with the law officers who came to their farms as they would any other threat to their household. Accustomed to the heft of an axe and the swing of a fence picket, they applied their strengths, skills, and inclinations to the problems at hand.

Those like McVarish who were on the receiving end of these responses were caught in an unenviable dilemma. On the one hand they were, often enough, dealing with women who possessed strength, endurance, physical tenacity, and the urge to cause considerable physical harm. McVarish's choice of targets when he levelled his pistol probably showed his appreciation of women's abilities. On the other hand, he and the other law officers on the front lines of the land war were, in one fashion or another, linked to a culture which saw women differently. According to increasingly dominant middle-class and upper-class views, women were revered as submissive nurturers of the domestic sphere.[35] Historians studying women's roles in collective action in other nineteenth-century contexts have suggested that plebeian protesters may have sought to exploit such perceptions when they challenged the status quo. Women, the argument goes, enjoyed some degree of immunity in violent confrontations, or at least believed that they did, and scattered evidence does suggest they were less likely than men to suffer harm or be prosecuted for their actions. This fact may help explain their prominence in illegal protest.[36] Might this have been the case with women's participation in the direct action associated with the Escheat movement?

The evidence bearing on this question is limited, but it supports an affirmative answer. Interestingly, despite the prominent role played by women in resisting the enforcement of landlords' claims in Kings and Queens Counties in the tense fall and winter of 1837–8, none was named in the law officers' reports nor were any indicted for their actions. Only men were tried. Such preliminary screening raises questions concerning how adequately indictments and court cases document women's participation in direct action or, indeed, in other sorts of activities of this type. Were law officers uncomfortable with admitting that their lumps and bruises were the work of women or that they had been chased or intimidated by women? And, other things being equal, did law enforcement take place in a cultural context where charges against males were preferable, if an example was to be made of a few members of a larger riotous assembly? Women, it would appear, were more likely to be indicted in household-level confrontations where the numbers involved were quite small. Even when charged, however, they sometimes fared better than men. Although two women were indicted for the assault on Donald McVarish, neither served a prison term or paid a fine. The charges were dropped against Nancy MacDonald, and Isabella MacDonald, though found guilty, was pardoned by the Island's governor, Aretas Young, on account of her 'being far advanced in pregnancy and having six young children'.[37] All three men involved were committed to prison.

The ways in which contemporaries referred to gender when assigning meaning to incidents of Escheat-related collective action provide another window on these issues. In the wake of the resistance to the sheriff at Robertson's farm in the fall of 1836, pressure was brought on the new governor, Charles FitzRoy, to send troops into the region to sustain the civil forces in their enforcement of landlords' claims. FitzRoy sent Charlottetown's mayor, Ambrose Lane, to the region as his personal emissary to inquire into the current state of the countryside and to conspicuously make arrangements for billeting soldiers. Seeking to downplay the seriousness of the incidents that had brought Lane to the region, Robertson and his family told him that the sheriff and his assistants had never been in any real danger as 'all the violence offered was by women and boys'. The law officers who had beaten a hasty retreat from the mob assembled at the farm had been 'unnecessarily alarmed'.[38] Similarly, a dispute over the significance of the Wood Islands incident of January 1838 came, in part, to revolve around the composition of the crowd which had assembled and fired shots over the heads of the rector's party. Those seeking to downplay the confrontation insisted that it had, in large part, been staged by women and boys. Those intent on seeing it as an indication of a broader spirit of rebellion threatening the status quo on the Island were equally insistent that the crowd had been 'composed chiefly of able-bodied men'.[39] What the disputants in these battles of words shared, or claimed to share, was the notion that females could not figure as real threats in violent confrontations. It is not clear whether exploitation of these perceptions of women figured into the strategic planning of household- and community-level rent resistance prior to confrontations or whether they were invoked only after the violence. Cases such as the rescue of Rose Hughes, where men were present but remained at a distance while women assaulted the constable, or the resistance at Robertson's farm, in which, according to reports, men were present but not active in the physical confrontation with law officers, suggest a conscious gendered strategy that made use of upper-class assumptions concerning women's behaviour.

. . . Charles Tilly has argued that [patterns of rural protest such as those on Prince Edward Island] fit within a broader category of 'reactive' collective action, locally focused efforts to protect existing rights or to uphold popular notions of justice.[40] John Bohstedt's term 'common people's politics' aptly captures another facet of this type of collective action. In contexts where ordinary people were excluded from participation in formal politics, direct action provided a means for articulating plebeian sentiments; it permitted them to act as 'proto-citizens'.[41] As Bohstedt and others have noted, women often participated extensively in this sort of political action. 'Common people's politics' tended to be an extension of plebeian life, and in locales where women 'worked shoulder to shoulder with men' they also 'marched shoulder to shoulder with men' in defence of their households and communities.[42] Such was the case with women's participation in the direct action associated with the Escheat movement. Local-level politics of this type was a matter for women and men alike.

This was not the case in the formal political arena. There the rules and norms that governed participation were extensions of elite and middle-class ways of life. In these circles, other notions of womanhood held sway. This would be of no small significance for the majority of women when, beginning in the late eighteenth century and extending across the nineteenth century and beyond, ordinary people about the Atlantic rim increasingly pushed themselves into, or were incorporated within, the field of formal politics. Lower-class entry into the sphere of political life was gained by compromise and by the acceptance of many of the modes of procedure that had been established by the upper classes. On the Island one thinks even of simple matters such as dress. When the Escheat leader John LeLecheur went off to Quebec to discuss the land question with Lord Durham, a fundraising campaign was necessary in order to buy him a new set of clothes. Such props were unnecessary for engaging in political debate in Murray Harbour, but they were a part of the basic entry requirements for being taken seriously in the governor general's circles.[43] Certainly, involvement in formal politics did lead to fundamental changes in the nature of plebeian politics. As historians have noted in other contexts, one of the many prices popular forces paid for entrance into the formal political arena in the nineteenth century was the relegation of women to a sphere outside direct participation in political life. A new mass politics was emerging at the time of the Escheat movement, but as it embraced larger numbers of previously excluded lower-class elements, it also denied political expression to women.[44] On the Island, women were legally disenfranchised on the eve of Escheat's electoral victory of 1838.[45]

The involvement of women in the local politics of direct action needs to be set in this larger context. While recognizing women's participation in the 'common people's politics' of the 1830s, it is important to note the transitional nature of the period and the immediate and long-term significance of the zone of political life in which women had a prominent place. Rural protest in Prince Edward Island had by the 1830s largely shifted away from direct action. A relatively broad franchise allowed many male tenants to vote; some even possessed sufficient wealth to meet the property requirements necessary for assuming a seat in the House of Assembly. The energy of the Escheat movement was directed toward exploiting the political possibilities these openings permitted. Escheat leaders sought to make agrarian voices heard in the formulation of state policy by achieving power in the legislature. This pursuit drew rural protest into an exclusively masculine sphere. The activities in which women had a substantial presence were not at the forefront of the Escheat movement, nor would they be central to the new politics that developed in the years which followed.

Notes

1. Minutes of Naufrage Trial, Colonial Office Records [CO] 226, vol. 52, 91–4, Public Record Office, Great Britain [microfilm copies in Harriet Irving Library, University of New Brunswick]. I would like to gratefully acknowledge the assistance of the Social Sciences and Humanities Research Council of Canada, whose financial support aided this research. Many thanks are due as well to Margaret McCallum for her comments on an earlier version of this paper.
2. *Royal Gazette* (Charlottetown), 24 June 1834, 3; Supreme Court Minutes, 25 June 1834; Indictments, 1834, RG 6, Public Archives of Prince Edward Island [PAPEI].
3. *Royal Gazette*, 23 July 1839, 3.
4. *Royal Gazette*, 16 Dec. 1834, 3.
5. *Royal Gazette*, 17 June 1834, 3.
6. *Royal Gazette*, 6 Jan. 1835, 3; 'Council Minutes', 7 Jan. 1835, CO 226, vol. 52, 330–2.
7. Executive Council Minutes, 5 Sept. 1837, RG 5, PAPEI; *Royal Gazette*, 5 Sept. 1837, 3.
8. Hodgson to Owen, 30 Sept. 1837, MS 3744, vol. 26, PAPEI.
9. George R. Young, *A Statement of the 'Escheat Question' in the Island of Prince Edward: Together with the Causes of the Late Agitation and the Remedies Proposed* (London: R. and W. Swale, 1838), 2; 'One of the Party' to the editor, *Colonial Herald* (Charlottetown), 27 June 1838, 3; 'O.P.Q.' to the editor, *Colonial Herald*, 23 Jan. 1841, 3; 'Plain Common Sense' to the editor, *Colonial Herald*, 6 Feb. 1841, 2–3; John Myrie Hall to the editor, *Colonial Herald*, 20 Feb. 1841, 2; 'The Only Clergyman Resident Within the Bounds of the District' to the editor, *Colonial Herald*, 20 Mar. 1841, 3; Charles Stewart and W.P. Grossard to the editor, *Colonial Herald*, 27 Mar. 1841, 3.
10. Statement of Angus McPhee, George Farmer, and Robert Bell, 27 Feb. 1838, CO 226, vol. 55, 176–80.
11. John Bohstedt, 'Gender, Household, and Community Politics: Women in English Riots, 1790–1810', *Past and Present* 120 (Aug. 1988): 88–122; Rudolf Dekker, 'Women in Revolt: Collective Protest and its Social Setting in Holland in the Seventeenth and Eighteenth Centuries', *Theory and Society* 16 (1987): 337–62; E.P. Thompson, 'The Moral Economy of the English Crowd in the Eighteenth Century', *Past and Present* 50 (1971): 76–136; George Rudé, *The Crowd in the French Revolution* (Oxford: Galaxy Books, 1959); George Rudé, *The Crowd in History: A Study of Popular Disturbances in France and England, 1730–1848* (London: Serif Publishing, 1964); Olwen Hufton, 'Women in Revolution', *Past and Present* 53 (1971): 90–108; John Stevenson and Roland Quinault, eds, 'Food Riots in England, 1792–1818', in *Popular Protest and Public Order: Six Studies in British History, 1790–1920* (London: St Martin's Press, 1974), 33–74; Natalie Zemon Davis, *Society and Culture in Early Modern France* (Stanford: Stanford University Press, 1975), 124–87; Kenneth J. Logue, *Popular Disturbances in Scotland, 1780–1815* (Edinburgh: Birlinn Publishers, 1979); Malcolm I. Thomas and Jennifer Grimmet, *Women in Protest 1800–1850* (London: St Martin's Press, 1982). A useful Canadian extension of this rich literature is Terence Crowley, '"Thunder Gusts": Popular Disturbances in Early French Canada', in *Readings in Canadian Social History*, vol. 1, *Economy and Society During the French Regime*, Michael Cross and Gregory Kealey, eds. (Toronto: McClelland and Stewart, 1983), 122–51.
12. Canniff Haight, *Country Life in Canada Fifty Years Ago: Personal Recollections and Reminiscences of a Sexagenarian* (1885; rpt. Belleville, Ont., 1971), 86.
13. Haight, *Country Life in Canada*, 46.
14. Robert Leslie Jones, *History of Agriculture in Ontario, 1613–1880* (1946; rpt. Toronto, 1977), 20–1.
15. Graeme Wynn, 'On the Margins of Empire', in *The Illustrated History of Canada*, Craig Brown, ed. (Toronto: Lester Publishing, 1987), 247.
16. Christopher Clark, *The Roots of Rural Capitalism: Western Massachusetts, 1780–1860* (Ithaca, NY: Cornell University Press, 1990), 274.
17. Alison Prentice et al., *Canadian Women: A History* (Toronto: Harcourt, 1988), 116. See also 76, 79, 83.
18. Hal Barron's call for the study of the extent, and timing, of the spread of the bourgeois ideals of the cult of domesticity among 'the less affluent and less "enlightened" strata of rural society' usefully indicates a single facet of a broader challenge, that of disaggregating and more closely examining rural experiences and rural change. John Faragher's critique of stereotypes in the writing of rural women's history, and call for moving beyond these, is to the point as well. Hal Barron, 'Listening to the Silent Majority: Change and Continuity in the Nineteenth-Century Rural North', in *Agriculture and National Development: Views on the Nineteenth Century*, Lou Ferleger, ed. (Ames: Iowa State University Press, 1990), 16; John Mack Faragher, 'History From the Inside-out: Writing the History of Women in Rural America', *American Quarterly* 33 (1981): 537–57.
19. There are, of course, exceptions to this characterization. Marjorie Griffin Cohen, for instance, notes

that farm women in early-nineteenth-century Ontario frequently performed 'men's work', though she tends to treat this as a temporary frontier phenomenon. *Women's Work, Markets, and Economic Development in Nineteenth-Century Ontario* (Toronto: University of Toronto Press, 1988), 69–71. As well, it is not unusual for contradictory evidence to be integrated with a more idyllic picture of the countrywoman's sphere. See, for instance, The Clio Collective, Roger Gannon and Rosalind Gill, trans., *Quebec Women: A History* (Toronto: The Women's Press, 1987), 89.

20. Rusty Bittermann, 'Farm Households and Wage Labour in the Northeastern Maritimes in the Early Nineteenth Century', *Labour / Le Travail* 31 (Spring 1993): 13–45.
21. When a Cape Breton farmer noted in the coal boom of 1871 that 'farmers and their sons by hundreds, nay, thousands, [were] leaving their farms to the women, and seeking employment at the collieries and railways,' he was describing the efflorescence of an older pattern. *Journal of Agriculture for Nova Scotia* (July 1871): 652.
22. Walter Johnstone, *A Series of Letters, Descriptive of Prince Edward Island* (1822) reprinted in *Journeys to the Island of St John*, D.C. Harvey, ed. (Toronto: Macmillan, 1955), 143.
23. Johnstone, *A Series of Letters*, 108.
24. John MacGregor, *British America* (Edinburgh: Blackwood, 1832), 329; George Patterson, *A History of the County of Pictou Nova Scotia* (1877; rpt. Belleville, Ont., 1972), 223.
25. MacGregor, *British America*, 346.
26. Johnstone, *A Series of Letters*, 109.
27. *Royal Gazette*, 28 Feb. 1832, 1.
28. *Prince Edward Island Register* (Charlottetown), 15 June 1830, 3.
29. *Royal Gazette*, 13 July 1830, 3.
30. *Prince Edward Island Register*, 15 June 1830, 3.
31. See also the case of Mary Prendergast v. Ellen Prendergast, *Royal Gazette*, 3 Jan. 1837, 3; and Isabella Stewart v. Edward Wilson, *Royal Gazette*, 13 July 1830, 3.
32. *Royal Gazette*, 21 Jan. 1834, 3; 22 September 1835, 3; 7 July 1840, 3.
33. For a good discussion of the tactic see John E. Archer, '"A Fiendish Outrage"?: A Study of Animal Maiming in East Anglia: 1830–70', *Agricultural History Review* 33, 2 (1985): 147–57.
34. *Royal Gazette*, 20 Dec. 1836, 3.
35. Barbara Leslie Epstein, *The Politics of Domesticity: Women, Evangelism, and Temperance in Nineteenth-Century America* (Middletown, Conn.: Wesleyan University Press, 1981), 67–87; Nancy F. Cott, *The Bonds of Womanhood: 'Women's Sphere' in New England, 1780–1835* (New Haven, CT: Yale University Press, 1977).
36. Malcolm I. Thomas and Jennifer Grimmet, *Women in Protest 1800–1850* (London: St Martin's Press, 1982), 54; Logue, *Popular Disturbances in Scotland*, 199–203.
37. Young to Hay, 20 Mar. 1835, CO 226, vol. 52, 89.
38. Hodgson to Owen, 30 Sept. 1837, MS 3744, vol. 26, PAPEI.
39. 'One of the Party' to the editor, *Colonial Herald*, 27 June 1838, 3.
40. Charles Tilly, *From Mobilization to Resolution* (Reading, Mass.: Rowman and Littlefield, 1978), 143–71.
41. John Bohstedt, 'The Myth of the Feminine Food Riot: Women as Proto-Citizens in English Community Politics, 1790–1810', in *Women and Politics in the Age of the Democratic Revolution*, Harriet B. Applewhite and Darline G. Levy, eds. (Ann Arbor, MI: University of Michigan Press, 1990), 21–60.
42. Bohstedt, 'The Myth of the Feminine Food Riot', 21. See also Thomas and Grimmet, *Women in Protest*, 54–5.
43. Rusty Bittermann, 'Escheat!: Rural Protest on Prince Edward Island, 1832–42' (PhD dissertation, University of New Brunswick, 1992), 321–8.
44. Useful views of the process are provided in Wayne Ph. te Brake, Rudolf M. Dekker, and Lotte C. van de Pol, 'Women and Political Culture in the Dutch Revolutions', in *Women and Politics in the Age of Democratic Revolution*, Applewhite and Levy, eds., 109–46; Joan B. Landes, *Women and the Public Sphere in the Age of the French Revolution* (Ithaca, NY: Cornell University Press, 1988); Allan Greer, 'La république des hommes: les patriotes de 1837 face aux femmes', *Revue d'histoire de l'Amérique française* 44, 4 (Spring 1991): 507–28; Bohstedt, 'The Myth of the Feminine Food Riot'.
45. They were disenfranchised by statute in 1836. John Garner, *The Franchise and Politics in British North America, 1755–1867* (Toronto: University of Toronto Press, 1969), 155.

Women at the Hustings: Gender, Citizenship, and the Montreal By-Elections of 1832

Bettina Bradbury

EDITORS' INTRODUCTION

What historians call the Whig view of history—the idea that history is a progressive, linear process invariably leading to a better and more just version of human society—can have enormous appeal for people interested in women's history. Seen through that lens, the story of women's history is one of a gradual but steady improvement in women's lot, beginning with oppression and drudgery and ending at the present, imagined as a time of relative equality and quality of life. The serious investigation of women's history challenges this Whig view. Historians have argued that taking account on women's experience prompts us to rethink the meaning of traditional signposts like the Renaissance, or, more recently, the Enlightenment.[1] In Canadian history, Jan Noel's pioneering article of women in New France prompted us to see that women had opportunities in pre-industrial, *ancient regime* society that would be absent from the allegedly more equitable societies of the later nineteenth and early twentieth-centuries. In this volume, Rusty Bitterman's analysis of women in the Escheat movement of Prince Edward Island shows us some particular ways that women's political possibilities were closed off in the middle years of the nineteenth-century. The republicanism that informed the Lower Canadian rebellions of the 1830s, as historian Allan Greer has explained elsewhere, did not extend their promises of greater liberty and equality to women.[2]

Bettina Bradbury's careful and insightful analysis of women's experience as voters in the Montreal by-election of 1832 also encourages us to question traditional signposts and rethink our assumptions about the progressive nature of historical change. She does not take the easy route by presenting this particular snapshot of history as a rosy 'golden age' for women. Instead, Bradbury treats Montreal in 1832 as a society as complicated and contradictory as our own. Under the laws of Lower Canada women could vote if they owned or rented property of the required value in their own name. This was allowed by Quebec's *coutume de Paris* derived legal code but prevented by the traditions of common-law used elsewhere in the British empire, including in the colonies that would, in 1867, form Canada.[3] In the particular by-election examined by Bradbury, some 226 women, or 14 per cent of the electorate, exercised their right to do so. While many historians of Quebec have portrayed these women as unthinking pawns in an intercene political struggle, Bradbury shows us that they were women who cared about politics, many of them hailing from families where politics ran in the blood.

That a substantial number of women had, and were able to use, a right that would be so resolutely and symbolically denied their daughters and granddaughters troubles our assumptions about history's progressive character. Yet Bradbury is clear that Lower Canada was no paradise for women in general and women voters in particular. Women were likely to have their votes contested and disqualified, and not infrequently had to risk their bodily safety and personal reputation in order to enter public space and cast their votes. In the following two decades the Roman Catholic church assumed a new influence, patriots were transformed into liberals who made claims to the universality of rights and freedom but denied basic liberties to women and enslaved people, and ethnic and national lines had hardened. Francophone women were valued by nationalists for producing families or by joining religious orders, but not for much else, a set of connections that reverberate through Denyse Baillargeon's essay in this volume. But when a bill of stripping women of the right to vote was introduced in the Lower Canadian legislature in 1848, it passed essentially without remark or protest.

Women regained the right to vote on less restrictive terms over the course of the twentieth-century and while a woman's basic right to vote is not now seriously questioned, women remain grossly under-represented in positions of political decision-making. Despite almost a hundred years of uninterrupted female voting, women remain radically under-represented in every level of Canadian decision making, with the sometime exception of local school boards. The 2004 federal election resulted in an almost 80 per cent male parliament. Women of colour and immigrant women are less likely than others to be appointed or elected to positions of responsibility in provincial or federal governments.[4] The presence of an Aboriginal majority in Nunavut sparked hopes that it might reject Euro-centric traditions and adopt two-member constituencies electing one female and one male MLA.[5] That proposal for gender equality ultimately failed; men remain massively over-represented in the new assembly, as they do in Band Councils throughout the Canadian south. Sociologist Cora Voyageur shows us some of the ways that women Chiefs pay the price for their willingness to take on what remains, despite Aboriginal traditions of female political authority, a male dominated political world.[6] When women do find their way into band council offices, provincial legislatures, or Parliament Hill, feminists are often disappointed at their apparent unwillingness or inability to make real change for women.

Local and regional political cultures matter to women in the 2000s as they did in the nineteenth-century world analyzed by Bradbury. Atlantic Canada, as Margaret Conrad shows, has an even more definitively male political scene. In 2000, only 7 per cent of the members of Nova Scotia's elected Legislative Assembly were female.[7] While Quebec was the last province to grant women the right to vote, it made up for lost time in the last quarter of the twentieth century, outdoing most others in the numbers of women elected both provincially and federally. Not unrelated was its leadership in the introduction of women-friendly public policy, such as the childcare policies discussed by Jane Jenson in this volume. The close, if sometimes contested, bonds between the women's movement and Québécois nationalism in general and the Parti Québécois in particular has buttressed women's claim to a fair share of the public sphere since the 1960s. Women represent about one-third of the of the decision-making bodies of the two main political parties in Quebec: the Liberal party and the Parti Québécois.[8] Thus the problems that Margeurite Paris encountered on the way to the polls in 1832 would not be wholly unfamiliar to three young women, identified only as Chloë R., Chi N., and Crystal G., who launched the '20,000 project' in 2004. They explained that their experience working on Ottawa's Parliament Hill had shown them that 'this place is still an old boys club.' The women created an impressive online campaign to encourage the 20,000 young women in Canada to vote in the federal election.[9] Now, as in 1832, it is not formal rules alone that keep women from relative equality in the political realm. Rethinking political history through women's history and understanding our current situation both require that we move beyond the simple question of whether women can or cannot vote to begin to think about how gender works in the homes, in the streets, and the corridors of power.

Notes

1. The pioneering formulation of such questions is Joan Kelly-Gadol's 'Did Women Have a Renaissance?' in *Becoming Visible: Women in European History,* Renate Bridenthal and Claudia Koonz, eds. (Boston: Houghton Mifflin, 1977).
2. Allan Greer, *The Patriots and the People: the Rebellion of 1837 in Rural Lower Canada* (Toronto: University of Toronto Press, 1993). Also see Micheline Dumont, 'Can a National History Include a Feminist Reflection on History?', *Journal of Canadian Studies* 35.2 (Summer 2000): 80–96.
3. See Bettina Bradbury, 'Colonial Comparisons: Rethinking Marriage, Civilization, and Nation in Nineteenth-Century White Settler Societies', in *Rediscovering the British World,* Phillip Buckner and Daniel Francis, eds. (Calgary: University of Calgary Press, 2005).
4. Linda Trimble and Manon Tremblay, 'Women Politicians in Canada's Parliament and Legislatures, 1917–2000: A Socio-demographic Profile', in *Women and Electoral Politics*, Manon Tremblay and Linda Trimble, eds. (Toronto: Oxford University Press, 2002).
5. For the possibilities see 'Appendix B. Two-member Constituencies and Gender Equality: a "Made in Nunavut" Solution,' in *In the Presence of Women: Representation in Canadian Governments*, Jane Arscott and Linda Trimble, eds. (Toronto: Harcourt Brace and Company, 1997).
6. Cora Voyageur, 'First Nations Women in Leadership in Canada', in *Unsettled Pasts: Reconceiving the West through Women's History,* Sarah Carter, Lesley Erickson, Patricia Roome, and Char Smith, eds. (Calgary: University of Calgary Press, 2005).
7. Margaret Conrad, 'Addressing the Democratic Deficit: Women and Political Culture in Atlantic Canada', *Atlantis* 27.2 (Spring/Summer 2003) 82–9.
8. Jocelyn Praud, 'The Parti Québécois, Its Women's Committee, and the Feminization of the Quebec Electoral Arena', in *Women and Electoral Politics in Canada*, Manon Tremblay and Linda Trimble, eds. (Toronto: Oxford University Press, 2003); Manon Tremblay, 'Quebec Women in Politics: An Examination of the Research' in *In the Presence of Women: Representation in Canadian Governments*, Jane Arscott and Linda Trimble, eds. (Toronto: Harcourt Brace and Company, 1997).
9. http://dawn.thot.net/election2004/issues9.htm.

Questions for Critical Reading

1. What does the experience of women in the Montreal by-election of 1832 tell us about women's social and economic roles in early nineteenth-century Canada?
2. In 1830s Lower Canada property qualifications and political culture kept many women from voting. What stops women from voting or running for office in the 2000s? Can informal barriers to political participation be as powerful as formal ones? Why? How might these informal barriers be changed?
3. How can women and gender be important to shaping political history even when—as in much of nineteenth- and twentieth-century Canada—women have been officially excluded from political life?

The polls had been open for six days when Marguerite Paris, the widow of a labourer, stepped up to proclaim her vote. Speaking loud enough for the male officials at the poll to hear, she publicly declared that the Patriot candidate, Daniel Tracey, was her choice in the by-election underway in Montreal West, Lower Canada.[1] It was the first of May 1832. The day before officials had moved the poll away from the Hall of the American Presbyterian Church—an alien place for French-speaking Roman Catholic Montrealers like Marguerite to enter—to a house behind it belonging to Patriot supporters. Surely even this illiterate widow knew that the hustings were particularly dangerous ground during this election? Just the day before she voted, the *Montreal Gazette*, the unabashed champion of the businessman and establishment candidate Stanley Bagg, had reported the 'most disgraceful riots and disturbances', complaining that 'several of our most respectable citizens have been most violently assaulted; beaten and otherwise maltreated.'[2] And, the same day, *La Minerve*, equally unwavering in its advocacy of his opponent, Daniel Tracey, the fiery Irish editor of the *Vindicator*, had described the insults and violence of drunken bullies who had seriously injured three of his supporters.[3]

In deciding to vote, the widow Marguerite Paris was stepping into a public space that was physically dangerous and politically and culturally contested. It was watched and commented on by the journalists of the city's highly partisan newspapers, and it was a space occupied by men and some women of all ethnic, religious, and class backgrounds. Even approaching the polls would later be described as a perilous act.[4] This danger did not deter Marguerite Paris and at least 225 other women from seeking to participate. Some 226 women made it to the hustings, seeking to express their political choice. Most were, like Marguerite, widows, but there were married and single women as well. These women do not seem to have accepted the understanding that politics and the public sphere were for men alone, though historians have argued that such ideas were increasingly prevalent across the western world, and in Quebec, by this period.[5] Nor was this particular by-election unique. Earlier that month over seventy women voted in the by-election to determine representatives for the other half of Montreal. Furthermore, Nathalie Picard has shown that women voted in at least 14 other districts in the British colony of Lower Canada between 1791 and 1849.[6]

This particular election is well known to Canadian historians for its length—twenty-three days—for its violence, and as a major flash point in the deteriorating relations between the predominantly French-speaking Catholic Patriots who controlled the elected Assembly, and the Conservative pro-Governor British group—the Tories—who dominated the appointed Legislative Council and the Executive of the colony of Lower Canada, later the Province of Quebec. The Patriots, like so many bourgeois reformers elsewhere, sought to increase the power of elected representatives. Their struggle was against the intransigence of colonial officials and their supporters, popularly known as the 'English party'. In retrospect the by-election of 1832 appears as an urban microcosm of the rebellions that pitted Patriot supporters against local militias and the British army in 1837 and 1838. And it is in this light that most historians have analyzed it. The conflict has, therefore, been interpreted mostly through the lens of ethnicity, linked partially to class and viewed as essentially a contest between English Tories and French-Canadian Patriots and hence as a key moment in the making of Quebec nationalism.[7]

This by-election was, indeed, a key moment in the production of divergent imaginings of nation in this colony that included a shrinking indigenous population, the descendants of the Canadiens conquered by the British in 1760, and growing numbers of English-speaking and other migrants. It was also a critical event in the contestation of colonial rule. And, as in all such imaginings of identity and nation, understandings of gender, class, and ethnicity interacted to shape and reshape practices and interpretations of the event. The experiences of the women who voted with Marguerite Paris offer historians a different thread in the burgeoning literature on gender, citizenship, and the changing contours of the public sphere. Historians of France, the United States, England, and Canada have explored the masculinization of citizenship in the wake of democratic revolutions and of the opening up of suffrage to a broader range of males. This paper builds on work by the Clio Collective, Fernand Ouellet, Nathalie Picard, and Allan Greer on women's involvement in politics in this period.

It joins studies of the regendering of the public and private in the late eighteenth and nineteenth centuries and the growing body of literature seeking to explore the complicated story of women's involvement in multiple publics, in the print media, in religious activism, or in politics. More specifically it responds to Jane Rendall's plea that historians pay more attention to the ways some nineteenth-century women exercised their franchise rights. It does so through a micro-history of women's participation in this particular by-election in a colony in which women's active participation in politics was not unusual and was recorded in documents that have survived.[8]

In what follows I seek to explore the links between women's involvement in this by-election and political attempts shortly afterward to exclude women from voting. After examining the characteristics of voting women,[9] the second section analyzes the ways understandings of class, ethnicity, gender, and citizenship were produced in the print media of the city. The third part concentrates on several of the outcomes of the election. One is the evidence given to the Patriot dominated House of Assembly committee that in late 1832 and early 1833 called on numerous witnesses to recount their experiences of the election. Here I look in some detail at the significant role played by one Montrealer, its future mayor, Jacques Viger, in producing knowledge about women's involvement in the election for the committee. The second is the brief debate in the same Assembly that led to the attempt to prevent women voting in 1834, and to their successful exclusion in 1849.

Widows and Other Women at the Hustings

Marguerite Paris and Emilie Tavernier were two of 141 widows who, along with much smaller numbers of single and married women, walked up to the poll and attempted to vote in the 1832 Montreal West by-election. Women made up 14 per cent of the citizens seeking to express their political choice in this tumultuous by-election. This, Nathalie Picard reports, was the highest proportion of women involved in any of the Lower Canadian elections for which she was able to locate the pollbooks.[10] As residents of Lower Canada, these women could imagine taking part in elections because the law did not explicitly prevent them and because other women had taken advantage of this right in various elections since 1791. That year, the Constitutional Act, which established the first elected Legislative Assembly and set out the property requirements for eligibility, had described voters as 'persons'. Only political candidates were referred to specifically by the pronoun 'he'. Persons admitted to vote had to be 21 years old, a 'natural citizen or subject' of His Majesty, and most importantly, to possess or rent land above a specified value. In these early decades of the nineteenth century that value was set pretty low.[11] The resulting franchise was much broader and more inclusive than in England, or than in some of the other colonies of British North America. Catholics could vote, and, after 1831, so could Jews. Just south of Montreal, across the Saint Lawrence River, at least 27 First Nations women from Caughnawaga voted in the 1825 election in Huntingdon county where they helped elect Austin Cuvillier, then a candidate for the Parti-Canadien, the precursors to the Patriots. He returns to the story of the 1832 election shortly.[12]

Thus, local legislation rooted in British constitutional government gave women rights as British subjects in the colony. The Custom of Paris, the French body of law, retained for all civil matters after the British conquest, determined women's property and inheritance rights. Like the civil law of much of Europe, and unlike the English Common Law prevailing in most of the States and other colonies of British North America, marriage created community property, shared equally by man and wife, but administered by the husband. If wives became widows, half of that shared property became theirs. They also had the right to use half their husband's inherited real property or land he had owned prior to his marriage as their dower. Widows thus had a greater likelihood of access to property than in common law jurisdictions. One English visitor considered these laws the reason 'that the fair sex have such influence . . . and even an air of superiority to the husband.'[13] English merchants railed against the way these rules deprived men of what they understood as their rights to freely accumulate property, and soon after the Conquest they were influential in securing legislation that gave all men and women freedom of willing, though this could not overturn a widow's right to dower. Migrants from elsewhere also quickly learned to use notaries to make marriage contracts that established either separate property for each spouse, or give husbands power closer to that of the English Common Law.[14]

In the broadest interpretation of election law, women should have been able to vote if they owned or rented property of the required value in their own name. This would include widows and single women who had inherited or purchased property, and wives who had kept their property separate at marriage by making a marriage contract to that effect. In practice, acceptance of voting women varied from region to region and election to election.[15] It was a dubious and contested right. Patriot supporter and future Montreal mayor, Jacques Viger, later told members of the House of Assembly investigating the Montreal West by-election that as the returning officer for the Montreal East by-election the same year, he had systematically 'refused the vote of all married women'. He also turned away all 'persons in a state of inebriety'. Though Viger assimilated wives' lack of independence to that of drunks, he did not contest widows and single women's right to vote. They had constituted over 9 per cent of the voters in that by-election.[16]

Election laws were inherited from the open voting methods of England, and modified somewhat by local legislation. Officials chose the polling places, candidates addressed the crowd, voters proclaimed their choices verbally. When one hour passed without anyone seeking to vote, the election was over and the leading candidate had won. Blocking opponents from the polls was therefore one way to attempt to secure victory for the man who had the most votes at any time.[17] Candidates and their supporters verbally challenged the right to vote of those choosing their opponent. In the rough politics of open voting, both sides engaged in verbal and physical intimidation. Assemblies in the predominantly male spaces of taverns, in which the champions of each candidate sought to recruit voters, released jostling and jeering bullies on to the streets. Violence became so much part of this election that the newspapers made a special point of remarking on the occasional peaceful day. They also reported on each day's tally. Such published counts gave the wider citizenry knowledge of who was ahead, much as opinion polls do today. In these nineteenth-century contests, the election campaign, the voting, and the publication of people's choices were concurrent, a potent mix that further fueled violence.

In this election, Stanley Bagg, the candidate closely linked to the colonial establishment, had the power to shape the running of the election in ways that Tracey could not. The opening of the initial poll in a Protestant church hall in this city in which Catholics were a majority, and most patriot supporters were Catholic, was one powerful sign of his influence. As the election continued, he and his supporters drew on their close links to the justices of the peace, swearing in additional constables from among his supporters to maintain the peace. Some of these constables were the very 'bullies' who intimidated Tracey supporters. On the second to last day of what turned into the longest election in the colony's history, as tempers and intimidation reached new heights, pro-Bagg magistrates called in the British troops garrisoned in the city. By the end of that day, three men in the crowd, all Canadiens had died at the hands of the soldiers. Canadiens quickly renamed the street 'La rue du Sang'—the street of blood.

All this was still in the future when Marguerite Paris proclaimed her vote on 1 May. It was, the newspapers would later report, a relatively peaceful day. The poll opened at 8 AM. Tracey was well ahead with 296 votes to Bagg's 220. When she stepped up to voice her choice, Stanley Bagg contested her right to vote. This labourer's widow was thus required to publicly affirm the authenticity of her claim to citizenship rights. She swore on oath that she did indeed possess the requisite property qualifications. Her vote was accepted. The male polling clerk inscribed her name in the poll book, indicated that she lived on Vallée Street in the Saint Lawrence ward, put a tally mark under Tracey's name and noted that Bagg had contested her right to vote. The returning officer then signed his name beside this entry.[18]

Women considering voting could anticipate a series of such contestations. The first was the very question of whether, as women, they should go to the polls, for the idea that such engagement in politics was improper for women had both its supporters and its detractors in the colony. Early in the 1820s the *Montreal Gazette* dismissed women's voting as 'absurd and unconstitutional' and derided the 'spiralling influence of women in Lower Canadian politics', predicting the dangers of a 'petticoat polity', should women continue to vote.[19] Shortly after the election, the same newspaper, the mouthpiece for the pro-British bureaucratic faction, reproduced the statement of an English novelist, Mrs Hemans, that a woman could 'never with consistency appear in the forum or the pulpit—in the senate or at the polls. . .without disparagement of her sexual character.' In direct contrast, a petition from Quebec electors in 1828 stressed women's intellectual equality with men. It argued that to vote was not a natural right of either men or women, but was based on their qualifications. The petition was reproduced approvingly in an article in *La Minerve*, which argued that widows with the proper qualifications were in all ways equal to men.[20] The year before *La Minerve* had lauded voting patriot women and reported favourably that they had crowned their winning candidate with flowers.[21]

Presence at the polls was sufficiently contested that it might risk tarnishing women's respectability. And yet they went to vote. On the way, many no doubt braved the derision of opponents of their candidates. As the election drew to an end, the Returning Officer requested that Montreal's Chief of Police provide 'six Constables with long Constable's staves', to prevent anyone from getting to close to the Hustings, unless they wished to vote or were accompanying Ladies.[22] In this protective move he both recognized women's presence and furthered the understanding that women voters were unlike male ones. Marguerite Paris was not alone in having to publicly affirm that she possessed the necessary qualifications to vote. Six of every ten women who dared to present themselves at the hustings during this election were either called upon by the opponent of their candidate to swear to their qualifications or were not allowed to vote. Women's votes were more frequently disqualified, contested, or an oath demanded than those of men. This was the experience of two of every five women who made it to the hustings.[23] Ambiguity about the propriety of women at the polls legitimated aggressive challenges to their claims. So did the suggestion voiced periodically in the press and later that women were sought after by candidates as susceptible to being told how to vote along with cripples, drunks, and other Montrealers represented as lacking independence and autonomy. How individual women were treated at the polls would depend on a complex mix of political expediency, personal networks, and gendered treatment in which some men sheltered some women as they entered the hustings while others engaged in hostile questioning.

In these contestations at the poll, women were not treated as a single category. Widows faced far fewer challenges than married and single women. None withdrew, fewer were required to swear an oath, and a greater proportion ended up voting than other women. As women no longer obviously under the patriarchal power of fathers and husbands, their claim to vote on the basis of independence and ownership of property had greater resonance than that of single women or of wives whose property was separate from their husbands. At the polls what mattered was whether they were known to hold property or would swear that they did. Thus, while half the widows were able to vote without any questioning of their right, this was true of about a quarter of the single women and half that proportion again of the wives.

The poll book records no challenge to the vote of the widow, Emilie Tavernier. She confirmed her family's close political ties to the Patriots by choosing Tracey on 9 May, the twelfth day of the election. Emilie's brother, François Tavernier, was an ardent supporter of Papineau and the Patriots. He had been her official guardian between the time her father died leaving her an orphan at the age of 14, and her marriage in 1823. Indeed at some point during the election François was arrested and charged with assaulting a Bagg supporter.[24] Her recently deceased cousin, Joseph Perrault, with whom she had been raised, had been elected as a member of the Assembly as a supporter of the Parti-Canadien. Emilie Tavernier also had close family links among some of the notable Canadien families who had broken with Papineau and thrown their support behind Bagg and his Tory supporters.

Emilie Tavernier become a widow in 1828 after just five years of marriage with the much older local merchant, Jean-Baptiste Gamelin. Her only surviving son died one year later. Although their marriage contract had provided that their property should remain separate, it had also stipulated that should the surviving partner outlive any offspring they could dispose of all the other's property as full owners.[25] As a result, Emilie faced widowhood with three small properties. These gave her the means to do what became her passion and eventually her profession—provide material, physical, and spiritual support to the poor. During her childhood and her short time as a wife she provided meals and support to the poor of the city who learned that hers was a door they could knock when hungry. After Jean-Baptiste's death she threw herself into this work. She was at the heart of many of the new ventures that the city's bourgeois Catholic women were organizing to care for orphans, the elderly, and the sick, to assist girls from the country seeking domestic work, and to redeem prostitutes. Her prime concern, however, was sick and elderly women. In 1829 she took four frail widows into her home on St Antoine Street. Needing more space she soon arranged to use a larger building in the St Lawrence suburb, where so many of her family and relatives lived.[26]

At the time of the election she had recently moved these elderly and infirm widows yet again, this time into a larger building that she rented at the corners of Saint Lawrence and St Phillip streets. This dwelling was large enough to house herself and up to twenty women. She and the friends, relatives, and the other women who were assisting her in this work and in organizing other charitable enterprises regularly traversed the streets of the city. They collected food, clothing, and money for their poor from the city's citizens, and visited others in their homes.[27] The streets of the city were familiar to them, and Emilie and her colleagues would have been well known figures on the streets. Catholicism, like Protestantism, translated readily in this period 'into a claim to enter the public world and contribute to the work which needed to be done', giving such women 'license to enter the public arena' in purposeful and empowering ways.[28]

Thus the widow Gamelin's family connections, her property, and her reputation as a devout Catholic widow working with the poor and elderly of the city likely guaranteed her immunity from harassment. A few days before she chose to vote, the poll was moved for the third time. The new poll occupied a much more welcoming Catholic space than earlier locations. It was very close to the new Catholic parish church, which was still under construction. Before her husband's death they had shared a keen interest in this project.[29] Situated between the Bank of Montreal and a building occupied by the church wardens of the parish on the North-West corner of the Place d'Armes,[30] it was also a bit closer to her shelter for women on St Philippe street, some six blocks north, than were earlier polls.

Some fifty-five people sought to vote the same day as Emilie Tavernier, the widow Gamelin. Ten of them were women. The fifth voter that morning was a widow, so was the eighth. Twenty-one men in a row then marched up to voice their choices. One Tracey supporter retired when Bagg objected to his vote.

A male labourer's vote was contested. He left, but came back later and voted. The nine men just ahead of Widow Gamelin all chose Stanley Bagg. Then the profoundly male face of the voters changed. Felicité Barbeau, a married woman, chose Stanley Bagg. Daniel Tracey demanded that she swear on oath that she did indeed own property. Two unmarried sisters, Charlotte and Margarite Leduc both chose Tracey and faced the objections of his opponent. Over the rest of the day four more women voted. Emilie's was the only women's vote that went uncontested.

The gender composition of voting citizens varied from day to day over the course of the election. Few came in the early days of voting, but by the fourth day the male face of the electorate was diluted. Every day between 28 April and 9 May between thirteen and twenty-nine women came to the poll. The peak day of female involvement occurred the day after Marguerite Paris's vote. Women must have been highly visible as electors that day, for they represented over a quarter of those endeavouring to express their political choice. Some women voted alone. Others, like Emilie Tavernier, voted with a small cluster of other women. They came from all parts of the electoral district—from the commercial streets of the old city and from the rougher streets of the suburbs of Saint Lawrence and Saint Joseph. Some were neighbours. In this relatively small colonial town many would have known each other. All in all 141 widows, 26 wives, and 54 single women as well as 5 women whose marital status was not indicated sought to vote, and nearly 200 of them did so.

When the press mentioned women voting, they represented them as the dupes of the candidates. Historians have not sufficiently critiqued the gendered underpinnings of such claims. The patterns of their voting and their family histories make it hard to imagine that all, or even many, of the women voted against their will. Few wives voted at the same time as their husbands, or daughters with their fathers. Politics permeated the culture of the colony and especially of Montreal the city in which the differences of language, religion, and culture between old and new colonizers were so apparent especially to visitors. Politics was hardly a foreign world for many of these women. Nathalie Picard has pointed out that many came from Quebec families with long traditions of female voting. The evidence of this in Emilie Tavernier's own extended family is striking. The aunt who had raised her, Marie-Anne Tavernier Perrault, voted as a widow in 1820, as did Barbe Castagnez, her brother's wife and her close friend. In the election of 1827 her cousin, Agathe Perrault, the widow of Maurice Nolan, voted for Louis-Joseph Papineau and Robert Nelson in the Montreal West election. Agathe voted again in 1832, three days after her cousin, Emilie, also choosing Tracey.[31]

The Quebec historian, Fernand Ouellet, has argued that the women who voted in Lower Canadian elections seem 'to have followed the major trends'. He suggests that this means they were 'swayed by pressure from the candidates'.[32] Such analysis downplays the cultural importance of political conflicts in this period. It allows no place for women embracing familial traditions of passionate involvement in politics. It is hard to imagine that either Emilie Tavernier or Agathe Perrault would have been 'swayed' by any arguments Tory candidates might make. Their families were so intimately involved in the emerging patriot movement that their minds would have been made up long before an election. Nor does it seem likely that even a fairly poor widow like Marguerite Paris would have been tempted by money or other offers to vote against the party so strongly supported by the largely Canadien 'craftsmen, farmers, carters, and day-labourers' in the Saint Lawrence suburb who were her neighbours and relatives.[33] Women supportive of the Patriots might be influenced to vote for their candidate, but it is highly unlikely they could be swayed in the opposite direction.

Similarly, given the growing identification of the Patriots with a nationalism that embraced Irish and some American supporters, but represented the British as coterminous with the ruling elite, there was little space for English speaking widows to imagine not voting for the group identified with Imperial rule. Anna Foster's 'gentleman' husband died just one year after their marriage in 1823. In 1827 she joined ninety other widows who voted in the Montreal West election that had pitted the Parti Canadien candidates Louis-Joseph Papineau and Robert Nelson against the establishment candidates, McGill and Delisle. The latter were her choice then, as was true of most of the widows with English names. When she voted again on 16 May 1832, she again chose the establishment candidate, Stanley Bagg. In such heated times, public, open voting ensured that if reluctant women were encouraged to vote, it would be by those whose politics they shared. Personal politics, forged in the crucibles of family discussions, family and ethnic culture, class interests, and empire, more than rhetoric or money would have shaped most women's allegiances long before they reached the polls.

More women voted in this by-election and they constituted a higher proportion of voters than in any others for which the poll books have survived despite the violence and the repeated contestations of their votes.[34] Whether they came willingly of their own initiative, reluctantly, or were bribed to do so, they stepped out publicly to assert their political choices in considerable numbers. And, if they possessed the required qualifications, they voted. Several widows returned after an initial refusal, voting successfully the second time. Furthermore, a significant proportion of the women whose property evaluations qualified them to vote seem to have done so. Historians have estimated that somewhere between one in four and one in eight family heads were eligible to vote in Lower Canadian elections. About 60 per cent of eligible male household heads voted in the two Montreal by-elections of 1832. Contemporary sources make it a challenge to venture similar estimates for women. As the majority of voters were widows, I have made three rough measures of the extent to which widows who were eligible to vote in this particular by-election and the one the same year in the other half of the city did so. Each suggests high rates of engagement. The first is based on the cohort of women who married in Montreal between 1823 whose lives I have been tracing as they made the transition from wife to widow. Around one in three of the women who were already widowed in 1832 and had not remarried voted in the by-elections of that year. Many others would not have fulfilled the property requirements. Comparing the proportion of propertied widows who voted in both by-elections to the number of such women listed in an enumeration of property owners made later that year for the first anticipated Montreal city election would suggest that nearly all eligible propertied widows voted. Thirdly, a comparison of the number of widows enumerated as heading households in the 1831 census and the number of voting widows suggests that nearly half the city's widowed female heads of household exercised their political rights in one of these two 1832 by-elections. These rough measures suggest then that somewhere between a third and nearly all of the relatively privileged widows of Montreal who possessed the qualifications to vote were willing to brave the public space and disorder of the hustings to elect either the Patriot or Tory candidate.[35]

Most of these female voters were property owners. In this city in which the vast majority of families rented their homes, women's claims to vote were more rooted in property owning than those of men. Yet, because of the low franchise, quite meagre holdings legitimated some widows' public voice, in addition to offering them a source of security in their widowhood. Voting widows like Marguerite Paris, could hardly be further removed from the hypothesis proposed by the political scientist, Diane Lamoureux, that most female voters in Lower Canada would have been the owners of seigneuries.[36] The property on which she staked her claim as a citizen was a small, one room, wooden house and lot on Vallée street in the St Lawrence ward. She and her labourer husband had succeeded in purchasing it through their joint labours during their marriage, and thus it formed part of the community property created by marriage on which she had a claim as his widow. It had provided her and her daughter, Marie-Marguerite, with shelter over her two years of widowhood at a time when their moveable possessions were minimal. It was valued for taxation purposes later that year as worth about £116, or as able to generate an annual revenue of just £7.0s.0d. This was very close to the minimum value necessary to vote.[37]

Privileged, as they were relative to widows without property, income, or support, these widows' modest properties pale beside the value of those of the city's largest male landowners or those of the wealthiest widows. Eleven widows, all with land assessed at a revenue of over £100 or around $333 a year, owned nearly half the total value of all the widows' properties that were evaluated. These wealthy widows included several who expressed their political choices during the by-election. The widow Oakes owned two properties assessed as worth over £300 annually in revenue. The widow Anne Platt, who was very active in the Montreal land market, owned two properties on the major thoroughfares, Saint Paul and Notre Dame streets in the Western section of the old city, worth some £180 annually. Both voted for the establishment candidate, Stanley Bagg. So did Anna Foster, as we have seen, and Sarah Campbell. Married between 1823 and 1826 to a 'gentleman', and a merchant, respectively, they, like Emilie Tavernier, were not affluent, but they lived in some comfort.

Marguerite Paris's husband had been a labourer. The deceased husbands of some of the other widows of modest means who voted in the 1832 by-elections had been masters and craftsmen in the artisanal trades that were so important in the local economy. Sarah Harrison, a tinsmith's widow who voted within two months of her husband's death, was described as renting the property on St Paul Street where she lived. Though she lived on this expensive street, and had been promised $1,000 outright instead of a dower, her husband was buried in the poor ground of the Protestant cemetery.[38] Mary Howard was the widow of a shoemaker, while Emilie Monjean who voted in Montreal East, was the widow of a master painter.[39] For widows, as for the wider population, the relatively low level of the franchise permitted those of modest means, especially those who had invested in real property, to have a say in elections. Yet Marguerite Paris was an exception among labourer's widows. Most had no property to soften the challenge of widowhood, let alone to provide a basis for voting.

Gender, Citizenship, and Election Coverage in the Press

Nearly 200 women successfully performed the act of citizenship in this by-election. More tried. They walked through supportive and hostile crowds, swore to their legitimacy as voters, and called out the name of the candidate of their choice. Over sixty did so in the election earlier in April Montreal East. Yet, in the day to day election reports of Montreal's newspapers, their presence at the polls was usually only mentioned to discredit the masculinity and behaviour of the opposing side, or to deride their inability to find more appropriate electors. Conflicting political visions of citizenship that built on and conjured up divergent forms of masculinity and nation took up much more space in reports of the election than acknowledgment of voting women. In its support of Stanley Bagg and the established order, the *Gazette* claimed a vision of masculine citizenship rooted in independence, industry, integrity, respectability, honour, class hierarchy, and benevolence toward the poor. His supporters stressed Bagg's residence in the colony since his childhood and lauded his contributions to agriculture and commerce and his loyalty to his King, country and the Constitution—political language that Cecilia Morgan has shown also represented all that was 'both British and manly' about Upper Canadian Conservatives at the same time.[40]

Conservatives belittled their opposition, representing Tracey and his largely Catholic supporters as uncontrolled, dishonest and desperate—the kind of rowdy, violence prone, lower-class men who did not deserve to exercise the vote, and who could be easily swayed by the words of eloquent, but misguided superiors, just as they were by their priests. These dismissals of his supporters frequently represented them as unruly Irishmen, rather than Canadiens, implying, for example, that many had recently arrived, had been dependent on charity to get through the winter, charity given by just the kind of men they were opposing. The clothes on their bodies were read to critique the breadth of the franchise, and to justify contesting their votes: 'The appearance of the great majority is sufficient to cast a doubt upon their claim.' Mistreatment of women was claimed as further evidence of their misguided manliness. That 'Mr Bagg's friends, particularly the ladies, when at the poll, are hooted and hissed at', was presented as proof that 'Tracey and his friends have disgraced themselves by their conduct so unworthy of BRITISH subjects, enjoying a free constitution.'[41]

In the equally fanatical criticism of 'la Bureaucratie', published daily in *La Minerve*, women's presence at the polls was usually linked with that of cripples, the elderly and the infirm as evidence that Bagg had few voters left in reserve and was getting desperate.[42] Women's presence, by implication, could only mean they were dragged to the polls. Patriot supporters claimed to be working for the 'public interest', the 'public good', and the 'rights of the people'. The people, in the columns of *La Minerve*, were not only Canadiens. At this time, the Irish and frequently Americans as well were explicitly embraced as supporters. Theirs was, at this point, a nationalist vision that embraced all those who espoused the cause of the people, of the Canadiens.[43]

Those with the capacity to vote were thus ascribed ethnic characteristics and were resolutely male. Despite the obvious presence of women at the polls, women as a category had little place in these competing understandings of the qualities of voters, articulated in the public sphere of assemblies and newspaper reporting. In this formative period of Lower Canadian politics, as in the revolutionary politics of the eighteenth century American colonies, France, or the constitutional politics of England, the citizen whose qualities were in the process of being elaborated discursively by Patriots and Tories alike could only be male. The reason, imagination, and independence that historians have identified as key characteristics of the individual constructed in emerging liberal theory were the very opposite of the emotionality and dependence attached to females or ascribed to political opponents. Widows and other women could vote, but the gendering of politics as masculine limited their visibility in the press.[44]

There was one major exception to this and it is an important one. On 19 May, Marie-Claire Perrault, the wife of Austin Cuvillier, and cousin of Emilie Tavernier, sought to vote for Stanley Bagg. As a young man, Cuvillier, a Montreal merchant and auctioneer, had been a critic of colonial policy and a committed member of the Parti Canadien. In the years leading up to the 1832 election, however, he and other more moderate nationalists, had increasingly distanced themselves from the politics of the Patriot party, finally breaking completely.[45] The fissure widened to a chasm when some 500 Montrealers met to determine who should be nominated to run in this by-election. Speaking in English, eventually to cries of 'Parlez français', Cuvillier had publicly nominated Stanley Bagg. He recommended support for him 'as a very respectable man' who had been long established in the colony, and dismissed Tracey as an inappropriate choice—too violent, and too prone to attacking 'the private character of individuals'.[46]

Cuvillier's new support for the colonial elite made him the prime target of patriot scorn during this election and in its acrimonious aftermath. When Marie-Claire sought to vote, patriots responded to her not as any woman, but as the wife of a Canadien who had chosen to defect from the 'national' party.[47] Her vote was allowed by the returning officer, who noted that she was married and that her goods were separate from her husband's as a result of a court decision. It was questioned in the patriot press. Assimilating domestic and political subterfuge, *La Minerve* challenged the validity of the separation of goods. This possibility offered by the Custom of Paris was one growing numbers of men in economically volatile positions like his, took advantage of to protect some of their property from creditors. *La Minerve* questioned Cuvillier's abilities as family provider and businessman by reminding readers of his bankruptcy, and mused more broadly on the implications of separate property for husbands' marital authority. Could two spouses vote if they were properly separate as to goods? If their separation was not valid, 'does she have the right that she was allowed to exercise?' If they were really separate as to property, why had she paid some of his creditors? This became a further occasion to criticize the independence of the Returning Officer, understood by all Patriots, to be controlled by Bagg and his supporters. Such tricky legal questions, the article, suggested, were best left to jurists, but the 'Returning Officer did not find this a tricky question. He decided Mme C. should 'vote without hesitation'.[48] In this commentary, *La Minerve* linked voting by wives, rather than women in general, to broader questions of domestic and political disorder in the colony and to the disruptions caused by choices like separate property that could be represented as of English origin and dubious propriety.

The public debate about Austin Cuvillier's wife's right to vote points to the significance of loyalty as a critical theme in this election. Patriots willingly integrated Irishmen like Tracey and his 'compatriots, our adopted brothers', into their fold. They were understood to embrace similar political goals and to readily embrace not just Catholicism, but a nationalism that was being built in opposition to the unjust implementation of British colonial rule. Much more troubling were Canadiens, like Cuvillier, who had 'fallen into the trap' of supporting the Bureaucracy, who had turned 'Brutus' on their people. In the public rhetoric of the election, as reported in the columns of the press, patriots wavered between derision and anguish over how such men could be brought back into a party that sought to speak for all Canadiens. In public anguishing over transgressions from the boundaries of the imagined nation they were building, Austin Cuvillier was the name most frequently mentioned. That his wife tried to vote, that their marital and monetary affairs were suspect, all signaled both Cuvillier's perfidy and the unmanly way Stanley Bagg neglected no strategy to muster as many votes as possible.[49] This also further diffused the understanding that it was the Tories who relied on women as voters, and further delegitimized women at the hustings.

Viger's Gaze: Producing Knowledge about Citizens

Widows and other women clearly voted. Yet, in the public press, citizens are largely presented as masculine. Women's presence denotes improper election behaviour or desperation for votes. This supports Greer's argument, that in the 1830s, understandings that politics were male were sufficiently widespread to justify their exclusion from the vote. Yet historians have inadequately explained why politicians decided in 1834 that the time had come to prevent women from taking to the hustings. True, similar legislation had already been passed in some American states, in England and would follow in most of the other colonies of British North America, though there is much less evidence of women using this right in those jurisdictions. Fernand Ouellet has suggested that the 1832 election played a role. His explanation that Papineau was upset because too many women had again voted for his opponent seems insufficient. Yet, in transforming Papineau into the sole author of the bill, and in rooting the explanation in the actual act of women voting, rather than any general set of ideas as the cause, Ouellet raised an important question that he failed to ask. How did anyone know how many women voted for each candidate? The English Montreal newspapers certainly speak disparagingly of Patriot leader, Louis-Joseph Papineau, lurking around the polls, and especially of his close surveillance during the subsequent Coroner's investigation.[50] Yet it is hard to imagine that he was keeping count of the votes for each candidate by their sex. Nor were the daily tallies in the newspapers ever broken down by the gender of the voters. Furthermore, if there is a connection between this election and the1834 bill, why and how did women's vote, so invisible in the print media during the election, become visible?

Here it is Papineau's cousin, Jacques Viger, who is central. At the time of the 1832 by-election, Viger would have been in his mid 40s. No Montrealer can have known the city's streets and people better than he did. No-one showed a greater interest in accumulating such knowledge. Whereas his more famous cousins focused on the future of Canadiens at the level of the colony, his passion was the city—its past, its people, and its future. In 1813 he was named surveyor of the highways, streets, lanes, and bridges of Montreal. In 1825 he was one of the two Census Commissioners for the whole Island of Montreal. In that capacity, as Jean-Claude Robert suggests, 'all the details of his fellow citizen's lives were known to him'. Three years later, he drew on his intimate knowledge of the social geography of the city to advise his patriot politician cousins on how best to allocate boundaries for the wards of the town and set the property qualifications low enough to ensure a Canadien majority in upcoming city elections. As politicians prepared a bill to incorporate Montreal, it was Viger who set out to assess the value of all property holdings in anticipation of the city's first election, which was predicted for the month of June. Early in April 1832, he had acted as Returning Officer in the Montreal East by-election. And when municipal elections were held in 1833, he was chosen as the city's first mayor.[51]

During the twenty-two days of the 1832 by-election, Jacques Viger was observing and practising what he called his 'habit of collecting matters of history'. His testimony to the House of Assembly after the election shows him playing multiple roles and in diverse locations. He went to the hustings on most of the days of the election. He acted as an intermediary between Papineau and his political adversaries. He repeatedly encouraged the High Constable to produce an accurate list of the constables sworn in and of those who were summoned but refused to appear. He eavesdropped on the whispered conversations of Bagg's Tory supporters about hiring and paying bullies, asked questions and offered advice.[52] Jacques Viger took on the role of official voyeur as he fixed his gaze on the electoral behaviour of Montrealers. Like a growing number of men of his times, Viger sought to make sense of the world through counting and categorizing. One of his ways of mastering this unruly political event, in which he had no official capacity, was to watch closely, to listen, and to intervene. Another was to make sure he had detailed information on people's voting at his fingertips. He did this, as he explained later to Austin Cuvillier, by transcribing the details from the Poll Book daily until he had produced his own 'entire copy' from one made by 'a writer in the Police Office of the Prothonotaries at Montreal'. He then made additional transcriptions of the entire poll book, organizing each one differently so that he could see at a glance how and when every Montrealer had voted, and identify voters by their ethnicity and sex.[53]

It is the statistics produced from his analyses and transcriptions of this poll book that have served as the basis of most of the published accounts of this election. More interesting are these transcriptions. For they were instruments that allowed him to answer many questions Patriot politicians later had about the running of the election. In one he included an alphabetical list of all the men and women who presented themselves at the hustings. On this list, he wrote the names of those who voted for Tracy in black, those for Bagg in red and those who were disqualified in blue. Widows and wives are cross-indexed by both their married names and their maiden names. With this colour-coded list, Viger could determine at a glance how anyone had voted. In the days of open voting, this is not as shocking an act as it would now seem. It was, however, extremely useful to a man intent on knowing his city, its people, and their politics.[54]

In his transcription of the larger poll book he assigned every person who attempted to vote a number and an ethnicity. The latter he determined from his own knowledge. The categories he chose divided voters into Canadiens, Americans, or Irish—those understood as patriot supporters—and 'English and others', into which the Scots, so significant in Montreal's Anglo community and economy disappeared. As he copied and added details on each citizen in this transcription, Viger changed his pen each time the voter was a woman. In the pages of this leather bound volume, the women, so barely visible in newspaper narratives of election events, jump off the parchment, their names inscribed in red rather than black ink. Beside any married men or woman whose spouse voted he indicated, also in red, what their polling number was. This colour coding was part of his method of ensuring accurate counts. It also rendered the number of women voters, and their daily presence, highly visible. It was through his careful counting, based on these transcriptions, and his frequent observation of the polls, that he legitimated his expertise at the investigations that followed the election.

From Red Ink, Redcoats, and the 'Street of Blood' to Male Citizens

In his leather bound volume, Viger's red ink marked out female voters as different kinds of citizens. On the streets of the city the shedding of Canadien blood brought this tumultuous election to a close, hardening the identification between Patriots and Canadiens and erasing for a while the significance of the presence of widows and other women at the hustings. On 21 May, after 22 days of voting, Daniel Tracey was three votes ahead of Stanley Bagg. It had been another conflict-ridden day. Tempers were high, and each side was using its power to try to shape the outcome. Tracey's supporters attacked their opponents with the weapons they had at hand. Umbrellas and stones from the newly macadamized roads are those most frequently mentioned. Bagg's powerful supporters among the city magistrates called in more constables and the troops. British soldiers and the cannons were set up at a discrete distance from the hustings. Jostling with sticks and stones continued. At some point the Riot Act appears to have been read, though when and where would be much disputed in the weeks and months that followed.

After the polls closed the soldiers shot into the crowd and killed three Canadien men. The news of their murder by British soldiers reverberated across the colony, exacerbating the tension between those seeking political change and the supporters of the status quo. The invective that already marked the journalism of the two city newspapers most closely associated with each side reached new heights, carving harder lines of ethnic difference and hatred between both sides and telling two very different tales of the day's events. The *Montreal Gazette* laid the blame squarely and disparagingly on 'Mr Papineau, and his political adherents resident in Montreal', casting Tracey as their dupe, as someone chosen in order to 'invite the Irish violently to uphold their course.'[55] In *La Minerve*, Duvernay reported that Bagg's partisans approached the corpses laughing, 'watching with ferocious joy the Canadien blood that flowed in the street', shaking hands, congratulating each other and regretting that they had not decimated the Canadiens. Soldiers were said to have been rewarded with abundant quantities of rum. The next morning the poll opened early. There was only one voter. Tracey was declared the winner. Bagg lodged an official protest against the result.[56]

Over the following days newspapers across the colony reported on the event. In Montreal the Coroner's inquest began immediately and there were calls on all sides for further investigations. On 24 May the public funeral for the three Canadiens attracted some 5,000 people in this city of 27,000. They were given a first class service, and then accompanied to the graveyard in a convoy with Papineau and other patriot politicians at the head behind the coffins. Whether any women were part of the crowd is impossible to tell from the press reporting on the event, though the suggestion that those present all wore black crepe on their hats dressed the crowd in masculine mourning attire.[57] Nor are women visible in most of the records generated by the events of 21 May. None were asked to testify at the coroner's inquest, which after many adjournments resolved in September that there was no basis for a charge of murder against the Colonel and the Captain of the troops.[58] Women may have attended the assemblies that met in parishes across the colony after church to discuss the 'horrors of the 21st of June', to deplore the actions of Canadiens like Austin Cuvillier, for having 'ignominiously abandoned the mass of the Canadiens to serve in a party that is not worthy of their support', to proclaim faithfulness to the King, disgust for the actions of the soldiers, magistrates and Bureacratic party, and to announce special church services to pray for the souls of the three victims. Yet no female names appear among the lists of local notables reported in attendance at the meetings in *La Minerve*. Such public assemblies, such meetings of citizens to discuss the affairs of their country, to engage in rational discourse, were the very essence of the new kind of 'bourgeois public' that the German scholar Jurgen Habermas has identified as typifying the politics of eighteenth and nineteenth century western states. They were resolutely male spaces.[59]

It is only in the evidence taken by the committee of the House of Assembly investigating the election that there is any mention of women as electors. And, of all the witnesses called, only Jacques Viger seemed interested in alerting the politicians to the question of women voting. He did so again and again, at first soliciting few reactions. Early in January 1833, he reported seeing a great many women voting on both sides. The next day he used the data he had so carefully collected to place women's voting in the public record. In authoritative, statistical detail he reported that:

> 225 women came to the Hustings, 26 of whom did not vote. There were 199 that voted; of whom 95 voted for Mr Tracey and 104 for Mr Bagg; that is to say 49 spinsters, 20 of whom voted for Mr Tracey, and 29 for Mr Bagg; 131 widows, 68 of whom voted for Mr Tracey, and 63 for Mr Bagg; and 19 married women, 7 of whom voted for Mr Tracey, and 12 for Mr Bagg.

Then, he gave committee members his listing that showed the numbers of women voting on each day of the election. He informed them that 'six married women voted. . . jointly with their husbands'. There was no immediate reaction to this information. The questioning turned to how the magistrates and Members of the House of Assembly had voted, and Viger could use his careful records to tell all.[60]

Yet once other issues had been investigated in depth these minute details and statistical tables about voting women finally provoked some interest among committee members, especially Mr Leslie, the main Patriot questioner. Early on, Viger informed him that as Returning Officer, he had refused to let married women vote during the Montreal East election.[61] Four weeks later, Leslie wanted to know which women 'were brought to vote toward the end of the hour, so as to feed the poll?' At this point widows, wives and spinsters no longer appear as statistical categories. Giving evidence that can only have been read from his transcription of the poll book in which the women were so visibly identified in red ink, he started naming individual female voters.[62]

Viger mentioned only women who had voted just after the Returning Officer proclaimed that the election would be over if no one voted in the next 60 minutes. This was easy for him to do, for he had identified such moments in his transcription with little stars. He did not mention all the women who had voted at other times. And, he failed to mention the many men who had voted at similar critical moments in the election process. Twenty-three women were mentioned by name—less than five per cent of the female voters. Fifteen of them were supporters of Bagg. This in itself led some credence to the accusation of Patriots that Bagg's supporters were pulling women in to the hustings to increase his chances.[63] James Leslie also wished to know which 'married women have voted as well as their husbands?' Again, Viger was able to be very specific. He named six couples, including 'Marie-Claire Perrault who voted on the 18th May for Mr Bagg; wife of Austin Cuvillier, Esquire, who had voted on the 18th for the same candidate'.[64] Viger mentioned Mme Cuvillier twice—as a woman voting to prevent the poll closing and as a wife voting the same way as her husband. He did so without casting any obvious judgment. Yet this publicity must have added to the broader discourse in newspapers and the assemblies throughout the province that castigated those Canadiens in general who had supported the 'Bureaucratic Party', and that named Austin Cuvillier in particular as the most prominent of the Canadiens 'wishing to crush their compatriots'.[65]

Viger, with his careful lists, numbers, and tracking of votes thus placed information about women's voting squarely on the floor of the Legislative Assembly, in the public record, and on the agenda of electoral reform in the colony. A year later, when the committee's lengthy investigation was over, the Patriot politician, John Nielson picked up the issue again, identifying a range of doubtful practices revealed at recent elections that should be dealt with. These included women's right to vote, how oaths should be sworn, and how to reduce tension and struggles at the polls. Not once was the possibility of a secret ballot raised, a choice that would have avoided many of the electoral problems, and that was already practiced in states south of the border.[66] A few days later Louis-Joseph Papineau rose in the Assembly pronouncing:

> As to women voting, that is something it is right to destroy. It is ridiculous, nay odious to see wives dragged to the hustings by their husbands, girls by their fathers, often even against their wishes. The public interest, decency, the modesty of the sex demand that these scandals should not be repeated any more. A simple resolution of the Chamber would exclude such people from the right to vote.[67]

This widely quoted statement has been read by historians as a general expression of the new understandings of gender and citizenship that the Patriots were articulating. Allan Greer quite rightly notes how little sense it made, given that most female voters were widows. He also shows how well it fitted with Rousseauian ideas about gender in which 'sexual disorder on the part of women, as evidenced by political self assertion, was considered deplorable.'[68] Yet Papineau's words were more than a succinct representation of the gender ideals of his times. They also continued the very personalized Patriot attacks on Austin Cuvillier as a traitor to the Canadien cause and the critique of his wife's vote during the election as a signifier of both domestic and political instability. Papineau was explicitly impugning the honour of Cuvillier and his wife in his reference to wives dragged to the hustings. Cuvillier, who was present in the Assembly at the time, was well aware of it. So, no doubt, were the other politicians. Cuvillier shot back expressing surprise that Papineau would 'accuse the women who vote of immodesty', when he had seen him 'receive their votes with pleasure'. The debate was brief. The only exchange in the Assembly on this subject was between these two men. Under attack from Cuvillier, Papineau wriggled between his language of gendered citizenship and individual critique, finally asserting unconvincingly that his were 'general and not individual reflections. . . . I was not accusing anyone.' The debate went no further. The motion to insert such a clause into the wider electoral reform bill was passed without amendment.

It was only because other parts of the bill were subsequently found unconstitutional[69] that the question of women's right to vote remained unresolved. It was not until after the discontent so evident in the 1832 by-election had mushroomed into rebellion, repression, rule by an appointed Special Council, and the amalgamation of the largely British province of Upper Canada with the mixed, but largely French-speaking province of Lower Canada, that the question was again addressed. In 1849, a year after American feminists had come together at Seneca Falls seeking greater rights for women, including the right to vote, politicians put the last nail in the possibility of widows and other women voting in another omnibus electoral reform bill. I have yet to find evidence that the clause excluding women was even debated.[70]

Conclusion

Two hundred women voting in this colonial city of some 27,000 inhabitants may not seem many. Yet, the widows and other women who stepped up to the polls over the twenty-three days of voting between April and May 1832 made up 14 per cent of the voters. On some days women were over a third of those voicing their choices at the hustings. Furthermore, a significant proportion of widows with the required property qualifications embraced the possibility of exercising the right to vote. What motivated these women to take part in this highly contentious election? Historians writing about other jurisdictions have suggested that candidates desperate to win were 'willing to ignore convention to secure as many supporters as they could'. Such arguments support the representations of the time, which downplayed women's initiative and interest by suggesting that women at the hustings had been dragged there. The women who braved the hustings in 1832 were taking advantage of a right that growing numbers of Canadiennes and immigrant women had embraced since the creation of an elected assembly in 1791. They followed the legacy of Patriot leader, Louis-Joseph Papineau's grand-mother, who, in an earlier bitterly contested Montreal election in1809, voted for his father. When asked for whom she wished to vote she is reported to have stated 'For my son M. Joseph Papineau, for I believe that he is a good and faithful subject.'[71]

The numbers of women involved, the patterns of their voting, and the courage involved in exposing their bodies and reputations at the hustings all suggest that politics mattered to them. These women voters were diverse in their class origins—they voted as the widows, daughters and occasionally the wives of labourers and craftsmen as well as of wealthy merchants. They were Jews, devout Catholics and committed Protestants. Outside the city they included First Nations women. Some came from families resident in Canada for centuries; others were relative newcomers, mostly from Scotland, the United States, England, and Ireland. Though many had very close to the minimum property required to be eligible to vote, this still marked them out among the privileged in this city where renters were rapidly outnumbering land-owners.

That so many eligible women chose to vote in 1832 is powerful evidence that the understanding that male and female spheres should be separate and that politics and citizenship required capacities found only in males was a contested one at this time in Lower Canada. If understandings about separate spheres for men and women, and about politics as a male domain were as powerful as Allan Greer has suggested, the presence of women like Marguerite Paris or Emilie Tavernier at the polls in 1832, women's attendance at the Legislative Assembly, or the passionate interest that the women in the family of Patriot leader, Louis-Joseph Papineau displayed in politics are difficult to explain.[72] Furthermore, women continued to vote between the 1834 attempt to exclude them and the successful law in 1849. In 1844 Agathe Perrault—the widow Nolan, Emilie Tavernier's cousin—voted again in a Montreal election, as she had done in 1827 and in 1832, though Emilie did not. Once again the widow Nolan chose the reform candidate, and once again she was joined by another woman from her family, this time her widowed sister-in-law.

Women challenged new understandings of citizenship, politics, and the public by choosing to vote. Yet their presence at the polls in such large numbers, especially during the 1832 election, did help to seal their fate. Louis-Joseph Papineau was no doubt influenced by ideas about gender deriving from Rousseau and more broadly from the growing hold of the idea of separate spheres in the Anglo-American world, as Allan Greer and Nathalie Picard have argued. There is ample evidence of these understandings in newspapers and other print media during the 1820s and 1830s. A commentary on a woman voter the Quebec Mercury in 1827 caricatured the idea of women voting by suggesting that they would also seek to enter the assembly where their presence would distract men from 'the affairs of State'. Worse, this English newspaper suggested, alluding to the particularly high birth rates among Canadien women, 'in this prolific country', pregnancies could mean that many would be unable to attend, 'and the natural consequence would be that the business of the state must be neglected whilst these family concerns were going forward.[73] This evocative image of a political institution both peopled and rendered empty by pregnant women promotes the desirability of the separation of home and politics and of men and women. It ignores the reality that single women, and especially widows were the usual voters, conflating all women with married women as became so common in the nineteenth century.[74]

The diffusion of new understandings of citizenship does not explain the timing of politicians' decision, or help interpret the minimal debate in the House of Assembly in 1834, when the first attempt was made to exclude women. Critical here were Viger and Cuvillier. Jacques Viger played a key role as the modern producer of knowledge who made the numbers known, pinned them down in statistical tables, and entered them into the public record, contributing more information about women voting in his testimony before the Select Committee investigating the election than did any elected politician.[75] Important too, especially in interpreting the brief debate in 1834, was the reaction of the Patriots to Canadiens like Austin Cuvillier who chose to support their enemies—the bureaucrats, Tories, 'the English Party', represented in this election by the merchant, Stanley Bagg. As Patriots struggled to articulate a new vision of nation and citizenship, the disloyal challenged their claim to speak for the conquered nation, exposing the fragility and constructed character of ethnicity as a boundary marker. The line between the public embarrassment of Mme Cuvillier in the newspapers during the 1832 by-election and the attempt by the Patriot controlled assembly to remove women's right to vote in 1834 was a direct one. Only constitutional errors in other sections of the bill prevented it becoming law.

In 1849, when the new bill to remove women's right to vote passed so quietly, the political and cultural context had changed. In the wake of the rebellions of 1837 and 1838 the Catholic Church gained a new hegemony over institutions and Catholic citizens. Patriots became reformers and liberals. The divisions between Canadien and others hardened into a less ethnically inclusive strand of nationalism which idealized francophone, Catholic women's contribution to the nation as mothers of large families. The numbers of Catholic women taking vows and working as teachers, nuns and charity workers within religious orders increased dramatically. Protestant Montreal women also became heavily involved as lay charity workers. Emilie Tavernier transformed her work with the elderly into a religious order, overseen by male religious authorities and took vows herself. When she died of cholera in 1851 she was the Mother Superior of the Sisters of Providence. Her order had housed over a hundred elderly and sick widows since their consecration in 1843 and it was one of the two major orders in the city that provided for the elderly and visited the poor in their homes.[76] Later they would establish institutions throughout much of the Canadian and American West.

Sarah Harrison, the tinsmith's widow remarried not long after the election. So did Marguerite Paris. Marguerite Gagnon, the mason's widow continued to live in the Saint Lawrence suburb where her wooden one-room house secured her shelter until her death in 1866. The last of the voting widows whose lives I have been following, Sarah Campbell, whose merchant husband had died shortly after going bankrupt in 1831, died in Montreal in 1884 at the age of 83. By that time, a new generation of Montreal women, Protestant and Catholic, English and French speaking were organizing to change women's rights. A year later the Canadian Prime Minister briefly proposed enfranchising widows and spinsters for federal elections.[77] In the pages and pages of Hansard recording the debates, women's involvement in earlier elections was not mentioned. The battle to regain suffrage in Quebec was long and difficult. Whereas early nineteenth century observers had commented on Quebec as a place where wives and widows had too much power, a century later Québécoises were generally viewed as being behind the rest of the country. In 1940, Quebec was the last Canadian jurisdiction to allow women to vote in provincial elections.

Notes

1. The MA thesis of Nathalie Picard, as well as her database on the widows who voted, have been invaluable in my writing of this article. 'Les femmes et le vote au Bas-Canada de 1792 à 1849', (MA, Université de Montréal, 1992); Nathalie Picard, 'Database of Women Voters'. So have Robert Sweeny's computerized version of a different transcription of the poll-book by Jacques Viger and his database derived from Viger's enumeration of six of the city's eight wards. Robert Sweeny, 'By-election of 1832'; 'A partial tax roll for the City and suburbs of Montréal, 1832', (St John's: MUN, 2002).
2. *Montreal Gazette*, 30 April 1832.
3. *La Minerve*, 30 April 1832.
4. Robert Rumilly, *Histoire de Montréal. Tome II* (Montreal: Fides, 1970), 83–4.
5. Allan Greer, *The Patriots and the People. The Rebellion of 1837 in Rural Lower Canada* (Toronto: University of Toronto Press, 1993); Jane Rendall, 'Women and the Public Sphere', *Gender & History* 11.3 (November 1999): 475–88; Joan Landes, ed., *Feminism, the Public and the Private* (Oxford: New York, 1998); Mary Ryan, *Women in Public. Between Banners and Ballots, 1825–1880* (Baltimore, Maryland, and London, England: The Johns Hopkins University Press, 1990); Leonore Davidoff, 'Regarding some "Old Husband's Tales": Public and Private in Feminist History', in *Worlds Between. Historical Perspectives on Gender and Class*, Leonore Davidoff, ed. (Oxford: Blackwell Publishers, 1995): 227–76; Leonore Davidoff, and Catherine Hall, *Family Fortunes. Men and Women of the English Middle Class, 1780–1850* (Chicago: University of Chicago Press, 1987).
6. Picard, 'Les femmes', (1992).
7. Fernand Ouellet, *Lower Canada, 1791–1840: Social Change and Nationalism* (Toronto: McClelland and Stewart, 1980), 226–9; France Galarneau, 'L'election partielle du quartier—ouest de Montréal en 1832: analyse politico-sociale', *Revue d'histoire de l'Amérique française*, (RHAF) XXXII.4 (mars 1979): 565–84; France Galarneau, 'L'élection pour le quartier Ouest de Montréal en 1832: analyse politico-sociale', (MA thesis, Université de Montréal, 1975); Gilles Boileau, *Le 21 Mai 1832 sur la Rue du Sang* (Montreal: Éditions de Meridien, 1999).
8. Ouellet, *Lower Canada*; Greer, *The Patriots*; Picard, *Les femmes*; Collectif Clio, *Quebec Women. A History* (Toronto: The Women's Press, 1987), 122–3; Joan B. Landes, *Women and the Public Sphere in the Age of French Revolution* (Ithica: Cornell University Press, 1988); Olwen Hufton, *Women and the Limits of Citizenship in the French Revolution* (Toronto: University of Toronto Press, 1991); Ryan, *Women in Public*; Joan Wallach Scott, *Only Paradoxes to Offer. French Feminist and the Rights of Man* (Cambridge, Massachusetts, and London, England: Harvard University Press, 1996); Anna Clarke, *The Struggle for the Breeches. Gender and the Making of the British Working Class* (Berkeley and Los Angeles: University of California Press, 1997); Eleanor Gordon and Gwyneth Nair, *Public Lives. Women, Family and Society in Victorian Britain* (New Haven and London: Yale University Press, 2003); Judith Apter Klinghoffer and Lois Elkis, '"The petticoat electors": Women's Suffrage in New Jersey, 1776–1807', *Journal of the Early Republic* 12.2 (1992): 159–93; Rendall, 'Women and the Public Sphere', 484–5; Kim Klein, 'A "petticoat polity?" Women Voters in New Brunswick Before Confederation, *Acadiensis* 26.1 (1996): 71–5.
9. Rendall, 'Women', 484–5. I draw here on biographical details of women's lives collected from parish registers, marriage contracts and other documents for my manuscript 'Wife to Widow: Lives, Laws and Politics in Nineteenth Century Montreal', and Picard 'Database.'
10. Picard, 'Les femmes', 72–3.Urban voters had to own a home or a plot of land with an annual revenue worth £5.11.s 1.5d local currency, or have lived as a tenant for twelve months prior to the election in a dwelling for which they had paid a minimum annual rent of double that amount £11.2s 2.5p
11. Lower Canada Statutes, 1825, cap XXXIII
12. Constitutional Act, 1791.
13. Hugh Gray, *Letters from Canada Written During a Residence There in the Years 1806, 1807 and 1808* (London, 1809; Toronto: Coles Pub. Co., 1971), 141–3.
14. Bettina Bradbury, *Wife to Widow: Class, Culture, Family and the Law in Nineteenth-Century Quebec, Grandes Conférences Desjardins, pamphlet No. 1* (Montreal: Programme d'études sur le Québec de l'Université McGill, 1997): 1–45; Bettina Bradbury, Alan Stewart, Evelyn Kolish, and Peter Gossage, 'Property and Marriage: The Law and Practice in early Nineteenth Century Montreal', *Histoire sociale/Social History* XXVI (May 1993), 9–39.
15. Picard, 'Les femmes.'
16. Journals of the House of Assembly of Lower Canada, (JHALC), 28 January, 1833.
17. *Montreal Gazette, La Minerve,* 25 April–25 May 1832; Galarneau, 'L'élection pour le quartier Ouest', 33.
18. ANQM, Poll Book, Montreal West By-Election, 1832. This is the official version.
19. *New Brunswick Royal Gazette*, 20 June 1820, citing

the *Montreal Gazette*, 25 April 1820, cited in Klein, 'A "petticoat polity"', 71.

20. *Montreal Gazette* 31 December 1833, cited in E.A. Heaman, 'Taking the World by Show: Canadian Women Exhibitors to 1900', *Canadian Historical Review* 78.4 (December 1997), 604; Petition of Pierre Faucher, Romain Robitaille et al., *Electors in the City of Quebec*, 3 December 1828, reprinted in *La Minerve*, 22 December 1828, cited in Picard, 'Les femmes', 48.
21. *La Minerve*, 13 August 1827, cited in Picard, 'Les femmes', 54–5.
22. H. St George Dupré to Benjamin Delisle, 15 May, 1832, cited in JHALC, 20 December 1832, 36.
23. Lower Canada, Statutes, 5 Geo IV, Cap. 33; Les archives du Séminaire de Québec (ASQ), P32 Fonds Viger-Verreau, 'Statistique de l'éléction de 1832, au Quartier-Ouest de la Cité de Montréal; JHALC, Appendix 1832–3; Evidence of Jacques Viger, 26 January 1833. Only 12 per cent of wives' votes were not contested in any way compared to 28 per cent of single women and 50 per cent of widow.
24. JHALC, 1833, Appendix, 91.
25. ANQM, Notary Doucet, Marriage contract of Emilie Tavernier and Jean-Baptiste Gamelin, 4 June 1823
26. Denise Robillard, *Emilie Tavernier-Gamelin* (Montréal: Éditions du Méridien, 1988), 101–4.
27. Robillard, *Emilie*, 101–4.
28. Gordon and Nair, *Public Lives*, 4.
29. Robillard, *Emilie*, 90.
30. Kathleen Jenkins, *Montreal. Island City of the St. Lawrence* (New York: Doubleday and Company, Inc., 1966), 285.
31. Nathalie Picard, 'Les femmes et le vote', 94–101.
32. Ouellet, *Lower Canada*, 25, 226.
33. France Galarneau, 'Daniel Tracey', DCB, VI.
34. Picard, 'Les femmes', 73.
35. These estimates were made based on my research into the women who married in Montreal between 1823 and 1826; Sweeny, 'A partial tax roll, 1832'; and a quick count of the numbers of widows heading households enumerated in the Census of 1831.
36. Among the 199 women who voted, 63 per cent of widows, 84 per cent of wives and 66 per cent of the single women owned property. Diane Lamoureux, *Citoyennes? Femmes, droit de vote et democratie* (Montreal: Remue-menage, 1989), 41.
37. ANQM, Notary Labadie, Inventory of the goods of Marguerite Paris and Joseph Guilbault, 3 March 1830; Bettina Bradbury, 'Itineraries of Marriage and Widowhood in 19th century Montreal', in *Mapping the Margins: Families and Social Discipline in Canada, 1700–1980*, Michael Gauvreau and Nancy Christie, eds. (Montreal and Kingston: McGill-Queen's University Press, 2004), 108–15; Sweeny, 'A partial tax roll, 1832.'
38. ANQM, Notary Cadieux, 6 November 1824; Mount Royal Cemetery records.
39. Sweeny, 'A partial tax roll, 1832;' ANQM, Notary Ritchot, Marriage contract of Emilie Moujeon and Antoine Laurent, 22 November 1824.
40. *The Gazette*, 16 April 1832, Cecilia Morgan, *Public Men and Virtuous Women. The Gendered Languages of Religion and Politics in Upper Canada, 1791–1850* (Toronto: University of Toronto Press, 1996), 6.
41. *The Gazette*, 16 April 1832; 30 April 1832; 5 May 1832, 17 May 1832.
42. *La Minerve*, 3 May 1832, 3.
43. For example, *La Minerve* 16 April 1832; 30 April 1832; 26 April 1832 and for an earlier formulation 23 April 1827.
44. Greer, *The Patriots*; Rendall, 'Women and the Public'; Scott, *Only Paradoxes*; Carole Pateman, *The Sexual Contract* (Stanford, CA: Stanford University Press, 1988).
45. Jacques Monet and Gerald J.J. Tulchinsky, 'Austin Cuvillier', DCB, VII, 224–8.
46. *La Minerve*, 16 April 1832.
47. *La Minerve*, 24 May 1832; Ouellet, *Lower Canada*, 226–9.
48. *La Minerve*, 21 May 1832, cited in Picard, 48.
49. *La Minerve* 26 April 1832; 14 May 1832; 21 May 1832.
50. Greer, *The Patriots*; Ouellet, *Lower Canada*, 226–9; *Gazette*, 24 May, citing the *Montreal Herald*.
51. Jean-Claude Robert, 'Jacques Viger', DCB.
52. JHALC, Appendix, 1832–3, 30 January 1833; 23 February 1833.
53. Robert, 'Jacques Viger;' Curtis, *The Politics of Population*; JHALC, 30 January 1833, Evidence of Jacques Viger; ANQM, P148, Collection Charles Phillips, 1770–1957, Livres d'élection à Montréal, quartier Ouest.
54. ANQM, Collection Charles Phillips, 1770–1957, 'Livres d'élection de 1832.'
55. *The Montreal Herald*, cited in *The Montreal Gazette*, 24 May 1832.
56. *La Minerve*, 24 May 1832.
57. *La Minerve*, 28 May 1832.
58. Galarneau, 'L'élection pour le quartier Ouest', 142–3.
59. Greer, *The Patriots*; Ruth Sandwell, 'The Limits of Liberalism: The Liberal Reconnaissance and the History of the Family in Canada', *Canadian Historical Review* 84: 3 (September 2003): 423–50.
60. JHALC, Appendix , 1832–3, Evidence of Jacques Viger, 25 and 26 January 1833.
61. JHALC, Appendix, 1832–3, Evidence of Jacques Viger, 28 January 1833, 23 February 1833.

62. ANQM, P148, 'Collection Charles Phillips, 1770–1957', transcribed poll book.
63. *La Minerve*, 3 May 1832.
64. JHALC, Appendix, Evidence of Jacques Viger, 23 February 1833. My translation.
65. *La Minerve*, 14 May 1832; 16 April 1832; 21 April 1832.
66. *La Minerve*, 3 February 1834, citing debate of 27 January 1834; L.E.Fredman, *The Australian Ballot: The Story of an American Reform* (Michigan: Michigan State University Press, 1968), 20–1.
67. *La Minerve*, citing debate of 3 February 1834.
68. Greer, *The Patriots*, 206, 202.
69. Debates, House of Assembly, Lower Canada, as reported in *La Minerve*, 3 February 1834; 'L'Acte pour régler la manière de procéder sur les contestations relatives aux élections des Membres pour servir dans la Chambre d'Assemblée et pour révoquer certains Actes y mentionnés', 4 William IV, C.28, 1834; Nathalie Picard, 'Les femmes', 1992, 58; Greer, *The Patriots*, 205 wrongly claims that women were no longer admitted to the hustings after the passage of this act.
70. Picard, 'Les femmes', (1992), 59; Catherine L. Cleverdon, *The Woman Suffrage Movement in Canada* (Toronto: University of Toronto Press, 1974), with intro by Ramsay Cook (1950), 158, 216; Collective Clio, *Quebec Women*, 122, 12; Victoria (1849), chap 27', Acte pour abroger certains Actes y mentionnés, et pour amender, refondre et résumer en un seul Acte les diverses dispositions des statuts maintenant en vigueur pour regler les éléctions des membres qui représentent le peuple de cette province a l'Assemblée Legislative', 30 mai 1849, article XLVI; Elizabeth Gibbs ed., *Debates of the Legislative Assembly of United Canada*, 1849, 6 March; 13 March; 16 March; 17 April; 18 April.
71. Klinghoffer, 'The petticoat electors'; 'Les femmes électeurs', *Bulletin de recherches historiques* (1947–58): 222.
72. Greer, *The Patriots*, 202; Picard, 'Les femmes', 1992; Nathalie Picard, 'Les femmes et le vote au Bas-Canada', in *Les Bâtisseuses de la Cité*, Evelyne Tardy et al, eds. (Montreal: Actes du Colloque, ACFAS, 1993): 57–64; Francoise Noel, *Family Life and Sociability in Upper and Lower Canada, 1760–1870* (Montreal and Kingston, McGill-Queen's University Press: 2003), 109–10, 127–8.
73. *Quebec Mercury*, 14 August 1827.
74. Karin Wulf, *Not all Wives. Women of Colonial Philadelphia* (Ithaca and London: Cornell University Press, 2000), 1.
75. Denise Robillard, 'Marguerite Lacorne, conseillère de Jacques Viger', in *Les Bâtisseuses de la Cité*, Evelyne Tardy et al, eds. (Actes du Colloque, ACFAS, Montréal, 1993): 57–64.
76. Bettina Bradbury, 'Elderly Inmates and Caregiving Sisters: Catholic Institutions for the Elderly in Nineteenth-Century Montreal', in *On the Case: Explorations in Social History*, Franca Iacovetta and Wendy Mitchinson, eds. (Toronto: University of Toronto Press, 1998): Huguette Lapointe-Roy, *Charité bien ordonnée. Le premier réseau de lutte contre la pauvrété à Montréal au 19e siècle* (Montréal: Boréal, 1987).
77. Veronica Strong-Boag, '"The Citizenship Debates": The 1885 Franchise Act', in *Contesting Canadian Citizenship: Historical Readings*, Robert Adamoski, Dorothy E. Chunn and Robert Menzies, eds. (Peterborough, Ontario: Broadview Press, 2002), 69–94.

'The Law Should Be Her Protector': The Criminal Prosecution of Rape in Upper Canada, 1791–1850

Patrick J. Connor

EDITORS' INTRODUCTION

The reality and threat of rape has a long and terrifying history for women and girls around the world. Scholars have convincingly documented that, despite its reputation as an uncommon, violent outburst on the part of deranged and disturbed individuals, rape is often used in times of national conflict and war as a measured, planned, and government-sanctioned weapon.[1] As Marlene Epp so poignantly shows in her essay in this volume and in her book, *Women Without Men: Mennonite Refugees of the Second World War*, rape has also been an integral weapon of power and control over female political refugees in the past. The use of sexual violence to control and disempower women and girls throughout history is a painful yet telling testament to the embodied consequences of patriarchal oppression.

Despite the enormous presence both the reality and the threat of rape represents, feminist historians in Canada have only a fragmentary understanding of how it affected the lives of women at different moments, and in different contexts, in the past. Karen Dubinsky's now classic article on the historical meanings attached to rape in nineteenth- and early twentieth-century Ontario, convincingly argued that the social shame visited upon victims of rape was central to the fear and dread it conjured for women and indeed its treatment in the courts.[2] The fact that victimized women needed to be concerned about their tarnished reputations in the aftermath of such extreme violence against their person is also highly suggestive of their place in the nineteenth century social order. Since women's fortunes traded so thoroughly on her 'respectability', the protection of sexual purity, unlike that of her male counterparts, was of major concern to entire families. This was true also, as Tamara Myers found, for girls who found themselves embroiled in disputes with the law in Montreal's Juvenile Court at the turn of the twentieth century and, indeed, well beyond.[3] In the case of some girls accused of breaking the law, as Myers and Sangster point out, however, attempts to sully reputations via association with sexual impropriety were also vigorously, if only imperfectly, resisted.[4]

The following essay by Patrick J. Connor enables us to significantly 're-think' what we know regarding women's experiences with rape in the past. The temporal setting of Connor's work is critical: Upper Canada between the late eighteenth and early to mid-nineteenth century. According to his findings, the treatment of both the rapists and the women who brought them to the attention of the courts unfolded very differently than would be the case a century later. Connor finds that justice for rape victims at this time was taken very seriously in the courts, demanded little invasive information from victims, and meted out extremely harsh punishments to the perpetrators, despite often desperate calls for leniency. As Connor argues here, 'in the first sixty years of the colony's existence, Upper Canadian women, backed by supportive kin and community networks, made use of a sympathetic legal system through which they were able to vigorously, and often successfully, assert their demands for sexual autonomy and personal safety.' Connor persuasively takes the reader through the legal processes involved in bringing rape charges against Upper Canadian men, the nature of women's accusations against them, the outcomes of trials, and the reaction of community members.

A critical question Connor explores is why were Upper Canadians seemingly more supportive, at least legalistically, of female rape victims? His answers to this question underscore the importance of the contextual forces that have always shaped women's lives in the Canadian past. From the point of view of colonial administrators, including the judiciary, rape was symptomatic of chaos, familial breakdown, and anarchy. In the interest of supporting a well-ordered, peaceable, and productive settler society, such crimes of moral depravity could not go uncontested. Upper Canadian women, he also argues, were for the most part at the centre of tight-knit communities of kit and kin and, as such, under the close watch of patriarchal protectors. An incidence of rape in such conditions would be hard to hush up or ignore. Another factor that Connor makes transparent is the youthfulness of many of the victims. That many victims were young, fourteen-years-old, for example, may well have encouraged the courts to seek the harshest of penalties. Given that historians still know very little about the attitudes towards children and youth in colonial Upper Canada, Connor's work on youthful female victims of rape provides important information. The other avenues of explanation Connor travels help us to understand that shifting attitudes towards not only women's and girls' roles, but to economic forces and trends in legal history have all had a profound impact on the history of sexual violence.

Students of women's history will also benefit from close attention to the way in which Connor deals with the problem of sources. Like Dubinsky and other historians concerned with piecing together an understandably fragmentary story, Connor is mindful here of both the limitations of his source base, and the need to read what is available with particular sensitivity to the subtleties of language and meaning. As Barrington Walker explains in his study of black women and spousal murder, the available records 'lay enmeshed within a white male legal apparatus' but still offer historians a valuable window into the lives of women.[5] What emerges from this delicate balance is an astoundingly rich narrative about how women, their families, and their communities coped, and still cope, with the reality and threat of male sexual violence.

Notes

1. Bülent Diken and Carsten Bagge Laustsen, 'Becoming Abject: Rape as a Weapon of War', *Body and Society* 11.1 (March 2005): 111–28; Anna M. Agathangelou, 'Nationalist Narratives and (Dis)Appearing Women: State Sanctioned Sexual Violence', *Canadian Woman Studies* 19.4 (Winter 2000): 12–22, and numerous essays in this volume of *Canadian Woman Studies*, subtitled 'Women in Conflict Zones'.
2. Karen Dubinsky, 'Sex and Shame: Some Thoughts on the Social and Historical Meaning of Rape', in *Rethinking Canada: The Promise of Women's History*, 4th ed., Veronica Strong-Boag, Mona Gleason, and Adele Perry, eds. (Toronto: Oxford University Press, 2002), 164–73.
3. Tamara Myers, 'Voluntary Delinquents: Parents, Daughters, and the Montreal Juvenile Delinquents' Court in 1918', *Canadian Historical Review* 80.2 (1999): 242–68.
4. Tamara Myers and Joan Sangster, 'Retorts, Runaways and Riots: Patterns of Resistance in Reform Schools for Girls, 1930–1960', *Journal of Social History* 34.3 (2001): 669–97.
5. Barrington Walker, 'Killing the Black Female Body: Black Womanhood, Black Patriarchy, and Spousal Murder in Two Ontario Criminal Trials, 1892–1894', in *Sisters or Strangers? Immigrant, Ethnic, and Racialized Women in Canadian History*, Marlene Epp, Franca Iacovetta, and Frances Swyripa, eds. (Toronto: University of Toronto Press, 2004).

Questions for Critical Reading

1. Despite the argument that rape was dealt with much more harshly in Upper Canada than later in the period, how does the author deal with the burden of social stigma associated with the crime? Was it still a factor for women in Upper Canada? Why or why not?
2. What kinds of sources does Connor use to prove his argument? What are some of the strengths and weakness of these sources? Could alternative readings of his sources be offered?
3. How did material conditions and economic realities of life in Upper Canada shape the incidence of rape and its outcome in the courts? How and why are these conditions still important in understanding the crime of rape today?

In April 1793, Colonel John Simcoe, Lieutenant-Governor of Upper Canada, issued a proclamation reminding the colonists of their 'indispensable duty . . . to suppress all Vice, Profaneness and Immorality', lest the province suffer 'the Divine Vengeance [of] Almighty God'. The proclamation was published in the colony's only newspaper, and Simcoe further ordered that it 'be Publickly read in all Courts of Justice [and] . . . immediately after Divine Service, in all places of Public Worship.' The proclamation stressed a concern for the promotion of virtue and raised the spectre of eternal damnation, but Simcoe's pronouncements also carried a purely secular message, ordering laws against various offences 'to be strictly put into Execution in every part of the Province' and urging 'Peace Officers and Constables, Judges, Justices and Magistrates' to 'exert themselves [in] putting the Laws against Crimes and Offences into execution.'[1] An analysis of Upper Canadian court records reveals the extent to which colonial officials did in fact exert themselves in the prosecution of one particular crime, that of rape. A close reading of trial reports and related accounts allows for an examination of the process by which rape was discovered, reported, and prosecuted, and the difficulties inherent for women in such an undertaking. The stories told by women, and the men who raped them, reveal that Upper Canadians regarded rape as a serious crime deserving of serious punishment. It was a crime that saw not only a woman violated, but also relations between the sexes disrupted, and well-understood modes of community interaction thrown into disarray. Attitudes toward rape, and its victims, grew less indulgent as the nineteenth century progressed, but in the first sixty years of the colony's existence, Upper Canadian women, backed by supportive kin and community networks, made use of a sympathetic legal system through which they were able to vigorously, and often successfully, assert their demands for sexual autonomy and personal safety.

Rape has traditionally been one of the most under-reported of all crimes, and the difficulty of estimating the true extent of sexual violence is particularly acute for Upper Canada. The colony was overwhelmingly rural in nature, economically dependant upon mixed agriculture, home production, and small-scale, local exchange networks. Settlement was sparse, communication awkward, and travel on the province's poor roads notoriously difficult. Consequently, the often arduous conditions of pioneer settlement affected routine enforcement of laws and the reporting of crime. Local magistrates, the most visible symbol of state power and the most basic form of law enforcement, were scarce and frequently difficult for the average settler to locate.[2] Once found, a magistrate might also have to be convinced that it was worth his time and expense to interfere in what sometimes turned out to be violent intra-community disputes.[3] For large blocks of settlers of French-Canadian, Scottish, German, or Native background, cultural differences—particularly that of language—could pose further difficulties in the detection and prosecution of crime. Although the province developed rapidly through the first half of the nineteenth century, many isolated areas retained a 'frontier mentality', with their world-view focused inward on the family, the domestic farm and the small, tight knit circle of close neighbours.[4]

As if physical and cultural barriers were not enough, those who did manage to make use of the colony's legal system found themselves facing a judicial apparatus that itself presented numerous hurdles. Colonial trials overwhelmingly attracted the supporters of the accused, and hissing, comments from the gallery, and even full-fledged brawls were not unknown. Architectural plans of the colony's early courthouses also reveal them to be rudimentary and purely functional spaces, with the principals of the case seated almost amongst the often hostile spectators.[5] Moreover, Upper Canadian courts, with their judge and associate judges, clerks, bailiffs and recorders, were entirely dominated by men. For a woman attempting to prosecute a charge of rape in such a setting, a trial could indeed come to resemble a second assault.

In spite of these difficulties, between 1791—when Upper Canada was established as a separate political and legal entity—and 1850, a total of 203 women left some record of their experiences as the victims of sexual assault. For the historian, the difficulty of recovering their voices is enormous. Countless rapes, of course, were never reported at all, and of the 203 for which some record exists, sources are often fragmentary or frustratingly vague. Upper Canadian newspapers rarely reported rapes—accounts of purely local news would have been redundant in such small communities—and when the topic was mentioned, it was often limited to the brief acknowledgement of a successful prosecution and exemplary punishment. Legal records offer a somewhat more detailed view, but here too, the gaps are large and information sketchy. Depositions taken before magistrates are almost entirely non-existent, and the official minutes of court sessions offer little more than the names of those involved and a record of the trial's outcome. A more detailed view can be gained from the benchbooks of the province's judges. These notebooks, kept during the trial, provide a verbatim transcript of testimony offered by prosecution and defence witnesses, as well as the judge's remarks and his charge to the jury. Once convicted, rapists frequently petitioned the Lieutenant-Governor for mitigation of their sentences, and these petitions also offer details of the crime not found elsewhere. Reliance on such sources necessarily results in a somewhat patchwork result: a victim without a name or a verdict with no apparent sentence. Nevertheless, a careful reading of what remains provides enough evidence to reconstruct the experience of rape in Upper Canada, to re-tell the stories of the women and men involved, and to assess how these stories were understood both by the participants and by the community at large.

As a British colony, Upper Canadian rape laws were identical to those in force in England, and colonial prosecutions were thus undertaken under the authority of 18 Eliz. I. c.7, a 1576 statute which declared rape to be a felony, punishable by death. The application of this statute was relatively straightforward, with Toronto attorney and legal writer W.C. Keele declaring that rape 'signifies the carnal knowledge of a woman, forcibly and against her will.'[6] While English jurists spilt much ink throughout the eighteenth century attempting to interpret this definition, the law in Upper Canada seems to have operated on a less strict evidentiary basis. The belief, prevalent in England, that if a women became pregnant she could not have been raped, was dismissed by Keele as a 'philosophy [which] may be very well doubted of', while the statutory requirement for the emission of seed was rarely, if ever, observed in the province.[7] At his March 1837 trial, Mary Ann Bullock stated simply that Patrick Fitzpatrick 'had done what he wanted before he let her go'.[8] In the summer of 1843, Courtland Travise was prosecuted for the rape of Susan Ann Still, with the court hearing testimony that 'he remained in witness till satisfied',[9] while at another trial later that same year, Julia Ann Wright merely declared that her assailant had 'effected his purpose'.[10] Such statements were good enough for a jury, which promptly convicted in each case, believing that penetration was in itself evidence of emission.

If the law was key in constructing definitions of rape, no less important were the impressions of victims themselves. Rape is by its very nature a secretive crime, and women's testimony necessarily plays a central role. Instructing potential jurors, W.C. Keele wrote that a victim's credibility depended upon whether she 'be of good fame; if she *presently* discovered the offence and made pursuit after the offender; shewed circumstances and signs of injury; if the place where the offence was committed was *remote* from habitation, [and] if the offender *fled* for it.' If such testimony could be corroborated by others, so much the better. 'On the other hand,' Keele continued, 'if she concealed her injury for any length of time, after she had the opportunity to complain; if the place where the offence was alleged to have been committed was *near* to inhabitants . . . and she made no outcry when the offence was perpetrated', jurors were to 'carry a strong presumption, that the testimony is false or feigned.' Overall, jurors were reminded that although rape was 'a most detestable crime', they should not be 'transported with indignation at the heinousness of the offence', but should instead pay close attention to the testimony and arrive at a verdict on the basis of evidence rather than outraged feelings.[11] Keele's fear that juries might be 'transported with indignation' was not an idle one. Widespread property ownership meant that Upper Canadian juries were composed of a far more representative cross-section of the (male) community than was the case in England, and if they felt a wrong had been done, they would often convict with little regard for legal hair-splitting.

Upper Canadian women were not always able to convince a jury of their claims, and many no doubt remained silent, ashamed of what had happened or fearful of further violence should they speak out. Those who refused to remain silent sought out other women for help, support and advice. The unique sexual nature of the crime made turning to a female relative, friend or neighbour seem an obvious choice, and seeking assistance from such quarters also highlights the female-centered social networks in which most Upper Canadian women moved.[12] The notion of female solidarity in the face of a sexual attack, however, should not be overstated, for just as many victims turned to men for aid, often appealing to a husband, father or brother. What mattered more than the gender of the listener was who was available close at hand, who was likely to be sympathetic, and who could most effectively set the wheels of justice in motion. Margaret Talbot testified in 1841 that 'the first she spoke of the ravishment was to her husband . . . but she did not tell the women.'[13] Fourteen-year-old Emma Sagerman, who was raped in a Windsor tavern, immediately told her brother, who was apparently so unconcerned by the news that he went back to sleep. Hearing the news the next morning, however, her father immediately 'took steps in the matter' and sought a warrant for the arrest of his daughter's attacker.[14] But if some women could rely on quick and sympathetic action from those to whom they turned for help, others were not so fortunate, as illustrated by the experience of Julia Ann Wright. Raped by her hired farm hand one morning in 1843, she testified that she was afraid to tell her husband of the attack, and only spoke out once she had been raped a second time.[15] Her case, and others like it, are stark reminders that for many women the stigma of rape deprived them of the support they otherwise expected, even from their own families.

Upper Canada had no public prosecutor, and for much of its history no formal system of policing. Consequently, how a rape was dealt with was left largely to the discretion of the victim and her family. There is slight evidence that compensation of some sort occasionally settled the matter, while at the other extreme, Margaret Talbot, mentioned above, turned down the offer of a friend to stab her assailant to death. Women could, however, follow the example of

Hannah Smith, who, only hours after she was raped in 1797 and in spite of the rapist's threats to kill her, sought out a nearby magistrate and filed a formal complaint. Her deposition described her assault in excruciating detail, telling how she had been interrupted while on a household errand, carried to 'a rogering place . . . in the thick woods' where she had been 'very much hurt and abused.'[16] Other accounts, like that of Cornwall spinster Ann Bills, were more formalistic, merely stating that Farquhar MacDonnell 'violently and feloniously did ravish and carnally know . . . against the will of her the said Ann Bills, and against the form of the statute in such case.'[17] The laying of a formal complaint was a collaborative effort between the victim and the magistrate. Whether laying the complaint alone or, as was the case with many women, with the support of a male family member, the victim engaged in a process of negotiation in the magistrate's parlour, as the details of her story were told and the magistrate decided whether the case was truly one which had 'offended the statute' and how this could best be expressed in the necessary legal terms.

Some women, likely on the advice of magistrates, chose to describe their assault as an attempted rape. Although many women who prosecuted in this manner had doubtless experienced much more than just an attempt, such a charge may have represented a necessary compromise. Unlike in England, which had removed the death penalty for rape in 1841, the crime remained a capital offence in Canada into the twentieth century. As John Beattie has noted, jurors in any capital case are notoriously reluctant to convict, and seeking a conviction for attempted rape might have represented a way for the prosecution to increase their odds of success.[18] If such a strategy was at work in Upper Canada, it seems to have been successful, although only moderately so. Of the 68 men who were charged with rape between 1791 and 1850, for whom a verdict is known, exactly half were found guilty as charged, while 43 per cent were found not guilty, and 7 per cent were convicted of a lesser charge. The conviction rate in 78 cases of assault with intent to rape was only slightly higher, at 52 per cent, with 29 per cent being acquitted and 18 per cent being found guilty of a lesser charge. Legal historian Constance Backhouse has called guilty verdicts 'atypical', declaring 'prosecutions for rape in Ontario rarely resulted in convictions in the nineteenth century', but this was clearly not the case before the mid-century mark.[19]

If the charge of attempted rape was a way in which to avoid the possibility of a jury hesitant to send a defendant to the gallows, such cases may also have been simply easier to prosecute. More successful rape prosecutions were those involving children, or in which the victims were severely injured or raped by several men in succession. Cases of attempted rape required no proof of penetration, and with a lower burden of proof, were often the favoured method of proceeding in cases with weak evidence or that relied solely on the uncorroborated testimony of the victim. Such cases, however, had their own drawbacks, for while a woman may have been quite sure of her assailant's intent, her attacker could argue the case was one of common assault, and it was not always possible to convince a jury otherwise. A charge of attempted rape also reminds us of the serious stigma associated with the crime throughout the nineteenth century, and the fact that although a woman may have desired justice she may not have been willing to admit that she had been raped. Ruth Trufflemier told a neighbour that Jack York, a black slave belonging to a local merchant, had broken into her home, 'treated her with great violence', and 'entered her body'. When the case finally went to trial in 1800, however, she testified that she had been unconscious and could remember nothing of the attack itself. Similarly unwilling to testify that she had been raped, Jane Lambert successfully prosecuted soldier William Newbury for robbery later the same year, claiming that he had stolen a piece of her dress in the woods. After sentencing Newbury to death, Judge William Dummer Powell informed the Lt Governor that 'the evidence respecting the robbery from her person had been concocted . . . to avoid the detail of the real crime, which was certainly an attempt to force her.'[20]

This articulated what was probably already understood by Lambert's neighbours, and emphasized the fact that even with a sympathetic jury, identifying oneself in a public court room as the victim of rape could be a difficult task with often unpleasant social consequences. Little had changed by mid-century, when a St Catharines newspaper reported the parents of a rape victim 'fairly begging to have the case kept out of print' and condemned rival newspapers which published the names as 'panderers to, and caterers for, a depraved public taste' in scandal.[21]

But, in spite of the potential for scandal, and the myriad of difficulties inherent in mounting a court case, women were no strangers to Upper Canadian courts. In criminal actions, women initiated approximately 11 per cent of prosecutions at the Quarter Sessions level and, despite significant restrictions, were also frequent participants in civil business. The seriousness with which women treated their experiences in court is also reflected in the manner in which their complaints were handled by magistrates. These men presided over the district Courts of Quarter Sessions, which had authority to try all non-capital crimes. Rape was not in their purview, but in theory they were able to try cases of assault with intent to commit rape. In most cases of attempted rape, however, magistrates saw the cases as serious enough to refer to the superior Court of King's Bench for trial. Local magistrates may have merely been making awkward cases disappear, not wishing to preside over problematic trials potentially involving acquaintances and neighbours. Whatever the reason for being referred to a higher court, doing so ensured that would-be rapists would be tried and sentenced by itinerant provincial judges with no connection to the community, and who would have no hesitation imposing harsh punishments. In deciding whether or not to believe a victim's story, the ultimate legal determination of whether a rape had occurred was the responsibility of the jury, but women exercised a fair degree of control over the handling of their own cases. Perhaps most important was the framing of the charge itself. Statutes covering seduction and breach of promise existed in Upper Canada, and the prosecution of such cases was common. But a criminal charge of rape was fundamentally different from a civil action undertaken on a woman's behalf by her husband or father. The cases discussed here are not those featuring scheming seducers or unfulfilled marriage proposals, but are instead those involving the forcible and often violent assault of a woman against her will.

It is impossible to speak of a 'typical' rape victim, for they were young and old, urban and rural, married and single, and from a variety of ethnic backgrounds. In terms of social standing, the women who were raped in Upper Canada ranged from domestic servants and farm help, to women like Margaret Ann Bultan, the wife of a man who styled himself simply as 'capitalist'.[22] There is little to distinguish these women from the rest of the province's inhabitants, for they shared little more than their gender and the experience of violation. The single commonality that does emerge is the seemingly disproportionate number of victims who were very young: one fifth of reported cases involved girls who were under the age of sixteen. Such a trend was by no means unique to Upper Canada. In her study of New York City cases in a similar time period, Marybeth Arnold has found that fully one-third of prosecuted rapes involved children under the age of fourteen, and in both places society reserved a special outrage for attacks on children.[23] Anna Clark has identified particular difficulties surrounding the prosecution of men who raped children. Very young witnesses sometimes lacked credibility, and due to their age and lack of sexual experience, often had no words in which to properly describe the attack.[24] This caution over children's testimony is evident in Upper Canada, where reports often made a point of stressing that young victims fully understood the nature of a criminal trial, and that they 'did not appear to have been tutored by anyone'.[25] Far from being a hindrance, the youth of the victim was often a favourable variable in a prosecution. Lacking a language of sex, young victims were able to avoid issues of reputation or consent, and instead stress the violence of the attack and the physical injuries sustained. Such factors worked in favour of the prosecution, and three-quarters of men tried for sexually assaulting women under sixteen were convicted. Well into the twentieth century, as Karen Dubinsky has shown, 'assaults against children were treated far more seriously than assaults against adult women.'[26]

The lack of a necessary vocabulary in which to explain rape was not an issue for the majority of Upper Canadian women, and their appearance in court provided them with an opportunity to give a clear account of their experiences in their own words. Such accounts reveal rape to be an incident that could occur at almost any time and in almost any place, as a woman went about her daily activities. The intrusion of rape into daily activities is well illustrated by the experience of Julia Ann Wright, who was thrown to the floor by her hired hand as she sat knitting in her parlour.[27] Lois Thomas of Elizabethtown was returning to her father's farm one evening in November 1833, when she was overtaken and assaulted by Nixea Walker. She was just one of several women who were attacked while walking on deserted country roads.[28] Women's participation in the household economy could also place them in positions of vulnerability. Picking berries—a task often carried out by young women working alone—could be especially dangerous. Such was the case for Vashty Waterhouse, who was picking strawberries 'on the Plains near Brantford' in 1831 when she was approached by John Standish. He spoke to her and departed, but returned an hour later and raped her.[29] Whether engaged in agrarian production, walking in one's immediate neighbourhood, or even working inside the family home, there were few areas in which a woman was immune from a potential attack.

The isolation of Upper Canada's farming communities, and indeed the overwhelming rural nature of the province as a whole, should not make it surprising that the majority of rape cases occurred in rural settings. What is startling is that, with the exception of two cases each in Hamilton and Kingston, and one each in London and Toronto, *all* the rapes examined in this study took place outside of an urban setting. Anna Clark has suggested that, by the early nineteenth century, rape in England was often used as a means of controlling the behaviour of working-class women, especially in public places. Only those women, argues Clark, who closely followed middle class expectations of modesty, chastity, speech, and public decorum, could expect any serious effort would be made to prosecute their rapists.[30] The relative absence of sexual assault cases in Upper Canadian cities may have been linked to this ideology, and it is possible that women raped in the urban environment encountered difficulties in mounting a successful prosecution that were not faced by their rural counterparts. Questions of a rape victim's reputation, her social status, and the public role of women in general may have created an atmosphere in which urban women, especially those who did not follow middle-class prescriptions of feminine behaviour, were discouraged from pursuing their cases in court.

But while middle-class English concepts of propriety, and especially female morality, certainly existed in Upper Canada, it would be a mistake to assume that the colony had wholly adopted the attitudes of the mother country in this sphere. Becoming the victim of a rapist was a very real possibility for any woman, but there is no evidence that the province's elites, or men in general, wielded this threat as a means of regulating women's public behaviour.[31] Perhaps the most compelling argument against such an idea lies in the location of reported rapes. While the majority of sexual assaults took place on farms, in fields, and in other rural areas, a substantial minority occurred in taverns. Many such cases involved excessive drink, but this should not obscure the much larger role played by taverns in Upper Canadian society. They provided food and lodgings for travellers, served as labour exchanges, and provided a meeting space for patriotic, literary, and other such groups. As polling places, taverns were at the center of every election and, in the early years of the colony's development, they provided a place for town meetings and even court sittings. Taverns in Upper Canada were thus more than mere places to take a drink; they were key sites of general sociability and ones that very much included women.[32]

Nonetheless, as a site of community interaction, taverns were also sites of sexual danger for women. An anonymous writer travelling between Ottawa and Kingston in 1830 recalled stopping at a roadside inn, where his travelling companion,

> under the predominating effects of gin, . . . or some other potent spell . . . entered the breakfast parlour when the maid was arranging the table. Her fresh complexion and ruby lip attracted his attention, and he commenced a chase with the desire of submitting to the sense of feeling what appeared so tempting to the sight. From this rude attack the fair one defended herself with the Tea Tray . . . and was rescued from her perilous situation by the abrupt entry of the Hoste with the bill which procured a diversion of hostilities in her favour.[33]

Fourteen-year-old Sarah O'Meara was not so fortunate. One rainy night in September 1845, while working as a serving girl at Mrs Gray's tavern outside of London, she was chased into the barn by a soldier named John English. Despite her screams, and attempts to defend herself with a shoemaker's knife, she was raped.[34] For female patrons, as well as employees, the tavern presented dangers. Hugh Kearney and his daughter Margaret were travelling home two days before Christmas in 1838, when they stopped for the night at the inn owned by Daniel Tiers of Springfield. While the father was drinking at the bar, Henry Cole entered the daughter's room and offered her ten dollars for a kiss. When she refused, he threw her down and 'abused her greatly'. A rape was only averted when her father and his drinking companions, hearing the commotion, returned to the room and attacked Cole.[35] The experience of Margaret Kearney was a fairly common one, and important for what it and similar cases reveal about women's experience of rape in Upper Canada. At the ensuing trial, the defence attempted to smear Margaret Kearney's reputation, but this attack centered on the fact that she was Catholic. No one even questioned what an eleven-year-old girl was doing in a tavern at night, and Henry Cole was easily convicted of attempted rape.[36]

Margaret Kearney may have avoided an attack on her reputation due to her age. Certainly, she was spared the sort of questioning endured by women in other jurisdictions, or which became increasingly common in late nineteenth century Canada, in which the victim's behaviour seemed on trial as much as was the accused rapist. Trial transcripts reveal that Upper Canadian women were rarely questioned in this manner, and that evidence of their character played at most a secondary role. Women who had been raped in taverns were asked if they had been drinking, but when the question was answered—invariably in the negative—the defence moved on. Questions concerning the victim's mode of dress, common even in modern rape trials, were entirely absent from Upper Canadian cases. As in the case of Margaret Kearney, questions about a woman's character were often unrelated to her sexual or moral behaviour, but focused on whether she was hard working, temperate, and a generally respectable member of the community. The court was concerned less with a victim's sexual history or reputation for modesty, than it was in simply determining whether it could give 'credit to her testimony'.[37]

Whether a woman's words could be credited depended upon a number of variables, many of which *were* related to her sexual behaviour. Sarah O'Meara called witnesses to testify that she was 'a modest, well behaved girl',[38] and similarly the trial of Patrick Fitzpatrick elicited comments from the judge that 'the whole of the witnesses were persons of good character'.[39] At the other end of the spectrum, however, was Laura McCan, who 'reluctantly' prosecuted John McCain only at the insistence of her husband. The court heard that 'all the girls [in the neighbourhood] were crazy about the prisoner' and McCan admitted that 'she was as bad as any'. Witnesses 'had seen them walking out at midnight' and had once even caught them together in bed in 'an intimate way'. The jury found a verdict of not guilty.[40] Frances Burgess, too, was unable to secure a conviction against Abel Conat for attempted rape in

1841. The court heard several hours of testimony in which details were exposed about her extra marital relations with several men—including her accused rapist—as well as illegitimate children, and sleeping arrangements that could only be described as irregular. The Attorney General abandoned the prosecution part way through the case, no doubt convinced that Burgess possessed no credibility as a witness.[41]

In spite of the Attorney General's frustration over his less than reputable witness, there were few all-out attacks on the character of the rape victim in Upper Canada. As the Kingston *British Whig* noted in 1835, 'the bad character of a woman ought to be no reason that she should be without the protection of the law; for once establish that maxim, and every woman of doubtful reputation will be assaulted with impunity.'[42] Judges were quick to limit testimony about the victim's reputation when in their view it was not materially related to the facts of the case. Nor were victims the only ones subjected to scrutiny over character, for just as often the court heard that the *defendant's* character was in some way lacking. At the 1839 trial of Ethan Card, the court heard much speculation about his reputation, including the fact that he 'does not bear a good character for chastity'.[43] Along the same lines, a would-be rapist named Tisdale had to defend himself from charges that he was 'a notorious nuisance in the neighbourhood in which he resides for his propensities for the feminine gender'.[44] A history of sexual immorality was important, and could often sway the jury one way or another, but it was seldom definitive. Chauncey Skinner introduced evidence that Mary Richie, who accused him of rape in 1829, was 'a person of most abandoned character, and one altogether likely to prefer such a charge from inclines very different from a wish to bring to justice the perpetrator of such a crime.' In spite of such damaging testimony, Skinner was convicted by the jury, and was sentenced to death.[45]

In 1849, the Kingston *British Whig* reported on the trial of Allan McInnis for the rape of Euphemia Brown. The newspaper commented that 'great effort was made to shake the testimony of the girl, but without success.'[46] Such efforts included questions about Brown's reputation and character, but this did not—and could not—represent the entire defence strategy. Clearly, defence lawyers understood that in Upper Canada, attacking a victim's reputation promised only limited success. The case of 'Jean Marie' of Brockville is an illuminating one. She was a prostitute, described as 'a Girl of ill-fame, and an inmate . . . of a Bagnio in this town'. In 1834 she swore out a complaint that Jonas Jones, a member of the local elite, had raped her. The charge was dismissed when she admitted that she had made up the story at the behest of Orange Order leader Ogle Gowan, in an attempt to ruin the reputation of Jones, his political rival. Nonetheless, it is clear that in Upper Canada, a charge of rape was one considered serious enough to ruin a man's career and reputation (if not end his life) and that even if such a charge came from a known prostitute it would not be considered to be without merit.[47] By the late nineteenth century, as Constance Backhouse demonstrates, testimony concerning a rape victim's character would come to dominate the trial procedure. This was seldom the case in Upper Canada, where even a prostitute expected, and could possibly even receive, a sympathetic hearing from a jury. Legal writer W.C. Keele echoed this sentiment, declaring, 'nor is it any excuse [for rape] that the woman is a common prostitute; for she is still under the protection of the law.'[48]

Rape trials were speedy affairs in Upper Canada, none lasting more than a day and most disposed of in an hour or two. Once in front of the court, the victim's testimony centered on describing for the jury the physical details of her rape. These narratives were clearly informed by the statute and, in addition to details of time and place, stress the victim's lack of consent and the resistance she made to the attack. The court repeatedly heard that the victim had 'refused', that 'she made all the resistance she could', or 'resisted as much as she was able'. Women 'screamed' and 'tried to holler', but, although only two of the rapists are reported to have used a weapon, victims were unable to prevent themselves from being 'thrown down on the floor' or being 'dragged into the woods' by the side of the road. Of all the elements that made up women's narratives of rape, it is the issue of violence that occupied center stage.

Garthine Walker has found that when rape victims in early modern England told their stories, they chose to emphasize violence and personal injury.[49] Framing the incident as a sexual crime, rather than a violent one, was potentially dangerous, for it might shift the trial's focus from the rapist's attack to the victim's sexual reputation. That women in Upper Canada were largely able to avoid sustained attacks on their reputation is perhaps an indication of the success of this approach. Another explanation for the emphasis on violence and injury in the court's records may be related to women's economic position in Upper Canada. Whether farm wives or tavern help, all the women examined in this study worked, and most made vital contributions to the household economy. When 18-year-old Euphemia Brown prosecuted her rapist in 1849, she made little overt reference to the sexual aspect of the crime. Instead, the court heard how after the rape she was 'much bruised', 'half-dead', and was 'three weeks recovering'.[50] Tavern keeper Mary Lee also testified that after the rape she experienced at the hands of Jacob Block, she 'was about dead'. She 'had been confined for three months' as a result of her injuries, and 'afterwards could hardly get up'.[51] Brown and Lee were not alone in bemoaning the loss of good heath, rather than the loss of virtue. In this regard, the women of Upper Canada may have shared concerns with the women of early national New York City studied by Marybeth Arnold, who noted that 'a physical injury or a pregnancy sustained in a sexual assault could incapacitate them for work and destroy the precarious sustenance they had managed to eke out.'[52]

With testimony relating to physical injury dominating Upper Canadian rape trials, the testimony of medical professionals could be of crucial importance. Particularly when the victim was a child, doctors confirmed cases of sexual assault, and provided evidence of injuries sustained. The same role was often played by midwives, who 'spoke from professional knowledge and experience' to draw similar conclusions for the court.[53] Such a common-sense basis for their knowledge seemed quite adequate for the jury, and neither were the statements of midwives challenged by physicians in cases where both were called to testify. The role of medical professionals in Upper Canadian rape trials differs sharply from that detailed by Anna Clark, who found that in early Victorian England, doctors' testimony was more useful to the defence than for the prosecution and that their moralistic pronouncements couched as scientific discourse often served to silence victims of rape.[54] Although physicians played an important role, particularly in cases involving children, it was a peripheral one, and there is no evidence that they were actively defining sexual assault. Summing up the attempted rape case of Alexander Greig for the jury in 1834, Chief Justice John Beverly Robinson noted that the victim 'did in direct terms swear that she *believed* his intention was to proceed to the extremity of violence'.[55] Although he further stated that the jury 'might properly doubt whether she was correct in this opinion', he did not question—nor did any other judge of this period—a woman's right to bring a charge based solely on her own belief that she had been raped.

The testimony offered by the prosecution provides details not only of the circumstances of the crime, but also the way in which women understood and responded to rape. These women were by definition victims, but the cases examined here show this to be only one aspect of their identities. When physical resistance to their assailants failed, women turned to the legal system as a means to assert their claim to personal safety and sexual autonomy. These claims were contested—sometimes successfully—by defendants who frequently had very different views on what constituted proper sexual behaviour. Nevertheless, the court provided Upper Canadian women with a public forum for expressing their strong views on what they considered acceptable sexual conduct.

The men accused of rape in Upper Canada were as varied as their victims, and it is equally difficult to generalize about them. Nevertheless, even the most cursory glance at the list of defendants reveals a startlingly disproportionate number of soldiers. Upper Canadians lived in perpetual fear of American invasion, and throughout its history the province was garrisoned by British regular troops. Soldiers were thus a common sight in Upper Canada, and residents generally appreciated their presence, but it was a situation that posed special dangers for the colony's women.[56] The men who guarded the colony were largely drawn from the age group statistically most likely to commit rape,[57] and it should come as no surprise that the violent, often alcoholic, homosocial world of the army barrack posed significant threats to the province's women. Commenting in 1800 on soldier and convicted rapist William Newbury, Judge William Dummer Powell remarked on 'his depravity and want of a proper education' and noted that he was 'a young man of bad character [who] was, I am told, enlisted out of the jail'.[58] It is possible that soldiers' status as single men, far from home, and without the ties of family and community simply made it easier to successfully prosecute them, but colonists were often convinced that soldiers inherently posed a special danger to local women. Writing in his diary in 1847, Marcus Gunn noted that his cousin Helen had been 'assaulted by two Brutal British soldiers' and commented that it was 'an instance of the danger of keeping together a hord of ignorant men'.[59]

The presence of soldier-rapists in the community presented particular problems to prosecuting victims. As Marcus Gunn continued in his diary the day after the attack on his cousin, he went to town the next morning 'and obtained faculty to identify the two soldiers who assaulted Helen last night, but could not'.[60] As Gunn and his cousin found, soldiers in uniform simply all looked alike, and were notoriously difficult to identify. This fact was also realized by Brigit Stokes, who was attacked by members of the 81st Regiment in 1846, but admitted 'all three soldiers were dressed alike' and she could not pick out the one who had attempted to rape her.[61] It is perhaps an illustration of the hostility felt by residents towards soldiers, and the threat they posed to local women, that in spite of Stokes' admitted inability to identify the prisoner as the man who had attacked her, the jury convicted him anyway. And, it was not just local residents who found such behaviour intolerable. 'The Commander of the soldiers' at London aided Marcus Gunn in his unsuccessful identification attempt,[62] while the 1843 case of Jane Edgar saw three members of the regiment stationed at Hamilton testify against one of their fellow soldiers on behalf of the prosecution.[63]

The soldier as rapist was not an uncommon phenomenon in Upper Canada, but what is notable is his status as an outsider in the community. Other than those who were victimized by soldiers, few women in the colony were raped by strangers. Indeed, there were very few true strangers in the closed agricultural communities of Upper Canada. A woman might not know her attacker's name, but she often recognized his face. He might be the man from the next farm, a local hired labourer, or perhaps had even attended the same school or church as the victim. Mrs Scott was returning home from Kingston in her wagon one morning in 1850 when she gave a lift to a local farmer, 'a resident of the same neighbourhood'. While on the road home, he 'begged she would favour him with a kiss' and then 'attempted some further liberties'.[64] Witnesses frequently testified at trial that the families of the victim and accused had known each other for years, sometimes even decades. This familiarity highlights the vulnerable position of women in the province, and certainly accounts for the large number of women who were attacked in places where they believed themselves to be safe.[65]

Previous familiarity between victim and accused could also complicate matters. It was relatively easy to convict a stranger, but the task could be made significantly more difficult if evidence could be introduced pointing to a previous relationship between the individuals concerned. Allan McInnis attempted to counter Effy Brown's charge of rape by calling witnesses who recalled seeing the two of them kissing at a school-yard frolic years before.[66] His strategy was not successful, but had the jury believed that Brown's rape had actually occurred within the context of an ongoing courtship, as the defence implied, McInnis might very well have been acquitted. Such was the case for Landon Henry, who was able to escape a rape conviction in 1832 by showing not only that he had been in a sexual relationship with Hannah Wheat for the past two years, but that she also had a child by him.[67] Pre-marital sex was not uncommon in rural Upper Canada, and it was generally tolerated if it took place within the confines of an established courtship in which the participants were expected to eventually wed.[68] Such attitudes allowed women in Upper Canada a great deal more sexual freedom than their daughters or granddaughters would come to expect in later nineteenth-century Canada, but it was a mixed blessing, for it afforded women little protection against unwanted advances from current, and even former, suitors.

It is difficult to say with certainty how Upper Canadian attitudes about sexual behaviour influenced attitudes toward rape. In spite of Lt Governor Simcoe's earnest proclamation against immorality, contemporary travellers claimed that the province was 'the most wicked and dissipated of any part of America'. In 1834 Belleville resident William Hutton 'was quite shocked at the depravity of young people generally . . . the tone of morals is low, low indeed, and almost frightening me for my children'. Newspapers occasionally reported on the presence of 'rowdies' and the fact that it was 'not safe for a female to walk the streets alone after nightfall'.[69] Nevertheless, it was not until the 1840s, and the rise of a self-conscious and aggressively activist middle class, that the courts began seeing large numbers of prostitution, vagrancy, and morals offences. Even then, this remained a predominantly urban phenomenon.[70] In the countryside, sometime resident E.A. Talbot wrote, one could find 'females who are destitute of virtue, as much respected, and as likely to make respectable alliances in the world, as if they were not merely its proud possessors, but its chaste and attentive guardians.' Indeed, he continued, 'the violation of chastity is not considered a crime of the first magnitude. And so far from this being the case, . . . that an unmarried female with a baby in her arms is as much respected and as little obnoxious to public animadversion, as she would be, had she preserved her virtue with a Vestal's fidelity.'[71]

In spite of such a free and easy approach to sex, the character of the libertine seems to have been largely absent from the Upper Canadian scene. Described by Anna Clark as a misogynist, sexually violent aristocrat, governed by 'uncontrollable passions', the libertine regarded any woman not under the protection of a father or husband as fair game, and would even boast about seducing other men's wives or daughters.[72] That such attitudes were unacceptable in the colony was discovered by John White, the provincial Attorney General, who was shot dead in a duel after spreading rumours that he had seduced the wife of a colleague.[73] The casual Upper Canadian attitude toward sex did *not* extend to the elite world within which John White moved. But even for the working classes, there were boundaries, one of which clearly involved the willing consent of one's partner. That these boundaries were understood differently by men and women is clear, for just under one quarter of the men charged with rape asked for the woman's consent at the outset. That after politely requesting a kiss, or asking permission to get into bed, they would proceed to violently rape their victims, points to a belief by some men that consent may have required a certain amount of 'persuasion'. For the women who ultimately laid charges, this was clearly *not* the case.[74]

It is extremely difficult to draw conclusions about men's attitudes towards rape, for of all the men prosecuted for this crime in Upper Canada, not a single one took the stand to testify in his own defence. Indeed, just under half the defendants called no witnesses whatsoever to speak on their behalf, relying instead on a mere cross-examination of the prosecution's witnesses. The absence of any serious defence on the part of the accused may, in part, be explained by the fact that in this period, the Attorney General undertook prosecutions personally. The accused rapist who chose to match wits with the Attorney

General was a foolish man indeed, and many may have hoped to escape a guilty verdict by remaining silent themselves and simply attempting to discredit the stories of prosecution witnesses. As a strategy, it was not a particularly good one. Of those who did mount a defence, two-thirds were found guilty, while those who called no witnesses of their own were convicted in 73 per cent of cases. The importance of a good defence, especially in cases where a guilty verdict could mean execution, was recognized by defendants, for while only 52 per cent of accused in attempted rape cases made a defence, this rose to 74 per cent in trials dealing with actual rape. Those men charged after 1836 could have taken advantage of the newly proclaimed Felon's Counsel Act, which allowed the accused the assistance of a lawyer to sum up his case to the jury. In practice, this seems to have made little difference. William Brass was 'ably defended' in 1837 by a young John A. Macdonald, yet despite his 'ingenious' efforts, the jury convicted Brass in less than half an hour.[75] The presence of lawyers in the courtroom may have been rather more beneficial to the victims, who at least no longer had to experience the ordeal of being cross-examined by the very man who was accused of raping them.

The punishment for rape in Upper Canada was death by hanging, and although many were convicted, few were actually hanged. The Lieutenant-Governor could, at his discretion, grant a pardon to a convicted felon, and while accused rapists were silent at their trials, they frequently included an explanation of their actions as part of their petition for a pardon. Men occasionally complained that they had been the victim of mistaken identity, or that the rape victim's testimony should not have been believed due to her poor character. Some even swore that they believed consent had been obtained. Most invoked transparent excuses that, while failing to impress the Lieutenant-Governor, reveal much about their attitudes toward rape. After being convicted for attempting to rape Margaret Kearney in 1838, Henry Cole felt 'compelled to confess that having been intoxicated on the occasion alluded to, he may have done some act' which gave the impression of sexual assault, but he further argued for 'the impossibility of his having entertained even an intention of committing a rape, when it is considered that it is alleged to have taken place in a public house, within a few feet of a number of individuals, and upon a child under the immediate protection of her father.'[76]

Another defence strategy, used both in petitions as well as at trial, was to raise the spectre of a false accusation. Upper Canadian jurist W.C. Keele, repeating earlier writers, noted that rape was 'an accusation easily to be made, and hard to be proved, and harder to be defended by the party accused, though never so innocent', and this was doubtless a dictum with which most accused were familiar.[77] Trial witnesses were often questioned at length about whether there had been any quarrels between the families of the prosecutor and the accused, and the possibility that a charge of rape might be a false one was exploited by the defence. Elias Anderson was acquitted in 1838 when he was able to produce witnesses who had seen the victim's father visit him in jail, and overheard threats to 'have his neck' if Anderson did not sign over a large tract of land.[78] Similarly, testimony at the trial of Ethan Card a year later reveals that Mary Switzer had concocted the charge of rape in an attempt to take revenge on the defendant. Since Switzer was seeking revenge for an earlier rape by Card which, all agreed, actually *did* happen, the jury convicted anyway.[79] Such initiative on the part of the jury was commonplace, but what is startling is the lack of direction from the trial judge in such cases. Perhaps Judge Macaulay was content to trust the instincts of the jurors, agreeing with the Kingston *British Whig*, which expressed surprise at an 1835 rape acquittal, but admitted, 'as the jury were mostly from the part of the country in which both parties reside, it is not unlikely that they knew more of the matter than appeared in open court.'[80]

False charges, mistaken identification, and imagined consent were all used, sometimes successfully, to escape rape convictions. But once a conviction had been secured, such arguments in a petition for pardon carried little weight. The Lieutenant-Governor was not a court of appeal, but rather a dispenser of royal mercy. Most petitioners understood this well, and in their petitions they admitted the justice of their conviction and simply begged for the chance of a reprieve. Their convictions were painted as an aberration in an otherwise exemplary life, and friends and neighbours were called upon to speak to the petitioner's previously unblemished character. Indeed, a good character was the key to securing a pardon, and as such, the Lieutenant-Governor and his staff, aided by reports from the trial judge and local magistrates, closely examined the convict's habits. If a woman's character played only a peripheral role in influencing the outcome of the trial, a man's reputation could well make the difference between whether he would live or die.

Many of the petitions submitted by convicted rapists are formulaic and repetitive, echoing arguments also found in petitions submitted by those convicted of other types of crime. Appeals such as that made by John Turnbull in 1826 lead the reader to question whether the petitioner fully understood the nature of the crime for which he had been convicted. After being found guilty of attempting to rape Elizabeth Welsh in Asphodel Township, Turnbull argued for a pardon by reminding the Lieutenant-Governor that he had a wife and child and, as 'no person is now with them, they are greatly in want of your Petitioner's protection.'[81] Such incongruity was not lost on the Lieutenant-Governor, who denied his request. The position of the state on such matters had been clearly articulated in 1820, when Robert McIntyre, a Kingston soldier, was hanged for the rape of Nancy Dick. Although McIntyre had submitted a petition for pardon that even included the support of his victim, Chief Justice William Dummer Powell recommended the execution proceed as planned. 'Example is necessary,' he wrote in his circuit report, 'to protect from similar outrage the Persons and habitations of that numerous class of females whose Occupations retain them alone in their houses the greatest part of their Time, in absence of their Husbands, fathers, and Brothers.'[82]

Such a clear statement of official views concerning rape and its punishment is rare in Upper Canada, but a similar case almost two decades later reveals a remarkable consistency. Convicted of raping nine year old Mary Ann Bullock in 1837, Patrick Fitzpatrick petitioned for a pardon 'On account of his previous good character, from the consideration of how easy the crime may be charged, and how hard it is to be disproved', and finally, 'On account of the disproportion of the punishment to the crime, which, however heinous, . . . ought not to be punished with death.' While on most petitions the head of state simply wrote 'granted' or 'not granted', in this case the government took the unprecedented step of responding to Fitzpatrick's plea point-by-point in the provincial press. The Lieutenant-Governor refused to overturn the decision of the jury, and closed by noting that as the victim 'was not strong enough to protect her[self,] it was deemed necessary that the law should be her protector.' 'Considering the inestimable advantages which society derives by this protection', he expressed his 'deepest regret' at being unable to 'extend to Patrick Fitzpatrick the Royal Mercy.' The newspaper editorialized 'the reasonings contained in this reply are unanswerable' and Fitzpatrick was hanged at Sandwich on 9 October 1837.[83]

The government's decision to publicly justify the execution of Fitzpatrick is a curious one, and raises important questions about Upper Canadian attitudes toward rape, and the extent to which the community at large shared official views. The fact that Fitzpatrick was able to collect the signatures of many of his most respectable neighbours seems to indicate a widespread consensus that execution was too harsh a penalty for rape. Other cases already mentioned show a similar trend. Twenty of his neighbours, as well as nine magistrates and several militia officers, signed Henry Cole's petition.[84] Dennis Russell's petition was signed by ten magistrates, a schoolmaster, and the commanding officer of Russell's militia unit,[85] while Chauncey Skinner managed to receive support from 106 'Sundry inhabitants of the Township of Whitby'.[86] The support that many of these men were able to garner in their pleas for clemency also highlight the dilemma faced by a woman who was prosecuting not only a rapist, but also a neighbour.

It is this status as neighbour that allows for an alternative reading of the petitions for pardon. Upper Canada had no poor law, and support for the indigent was dependant upon informal charity. A husband or father who was executed or subjected to a lengthy imprisonment would place a burden on the entire community for the support of their families. This eventuality was especially feared by magistrates, who would have had to draw on limited district funds for the provision of assistance. An ongoing drain of limited resources was likely uppermost in the minds of six Cornwall magistrates who signed a petition in favour of George Burns in 1826. They argued that he had already served one year of a seven-year sentence for attempted rape in their small district jail, and it seemed enough. Whether they meant enough punishment, or enough of an expense, is left unsaid.[87] While John Turnbull may have displayed an uncommon degree of insensitivity by arguing for his release on the basis of having a wife and family in need of his protection, on another level, this argument shows he was quite attuned to the priorities of the magistrates he convinced to sign his petition. More than this, he attempted—albeit unsuccessfully—to tailor his own situation to fit a larger discourse on the role of men, and the state, in the protection of the colony's women.[88]

In spite of occasional grumbling over sentences, rape was considered a serious crime in Upper Canada, and was harshly punished. Although most convicted rapists had their death sentences commuted, this reflects more a general distaste for executions than any feeling that rapists deserved leniency. In a larger context, of the 394 men and women sentenced to death in Upper Canada for all crimes between 1791 and 1841, only 88 were actually executed. For those who escaped the gallows, punishment was nevertheless harsh, and was meant to be exemplary. Those pardoned could still expect to be transported or, after 1835, spend prolonged terms in Kingston Penitentiary. While a rape conviction required a death sentence at least be pronounced, judges routinely sentenced those convicted for attempted rape to lengthy prison terms or fines far in excess of those assessed on other criminals. In 1834, a jury found Alexander Greig, charged with attempted rape, guilty of simple assault. The Chief Justice sentenced him to pay the enormous fine of 50 shillings and to stay in jail until it was paid.[89]

While harsh sentences were the rule, they generally reflect elite attitudes toward crime. But there is also evidence that ordinary community members shared such attitudes. Petitions for pardon were common, but rape was one of the few crimes in which petitions were *not* signed by members of the convicting jury, and which also generated counter-petitions—appeals from the community that a rapist *not* be released from jail. John Standish had been sentenced to death for rape in 1831, and quickly set about petitioning for royal mercy. His appeal arrived at Government House in September, but five weeks later was followed by a petition from Vashty Waterhouse, his victim, who expressed her 'unfeigned satisfaction' at the idea of Standish being pardoned, but nevertheless urged that he be transported. As long as he was in Upper Canada, she argued, she and her husband did 'not consider themselves safe from personal injury, nor their property from danger of being destroyed'. The administration apparently took Waterhouse's fears to heart. Standish was left to languish in the Hamilton jail, without an answer to his own petition, for sixteen months. He was the only prisoner who was not released during the 1832 cholera epidemic, and was ultimately transported to a penal colony in Bermuda, where the likelihood of him revenging himself on his prosecutor dimmed next to his chances of contracting malaria.[90] Standish's case is but the most egregious of several in which community members urged even harsher punishments, officials deliberately delayed news of pardons, or convicts unable to pay high fines remained imprisoned for months or even years. A rape conviction was considered so distasteful that support could not always even be counted on from one's own family. Convicted of an attempted rape, a man named Tisdale petitioned for release from jail, but was unsuccessful when his own father informed the Lieutenant-Governor that he was 'well pleased that he should remain where he is' and 'had no objection if he had been sent to the Penitentiary'.[91]

Community sanction could also be expressed outside of official channels, and Upper Canadians had little hesitation in resorting to vigilante justice.[92] An 1822 incident in Kingston is uncommonly revealing. Accused of abusing—although not specifically raping—his wife, 'a certain man' was approached by about twenty of his neighbours who, with their faces blackened to avoid recognition, 'tore [him] from his horse and mounted him on a rail, carrying him by force upwards of a mile, thereby bruising and injuring him very materially'.[93] Such instances rarely entered the official record, but nevertheless represented a manner in which justice of a sort might be served, and community outrage expressed. More common were extra-judicial financial settlements. Many cases offer details of defendants who offered cash payments to victims if only prosecutions would be abandoned. Although there are several fairly obvious attempts to bribe both prosecutors and prosecution witnesses to remain silent, many also seem to represent a serious effort to arrive at some sort of settlement. Nancy Dick attempted to halt the execution of the man who raped her in 1820 by petitioning the Lieutenant-Governor with news that Robert McIntyre had 'attoned' for his crime.[94] Although Anna Clark has linked such payments to a corrupt English justice system,[95] a cash settlement may have seemed far more useful to a victim of rape, and done much more to preserve community harmony, than seeing her assailant 'launched into eternity'.

Rape cases in Upper Canada involved much more than a victim and assailant. Issues of sexual violence influenced, and were influenced by, the communities in which it occurred. Questions of reputation, one's standing in the community, and understandings of often class-based codes of sexual behaviour ensured that such cases were very much rooted in the problems and preoccupations of larger society. Within such communities, men were expected to protect women—particularly the women of their household—from unwanted advances and sexual danger. In the absence of such protection, Upper Canadian women could rely on the colony's criminal justice system, if not to protect them, then at least to address the wrong done to them by their attackers. Mounting a prosecution was not a painless affair, and the colony's courts were themselves infused with a paternalistic ethos, but by and large women were able to prosecute men who raped, within a legal system that took their complaints seriously and made prosecution relatively simple.

Notes

1. *Upper Canada Gazette*, 18 April 1793.
2. On the rarity of magistrates and the incompetence of those who did act, see *Niagara Gleaner*, 23 August 1823; *Colonial Advocate*, 21 March 1833; *St Thomas Liberal*, 22 August 1833; *Canadian Emigrant*, 19 July 1834; *Kingston Spectator*, 23 July 1835; *Bytown Gazette*, 21 March 1838 and 19 July 1840. Hundreds of petitions from settlers, begging for the appointment of local magistrates, can be found in the National Archives, RG 5, A-1, *Upper Canada Sundries* [hereafter: *Sundries*].
3. Susan Lewthwaite, 'Violence, Law, and Community in Rural Upper Canada' in *Crime and Criminal Justice: Essays in the History of Canadian Law* Vol. 5, Jim Phillips, Tina Loo, and Susan Lewthwaite, eds. (Toronto: University of Toronto Press, 1994). See also *Colonial Advocate*, 26 September 1833.
4. On the lives of ordinary women in Upper Canada, especially their physical and social isolation, see Jane Errington, *Wives and Mothers, School Mistresses and Scullery Maids: Working Women in Upper Canada, 1790–1840* (Kingston: McGill Queen's University Press, 1995).
5. *Brockville Gazette*, 21 May 1840; Lorne Pierce, *William Kirby: The Portrait of a Tory Loyalist* (Toronto: Macmillan, 1929), 42; P.J.R. King, '"Illiterate Plebeians, Easily Misled": Jury Composition, Experience, and Behaviour in Essex, 1735–1815' in *Twelve Good Men and True: The Criminal Trial Jury in England, 1200–1800*, J.S. Cockburn and Thomas A. Green, eds. (Princeton: Princeton University Press, 1988), 298; *Sundries*, 127544; Kenneth W. McKay, *The Court Houses of a Century* (St Thomas, ON: Times Printing Company, 1901); Marian MacRae and Anthony Adamson, *Cornerstones of Order: Courthouses and Town Halls of Ontario, 1784–1914* (Toronto: Clarke and Irwin, 1982).

6. W.C. Keele, *The Provincial Justice*, 2nd ed. (Toronto, 1843), 516–21.
7. Ibid. On the difficulty of obtaining convictions in English cases without proof of ejaculation, see Anna Clark, *Women's Silence, Men's Violence: Sexual Assault in England, 1770–1845* (London: Pandora, 1987), 55, 61–3.
8. *Sundries*, [Judge] Archibald McLean to Lt Governor, 26 September 1837, 98163.
9. Archives of Ontario, RG 22, 390–1, Benchbooks of James Buchanan Macaulay [hereafter: Macaulay's Benchbooks]. Gore District Assizes, 27 September 1843.
10. Macaulay's Benchbooks, Newcastle District Assizes, Spring, 1844.
11. Keele, *Provincial Justice*, 518. Much of Keele's commentary on rape was lifted directly from earlier English sources. Cf. Constance Backhouse, 'Nineteenth-Century Canadian Rape Law, 1800–92' in *Essays in the History of Canadian Law*, Flaherty, ed. 2: 202–3.
12. Marybeth Hamilton Arnold, '"The Life of a Citizen in the Hands of a Woman": Sexual Assault in New York City, 1790–1820' in *Passion and Power: Sexuality in History*, Kathy Peiss and Christina Simmons, eds. (Philadelphia: Temple University Press, 1989), 148.
13. Macaulay's Benchbooks, Talbot District Assizes, 6 May 1841.
14. Macaulay's Benchbooks, Western District Assizes, May 1846.
15. Macaulay's Benchbooks, Newcastle District Assizes, Spring, 1844.
16. Archives of Ontario, RG 22–94, Home District General Quarter Sessions of the Peace, Misc. Filings, 1797.
17. Archives of Ontario, RG 22–49, Cornwall General Quarter Sessions of the Peace, Misc. Filings, 1794–6.
18. John Beattie, *Crime and the Courts in England, 1660–1800* (Princeton, NJ: Princeton University Press, 1986), 423–30.
19. Constance Backhouse, *Petticoats and Prejudice: Women and the Law in Nineteenth-Century Ontario* (Toronto: Women's Press, 1991), 99. Between 1791 and 1841, the assize conviction rate for all crimes was: 29 per cent convicted as charged; 4 per cent pleading guilty; 4 per cent convicted of lesser charges; and 25 per cent acquitted.
20. On York, see Robert Fraser, 'Jack York' in the *Dictionary of Canadian Biography*, Vol. IV, (Toronto: University of Toronto Press, 1979). On Newbury, see: *Sundries*, W.D. Powell to Lt. Governor, 8 August 1800, 443.
21. St Catherines *Daily Times*, 8 July 1858.
22. John Beverly Robinson's Benchbooks, Home District Assizes, Spring, 1834.
23. Arnold, 'The Life of a Citizen in the Hands of a Woman', 42–4.
24. Clark, *Women's Silence, Men's Violence*, 42. Also, Garthine Walker, 'Rereading Rape and Sexual Violence in Early Modern England', *Gender and History* 10.1 (April 1998): 7.
25. See, for example, the prosecution of Dennis Russell for the rape of an unidentified nine-year-old girl in *Sundries*, [Judge] L.P. Sherwood to Lt Governor, 15 September 1828, 49922. Also, prosecution of William Brass for rape of eight-year-old Mary Ann Dempsey, in *Kingston Chronicle*, 11 October 1837.
26. Karen Dubinsky, *Improper Advances: Rape and Heterosexual Conflict in Ontario, 1880–1929* (Chicago: University of Chicago Press, 1993), 23.
27. Macaulay's Benchbooks, Newcastle District Assizes, Spring 1844.
28. Macaulay's Benchbooks, Jonestown District Assizes, 8 August 1833. See also Ibid, Sandwich Assizes, 30 July 1832; Niagara District Assizes, October 1843;
29. There is a large amount of material relating to this case, including petitions to the Lt Governor from both Standish and Waterhouse. See *Sundries*, 62203, 62208–18, 65511–17, 67504–24; Minutes of the Court of King's Bench, Gore District, 1831. Picking berries continued to be a dangerous occupation for women into the twentieth century, as illustrated by Dubinsky, *Improper Advances*, 38. For more such cases in Upper Canada, see *Dundas Weekly Post*, 18 August 1835, and Macaulay's Benchbooks, Colbourne District Assizes, October 1849; Gore District Assizes, 27 September 1843.
30. Clark, *Women's Silence, Men's Violence*, 110.
31. There is no evidence of such a conspiracy in Upper Canada, but Carolyn Strange shows this had changed by the early twentieth century. See her 'Patriarchy Modified: The Criminal Prosecution of Rape in York County, Ontario, 1880–1930' in *Crime and Criminal Justice*, Phillips, ed.
32. Indeed, many Upper Canadian taverns were owned and operated by women.
33. Erin Welch, ed., Anonymous (A.J. Christie?), *Yankies and Loyalists: A Trip from Bytown to Kingston in February 1830* (Ottawa: Historical Society of Ottawa, 1979), 12.
34. Macaulay's Benchbooks, London District Assizes, May 1846.
35. *Kingston Spectator*, 4 July 1839; *Sundries*, Case of Henry Cole, 117141–42, 117860–63, 122048–71; Macaulay's Benchbooks, Home District Assizes, July 1839.
36. For other cases in which women's presence in taverns is treated in such a matter-of-fact way, see *Sundries*,

[Judge] L.P. Sherwood to Lt Governor, 31 December 1833, 74589–92, 74714–17; Macaulay's Benchbooks, Western District Assizes, May 1846, and Wellington District Assizes, May 1846.

37. It should be kept in mind that issues of 'character' were always key elements in any trial before the advent of modern forensic evidence.
38. Macaulay's Benchbooks, London District Assizes, May 1846.
39. *Sundries*, [Judge] Archibald McLean to Lt Governor, 26 September 1837, 98159–72, 98245–55.
40. Macaulay's benchbooks, Midland District Assizes, July 1833.
41. Macaulay's Benchbooks, Home District Assizes, October 1841. With enough credibility, a victim's uncorroborated testimony was occasionally enough to secure a conviction. See *Sundries*, John Turnbull to Lt Governor, 12 January 1826, 40532; Kingston *British Whig*, 3 August 1850.
42. Kingston *British Whig*, 12 August 1835, commenting on the attempted rape of Margaret Fair.
43. Macaulay's Benchbooks, Prince Edward District Assizes, Fall 1839.
44. *Sundries*, B. Biddell, MP to Lt Governor, n.d., 139046–48.
45. Robinson's Benchbooks, Home District Assizes, 21 October 1829; *Sundries*, 54088–91, 55090–92, 55771–73. Skinner was pardoned for this rape but he was hanged for murder in June 1840, demonstrating that however bad Mary Richie's character was, his was far worse. For other case where a jury convicted in spite of testimony concerning the victim's bad character, see: Macaulay's Benchbooks, Newcastle District Assizes, Spring 1844, and April 1842.
46. Kingston *British Whig*, 3 November 1849. For details of this case, see Macaulay's Benchbooks, Colbourne District Assizes, October 1849.
47. *Sundries*, Ogle R. Gowan to Lt Governor, 10 February 1834, 75362–64. Ironically, Gowan's own political career came to a halt in 1861 when he was charged with criminal assault for his sexual relations with a 12-year-old Toronto girl. See Donald H. Akenson, *The Orangeman: The Life and Times of Ogle Gowan* (Toronto: James Lorimer, 1986), 155–6, 295–307.
48. Keele, *Provincial Justice*, 517. For a later nineteenth century case involving the rape of a prostitute, with a decidedly unsympathetic jury, see Backhouse, *Petticoats and Prejudice*, 81–101.
49. Walker, 'Rereading Rape and Sexual Violence', 8. See also Clark, *Women's Silence, Men's Violence*, 55.
50. Macaulay's Benchbooks, Colbourne District Assizes, October 1849.
51. Macaulay's Benchbooks, Wellington District Assizes, May 1846.
52. Arnold, 'Life of a Citizen in the Hands of a Woman', 47.
53. For cases involving midwives and doctors, see *Sundries*, [Judge] Archibald McLean to Lt Governor, 26 September 1837, 98159–72; [Judge] Jonas Jones to Lt Governor, 31 October 1837, 98350–61; Macaulay's Benchbooks, Gore District Assizes, September 1843; Home District Assizes, 23 October 1838. For doctors' unwillingness to testify for the defence, see Macaulay's Benchbooks, London District Assizes, May 1846.
54. Clark, *Women's Silence, Men's Violence*, 5.
55. Robinson's Benchbooks, Home District Assizes, Spring 1834. Emphasis in original.
56. For a view of the convivial relations between residents of London, and the local troops, see in particular Robin S. Harris and Terry G. Harris, eds., *The Eldon House Diaries: Five Women's Views of the Nineteenth Century* (Toronto: The Champlain Society, 1994), passim. For evidence of a less hospitable relationship, see *Kingston Gazette*, 15 and 29 March 1817; 5 April 1817. One's relationship with the local military establishment seems to have been very much dependent on one's class status and, clearly, on one's gender.
57. Brownmiller, *Against Our Will*, 176, 182. Precise ages are not always given for Upper Canadian rapists, but most were young men, a few only teenagers. The exception seems to have been those charged with raping small children. For rape by soldiers in general, see also Brownmiller, *Against Our Will*, 31ff.
58. *Sundries*, W.D. Powell to Lt Governor, 8 August 1800, 443–5.
59. Archives of Ontario, MU 1182–1186, Marcus Gunn Diary, 29 January 1847.
60. Ibid, 30 January 1847.
61. Macaulay's benchbooks, London District Assizes, May 1846.
62. Gunn Diary, 30 January 1847.
63. Macaulay's Benchbooks, Gore District Assizes, 27 September 1843.
64. Kingston *British Whig*, 3 August 1850. She gave him 'a slap in the chops', turned the wagon back to Kingston, and had him arrested. He was fined ten shilling plus costs.
65. This trend (which continues to the present day) was also found by Arnold, 'Life of a Citizen', 38.
66. Macaulay's Benchbooks, Colbourne District Assizes, October 1849. Brown responded, 'he only kissed like a neighbour-boy, not like a lover'.
67. Macaulay's Benchbooks, Sandwich Assizes, 30 July 1832.
68. There is little work on Upper Canadian sexual behaviour. The most accurate picture would probably be John Gillis, *For Better, For Worse: British Marriages,*

1600 to the Present (Oxford: Oxford University Press, 1985), esp. 126–30.

69. Cited in John Carroll, *Case and His Contemporaries*, (Toronto: Wesleyan Conference Office, 1877), 1, 182; Gerald E. Boyce, ed., *Hutton of Hastings: The Life and Letters of William Hutton, 1801–1861*, (Belleville, ON: Hastings County Council, 1972), 14; *Bathurst Courier*, 10 December 1852.
70. John Weaver, 'Crime, Public Order, and Repression: The Gore District in Upheaval, 1832–1851' in *Ontario History*, 78.3 (September 1986).
71. E.A. Talbot, *Five Year's Residence in the Canadas. . .* (London, 1824), 11, 38–40. While Talbot is doubtless exaggerating for effect, it is interesting to note the experience of unwed mothers who were the victim of rape in Upper Canada. By the turn of the century, Dubinsky notes that charges were dismissed 'in every case in which the woman was found to have had illegitimate children', yet several such women in Upper Canada were able to see their rape prosecutions through to a conviction. See Dubinsky's *Improper Advances*, 27, and Macaulay's Benchbooks, Newcastle District Assizes, 27 April 1842.
72. Clark, *Women's Silence, Men's Violence*, 23–4.
73. The best description of this affair is found in Katherine M.J. McKenna, *A Life of Propriety: Anne Murray Powell and Her Family, 1755–1849* (Montreal & Kingston: McGill-Queen's University Press, 1994), 70–2.
74. Transcripts reveal 21 cases where men asked permission before raping, although the actual number is certainly higher. See also Arnold, 'Life of a Citizen', 39.
75. Kingston *Chronicle*, 11 October 1837. Brass was hanged at Kingston.
76. *Sundries*, Henry Cole to Lt Governor, 8 June 1839, 122057.
77. Keele, *Provincial Justice*, 518.
78. Macaulay's Benchbooks, Home District Assizes, October 1838.
79. Macaulay's Benchbooks, Prince Edward District Assizes, Fall 1839. Macaulay tried a similar case at the Wellington District Assizes, May 1846.
80. Kingston *British Whig*, 12 August 1835.
81. *Sundries*, John Turnbull to Lt Governor, 12 January 1826, 40532.
82. *Sundries*, W.D. Powell to Lt Governor, 22 September 1820, 24195–99, 24224–25.
83. *Sundries*, 98159–72, 98245–55. The reply to Fitzpatrick's petition was published verbatim in various papers, including the *Bytown Gazette*, 29 November 1837.
84. *Sundries*, Inhabitants of the Township of Toronto to Lt Governor, March 1840, 132260–62.
85. *Sundries*, Dennis Russell to Lt Governor, 9 September 1828, 49920–26, 50291.
86. *Sundries*, Inhabitants of the Township of Whitby to Lt Governor, 4 November 1829, 54088–91.
87. *Sundries*, Six magistrates to Lt Governor, 28 January 1826, 40707–08. Burns was also sentenced to stand in the pillory. See also Assize Minute Books, Eastern District, 9 August 1825. Due to its expense, imprisonment for more than 90 days was extremely rare in Upper Canada, until the opening of Kingston Penitentiary in 1835.
88. This was a common, and often successful, argument. See *St Catharine's Journal*, 30 September 1829.
89. Robinson's Benchbooks, Home District Assizes, Spring 1834. Average fines for simple assault were generally well under twenty shillings.
90. *Sundries*, John and Vashty Waterhouse to Lt Governor, 17 October 1831, 62203–17, 65511–17, 67505–7, 67822–5
91. *Sundries*, B.Biddell, MP to Lt Governor, n.d., 139046–48. It also seems likely that Allan McInnis, convicted of rape in 1849, was turned in by his own father. See Macaulay's Benchbooks, Colbourne District Assizes, October 1849.
92. Threats are detailed in many trial transcripts. See also *Kingston Spectator*, 5 October 1835.
93. *Sundries*, [Judge] D'arcy Boulton to Lt Governor, 10 October 1822, 29985; Petition of Master and Journeymen Shoemakers of Kingston to Lt Governor, 1 October 1822, 29900–02
94. *Sundries*, W.D. Powell to Lt Governor, 18 September 1820, 24195–99, 24224–5. See also Macaulay's Benchbooks, Midland District Assizes, July 1833.
95. Clark, *Women's Silence, Men's Violence*, 21–2.

From 'Marrying-In' to 'Marrying-Out': Changing Patterns of Aboriginal/Non-Aboriginal Marriage in Colonial Canada

Sylvia Van Kirk

EDITORS' INTRODUCTION

Acknowledging the role that women played in the past does more than simply add a new dimension to our history; it fundamentally alters it. Within Canadian history the revolutionary potential of women's history is made abundantly clear in fur-trade historiography. For generations, historians explained the Canadian fur trade as an overwhelmingly, if not entirely, male phenomena. In 1980, two books—Sylvia Van Kirk's *'Many Tender Ties': Women and Fur Trade Society, 1670–1870* and Jennifer S.H. Brown's *Strangers in Blood: Fur Trade Families in Indian Country*—conclusively challenged the prevailing vision of the fur trade by marshalling evidence of the important work Aboriginal women performed as translators, guides, and producers of food, moccasins, and other goods essential to the trade. Van Kirk and Brown also shifted our understanding of the fur trade by highlighting the enormous importance of marriages, families, and relationships forged between Indigenous women and European men. The primary evidence used by Brown and Van Kirk was not new, but their interpretation of it was: they saw women where others had not and while this work did not always impress scholars interested in addressing negative stereotypes of Aboriginal women,[1] it did profoundly shift how historians perceived the fur trade era and remains some of the most widely read works of Canadian women's history internationally.

In this article Van Kirk revisits fur trade marriages and places them within the shifting terrain of settler–Aboriginal relationships in Canada before 1885, the date Van Kirk assigns as the end of 'colonial Canada'. She notes that the notion that New France would be a society rooted in unions of European and Aboriginal was essentially dropped in the 1660s. Yet mixed relationships continued to occur alongside the settler marriages discussed in Josette Brun's article and the Aboriginal conversions analyzed by Nancy Shoemaker. In New France's fur-trade frontier Indigenous women used marriages with French men to integrate European men into Indigenous kinship and community. Aboriginal women did not 'marry out' of Indigenous communities as much as French men 'married in', and in doing so, helped to knit together fur trade communities throughout the Great Lakes.[2]

It would be from these communities, and the women that anchored them, that Métis communities and identity would be born.[3] It was in present-day Manitoba and Saskatchewan that the Métis nation was most clearly articulated and, after the Red River Resistance of 1868–9 and the North-West Rebellion of 1885, most challenged. Historian Diane Payment has shown that women were present in both of these struggles as well.[4] Throughout the nineteenth century the increasing ascendancy of Euro-Canadian settlement and the growing influence of popular notions of the dangers of racial mixing combined to create an increasingly hostile environment for mixed-marriages.[5]

This changing climate for intermarriage is inseparable from the changing experience of Indigenous women. As Van Kirk explains, discussions about intermarriage were, in effect, discussions about Aboriginal women and European men. This was codified with the Indian Act, first passed in 1876 and still in effect today. The Indian Act created a male-dominated political structure in which a range of Indigenous possibilities had existed, some of which, like the Mohawk Confederacy of central Canada or the Haida and Tsimshian of coastal British Columbia, had accorded meaningful political authority or possibility to women. More particularly, it stripped Aboriginal women of their status as 'Indians' if they married non-Indian men, and specified that any children they had with non-status men would be denied 'Indian status' and the rights it conferred. In this volume, Jo-Anne Fiske's study of Carrier women and the politics of mothering shows us some of the ways that Indigenous women sought and found roles of power, authority, and autonomy within the constrained contexts governed by the Indian Act while haunted by poverty and cultural dislocation.

Almost a century would pass before Indigenous feminists, with scant support from the male-dominated Aboriginal rights movement, successfully used the newly minted Canadian Charter of Rights and Freedoms to challenge the Indian Act as sexist. In response Ottawa was forced to pass Bill C-31 in 1985, which rendered the Indian Act putatively gender neutral.[6] The Aboriginal Women's Action Network's participatory research project has found that the majority of people applying for status under Bill C-31 are women, and suggest that the laws of 'Indian Status' continue to function in highly gendered ways.[7] The contentious history of the Indian Act and Bill C-31, like the history of the fur-trade itself, is one that cannot be properly understood unless we pay adequate attention to the roles of women and the work of gender.

Notes

1. See Janice Acoose/Misko-Kìsikàwihkwè (Red Sky Woman), *Iskwewak—Kah' Ki Yaw Ni Wahkomakanak: Neither Indian Princesses Nor Easy Squaws* (Toronto: The Women's Press, 1995).
2. Susan Sleeper-Smith, *Indian Women and French Men: Rethinking Cultural Encounter in the Western Great Lakes* (Amherst, MA: University of Massachusetts Press, 2001).
3. Jacqueline Peterson and Jennifer S.H. Brown, eds., *The New Peoples: Being and Becoming Métis in North America* (Winnipeg: University of Manitoba Press, 1985).
4. Diane P. Payment, '"La vie en rose"? Métis Women at Batoche, 1870 to 1920', *Women of the First Nations: Power, Wisdom, and Strength*, C. Miller and P. Chuchryk, eds. (Winnipeg: University of Manitoba Press, 1996).
5. Sarah Carter, *Capturing Women: The Manipulation of Cultural Imagery in the Prairie West* (Montreal and Kingston: McGill-Queen's University Press, 1997); Adele Perry, *On the Edge of Empire: Gender, Race, and the Making of British Columbia, 1849–1871* (Toronto: University of Toronto Press, 2001).
6. As told to Janet Silman, *Enough is Enough: Aboriginal Women Speak Out* (Toronto: The Woman's Press: 1987); Lynn Gehl, 'The Queen and I: Discrimination Against Women in the Indian Act Continues', *Canadian Woman Studies/Les cahiers de la femmes* 20.2 (Summer 2000): 64–9.
7. Audrey Huntley and Fay Blaney, *Bill C-31: Its Impact, Implications and Recommendations for Change in British Columbia*, Final Report (Vancouver: Aboriginal Women's Action Network, 1999).

Questions for Critical Reading

1. Why are historians of women interested in the history of marriage and the family? What can the changing history of marriage tell us about women's experience and expectations?

2. We usually think of the late nineteenth-century and early twentieth-century as a time of increasing rights for women. How can analyses like Van Kirk's and Bradbury's challenge that perspective?
3. Van Kirk accesses what historians have learned about white-Aboriginal marriages in the last few decades. What does she think we still need to study and why?
4. What might Aboriginal women have lost by marrying a non-Aboriginal man? What might they gain? How could these losses and gains have varied? Why?
5. View Christine Welsh's powerful documentary Women in the Shadows (NFB, 1991). How does the scholarship on women in the fur trade impact Welsh and her family? Why?

Although considerable work has been done on the nature of intermarriage in fur trade society there has been little attempt to fit these patterns into the larger colonial context or to examine their legacy for settler/Aboriginal relations. This article offers a broader analytical framework and raises some of the fundamental questions that need to be asked. It argues that over the course of the colonial period, from the early seventeenth to the late nineteenth centuries, the practice of Aboriginal/non-Aboriginal marriage shifts from 'marrying-in' to 'marrying-out'.[1] I deliberately use the term 'marrying-in' to focus on the host Aboriginal societies whose homelands at the time of European contact later became Canadian territory. Especially in the fur trade context, a major impetus for such unions came from Aboriginal groups themselves. The idea was to create a socio-economic bond that would draw the Euro-Canadian male into Native kinship networks. However, by the end of the colonial period, intermarriage had been transformed by settler society into 'marrying-out'. Aboriginal women lost their Indian status if they married non-status males. Aboriginal groups were deprived of any say in the matter and their kinship structures were ignored.

Charting the course of how this happened over several centuries raises challenging questions and demonstrates how such a study must be nuanced in terms of the intersection of race and gender. Historically, much concern was expressed by colonizers over such unions because of their cultural and racial implications. The marital union of European and Aboriginal was perceived as problematic because it symbolized the mixing of irreconcilable dichotomies: civilized versus primitive and Christian versus heathen. It must be remembered that even though such notions are discredited today, Europeans in the past were quite apprehensive about mixing with those they categorized as being of a different and lesser race and whose 'degenerate' qualities they thought could be transmitted by blood.[2] In the context of colonial Canada it also becomes apparent that the phenomenon of intermarriage was not gender neutral. In the majority of cases the union was between a Euro-Canadian *man* and an Aboriginal *woman*. This pattern has been accepted as a given while the racial and gender hierarchies that are embedded in this dynamic have not been subject to much analysis. This is starkly revealed in the rarity of the reverse union (that is, Aboriginal man married to a Euro-Canadian woman) and the negative reaction to such an occurrence.

Given the complexities of cross-cultural sexual and marital practices it is necessary to explain how I am defining 'marriage' throughout this study. European commentators, especially religious ones, were quite certain that only *their* marital practices had legitimacy and were adamant that Aboriginal people adopt them.[3] Aboriginal people, of course, thought otherwise; for them, polygamy and divorce were widely accepted concepts. In the Canadian fur trade one finds European men willing to accept or tolerate Aboriginal marital practices to an unusual extent. This becomes quite a complicated social and legal context, but it is significant that a fascinating Canadian court case in 1867 highlighted the essential components of a marital union that were adhered to in *both* Aboriginal and Euro-Canadian societies: a marriage was defined as being openly recognized and characterized by mutual consent, cohabitation, and public repute as husband and wife.[4]

In Canada the widespread and long-lasting phenomenon of the fur trade assumes great importance in accounting for the frequency of Aboriginal/non-Aboriginal marriage. This is in contrast to contexts where a settler agenda is more explicit, such as in New England for example. In Acadia and New France, fur trade and military concerns were intertwined with small-scale settlement projects, which contributes to the perception that intermarriage was more commonplace than it actually was. There is a general impression that intermarriage was widespread in New France and that Frenchmen had a natural predilection for Aboriginal women. Upon closer scrutiny, however, the French Canadian experience can be differentiated in terms of context: the settler colony along the St Lawrence was ultimately far less enthusiastic about intermarriage than were fur traders in the hinterland. At the beginning of the colonization of New France during the early seventeenth century, it appears that intermarriage might have been a key component of French colonization policy. This stems from Champlain's famous remark, 'Our young men will marry your daughters and we shall be one people,' but far too much can be made of this.[5] By the time a Crown Colony was established in 1663, it was acknowledged that intermarriage had failed to produce a stable demographic base. The new approach was to begin state-supported importation of French women, the *filles du roi*.

One of the reasons that intermarriage had failed was that French colonizers had explicitly different motives in promoting it than did their Aboriginal allies. This becomes clear in a fascinating debate about the terms of intermarriage between French Jesuits and a delegation of Huron chiefs in 1637. The Hurons declared themselves to be favourably disposed toward intermarriage because the French traders were proving to be quite good Hurons, but they had some temporal concerns that focused on questions such as bride price and the woman's right to property and divorce. The Jesuits were shocked by these views; the Hurons had to be made to understand that the purpose of these marriages was to work in the opposite direction: 'to make them like us, to give them the knowledge of the true God, . . . and that the marriages . . . were to be stable and perpetual'.[6] To the extent that intermarriage was to be encouraged, it was to be a vehicle for missionization and Frenchification. Only Aboriginal women who had been Christianized and introduced to a gender-role similar to that of French peasant women would make acceptable wives for French settlers. As one colonial administrator emphasized, the introduction of a new gender role was as important as religion: 'One must teach them to live like villagers in France, meaning to teach them to spin, sew, knit and take care of animals.'[7] But in spite of the efforts of the Ursuline nuns, only a small number of Native women were exposed to this kind of acculturation program, and not many were interested or successfully converted. In any event, Aboriginal women would not likely have been accepted as the 'founding mothers of New France'. Inherent in the settler project was cultural replication: women of another culture were not really deemed appropriate to play the vital female social and reproductive roles necessary for this. Indeed, the lack of French women signals the beginning of a refrain that will be repeated on several Canadian frontiers—that *white* women are vital to a colony's demographic stability and cultural success. It does seem, however, that in this early period Aboriginal women were found unsuitable as settlers' wives more on cultural grounds rather than on racial or biological grounds. If contemplated at all settler society only conceptualized intermarriage as a vehicle of 'marrying-out', but such unions really did not advance the settlers' agenda or destabilize their

Eurocentric conventions. From the early days of New France, it can be argued, settler society was deeply ambivalent about whether this practice should be encouraged at all.

This was not so in the fur trade, however, where very different motives were at play. One of the reasons that French colonial officials came to discourage intermarriage was that they were alarmed at the propensity of Frenchmen to 'go Native'. The success of the fur trade (unlike settlement) depended on intricate social and economic interactions with Aboriginal people and intermarriage very much facilitated this process. From the Aboriginal point of view, crosscultural unions were a way of integrating the Euro-Canadian stranger into Native kinship networks and enmeshing him in the reciprocal responsibilities that this entailed. The Native woman's gender role was also complementary; indeed, her work was vital to the functioning of the trade as she supplied indigenous clothing, food, and means of transportation. For well over a century, intermarriage in the vast domains of what is today Western Canada was subject to regulation by Aboriginal custom and fur trade company policies alone. Initially the Hudson's Bay Company (HBC), which was founded in 1670, had tried to forbid intermarriage with Native women, but this policy soon proved unenforceable. In contrast, during the late eighteenth century the North West Company, with its headquarters in Montreal, inherited the French traders' appreciation of the benefits of intermarriage.

It was within the context of the Northwest fur trade that the indigenous (indeed, unique) marital rite known as marriage 'after the custom of the country' reached its height. Only its main elements need to be summarized here.[8] Initially fur trade marriages were most influenced by Native attitudes and customs, which included payment of a bride price and did not necessarily entail a lifetime commitment. Some HBC officers even went so far as to adopt the Aboriginal custom of polygamy, which was seen as a mark of prestige for a husband. This is not to say that all traders appreciated the reciprocal obligations they had incurred or were above exploiting what appeared to be a more open Native sexuality, but marriage 'after the fashion of the country' was *the fundamental social relationship* through which a fur trade society developed. As fur trade society became more endogamous, marriage rites evolved more toward European custom. During the era of the HBC's monopoly after 1821, the company actually introduced marriage contracts that emphasized the husband's financial responsibility and the monogamous bond. But fur trade society was not autonomous. Within this specific social context, Euro-Canadian males had proved themselves adaptable to Aboriginal custom, but many felt ambivalent, and the pull of their own cultural norms remained strong. When they retreated from this fur trade world, their unions, which had not been sealed by European religious ceremony—and, by extension, their wives and families—were vulnerable to the differing attitudes of settler society, where retiring traders might renege on their commitments.

This is why the court case alluded to earlier is so intriguing. The validity of marriage 'after the fashion of the country' was tested in the Canadian courts in 1867 after the death of Chief Factor William Connolly, who, upon retiring to Montreal in 1830, had repudiated his Cree wife of nearly thirty years and married a cousin according to Catholic rite. After Connolly's death the children by his Cree wife sued for what they believed was their legitimate inheritance. The transcript of the Connolly case is a fascinating source of firsthand testimony as to what constituted 'the custom of the country'. In a remarkably balanced judgment, Chief Justice Coram Monk ruled that William Connolly's union with the Cree Suzanne constituted a valid marriage in both cultures—on the one hand because Suzanne had been married according to the customs and usages of her own people and, on the other, because the consent of both parties, the essential element of 'civilized' marriage, had been proved by twenty-eight years of repute, public acknowledgement, and cohabitation as man and wife.

Given the widespread and long-lasting nature of the fur trade in the history of Canada, one might speculate that it should have had more of an impact on settler society. The mutual interdependence inherent in fur trade relations might have provided an alternative to conflict-ridden settler/Aboriginal relations. But there is no evidence that this was so. In spite of the progressive cultural relativity shown by the chief justice, this was not the prevailing norm in the settler colonies that developed in Eastern Canada. In Upper Canada, in spite of the importance of Aboriginal allies in the early years of the colony, intermarriage does not appear to have ever been articulated by any colonial official as a useful means of securing good relations with the Indians or enhancing the demographic base of the colony. By the early nineteenth century, intermarriage was reported to be quite rare.[9] Isolated comments suggest that miscegenation was only a symptom of the widespread degradation of the Native population, which, although relegated to the margins of colonial society, was nevertheless becoming an expensive burden for colonial administration.[10] As a result the prospect of transferring economic responsibility from the state to a white husband became one of the few reasons advanced for sanctioning the marriage of an Aboriginal woman outside her band. The Bagot Commission, which investigated Indian affairs in the Canadas in the 1840s, noted approvingly: 'The principle has been lately sanctioned by the Governor General, who has directed that no Indian woman, living, married or otherwise, with a white man shall receive presents.'[11] Both the desire to save money with regard to treaty obligations and the desire to assimilate Native people were consolidated in subsequent Indian Acts. By the Indian Act of 1869, an Indian was defined in patriarchal terms as 'as any male person of Indian blood reputed to belong to a particular band'; a wife's status was determined solely by that of her husband's. An Indian woman who married a nonstatus male legally ceased to be an Indian and lost all rights related to Indian status, as did her children.[12] Thus, by the mid-nineteenth century, the process of intermarriage had become effectively colonized. Intermarriage was seen as a vehicle for removing Aboriginal women from their own cultures.

The patriarchal assumptions inherent in the Indian Act, however, contained a peculiar irony. Should a Euro-Canadian woman marry a status Indian, she would become an Indian! One might ask why, given their Eurocentric assumptions, settler society would permit its own women to sink to the status of Aboriginal. It seems that the likelihood of this happening was too appalling to contemplate; there is no evidence that this corollary was even discussed, much less sanctioned. Intermarriage, as we have seen, had been shaped by its own gender dynamics: there was no symmetry in the pattern of these relationships. In the process of colonization, males of the dominant society might form sexual and marital unions with subordinated females, but such men revealed little tolerance for the possibility of their own race and gender hierarchies being challenged.

It is significant that there were very few examples of an Aboriginal man marrying a Euro-Canadian woman in colonial Canada. This was not just because of demographics. Two cases from Upper Canada underscore the fact that, although the men in question were Christian and held positions of prestige, the very idea that *red* men should marry *white* women was anathema to colonial society. The first case was the marriage of Mississauga leader Peter Jones to a middle-class British woman, Eliza Field. Jones, who was also a Methodist preacher, had met his future wife when he was on a fund-raising trip to England in the early 1830s. The couple was forced to overcome severe criticism from her relatives, but they persisted, as their touching correspondence reveals, and they finally married when Field came out via New York in 1833. But instead of congratulations, they were faced with humiliating public condemnation. A scurrilous account published in the *New York Spectator* portrayed Jones as a conniving savage who had somehow managed to dupe an innocent Englishwoman, who could have had no idea of the fate that awaited her. The author decried the way in which an Indian man had transgressed racial boundaries: 'We heard the Indian and herself pronounced man and wife! It was the first time we ever heard the words . . . sound hatefully . . . . The idea is very unpleasant with us, of such ill-sorted mixtures of colors.'[13] To Jones's great distress, the article was circulated widely in the papers in Upper Canada and, although some supporters attempted to refute these accusations, he continued to be the target of criticism and plagued by rumours that the marriage had foundered.

Similar criticism was expressed in the second case in 1859, when George Johnson, a prominent Mohawk chief of the Six Nations, married the Euro-Canadian Emily Howells. Her brother-in-law, who was an Anglican clergyman, declared, 'I'll have no Indian come here after my wife's sister,' and refused to acknowledge the couple for many years.[14] While the Johnsons apparently did find some sympathetic support, it is important to probe the sense of outrage that accompanied the actions of these Aboriginal men, who were both community leaders. In these cases the fear that civilized white women would be returning to the primitive was not at issue. Both of these women were marrying into a highly acculturated Aboriginal elite. Emily Howells actually improved her living conditions; her home, 'Chiefswood', on the Six Nations reserve was a Victorian mansion much superior to many Upper Canadian settlers' homes. Nor were these women's prescribed gender roles as bearers of European civilization challenged; indeed, Eliza Field was to assist her husband in his missionizing endeavors. Such marriages might have been promoted as a way of furthering assimilation, but the colonial reaction illuminates deeply rooted anxieties about the potential threat to white male dominance in these transplanted societies. Both the Aboriginal man and the Euro-Canadian woman were deemed to be behaving inappropriately. Aboriginal men were seen to be usurping Euro-Canadian male prerogatives; and it was not acceptable for a white woman to be subordinate to an Aboriginal man. On the other hand, 'whiteness' could not prevail in the person of a woman; for any man to be subordinate to a woman was unthinkable. These cases bear out the findings of historians analyzing the intersection of race and gender in other contexts. In colonizing patriarchal societies exclusive control of women goes hand in hand with the subordination of the 'racial' Other, both male and female.[15]

Nevertheless, Euro-Canadian hegemony could not be taken for granted; it had to be built. As settler society spread west, the reification of racial and gender hierarchies was used to gain control, throwing all patterns of miscegenation into disrepute. In British Columbia, the fur trade frontier was rapidly transformed into a settler colony as a result of the gold rush in the late 1850s. Given the demographic imbalance incoming white men continued to have sexual relations with Native women, although these appear to have been more transient and exploitative than they were previously during fur trade society. As Adele Perry's recent book *On the Edge of Empire* shows, the colonial discourse was virulently hostile to Aboriginal people and race-mixing. Miscegenation was denounced as a 'vice', and the old refrain—harkening back to the days of New France—about the necessity of importing marriageable white women was given new urgency.[16] However, due partly to the legacy of the fur trade, which meant that several HBC/Native families were prominent in the early colonial elite, British Columbia never went as far as the new states south of the border in passing anti-miscegenation laws.[17]

In the Prairie West racism and prejudice against intermarriage had been growing since the latter days of the fur trade, with the intrusion of agents of settler society in the persons of the missionary and the Euro-Canadian woman. For the new homestead west of the prairies, with its renewed emphasis on replicating Euro-Canadian family structures, Sarah Carter has effectively shown how the Aboriginal woman was constructed as the sexually permissive Other: someone with whom Euro-Canadian males might have clandestine sex, but definitely not someone to marry.[18] Symbolic of this hardening of colonial attitudes is another court case in 1886 that negates the judgment of the original Connolly case. In adjudicating another test of marriage 'after the fashion of the country', an eastern Canadian court ruled that it could *not* accept that 'the cohabitation of a civilized man and a savage woman, even for a long period of time, gives rise to the presumption that they consented to be married in our sense of marriage.'[19] This represents the consolidation of the Eurocentric privileging of who gets to define what constitutes marriage. It is no accident that this coincides with the rise of racist attitudes that focus more explicitly on the degenerate consequences that were supposed to result from 'the mixing of blood'.[20]

The physical legacy of fur trade intermarriage, which had produced the Métis people of Western Canada, was further discredited by the North-West Rebellion, which had been ruthlessly crushed by the Canadian government in 1885. Increasingly racist rhetoric condemned the product of miscegenation as degenerate. Even the highly acculturated mixed-race families of the colonial North West found their progenitors' choice of marriage partners disparaged. In the first official history of the Pacific Northwest the American historian Hubert Howe Bancroft denounced miscegenation as 'the fur trader's curse'. He lamented that the distinguished officers of the Hudson's Bay Company had stooped to marrying Indian and 'half-breed' women, for, by doing so, 'their own old Scotch, Irish and English blood would . . . be greatly debased'.[21]

By the end of the colonial period the legacy of fur trade intermarriage had effectively been negated, and the place of Aboriginal/non-Aboriginal marriage in Canadian society had undergone a major transformation. Because of the importance and longevity of the fur trade in the Canadian experience, it had at one time been a widespread and vital phenomenon, but settler society had always been ambivalent about its desirability, and, as Euro-Canadian patterns of settlement were solidified, intermarriage was increasingly denigrated and marginalized.

In the late nineteenth and early twentieth centuries few voices were raised in opposition to the construction of an increasingly racist discourse. Significantly, one important antidote was the voice of Native writer E. Pauline Johnson, herself a product of the aforementioned Johnson marriage whose own marital prospects were apparently blighted by these attitudes. In several of Johnson's short stories she has her strong Native heroines take on the hypocrisy of Euro-Canadian society. In her story 'A Red Girl's Reasoning' the heroine gives a passionate defence of the sanctity of Aboriginal marriage rites and leaves her white husband because his bigoted attitudes have dishonoured her and her parents. In 'As It Was in the Beginning', Johnson exposes the hypocrisy of the priest who counsels his nephew not to marry the Métis woman Esther. The language used is worth quoting, as it was to be repeated many times. 'The blood is a bad, bad mixture', says Father Paul. Although Esther might be a modest, Christian young woman, she is forever tainted by her Native blood. Father Paul declares that, although he has devoted himself to the betterment of his Native flock, 'It is a different thing to marry with one of them.'[22] We now know that concepts such as 'Native blood', even 'race' categories, are artificial constructions. Nevertheless, the legacy of the patriarchal and racist structuring of intermarriage continues to have serious repercussions in Aboriginal communities and for Native identity today.[23]

Notes

I would like to thank all those whose stimulating comments and suggestions contributed to the development of this paper in various venues. It was originally presented at a comparative session on intermarriage at the Berkshire Conference on Women's History in June 1999. The gender dimension was highlighted at the workshop on Gender Issues in Atlantic History at Harvard University in the spring of 2001. Further reflections emerged from my presentation at the Women's History Discussion Group at the University of Toronto in the fall of 2001.

1. I consider 1885 a more appropriate date for the end of the colonial era in Canada, rather than the usual date of Confederation in 1867. It was not until 1885 that the Plains Indians had been subjugated and the first transcontinental railway, the Canadian Pacific, was completed.
2. For a general discussion about attitudes toward miscegenation in North American, a good place to start is the collection of essays edited by Martha Hodes, *Sex, Love, Race: Crossing Boundaries in North American*

History (New York: New York University Press, 1999); see especially the essays by Richard Godbeer, 'Eroticizing the Middle Ground: Anglo-Indian Sexual Relations along the Eighteenth-Century Frontier', and Jennifer Spear, '"They Need Wives": Métissage and the Regulation of Sexuality in French Louisiana, 1699–1730'.

3. For a fascinating discussion of such missionary endeavors in an American colony, see Ann Marie Plane, *Colonial Intimacies: Indian Marriage in Early New England* (Ithaca NY: Cornell University Press, 2000).
4. See 'Connolly *v.* Woolrich, Superior Court, July 9, 1867', *Lower Canada Jurist,* II, 197–265.
5. Reuben G. Thwaites, ed., *The Jesuit Relations and Allied Documents: Travels and Explorations of the Jesuit Missionaries in New France, 1610–1791* (New York: Pageant Book Co., 1959), vol. 9 (1633), 211.
6. Thwaites, *Jesuit Relations,* vol. 14 (1637), 15–21.
7. Intendent de Meulles in 1682, as quoted in Alfred G. Bailey, *The Conflict of European and Eastern Algonkian Cultures, 1504–1700: A Study in Canadian Civilization* (Toronto: University of Toronto Press, 1969), 108, quotation translated by Annie Forget.
8. For a fuller discussion of fur trade marriages, see my article, Sylvia Van Kirk, '"The Custom of the Country": An Examination of Fur Trade Marriage Practices', in *Canadian Family History: Selected Readings,* Bettina Bradbury, ed. (Toronto: Copp Clark Pittman, 1992), 67–92.
9. Peter Jones, *History of the Ojebway Indians* (London: A.W. Bennett, 1861), 240–1.
10. Francis Bond Head, 'Memorandum on the Aborigines of North America', published as an appendix in *A Narrative* (London: J. Murray, 1839).
11. As quoted in Sylvia Van Kirk, 'Toward a Feminist Perspective in Native History' (Toronto: Ontario Institute for Studies in Education, Occasional Paper 14, 1987), 6.
12. See Kathleen Jamieson, *Indian Women and the Law in Canada: Citizens Minus* (Ottawa: Minister of Supply and Services, 1978) for a further discussion of the ramifications of loss of status for Indian women who 'married out'.
13. *The New York Spectator,* Peter Jones Collection, Victoria University Archives, University of Toronto. For a biography of Peter Jones, see Donald B. Smith, *Sacred Feathers: The Reverend Peter Jones (Kahkewaquonaby) and the Mississauga Indians* (Lincoln: University of Nebraska Press, 1987).
14. E. Pauline Johnson, 'My Mother,' in *The Moccasin Maker* (1913; Tucson: University of Arizona, 1987), 23–85.
15. See, for example, the perceptive analysis of Vron Ware in *Beyond the Pale: White Women, Racism and History* (London: Verso, 1992).
16. Adele Perry, *On the Edge of Empire: Gender, Race, and the Making of British Columbia, 1849–1871* (Toronto: University of Toronto Press, 2001).
17. See Carlos Schwantes, *The Pacific Northwest: An Interpretive History* (Lincoln: University of Nebraska Press, 1996). For my study of the elite fur trade families of colonial Victoria, see Sylvia Van Kirk, 'Tracing the Fortunes of Five Founding Families of Victoria,' *BC Studies* 115/116 (1997/1998): 148–79.
18. Sarah Carter, *Capturing Women: The Manipulation of Cultural Imagery in Canada's Prairie West* (Montreal: McGill-Queen's University Press, 1997).
19. As quoted in Sylvia Van Kirk, *'Many Tender Ties': Women in Fur Trade Society in Western Canada, 1670–1870* (Winnipeg: Watson & Dwyer, 1980), 241.
20. For an excellent discussion of the construction of racist hierarchies and the growing fear of miscegenation in the later nineteenth century, see Robert Young, *Colonial Desire: Hybridity in Theory, Culture, and Race* (London: Routledge, 1995).
21. Hubert Howe Bancroft, *History of the Northwest Coast,* vol. 2 (San Francisco: A.L. Bancroft and Company, 1886), 650–1.
22. These stories are published in Johnson's book *The Mocassin Maker.* The most recent and insightful biography of Johnson is Veronica Strong-Boag and Carol Gerson, *Paddling Her Own Canoe: The Times and Texts of E. Pauline Johnson (Tekahionwake)* (Toronto: University of Toronto Press, 2000).
23. In 1985 the discriminatory clause against Aboriginal women 'marrying-out' was removed from the Indian Act. For details of the Aboriginal women's campaign, see *Enough is Enough: Aboriginal Women Speak Out,* Janet Silman, ed. (Toronto: Women's Press, 1987). However, the complicated formula for the reinstatement of Aboriginal women and their descendants and the lack of financial support to bands has created many new problems. See Val Napoleon, 'Extinction by Number: Colonialism Made Easy', *Canadian Journal of Law and Society* 16.1 (2001): 113–45.

'A Fragment of Heaven on Earth'? Religion, Gender, and Family in Turn of the Century Canadian Church Periodicals

Lynne Marks

EDITORS' INTRODUCTION

Few historians of women would dispute the fact that religion was of enormous importance to Canadians in the past. Yet historians of women in Canada have been inexplicably loath to provide a sustained investigation of how religion works in women's lives. In the 1980s and 90s a handful of works treated the topic, the bulk arguing that religion offered women, whether Roman Catholic nuns in late-nineteenth or early twentieth-century Quebec or Protestant missionaries to Canadian Indigenous people and non-Christians abroad, an avenue for self-expression and autonomy denied them in secular society.[1] Yet outside these works, religion was not much discussed. Historian Ruth Compton Brouwer argued that there was an 'unacknowledged quarantine' that kept religion out of Canadian women's history, one that did enormous damage to our ability to understand and analyze women's pasts.[2] Some recent publications suggest that this is changing, at least with regards to Christianity.[3] Lynne Marks's essay, which studies gender and the family in church periodicals in turn-of-the-century Canada, provides another example of how historians of women are also historians of religion.

In keeping with much of the secondary scholarship, Nancy Shoemaker's analysis of the 'Mohawk Saint' Kateri Tekakwitha in this volume stresses women's ability to transform patriarchal religious institutions to suit their own agendas. Marks offers a less cheerful evaluation of what Protestant and Roman Catholic churches offered to women in the closing years of the nineteenth-century and the first years of the twentieth. Church periodicals, she argues, offered readers an idealized vision of the 'Christian family' anchored in ideas of domestic, caring, and subservient motherhood. Roman Catholic women were provided with a slightly wider range of alternatives rooted in the Marian ideal of motherhood and the notion that women owed obedience not simply to their husbands and fathers, but to God and the Church as well. But in all the periodicals Marks finds women were offered a highly circumscribed role in which they were imagined as largely, if not wholly, responsible for the production of respectable Christian sons and daughters.

Marks's findings remind us that there is good reason for historians of women to have spilled so much ink on the concept of 'separate spheres', that powerful nineteenth-century idea of men and women as separate and distinct creatures, each with their own 'sphere'—men's public, economic, and political, and women's domestic, private, and nurturing. As historians Suzanne Morton and Janet Guilford's edited collection on women's history in the Maritimes makes clear, 'separate spheres' was at best an idea, one that the vast majority of men and women could not and would not live up to.[4] Yet it was an incredibly powerful ideal that had real power to shape social expectations and experiences. Thus working-class women, unable to live up to the ideas of Christian, domestic motherhood offered them in Church periodicals, were judged harshly for failing to do so.

It is worth noting that Marks is studying both women and men. She finds that church periodicals were worried about men, fearing their descent into a reckless, Godless manhood and encouraging them to be involved, Christian fathers who would lead their families in prayer. In recent years historians have struggled over whether our goal should be 'women's history', or an alternative history rooted in a critique of women's oppression, or 'gender history', or a study of how both masculinity and femininity shaped and were shaped by historical change.[5] Here, Marks takes the latter route, as does Josette Brun in her investigation of widows and orphans in New France in this volume. Women do not disappear as topics, but they are reimagined as part (albeit a highly important one) of a larger and more complicated gender history.

Marks's discussion also reminds us that what might seem to be a shopworn category of Canadian history—region—has real relevance to historians of women and gender. She found that the church periodicals from Catholic, Anglican, Methodist, Baptist, and Presbyterian faiths all concurred on the idealization of the Christian home and a 'profoundly unrealistic idealization of the Christian role of mothers'. And none were especially concerned about marriages between different denominations, in sharp contrast to the concern for marriages across racial lines discussed by Sylvia Van Kirk. But region did matter. Francophone Catholics were concerned with the absence of men from the churches. But anxieties about men's religious roles (or lack thereof) were strongest in British Columbia, a province home to an overwhelmingly young and male settler community that was likely, in the minds of their church going neighbours, to run afoul of the conventions of Christian, respectable manhood. Like Margaret Little's essay on mother's allowances in this volume, Marks suggests the need to keep in mind how different demographies, cultures, and societies could and did create different gendered histories within Canada. This is perhaps one of the reasons that women's and gender history have developed so differently in Canada's various regions, and why we know so much about some things in some places and so little about those same things elsewhere.[6]

Notes

1. Marta Danylewycz, *Taking the Veil: An Alternative to Marriage, Motherhood, and Spinsterhood in Quebec, 1840–1920* (Toronto: McClelland and Stewart, 1987); Ruth Compton Brouwer, *New Women for God: Canadian Presbyterian Women and Indian Missions, 1876–1914* (Toronto: University of Toronto Press, 1990); Rosemary R. Gagan, *A Sensitive Independence: Canadian Methodist Women Missionaries in Canada and the Orient, 1881–1925* (Montreal and Kingston: McGill-Queen's University Press, 1992).
2. Ruth Compton Brouwer, 'Transcending the "unacknowledged quarantine": Putting Religion into English-Canadian women's history', *Journal of Canadian Studies* 27 (Fall 1992): 3.
3. Nancy Christie, ed., *Households of Faith: Family, Gender, and Community in Canada, 1760–1969* (Montreal and Kingston, McGill-Queen's University Press, 2002).
4. Janet Guildford and Suzanne Morton, eds., *Separate Spheres: Women's Worlds in the 19th Century Maritimes* (Fredericton: Acadiensis Press, 1994).
5. Joan Sangster, 'Beyond Dichotomies: Re-Assessing Gender History and Women's History in Canada', *Left History* 3.1 (Spring/Summer 1995): 109–21; Karen Dubinsky and Lynne Marks, 'Beyond Purity: A Response to Sangster', *Left History* 3.2, 4.1 (Fall 1995–Spring 1996): 205–20; Franca Iacovetta and Linda Kealey, 'Women's History, Gender History and Debating Dichotomies', in ibid., 221–38; Kathryn McPherson, Cecilia Morgan, and Nancy M. Forestell, 'Introduction: Conceptualizing Canada's Gendered Pasts', in *Gendered Pasts: Historical Essays in Femininity and Masculinity in Canada*, Kathryn McPherson, Cecilia Morgan, and Nancy M. Forestell, eds. (Toronto: Oxford University Press, 1999).
6. See *Atlantis*, Special Issue on 'Feminism and Canadian History', 25.1 (Fall/Automne 2000).

Questions for Critical Reading

1. Even though organized religion often seems to have perpetuated negative images of women, many women have been drawn to it. What has religious faith and practice offered women?
2. Marks's sources are what historians call 'prescriptive' in nature, meaning they aimed to tell people what they should do, rather than describe what they were doing. What are the limits and possibilities of using prescriptive sources to study the past?
3. Why have historians of women in Canada been slow to embrace the study of religion?
4. Marks studies what are often called 'mainstream' Christian churches in Canada. How might the relationship between gender and religion work differently in Jewish, Muslim, Hindu, or Buddhist faiths? How might it be different in evangelical Christian churches?

Today's conservatives bemoan the apparent fragmentation of the family in late-twentieth and early-twenty-first century North America. Many among them lay much of the blame for contemporary family difficulties on an apparent decline of religious faith. Christian belief and practice within the family is heralded as a bulwark of stability for both the family and society. In advocating family prayer and, increasingly, home schooling in Christian values, contemporary conservative Christians hark back to an earlier era when religious faith was assumed to be integral to family life and to help keep families strong. While historians in both Canada and the United States have convincingly challenged conservatives' happy picture of the unified nuclear family of past eras, there has been little exploration of the role of religion in family life, particularly in the Canadian context.[1] Most Canadian family historians ignore religion. The social history of religion is not well developed in this country, particularly in English Canada, and the relationship between religion and family is not studied in most existing works in this field. Those studies that at least touch on this topic tend to focus on one region or community or on a single denomination.[2]

It is unfortunate that Canadian scholars have largely ignored the relationship between religion and family, since British and American historians have clearly demonstrated the significant impact that shifting religious discourses can have on gender and family ideals and relationships.[3] Canadian historians have provided in-depth analyses of the manner in which scientific and social scientific discourses influenced dominant family and gender ideals and behaviors over the course of the twentieth century.[4] At most, such scholars sometimes briefly acknowledge the comparative impact that religious discourses may have had in the nineteenth and early twentieth centuries.

This article looks at the relationship between gender, family, and religion at the turn of the century, the period just before scientific discourses began to overshadow religious ones in defining hegemonic ideals of gender and family.[5] The article examines how the relationship between Christianity and family is presented in Canadian Christian periodicals. It is based on research in nineteen religious periodicals. Eleven of the journals have a national or regional focus, with the remainder being local church journals. The periodicals cover all mainstream Protestant denominations and include two Catholic journals (one English Canadian and the other French Canadian).[6] Given the many religious journals published at this time, this article cannot reflect all Christian perspectives on issues of religion and family. However, it does provide a sense of both diversity and common themes across regions and denominations. The commonalities in both ideals of religion and family and anxieties around these issues discovered between Catholics and Protestants and, indeed, between French Catholics and English Protestants were somewhat surprising in this era of deep Catholic-Protestant divisions.[7] While some denominational differences can be identified, the most significant differences are regional. Shared anxieties about religion and family took on a particular form and intensity in British Columbia, a province that in this period had a dramatic under-representation of European women and thus a relative lack of the white, Christian nuclear families that were deemed crucial to maintaining both Christianity and social order.[8]

Of course, a focus on church periodicals presents the official perspective on both ideals and anxieties regarding religion, gender, and family. Particularly among Protestants, this official perspective was very much that of the white middle classes who dominated the leadership of the churches at this time.[9] Although women were gaining more power, particularly within the more evangelical churches, this official voice was primarily male. Nonetheless, it seems that women made up the majority of the readers of these journals, particularly those that billed themselves as family papers or journals for the home.[10] For women, particularly middle-class women who may have been looking for advice literature in their roles as mothers, the church journals provided one of the central sources for such information in this period. While we cannot know exactly how seriously the ideals presented in these journals were taken by the readership, studies of women primarily but not exclusively middle-class women) in both English and French Canada make it clear that the values and patterns of faith and religious practice promulgated by the churches were central to the lives of many of these women. Existing research also makes clear that while not everyone attended church every week, the churches were a central institution in Canadian society at this time. While this was particularly true in Quebec, throughout Canada the values and ideals of both the Protestant and Catholic churches had considerable hegemonic power.[11] Quantitative research currently being undertaken regarding patterns of family religious involvement will complement the findings of this article, but a study of these periodicals provides valuable insights into dominant discourses of Christianity and family as well as useful clues as to the nature of popular belief and behavior.[12]

Gender and the Ideal Christian Family

The ideal relationship between family and religion appears to have been relatively similar between the various denominational periodicals examined for this study. This ideal relationship worked in two directions. Christianity was presented as essential to the creation and preservation of happy, harmonious, and closely knit families, while such Christian families were seen as crucial to the survival of the church and of Christian society more generally. The Christian families presented in these ideal visions were almost always heterosexual nuclear families. Very rarely, an older image of the family as a broader household including servants was presented.[13]

Religion within the home was to create joy among family members and bring them together in warm, loving Christian domesticity. All of the journals surveyed offered variations on the *Western Methodist Recorder's* comment that religion 'glorifies and beautifies the home life' and, as the *Canadian Churchman* stated, makes the home 'a fragment of heaven on earth'.[14] Arguments that the practice of Christianity was essential to the creation of happy homes and families were reinforced by comparisons between Christian families and the 'other'. The 'other' in these contexts was generally the non-Christian, and usually non-white, families. The evils and miseries of such families, and particularly women's supposedly degraded position in 'heathen' homes, were commonly mentioned. For example, an article in the *Western Methodist Recorder* encouraged women to be grateful that they live in a Christian country.

> Visit a heathen country and you will appreciate to the full all that Christianity has given to us of privilege and of honor. In all this wide world no

> women are more happily situated, none occupy a more exalted position, loved and honored in the home.[15]

Historians have noted that in some contexts Protestants have similarly compared happy Protestant home life with the evils of Catholic celibate religious life, with lurid tales of nuns being 'unnaturally' torn away from the joys of wifehood and motherhood, while Catholic priests are represented as sexually preying on young girls and married women and thus destroying many happy homes.[16] Catholics vehemently countered such bigotry and also counterposed the happy Catholic family, and particularly the position of women, to the non-Christian 'other'. An article in the *Catholic Register* appealed to wives and mothers to remember that they owed to the Catholic Church the fact that 'they are not the slaves of men and the toy of their caprice, but the partners of their husbands and queens of their homes.'[17]

The very clear message was that women were to be grateful to the Christian churches for making women's exalted role in the home possible. Such a message, of course, papered over the very real inequalities these 'queens of the home' faced in turn-of-the-century Christian North America. It also provided the context for the range of directives issued by these journals as to how women had to behave in order to create those warm, loving Christian families in which they were to be so honoured. Historians have written extensively about how the nineteenth-century middle class placed considerable emphasis on women's role in creating a haven of domestic bliss in a harsh industrial capitalist world.[18] The journals surveyed focus on the centrality of Christian values to women's ability to create such homes. A key Christian virtue—self-sacrifice—was an essential part of these womanly roles, especially for mothers. This was particularly explicit in the Catholic papers. *Le Messager Canadien* frequently compared ideal mothers to Mary, mother of Jesus, who made 'the home of Nazareth a sanctuary of peace, pleasing gentleness, attractive and sweet piety'.[19] The idealization of motherhood in both English and French Catholic papers was particularly powerful in the late nineteenth century, in part because of the particular popularity of the devotional cult of Mary in this period and because of the general valorization of bourgeois motherhood in the larger culture at this time.[20] While the Catholic papers include many stories of saintly mothers who somehow lived up to the Marian ideal, it was no easy task. Loving one's children and always putting them first was not enough. Concern for their eternal souls was to be as important as day-to-day self-sacrifice on their behalf. One story in *Le Messager Canadien* blamed the mother of a young boy who apparently went to hell because his mother, 'blind with tenderness', refused to tell him that he was dying. Because his mother did not provide him with the opportunity to repent of his sins before death, he was 'Damned!'. While the emotional intensity is a bit lower in the Protestant journals, the ideal mother is similarly presented as one who has no thought for herself but only cares for the physical, emotional, and spiritual well-being of her children. For example, a story in the *Western Methodist Recorder* speaks of 'a kind and devoted mother. Her children were her whole object for living and it was the delight of her daily life to see them assuming the responsibilities of a broad and useful life.' An obituary in the same journal speaks of a wife and mother who was 'kind, devoted and self-sacrificing'.[21]

By the late nineteenth century, most denominations sanctioned some roles for women beyond motherhood, but such roles remained extremely limited and had to include at least some religious component. Baptist and Methodist periodicals conceded that women could spend some of their energies outside the home if they were involved in church societies. Presbyterians saw work as a missionary as being one of the only sanctioned roles for women, beyond the home.[22] Despite the veneration of motherhood among Catholics, vocation as a nun was viewed as an even more valued option. If they did not become nuns, however, women were to remain in the home. The *Catholic Register* informed women that 'the good that a woman can do toward the great world at large is nothing compared to her possibilities in her own home if she be a wife or mother.'[23]

While for Catholics being a nun was seen as a higher calling than that of wife and mother, for Protestants nothing was considered more important than a woman's role in the home. Church associations were at best secondary to home life. This was as true for daughters as for mothers. As the story 'That Provoking Brother' in the Baptist *Religious Intelligencer* demonstrates, the sister who puts her energies into her church society while her brother is abandoning family life for 'bad companions' must discover that 'the first place to begin Christ-like living is at home, and about one's daily duties' if one wishes to bring one's brother back to God and the family.[24] Other articles in Protestant church papers also focused on a sister's responsibility to help ensure her brother's moral and spiritual well-being.[25]

Women, as mothers, wives, and sisters, were to be primarily responsible for creating havens of domestic bliss and Christian morality, but turn-of-the-century Christians also believed that fathers should play an important role here. An old style, rigid Christian patriarchal version of fatherhood was rejected by most denominations. There was some recognition that a punitive, narrow-minded, bigoted version of belief was inappropriate and would only turn family members away from Christianity.[26] At the same time, the Anglican *Canadian Churchman* did express concern that the growing emphasis on women's role as nurturer and educator in the home was taking away from men's crucial responsibility in providing Christian guidance and education for their children.[27] While most papers were more interested in valorizing women's role as nurturer and religious educator than in critiquing it, there was also a strong sense that men should play an active role in religious leadership and education in the home. As well, all journals, even those of the more liberal denominations, such as the Methodists, were in agreement that men were to remain masters in their own homes and that in cases of disagreement between husband and wife, women were to obey.[28]

The only possible exception to wifely obedience occurred in cases where one's obedience to a husband conflicted with one's obedience to God. More evangelical Protestant denominations, which strongly valued the close, direct relationship between an individual and God, were particularly likely to sanction the disobedience of women and children in such cases. This was true, for example, of the Methodists earlier in the nineteenth century or of the Salvation Army in the latter part of the century. Women who remained faithful to religious belief and practice, even in the face of hostility and abuse from non-believing husbands, were valorized as heroines to their faith and were not challenged as disobedient wives. Non-evangelical Protestants, such as the Anglicans, were much less likely to sanction such disobedience, even in the name of obedience to a higher authority. In their view, tampering with earthly patriarchal authority undermined both spiritual and secular order and could only lead to chaos and evil.[29] While one might assume that Catholics would be among the strongest in upholding patriarchal authority within the family, the Catholic position on these issues was somewhat more complex. In most cases, the obedience of wife and children was considered essential. However, in addition to one's own flesh-and-blood family, the Catholic Church also provided the faithful with other relationships, defined in familial terms, that also demanded obedience, an obedience that could at times conflict with obedience to husband and father. Both the *Catholic Register* and *Le Messager Canadien* frequently spoke of the obedience that Catholics owed the 'mother' church, as well as speaking about the role of the Pope as father, to whom obedience was also owed. Priests, of course, were also spiritual fathers at a more local level. 'Supernatural' parents, in particular Jesus and Mary but also the various saints, were also owed loyalty and obedience. While such Catholic familial language is of course not unique to this period, scholars have suggested a heightened focus on such language in the mid to late nineteenth century as part of valorization of family and domesticity in the larger culture.[30]

Stories about disobedience to earthly fathers in the name of a higher obedience are occasionally found in the Catholic journals studied here. In one example, a boy who chooses to join a choir at a priest's request but against his father's explicit instructions is beaten by his father for his disobedience, with the journal disapprovingly noting that the beating 'had nothing of the paternal about it'. In this case, the son's behaviour is praised, especially as his example ultimately brings his father back to the church. Such direct disobedience is rarely explicitly featured, however. Wives and children are more commonly praised for more subtle ways of bringing husbands and fathers back to the church. The church may not have wanted to obviously undermine patriarchal authority, but the spiritual filial obedience owed beyond the biological family did complicate the Catholic family picture. Catholic parents were frequently chastised in these journals for not willingly accepting their children's vocations as priests and nuns. Parents were expected to happily accept the fracturing of the biological family that occurred when a child entered the alternative family of the religious order and are told to give their children 'generously, without waiting and joyously'.[31]

While alternative spiritual loyalties could take precedence over Catholic family life, for those Catholics who chose family life, spirituality within the family, particularly through family prayer, was seen as essential. Catholic and Protestant journals were in full agreement that daily family prayer was crucial, not only to keep the family Christian but to maintain harmony and strengthen domestic ties. By family prayer the journals did not mean simply grace before meals. Family prayer, which ideally was to occur morning and evening, but at least once a day, was the gathering of the family together in prayer and, in Protestant families, in reading from the Bible. The warmth and delights of such family practice is frequently mentioned. The Baptist *Messenger and Visitor* spoke of 'the sweetness, the sunshine, the melody, the unity of . . . a home' which had a 'family altar' (i.e., family prayer).[32] Colleen McDannell suggests that until the late nineteenth century family prayer was much less important in American Catholic families than in Protestant ones, being seen by the Catholic hierarchy as very much secondary to church- and parish-centred religious practice. However, by the turn of the century, Canadian Catholic religious leaders certainly valued family prayer. Praise of family prayer appeared in the English Canadian *Catholic Register* but was particularly common in *Le Messager Canadien*, which assured its readers that family prayer restores domestic harmony and erases all signs of strife within the family.[33] Within all denominations, family prayer was thus explicitly advocated as a means of creating domestic harmony and happiness for all classes.

While family prayer was very important, family church attendance, which brought the family together outside the home in a public affirmation of Christian belief, was also assumed to both reflect and reinforce family unity and domestic bliss.[34] The most concrete manifestation of the value of family togetherness in church was the idealization of the family pew, which was found in some Protestant periodicals. All members of the family were to be present on Sunday morning in the 'old-fashioned family pew', which not only reinforced Christian belief and domestic ties in the present but also provided a linkage to family members long gone who had once also shared the family pew.[35] Catholic journals also argued that attending mass together brought families together. For example, *Le Messager Canadien* informed its readers that after mass the home is happy, the family reunited, and 'affection, confidence, gaiety reappear in homes'.[36]

While Christian belief, family prayer, and church involvement were ideally to produce happy, united families, church periodicals focused more attention on the centrality of Christian families to the creation of strong churches and a moral, ordered society. Various articles suggested that Christian family life was more important in this regard than any church institution, including Sunday school. Family prayer, once again, was considered crucial in fostering a strong sense of Christian belief, particularly among children.[37] More generally, as the *Religious Intelligencer* argued,

> religion in the home, in early life, is one of the safeguards for our children when they arrive at manhood or womanhood . . . . The true religious spirit instilled into the child mind, under the divine blessing, abides and brings about glorious results.[38]

Parents played an important role, but mothers, again, were key. As the *Catholic Register* argued, 'The devout Christian mother is called to be an apostle. The family is her field of labour; the members of the household are the souls committed to her ministry.'[39] A range of denominational papers focus on the influence mothers could have, particularly in training their sons to avoid the moral pitfalls of the world and to become good Christians. Such articles speak of young men who are tempted by drink and other 'dissolute' pursuits, but who remain firm, in memory of a godly mother.[40] Biographical sketches and obituaries of prominent men also point to the role Christian mothers played in shaping their characters.[41] Such tales suggested that the power of a pious mother transcended class divisions, as seen in a story of a woman who lived in the direst poverty in Scotland but through her piety and cheerfulness was able to raise seven godly (and ultimately successful) sons.[42]

Gender, Region, and Christian Anxieties

Ideal Christian mothers were granted much influence in creating stable, moral families and in producing Christian sons. However, this ideal placed enormous responsibility on mothers and led to a great deal of mother-blaming when young men did not live up to Christian ideals. One of the central anxieties of the church papers surveyed was the fate of young men from Christian homes. The moral ruin of young men who failed to become Christians—who entered a 'fast' crowd, got involved in drinking and gambling, and ultimately ended up in poverty and misery—was frequently sketched out in church papers. Mothers were blamed for the moral ruin of young men, not only in cases where women did not live up to their responsibilities of training and educating sons in Christian values but also for simply taking other aspects of their ideal feminine role too seriously. In particular, women were often chided about the need to not let concerns about their associational work, or even their housekeeping, take precedence over the attention they needed to pay to their sons. Mothers were told not to make sons unwelcome in the house in order to preserve a tidy or 'dainty' home and not to ignore boys' childish interests for other housewifely responsibilities. The results of such maternal behaviour were viewed as dire indeed: the young boy would find interests outside the home, if he did not find them within, leading to involvement with a bad crowd and the ultimate downward slide.[43] For middle-class mothers, such advice would have led to much maternal guilt, given the major time and effort involved in maintaining a household, even among middle-class women in this period. For working-class mothers struggling to survive, such advice was completely unrealistic.[44]

The religious journals focused less attention on advising mothers on raising their daughters than they did regarding sons. This was largely because of the value placed on young men in this culture. At the same time, young women were also seen as less of a problem. Mothers, of course, were to train their daughters in proper Christian behaviour and teach them to avoid selfishness, laziness, and worldliness. However, there was much less concern expressed in the church papers about the potential dangers of young women moving away from the church toward ruin. It was believed that young women would naturally assume a moral, Christian lifestyle. They were addressed far more as the potential saviours of young men (as sisters, sweethearts, and future mothers) than as being at risk themselves.[45]

While women (particularly mothers) were granted primary responsibility in safeguarding young men, the churches realized that they, too, needed to do something about this problem. Protestant churches were well aware that few young men remained in Sunday school classes in their late teens, and they were concerned that most did not become church members or active churchgoers.[46] As one minister noted,

> That [the young man] is not with us is only too evident in every city and town the world over. Other circles gain his presence and the influence of his energy, but the Church is looked upon as only the abridgement of his liberties.[47]

The *Canadian Epworth Era*, the paper of the Epworth League, the main young people's society within the Methodist church, published, not surprisingly, many articles about the need to bring more young men into the league and into the churches. The fact that young women made up two-thirds of league membership was viewed as a cause for concern.[48] The anxieties about the absence of young men from the Epworth League and the churches were partly concerns for the churches themselves, for they needed the involvement of young men. However, concerns more commonly focused on the fate of young men who stayed away from the churches. Many fears were expressed that these young men would choose immoral, un-Christian lifestyles of drinking, gambling, and sexual promiscuity. The fear again was of the slide to ruin, if not protected by conversion and church involvement.

While concern regarding young men runs through all denominational papers, the *Western Methodist Recorder* focused the most attention on this issue.[49] This is not surprising given the fact that this was a British Columbia paper and that among the non-aboriginal population in British Columbia at this time men dramatically outnumbered women.[50] Young, single men who had come west to seek their fortunes were particularly over-represented. There was a general sense that this demographic fact played a major role in explaining the low levels of religious involvement in the province.[51] As a result, churchgoers in British Columbia created a number of missions and clubs that were intended to keep young men in the Christian fold or to bring back those who had strayed. For example, the work of the Women's Christian Temperance Union's Mission Hall in Victoria is described as coming into existence because

> in the hearts of some mothers there was a strong, earnest desire to reach the hitherto un-reached portion of the population of the city, the non-church goers . . . [and create] a place . . . where men would come in touch, and be to a certain extent under the influence of a kind Christian woman who would take a real personal interest in them, such an interest that none could go away from the Mission . . . and say in moments of loneliness 'nobody cares how I go or what I do.' Words that have been echoed in many a poor fellow's heart when far way from home and those he loves; surrounded only with such influences as tend to drag him down, deeper and deeper into a life of reckless sinful pleasure from which alas, he so surely reaps in the future the fruit of sin.[52]

The *Western Methodist Recorder* noted a few years later that, following a Vancouver church's example, Victoria's Centennial Church had organized a Young Men's Club. The editor asked,

> Why should we not by every legitimate means make the Church the chief place of attraction for the young men all week round? . . . We have much yet to learn in competing with the Devil and his agencies for the lives of the young men, but we believe that conducted under broad though careful regulation, the clubs may be made a powerful instrument of saving grace.[53]

While the *Western Methodist Recorder* was the most vocal on the subject of the dangers facing young men in British Columbia, two Presbyterian papers, the *Presbyterian* and the *Westminister*, which had a significant Western Canadian focus, also provided considerable discussion about the absence of young men from British Columbian churches. Like the

Western Methodist Recorder, the Presbyterian papers raised concerns about the 'immoral' lifestyle of many young men, especially in the mining towns of interior British Columbia, where the gender ratios were particularly skewed and 'profanity, drink, gambling and lewdness seem to have the upper hand and the church and her services are very generally ignored.'[54] The move away from the churches to immoral lifestyles was explained partly by the nature of young men, who were considered more susceptible to such temptations, but it was the absence of adequate numbers of white women and, therefore, the distance of most of these men from the Christian influences of home and family that was seen as the real culprit.[55] Relationships with First Nations women, even if they were Christian, were seen as part of the problem of immorality facing young men in the West and were not considered part of the solution. It was believed that interracial marriages did not provide the appropriate 'civilized' Christian family life for European men.[56]

While most articles decrying the perils facing young men in the West focused on immorality and religious indifference, a few articles in the Presbyterian papers also recognized that at least a minority of British Columbian men were actively hostile to the churches and defined themselves as atheists or freethinkers, often as part of a socialist ideology that was particularly common in the mining communities of British Columbia.[57] The fact that some British Columbia papers were willing to raise this issue is not surprising, since atheism was indeed far more common in the westernmost province then elsewhere in Canada.[58] There is evidence, however, that even beyond British Columbia a tiny but growing number of young men, and men generally, were defining themselves as atheists.[59] However, the question of free thought was not commonly raised in most Canadian Christian papers' discussions of the 'young man problem'. While a few dark hints suggest the possibility that secularism may have been one of the many evils waiting to ensnare young men who remained outside the churches, the lack of discussion in most church periodicals may simply mean that the churches did not wish to raise ideas in their readers' minds.

Perhaps surprisingly, given French Canada's reputation for piety in this period, the only other paper to raise the specter of atheism or free thought was the francophone Catholic paper *Le Messager Canadien*. Although by the early twentieth century the periodical sometimes raised concerns about young men that were very similar to those of the Protestant papers, it was much more anxious about the relative absence of adult men, especially husbands and fathers, from the churches.[60] Some of this concern reflected Quebec's religious patterns, since women were much more overtly pious than men. Women took communion at least several times a year, while men were much more likely to fulfill only the minimal requirement of Easter communion. While the journal's concern partly reflected the religious hierarchy's desire to increase Quebec men's piety, the fears expressed are also based on the specter of what was happening in France, where many men were abandoning the churches.[61] Articles decrying the power of free thought among men focus primarily on the evils of the French example and the need to protect Quebeckers from such contagion. There was considerable fear that atheistic men could corrupt their families and challenge the church. 'What good can come, for instance, of a family in which the father teaches error and impiety and gives the example of vice?'[62] While free thought among men was clearly a worry to the church hierarchy, most articles about men's reluctance to attend church focused not on atheism but rather on men's preference for leisure and associational activities beyond the churches. For example, one article chided men for finding pleasure 'in the crowd and noise, among false friends, in cabarets, in theatres', rather than with their families.[63] Particularly after the turn of the century, *Le Messager Canadien* expressed considerable anxiety about the relative absence of men from the churches. Women—as pious mothers or nuns—were frequently idealized in the pages of this journal, reflecting the more general idealization of pious women and the feminine in Quebec religious culture in this period, as identified by Christine Hudon. Men were more likely to appear as a problem—a problem that could at least sometimes be solved by female piety. There are many stories in the paper of irreligious husbands and fathers being brought back into the church by pious wives or children.[64]

The Protestant and English Catholic papers did reflect some concern about the absence of fathers and husbands from the churches, although such concern was less extreme than in *Le Messager Canadien* and tended to vary by denomination. Existing research for Ontario suggests that women predominated less in the Baptist churches than in those of other denominations.[65] It is therefore perhaps not surprising that the three Baptist papers consulted expressed less concern about the relative absence of men from the churches than did other church periodicals.

Like *Le Messager Canadien*, most English-Canadian papers blamed men for their absence from church. Men were accused of being lazy and worldly or of preferring more entertaining alternatives, such as lodges and saloons, to church services. Such preferences were seen as damaging not just to the men themselves but to the preservation of Christian families.[66] Anglicans, with particularly high levels of feminization within congregations, and with very narrow definitions of women's appropriate roles, tended to lay the blame for men's absence from the churches not just on men but on women as well. By becoming so active in the churches, particularly in church associations, it was suggested that women were pushing men out. Writers also argued that if women spent more time at home they would be more able to influence their sons and husbands to become involved in the churches. A letter writer to a British Columbia Anglican paper argued that young men may not feel welcome enough in British Columbia's Anglican churches not because there were not enough church societies to interest them but because not enough women remained in their homes to provide much needed hospitality to young men who were new to the parish. The letter writer argued that

> if a little of the time expended in, say the Women's Christian Temperance Union, or any such organization which draws away members from their homes, were spent in making those homes a little more attractive and available to the men kind and their friends, something successful might be done towards keeping our stray brothers within the Family of Christ's Church.[67]

The Anglican papers did not just blame women directly for men's absence from the churches. They also saw women's presence as damaging to the strength and power of Anglicanism and as creating an increasingly soft, weak, and feminized religion that would not attract men into the churches. One writer to the *Canadian Churchman* attacked clergymen for preaching 'insipid' sermons. He suggests that therefore 'it is not to be wondered at that four-fifths of our congregations are women.' Other articles in the *Canadian Churchman* attacked the 'effeminate easiness' of the Church of England or called for 'strong, masculine prayer' within the church.[68] As scholars have noted, anxieties about the feminization of the churches and of church doctrine were common across denominations at this time and led to various calls for a more 'manly' Christianity. For example, an article in the *Western Methodist Recorder* noted the importance of ministers' speaking simply, 'without the theological millinery, the true, straight manly principles of the kingdom of God'.[69] *Le Messager Canadien* assured its male readers that they would 'recover virility in re-making contact with that Heart [of Jesus] that loves you so', while the *Catholic Register* pointed out that the most manly of men—soldiers—were attracted to the priesthood.[70] However, neither the Methodists nor the Catholics directly blamed women for men's absence, as some Anglicans appeared to do.[71] Methodists provided women with at least somewhat greater freedom to be involved in church work beyond the home than Anglicans did. Catholics were not interested in sanctioning women's role beyond the home, unless they became nuns, but for Catholics in this period the emphasis on Mary, Mother of Jesus, and the resultant idealization of mothers and motherhood meant that women (who fulfilled their ideal roles) were seen far more as part of the solution to men's impiety than as part of the problem.[72]

While the Anglicans were more likely than other Protestants to hark back to a golden age of patriarchy, where men ruled their homes and ran their churches, even they were willing to grant women a central role in one religious function that of family prayer. Family prayer was a source of considerable anxiety among all denominations since there was general agreement that the practice had declined significantly in recent decades. This rhetoric of decline from an earlier golden age of family prayer was echoed in the 1950s and is still echoed today, suggesting the continuing power of such anxieties and of associated historical myths of the ideal Christian family.[73] The decline of family prayer at the turn of the century was viewed as a threat to family unity and social order. The hand-wringing engaged in over this subject underlines just how important the churches saw the Christian family as being in providing the basis for strong churches and a Christian society. The powerlessness of turn-of-the-century churches in reinstituting (or instituting) family prayer may be explained (as it was by the churches) as the impact of a more fast-paced, industrial capitalistic lifestyle, with its attendant 'worldly' values, on the sacred world of the family. There were frequent complaints that people were no longer willing, or able, to make time for family prayer.[74] The impact of industrialization can also be viewed in another way: as having increased the divisions between public and private, with the family increasingly being considered a private sphere, ultimately beyond the control of the more public world of the church. It is interesting to note a Baptist writer observing that in the past pastors visited families and asked whether family prayer occurred regularly. The article notes that 'it would seem now as though this were going too far. Perhaps the present generation would not tolerate such inquiries.'[75]

Whatever the reason for the decline of family prayer, it was seen as a serious crisis. And in times of crisis, some compromises may be accepted. The ideal image of a family at prayer was a patriarchal one. This image was sketched out in *Le Messager Canadien:* 'Each night, at the determined hour, the father assembles his children and servants . . . and says to them, "we will pray all together".'[76] However, even in this paper, other images of family prayer involve mothers leading the family in prayer.[77] While the Anglican *Canadian Churchman* at one point argued that it was the responsibility of both father and mother to ensure that family worship occurred daily, at other points the editors placed the responsibility for arranging family worship on mothers.[78] The *Western Methodist Recorder* urged men not to be 'humiliated' by family prayer, suggesting that while male leadership of family prayer may have been a religious ideal, it did not fit well with dominant notions of manhood, especially as religiosity was increasingly associated with the feminine and as antithetical to the public, masculine world of business. Again we see a public-private division, but here the division is between the private world of home and religion and the public, secular world of commerce. It is certainly clear that most men who were willing to lead family prayer were not willing to extend their private religiosity into the public world. In this regard, the story told of lawyer McLean in the *Baptist Religious Intelligencer* is instructive. Upon being converted, McLean apparently insisted upon instituting family prayer in front of visiting fellow lawyers, regardless of what they might think of him. He was lauded as a courageous Christian by editors who felt it necessary to make the point to their male readership that leading family prayer, and especially being public about it, was a manly act.[79] Similarly, the editors of *Le Messager Canadien* urged their readers, particularly their male readers, to be willing to place religious symbols for the home in public spaces in the home, such as the salon, rather than hiding them in the kitchen or bedroom.[80] They were told that God wanted such images in the public eye and that one could not compartmentalize life and only be religious in the private world, where business associates could not see their behavior.[81] A similar message about the need to demonstrate one's belief in God not just in private but also in the public commercial and social worlds was common within evangelical denominations.[82]

Despite admonitions from the churches, however, the reality was that by the turn of the century the ideology of public and private was dominant, making women, who were already associated more strongly with religion and with the home, particularly suited for conducting the family devotions of domestic religion. The importance placed on women as nurturers and educators of children in this period, and the increasing emphasis on family prayer as a way of moulding and training children's religious sensibilities, further strengthened women's association with family prayer.[83] As a result, many editors urged on mothers the responsibility of family prayer. One article spoke of a mother whose family was too busy for family prayer, so she 'sometimes conducted family prayers in the parlor alone. But the children who were preparing for breakfast could hear her voice in prayer, and it was not in vain.[84] The churches may have preferred to hark back to an age where the father led family prayer. However, their fear that the practice of 'the family altar' was dying out led them to attempt more pragmatic solutions. The nature of such solutions suggests that they believed that men took little interest in active piety within the home and that women as the religious mainstay of the home were the only ones that could be trusted to maintain family prayer. Of course, by encouraging women to lead family prayer, the churches were reinforcing the already existing association of religiosity with the feminine, making it yet more difficult to convince men that leading the family in prayer, or even attending church, were manly practices.[85]

While the decline in family prayer was viewed as a serious threat to the unity of the Christian family, religious intermarriage, which one might think would be seen as a much more serious threat, was rarely mentioned in the Protestant papers.[86] This may have been because rates of religious intermarriage appear to have generally been relatively low. In most provinces in 1901, religious endogamy rates (marriage to a partner of the same religion) were over 90 per cent. While rates of endogamy were generally particularly high among Catholics, an exception to this pattern appears to have been Catholic–Protestant marriages in Ontario.[87] Rates of intermarriage in Toronto in particular were quite high (at up to a quarter of all Catholic marriages), reflecting the fact that the second- and third-generation Irish Catholic community in that city was becoming increasingly less culturally isolated from the larger Protestant society.[88] This helps to explain the significant anxiety about mixed Catholic–Protestant marriages that was commonly featured within the Toronto-based English Canadian *Catholic Register*. One writer for this journal put the case against intermarriage particularly clearly:

> [Mixed marriages] involve a peril to the faith of the Catholic spouse; they are an obstacle in the way of the education of the children; and they often persuade the mind to grow accustomed to a sense of equality among all religions, by the removal of a real distinction between the true and the false.[89]

The fact that English Canadian Catholics were a minority in a Protestant culture, and were indeed at considerable risk of intermarriage, makes such concern quite predictable. The lack of concern about this issue in *Le Messager Canadien* is not particularly surprising given the dominance of francophone Catholics in Quebec and the almost 98 per cent endogamy rates in the province. By the 1920s and 1930s, anxiety levels rise significantly, however, as fears of intermarriage become part of francophone Catholic nationalist rhetoric.[90]

The apparent lack of concern about intermarriage in the Protestant papers is a bit more surprising. It is true, however, that while denominations such as the Methodists were officially opposed to marriages with those of other denominations, religious leaders of Protestant denominations have historically been less concerned with intermarriage than has the Catholic hierarchy.[91] The lack of major public concern about marriages between Protestants of different denominations may also reflect the softening of denominational boundaries between evangelical denominations that was occurring in this period. While denominational differences certainly remained, there were increasing efforts at cooperation and a recognition of shared beliefs that would ultimately help lead to the union of the Methodists and Presbyterians in the United Church in 1925. Given the continued force of anti-Catholicism in this period, however, the relative absence of discussion of Catholic–Protestant intermarriage is more surprising. Such marriages would seem to strike at the heart of the ideal Christian family of the time, united in shared Christian belief and practice.[92] Of course, while levels of Catholic–Protestant marriages may have appeared high to an embattled Catholic minority, the numbers involved would have seemed much less significant to the majority culture. At the same time, more concern might have been expected. Apparently, among Protestants, the Catholic threat to the family lay more in the external threat posed by the 'predatory' priests and 'unnaturally' celibate nuns of contemporary anti-Catholic rhetoric than in fears of Catholics within the Protestant family.

Conclusion

This study of the ideals and anxieties presented in Christian periodicals provides important insights into the relationship between religion, gender, and family in turn-of-the-century Canada. This article reveals the existence of a range of common ideals across denominations. Idealization of the Christian home was shared, as was a profoundly unrealistic idealization of the Christian role of mothers. For rather different reasons, Catholics and the more liberal evangelical denominations, such as the Methodists, provided women with more options beyond the family than did the Anglicans. While religious anxieties were similar in many ways across denominations and regions, they did differ in both expected and more surprising directions. Anxieties about men's religious roles were strongest in British Columbia, where a skewed gender ratio left many men without the 'civilizing' and Christianizing influence of white women. While young men were the focus in British Columbia, francophone Catholics tended to focus more attention on the religiously delinquent husband and father. Further quantitative research is needed to determine the extent to which these anxieties were based in actual social practices and beliefs (or non-beliefs) of the groups that were the focus of concern.

Among Catholics, a particular emphasis on idealized Marian motherhood in this period made women part of the solution in dealing with irreligious men, while Anglicans were more likely to see women's active religiosity as part of the problem in keeping men out of the churches. All churches tried to bring men back into the churches and religious practice more generally, with a focus on a more manly Christianity, but such efforts had little success. Despite efforts to draw men into family prayer, most denominations recognized the increasingly strong association between women, Christianity, and the home and granted women Christian leadership roles in this important sphere. The anxieties expressed over male impiety and the decline of family prayer, and the fears of the challenges this apparently posed to both family unity and social order, demonstrate clearly that the efforts of today's evangelical churches to hark back to a golden age of Christian family piety and harmony lack any sense of historical memory.

Notes

I would like to express my sincerest appreciation to Lorraine O'Donnell for her excellent research and translation work on *Le Messager Canadien*. I would also like to thank Tina Block, Lana Castleman, John Threlfall, and Kelley Finney for their diligent research assistance. This research was funded by the Social Sciences and Humanities Research Council of Canada SSHRC-funded Canadian Families Project, by University of Victoria work-study positions, and by an internal SSHRC grant. I would like to thank John Blakely, Nancy Forestell, Ruth Frager, and Peter Gossage for their most helpful comments on earlier drafts of this article, and Christine Hudon for her advice.

1. For challenges to myths of the family in earlier eras, see Stephanie Coontz, *The Way We Never Were: American Families and the Nostalgia Trap* (New York: Basic Books, 1992), and Eric Sager, 'Canada's Families: An Historian's Perspective', in *Profiling Canada's Families II* (Ottawa: Vanier Institute of the Family, 2000).
2. Bettina Bradbury, 'Feminist Historians and Family History in Canada in the 1990s', *Journal of Family History* 25.3 (2000): 362–83; Cynthia R. Comacchio, *The Infinite Bonds of Family: Domesticity in Canada, 1850–1940* (Toronto: University of Toronto Press, 1999); Bettina Bradbury, ed., *Canadian Family History: Selected Readings* (Toronto: Copp Clark Pitman, 1992); and Lori Chambers and Edgar-Andre Montigny, *Family Matters: Papers in Post-Confederation Canadian Family History* (Toronto: Canadian Scholars Press, 1998). The social history of religion is much better developed in Quebec than in English Canada. See, for example, Lucia Ferretti, 'L'Église de Montréal (1900–1950) dans les mémoires et les thèses depuis 1980', *Etudes d'Histoire Religieuse: Societé Canadienne d'Histoire de l'Eglise Catholique* 59 (1993); Jean Hamelin and Nicole Gagnon, *Histoire du Catholicisme Québécoise,* vol. 3 (Montreal: Boreal Express, 1984); Louis Rousseau, 'À Propos du 'Réveil Religieux' dans le Quebec du XIXieme siécle: Où se loge le vrai d ébat?' *Revue d'histoire de l'Amerique française* 49.2 (1995): 223–45; and Jean Roy, 'Quelques influences françaises sur l'historiographie religieuse du Québec des dernières décennies', *Revue d'histoire de l'Amerique française* 51.2 (1997): 301–16. For regional work and community studies on the social history of religion that include some analysis of family, see, for example, Marguerite Van Die, '"The Marks of a Genuine Revival": Religion, Social Change, Gender and Community in Mid-Victorian Brantford, Ontario', *Canadian Historical Review* 79.3 (1998); Cecilia Morgan, *Public Men and Virtuous Women: The Gendered Languages of Religion and Politics in Upper Canada, 1791–1850* (Toronto: University of Toronto Press, 1996); Lynne Marks, *Revivals and Roller Rinks: Religion, Leisure and Identity in Late Nineteenth Century Small Town Ontario* (Toronto: University of Toronto Press, 1996); Andrée Lévesque, *Making and Breaking the Rules: Women in Quebec, 1919–1939* (Toronto: McClelland & Stewart, 1994); and Brian Clarke, *Piety and Nationalism: Lay Voluntary Associations and the Creation of an Irish-Catholic Community in Toronto, 1850–1895* (Montreal: McGill-Queen's University Press, 1993). For work that focuses on a single denomination and addresses family issues, see, for example, Neil Semple, *The Lord's Dominion: A History of Canadian Methodism* (Montreal: McGill-Queen's University Press, 1996); Hannah Lane, '"Wife, Mother, Sister, Friend": Methodist Women in St. Stephen, New Brunswick, 1861–1881', in *Separate Spheres: Women's Worlds in the 19th Century Maritimes,* Janet Guildford and Suzanne Morton, eds. (Fredericton, New Brunswick: Acadiensis Press, 1994); Christine Hudon, 'Des Dames Chretiénnes: La Spiritualité des Catholiques Québécoises au XIX Siècle', *Revue d'histoire de l'Amérique français* 49.2 (1995): 169–94; and Micheline Dumont-Johnson, Nadia Fahmy-Eid, and Johanne Daigle, *Les couventines: l'éducation des filles au Québec dans les congrégations religieuses enseignantes, 1840–1960* (Montreal: Boreal Express, 1986). For a slightly earlier period, see Serge Gangnon, *Mariage et Famille au Temps de Papineau* (Sainte-Foy, Quebec: Presse de L'Université Laval, 1993).
3. See, for example, Mary Ryan, *Cradle of the Middle Class: The Family in Oneida County, New York, 1790–1865* (Cambridge, UK: Cambridge University Press, 1981); Nancy Cott, *The Bonds of Womanhood: 'Woman's Sphere' in New England* (New Haven, CT: Yale University Press, 1977); Leonore Davidoff and Catherine Hall, *Family Fortunes: Men and Women of the English Middle Class* (London: Routledge, 1987); and Robert A. Orsi, *Thank You, St. Jude: Women's Devotion to the Patron Saint of Hopeless Causes* (New Haven, CT: Yale University Press, 1996).
4. Kathy Arnup, *Education for Motherhood: Advice for Mothers in Twentieth-Century Canada* (Toronto: University of Toronto Press, 1994); Mona Gleason, *Normalizing the Ideal: Psychology, Schooling, and the Family in Postwar Canada* (Toronto: University of Toronto Press, 1999); Cynthia Commachio, *'Nations Are Built of Babies': Saving Ontario's Mothers and Children 1900–1940* (Montreal: McGill-Queen's University Press, 1993); and Mary Louise Adams, *The Trouble with Normal: Postwar Youth and the Making of Heterosexuality* (Toronto: University of Toronto Press, 1997).
5. Scientific ideals were certainly beginning to gain more prominence in public and religious discourse from the latter part of the nineteenth century. In Canada, however, it was not until the First World War and the 1920s that religious discourse started to clearly be on the defensive in the face of the rising popular influence of scientific ideas. The extent to which the churches were able to either incorporate the new scientific worldviews into their own discourse or lose legitimacy as a result of the increasing dominance of scientific discourse is the subject of ongoing debate. See, for example, Ramsay Cook, *The Regenerators* (Toronto: University of Toronto Press, 1985); Nancy Christie and Michael Gauvreau, *A Full-Orbed Christianity: The Protestant Churches and Social Welfare in Canada, 1900–1940* (Montreal: McGill-Queen's University

Press, 1996); and Mariana Valverde, *The Age of Light, Soap, and Water: Moral Reform in English Canada, 1885–1925* (Toronto: McClelland & Stewart, 1991).

6. The journals studied are the following: *Christian Guardian* (Methodist, national, central Canadian), *Western Methodist Recorder* (Methodist, British Columbia), *The Canadian Churchman* (Anglican, national, central Canadian), *Catholic Register* (Catholic, English Canadian), *Le Messager Canadien du Sacre-Coeur de Jesus* (Catholic, French Canadian), *The Religious Intelligencer* (Baptist, Maritimes), *The Messenger and Visitor* (Baptist, Maritimes), *The Westminister* (Presbyterian, national but primarily central Canada and the West), *The Presbyterian* (Presbyterian, national but primarily central Canada and the West), *The Church Record* (Anglican, British Columbia), *The Canadian Epworth Era* (Methodist, official paper of the young people's association, the Epworth League), *The Aylesford Union* (Baptist, local, Nova Scotia), *The Church Observer* (Anglican, local, Nova Scotia), *Church and Home* (Presbyterian, local, New Brunswick), *Salt Spring Island Parish and Home* (Anglican, local, British Columbia), *Stratford Parish Magazine* (Anglican, local, Ontario), *Parish and Home* (Anglican, local, Ontario), *The Diocesan and Parish Magazine* (Anglican, local, British Columbia), and *Home and Youth* (interdenominational). These journals were studied for various years between 1893 and 1908. While all of these periodicals included selections from other journals as well as original articles, I assumed that the reprinted articles were selected to fit with the editorial approach of the journal.

   In addition to the journals listed above, Vanessa McKenzie's master's thesis, 'This Vexed Question: Womanhood and the "Woman Question" in the Methodist Christian Guardian, Presbyterian Record, Anglican Canadian Churchman and Canadian Baptist, 1890–1914' (Queen's University, 1996), provided a valuable study of gender roles (both masculine and feminine) in two religious journals that were not included in this study (i.e., the *Presbyterian Record* and the *Canadian Baptist*, both central Canadian journals of their respective denominations). The fact that I have only included one French Canadian Catholic journal makes me particularly cautious about making generalizations about French Canadian Catholic attitudes. *Le Messager Canadien* is the journal of a particular devotion—to the Sacred Heart (of Jesus). The growing popularity of this devotion over this period, and of the journal as a 'family paper', does, however, make this journal an appropriate choice. The study of this journal is useful in providing at least some clues regarding commonalities and differences between English and French Canadian attitudes regarding religion and family.

7. See J. R. Miller, 'Anti-Catholic Thought in Victorian Canada', *Canadian Historical Review* 66.4 (1985).

8. Adele Perry has discussed concerns about the relative absence of European women and thus heterosexual families in the earlier period of colonial British Columbia. However, she does not address the issue of religion directly. See Adele Perry, '"Oh I'm Just Sick of the Faces of Men": Gender Imbalance, Race, Sexuality and Sociability in Nineteenth-Century British Columbia', *BC Studies* 105–6 (Spring–Summer 1995): 27–43.

9. See Marks, *Revivals and Roller Rinks*, chaps. 2 and 3, and Semple, *The Lord's Dominion*, chap. 13. Among Catholics, the church hierarchy had primary control over the content of the journals.

10. See Colleen McDannell, *The Christian Home in Victorian America, 1840–1900* (Bloomington: Indiana University Press, 1986), 55–6. Journals for the home can be contrasted with those more learned religious journals that focused more of their attention on theological controversies, although such issues were not necessarily absent from the journals discussed here.

11. For specific discussions of the way women (particularly middle-class women) in both English and French Canada took the teachings of the church very seriously, see Hudon, 'Des Dames Chretiennes'; Marguerite Van Die, '"A Woman's Awakening": Evangelical Belief and Female Spirituality in Mid-Nineteenth Century Canada', in *Canadian Women. A Reader*, Wendy Mitchinson et al, eds. (Toronto: Harcourt Brace, 1996), 49–67; and Sharon Cook, 'Beyond the Congregation', in *Aspects of the Canadian Evangelical Experience*, George Rawlyk, ed. (Montreal: McGill-Queen's University Press, 1997). In *Piety and Nationalism*, Brian Clarke also provides some compelling evidence of working-class Catholic women's piety. For works that examine the relative hegemonic power of the churches at this time, see, for example, Clarke, *Piety and Nationalism*; Lucia Ferretti, *Entre Voisins: La societe paroissiale en milieu urbain Saint-Pierre Apotre de Montréal, 1848–1930* (Montreal: Boreal, 1992); Christie and Gauvreau, *Full-Orbed Christianity*; and Marks, *Revivals and Roller Rinks*.

12. As part of the Canadian Families Project, I am conducting quantitative research projects on questions of religious involvement and noninvolvement that will be linked to the findings of this article. See, for example, Lynne Marks, 'Exploring Regional Diversity in Patterns of Religious Participation', *Historical Methods* 33.4 (Fall 2000): 247–55. and 'A Godless Province? A Gender, Family, Race and Class Analysis of Non-Belief in British Columbia in 1901', a paper presented at the Canadian Historical Association meeting, Sherbrooke, Quebec, June 1999.

13. *Le Messager Canadien*, August 1899, 370. However, most images of the family in this journal were of the heterosexual nuclear family.
14. *Western Methodist Recorder*, October 1901, 7, and *Canadian Churchman*, 2 February 1899, 76. Also see *Canadian Churchman*, 27 April 1899, 268, and *Messenger and Visitor*, 3 August 1898, 2.
15. *Western Methodist Recorder*, 20 December 1899. Also see *Western Methodist Recorder*, July 1904, 1–2; *Canadian Churchman*, 2 February 1899, 78; *Canadian Epworth Era*, 14 November 1900; *Religious Intelligencer*, 24 January 1900, 1; and *Church and Home*, April 1897, 47. For a more detailed discussion of this issue, see Mariana Valverde, 'When the Mother of the Race Is Free', in *Gender Conflicts*, Franca Iacovetta and Mariana Valverde, eds. (Toronto: University of Toronto Press, 1992), and Antoinette Burton, *Burdens of History* (Chapel Hill: University of North Carolina Press, 1994).
16. Marie Anne Pagliarini, 'The Pure American Woman and the Wicked Catholic Priest: An Analysis of Anti-Catholic Literature in Antebellum America', *Religion and American Culture* 1999 (Winter). While such stories were not found in the religious literature examined here, they were circulating widely in Canada in this period through the literature and travelling speakers of such organizations as the Protestant Protective Association. See, for example, Miller, 'Anti-Catholic Thought', and Marks, *Revivals and Roller Rinks*, 37–42.
17. *Catholic Register*, 28 September 1893, 1.
18. See, for example, Cott, 'Bonds of Womanhood', and Davidoff and Hall, 'Family Fortunes'.
19. *Le Messager Canadien*, March 1896, 77–81. Translation by Lorraine O'Donnell (who did all translations of *Le Messager Canadien* cited in this article). Also see *Le Messager Canadien*, November 1898, 505–6; June 1899, 251; and July 1899, 328–9. While the *Catholic Register* is much less likely to make explicit comparisons between ideal mothers and Mary, the image of the ideal mother as completely self-sacrificing is also clear. See, for example, *Catholic Register*, 14 May 1893, 6; 4 May 1893, 2; and 27 July 1893, 7. For images of Mary as the ideal mother in American Catholicism, see McDannell, *Christian Home in Victorian America*, 142–5.
20. See Hudon, 'Des Dames Chretiennes', 174; McDannell, *Christian Home in Victorian America,* 15; and Clarke, *Piety and Nationalism*, 78–9.
21. *Le Messager Canadien*, July 1898, 331; *Western Methodist Recorder*, December 1906, 10–13, and August 1904, 7.
22. McKenzie, 'This Vexed Question', chaps. 3 and 4, points out that Anglicans believed that women should remain in the home, while for Presbyterians the only sanctioned role beyond the home was as a missionary.
23. *Catholic Register*, 1 June 1893, 7. Regarding the choice to enter a convent and the large number of Quebec women making this choice in this period, see Marta Danylewycz, *Taking the Veil: An Alternative to Marriage, Motherhood, and Spinsterhood in Quebec, 1840–1920* (Toronto: McClelland & Stewart, 1987).
24. *Religious Intelligencer*, 12 August 1896, 7.
25. Also see ibid., 21 March 1900, 3; *Canadian Epworth Era*, 31 March 1899; and *Christian Guardian*, 11 October 1893, 642, and 16 September 1908, 14.
26. See, for example, *Canadian Churchman*, 19 March 1899, 172; *Religious Intelligencer*, 29 August 1900, 2; *Christian Guardian*, 21 June 1893.
27. McKenzie, 'This Vexed Question', chap. 3.
28. *Messenger and Visitor*, 4 May 1898, 3; *Religious Intelligencer*, 29 August 1900, 6; *Christian Guardian*, 13 September 1905, 5, and 10 December 1902, 790–1.
29. See, for example, Morgan, *Public Men and Virtuous Women,* 126–7, and Marks, *Revivals and Roller Rinks,* 174–5.
30. *Le Messager Canadien*, June 1897, 222–7, and January 1898, 24. *Catholic Register*, 16 February 1893, 5; 11 May 1893, 7; 17 September 1896. Also see Ann Taves, *The Household of Faith: Roman Catholic Devotions in Mid-Nineteenth-Century America* (Notre Dame, IN: University of Notre Dame Press, 1986), chaps. 3 and 4; Hudon, 'Des Dames Chretiennes'; and McDannell, *Christian Home in Victorian America.* While there are very occasional references in the Protestant journals to God as Father and to the local church as home or family (suggesting again the impact of dominant familial and domestic imagery), there is nothing really comparable in the Protestant literature to the Catholic 'alternative family' metaphor.
31. *Le Messager Canadien*, July 1897, 247–54; see also January 1897, 9–15, and January 1896, 28. *Catholic Register,* 14 September 1893, 6 and 9.
32. *Messenger and Visitor*, 24 August 1898, 10, and *Religious Intelligencer*, 28 March 1900, 2. Also see *Canadian Churchman*, 19 January 1899, 44.
33. *Le Messager Canadien*, August 1899, 370–1; October 1896, 328; May 1899, 222–5; and August 1899, 369–71. Also see *Catholic Register*, 9 March 1893, 6. McDannell, *Christian Home in Victorian America*, chap. 4.
34. See, for example, *Canadian Epworth Era*, March 1901, 5.
35. *Canadian Epworth Era*, February 1900, 17, and April 1901, 16, and *Church and Home,* January 1897, 10–11. Also see Marks, *Revivals and Roller Rinks*, 33.

36. *Le Messager Canadien*, August 1901, 342.
37. See, for example, *Religious Intelligencer*, 13 July 1900, 2.
38. Ibid., 1 August 1900, 2. Also see *Western Methodist Recorder*, January, 1900, 1, and *Catholic Register*, 4 May 1893,8.
39. *Catholic Register*, 2 May 1901, 6. Also see Hudon, 'Des Dames Chretiennes', 178.
40. See, for example, *Canadian Epworth Era*, August 1899, 28, and July 1901, 10–11. In 'Beyond the Congregation', Sharon Cook discusses the ideal relationship between evangelical mothers and their sons.
41. See, for example, *Western Methodist Recorder*, August 1900, 3; *Catholic Register*, 24 January 1901, 6; McDannell, *Christian Home in Victorian America*, 129; and McKenzie, 'This Vexed Question'.
42. *Messenger and Visitor*, 22 June 1898, 10.
43. See, for example, *Catholic Register*, 23 July 1896, 6; *Religious Intelligencer*, 20 May 1896, 3; *Messenger and Visitor*, 7 September 1898, 10; *Parish and Home*, April 1897, 46; and *Canadian Epworth Era*, April 1901, 31.
44. For studies of women and housework, see, for example, Susan Strasser, *Never Done: A History of American Housework* (New York: Henry Holt, 2000), and Ruth Schwartz Cowan, *More Work for Mother: The Ironies of Household Technology from the Open Hearth to the Microwave* (New York: Basic Books, 1983). For discussions of Canadian rural and working class women's work, see Marjorie Cohen, *Women's Work, Markets and Economic Development in Nineteenth-Century Ontario* (Toronto: University of Toronto Press, 1988), and Bettina Bradbury, *Working Families: Age, Gender; and Daily Survival in Industrializing Montreal* (Toronto: McClelland & Stewart, 1993).
45. See, for example, *Religious Intelligencer*, 12 August 1896, 7; *Canadian Epworth Era*, 31 March 1899; and *Canadian Churchman*, 29 June 1899, 414.
46. See, for example, *Catholic Register*, 4 May 1899, 3; *Religious Intelligencer*, 24 March 1896, 4; *Canadian Churchman*, 19 March 1899, 172; *Church Record*, June 1897, 63–4; and Marks, *Revivals and Roller Rinks*, 30–7.
47. *Presbyterian*, 6 June 1903, 736.
48. Semple, *The Lord's Dominion*, 385. See, for example, *Canadian Epworth Era*, February 1899, 14; May 1899, 8; March 1900, 25; and April 1900, 23.
49. See *Western Methodist Recorder*, December 1899, 12 and 19; January 1900, 9; December 1900, 6.
50. Men made up 71 per cent of the adult (fifteen years or older) non-aboriginal population in 1901 (men n = 81,946, women n = 33,687). Perry, 'Sick of the Faces of Men', 36.
51. See Marks, 'A Godless Province?'
52. *Western Methodist Recorder*, December 1900, 6.
53. Ibid., February 1904, 7. For the creation of another club, see October 1901, 14.
54. *Westminister*, 6 January 1900, 14.
55. *Presbyterian*, 20 September 1902, 361, and 11 June 1904.
56. See Sylvia Van Kirk, *'Many Tender Ties':Women in Fur-Trade Society in Western Canada, 1670–1870* (Winnipeg: Watson and Dwyer, 1980), and Sarah Carter, 'Categories and Terrains of Exclusion: Constructing the "Indian Woman" in the Early Settlement Era in Western Canada', in *Gender and History in Canada*, Joy Parr and Mark Rosenfeld, eds. (Toronto: Copp Clark, 1996).
57. Marks, 'A Godless Province?'; A. Schwantes, *Radical Heritage: Labor, Socialism and Reform in Washington and British Columbia, 1885–1917* (Vancouver: Douglas and McIntyre, 1979); A. Ross McCormack, *Reformers, Rebels and Revolutionaries: The Western Canadian Radical Movement, 1899–1919* (Toronto: University of Toronto Press, 1977); and Allen Seager, 'Socialists and Workers: The Western Canadian Coal Miners, 1900–1921', *Labour/Le travail* 16 (Fall 1985).
58. See Marks, 'A Godless Province?' and Bob Stewart, '"That's the BC Spirit!" Religion and Secularity in Lotus Land', *Canadian Society of Church History*, Papers (1983).
59. Marks, *Revivals and Roller Rinks*, chap. 2, and Cook, *Regenerators*.
60. For a discussion of the moral dangers facing young men, see, for example, *Le Messager Canadien*, April 1901, 145–9; October 1903, 434; June 1904, 257; and October 1905, 437–8.
61. Ibid., February 1903, 50–4. Also see Hudon, 'Des Dames Chretiennes', 172, and Christine Hudon, *Pretres et fideles dans le diocese de Saint-Hyacinthe, 1820–1875* (Sillery, Quebec: Septentrion, 1996), 398–400.
62. *Le Messager Canadien*, February 1903, 51.
63. Ibid., March 1901, 120. Also see October 1902, 451.
64. See, for example, ibid., August 1898, 353; June 1899, 248; and June 1901, 278–80. Also see Hudon, 'Des Dames Chretiennes', 178.
65. Marks, *Revivals and Roller Rinks*, 29.
66. See, for example, *Messenger and Visitor*, December 7, 1898, 5; *Stratford Parish Magazine*, 1 December 1894, 2; and *Parish and Home*, March 1897, 26.
67. *Church Record*, June 1897, 63–4. Also see McKenzie, 'This Vexed Question', chap 4.
68. *Canadian Churchman*, 10 December 1896, 770; March 28, 1895, 201; and January 17, 1895, 38.
69. *Western Methodist Recorder*, August 1906, 3; see also

February 1900, 6. *Messager Canadien*, April 1905, 145, and *Religious Intelligencer*, 29 August 1900, 4. Norman Knowles also speaks of the churches' recognition of the need for a more 'manly' discourse to attract men in the mining communities of British Columbia and Alberta. See Knowles, 'Christ in the Crowsnest: Religion and the Anglo-Protestant Working Class in the Crowsnest Pass, 1898–1918', in *Nation, Ideas, Identities: Essays in Honour of Ramsay Cook*, Michael D. Behiels and Marcel Martel, eds. (Toronto: Oxford University Press, 2000). For a discussion of concerns about the feminization of the Protestant churches in Canada and the United States, see, for example, Ann Douglas, *The Feminization of American Culture* (New York: Knopf, 1977); Marks, *Revivals and Roller Rinks*; and Susan Curtis, 'The Son of Man and God the Father', in *Meanings for Manhood: Constructions of Masculinity in Victorian America*, Mark Carnes and Clyde Griffen, eds. (Chicago: University of Chicago Press, 1990).

70. *Le Messager Canadien*, August 1904, 363, and Catholic Register, 6 July 1893, 10. Also see *Le Messager Canadien*, January 1903, 3, and April 1905, 145.
71. The anxiety of Methodists and Presbyterians regarding the feminization of the churches was seen more implicitly, for example, in their opposition to women-run church socials. (See Marks, *Revivals and Roller Rinks*, chap. 3.) The particularly conservative message put forth by the Anglicans might be explained in part by the fact that the main Anglican periodical examined for this study was the *Canadian Churchman*, which was the organ of the High Church group within the denomination. The Low Church, or more evangelical group, may have been more willing to accept women's active involvement in the church, as did the other evangelical denominations.
72. This idealization of motherhood appears to have been particularly powerful at the turn of the century, because both earlier in the nineteenth century and later in the twentieth century there was far more emphasis in Catholic ideology on the weaknesses and potential wildness of women. See McDannell, *Christian Home in Victorian America*, and Orsi, *Thank You, St. Jude.*
73. Tina Block, '"Housewifely Prayers" and Manly Visions: Gender, Faith and Family in Two Victoria Churches, 1945–1960' (Master's thesis, University of Victoria, 1999).
74. For concerns regarding the decline of family prayer, see, for example, *Canadian Epworth Era*, October 1900, 4–5, and June 1901, 15; *Canadian Churchman*, April 27, 1899, 268; and *Religious Intelligencer*, 9 September 1896, 1, and 28 March 1900, 2.
75. *Religious Intelligencer*, 13 June 1900, 2. Also see Lynne Marks, 'Railing, Tattling, and General Rumour: Gossip, Gender, and Church Regulation in Upper Canada', *Canadian Historical Review* 81 (2000): 380–402, for a discussion of churches' shift away from control over what we would now define as private behaviour.
76. *Le Messager Canadien*, August 1899, 370. Also see *Religious Intelligencer*, 13 June 1900, 2. This was the earlier ideal in Upper Canadian Protestant denominations. See Morgan, *Public Men and Virtuous Women*, 127. The image of the father leading family prayer remained important in the Quebec tradition of the father's New Year's Eve blessing to his family. (Thanks to Peter Gossage for this reference.)
77. *Le Messager Canadien*, May 1899, 223–4, and October 1896, 328.
78. *Canadian Churchman*, 27 April 1899, 268, and 17 August 1905, 529.
79. *Religious Intelligencer*, 2 September 1896, 2.
80. *Le Messager Canadien*, October 1901, 457, and March 1902, 98–9.
81. Ibid., June 1904, 251–2.
82. Marguerite Van Die, 'Marks of a Genuine Revival'.
83. McDannell, *Christian Home in Victorian America*, chap. 6.
84. *Religious Intelligencer*, 13 June 1900, 2.
85. Also see McDannell, *Christian Home in Victorian America*, chap. 5 and 6.
86. One of the very few cases found was in the *Western Methodist Recorder*, July 1906, 3–5.
87. Stacie D.A. Burke, 'Marriage in 1901 Canada: An Ecological Perspective', *Journal of Family History* 26 (2001): 189–219, and Madeline Richards, *Ethnic Groups and Marital Choices: Ethnic History and Marital Assimilation in Canada, 1871 and 1971* (Vancouver: UBC Press, 1991), 115–16.
88. Mark McGowan, *The Waning of the Green: Catholics, the Irish, and Identity in Toronto, 1887–1922* (Montreal: McGill-Queen's University Press, 1999), chap. 3. The rate of intermarriage is, however, difficult to quantify exactly, given the limitations of the sources. The Catholic intermarriage figures provided by McGowan are difficult to compare to the endogamy statistics of Burke, since McGowan is using various sources that count the religion of spouses at time of marriage, while Burke is studying the religion of spouses who are already married (at which point, one spouse may have converted to maintain religious homogeneity in the marriage).
89. *Catholic Register*, 21 September 1893, 5. Also see 22 June 1893, 3; 24 October 1893, 4; 9 January 1896, 2; and 10 January 1901, 4.
90. For 1901 endogamy rates in Quebec, see Burke, 'Marriage in 1901 Canada', 189–219. For Catholic nationalist rhetoric against intermarriage, see, for

example, Lionel Groulx, *L'appel de la race* (Montreal: Bibliothéque de l'Action française, 1922).

91. Peter Ward, *Courtship, Love and Marriage in Nineteenth-Century English Canada* (Montreal: McGill-Queen's University Press, 1990), 23–4.
92. See J.R. Miller, 'Anti-Catholicism in Canada: From the British Conquest to the Great War', in *Creed and Culture*, Terrence Murphy and Gerald Stortz, eds. (Montreal: McGill-Queen's University Press, 1993).

Rediscovering our Foremothers Again: Racial Ideas of Canada's Early Feminists, 1885–1945

Janice Fiamengo

EDITORS' INTRODUCTION

Over the past decade English Canadian literature has assumed an unprecedented popularity and recognition both within Canada and internationally. Women have played a remarkably significant role in this literary resurgence. Short stories, novels, and plays by established authors like Margaret Atwood, Alice Munro, and Carol Shields are explicitly feminist in content and throw new light on the modern Canadian experience. Authors like Dionne Brandt, Ann Marie McDonald, Miriam Toews, Shani Mootoo, and Eden Robinson explore the gendered landscape of multicultural and multiracial Canada, with Brandt, McDonald, and Mootoo placing lesbian experience firmly on that map. This article by literary scholar Janice Fiamengo reminds us that these authors can lay claim to a long history of popular writing by Canadian women and shows us that this is by no means an uncomplicated legacy.

Here Fiamengo addresses how race worked in the fiction and non-fiction writing of what historians call 'first wave feminists'. As Brenda O'Neill explains in her article in this volume, the 'first wave' of feminism took place in the late nineteenth and early twentieth centuries and was especially concerned with addressing women's exclusion from formal political decision-making and authority, symbolized most concretely by the vote. The small spaces for women's political agency, so ably captured by Bettina Bradbury's analysis of politics in early nineteenth-century Montreal, had been sealed up entirely by the closing years of era. By launching highly organized, well-orchestrated, and eventually successful campaigns demanding women's right to vote, organizations like the Dominion Women's Enfranchisement League fundamentally challenged the undeniable and systemic sexism of Canadian political life. First-wave feminism owed no small part of this success to its manifold connections to what historians have variously called the social reform, progressive, or social purity movement. This loosely connected group of largely urban, protestant, and middle-class activists called for a more compassionate, rational, and moral society, one where poverty, alcohol and drug use, illness, uncleanliness, and ignorance would no longer threaten Canadians in general and women and children in particular.

The role of race and racism in first-wave feminism has been a vexed question for historians. The pioneering scholarship of historian Catherine Cleverdon positioned Canada's suffragists as heroines and this view, to the extent that anyone paid much attention, held sway until women's history emerged as a field of study in the 1970s.[1] In 1983 Carol Lee Bacchi argued that the campaign for women's right to vote was irreparably flawed by an inadequate analysis of capitalism's economic and social consequences and led by arrogant and self-interested champions who endeavoured to impose social and moral controls on immigrants, the working class, and rural peoples.[2] In the next decade historians created a critical re-evaluation that did not, *à la* Bacchi, deny the radicalism of first-wave feminists, but they did confirm that ideas of racial specificity and superiority were central to the thinking and action of these activists.[3] In French Canada, studies of the suffrage pioneers Marie Gérin-Lajoie and Idola St Jean continued to emphasize the value of the contribution to women's rights and the modernization of the community.[4]

In English-Canada the old agreement about the essential heroism of the first-wave feminist activists had essentially disappeared by the 1990s. Take Emily Murphy, a judge and member of the 'famous five' who successfully challenged the exclusion of women from category of 'persons' in the British North America Act in 1929. Murphy, celebrated as a tireless advocate and a role model for women, lost her place in the feminist pantheon and, in 1998, a women's shelter in British Columbia took her name off its door.[5] These shifts reflected, as scholarly trends so often do, a changing contemporary climate. As O'Neill points out, feminists of the 'third-wave' squarely rejected the 'universal woman' of earlier generations, calling instead for a feminist politics that recognizes all identities, including gender, as multiple. The increasing vocality and visibility of anti-racist feminism in the 1980s and 1990s further suggested that feminists not only needed to acknowledge the importance of race to the present, but critically examine the legacies of earlier generations of Canadian feminists.[6]

In this article Fiamengo offers a sophisticated and nuanced evaluation of race in the thinking of Sara Jeanette Duncan, Agnes Maule Machar, Nellie McClung, and Flora MacDonald Denison. Instead of celebrating these women as heroines or blasting them as unmitigated bigots, she uses the insights of post-colonial scholarship to explore how race functioned in their writing. Ideals of racial difference, she concludes, were central to the thinking of early Canadian feminists, but seldom in a straightforward way. Fiamengo argues that there was a variety of 'white feminist conceptions of racial difference', and that feminist ideals of equal justice complicated acceptance of racial hierarchy.

That Fiamengo reaches this conclusion through a study of literature seems worth nothing. Women played a central role in the development of Canadian literature since the early nineteenth century when authors like Susanna Moodie and Anna Jameson began to offer a vision of Canadian womanhood in print. Women like McClung were known as much for the writing—which sold remarkably well in its day—as they were for their activism. Mohawk Pauline Johnson was famous in early twentieth century Canada for performances, but also for her enormous literary output.[7] In the last ten years, literary scholars like Carole Gerson, Misao Dean, and Jennifer Henderson have offered sophisticated and unsentimental analyses of the body of Canadian women's writing, ones that, like Fiamengo's, have much to offer historians.[8]

Notes

1. Catherine Cleverdon, *The Woman Suffrage Movement in Canada* (Toronto: University of Toronto Press, 1950; rev. edn., 1974).
2. Carol Lee Bacchi, *Liberation Deferred: The Ideas of English Canadian Suffragists, 1877–1918* (Toronto: University of Toronto Press, 1983).
3. Mariana Valverde, *The Age of Light, Soap and Water: The Social Purity Movement in English Canada, 1885–1925* (Toronto: McClelland and Stewart, 1991); Mariana Valverde, '"When the Mother of the Race is Free": Race, Reproduction, and Sexuality in First-Wave Feminism', in *Gender Conflicts: New Essays in Women's History*, Franca Iacovetta and Mariana Valverde, eds. (Toronto: University of Toronto Press, 1992); Angus McLaren, *Our Own Master Race: Eugenics in Canada, 1885–1945* (Toronto: McClelland and Stewart, 1990).
4. See H. Pelletier-Baillargeon, Marie Gérin-Lajoie, *De mère en fille, la cause des femmes* (Montreal: Boréal,

1985); Karine H´bert, 'Une Organisation maternaliste au Québec. La Fédération nationale Saint-Jean-Baptiste et la bataille pour le vote des femmes', *Revue d'histoire d'Amérique française* 52.3 (Hiver 1999): 315–44.
5. 'Famous Suffragists Honoured', *Globe and Mail*, 19 October 2000.
6. See Enakshi Dua and Angela Robertson, eds., *Scratching the Surface: Canadian Anti-Racist Feminist Thought* (Toronto: The Women's Press, 1999).
7. See Veronica Strong-Boag and Carole Gerson, *Paddling Her Own Canoe: The Times and Texts of E. Pauline Johnson* (Toronto: University of Toronto Press, 2000); Carole Gerson and Veronica Strong-Boag, eds., *E. Pauline Johnson Tekahionwake: Collected Poems and Selected Prose* (Toronto: University of Toronto Press, 2002).
8. Carole Gerson, 'Nobler Savages: Representations of Native Women in the Writings of Susanna Moodie and Catherine Parr Traill', *Journal of Canadian Studies* 32.3 (Summer 1997): 5–21; Misao Dean, *Practising Femininity: Domestic Realism and the Performance of Gender in Early Canadian Fiction* (Toronto: University of Toronto Press, 1998); Jennifer Henderson, *Settler Feminism and Race Making in Canada* (Toronto: University of Toronto Press, 2002).

Questions for Critical Reading

1. In her essay in this volume Lynne Marks argues that historians of women pay insufficient attention to religion. How did religion shape the thought of the feminist authors discussed by Fiamengo?
2. Fiamengo argues that white supremacy was not simply 'in the air' of early twentieth-century Canada, but was something chosen or not chosen from a range of different discourses available. What kind of choices did early twentieth-century women have to think about human difference? Why might they chosen one set of ideas above another?
3. Why did historians writing in the 1970s see suffrage activists as heroines? Why did historians writing in the 1990s want to reconsider their legacy?
4. Compare the feminism of McClung, Machar, Duncan, and Denison to that of the 'third-wave' women discussed by O'Neill. How are they different? How are they the same?

The past decade witnessed a sea change in scholarship on the early Canadian women's movement as feminist scholars came to recognize (or were forced to see[1]) the racism of white feminist 'foremothers' and wrestled with its implications for critical practice. Whereas scholars in the 1970s and 1980s tended to celebrate the achievements of early suffrage and reform activists, often 'white-washing' (Smith, 1995: 93) their ideological impurities so that they might stand as icons of resistance, more recent scholarship by Carol Lee Bacchi, Angus McLaren, Mariana Valverde, and others has emphasized the imperialist and racist foundations of early Canadian 'feminism'.[2] Such work has been crucial in redressing the errors and omissions of white feminist scholarship. Critical reassessment, however, has often shaded into outright dismissal, and in the process some of the complexities of early feminist discourse have been lost in the reductive conclusion that all first-wave feminist writing promoted a monolithic racism. Investigation of Canada's past is, as Veronica Strong-Boag has suggested, an ongoing and open-ended process of reexamination guided by current concerns and theoretical perspectives, and it is perhaps time to take another look at early feminist engagements with race. As I hope to demonstrate, the differences between and within early white feminist writers are worth exploring for a number of reasons.

Recent developments in postcolonial and critical race theory, especially Homi Bhabha's emphasis on 'the ambivalence of colonial discourse' point the way to a nuanced reading of this complex archive. Particularly important for my purpose is the recognition that ideological formations such as white supremacy are rarely stable or coherent (Hall, 2000: 15). John Comaroff (1997) has stressed that scholars studying colonialism's history do well to pay attention to its 'moments of incoherence and inchoateness, its internal contortions and complexities' (165), because they often provided the points where resistance came to be focused.[3] Race was always a contested subject in nineteenth- and early-twentieth-century Canada,[4] and competing understandings of race within Social Darwinism and evangelical Christianity made the term itself highly unstable.[5] Scientific debate raised unanswered questions about how profound racial differences were and whether they were primarily biological or cultural (Anderson, 1991: 40–4). Furthermore, early white feminism also contained competing claims. Although Darwinian beliefs about the superiority of the Anglo-Saxon race and evangelical emphasis on the civilizing mission often fit smoothly with white feminist self-positioning as 'mothers of the race' (Valverde, 1992: 1) and 'crusaders for Empire' (Carty, 1999: 37), feminist rhetoric of equal justice for all complicated acceptance of racial hierarchy and made possible statements of empathy and solidarity with nonwhite people. Race ideologies are mobilized and contested in the fiction and nonfiction of four widely read writers of the late nineteenth and early twentieth centuries: Sara Jeannette Duncan, Agnes Maule Machar, Nellie McClung, and Flora MacDonald Denison. This preliminary overview of their race thinking is intended to encourage further consideration of their work and of the myriad associations between early feminism and discourses of race.

Emphasizing the variety of white feminist conceptions of racial difference is useful because it demonstrates that white supremacy, undeniably the dominant ideology during this period,[6] was nonetheless not absolute in Canadian society before the Second World War. Recognizing the diverse positions that whites could occupy in those years is crucial in avoiding extremes of apology (everyone thought like that, so we can't judge them for it) or disavowal (they were all racist, so their work isn't worth reading carefully) in order to understand how well-intentioned individuals negotiated the racial and racist discourses of their day. In this discussion, I follow Kwame Anthony Appiah and David Theo Goldberg in distinguishing between racism and racialism, problematic as such a manoeuvre is. Because the writers considered in this paper used a racial discourse, it is necessary to attempt a distinction in order to notice where racialism does not lead to racism. Put simply, racialism is the belief that particular races share certain inherited traits and characteristics (whether produced through culture or biology) that define 'a sort of racial essence' (Appiah, 1990: 5). Racism, in contrast, uses these traits to create a physical, intellectual, and moral hierarchy. It is probably safe to say that, because racialism was a constituent part of the formation of Western subjects, few white persons could have escaped racialist thinking; as Kay Anderson (1991) has argued, by the end of the nineteenth century, most white Canadians believed 'that the mental, moral, and physical differences between "the races" were profound' (61). Just how they understood those differences in relation to their own whiteness is the question that I explore in the following pages.

The feminist writer concerned most explicitly throughout her career with race and its connection to the British empire was Sara Jeannette Duncan (1861–1922). After her marriage to Everard Cotes, Duncan left Canada permanently in 1891 to live in India, thus exchanging one colonial society for another, and her experience of these two different colonies provided a complex subject for much of her writing. She had begun her Canadian career as a witty young journalist covering women's and social issues for the *Week*, the Toronto *Globe*, and the *Montreal Star*, and later she became a moderately successful novelist;

her articles and fiction explore national types, elaborate the significance of the imperial connection for Canada, and examine the British presence in India. Because her ongoing focus is the collision between the ideal and the real,[7] imperialism's founding narrative of justice and good government occupies much of the narrative energy. Emerging out of two decades of intense debate over Canada's future national existence, *The Imperlialist* (1904) is Duncan's impassioned tribute to an ideal of Canada inheriting the best of British civilization, 'rich with character and strong with conduct and hoary with ideals' (90), and then investing that best with its own 'bright freedom' (38). The novel also depicts the violent racial exclusions necessitated by that ideal. Painting an affectionately ironic portrait of the 'hard-working folk' of Elgin (37), a small manufacturing town in southern Ontario, the novel makes this developing community stand in for the social and political situation of the new nation as a whole, as old social barriers crumble and a spirit of independence and enterprise develops in the last decades of the nineteenth century. It is testimony to the power of Duncan's representation—and perhaps to the manner in which it has mirrored the self-conception and biases of the scholarly community—that until recently the novel has been celebrated as a text of colonial resistance because it claims a place for Canada within the empire and deplores the influence of American materialism.[8] Few scholars, myself included, have examined Duncan's blunt portrayal of Canada's racial hierarchy. Exiled from the largely Scots-Presbyterian and middle-class national community (Hubel, 1996; Thomas, 1996) are the reserve Indians of Moneida, who figure only as remainder in Duncan's chronicle of 'the making of a nation' (37). Duncan's Indians are thoroughly marginalized by the narrative as, at best, spectacle (the 'drunken Indians vociferous on their way to the lock-up' [3] or the papoose that a sensitive young Advena attempts to rescue from a 'drunken squaw' [35]); however, Indians are also necessary to the narrative as rationale for the text's political agenda. It is no accident that the election scandal that derails the hero's political career, aimed at strengthening ties with England, involves the bribery of Native voters. The narrator tells us (that) 'civilization had given him [the Indian] a vote, . . . and he has not yet learned to keep it anywhere but in his pocket' (240). Inability to govern themselves distinguishes the Moneida Natives, for whom the principles of democratic representation are meaningless. Remnants of a deservedly dying race, these historical relics resemble Homi Bhabha's colonial mimics, aping but never quite equaling civilized people. Duncan emphasizes how the Indian almost, but not quite, blends into the crowd of poor whites. He has 'taken on the sign of civilization' such that one might mistake his heritage but a closer look reveals 'the brown skin . . . and the high cheek-bones and the liquidly muddy eye' of the impostor' (239). Mrs Murchison remarks that she 'thought they were all gone long ago' (239), and the narrative makes it clear that the disappearance of the Indian is a necessary accompaniment to the regeneration of the British ideal in the New World. Canada's difference from the Old Country—summarized in Lorne's appreciative remark that 'there's room here' (120)—is predicated on Native absence.

Duncan's calm acceptance of the disappearance of Native peoples in *The Imperialist* seems to have been fairly widespread among white Canadian feminists in the late nineteenth century. Like their American counterparts, many white middle-class Canadian women came to recognize how industrial capitalism—which cosseted them in domesticity—depended on the difficult labour of their white working-class sisters. Agnes Maule Machar frequently identified 'the relation of rich and poor, or of employer and employed' (1893b: 1138), as *the* pressing social question requiring every Christian's earnest action; conviction of obligation leads her to quote approvingly the Social Gospel truism that 'We do not *own* our wealth, we *owe* our wealth' (1138) and to suggest that the capitalist needed state assistance in the form of protective labour legislation to 'wash the blood of guilt from his own garment' (1139). There was no similar widespread awareness of racial privilege, white feminists had coherent recognition that their wealth and comfort were purchased at the expense of Native peoples. The racial hierarchy that they saw, and in some cases deplored, seemed to them to have evolved naturally rather than to have constructed through conquest and pillage. Nellie McClung, for example spoke frequently of how Canadian egalitarianism had been born in the mutual struggle and cooperative ethic of white settlement. The absence of Native people from her myth of origins assumes the prior emptiness of the continent and reflects her belief that egalitarian community began with the arrival of whites. As late as 1942, McClung could write with pride of Canada that 'we have never coveted any people's land, nor stolen their food, nor sought to enslave their people.' Belief in Anglo-Saxon superiority mandated Canadians' twofold mission to civilize Native peoples and to Canadianize foreigners. In a biography of a fellow Christian and reformer, Machar referred to the good work of 'labouring by any method to humanize and Christianize the heathen at home' (1887: 759). Her conviction that certain human beings needed humanizing opened a wide field for her reform energies. Where these reformers saw racial injustice and suffering, they tended to believe that a more rigorous application of Christian and British ideals—rather than a change in the social order—was the solution. Belief in the civilizing mission of Anglo-Saxon Christianity was strong enough that even E. Pauline Johnson praised the work of missionary women, dedicating her poem 'A Request' to 'the noble society known as "the Woman's Auxiliary of Missions of the Church of England in Canada"—who are doing their utmost in the good work of sending missionaries to the Crees and Blackfeet' (821). The poem criticizes the brutal suppression of the Northwest rebellion and recommends the salvation of souls over military conquest.

Occasionally, however, Canada's racial hierarchy was, at least momentarily questioned. In an article for the *Week*, Duncan contemplated the unveiling of a bronze memorial monument to Joseph Brant, the Mohawk chief whose 'probity and prowess' (1886: 756) in aiding British forces during the American War of Independence caused the city of Brantford (Duncan's hometown) to be named after him. On the day of the unveiling, a group of Six Nations peoples attended the ceremony and danced to honour Brant. Duncan records a moment of pained recognition of Euro-Canadians' role in dispossessing Native peoples of their land and sovereignty. She admits with some embarrassment that 'One felt in a vaguely sentimental way the pang of the usurper at the sight of these early Indian freeholders of the soil, joining to honour him who had given allegiance to a power that robbed them of their right of tenantry, and all their wild ancestral life' (757). In speaking of the British as those who had 'robbed' Indian people 'of their right of tenantry' Duncan refers with unusual frankness to colonial history. At least for a moment, the violence of Canada's past presses itself upon her consciousness as she regards Brant's Iroquois descendants not as a backward and 'foreign' people but as the original and rightful tenants of the North American continent, deceived and betrayed. Experiencing 'the pang of the usurper', she is for a moment uncomfortable and guilty. In the final sentences of the article, Duncan emphasizes the irony of the monument, which pays tribute where it enforces submission. Imagining the future extinction of Native peoples—which she believed would occur in a few centuries—Duncan targets the monument's hypocrisy, trying to see it from the Native point of view: 'Shall liberty be any the less dear because fetters are of bronze and of honour? Shall extinction be any more acceptable because of carven memory? The strength and agility and endurance of the red man are set up before us in a graven image to his everlasting renown—but at what price?' (757).

Duncan's moment of usurper guilt nevertheless reveals how myths of empire work to contain a potentially disruptive empathy. In reflecting on the 'element of pathos' in the ceremony honouring 'the warrior of his race who did most to dispossess it of its great inheritance' (757), Duncan rewrites Aboriginal history as the surrender of a passive people. She does not mention that, far from simply giving allegiance to the British (and thus perhaps betraying his own people, as she obliquely suggests), Brant consistently demanded compensation for Iroquois contributions to British defence and was instrumental in securing the land near Grand River for his people. Moreover, her sympathy for Aboriginal peoples is limited by her emphasis on British honour, as Duncan reflects with pride on British justice in its dealings with this 'subject and alien race' (756), distinguishing Canadian compassion from the notoriously brutal treatment of Natives in the United States. 'And by no means least among British glories', she writes, 'should be the fact that whenever the Sovereign of the United Empire has by direct representation entered into treaty with, or received allegiance from, previously hostile tribes, the representative has been invariably reverenced, the treaty kept, and the allegiance recognized' (756). Although Duncan recognizes their painful dispossession, she asserts, paradoxically, that Native peoples have been relatively well treated by the British government. The contradiction between her exposure of British violence and her assertion of British benevolence is left unresolved.

Another writer in whom the claims of justice and the civilizing mission produced a complex blend of racial chauvinism and empathy was Agnes Maule Machar (1837–1927), a Protestant intellectual and reformer based in Kingston who was one of the first in Canada to argue for a socially oriented Christianity.[9] Often writing under the pen name 'Fidelis', Machar published poetry, novels, popular history, and essays revealing her commitment to women's education, poor relief, wilderness conservation, the rights of labour, and many other contemporary issues that were, for her, 'the integral human side of the Christian religion' (1891: 169). Machar shared Duncan's idealism, rejecting the materialism of the age and seeking a Canadian nationality founded on pure ideals rather than self-interest; like Duncan, she saw the greatest possibility for such a national identity in continued connection with Great Britain. Yet Machar's understanding of the imperial project was informed more explicitly than Duncan's by Christian evangelism, which led to a deeper commitment to social regeneration and moral citizenship. Machar's Christian sociology often constrains and sometimes radically broadens her race sympathies. In her narrative of empire, Canada is evidence of God at work in history, and the Anglo-Saxons are a kind of chosen people spreading moral truth and civilization. As James Greenlee and Charles Johnston explain, Christian imperialists often articulated empire not primarily in terms of the spread of railways, irrigation systems, and good government but as the fulfillment of a moral trust to evangelize the world. Evangelical Christianity was always at least potentially radicalizing because it—demanded that adherents think about justice and mercy. In 'Voices Crying in the Wilderness', 'Our Lady of the Slums', and many other essays, in which Machar held the Christian churches accountable for the human misery caused by industrialization, she spoke as one of Canada's most eloquent apostles for the Word made flesh—in other words, the Christian mandate to establish God's kingdom on Earth through practical social reforms.

At least in theory, Christianity was committed to 'the great truths of human brotherhood and human equality', as Machar frequently emphasized (1893b: 1138). In her understanding, missionaries had brought a materially better life and the priceless gift of salvation to the Indians of North America. Occasionally, as in her poem 'The Passing of Père La Brosse', Machar eulogizes the best French Canadian missionaries as those for whom 'White men or red, 'twas all the same' (1899: 27): race was irrelevant. But more often, in seeing non-Christians as heathens who needed to be saved, she positions nonbelievers, especially Native peoples, at a lower order of humanity.[10] In *Marjorie's Canadian Winter: A Story of the Northern Lights* (1893), Machar responds to tensions between French and English in Canada by stressing the essential unity of white people in North America—French Canadians, English Canadians, and Americans—through emphasis on their shared Christian errand. As Dianne Hallman (1997) points out, the organizing metaphor of the 'northern lights' equates Christianity with bringing light to a previously dark part of the world, necessarily aligning Native peoples with spiritual blankness and incomprehension (38–9). Hearing stories about Jesuit efforts to convert the Algonquins and Hurons, the novel's young heroine remembers the text 'The light shineth in darkness, and the darkness comprehendeth not', concluding that 'the Indians didn't comprehend' their teachers (225). Many of the novel's didactic tales highlight the heroic martyrdom of the Jesuits at the hands of their 'savage tormentors' (138). The best that the novel can manage seems to be peaceful interaction between fatherly whites and receptive Indians, as when we are told that 'They [the Indians] were very much like children, and in Champlain they always found a fatherly friend' (183). In this vision, conversion to the civilizing mission confers heroism on white men and women but only infantilized innocence and dependency on Native peoples. Machar's penchant for military metaphors has ominous overtones also. Machar speaks, for example, of the church's duty to fulfill its 'marching orders' (1887: 759) and praises the 'battle spirit' of the missionary enterprise in 'combating sin and darkness' on the way to 'the final victory' (1893b: 1140); such imagery implies and justifies harsh methods in the service of God.

Faith in the divine significance of British conquest did not blind Machar to the pain and violence that it involved, however, and a number of her evangelizing poems in *Lays of the 'True North' and Other Canadian Poems* (1899) render the suffering of the colonized in great detail and emotional intensity. Such suffering is sanctified by the overarching Christian plan but still dominates the text. For example, in 'The New World' (1899: 9), Machar includes twenty-two lines that describe the devastation of Indigenous peoples at the hands of white men, while eight lines justify the violence as providential. The first section of the poem is told from the perspective of the 'red men'; the word *strange* is used twice to describe the white invaders, whose white sails are characterized as 'omens dark of misery'. They bring 'strife and blood and tears' and 'desolation, death and pain'. Some of the suffering is the result of changes that most of Machar's readers would have regarded positively—for example, the imposition of agriculture—but other changes inflicted on the Indians, such as '[t]heir lodges leveled and their forests burned', are clearly wanton and un-Christian acts of colonial violence. Although there can be no doubting Machar's sincerity in celebrating the spread of Christianity, the poem's conclusion does not convey a convincing vision of peace and justice to offset its earlier violence.

Moreover, while Christian triumphalism may have helped Machar to rationalize violence in the past, her Social Gospel vision made her aware of suffering in the present and alert to opportunities to alleviate it. In 'Quebec to Ontario: A Plea for the Life of Riel, September, 1885' (1899: 36–7), Machar writes a sympathetic account of Louis Riel's leadership of the North-West Rebellion and an appeal for clemency. She characterizes Riel approvingly as 'one whose heart was fired at sight / Of suffering and wrong' (36), which for her were words of the highest praise. To praise Riel at all was to adopt a radical position at a time when many journalists were too apt to comment flippantly that 'The only defence which his best friends could make for his extraordinary conduct was to suggest that he was insane' (An Anglo-Canadian, 1886: 396). 'Quebec to Ontario' is not an explicit appeal for Métis rights and is written from the point of view of Quebec, suggesting that Machar understood the Northwest Rebellion primarily in terms of the historic tension between the two 'founding nations'. However, we can conclude that she followed news of the rebellion closely and believed that the Métis had legitimate grievances. In *Marjorie's Canadian Winter*, for example, the Northwest Rebellion is described as a case in which the Indians 'had real reason to complain of their treatment under the British flag' (1893: 335). The poem reveals Machar's sympathy for the weak and dispossessed. Emphasizing that past injustices fuel present bitterness, Machar hopes that greater awareness of suffering may pierce previously deaf ears as a result of the rebellion, and she ends the poem by stressing compassion as the best policy for a conquering nation:

> Pity the captive in your hand,
> Pity the conquered race;
> You—strong, victorious in the land—
> Grant us the victor's grace! (37)

Despite, or alongside, her fervent Christian faith, Machar's wide learning and capacity for sympathy sometimes contributed to assertions of the dignity of all races. In 1893, Machar wrote four articles for the *Week* reporting her 'Impressions of the Parliament of Religions' in Chicago at the World's Fair. Her response to the congress can be read within a number of contexts, including the growing secularism of Canadian society, which prompts her declaration that, 'Whatever agnostics may say, religion has not lost its interest as a paramount concern of our race', and the failure of Christian missions overseas, which Machar attributes to missionaries' 'failure to recognize' the spiritual value of Eastern faiths (1115). The gathering provided her with the opportunity, over a period of seventeen days, to listen to representatives from the world's major religions present the best cases for their faiths; it also enabled her to gaze with interest and admiration on 'the darker but not less earnest faces of the Wise Men of the East, swarthy, turbaned Hindoos, white-robed Cingalese, shaven, yellow-robed monks from Japan, Moslem and Brahmin and Chinese drawn from their distant homes . . . by their common interest in those sublime questions which are of such momentous importance to humanity' (1114). Inspired by the liberal spirit informing the congress, Machar enthuses that it testifies to 'the common basis of faith . . . [and] the common bond of brotherhood' across religions and races (1114). One can discern in these articles an interesting tension between two strands of her Christianity, as ecumenism pulls her to celebrate the 'core or kernel of spiritual truth' in every religion while Christian evangelicalism pulls her to emphasize 'the fuller and clearer light of Christianity' (1115). For Machar, an important object of the congress was the aid that it would give to the Christian church in its 'glorious mission to the human race' (1115). Learning to respect other peoples would assist missionaries in converting them. Yet Machar was so moved by the moral and intellectual force of the presentations that she also argues that the greatest aim of the congress should be a 'universal religion' combining the best of all faiths (1115). She was particularly intrigued by the papers on Buddhism and the concept of Nirvana, and she postulates that certain aspects of Buddhism, especially the release of the self from materialistic desires, might have a purifying influence on Christianity. Suggesting the remarkable conclusion that Christianity is only one form of truth—even if a more highly developed form than other religions—liberal ecumenism led Machar away from a Christian chauvinism that divided faiths into pure light and pure dark. At a time when Christian denominations competed for converts in all corners of the globe, and when many orthodox Christians thought that the congress endangered the dignity of Christianity,[11] Machar's respect for non-Christian faiths signalled the liberal dimension of her Christian humanism.

These articles are notable because they contain little of the Orientalism and condescension that one might expect in a text written by a devout, nineteenth-century Christian about Eastern peoples. Machar speaks in strong terms about the necessity of 'respect and justice to other forms of faith and those who hold them' (1116). Religious toleration is far more than the absence of coercion, she declares; rather, it 'recognizes the sacred and inalienable right of man to worship God according to his conscience, and which is quite compatible with the most ardent and tenacious grasp of what we ourselves hold for truth' (1116). Impressed with the conviction evidenced by the delegates and the worth of their conceptions, Machar even ironizes the term *heathen,* declaring that 'these heathen' orientals might teach many professing Christians a needed lesson' (1116). She takes seriously the rebuke by representatives from India and Japan that Christians too often fail to 'practice the 'teachings of Jesus', quoting in particular the criticism of a 'Hindoo monk' who delivered 'a not undeserved reproach' to overzealous missionaries indifferent to the cultural beliefs and social circumstances of those whom they wish to convert (1893b: 1140). She receives with respect a lecture by a 'Hindoo lady—Miss Jeanne Serabjiattir—who 'told in a soft voice and pleasing manner of the great and growing intellectual progress of "TheWomen of India"' (1140). And she notes particularly 'the stirring demonstration in celebration of Lincoln's proclamation of Negro emancipation, which brought out a large assemblage of African descent' (1893a: 1116).

In a separate article entitled 'Sidelights on the Columbian Exposition', Machar chronicles the other great opportunity presented by the conference: the chance to observe peoples and cultures from all over the world. She describes in reverent terms her sense of the significance of this spiritual and racial communion. '[T]he sight of this mingling and intermingling of races from north and south, from east and west, seem[s] to give a new sense, both of the essential oneness and outward diversity of our wonderful human family' (1209). Her description of the cultural fair along the Midway, though coloured by racial stereotype and a touch of condescension in her reference to these 'strange peoples', is remarkable for its delighted cataloguing of difference and its disinclination to hierarchize: 'Sable Africans and swarthy Arabs—looking, in their, long burnouses, like our ideals of sheikhs or Bible patriarchs— turbaned Hindoos, Javanese with their twisted kerchiefs for head gear, the Turkish fez and the Chinese pig-tail, blend with our commonplace European attire in a medley that is full of color and interest even to the careless observer' (1209). One could read her account as an example of the imperial gaze, delighting in its consumption of a 'medley' of exotic cultures laid out for its delectation.[12] Assumption of a natural hierarchy is suggested by Machar's 'complaint about the lack of an organizing scheme in the Midway, objecting to the dissonance created by 'the quaint melancholy clangour of Chinese gongs and drums' mingling strangely 'with the melodious strains of an Austrian band', while the 'pure orientalism' of a Cairo street sits uneasily beside 'the castellated gateway of Donegal Castle' (1210). Overall, though, Machar's account emphasizes the mutual enrichment and interdependence of cultures and religious traditions, as her final thoughts return not to the differences between races but to 'the close relationship of our human family, and the importance of drawing closer the ties of brotherhood' (1210). Finding evidence everywhere of the 'essential oneness' of human nature (1209), Machar concludes by hoping that all who visit the fair will come away with a 'realization of the long-reaching and many-colored web of humanity, stretching its unity in diversity from century to century' (1210). Her emphasis on ultimate unity is a significant break with the scientific racism of much late nineteenth-century thought, with its stress on hierarchizing difference. Machar's response to the World Congress of Religions reveals that, while her Christian triumphalist vision of Canada tended to position racial Others, particularly Native people, as lesser beings who needed to be made wholly human, her liberal ecumenical program for world citizenship made it possible for her to begin to understand white Canadians as only one group of truth seekers among many and one human strand in a vibrant and colourful tapestry.

Such endorsements of racial diversity also occur—and much more explicitly—in the writing of Prairie reformer Nellie McClung (1873–1951), who belonged to a later and more radical generation of Social Gospel activists. A tireless campaigner for temperance, women's suffrage, peace, democracy, and church reform, McClung was an effective leader who saw herself as a 'voice for the voiceless' (1935: 281).[13] Her vision of social reform developed at a time of expanding white settlement on the Prairies, racist fears about the immigration to Canada of 'foreigners', and developing international tensions between imperial powers. As previous references have indicated, Christianity and love for the British Empire (McClung once wrote 'My heart has been thrilled with what it is to be a citizen of the British empire'[14]) underpinned much of her thought; she was committed to Methodism (later the United

Church) and to British justice even though a critic of their failings. Her commitment to justice was at least partly forged by the hard conditions of rural life, especially the poverty and government neglect that destroyed struggling white settler families on the Prairies. The two ideological strands of ethnocentrism and a commitment to democratic citizenship produce a complex racial ideology in which racism and antiracism are difficult to separate. Arun Mukherjee (1995) and, to a lesser extent, Mariana Valverde (1991) have highlighted the racist and imperialist assumptions in McClung's fiction and essays, showing how belief in Christian mission work led McClung to dismiss the civilizations of non-Christian peoples and to mobilize racist stereotypes, particularly her association of Chinese men and opium. Valverde notes that 'the very origins, as well as the form of McClung's feminism are shaped by ethnocentric ideas' (120). Mukherjee's discussion indicates the difficulty of defining McClung's beliefs about race as Mukherjee shows, nearly every 'politically incorrect' (20) statement can be countered with a more progressive one. Here I will concentrate on some of McClung's uncollected writings in order to consider lesser known aspects of her thought and activism. These writings indicate that McClung struggled with the meaning of race throughout her life and showed herself capable of rethinking racist assumptions when the occasion demanded it; her sympathetic interest in racial Others highlights the progressiveness of her feminism even while she continued to rely on racial and racist discourses to frame her arguments.

The paradoxes of Christian commitment are everywhere in McClung's writing. Her belief in the ideals of Christian civilization limited her apprehension of the damage that settlement and government policies inflicted on Native peoples, yet that very commitment to Christian justice also galvanized some empathy for Native struggles. In *Clearing in the West* (1935), for example, McClung recounts how, as a child, she defended Métis and Indian rights to land and autonomy during the Riel Rebellion, arguing with her parents that the Métis had 'a grievance, a real one' (168). At the same time, her adult conception of Canada as a new country ('a great blank book' with 'no precedents to guide us' [1915: 96]) dismissed the First Nations entirely. A scene from *The Stream Runs Fast* (1945) demonstrates McClung's willingness to extend membership in the British imperial family to a Native father whose son is fighting in the First World War; McClung recognizes that 'He was one of us—and one who had made a big contribution. We were all citizens of the British Empire; we were all of the great family of the Next-of-Kin' (158). Family membership in the empire is clearly negotiated on white terms in this scene. Equal citizenship meant assimilation to Britishness, an inclusive alternative to the early-twentieth-century assertion of Native biological inferiority. At the same time, McClung often characterized Native peoples using more or less benign racial stereotypes invoking inherent difference. For example, she records how she was prevented from being lost in London's streets while attending a Methodist conference by a young Native woman (also attending the conference) who had the 'blessed native instinct' for direction (1945: 224); in linking this young woman's ability to negotiate direction with a wild bird's homing instinct, she betrays a tendency to equate Native peoples with God's lesser creatures. The autobiography in which these passages occur was the last book that McClung published, making it difficult to argue, as one might be tempted, that her racial beliefs progressed unidirectionally toward antiracism as she grew older. However, evidence from her papers reveals that she participated actively in antiracist causes toward the end of her life, most notably in defence of Japanese Canadians before and during the Second World War when she was nearing seventy years of age. McClung was more concerned about racial injustice than many of her white feminist contemporaries, and her belief in the God-given common humanity of all people anchored the liberating potential of her Social Gospel activism.

McClung was unusual in her stress on a multiracial vision of the country at a time when most whites took for granted that Canada would always be a white nation. At the London Methodist meeting cited above, she reacted with anger when southern American delegates refused to sit with the 'coloured people' of the African Methodist Church. 'We were seated near the malcontents, and quickly changed seats with them, wondering if they would carry their race prejudices to heaven,' she records sarcastically, reflecting that 'my soul was scorched with shame for my race' (1945: 221). From the early years of her career to the end of her life, McClung articulated a vision of Canada based on equal justice for all. 'One of my most glorious dreams,' she wrote famously for the Ottawa *Citizen* in 1915, 'is that Canada shall be known as the land of the fair deal.'[15] When she defined that phrase for *In Times like These* (1915), she listed racial justice as her first criterion of fairness: 'Canada should be a place where every race, colour and creed will be given exactly the same chance' (97). Living in a country that blended many peoples, Canadians, she believed, had an unprecedented opportunity for interracial understanding.[16] Too often, 'however, we are a pretty self-centred race, we Canadians', she lamented. [17] During the Second World War, McClung held on to the hope that a new world order might emerge from the fight against Hitler, dreaming of a regenerated society in which it would be recognized that 'all men are equal in God's sight, irrespective of race or colour. There are no superior races.'[18] The confusing elasticity of her use of the term *race* (which is sometimes synonymous with ethnicity, sometimes linked with colour, and at other times identified with nation) makes precise analysis of her meaning difficult but also seems to have enabled McClung to think flexibly about Canadian national identity. Her faith that all peoples could find a 'spiritual cement' to bind them together in communities of fellowship helped her to avoid the racist extremes of some fellow reformers.

As Mukherjee (1995) has stressed, such idealistic statements need to be considered in the context of McClung's racist and imperialist culture and weighed against her complicity with or opposition to the racism that McClung encountered in her daily life. For example, Mukherjee notes that McClung supported overseas Christian mission work, campaigned for women's suffrage with American racists, and wrote nothing about racial inequality when she travelled through the southern United States. 'Would it not seem interesting to know how McClung responded to the Jim Crow south and the racist feminism of the southern suffragists?' she asks (22). Indeed. While some of Mukherjee's queries about the extent to which McClung challenged friends and colleagues (e.g., Emily Murphy) on their racism may never be definitively answered, Mukherjee signals important future directions for work on McClung. Uncollected newspaper articles in McClung's personal papers give evidence of some of her more decisive and public antiracist stands and answer a few of Mukherjee's questions about McClung's antiracist practice.

Unlike some white suffragists, who voiced bitterness that they were denied the vote, while it was granted to ignorant men such as 'untutored Ruthenians and Galicians' [Ukrainians] (Bacchi, 1983: 53), McClung largely refused such postures of wounded racial superiority. In 1915, on the suffrage trail, she managed to avoid being drawn into racist arguments. The *Winnipeg Free Press* reported that McClung 'spoke passionately in defence of the foreign women' on the question of suffrage. 'Let it be remembered,' the newspaper quoted McClung, 'that there are far more foreign men than women in the country and there is no objection to their voting. It has even been urged that the vote should be taken from these foreign men because corrupt politicians have bought their votes. I wouldn't take away their vote, but I would remove their ignorance. There is no menace to be feared from the foreign women.'[19] In this instance, McClung does not refute the charge that 'foreign' men, mainly, it seems, Eastern and Southern Europeans, were particularly vulnerable to corrupt voting.[20] Her assumption that foreigners probably did need education betrays the paternalistic racialism of her thinking, but she does not call for exclusions, preferring a rhetoric of inclusivity and possibility. A number of newspaper articles from this period report McClung's '[s]tirring defence of foreign women'[21] during her wartime suffrage campaigns. In

1917, McClung seemed to contradict her earlier position by calling for the vote to be given to Canadian and English-born women first, as a special war measure however, she withdrew this suggestion and publicly acknowledged her error when Francis Marion Beynon criticized the idea in the pages of the *Grain Growers' Guide*.[22] While McClung likely believes that not all people understood democracy as well as the British, she rarely allowed that thinking to limit her commitment to voting rights for all citizens.

Angus McLaren has noted that racist and anti-immigrant mobilizing reached a peak during the Depression years, when economic hardship and the threat to public order caused by hordes of unemployed people exacerbated the racism of many Canadian officials, politicians, and business leaders. McClung's public statements during the 1930s on behalf of the Doukhobors in British Columbia, European Jews, and Chinese and Japanese Canadians reveal resistance to the fear-mongering of public officials and community elders, who frequently warned of racial threats to Canadians by unassimilable aliens (Valverde, 1991: 104–28). In fact, McClung was one of the few commentators to argue that the danger lay not in racial contamination by these others but in Canada's failure to fulfill its Christian obligation to people seeking refuge. Commenting on Canada's humanitarian obligation to accept Jews fleeing Hitler, she charged that 'in spite of our broad territory Canada has not been generous with the 'stranger at our gates' and insisted that 'unless we adopt a new policy . . . the verdict of history will be that the Canadian people were both short-sighted and hard of heart.'[23] She chided 'narrow racial groups of great political power', clearly naming and deploring the racism of whites.[24] 'Noted Author Bursts Bomb at City Rally' was the title of a Vancouver newspaper report for 10 October 1935, when McClung addressed a Liberal Party rally at the Empress Theatre in Vancouver to disagree explicitly with the Liberal MP's opposition to Oriental franchise. 'In my opinion every class and every creed of people should have equal rights,' McClung was reported to have said in explanation of her disagreement with Ian Mackenzie, Liberal MP for Vancouver Centre.[25] Two years later, when Japanese military aggression in China, combined with economic tensions at home, seemed to validate anti-Japanese discourse, McClung was urging Victoria residents to maintain justice in their dealings with the local Japanese Canadian population. 'It was a time,' the *Colonist* reported McClung as saying on 9 October 1937, 'to show kindness and understanding and not blame those who are powerless to help what is being done by the militia party.'[26] These statements reveal that, although her conception of the nation was ethnocentric in its celebration of British heritage, faith in British justice led her to oppose racial exclusivity and persecution.

After the bombing of Pearl Harbor by the Japanese on 7 December 1941, McClung's insistence on fairness was even more unusual and difficult to maintain.[27] Although a few individuals and newspaper editors counselled calm and consideration for the difficult position of Japanese Canadians, 'those voices advocating either a "tolerant" or even a "moderate" attitude were quickly submerged in the wave of anti-Japanese protest' (Adachi, 1976: 201). At this time, McClung wrote some of her most notable newspaper columns on Canadian race relations, revealing a commitment to justice in troubled times.[28] Her providential view of history enabled her to understand the so-called problem of Japanese Canadians in British Columbia as an opportunity for Canadians to test their commitment to justice. 'We have in this province of British Columbia 23,000 Japanese people, many of them natives of Canada and some of the second generation,' she wrote on 3 January 1942[29]

> We have an opportunity now of showing them that we do respect human rights and that democracy has a wide enough framework to give peace and security to all people of goodwill irrespective of race or colour. I believe that all precautions must be taken at this time, but we must not sink into Hitler's ways of persecution. We must not punish innocent people.

> The Canadian Japanese are not to blame for the treacherous attack on Pearl Harbor, nor for the other misdeeds of their misled people.

McClung went on to ask readers to remember that Canada's treatment of its citizens would be judged by history. 'A great opportunity is ours today to show a kindly spirit of watchful tolerance. Let us guard well, not only our bridges and our plants, but our good name for fair dealing. We must have precautions, but let us think of our Japanese, as human beings, not as enemy aliens.' 'Our Japanese' has a ring of paternalism but *also* stresses Japanese Canadian inclusion in the national family. The call to think outside racial categories and to see the full humanity of Japanese Canadians indicates the extent to which McClung could mobilize patriotic myth ('our good name for fair dealing') to oppose xenophobia. Given that, as a resident of Victoria, she believed herself to be in imminent danger of an air attack, this was no small achievement. Two weeks later, McClung returned to her theme of Canada's moral obligations. 'Last week I made a plea for the individual Japanese, that they should be treated fairly,' she reminded readers,

> and I know these sentiments will be challenged, for this is a time of excitement, when prejudices run riot. But we must remember we are a Christian people. On New Year's Day we confessed our sins and asked God to guide us. If we are to merit that guidance we must not allow hate centers to develop here . . . . Let us, the free people, do all in our power to keep open the gates of mercy, no matter what comes. A great purpose and design for humanity is being worked out in the world now before our eyes and we must not blot our part of the pattern.[30]

McClung's insistence that God's hand was guiding history and that Canadians had a vital role to play in its unfolding show her use of a Christian narrative of good warring against evil that made the protection of racialized victims a cornerstone of Canada's wartime mandate.

Mary Hallett and Marilyn Davis, authors of McClung's biography, have suggested that outright criticism of government policy would have been censored at this time. It certainly seems that McClung was under orders from her editor to avoid 'political' matters. In one article, she prefaced a few remarks on conscription with the injunction 'now don't be nervous, Mr Editor, I am not dealing with it in a political way.'[31] Whatever the reason, there is no record that McClung protested the internment of Japanese Canadians, which occurred shortly after these columns were published; the announcement of partial evacuation occurred on 14 January 1942; total evacuation of all persons of Japanese ancestry was announced on 26 February 1942. Rather than focusing on the internment, McClung turned her sights to the future, imagining the better Canada that should be built after the war, hoping that the Oriental franchise would be implemented immediately once the war ended as evidence that Canada would finally be 'through with racial antipathies' and characterizing the war as 'a war against all racial superiorities'.[32] Even to McClung, such statements must have seemed optimistic. As the war dragged on, many of her columns were devoted to strengthening morale: she urged all-out support for the war effort, with boosterish articles on conserving sugar, sharing food, making sacrifices, and salvaging useful materials. She continued to devote a good deal of print space to intemperance, which she occasionally targeted as one of the causes of the war. Her attention to wartime racial injustice was, in the end, weakened by her belief that God was on the Allies' side and that Canadians' moral energies should be fully concentrated on the war effort. Nonetheless, her articles on fair treatment for Japanese Canadians reveal that, unlike the majority of white Canadians in Western Canada, McClung was not swayed by wartime propaganda. Ultimately, her emphasis on Canada as a nation of immigrants and her belief in Christian democracy meant that she did not appreciate the unique situation of Native peoples; she promoted assimilation to British civilization as the answer to racial conflict. Nevertheless, her sense of her role in an unfolding Christian narrative often prompted concern for racial justice and explicit anti-racism work.

Christianity was such a powerful force behind social reform in the period under consideration that I will conclude by briefly considering another reformer whose feminism was animated by wide democratic sympathies but who moved away completely from Christianity to embrace Theosophy and the (so-called) brotherhood of races. Flora MacDonald Denison (1867–1921), based in Toronto was a leader in the Canadian Suffrage Association from 1906–14, a popular columnist for the Toronto *Sunday World* and *Saturday Night* during the same years, and later the founder of the Whitmanite Fellowship of Canada. As Deborah Gorham has argued Denison's precarious class status made Denison unusually sensitive to the way that gender and other determiners of social status worked in concert to disadvantage many Canadian women. In addition to being one of Canada's most radical suffragists (one of the few who supported the militant tactics of England's suffragettes) she was a spiritualist and a critic of social inequality whose unorthodox thinking about socialism, divorce, and the occult eventually caused an irreparable rift between her and fellow suffragists in Toronto.[33] Much of Denison's philosophy was influenced by Theosophy's combination of Darwinian science and Eastern mysticism.[34] With roots in Hinduism and Buddhism, and claiming that the mixing of races was integral to the next evolutionary plane of human existence. Theosophy explicitly rejected Anglo-Saxon and Christian chauvinism, promoting interracial harmony and a 'world-wide super-religion' (Lacombe, 1982: 102).[35] Early in her writing career, Denison published a novel entitled *Mary Melville, the Psychic* (1900), a fictional biography of her younger sister, whom Denison believed to have been psychically gifted. The novel is an important document of Denison's rejection of orthodox Christianity for its failure to implement Christ's teachings and its doctrine of eternal damnation. For my purpose here, it also contains suggestions of her antihegemonic thinking on race.

In the course of the novel, the precocious Mary Melville has a revelatory dream that indicts Christian missionary activity and reveals that social and religious truth is to be found in a society of 'dark-skinned people' who reject authoritarianism and hierarchy in favour of egalitarianism. In the dream, Mary is 'with a tribe of strange, dark-skinned people in a lovely valley' (148). A spiritual leader of the people is presenting an oration on 'Christianity in Christendom', a sweeping condemnation of Christian nations' greed and perpetual warfare. The speaker argues that Christianity has failed to lead the evolution of the human race, enumerating the suffering, poverty, and injustice of Christian nations, noting that, 'If half the energy spent in imposing ceremonies, in palatial cathedrals were spent bettering the social conditions of the people, there would be no starvation' (148). The speaker ends by castigating the arrogance of missionaries who assume that they have something to teach the peoples of non-Christian nations:

> Now these people call us heathens, because we do not know their Christ, who they claim, has done so much for them. We work away and all goes into the general coffers. We draw on that wealth as required for our support and comfort. One of the greatest crimes among us is to take more than we would give our brother. The greatest virtue among Christians is to grab all within reach, and the more 'you are able to control, the greater will be the homage paid you. These people propose to send us a missionary to teach us to live as they do,' and there arose a great cry, 'Keep him out! Keep him out!' (149)

Denison's rejection of Christianity in favour of an all-embracing world religion makes possible at least the beginnings of an anti-colonial critique of the racial politics of evangelical Christianity. This critique is not fully developed in the novel, but resistance to Christian chauvinism certainly places Denison outside mainstream cultural opinion. During and after the First World War, she operated a nature retreat called Bon Echo in the Ontario highlands, where followers of Walt Whitman gathered to consider the master's ideas, eat vegetarian food, and enjoy the natural surroundings. According to Michèle Lacombe (1998), activities at the retreat included discussion of Native spirituality. Lacombe has argued that Denison's appropriation of Native culture and her questionable treatment of Native staff at Bon Echo warrant criticism and deserve further investigation; nonetheless, the fact that Denison's writing rejects Anglo-Christian superiority and imagines the locus of truth in non-white and non-Christian cultures deserves to be recognized. Her unorthodox feminism demonstrates that at least some suffragists and reformers explicitly distanced themselves from the racist underpinnings of social reform ideology.

Constance Backhouse ends her study of the legal history of racism in Canada by noting that cases of resistance demonstrate that 'Those who espoused philosophies of white supremacy were not speaking in a moral vacuum' (278). Although racism was the dominant ideology in the period under consideration, it was not simply the air that early Canadians breathed, as is often asserted. Feminist reformers, like others, made choices from among a range of discourses, some of which enabled antihegemonic thinking about race. In particular, Machar's liberal ecumenism, McClung's fair deal, and Denison's Theosophy all seem to have favoured the development of inclusive understandings of race that saw difference as at least potentially an opportunity rather than a threat. Because of space constraints, I have only scratched the surface of their writing, and therefore my conclusions are tentative rather than definite. Important work remains to be done to contextualize and analyse the ideologies that frequently limited, but occasionally furthered, a racially inclusive white feminist vision in the early years of the Canadian women's movement.

Notes

I am grateful to the Social Sciences and Humanities Research Council of Canada for supporting the research upon which this paper is based. I would also like to thank Susan Gingell, Gabriele Helms, Joel Martineau, and Francis Zichy for giving of their time so generously to read and comment on earlier versions of this essay. The paper is much improved as a result of their suggestions; the limitations that remain are solely my responsibility.

1. Women of colour and Native women in Canada have been primarily responsible for prodding white feminists into this realization. As Donna Haraway has noted, to say that white women 'discovered' or 'came to 'realize' their complicity in racism really means that they 'were forced kicking and screaming to notice it' (157)! For a good example of such prodding, see Mukherjee, 'Right', on white feminist silence about Charlotte Perkins Gilman's racism.
2. McLaren see Valverde (1991), Perry (2001), Newman (1999), Gerson (1997), and Devereux (2000).
3. For an overview of scholarly interest in the tensions and contradictions of empire, see Stoler and Cooper (1997).
4. For an overview of Canadian thinking about race and national identity, particularly the relationship between Aboriginal peoples and Euro-Canadians, see Strong-Boag and Gerson, 2000: 19–32.
5. The instability of race in the late nineteenth century was exacerbated because it could mean 'different things simultaneously' (Valverde, 1992: 5). As Louise Michele Newman has suggested in her analysis of early American feminism, race often 'functioned as an absent presence' in white women's suffrage arguments (57). I deliberately keep the waters muddy by following the usage of my writers, evoking 'race' when referring to any people defined as foreign, non Anglo-Saxon, or nonwhite in situations where power and exclusion are at issue. I intend such conceptual muddiness to signal my disbelief in any immutable or absolute basis for racial distinction following recent theorists in understanding race not as a biological given but as a historically inflected idea produced through representation and constantly being remade in particular discursive situations. For an overview of central issues in race thinking, see Cornell and Hartmann, 1998: 15–38; for a history of race thinking, see Anderson, 1991: 38–44, and Bernasconi and Lott, 2000: vii–xviii.
6. See Backhouse for a study of 'the central role of the Canadian legal system in the establishment and enforcement of racial inequality' (15). For a discussion of moves to prevent the immigration of 'inferior' races, including Slavs, Jews, Southern Europeans, Orientals, and Blacks, see McLaren, 1990: 46–67.
7. See Dean, 1991, 46–53, for a discussion of Duncan's philosophical idealism.

8. See, for example, Heble (1996).
9. See Brouwer, (1984), Brouwer (1985); see Hallman (1997); see Cook (1985).
10. For a discussion of the racist judgments of Methodist missionaries on Eastern European immigrants and Native peoples in Canada, see Gagan, 1992: 178–203.
11. See Machar's defence of the congress against the 'shallow criticism and shallower sneers it met with in advance' (1893a: 1115).
12. According to Newman, the *Midway* at the World's Fair was constructed so that white Americans (and Canadians) could gawk at racialized human exhibits; the fact that these 'foreign' peoples were on display for white viewers affirmed white subjectivity and the othering of nonwhites (7). Machar's reaction suggests that it was possible for whites to choose subject positions other than that of racial superiority.
13. For a biography that discusses McClung's activism, see Hallett and Davis (1993); for a 'scrapbook' with extensive quotations, see Savage (1979). For an analysis of McClung's fiction from a feminist perspective, see Warne (1993).
14. Unidentified clipping, Nellie McClung Papers, PABC, vol. 17.
15. Untitled clipping, Nellie McClung Papers, PABC, vol. 17.
16. Untitled clipping, Regina *Star,* 9 November 1937, Nellie McClung Papers, PABC, vol. 17.
17. 'How Should We Celebrate July 1?' *Western Home Monthly,* July 1927, Nellie McClung Papers, PABC, vol. 15.
18. 'What Holds the British Empire Together'. Unidentified clipping; Nellie McClung Papers, PABC, vol. 14.
19. Unidentified clipping, Nellie McClung Papers, PABC, vol. 17.
20. But McClung also recorded how 'in our blind egotism we class our foreign people as ignorant people, if they do not know our ways and our language. They may know many other languages, but if they have not yet mastered ours they are poor, ignorant *foreigners.* We Anglo-Saxon people have a decided sense of our own superiority, and we feel sure that our skin is exactly the right color' (1915: 53).
21. Undated clipping, Nellie McClung Papers, PABC, vol. 17.
22. Untitled clipping, *Grain Growers' Guide,* 24 January 1917, Nellie McClung Papers, PABC, vol. 17.
23. Unidentified clipping, Nellie McClung Papers, PABC, vol. 17.
24. For a discussion of Canada's protracted unwillingness to offer refuge to European Jews, see Abella and Trooper (1982).
25. Unidentified clipping, Nellie McClung Papers, PABC, vol. 17. In the federal election campaign of 1935, the Liberals opposed the newly created CCF's stand on enfranchising Chinese and Japanese Canadians, vowing to defend the white electorate.
26. 'Urges Women to Consider Local Japanese People', *Victoria Colonist,* 9 October 1937, Nellie McClung Papers, PABC, vol. 17.
27. Within a week of the attack, demands were being made across British Columbia that all people of Japanese heritage be interned, and soon newspaper editorials began to support the majority public opinion. See Adachi, 1976: 201–2.
28. Mary Hallett and Marilyn Davis (1993: 274–6) also discuss these columns.
29. 'What Did We Learn in 1941?' Unidentified clipping, 3 January 1942, Nellie McClung Papers, PABC, vol. 52.
30. Unidentified clipping, 17 January 1942, Nellie McClung Papers, PABC, vol. 52.
31. Unidentified clipping, 21 February 1942, Nellie McClung Papers, PABC, vol. 52.
32. 'That We May Not Forget,' *Winnipeg Free Press,* 14 November 1942, Nellie McClung Papers, PABC, vol. 53.
33. See Gorham (1979); see also Cook, 1985: 78–84.
34. A fuller analysis of Denison's thinking on race may be gleaned from an examination of her papers, which I will soon undertake; Michèle Lacombe has a forthcoming biography that will likely explore the subject.
35. See Lacombe (1982) For a discussion of Denison's resort at Bon Echo, see Lacombe (1998).

References

Abella, Irving, and Harold Trooper. 1982. *None Is Too Many: Canada and the Jews of Europe, 1933–1948.* Toronto: Lester.

Adachi, Ken. 1976. *The Enemy That Never Was.* Toronto: McClelland.

An Anglo-Canadian. 'Teutons and Celts—1'. *Week* (20 May 1886): 395–6.

Anderson, Kay J. 1991. *Vancouver's Chinatown: Racial Discourse in Canada, 1875–1980.* Montreal: McGill-Queen's University Press.

Appiah, Kwame Anthony. 1990. 'Racisms', pp. 3–17 in *Anatomy of Racism*, D. Goldberg, ed. Minneapolis: U of Minnesota Press.

Bacchi, Carol Lee. 1983. *Liberation Deferred? The Ideas of the English-Canadian Suffragists, 1877–1918.* Toronto: University of Toronto Press.

Backhouse, Constance. 1999. *Colour-Coded: A Legal History of Racism in Canada, 1900–1950*. Toronto: University of Toronto Press.

Bernasconi, Robert, and Tommy L. Lott, eds. 2000. *The Idea of Race*. Indianapolis: Hackett.

Bhabha, Homi. 1997. 'Of Mimicry and Man: The Ambivalence of Colonial Discourse', pp. 152–60, in *Tensions of Empire: Colonial Cultures in the Bourgeois World*, F. Cooper and A.L. Stoler, eds. Berkeley: University of California Press.

Brouwer, Ruth Compton. 'The 'Between-Age' Christianity of Agnes Machar', *Canadian Historical Review* 65.3 (1984): 347–70.

———. 'Moral Nationalism in Victorian Canada: The Case of Agnes Machar', *Journal of Canadian Studies* 20.1 (1985): 90–108.

Carlin, Deborah. 1993. '"What Methods Have Brought Blessing": Discourses of Reform in Philanthropic Literature', pp. 203–25, in *The (Other) American Traditions: Nineteenth-Century Women Writers*, Joyce W. Warren, ed. New Brunswick, NJ: Rutgers University Press.

Carty, Linda. 1999. 'The Discourse of Empire and the Social Construction of, Gender', pp. 35–47 in *Scratching the Surface: Canadian Anti-Racist Feminist Thought*, Enakshi Dua and Angela Robertson, eds. Toronto: Women's Press.

Comaroff, John L. 1997. 'Images of Empire, Contests of Conscience: Models of Colonial Domination in South Africa', pp. 163–97 in *Tensions of Empire: Colonial Cultures in the Bourgeois World*, F. Cooper and A.L. Stoler, eds. Berkeley: University of California Press.

Cook, Ramsay. 1985. *The Regenerators: Social Criticism in Late Victorian English Canada*. Toronto: University of Toronto Press.

Cooper, Frederick, and Ann Laura Stoler, eds. 1997. *Tensions of Empire: Colonial Cultures in the Bourgeois World*. Berkeley: University of California Press.

Cornell, Stephen, and Douglas Hartmann. 1998. *Ethnicity and Race: Making Identities in a Changing World*. Thousand Oaks, CA: Pine Forge.

Dean, Misao. 1991. *A Different Point of View: Sara Jeannette Duncan*. Montreal: McGill-Queen's University Press.

———. 'The Paintbrush and the Scalpel: Sara Jeannette Duncan Representing India', *Canadian Literature* 132 (1992): 82–93.

[Denison], Flora MacDonald. 1900. *Mary Melville, the Psychic*. Toronto: Austin.

Devereux, Cecily. 'Writing with a "Definite Purpose": L.M. Montgomery, Nellie L. McClung, and the Politics of Imperial Motherhood in Fiction for Children', *Canadian Children's Literature* 26: 3 (2000): 6–22.

Duncan, Sara Jeannette. 'Saunterings'. *Week* (21 October 1886): 756–7.

———. [1904] 1996. *The Imperialist*. Ottawa: Tecumseh.

———. [1906] 1996. *Set in Authority*, Germaine Warkentin, ed. Peterborough, ON: Broadview Press.

———. [1909] 1919. *The Burnt Offering*. London: Methuen.

Gagan, Rosemary R. 1992. *A Sensitive Independence: Canadian Methodist Women Missionaries in Canada and the Orient, 1881–1925*. Montreal: McGill-Queen's University Press.

Gerson, Carole. 'Nobler Savages: Representations of Native Women in the Writings of Susanna Moodie and Catharine Parr Traill', *Journal of Canadian Studies* 32.2 (1997): 5–21.

Goldberg, David Theo, ed. 1990. *Anatomy of Racism*. Minneapolis: University of Minnesota Press.

———. 1990. 'The Social Formation of Racist Discourse', pp. 295–318 in *Anatomy of Racism*, David Theo Goldberg, ed. Minneapolis: University of Minnesota Press.

Gorham, Deborah. 1979. 'Flora MacDonald Denison: Canadian Feminist', pp. 47–70 in *A Not Unreasonable Claim: Women and Reform in Canada, 1880s–1920s*, Linda Kealey, ed. Toronto: Women's Press.

Greenlee, James G., and Charles M. Johnston. 1999. *Good Citizens: British Missionaries and Imperial States, 1870–1918*. Montreal: McGill-Queen's University Press.

Hall, Catherine. 2000. 'Introduction: Thinking the Postcolonial, Thinking the Empire', pp. 1–33 in *Cultures of Empire: A Reader*, Catherine Hall, ed. New York: Routledge.

Hallet, Mary, and Marilyn Davis. 1993. *Firing the Heather: The Life and Times of Nellie McClung*. Saskatoon: Fifth House.

Hallman, Dianne M. 1997. 'Cultivating a Love of Canada through History: Agnes Maule Machar, 1837–1927', pp. 25–50 in *Creating Historical Memory: English-Canadian Women and the Work of History*, Beverly Boutilier and Alison Prentice, eds. Vancouver: UBC Press.

Haraway, Donna J. 1991. *Simians, Cyborgs, and Women: The Reinvention of Nature*. New York: Routledge.

Heble, Ajay. 1996. '"This Little Outpost of Empire": Sara Jeannette Duncan and the Decolonization of Canada', pp. 404–16 in *The Imperialist*. By Sara Jeanette Duncan, Thomas Tausky, ed. Ottawa: Tecumseh.

Hubel, Teresa. '"The Bride of His Country": Love, Marriage, and the Imperialist Paradox in the Indian Fiction of Sara Jeannette Duncan and Rudyard Kipling'. *Ariel* 21.1 (1990): 3–19.

———. 1996. 'Excavating the Expendable Working Classes In *The Imperialist*', pp. 437–55 in *The Imperialist*. By Sara Jeanette Duncan, Thomas Tausky, ed. Ottawa: Tecumseh.

Johnson, E. Pauline. 'A Request'. *Week* (18 November 1886): 821.

Lacombe, Michèle. '"Songs of the Open Road": Bon Echo, Urban Utopians and the Cult of Nature', *Journal of Canadian Studies* 33.2 (1998): 152–67.

———. 'Theosophy and the Canadian Idealist Tradition: A Preliminary Exploration', *Journal of Canadian Studies* 17.2 (1982): 100–18.

Lawn, Jennifer. '*The Simple Adventures of a Memsahib* and the Prisonhouse of Language'. *Canadian Literature* 132 (1992): 16–30.

Machar, Agnes Maule. 1887. 'Prominent Canadians—III', *Week* (20 October): 758–9.

———. 1893. *Marjorie's Canadian Winter: A Story of the Northern Lights.* Boston: Lothrop.

———. 1893a. 'Impressions of the Parliament of Religions', *Week* (20 October): 1114–17.

———. 1893b. 'Impressions of the Parliament of Religions—II', *Week* (27 October): 1138–41.

———. 1899. *Lays of the 'True North' and Other Canadian Poems.* Toronto: Copp.

———. 1891. 'Our Lady of the Slums', *Week* (13 March): 234–5.

———. 1891. 'Voices Crying in the Wilderness', *Week* (13 February): 169–70.

McClung, Nellie. [1915] 1972. *In Times like These.* Toronto: University of Toronto Press.

———.1935. *Clearing in the West.* Toronto: Allen.

———. 1945. *The Stream Runs Fast.* Toronto: Allen.

McLaren, Angus. 1990. *Our Own Master Race: Eugenics In Canada, 1885–1945.* Toronto: McClelland & Stewart.

Mukherjee, Arun P. 'In a Class of Her Own', *Literary Review of Canada* (July–August 1995): 20–3.

———. 1993. '"Right our of 'Herstory": Racism in Charlotte Perkins Gilman's *Herland* and Feminist Literary Theory', pp. 159–75 in *Returning the Gaze: Essays on Racism, Feminism, and Politics*, Himani Bannerji, ed. Toronto: Sister Vision.

Newman, Louise Michele. 1999. *White Women's Rights: The Racial Origins of Feminism in the United States.* New York: Oxford University Press.

Perry, Adele. 2001. *On the Edge of Empire: Gender, Race, and the Making of British Columbia, 1849–1871.* Toronto: University of Toronto Press.

Savage, Candace. 1979. *Our Nell: A Scrapbook Biography of Nellie L. McClung.* Saskatoon: Western Producer Prairie.

Smith, Susan L. 'Whitewashing Womanhood: The Politics of Race in Writing Women's History', *Canadian Review of Comparative Literature* 22.1 (1995): 93–103.

Stasiulis, Daiva, and Nira Yuval-Davis. 1995. 'Introduction: Beyond Dichotomies—Gender, Race, Ethnicity, and Class in Settler Societies', pp. 1–37 in *Unsettling Settler Societies: Articulations of Gender, Race, Ethnicity, and Class*, Daiva Stasiulis and Nira Yuval-Davis, eds. London: Sage.

Stoler, Ann Lama, and Frederick Cooper. 1997. 'Between Metropole and Colony: Rethinking a Research Agenda', pp. 1–56 in *Tensions of Empire: Colonial Cultures in the Bourgeois World*, F. Cooper and A.L. Stoler, eds. Berkeley: University of California Press.

Strong-Boag, Veronica. 'Contested Space: The Politics of Canadian Memory', *Journal of the Canadian Historical Association* 5 (1994): 3–18.

Strong-Boag, Veronica, and Carole Gerson. 2000. *Paddling Her Own Canoe: The Times and Texts of Pauline Johnson (Tekahionwake).* Toronto: University of Toronto Press.

Tausky, Thomas. 1980. *Sara Jeannette Duncan: Novelist of Empire.* Port Credit, ON: Meany.

———, ed. 1996. *The Imperialist.* By Sara Jeannette Duncan. Ottawa: Tecumseh.

Thomas, Clara. 1996. 'Canadian Social Mythologies in *The Imperialist*', pp. 356–68 in *The Imperialist.* By Sara Jeannette Duncan, Thomas Tausky, ed. Ottawa: Tecumseh.

Valverde, Mariana. 1991. *The Age of Light, Soap, and Water: Moral Reform in English Canada, 1885–1925.* Toronto: McClelland & Stewart.

———. 1992. '"When the Mother of the Race Is Free": Race, Reproduction, and Sexuality in First-Wave Feminism', pp. 3–26 in *Gender Conflicts: New Essays in Women's History*, Franca Iacovetta and Mariana Valverde, eds. Toronto: University of Toronto Press.

Warkentin, Germaine. 1996. 'Introduction', pp. 9–60 in *Set in Authority.* By Sara Jeanette Duncan, G. Warkentin, ed. Peterborough, ON: Broadview Press.

Warne, Randi R. 1993. *Literature as Pulpit: The Christian Social Activism of Nellie McClung.* Waterloo: Wilfrid Laurier University Press.

Claiming a Unique Place: The Introduction of Mothers' Pensions in British Columbia

Margaret Hillyard Little

EDITORS' INTRODUCTION

Contemporary feminist scholarship has much to say about the gendered and racialized nature of citizenship in Western democracies where white, able-bodied males have been widely regarded as the measure of normalcy. As the contributors to a recent collection of essays entitled *Contesting Canadian Citizenship* demonstrate, citizens have largely been evaluated as either wanting or satisfactory by reference to a criteria associated with presumed male characteristics in the public sphere, namely independence and autonomy.[1] Historically privatized within the household and dependent upon male relatives, women have rarely been regarded or treated as equal. Ideally, men, whether self-employed or freely contracting their labour to others, were to be able and willing to support their families on their own and to contribute to the public good. Since the early twentieth century men's citizenship claims upon the state have been based on the premise that their real or potential employment, military service, and taxpayer status have given them particular rights to support at times when they are unable to work for wages. Legislation providing workers compensation and veteran benefits enshrines the success of this argument.

In contrast, women's claims for assistance have more often been made from their position as dependents of men rather than as contributors to the larger community. In order to justify what are commonly regarded as their privileges—not rights—they have regularly had to prove that they are morally deserving of the state's support. In other words, the modern welfare state operates differently for men than it does for women. The frequency with which Canadians have had to call on this state for support suggests that the male breadwinner model, like separate spheres, was more ideal than reality. Many Canadian families have not fit into the pattern of male breadwinning. Some mothers never had husbands. Many working men have died in war, or of illness or work-related injuries, or have become too sick or disabled to earn a living. Others have deserted women and children. Some have been hard put to earn enough money to support their families on their own. Consequently, private individuals and groups and, increasingly, the state have been called on to deal with the breakdown or non-existence of the self-supporting male-headed family. They have done so in ways that reflect assumptions about the proper roles of women and men both at home and in the public world.

At the turn of the last century, feminist middle-class activists and their allies responded to poverty by demanding social and legal recognition of women's primary role as parents and men's responsibilities as breadwinners. As Little describes in detail in *'No Car, No Radio, No Liquor Permit': The Moral Regulation of Single Mothers in Ontario, 1920–1997* (1998), working-class clients of initiatives such as mothers' pensions, were similarly insistent on winning acknowledgment of women's claims to state support for parental duties. Such cross-class agreement anchored the social welfare state, first in its adoption of mothers' pensions or allowances and, later, of family allowances.[2]

Gender alone cannot explain the evolution of the welfare state. Little's assessment of British Columbia's mothers' pensions provides an important discussion about how gender, race, and class interacted to produce a particular policy environment at the dawn of Canada's experiment with social security. As Lynne Marks also points out in this volume, British Columbia can claim a particular and specific gendered past. Because of its unusual combination of anti-Asian politics, weakness of conventional church leadership, and strength of both the middle-class women's movement and of organized labour, early twentieth century British Columbia created a rights-based program for women that was more inclusive than any other in Canada and most others in the United States. Anglo-Celtic mothers, whether single or married, became the beneficiaries of policies that, implementing the goals of middle-class activists such as Mary Ellen Smith, were intended to ensure one of the British Empire's frontiers of settlement stayed White. Different exclusions in different provinces are suggestive about prevailing social patterns and fears. In Manitoba, women who had not been resident in the province for two years or who were married to men who were not Canadian citizens were denied mothers' allowances.[3] Making sense of the connections between gender, race, class, and their relationship to the development of public policy is a critical theme of much new feminist scholarship.

Mothers' pensions, or allowances, an important distinction with policy implications as Little makes clear, introduced the modern Western state's first systematic effort to address the long-standing vulnerability of women who were the sole support of children. White feminists were among the leading champions of this assistance, arguing that mothers served the public good in ways that were the equal to waged workers and servicemen. Just as workers' compensation and veterans' pensions compensated those who had put themselves at risk, social assistance performed the same role for mothers who could not count on breadwinner husbands. As in Australia, feminists argued that mothers were political subjects with rights: child-bearers, to them, were rights-bearers.[4]

This maternalist interpretation of citizenship, with its demand for official recognition for mothers' work in the creation of moral and responsible adults, floundered during the 1930s. The Great Depression's particularly harsh times saw mothers' rights largely superseded by a set of entitlements founded on the men's workplace rights. By the Second World War, as Nancy Christie reminds us in *Engendering the State: Family, Work, and Welfare in Canada* (2000), 'motherhood no longer constituted an independent claim on the State'. Instead, 'waged labour' had won the battle to become the 'fundamental criterion for welfare entitlements'. That defeat, with its decisive gendering of 'definitions of citizenship rights and welfare entitlements' remains.[5] Ann Porter's recent prize-winning study of gender and unemployment insurance policy explains that the construction of women and youth as 'secondary workers' was central to the restructuring of unemployment insurance into the less-generous 'employment insurance' in 1996.[6]

In January 2000 the federal government introduced twelve-month parental leaves for parents who qualified under federal 'employment insurance' regulations. This move was widely heralded as a bright spot in an era otherwise remarkable for rolling back benefits and privileges offered to women, and more particularly mothers, including the transformation of the once-universal family allowance programme into the means-tested Child and Family Tax Benefit programme. Yet many women whose lives do not fit the model of a full-time, life-long wage-worker do not qualify for federal parental-leave benefits. Provincial welfare policies directed towards women as mothers continue to be less generous and more intrusive than the rights-based programmes stemming from workplace or military contributions. The fact that a significant number of women and children remain among the most desperate of the nation's poor continues to raise fundamental questions about effective equality of citizenship at the beginning of the twenty-first century.[7]

Notes

1. See, especially, essays by Veronica Strong-Boag, Denyse Baillargeon, Lorna R. McLean, Katherine Arnup, Mary Louise Adams, Bernice Moreau, Joan Sangster, and Dorothy E. Chunn in *Contesting Canadian Citizenship: Historical Readings*, Robert Adamoski, Dorothy E. Chunn, and Robert Menzies, eds. (Peterborough, ON: Broadview Press, 2002). See also Katherine Scott, 'The Dilemma of Liberal Citizenship: Women and Social Assistance Reform in the 1990s', *Studies in Political Economy* 50 (Summer 1996): 7–36; Margaret Hillyard Little, 'The Limits of Canadian Democracy: The Citizenship Rights of Poor Women', *Canadian Review of Social Policy* 43 (Spring 1999): 59–76; Sedef Arat-Koç, 'Immigration Policies, Migrant Domestic Workers and the Definition of Citizenship in Canada', in *Deconstructing a Nation: Immigration, Multiculturalism and Racism in '90 Canada*, V. Satzewich, ed. (Halifax: Fernwood Books, 1992).
2. Dominique Marshall, *Aux origins sociales de l'état-providence* (Montreal: Les presses de l'Université de Montréal, 1998).
3. See 'Manitoba Mothers Allowance Act and memoranda for the Guidance of Applicants and Beneficiaries Under the Act, 1920'. This is discussed in Esyllt Jones, *Influenza 1918: Women, Families, and Worker Militarism in Winnipeg* (Toronto: University of Toronto Press, forthcoming).
4. Marilyn Lake, 'Childbearers as Rights-bearers: Feminist Discourse on the Rights of Aboriginal and Non-Aboriginal Mothers in Australia, 1920–1950', *Women's History Review* 8.2 (1999): 347–63.
5. Nancy Christie, *Engendering the State: Family, Work and Welfare in Canada* (Toronto: University of Toronto Press), 16.
6. Ann Porter, *Gendered States: Women, Unemployment Insurance, and the Political Economy of the Welfare State in Canada, 1945–1997* (Toronto: University of Toronto Press, 2003).
7. Monica Townson, *A Report Card on Women and Poverty* (Ottawa: Canadian Centre for Policy Alternatives, 2000).

Questions for Critical Reading

1. Compare the conception of motherhood in Little's article with that in Fiske's. How can motherhood become political in different contexts?
2. What does it mean to be the family 'breadwinner'? What kind of power and resources flow from bringing in a paycheque? What power and resources are associated with family members who do not do paid work?
3. What role might the type of publicly funded daycare discussed by Jenson play in the solution to the problems experienced by poorer women discussed in Little's article?
4. The Newfoundland feminists discussed by George connect violence against women with poverty. Why is that?

At the turn of the century, an international child-saving movement lobbied governments throughout the industrialized world for protective labour legislation and welfare reforms.[1] One of the centrepieces of this movement was the promotion of Mothers' Pension or mothers' allowance legislation for needy single mothers and their children. Through such legislation social reformers made new claims upon the state. By examining these early claims, we can better understand women's unique relationship to the state.

The relationship between citizenship rights and the welfare state has been an ongoing discussion in the welfare state literature. T.H. Marshall initiated the debate with his now famous typology of rights: civil, political, and social. He believed that civil (legal) and political rights (primarily suffrage) were precursors to social rights. Social rights encompassed the guarantee of economic security but also 'the right to share to the full in the social heritage and to live the life of a civilized being according to the standards prevailing in the society'. The latter was to develop in the twentieth century with the emergence of public education and the welfare state.[2] Feminist scholars have found Marshall's typology and evolution of rights to be gender-blind.[3] Women achieved a number of social provisions, such as Mothers' Pensions and War Pensions, prior to their successful struggle for the political right to vote. American political scientist Barbara Nelson has also argued that women's early claims upon the state were distinct from men's; while men claimed social legislation, such as Workers' Compensation, as a right, women argued for Mothers' Pension as a privilege to be granted to the most deserving. According to Nelson, these different claims created a two-tiered welfare state, with one tier establishing rights predominantly for working men and the other tier creating a number of charity-styled welfare programs, namely for low-income women, based on privileges rather than rights.[4]

An examination of BC Mothers' Pensions adds further nuance to this citizenship debate and to the study of women's relationship to the welfare state. On 14 April 1920, following an aggressive lobby effort, the British Columbia Legislature adopted Mothers' Pensions; 39 states in the United States and 3 other Canadian provinces had previously done so. But the BC lobby and subsequent policy reveals a distinct notion of citizenship. During the lobby effort, advocates embraced a rights-based discourse, claiming that single mothers had a right to the proposed pension. Not all single mothers were able to make this claim to entitlement. As in many jurisdictions, claims to citizenship rights in British Columbia occurred simultaneously with the exclusion of racial minorities. While advocates extended this right to all Anglo-Celtic single mothers, they simultaneously and vehemently excluded others, namely Asian mothers. Mothers' Pensions were understood as a state payment fee in exchange for mothering service provided by Anglo-Celtic single mothers.

This is not to overstate the case; BC Mothers' Pensioners were never as entitled to payment as those claimants of employment-related benefits, such as Workers' Compensation. Workers' Compensation rates were more generous and the terms of entitlement more clearly established. Given this distinction it is still important to distinguish BC Mothers' Pensions from other similar legislation of the era. Unlike most North American Mothers' Pension legislation, this policy, premised upon a rights-based discourse, was more inclusive and more generous to Anglo-Celtic single mothers while simultaneously excluding most racial minorities.[5] In an effort to provide a better understanding of this unique legislation, this article will explore the lobby effort which preceded the policy and the characteristics of the policy during its first decade, and will culminate with an explanation of why this BC policy has a unique place in the history of Mothers' Pensions.

The Lobby for Mothers' Pensions in British Columbia

Welfare policies are not created in a vacuum. Too often, welfare state scholars have ignored or paid scant attention to the origins of particular welfare policies. Generally, the introduction of Mothers' Pensions in Canada has been underexamined. Historian Veronica Strong-Boag has explored the general features of this policy in relation to other early welfare programs. In the BC case, Megan Davies has provided a brief analysis of BC Mothers' Pensions.[6] But neither of these scholars adequately compares the BC legislation with other Mothers' Pension policies of the era. As a result, they are unable to account adequately for the nature of a specific policy. In order to understand the progressive nature of the BC Mothers' Pension policy, it is important to locate the emergence of a number of lobbyists, their interests, and the alliances they formed.

In most North American jurisdictions at the turn of the century, much of the available welfare assistance was provided by private organizations, be they charities, women's groups, or religious associations.[7] With expertise gained from this private welfare work, these organizational leaders were well placed to lead the lobby for state welfare programs. In the BC case, women's organizations played an even more prominent role in private welfare activity than in many other areas of North America. A number of women's groups, such as the Friendly Aid Society (FAS), gave money or aid to individual families in need.[8] Besides charitable organizations such as the FAS, a vast array of women's organizations donated a portion of their time to charitable duties. These included the Vancouver Women's Forum, the New Era League, the University Women's Club, and the Local Council of Women.

While women's social reform and suffrage activities did overlap throughout the country in this period, this appears to have been even more true among BC women than elsewhere in Canada. In British Columbia those who led the suffrage movement were also leaders in social reform.[9] As a result, their alliances were strong and their lobbies persuasive. One concrete example of their political force and cohesiveness is the successful struggle to obtain a Women's Building in which a wide array of women's groups were housed. Consequently, these women were able to lead a unified campaign to ensure minimum-wage legislation for women, the raising of the marital age to 16 years, women's suffrage, compulsory school legislation, prohibition laws, and the establishment of the Children's Aid Society.

The Mothers' Pension lobby was an outgrowth of other social reform and political work. There were many reasons why Mothers' Pensions became one of the most popular political lobbies of this period. This era was one of rapid industrialization and large-scale immigration. Many men who worked in the lumber camps and mines were separated for months from their families. These dangerous working conditions resulted in incapacitation or early deaths for many male breadwinners. Death, disability, and long distance resulted in the dissolution of many families. World War I and the 1918 influenza epidemic only exacerbated these trends. Consequently, the number of widows, deserted wives, and unwed mothers increased, as did the accounts of neglected and delinquent children. Women and children were often forced to work at unhealthy and dangerous jobs. Orphanages were overcrowded.[10] There was a great fear that the family unit was being destroyed. One prominent Mothers' Pensions advocate explained,

> We are told that 'the hand that rocks the cradle rules the world.' If that be true, what is to come of the cradle-rocking, when the grim reaper gathers in the stalwart provider and protector of many a little family group, and the mother must leave the cradle-rocking to someone else, and herself become the bread-winner. . . .[11]

The migration of thousands of immigrant workers also greatly altered the social and economic fabric of the province. From 1885 to 1914 the provincial population more than quadrupled in size, mainly as a result of immigration.[12] In 1910, approximately one-third of the BC population was non-British.[13] Fears, prejudices, and emotions ran high as a result. There were concerns that ethnic-minority immigrants had higher fertility rates and would overwhelm the white Anglo-Celtic population. For instance, the Women's Canadian Club of Vancouver advocated that 'there should be four children in each Anglo-Saxon family if the race is to perpetuate itself. . . .'[14] As historian Angus McLaren states, 'No one was embarrassed to speak of the need to protect the race. . . .'[15] Consequently, there were demands for state intervention in an effort to bolster the white Anglo-Celtic population against potential 'race suicide'.[16]

This hostility towards foreigners was particularly directed at Asian immigrants. In Canada at this time there was a clear racial hierarchy: immigrants from

Britain and the United States were considered the most desirable, Northern and Western Europeans were relatively acceptable, Central and Eastern Europeans were somewhat less so, while the 'non-assimilable' Asians and blacks were not wanted by most white Anglo-Celtic Canadians. However, since Canadian capitalists required a cheap pool of labour to build the necessary infrastructure for the province's industrialization, they supported Asian immigration. Chinese labour, in particular, was utilized extensively for the short-term, low-paid, dangerous jobs.

Anglo-Celtic residents responded to Asian immigration with virulent racism, expressed through fears about jobs, health, and the moral environment. Working men and their unions feared 'unfair job competition' from the influx of Asian 'hordes' and called for restrictive labour legislation. Social reformers were concerned about the health and moral risks supposedly caused by the Asian population and feared the 'moral degeneration' of society generally. One of the most popular moral tales was that of the Chinese opium peddler enslaving innocent white young women into prostitution. Despite federal and provincial laws passed in the late nineteenth and early twentieth centuries, which limited Asian immigration, stripped all naturalized and Canadian-born Asians of their political citizenship rights (enfranchisement), and attempted to limit Asian employment opportunities, Anglo-Celtic fear and racism remained strong.[17] The fact that in 1910 the Asian population was 8 per cent while the British population was more than eight times that also failed to calm fears of 'race suicide'. Reformers continued to call for 'solutions' to the presence of Asians in BC society.

A number of reformers advocated eugenics as a method to rid Canada of morally corrupt races. For social reformers 'the two seemingly paradoxical urges—the one to do good, the other to exclude—cheerfully co-existed. . . .'[18] They argued in favour of school segregation and exclusion from charitable aid in an effort to bolster and protect the moral purity of the Anglo-Celtic race. According to the reformers, 'mixed' education would expose innocent Anglo-Celtic children to corrupting influences, while access to charity would increase the ability of Asians to compete with their fellow citizens.[19] As a result of the propagation of these myths and prejudices, BC's early history was dotted with riots, rallies, and petitions—all in an effort to control or limit the rights of Asians.

In turn-of-the-century British Columbia, large-scale immigration was accompanied by significant urbanization and industrialization. The vast majority of immigrants and BC citizens resided in urban areas in the lower mainland region, Victoria, and the Saanich Peninsula.[20] In British Columbia, as in North America more generally, the combined effect of urbanization and industrialization made the poor more visible and simultaneously produced the emergence of a middle class who were anxious to solidify their new-found socioeconomic position. But their declining birth rate in relation to the working class caused them considerable anxiety. They believed this could lead to 'degeneration' or a deterioration in the moral fibre of the province's citizens. These changing class relations had a particular impact upon women. With industrialization came the separation of home from work, and the removal of at least bourgeois women from productive activities. As a result, women's identity increasingly came to be focused on their role as mothers. Some middle-class women used the increasing social emphasis on motherhood to assert a position for themselves in the public sphere. Welfare reforms such as Mothers' Pensions provided an opportunity for them to establish themselves as maternal experts and promote their version of the ideal family, with husbands as the sole breadwinner and mothers and children in the home. This new familial ideology was influential, even though most working-class families were not able to adhere to it.

Support for Mothers' Pension legislation in British Columbia can be viewed as a response to the socioeconomic and cultural concerns of the period. In response to the concerns engendered by industrialization, urbanization, and massive immigration, a number of organizations joined forces to help enact the Mothers' Pension policy. Most prominent were the many women's organizations that played a central role in lobbying for Mothers' Pensions. As early as 1901, the Local Council of Women in Vancouver promoted the issue.[21] As a member of the National Council of Women, the Local Council was well situated to lead the Mothers' Pension lobby. The National Council of Women was modelled after other national women's associations established in a number of industrialized countries at the turn of the century. As an umbrella organization, it represented a wide cross-section of middle-class women's interests, including the Victorian Order of Nurses, women's church groups, and literary societies. This council had national and international contacts and was informed about the successes and failures of other social reform lobbies elsewhere.[22]

A second women's group that was instrumental in the BC Mothers' Pension lobby was the University Women's Club, an organization which both acted as a social club for university women graduates and pursued the advancement of women's rights. In the BC case, this association provided the legal expertise for the Mothers' Pension lobby. Club member Helen MacGill conducted a painstaking exploration of all laws affecting women and children and persuaded the club to endorse and lobby for legislative change.[23] As the first woman judge in the province, MacGill was particularly concerned about delinquent children and unwed mothers who ended up in her courtroom, and desired both social policy and legal measures which would benefit them.[24]

While women's groups led the Mothers' Pension delegation, the BC labour movement was also involved. It is important to recognize that members of the labour movement had previously called for a number of social reforms, including Mothers' Pensions. In 1914, the president of the Trades and Labour Congress argued that assisting widows with small children was more important than financing the building of railways.[25] A year later, well-known BC labour activist Helena Gutteridge persuaded the Vancouver Trades and Labour Council to lobby for a national Mothers' Pension.[26] The labour movement had lobbied for a number of social reforms previously with little effect. Once the newly aware middle-class reformers who had access to political power became interested in these issues, the possibilities for social legislation improved immeasurably. The ties between labour and various women's organizations were strong partly as a result of Gutteridge's previous work. She had worked with women's organizations, such as the University Women's Club and the Local Council of Women, to improve women's relief and employment conditions.[27] Gutteridge and these middle-class women saw Mothers' Pensions as a way to reduce the heavy burden placed on single mothers, who had to both raise their children and financially provide for them through paid work. With Mothers' Pensions, single mothers could spend more time at home with their children, thus more closely approximating the dominant familial ideal.

Religious leaders were also involved in the BC Mothers' Pensions coalition. Generally, religious organizations do not appear to have had the social or moral influence in British Columbia which they enjoyed in other regions of the country. BC historians have demonstrated that the social gospel movement in the Christian churches, which advocated a number of private and public welfare reforms, tended to be less popular in British Columbia than elsewhere in Canada.[28] Consequently, religious leaders performed a back-seat role in the BC Mothers' Pension lobby, whereas they helped lead similar coalitions in other provinces. For example, Reverend Peter Bryce, an influential Methodist minister, played a key role in the Ontario Mothers' Pension lobby. He effectively mobilized the church community, made a strong alliance with the women's organizations, and became the leader of the lobby effort. His views were so influential that he was nominated as the chief administrator once the policy was enacted.[29] No prominent religious leader or church coalition played such a significant role in the BC lobby.

In 1918, following years of discussion and coalition building, a large delegation, including representatives from women's charity, labour, and religious organizations, approached the government. Led by

BC's first woman MLA, Mary Ellen Smith, the delegation also included a number of other powerful women leaders, most notably Cecilia Spofford, a Children's Aid Society administrator and WCTU member; Maria Grant, also of the WCTU; and Helen MacGill, representing the University Women's Club.[30] Premier John Oliver considered it the most businesslike and representative delegation that had ever appeared before the government. So persuasive was the lobby that the government appointed a commission to investigate the matter.[31] Cecilia Spofford, of the WCTU and part of the 1918 lobby, was appointed as one of the commissioners.

The commission held hearings in 17 locations throughout the province.[32] During the hearings there was unanimous support for Mothers' Pensions. The legislation was endorsed by 77 organizations, 24 fraternal societies, 34 labour organizations, 6 other groups, 10 religious leaders, 13 medical doctors, 4 insurance agents, and 46 private individuals. Notable among these advocates was the strong voice of women, for almost every women's organization in the province participated in these hearings.

The overwhelming support for Mothers' Pensions was not unique to British Columbia; this legislation was considered the most popular legislation of its era. But what is distinctive is the content of this support. In most other locales, Mothers' Pension advocates were quick to distinguish between 'suitable', moral mothers—most particularly widows—who should be eligible for Mothers' Pensions, and 'unfit', immoral mothers, who should not be eligible. During the BC hearings, lobbyists argued that many different types of mothers should be eligible for Mothers' Pensions. This endorsement was particularly unique in the discussion of unwed mothers during the hearings. In the BC case, almost every women's organization supported the inclusion of unwed mothers. Representations of labour, war veterans, local politicians, religious leaders, and nurses also supported the eligibility of unwed mothers. As one women's organization representative explained, 'We feel that many unmarried mothers have children who are just as good as those who are married; why should she be deprived of support, if she is your daughter or my daughter—let us stick together.'[33] Another advocate stated, 'Your statistics will prove that there will not be one in 500,000 [unmarried] girls who will not prove true—you not only save the mother but the child has the love and protection of its mother.'[34] And more than one WCTU member believed that if an unwed mother was eligible for Mothers' Pensions, she would be encouraged to keep the child and this would act as a safeguard from further illegitimate pregnancy; a rather novel form of birth control.[35] Finally, one worker who spoke on behalf of unwed mothers reminded the commissioners that 'Jesus Christ himself was born out of wedlock'.[36]

A comparison of the BC and the Ontario Mothers' Pensions hearings, held in the same year, reveals how significant a difference there was in attitudes towards unwed mothers. In the Ontario case, women's organizations, the CAS, charities, and church groups all opposed the inclusion of unwed mothers. The Local Council of Women in Ontario generally believed that unwed mothers with one child should seek financial support from the father and argued that unwed mothers with two or more children should be institutionalized, for these women were considered 'weak intellects'. Labour representatives were the only ones in the Ontario case who acted on behalf of unwed mothers, and did so with little effect. And the Ontario policy which resulted reflected the majority views and initially excluded all but widows.[37]

The BC lobby and hearings also demonstrated a particular position regarding the racial origins of recipients. While Mothers' Pension advocates in many jurisdictions perceived the policy as a method to support white Anglo-Celtic offspring at the expense of other less valuable babies, there was greater unanimity for this position in the BC case. As previously documented, British Columbia was characterized by great racial prejudice and fear at the turn of the century, and these fears imbued the Mothers' Pension hearings. One Mothers' Pension supporter argued that the 'Anglo-Saxon race . . . [is] becoming exterminated'.[38] Another asserted that, 'You are going to find in BC inside of 30 years that you will have nothing but Orientals. . . .'[39] The position was unanimous; while some were willing to extend the pension to British subjects and other white mothers who swore allegiance to the crown, no one supported the inclusion of immigrants who were non-British subjects.

Following the hearings, the commissioners reported that they were unanimously in favour of legislation which reflected the views expressed during the hearings. When the proposed legislation came before the provincial legislature, Mary Ellen Smith was there to see it through. During her time in the legislature, Smith was credited as the force behind a number of social reforms, including the Female Minimum Wage Act, the Deserted Wives Maintenance Act, and the Equal Guardianship Act. But she was perhaps most influential during the campaign for Mothers' Pensions. During the 1917 provincial election campaign, she had promised her supporters a Mothers' Pensions Act.[40] She was part of the Mothers' Pension delegation to the premier in 1919. And when the bill came before the legislature for the second reading, she argued for a generous policy which would include many types of single mothers. She is remembered particularly for her support for unwed mothers and her now famous speech before the legislature on their behalf: 'Mr Speaker, there are no illegitimate children. It may be there are . . . people who will contend there are illegitimate parents but in God's name, do not let us brand the child.'[41]

Once Enacted: Policy Development and Administration

With Smith's help in the legislature, the Liberal government under Premier Oliver passed the BC Mothers' Pension Act on 17 April 1920.[42] Immediately the government received high praise, numerous letters of support, and a flood of applications.[43] Within a year, the government announced that the individual pensions would have to be reduced because the demand had exceeded the $400,000 allotted.[44] During the first decade, there were a number of amendments made to the original Act in an attempt to curb the number who qualified.[45]

Despite these amendments, this popular legislation continued to be the most progressive Mothers' Pension policy of its era in North America. Three traits of the policy distinguish it from other Mothers' Pension programs of the 1920s. First, it was the most inclusive. Whereas other Mothers' Pension policies generally restricted eligibility to widows, the BC legislation included not only widows but also mothers whose husbands had deserted, were imprisoned, or were incapacitated. British Columbia also included mothers with one child, while many other policies restricted eligibility to mothers with two or more children.[46]

Even more noteworthy was the discretionary clause within the BC legislation. No other jurisdiction in North America had such a clause. This clause permitted any other case not covered by the Act to be eligible provided the Superintendent of Neglected Children deemed the case to be 'a proper one for assistance'.[47] Through this discretionary clause divorced and unwed mothers also received the pension.[48] In 1920, when the legislation was passed, British Columbia was one of only three jurisdictions in North America to include divorced mothers and the only one, except Hawaii, to include unwed mothers (see Table 1).

Not only was the BC policy more inclusive, it also provided more pensions per capita than anywhere else in North America. Given the breadth of the BC policy, no sooner was the program announced than the applications began to pour into the office. Within seven months, the office had received more than 1,000 applications—almost five times more than the number predicted during the commission hearings.[49] As the applications increased, so did the acceptance rate. During the first decade, British Columbia had second highest acceptance rates per capita in all of North America at 212 families per 100,000 population. As a result, the total pension costs per population were the highest in North America at $1.40 per person, whereas the second highest rates were Manitoba and New York State at 71 cents per person.[50]

Table 1: Comparison of Mothers' Pension legislation in Canada, 1920

Province	Persons benefited
Alberta	Widow or woman whose husband is in insane asylum, leaving boys under 15 and girls under 16.
British Columbia	Widow or woman whose husband is in prison or asylum; or whose husband is incapacitated; or whose husband has deserted; or 'any other person whose case . . . is a proper one for assistance'. The latter clause can include divorced and unwed mothers. In all the above cases the mother must have 1 or more children under 16 years.
Ontario	Widowed leaving 2 or more children under 16 years. The mother must be a fit and proper person. During 1920 this act was expanded to include a woman with 2 or more children under 16 years who had not seen nor heard from her husband in seven years.
Manitoba	Widowed mother or if husband is in prison or asylum or physically disabled.
Saskatchewan	Dependent widowed mother, who is proper person to have custody of children.

Even the very discourse of the BC policy was distinctive. Most other jurisdictions enacted a Mothers' Allowance policy—to be allowed when a mother was deemed both financially and morally worthy. Such an allowance connoted a sense of privilege which had to be earned, as in the case of charitable welfare. The BC legislation, on the other hand, was a pension. Pensions were associated with Workers' Compensation and later Old Age Pension, and were considered a payment for recognition of services rendered. During the commission hearings, many participants spoke about the right of mothers to bring up their children and argued for a policy based on rights. The Act, in turn, reflected this rights-based discussion. It stated that this was a measure to provide pensions for mothers, whereas other similar programs stated that the allowance was restricted to mothers who demonstrated their financial and moral worthiness to care for their children.[51] In 1921, the administration of Mothers' Pensions was transferred from the Superintendent of Neglected Children to the Workers' Compensation Board, further emphasizing the notion that Mothers' Pensions were a right.[52]

This rights discourse was also reflected in the administration of the policy once enacted. Letters written by applicants and lobbyists, as well as government correspondence and annual reports, all demonstrated that the majority of BC citizens viewed Mothers' Pensions as a statutory right to which recipients were unquestionably entitled if they met the purely technical qualifications spelled out in the legislation.[53] There are numerous letters from applicants demanding that it is their right to receive Mothers' Pensions. For instance, one young mother with one child was rejected because she had refused full-time work at a school. The Pension Board found her 'healthy and vigorous, who spends a great deal of energy in pursuing what she conceives to be her legal right to a Mothers' Pension . . . ,' when she should be looking for work. In response, the mother wrote the premier to complain: 'Mr Winn [chairman of the Mothers' Pension Board] argued along such small mean lines and seemed far more anxious to steer the conversation to some unimportant detail over which he might sneer with pleasure than to try to understand my problem.'[54] This notion of entitlement was widely accepted by other applicants. In 1931, a report investigating the policy condemned British Columbians for their 'socially disturbing attitude to regard this and other forms of public aid as an inalienable statutory right, to which the recipient is unquestionably entitled. . . .'[55]

The rights-based discourse of BC Mothers' Pensions refutes some of the previous feminist literature on the early welfare state. As discussed earlier, Barbara Nelson has argued that the welfare state is fundamentally divided into two tiers. One tier, developed mainly to support male workers, was based on a notion that welfare was a right which must be earned through paid labour. Eligibility was determined in a scientifically ordered fashion and generally based on financial need. Administration of such policies was for the most part routinized. The second tier was based on a notion that welfare was a privilege rather than a right and had to be continually earned. Recipients tended to be poor women who were, for the most part, outside the wage-labour relationship. This latter charity-styled welfare did not have clearly defined criteria based on economic need. Rather, these programs required applicants to prove that they were morally as well as financially deserving. To determine the deservedness of the applicant required a great deal of intrusive investigation and opened the door for much discretionary decision-making. It is Nelson's belief that Workers' Compensation sets the tone for the first tier of the welfare state and Mothers' Allowance for the second.[56] Clearly, the evidence provided here suggests that BC Mothers' Pension was a hybrid between the two tiers. The discourse surrounding the BC policy implies that it was considered a right rather than a privilege. Given the different types of single mothers clearly defined as eligible for the program, the investigation of moral worthiness was certainly much less significant in the BC case than in other jurisdictions.

This is not to imply that the BC program was entirely inclusive and generous. While rights were claimed for Anglo-Celtic mothers, they were carefully and consciously denied for other racial minority groups. The policy clearly excluded immigrants who were non-British subjects, and a number of naturalized immigrants were also refused the pension. As one Mothers' Pension administrator explained, 'There were such an endless number of non-British subjects applying . . . that it was necessary for the Legislature to tighten up the Act very materially, with the result that a few deserving cases on the border line have been excluded from the benefits.'[57] It was generally believed that those of non-Anglo-Celtic blood could take care of themselves. This was particularly true of applicants of Asian background. For example, Mrs Wong married Charlie Wong while he was in prison. Because Charlie Wong was a second-generation Chinese Canadian whose father had been naturalized, Mrs Wong legally became a British subject through this marriage. As a poor mother of six children she applied for the Mothers' Pension. The Mothers' Pension administration was adamant in its refusal:

> We now have on our list three cases of Chinese, together with three other cases whose applications we have not yet accepted. In all they represent potential liability to the Province of between $35,000 and $40,000. This, we believe, is but the thin edge of the wedge. . . . Heretofore, the Chinese people have looked after their own cases. In the many thousands of those receiving relief from the City of Vancouver in past years there was only one Chinese case and that was by reason of a Tong War which practically ostracized that particular family.[58]

Thus, the administration refused to acknowledge Mrs Wong's naturalization and concluded that 'there is no reason to believe that Mrs Wong will go uncared for if she remains a Chinese citizen'.[59]

Although the BC Mothers' Pension rates were more generous than most Mothers' Pension policies, they still remained inadequate. Like other Mothers' Pension rates, the BC rate remained well below subsistence.[60] In comparison to the Veterans' Allowances, the BC pension payments were inadequate. Veterans' Allowances, established in 1916, provided a soldier's dependants with a supplement beyond his soldier's pay. The Veterans' Allowance paid a widow $55 a month, whereas the Mothers' Pension rate for a widow was $35. As well, the Veterans' Allowance paid $12 for the first child, $10 for the second, and $8 for each additional child, while Mothers' Pensions paid $7.60 per child.[61]

The pension policy was also characterized by an intrusive administrative structure. Like other Mothers' Pension policies, the BC program hired investigators who came into the homes of the applicants, much as charitable women had done previously, and carefully scrutinized all aspects of the home.[62] The discretionary clause, which allowed many types of single mothers not covered under the Act to apply, also permitted the administration to determine eligibility on a case-by-case basis. Consequently, this provided the possibility of subjective decision-making.[63]

Conclusion

Several factors help to explain the unique claims made upon the BC state by Mothers' Pension lobbyists and the policy which resulted. First, racism played a strong hand in the Mothers' Pension lobby and in the subsequent policy. The white Anglo-Celtic population of British Columbia was small in comparison to that of other provinces, and certainly the hearings demonstrated that members of this racial group were concerned about their numbers. A much higher level of racism was exhibited during the hearings in British Columbia than during the Ontario hearings of the same year. During the BC hearings, no one advocated that non-British subjects should be eligible for Mothers' Pensions. Several said they feared for the survival of the white Anglo-Celtic race. Several women's charitable organizations had a prior history of giving relief to white Anglo-Celtic citizens and sending immigrant families back to their homeland. Labour representatives were concerned that immigrant workers would threaten the competition for jobs. It seems possible that BC lobbyists were willing to include all types of white Anglo-Celtic mothers (be they widowed, divorced, or unwed) in an effort to increase this racial group at the expense of other racial/ethnic groups.

Also not to be dismissed is the limited role of churches. In British Columbia, the churches played a smaller role both in charity work prior to the Mothers' Pension lobby and in the lobby effort itself than was generally the case in other provinces. BC church organizations did not have a century of experience in the field of welfare, and consequently church leaders were unable to establish themselves as the moral authorities on this question. In the Ontario case, however, church representatives played a leadership role in the debate and asserted themselves as experts on the question of welfare administration.

Thirdly, women's organizations filled the vacuum left by the churches. Middle-class women's organizations initiated and led the BC Mothers' Pension lobby. In 1921, following the enactment of the legislation, the Civilian Mothers' Pension Association (CMPA) of Vancouver was established both to help individual single mothers and to lobby the government collectively for further reforms to the policy. Along with other women's organizations, the CMPA was extremely influential in the ongoing administration of this policy.[64] There is no record of a similar organization in any other province of the country. In fact, historical records demonstrate that women's groups in most provinces lost interest in Mothers' Pensions once the program was established.

The unique nature of the BC Mothers' Pensions Act was not to last. During the 1920s, most British Columbians were proud of this progressive policy, and numerous newspaper stories boasted of the province's generosity towards single mothers. But by the end of the decade this support had waned, and opposition from both inside and outside of the province mounted. Increasingly, both the public and the government became concerned that British Columbia was becoming 'a dumping ground' for people who would not have been eligible for Mothers' Pensions in other provinces.[65] The erosion of the inclusive elements of this policy occurred during the difficult Depression years, a subject that requires separate examination.

Notes

An earlier version of this paper was presented at the BC and Beyond: Gender Histories Conference, University of Victoria, Victoria, BC, 17 June 1994. This research was made possible by the Ruth Wynn Woodward Postdoctoral Fellowship at Simon Fraser University. I would like to thank Susan Johnson for her archival assistance and expertise and the guest editors of *BC Studies* 105–6 (Spring/Summer 1995) and the anonymous reader for their helpful comments on an earlier version of this paper. I am indebted to Jacquie Buncel, Lykke de la Cour, Marty Donkervoort, Nancy Forestell, Judy Hill, Susan Prentice, and Carolyn Whitzman for their constant support; to Rhonda Chorney, Janice Ristock, and Catherine Taylor who kept me laughing; and a special thanks to Lynne Marks for always being there. Each of them, in their own way, helped me through a very difficult transition.

1. This reform took the form of both state legislation and private welfare activities. Legislation such as compulsory school attendance, restrictive child labour laws, and Mothers' Pensions were enacted to provide and guide mothers and children. Many new social clubs, charities, and women's organizations, such as Brownies, Girl Guides, and the Red Cross, focused on the proper guidance of children in their leisure pursuits and the development of a mother's parental skills. Other associations such as the Children's Aid Society were an amalgam of public and private welfare activities. For a more detailed discussion of this mixture of public and private welfare reform, see Margaret Hillyard Little, 'The Blurring of Boundaries: Private and Public Welfare for Single Mothers in Ontario', in *Studies in Political Economy* 47 (Summer 1995), 89–102.
2. T.H. Marshall, 'Citizenship and Social Class', *Class, Citizenship and Social Development* (New York: Doubleday, 1964), 65–126, esp. 71.
3. Feminist critiques of Marshall's notion of citizenship rights include articles by Linda Gordon, Diane Pearce, and Barbara Nelson in Linda Gordon, *Women, the State and Welfare* (Madison: University of Wisconsin Press, 1990); Nancy Fraser and Linda Gordon, 'Contract Versus Charity: Why is There No Social Citizenship in the United States?' *Socialist Review* 22.3 (July–Sept. 1992); and Gillian Pascall, 'Citizenship: A Feminist Analysis', *New Approaches to Welfare Theory* (Brookfield: Edward Elgar Publishing, 1993), 113–26.
4. For a more detailed discussion of this argument see Barbara Nelson, 'The Origins of the Two-Channel Welfare State: Workmen's Compensation and Mothers' Aid', in *Women, the State and Welfare*, 123–51.
5. Recent study of the development of American Mothers' Pension legislation has revealed that certain lobbyists did use a rights-based discourse but that this was very much a minority view. A few state policies briefly included a number of types of single mothers, but these groups were quickly excluded prior to 1920. Molly Ladd-Taylor, *Mother-Work: Women, Child Welfare, and the State, 1890–1930* (Urbana: University of Illinois Press, 1994), 148–9 and Table 1.
6. See: Veronica Strong Boag, 'Canada's Early Experience with Income Supplements: The Introduction of Mothers' Allowance', *Atlantis: A Women's Studies Journal* 4.2 (Spring 1979): 35–43; Strong-Boag, 'Wages for Housework: Mothers' Allowances and the Beginnings of Social Security in Canada', *Journal of Canadian Studies* 14.1 (Spring 1979): 24–34; and Megan Davies, 'Services Rendered, Rearing Children for the State: Mothers' Pensions in British Columbia, 1919–1931', Barbara Latham and Roberta Pazdro, eds., *Not Just Pin Money: Selected Essays on the History of Women's Work in British Columbia* (Victoria, BC: Camosun College, 1984), 249–64.
7. Most of the limited state welfare assistance then available was provided by municipal governments. In British Columbia, however, the provincial government did provide some welfare assistance in non-urban areas through the Provincial Secretary's Indigent Fund.
8. Founded in 1894, the Friendly Aid Society is the most notable welfare agency in the province, for it attempted to co-ordinate and centralize relief to the poor. This society received money from city councils in exchange for relieving the city of any responsibility to care for the poor. City of Vancouver Archives (VA), Series 447, Social Service Department, City of Vancouver, vol. 106 A1, The Friendly Aid Society; and Victoria City Archives (VCA), M98308-01, Friendly Help Association, 1895–1933, Minute Book, 1890–1900.
9. Whereas Carol Bacchi has argued that suffrage women and social reformers were somewhat distinct, Michael Cramer suggests that these efforts were closely aligned in the BC case. Leaders of the Mothers' Pension lobby, Cecilia Spofford, Helena Gutteridge, and Helen MacGill,

were also well known for their suffrage and other political work. See Carol Bacchi, *Liberation Deferred?: The Ideas of English-Canadian Suffragists, 1877–1918* (Toronto: University of Toronto Press, 1983), 24–39; Michael W. Cramer, 'Public and Political: Documents of the Women's Suffrage Campaign in BC, 1871–1917: The View from Victoria', in *In Her Own Right: Selected Essays on Women's History in B.C.*, Barbara Latham and Cathy Kess, eds. (Victoria, BC: Camosun College, 1980), 79–100; British Columbia Archives and Records Services (BCARS), GR 517, Box 1, file 1, Lillian Nelson, 'Vancouver's Early Days and the Development of Her Social Services'; and VA, Helen MacGill, 'Story of Vancouver Social Service'.

10. For example, in 1908, the Children's Aid Society Home in Vancouver had almost doubled the acceptable occupancy level. VA, MS 351, Children's Aid Society, vol. 1, file 2.
11. VA, MS 822, vol. 1, file 5, p. 16, citation by Mrs Chippendale.
12. Peter Ward, *White Canada Forever: Popular Attitudes and Public Policy toward Orientals in British Columbia* (Montreal and Kingston: McGill-Queen's University Press, 1978), 53.
13. The ethnic composition of the province's population in 1910 was: British—68 per cent, Continental European—18 per cent, Asian—8 per cent, and Aboriginal—5 per cent. See Jean Barman, *The West Beyond the West: History of British Columbia* (Toronto: University of Toronto Press, 1991).
14. VA, 'Saving Babies Subject of Canadian Club Address', *The Vancouver Daily World*, 16 Apr. 1919, MS 272, Women's Canadian Club of Vancouver, vol. 3, file 2.
15. Angus McLaren, *Our Own Master Race: Eugenics in Canada, 1885–1945* (Toronto: McClelland and Stewart, 1990), 48.
16. For a discussion of the racial tensions in British Columbia during this era, see Patricia E. Roy, *A White Man's Province: B.C. Politicians and Chinese and Japanese Immigrants, 1858–1914* (Vancouver: UBC Press, 1989); and Ward, *White Canada Forever*.
17. A federal head tax limited Chinese immigration. During the early 1900s this head tax was increased from $50 to $500 to further limit entry of this group. In 1908 the federal government restricted the immigration of Japanese and East Indians through the bureaucratic rule that only those with a continuous journey ticket were permitted to enter Canada. This eliminated many Asians who travelled through Hawaii before journeying on to Canada. The Chinese were provincially disenfranchised in the 1870s, the Japanese in the 1890s, and the East Indians in 1908. Ward, *White Canada Forever*, 55 and 76.

    The BC Alien Labour Act, 1897, banned Chinese and Japanese on a variety of private works conducted under the provincial government's charter (i.e., the construction of railways, roads, telephone lines, harbours, canals, and dams). The federal government, however, struck this type of legislation down. Ward, *White Canada Forever*, 55.
18. Barman, *The West Beyond the West*, 233. See McLaren, *Our Own Master Race*, for further discussion of the popularity of eugenics ideas among social reformers.
19. Roy, *A White Man's Province*, 24–8.
20. In 1911, 50 per cent of British Columbians lived in the Lower Mainland while another 10 per cent lived in Victoria or the Saanich Peninsula. The remaining 40 per cent were spread throughout the province in tiny resource-based communities. Barman, *The West Beyond the West*, 194.
21. VA, MS 438, Local Council of Women, Vancouver, Historical Pamphlet.
22. For a detailed discussion of the history of the National Council of Women, see Veronica Strong-Boag, *The National Council of Women, 1893–1929* (Ottawa, 1976).
23. Some examples of Helen MacGill's investigative legal work include: 'The Child in Industry', 1926; 'Daughters, Wives and Mothers in B.C.', 1913; 'The Juvenile Court in Canada: Origin, Underlying Principles, Governing Legislation and Practice', 1925; Oriental Delinquent in the Vancouver Juvenile Court', 1938; and 'Laws for Women and Children in B.C.', 1925. For MacGill's role in the Mothers' Pension lobby, see Elsie Gregory MacGill, *My Mother the Judge* (Toronto: Ryerson Press, 1955), 169–78.
24. For a discussion of unwed mothers and juvenile delinquency, see MacGill, 'The Juvenile Court in Canada: Origin, Underlying Principles, Governing Legislation and Practice'.
25. VA, MS 307, Vancouver Trades and Labour Council, Reel #1, 'Congress Report Presented Last Night', Nov. 1914.
26. VA, MS 307, Resolution from the Vancouver Trades and Labour Council to the Trades and Labour Congress Convention, 7 Feb. 1915.
27. As a member of the University Women's Club Committee to Aid Unemployed Women and also the Women's Employment League of the Vancouver Local Council of Women, Helena Gutteridge had worked with middle-class women to give destitute women meal tickets, groceries, emergency funds, and employment advice. Gutteridge was also well known for her suffrage work with both the women's organizations and the trade union movement. See Irene Howard, *The Struggle for Social Justice in British Columbia: Helena Gutteridge,*

the Unknown Reformer (Vancouver, UBC Press, 1992); Tami Adilman, 'Evelyn Farris and the University Women's Club', in *In Her Own Right*, 147–66; and Susan Wade, 'Helena Gutteridge: Votes for Women and Trade Unions', in *In Her Own Right*, 187–203.

28. For a discussion of the limited influence of religious organizations in British Columbia, see Diana Matters, 'The Development of Public Welfare Institutions in Vancouver, 1910–1920', honours essay, History Department, University of Victoria, Apr. 1973, 86–7; and Bob Stewart, 'That's the B.C. Spirit: Religion and Secularity in Lotus Land', *Canadian Society of Church History Papers* (1983): 22–35.
29. See Margaret Hillyard Little, 'No Car, No Radio, No Liquor Permit: The Moral Regulation of Single Mothers in Ontario, 1920–93' (Ph.D. thesis, York University, 1994), ch. 1.
30. For further discussion of the work of Cecilia Spofford and Maria Grant in the WCTU, see Lynn Gough, *As Wise as Serpents: Five Women and an Organization That Changed B.C., 1883–1939* (Victoria: Swan Lake Publishing, 1988).
31. This was not the first inquiry which included the study of Mothers' Pensions. In 1912, the Royal Commission on Labour had conducted a report on the subject but without public hearings or legislative results. In 1920, the Health Insurance Commission chaired by E.S.H. Winn, newly appointed chair of the Workmen's Compensation Board, was 'to enquire as to the laws relating to the subjects of Mothers' Pensions, Maternity Insurance, Health Insurance and Public Health Nursing. . . .' Because of the tremendous support for Mothers' Pensions, the Commission was asked to report separately and promptly on this subject. BCARS, GR 684, Ministry of Labour, Box 4, Royal Commission on Labour, 1912, 'Report of Information in Regard to Mothers' Pensions'; and BCARS, GR 706, BC Commission on Health Insurance, 1919–21, Box 1, file 2, 'Letter to Lieutenant Governor in Council, Victoria, B.C., Mar. 18, 1921'.
32. These hearings were held in Chilliwack, Cranbrook, Fernie, Golden, Grand Forks, Kamloops, Nanaimo, Nelson, New Westminster, Prince Rupert, Princeton, Revelstoke, Rossland, Trail, Vancouver, Vernon, and Victoria. BCARS, GR 706, Box 1, file 3, 'Report of the Health Insurance Commission'.
33. BCARS, GR 706, Box 1, file 3, Mrs E.J. Carson, Women's Forum, Vancouver, 511.
34. BCARS, Box 1, file 3, Mrs H.G. Taylor, New Era League and Local Council of Women, Vancouver, 544.
35. BCARS, GR 706, Box 1, file 3, Mrs William Grant, WCTU, Nanaimo District, 409 and Mrs J.A. Gillespie, WCTU, Vancouver District, 709–10.
36. BCARS, GR 706, Box 1, file 3, George H. Turner, shipwright by trade and secretary of The Fire Clay Company, 725–6.
37. Little, 'No Car, No Radio, No Liquor Permit', ch. 1.
38. BCARS, GR 706, Box 1, file 3, Dr Ernest Hall, 414.
39. BCARS, GR 706, Box 1, file 3, F.W. Welsh, President, Vancouver Trades and Labour Council, 631.
40. VA, MS 822, Mrs Sheyla Scott Chippendale, Box 1, file 5, 'Vancouver Women's Building, Year Book, 1922', 3.
41. Quotation cited in Elizabeth Norcross, 'Mary Ellen Smith: The Right Woman in the Right Place at the Right Time', in *Not Just Pin Money*, 361–2.
42. BCARS, GR 441, Premier's Office, Series 14, vol. 427, Legislature Scrapbook, 1921–1923, 'Many Wives Left, but Pensions Bring Back Happy Homes', *Times*, 16 Feb. 1921.
43. Letters of support included correspondence from the Liberal Association, Nelson; the University Women's Club, Methodist Parsonage, Cloverdale; City Clerk, Rossland; and other private individuals. BCARS, GR 541, Provincial Secretary, Letter Book, vol. 2, 1920.
44. BCARS, GR 441, Series 14, vol. 427, 'Too Many Mothers Ask for Pensions', *Times*, 1921.
45. In 1921, the government announced that women who had independent incomes or some type of employment would receive less than those who had nothing. BCARS, GR 441, Series 14, vol. 427, 'Too Many Mothers', *Times*, 1921.

    Other amendments to the Act were made during the first decade:

    1921 — clarified that the male breadwinner must be totally disabled.
    — stipulated that the applicant whose husband had deserted, was imprisoned, or was incapacitated had to have resided in the province at the time of the difficulty.
    1924 — stated that the disability must not only be total but be 'reasonably be expected to continue for at least one year'.
    — the deserted applicant must be deserted for at least two years, and her husband must not reside or own property in British Columbia at the time of the application.
    — applicant must own less than $500 cash and hold property valued less than $1,500.

    'An Act to amend the Mothers' Pensions Act, 1921', *Statutes of B.C.*, King's Printer, Victoria, BC, 1921, c. 43, s. 2, ss. b, c, and d; 'An Act to amend the Mothers' Pensions Act, 1924', *Statutes of B.C.*, 1924, c. 32, s. 2, ss. c and d.

46. Other provinces included one-child families only in exceptional cases. BCARS, GR 100, Box 1, file 1, Charlotte Whitton, Executive Director of The Canadian Council on Child and Family Welfare, 'Full Report re: The Operation of Mothers' Pensions in British Columbia, 1920–21 to 1930–31', 60–73.
47. 'An Act to Provide Pensions for Mothers, 1920', *B.C. Statutes*, King's Printer, Victoria, BC, c. 61, s. 2, ss. 3.
48. By the end of the decade divorced mothers accounted for 5 per cent of the total BC Mothers' Pension cases, and unwed mothers represented 3.5 per cent. BCARS, GR 100, Box 1, file 1, Whitton, 'Full Report', 48.
49. BCARS, GR 441, Series 14, vol. 427, 'Many Wives Left', *Times*, 16 Feb. 1921.
50. BCARS, GR 497, Box 7, file 7, Charlotte Whitton, 'Report on the Administration of Mothers' Pensions in British Columbia, 1920–21 to 1930–31, Summary of Findings and Recommendations', 2–4. A table in the original article, showing the eligibility requirements for mothers' pensions in every state in the United States in 1920, has been deleted for this volume.
51. 'An Act to provide Pensions for Mothers, 1920', *B.C. Statutes*, 1920, c. 61.
52. Charlotte Whitton also emphasized this distinction between mothers' allowances and mothers' pensions in her 1931 report. BCARS, Annual Report of the BC Mothers' Pension Act, 30 Sept. 1922, 1; and BCARS, GR 497, Box 7, file 7, Whitton, 'Summary Report', 20.
53. Government reports bemoan the fact that applicants believe they are entitled to the pension. Annual reports and applications demonstrate that many single mothers who were not impoverished believed themselves to be eligible for the pension. BCARS, Annual Report of Mothers' Pensions, 30 Sept. 1922, 5.
54. BCARS, GR 1323, Attorney General Correspondence, 1902–1937, Reel B2320, 'Letter from The Workmen's Compensation Board to the Provincial Secretary', 16 Nov. 1928; 'Letter from Applicant to Premier', 26 Nov. 1928; and 'Letter from Deputy Attorney-General', 10 Jan. 1929.
55. BCARS, GR 497, Box 7, file 7, Whitton, 'Summary Report', 19.
56. Nelson, 'The Origins of the Two-Channel Welfare State', 123–51.
57. In one case the applicant and her husband were both naturalized, had lived in British Columbia for more than a decade, had voted in the provincial elections, and yet were refused the pension because the naturalization papers were lost. BCARS, GR 1323, Reel B2211, 'Letter to E.S.H. Winn, Chairman, Workmen's Compensation Board', 3 Dec. 1931. Citation from BCARS, GR 1323, Reel B2211, 'Letter from A.M. Manson to Mrs H.', 5 Sept. 1923.
58. Please note that Mrs 'Wong' is a pseudonym. BCARS, GR 1323, Reel B2320, 'Letter from E.S.H. Winn, Chairman of Workmen's Compensation Board to R.H. Pooley, Attorney General', 14 July 1930.
59. BCARS, GR 1323, Reel B2320, 'Letter from E.S.H. Winn, Chairman of Workmen's Compensation Board to Col. C.E. Edgett, Warden, B.C. Penitentiary', 25 June 1930.
60. Government officials publicly admitted that the Mothers' Pension was not sufficient to live on. BCARS, GR 441, Series 14, vol. 461, Scrapbook, Provincial and Public Affairs, 1919–1920, 'Four Hundred Acts Show Work of Legislature', *Colonist*, 23 June 1920; BCARS, Annual Report of BC Mothers' Pensions, 30 Sept. 1922, 3; and Annual Report of BC Mothers' Pensions, 30 Sept. 1925, 2.
61. BCARS, GR 441, Series 14, vol. 427, 'Mothers' Pensions Charges of Canon Proved Unfounded', *Times*, 8 Dec. 1922.
62. When the Act was established four trained investigators were hired to conduct this work. BCARS, Annual Report of BC Mothers' Pensions, 30 Sept. 1922, 2.
63. Unfortunately there is no statistical data to adequately assess the types of applicants rejected. BCARS, GR 100, Box 1, Whitton, 'Full Report', 48.
64. Mrs T. Chippendale of the Chippendale furniture family was founder and president of the CMPA during its early years. While the CMPA devoted itself exclusively to the issue of Mothers' Pensions, a number of other women's organizations also continued to lobby the government to amend this policy. They included the New Era League, the WCTU, and Local Councils of Women. BCARS, GR 1323, Correspondence, 1902–1937, Reel B2211.
65. BCARS, GR 1323, Correspondence 1902–1937, Reel B2211, 'Letter from E.S.H. Winn, The Workmen's Compensation Board to the Attorney General', 23 Feb. 1923.

Indispensable But Not a Citizen: The Housewife in the Great Depression

Denyse Baillargeon

EDITORS' INTRODUCTION

The history of women in Canada is rife with contradiction. For example, First Nations women were critical to the success of the fur trade—they acted as scouts, wives, and go-betweens for White traders—but came to be dismissed by White society as primitive and wanton savages.[1] As Sylvia Van Kirk explores in this volume, by the mid-nineteenth century intermarriage was effectively 'colonized' and became a means primarily of taking Aboriginal women out of their own cultures, not of solidifying and improving First Nations–white relations. In the nineteenth-century white Christian wives and mothers were expected to create homes that were 'heaven on earth' for family members, as Lynne Mark's essay explores, yet they were to do so amidst the deepening inequalities of industrializing society. Women were likewise praised for being their children's 'most important teacher' but found themselves buried under a mountain of expert advice, often from men, which suggested mothers were incompetent and dangerous.[2] This contribution from Denyse Baillargeon explores another revealing contradiction that characterized the lives of poor and working class women in Montreal during the Great Depression: they were indispensable to the survival of their families, yet because they were lacking the vote and subject to the patriarchal hand of both their husbands and the Catholic Church, they were not considered full citizens of the society their labour shored up.[3]

Like the efforts of other scholars in this volume, among them Rusty Bitterman and Bettina Bradbury, Baillargeon takes on a seemingly exhausted topic in Canadian history and resuscitates it using the insights of feminist analysis. Her work demonstrates that when we pay attention to what women did in any historical context, taken for granted interpretations are often fundamentally challenged. Historians, for example, have asked why was there no serious revolt on the part of the working class in Montreal during the Great Depression. Terry Copp, as Baillargeon argues, concludes that the members of the working class were better off during these difficult years than is usually acknowledged and thus widespread unrest was effectively avoided. Foregrounding a feminist analysis that challenges how Copp determined this relative stability, Baillargeon asks us to look more closely and critically at the domestic management of Montreal housewives for more satisfactory answers to this appearance of stability.

The well-worn axiom 'a woman's work is never done' takes on a heightened meaning in the context of working class women who lived through the Depression years. Using oral histories, a methodology also employed by Epp, Chenier, and Sugiman to great effect in this volume, Baillargeon centrally positions domestic contributions made by women, particularly those of the working class, that often go undocumented and thus unacknowledged in the historical record. Not only does she give these contributions visibility, Baillargeon effectively links the domestic to more traditionally public questions of who has had the privilege historically of being acknowledged as 'citizen'.[4] How did women cope with little or no money being made by un- or underemployed husbands? What domestic strategies for survival did they marshal? How did gendered attitudes towards women's work to constrain their contributions? Baillargeon finds that, perhaps unsurprisingly, the labour of Montreal working class housewives not only spared their families from complete devastation during the Depression, but, in so doing, helped preserve their husband's masculine identity. Not entitled to access social welfare programmes in their own right, women's domestic skill was nonetheless critical to their husband and family's eligibility for help. Thus, the public welfare system, acknowledging only men as recipients of relief as heads of households, fostered and perpetuated women's second-class citizenship status. As Baillargeon points out, 'relief payments were as a rule largely contingent on good housekeeping', and women, as wives and mothers, were expected to ensure this was the case.

In order to comply, women employed a wide and inventive range of strategies to keep both bill collectors and hunger at bay. Some worked for meager pay outside the home (when husbands didn't object), others took in laundry, sewing, boarders, or provided childcare. They drew upon immediate and extended kinship circles for help and tried to negotiate a terrain of deprivation often not softened by the powerful Catholic Church. In fact, as Baillargeon found through her oral history interviews, the pressure on married women to continue to have babies throughout the crisis was a source of considerable emotional, physical, and economic stress. Religiously-backed, socially-sanctioned notions such as the conjugal rights of husbands, the mortal sin of birth control and abortion, and the association between motherhood and the feminine sense of self in Quebec society at this time, worked to severely constraint women's life choices. Whereas some couples certainly did work self-consciously to limit family size during these years, others conceded to the demands of Catholic dogma. In yet another contradiction with which women had to contend, large families could mean enduring a hell on earth to secure a place in heaven. In striving not only to 'make do' but to avert the violence associated with social desperation, Montreal's working class depended fundamentally on the wits and strengths of women.

Notes

1. Sylvia Van Kirk, 'The Role of Native Women in the Fur Trade Society of Western Canada, 1670–1830', in *Rethinking Canada: The Promise of Women's History,* 3rd ed., Veronica Strong-Boag and Anita Clair Fellman, eds. (Toronto: Oxford University Press, 1997), 70–8. Carol Cooper has shown that some Native women were also traders in their own right. Carol Cooper, 'Native Women and the Northern Pacific Coast: An Historical Perspective, 1830–1900', *Journal of Canadian Studies* 27.4 (Winter 1993/3): 44–75.
2. Katherine Arnup, Andrée Lévesque, Ruth Roach Pierson, eds., with assistance of Margaret Brennan, *Delivering Motherhood: Maternal Ideologies and Practices in the 19th and 20th Centuries* (London, New York: Routledge, 1990); Katherine Arnup, *Education for Motherhood: Advice to Mothers in Twentieth-Century Canada* (Toronto: University of Toronto Press, 1994).
3. This chapter is part of a larger study by Baillargeon entitled *Making Do: Women, Family, and Home in Montreal During the Great Depression,* trans. Yvonne Klein (Waterloo: Wilfrid Laurier University Press, 1999).
4. On 'citizenship' as contested terrain in Canadian history, see Robert Adamoski, Dorothy E. Chunn, and Robert Menzies, eds., *Contesting Canadian Citizenship—Historical Readings* (Peterborough: Broadview Press, 2002); See also a special issue of *Canadian Woman Studies/Les cahier de la femme* 20.2 (Summer 2000).

Questions for Critical Reading

1. Women have long been considered less worthy of political citizenship than their fathers, husbands, sons, and brothers. Who else has been denied citizenship in Canadian history? What has this exclusion been based upon? How are constraints based on gender, class, sexuality, race, able-bodiedness, and ethnicity implicated in the historic denial of citizenship in Canada?
2. Baillargeon's essay reminds us that the domestic labour of women has been traditionally undervalued throughout Canada's history. Compare Baillargeon's findings with Sedef Arat-Koç's essay in this volume. What parallels, if any, can be drawn between poor working-class women in Depression-era Montreal and the experienced of foreign domestics from deemed to be from 'less desirable' backgrounds? How is race implicated in this?
3. In some ways the Québécois women studied by Baillargeon cope with poverty in much the same way as the Carrier women analyzed by Fiske. Yet what empowers the Aboriginal women seems to disempower the Montreal housewives. What accounts for this discrepancy?

In an article published in 1975, the historian Terry Copp, after describing the difficult conditions that the Montreal working class endured during the Great Depression, concluded, 'One of the great mysteries of the depression decade is the reason for the relatively low level of social unrest . . . that these conditions produced.'[1] It is true that, despite especially high rates of unemployment, the 1930s did not see any extraordinary incidence of working-class mobilization. Leaving aside the On to Ottawa Trek that was staged by young single men who were inmates in the Bennett government's labour camps, it must be said that mass demonstrations were extremely few and that protests by the unemployed did not seriously threaten the foundations of the liberal economy or the capitalist social order.[2] Addressing himself to the task of elucidating this mystery, Copp attributes the relatively stable social climate first to the fact that only a minority of wage-earners, which he estimates at twenty per cent, were profoundly affected by the Depression, and second to the decrease in the cost of living which would have more than made up for reductions in wages. As a result, 'many working-class families were, in fact, better off during the 1930's than they had been in the 1920's.'[3] In essence, Copp suggests that the times were not 'hard' enough to provoke revolt.

Copp may be correct, but the arguments he advances are certainly not sufficient to explain a phenomenon such as this. In the years since Copp wrote this article, a number of feminist historians have made the point that the economic indicators he cites to explain the weak level of social protest actually turn out to be quite imperfect instruments for evaluating working-class standards of living. Hence it would be risky to draw conclusions from these indicators concerning the revolutionary potential of such social conditions. Indeed, if we consider underemployment, small business and shop bankruptcies, and the extraordinary length of time that certain groups of labourers were without work, especially in the building trades, we might just as easily conclude that the Depression generated a measure of poverty and of economic, social, and psychological insecurity much greater than that revealed by official statistics. Wages were not, however, the sole resource upon which families depended for their support. From the beginning of industrialization, working-class families had employed a range of survival tactics that were based as much on the labour of women in the home as on that of male breadwinners and of children.[4] The responsibilities undertaken by women within the home were indispensable even during 'prosperous' times such as the 1920s; they turned out to be even more crucial during the Depression when government relief measures were far from making up for losses in wages.[5] For this reason, these women are unquestionably one of the key elements we must take into account if we are to understand properly the weakness of social protest in the period compared with the economic collapse that characterizes it.

More recently, several feminist historians have also observed that the Great Depression has appeared, both at the time and in retrospect, as an essentially 'masculine' crisis, as a crisis of masculinity, in fact, because it undermined the breadwinner status that constituted the foundation of male power and identity.[6] All the same, the aid programs, home relief, and public works established by the nascent Canadian welfare state operated to support the prerogatives of the male heads of the household, as married women, seen as the economic dependants of their husbands, could not avail themselves of such relief programs directly.[7] The intervention of the Canadian government may have been reluctant and largely inadequate, but it did confirm the privileged access men had to a source of income, a proof of both their independence and their status as citizens. In so doing, state policies simultaneously consolidated patriarchal family structures and encouraged men to remain faithful to their role as breadwinner.[8] Housewives, excluded as they were from the job market and subordinate to the man of the house, were not regarded as citizens of the developing welfare state even if, implicitly, the state recognized women's contribution to family maintenance.[9] In fact, relief payments were as a rule largely contingent on good housekeeping, which state representatives checked up on through home visits to recipients; likewise, the allocation of tracts of land to aspiring 'pioneers' in the 'colonization areas' depended upon the ability of their wives to adapt to a life on the farm.[10] Thus the state expected women to make a specific contribution to their families' welfare as a complement to whatever public assistance it might extend. Governmental measures and the unpaid labour of women in the home combined to cushion the worst effects of the Depression not only on the economic scheme, but also on patriarchal social and family organization. Placed under severe strain in the public marketplace, the bases of masculine identity were thus preserved in the domestic sphere, which probably contributed to calming any rebellious urges on the part of married workers and fathers.

On the basis of thirty interviews undertaken among francophone women from Montreal,[11] in this chapter I will examine the dynamics of gender relationships and the contribution made by women to the survival of workers' families during the Great Depression. In the 1920s or at the beginning of the 1930s, these women, from poor backgrounds, married labourers, white-collar workers or small businessmen who, for the most part, would suffer from periods of joblessness or underemployment.[12] This 'feminine' take on the economic crisis will bring to light the dependence of both society and the state upon these 'non-citizens', providing an excellent example of the inter-relation between the public and private spheres as well as of the ways in which social policies and private welfare activities are articulated. The latter rely, in particular, on the failure to acknowledge the citizenship of housewives in the same way as that of men.

The Gender of Work

When women married, it was understood that they would quit work in order to take care of the house and the children, while their husbands would work outside the home to earn the money needed for the household. The ideology of separate spheres was so entrenched that this gendered division of labour seemed to spring from immutable natural law, and so the question would never even arise as a topic of discussion between engaged couples. Almost by instinct, these women knew that the male identity depended on the ability of the husband to 'support' his wife and they were perfectly aware of the social prohibitions against paid work for married women. As one respondent said, 'Married women weren't allowed to work in those days. My husband did not marry me for me to support him . . . . Men had their pride. They didn't want their wives working' (I23).[13]

Though the breadwinner/homemaker model was rigid, it could allow certain accommodations. In fact, almost two-thirds of these women worked for a salary or wages even before their husbands fell victim to unemployment or cuts in pay due to the Depression.[14] In reality, at the time of their marriage, only five of the husbands earned more than twenty-five dollars a week, the level that could be termed a decent salary; more than half were earning less than twenty dollars a week and a few were making less than ten dollars. According to the figures of the federal Department of Labour, it would require $20.18 a week in Quebec merely to cover the costs of food, heating, light, and rent, these outlays representing approximately 65 per cent of the expenses needed by a family of five.[15] From all the evidence, the image of the homemaker wholly dependent on the male wage and exclusively dedicated to housework and child care represented a virtually unattainable ideal for the majority of these poor working-class households. In the absence of a genuine 'family wage', family survival depended by necessity on intensive domestic production and the extremely close management of the household budget, to which were often added the earnings from paid work of the mother of the family.

Unable to make ends meet, especially after the birth of their first children, several of these women sought sources of supplementary income. Five of them worked at jobs outside the home for brief periods; the others worked at home in one or more paid capacities, sometimes several at a time, in addition to carrying out their household responsibilities. They did sewing, knitting or took in laundry, they took care of boarders, they worked as domestics, managed a small business, sold home-made baking—all ways of transforming their 'feminine' expertise into hard cash. While the amounts they were able to earn from these activities varied considerably—depending on how much they charged and on the customers who used their services (if they were working for themselves, for example), or on the amount of work they did for their employers in a given week—this monetary contribution on the part of women might represent a considerable part of the household income: 'We didn't have enough money. I used to smock baby clothes. Then I had my boarder who gave me six bucks a week. That helped a little, my husband was making ten dollars a week' (I13). Without always representing such a large proportion of the total family income, the money these women earned in their 'spare time', as they put it, often made the difference between living below or just a little above the poverty line. It also allowed them to avoid going into debt: 'It didn't pay a helluva lot, but it was only that it gave me a little something at the end of the week. . . . When [my husband] didn't have enough, then I was the one who paid, I would put it toward the rent or to buying clothes for the kids. . . . It meant that we stayed out of debt' (I17).

If male salaries were largely inadequate before the Depression the financial situation of the majority of families deteriorated even further during the 1930s. Unemployment, underemployment, and pay cuts affected the great majority of heads of households, forcing more than half of them to fall back on relief payments. This circumstance did not, however, lead to a major disruption in attitudes, limited by the patriarchal social norms in force, toward the financial contribution of wives to the family economy. Thus only two women became the principal support of their families while their husbands were unemployed. On the other hand, nine of the men lost their jobs for periods ranging from several months to several years without there being any question of their wives looking for work. Full-time homemakers since the day they married, they pointed to various obstacles to explain this paradox, such as the number of children at home, the impossibility of finding work, even work at home, but also, and

women doing jobs

perhaps chief of all, the opposition of their husbands. 'I would have liked to go to work,' one of them maintained, 'but [my husband] didn't want me to. Anyway, the children were too little, I couldn't leave them. In those days, you didn't leave your babies with someone else' (I20).

For this woman, as for several others, having young children seemed to present a major barrier to her entry into the job market, even if the father, who was unemployed, would have been available to take care of them.[16] Mothering was so profoundly identified with femininity that it seemed unthinkable that it could become a male responsibility. Most of these women also asserted that there was no employment to be had, even if they had not actually looked for work, or that jobs were strictly reserved for men, a discourse that was an article of faith during the Depression.[17] As one woman mentioned, 'There wasn't any more work for girls than there was for men in those days. . . . And I'd never had a job,[18] let me tell you I'd have had a lot of trouble finding work too' (I19). Another declared: 'Married women did not have the right to go to work. . . .There was too much unemployment. . . .they would rather hire heads of families' (I6).

Underneath these arguments, one detects a strong reluctance, as much from the women as from their husbands, against bringing about a reversal in roles that would be incompatible with defined and accepted social norms[19]—indeed, in these instances, the sexual division of labour was integrated in so rigid a manner that it precluded any possibility of redefining, even briefly, how responsibilities were shared within the home. The opposition of a husband resolved to preserve his dominant status was probably the determining factor in most cases, but, as Margaret Hobbs suggests, some of these full-time homemakers perhaps were fearful that if they were to stand in for the male breadwinner, they might encourage their husbands to lose interest in their family obligations.[20] In this connection, moreover, the women were anxious to stress that it was the husband's assignment to apply for government aid, a chore they were happy to leave to him: 'It wasn't me who would have gone—I would have starved to death before going to ask for home relief . . . He knew perfectly well that he was the man of the family—it was up to him to go see them. It wasn't up to me' (I19). In this very special circumstance, where it was a question of publicly admitting an inability to take care of his family, having breadwinner status was nothing to envy. The men who had this experience suffered a profound assault on their masculine dignity and came out of it feeling humiliated. Nevertheless, remitting aid to the head of the family left power relationships within the family intact. Those wives who were economically dependent on husbands who refused to shoulder their responsibility to provide for their families, perhaps because they drank or gambled for example, had to stand by while the resources necessary for their survival and that of their children were continually squandered: 'The dole was given in the husband's name, not the wife's. So that meant that he went to collect it and if he spent it, then you had nothing. It happened a lot—he went to get the relief money and when he came home, he didn't have a penny left' (I22).[21]

The women who had engaged in one or several paid occupations at home before their husbands lost their jobs continued and even augmented their work as far as was possible.[22] But none of them imagined replacing the work they did in the home with an outside job, which, by their own admission, their husbands would never have stood for: 'During the Depression, I took in sewing to bring in some money. I was a big help to my husband—he did the best he could and so did I,' one of them remarked. But when she was asked if she had thought about looking for a paying job, she answered, 'My husband would never have let me, not at all' (I22). Just like the men whose wives made no financial contribution to the household before they were unemployed, those who agreed to their wife's working at home for pay would never have put up with her finding a job outside the home. This reversal of roles would have been a direct threat to their superior position as man of the house and would have represented too stern a blow to their pride, which had already been sufficiently shaken by their failure to fulfill this role adequately.

Just as the wives did not attempt to take over their husbands' place as breadwinner, the men were not prompted to participate more fully in the housework because their unemployment gave them more time on their hands, even if they already were in the habit of doing certain chores, like going to the store or washing the floors. Undeniably, the majority of the women considered the house their domain and they themselves did not ask for any additional help. To ask for help was the same as admitting that they were not able to carry out their part of the husband-wife contract, and that would bring their own femininity into question: 'We didn't ask them to help us—as far as we were concerned, it was our work.' We said, 'We don't want to have them in our pots and pans.' We were the ones who looked after that' (I29). Many others agreed: 'When you're married you each have your own job' (I7). Additionally, a number of these men spent most of their time outside the house. Some of them were employed for short periods on public works projects or were doing various kinds of odd jobs,[23] but others stayed away regularly, claiming to look for work. In this way, they could escape the 'female' universe in which they had difficulty situating themselves and which could seem to threaten them—constant immersion in the world of women could be seen as yet another attack on their already shaky male identity, weakened as it was by their being out of work.[24] The women themselves preferred their husbands to get out of the house, as they found their unaccustomed presence rather annoying or even a bit abnormal, since men did not belong in the domestic space: 'Oh, sometimes, I'd really get fed up. I used to think, this is not his place. A man's place is to go to work, not to hang around the house' (I19). Even if the wives sometimes expressed impatience at having their husbands underfoot, they rarely complained about it to them. Part of their wifely role was to maintain their husbands' morale and preserve their self-respect; they fulfilled this by not seeking to become the principal breadwinner and by avoiding reminding the men of their failure to provide properly for the family. Some of these women insisted that their husbands had also tried to cheer them up. It is certainly possible that some of these men had kept their feelings of insecurity or desperation to themselves in order to preserve their image as a protector able to cope with any situation. Still, one of the few men who did participate in part of the interview with his wife acknowledged that he had often cried in secret.

Making Ends Meet

According to a tradition that was deeply rooted in the working class in Quebec as well as elsewhere, it was most often the wife who was responsible for managing the family budget. As several feminist historians have observed, giving over the pay envelope to the wife, far from representing a real delegation of power, allowed the men to avoid the trial of having to manage on insufficient wages (a reality that called their status as breadwinner into question) without having to go so far as to renounce the definite privileges which that status conveyed.[25] Most of the men in fact kept back a certain amount for their own expenses or expected that there would be something left over for them if they said they needed it. For their part, the women were explicitly aware that they were managing money earned by someone else and clearly felt that it was not theirs by right. Their economic dependence thus induced women to get by on the amount available without complaining about not having enough money, which in turn contributed to maintaining the myth that their husbands continued to be adequate providers.

Despite the additional amounts that women's paid work provided, their families' income was still generally very low because these extras most often added to only the lowest of wages. Making ends meet represented a daunting challenge confronting most of these women. To respond to it, they committed themselves to an extremely strict set of priorities to which they made every effort to conform, no matter what. At the top of the list came the irreducible expenses like electricity and rent, seen as 'debts' that

they made a point of honour to pay regularly. The remainder of the money went for food, for wood or coal for the stove, and, in last place, clothing, transportation, and insurance, if there were a few pennies left. Very few among them were able to save anything at all. Households that had succeeded in accumulating any savings had to nibble away at them before resigning themselves to signing on for the dole.

Checking prices, buying only what was strictly necessary, wasting nothing, and not going into debt were watchwords that recurred constantly in their oral testimonies: 'I never wasted anything' (I1); 'You had to really know not to buy anything you didn't need. We didn't waste a thing' (I26). What they got in return for this dedication was the most intense household labour, with a bare minimum of domestic appliances and in housing conditions that were often substandard. On their coal or wood stoves, which were also the only source of heat, they cooked every meal, from soup to dessert, not to mention pickles, jams, and jellies. Those who had learned how to sew made most of the clothing, at least for the children, often out of old clothes they altered to fit. Most of them sewed the household linen—sheets, tablecloths, dishcloths, bedspreads, and curtains. As well, most of these women had a sewing machine, if only to repair rips and tears. This purchase, more advantageous because it represented a source of savings, often came before a washing machine, and it seems that the majority delayed until the second or third child appeared before buying one of these. Despite the absence of this convenience, very few of the women patronized commercial laundries and none used their services on a regular basis. What this meant was that for some significant time almost all the women did the washing on a washboard in a laundry sink or bathtub, if there was one in the flat.

The amounts that the women could spend on rent, between twelve and eighteen dollars a month, restricted them to substandard accommodations, that is, to flats that were poorly lit, badly insulated, with softwood floors that were difficult to keep clean, and sometimes infested with rats and cockroaches.[26] All these lodgings were connected to the municipal water mains and had electricity, but rarely were they supplied with gas; less than half of the women interviewed had always lived in quarters that were equipped with a bathtub and almost none of them could afford to buy or rent a hot-water heater. Their inadequate incomes often meant that these families had to make do with accommodations that were too small, even if it meant sacrificing the living room in order to make an extra bedroom. Some of the children might have to sleep in the kitchen or in the hallway on a folding bed that was put up and taken down daily.

This brief sketch reveals that, for these women, managing the family expenses proved to be an almost obsessive concern, while housework represented a trying, physically exhausting obligation that they had to carry out in difficult circumstances, without always having the household conveniences they needed to do it. Faced with the consequences of unemployment and shortened work weeks, they had very little room to manoeuvre, considering what they were already providing for their families. Indeed, their domestic production encompassed such a range of products and services that, when the Depression hit, it was difficult for them to add new tasks to those that they were already doing. But since they were already consuming no more than necessary, reductions in wages and, even more, the low level of state assistance obliged them to reduce their expenditures in vulnerable areas, which translated into an increase in and intensification of their workload and ever-greater deprivation, which they were often the first to experience.

Buying the least possible was already one of the habitual consumer strategies of these housewives. Particularly when it came to food, however, they often found it hard to cut back on quantities. Therefore, the housewives sought new ways to economize by purchasing lower quality goods and by procuring their groceries in new ways. For instance, some of the women began to buy their meat directly from the abattoir rather than from the local grocery, which permitted them to obtain greater quantities at the same price though they had to travel longer distances to get there. It was also possible to get cut-price meat by buying it late on a Saturday evening, just before the stores closed;[27] a number of grocers who did not have refrigeration preferred to get rid of their stock rather than risk losing their merchandise by storing it until Monday morning. Some of the women would get fruits and vegetables that were on sale or even being given away because they were wilted or beginning to rot, even if it meant taking a little more time to prepare them: 'It was a lot of work to make them all right to eat. Sometimes they were starting to go. But if you picked out what was edible . . .' (I5). Just one of the respondents tried several times to make bread, but, as she pointed out, it was a long and complicated process, not to mention that her inexperience made it more likely that there would be waste. It was cheaper to go directly to the bakery at the end of the day: 'We would go there at four o'clock in the afternoon when the bread runs came back. We could fill up a whole pillowcase with bread for twenty-five cents. You'd see everybody there—I would see them on the corner, they all had a pillowcase folded up under their arm or some of them had bags . . .' (I20).

Preparing the same amount of food with fewer means and from inferior quality products required a good pinch of ingenuity to create appetizing meals. Sausage, minced meat, spaghetti, and noodles appeared very often on the table, prepared in every imaginable way. Dishes in sauce, made with a base of flour and water, were also an economical solution, since they generally did not contain meat: 'I made potatoes and white sauce, eggs and white sauce, beans and white sauce, and tinned salmon and white sauce. We ate a lot of paste!' (I25).[28] Desserts were skipped altogether or consisted of 'broken biscuits' sold cheaply in bulk or made from recipes that did not ask for expensive ingredients, like the famous 'pouding chômeur' (literally, unemployed pudding, poor man's pudding).

Despite all of these strategies, some of the informants and even their husbands simply had to deprive themselves of food so their children could eat: 'I would make a stew, as we called it. . . . I would make it out of spaghetti and whatever stuff was the cheapest and the most nourishing. But that doesn't mean we were well fed. . . . All it meant is that we had something to eat and even then sometimes we had to leave it all for the children' (I27). One couple often made do with macaroni and butter and sugar spread on bread, while another informant admitted that she had often eaten sugared bread dampened under the faucet. Another explained, 'We often ate mustard sandwiches . . . before the next cheque would come. When we got to the last stretch, we had a little jar of mustard and a few slices of bread and we would say, we're going to have to be happy with that—what do you want, there isn't anything else. . . . My mother-in-law would come and take my little girl. As long as I knew my little girl would have something to eat, it was all right, I knew we'd get by' (I19).

During spells of unemployment, buying clothing was the first thing to go. Women, whose wardrobes were already strictly limited, were the most likely to pass up new garments in favour of devoting whatever resources were available to clothing for their growing children or for their husbands who had to go out of the house more often. One of them recalled that during the Depression she had only two dresses to call her own: 'I only had two dresses—wash the dress, iron the dress. Two days later—wash the dress, iron the dress. . . . Me, who hates to iron!' (I26). Some respondents patronized the outlets run by the Salvation Army or St Vincent de Paul, while others, who had never previously done any sewing, had to resign themselves to learning how: 'That's when I learned to sew because I used to buy ready-made clothes for my kids in the beginning but later on, I couldn't. . . . You had to make new clothes out of old ones. Everybody gave me clothes—I'd take them apart and make them up for the kids. I didn't have a machine—I'd go to my mother's to use hers' (I12).

Half of the families also moved, sometimes several times, into ever cheaper housing, which meant smaller, less comfortable, and less well-equipped accommodations.[29] Women were thus forced to give up what little comfort and convenience they had enjoyed. If the whole family suffered from the deterioration in their housing conditions, it was the women, for whom the house represented both their workplace and their living space, who were the most affected. For women, moving to new accommodations represented an increase in their work as well. Not only did they have to find the new flat and pack and unpack the family's belongings, but they also had to clean it from top to bottom and, if they had the money, repaint or repaper, run up new curtains, and the like.

The Depression likewise deprived a number of these women of their customary amenities, for a number of reasons. One of them, for example, did the laundry for several months in the bathtub because she did not have the money to get her machine fixed: 'I had a wooden agitator with a handle in the side and the wringer was broken, which meant I had to do the wash in the bathtub. And it was only something that cost thirty-nine cents. I did the laundry for I think five or six months in the bathtub like that' (I27). Others avoided using their electrical appliances, especially the iron or the washing machine, in order to save on electricity. Those who had their lights cut off because of unpaid bills reported doing some of their chores in the evening, when they could reconnect illegally without worrying about inspectors from the company coming by, but this seriously complicated their housework schedule.[30] Finally, two of the women went back to live in the countryside because their husbands were not able to find jobs and could not reconcile themselves to going on the dole. Without electricity or running water, they had to give up their washing machines and other electric appliances and return to making a good number of items at home, like bread and soap, which they had previously bought. These two women had already experienced this kind of life, which made it easier for them to adapt to their new situation. All the same, it represented a net loss in the standard of their working conditions.

In short, even though these women were already doing practically everything they already could to balance their budgets and could only with great difficulty do more, the Depression nevertheless meant an increase in the burden of their household tasks, since they had to accomplish them with less money, less space, and fewer conveniences. Without any extra help from their husbands, they had to shoulder the additional labour occasioned by loss of income all by themselves and they were generally the first to leave the table hungry or to manage without decent clothing. The unequal distribution of resources within the home, already a present reality for these families before the Depression, was only heightened in the absence of a wage.[31]

Motherhood

More than other Canadians, Québécoises at the beginning of the century were the target of religious and medical pronouncements that exhorted them to have children in order to insure the future of the 'race'.[32] This pro-birth rhetoric, reinforced by legal prohibitions on birth-control devices and by the notion of 'conjugal duty', which presumed the husband's unlimited and unconditional access to his wife's body, varied by not a single syllable during the Depression. For women starting their families in this period, the intransigence of the Church, which could impose individual control over their behaviour through the agency of the confessional, meant they had but two choices: they could either live in the perpetual anxiety of 'getting caught' or employ 'artificial contraception' and experience a profound sense of guilt.

From their wedding day, these women deeply desired to have a baby, since motherhood represented one of the fundamental elements of their feminine identity. As one of them said, 'Life was having children' (I24). The daily responsibilities of taking care of them and raising them did, however, become a heavy load to carry, especially when money was short. Repeated pregnancies represented a considerable burden for women whose strength was being sapped at the same time that they had to undertake greater toil. If her husband lost his job, she would spend her pregnancy in conditions that were worse for her own health and that of the child she was carrying, as she would not be eating properly or receiving adequate medical supervision. From the strictly monetary point of view, the arrival of another child might turn out to be simply a catastrophe. The doctor's fees alone for a delivery amounted to at least ten dollars, an astronomical sum in view of the fact that this was the equivalent of a week's wages for the poorest worker. Then there would be another mouth to feed at a time when there wasn't enough money as it was. A birth represented such a drain on the family finances that *Assistance maternelle* of Montreal, a female philanthropy founded in 1912 with the aim of offering material aid and free medical care to poor mothers, was rapidly overwhelmed by the demand: whereas in the 1920s it helped an average of 800 women a year, in the 1930s it aided between 3,000 and 4,000 expectant mothers annually.[33]

After the birth of two or three children, a number of these women wished to space out their pregnancies and, despite the fulminations of the Church, fifteen of the couples[34] did indeed take steps to prevent conception. The economic situation certainly played a considerable role in their desire to limit the size of their families, but it should be noted that economic difficulties were not the only motivation underlying this decision and did not always lead to the use of contraception. In fact, if the majority of couples using birth control did rely on home relief for a greater or lesser period of time or suffered from cuts in income, the women also offered other reasons to justify their choice, like the workload involved in a large family and the desire to pay enough attention to each of the children and bring them up properly: 'I told the good Lord to send me children, but that I did not want them to suffer afterwards. Large families always have problems. Someone is always overlooked in a big family, even if it isn't meant. . . . I said, I'd rather have a small family and be able to give them what they need. It was their education that I was thinking about for later' (I16).

On the other hand, other couples, equally affected by serious financial problems, never imagined the possibility of limiting the size of their families. One of the women, who was pregnant sixteen times and bore eleven children although her husband rarely worked and drank up a portion of what he did earn, stated, 'I thought that's the way it always was, since I came from a big family' (I22). Another said, 'There wasn't anything, you never heard of anything that would prevent a baby. . . . You'd often think, if I only had something. . . . Some had ways that they talked about, but I only learned about them later' (I3), while a third woman maintained, 'Birth control was out of the question. It was the law of the Church. You had to have babies' (I29).

Ignorance of contraceptive practices and the internalization of religious values could therefore lead to an almost fatalistic acceptance of successive pregnancies, despite precarious economic circumstances. But more often than not, it was those couples whose relationships were the most hierarchical, where the husband's authority was the most heavily felt, and where all discussion between husband and wife was absent who were the least likely to control their fertility. In view of the contraceptive means available—condom, withdrawal, and the rhythm method[35]—the women could not manage without the agreement and cooperation of their husbands. It was the men who had all the freedom to decide how and how often sexual relations would take place and they could easily decide not to worry about any possible consequences. Women who had not sought to limit their families and who were confronted with particularly trying economic conditions spent their pregnancies in anxiety and dread lest they not be able to provide sufficiently for their babies: 'He was working up until 1933. . . . After that there wasn't any more construction. And the little ones kept coming every year. That was really hard. They have to eat, eh? But when the man isn't working . . .' (I12).

On the other hand, given the religious climate of the period, women who did turn to contraception had guilt and reproach to deal with. Even when they were convinced of the logic of their decision, most of the women who limited the size of their families felt they were in the wrong in breaking the rules

How did the Depression affect Motherhood?

of the Church and continued to confess their sin, at the risk of being refused absolution, something that happened to more than one of them: 'Oh, yes, madame, I was refused absolution, yes, indeed, that happened to me. I didn't repent because I was using my head. In my opinion, the priests were there to inform us, but they weren't there to raise our kids. And in those days, it wasn't easy. . . . You know, women always felt guilty because in those days . . . when you went to the retreat . . . we had one evening in the week about it, you were going to go straight to hell. . . . When you came away, you were shook up, let me tell you' (I16). Even if it was the men who actually employed the contraceptive, it was the women who were condemned by the Church. Men seemed to have a much more elastic conscience and, in order to be left in peace, did not hesitate simply to hide the facts from their confessor. One husband recommended that, if his wife wanted absolution, she not tell 'what we do in our own bed' (I6). Another felt fully justified in limiting the size of his family in the light of his income: 'My husband said, I'm the one who earns the money. It doesn't make sense to live like the animals, neither better or worse' (I5). Used to enjoying a large measure of autonomy and to exercising both their free will and their authority, men easily convinced themselves that they were well within their rights, especially as their earning capacity was objectively demonstrable.

For women, more children certainly meant more work, more worries, and greater risks to their own health, but the Church and patriarchal society had taught them that their needs and even their lives counted for little in the scheme of things: 'It was cruel when you went to confession. It was not a small thing to say that you had used birth control. . . . The priests would scold us. . . . We would tell them, 'The doctor said that I mustn't have any more children.' They didn't care—the baby would live even if the mother died. That's all they had to say to us. It wasn't right' (I5). Whether or not these couples used contraception, their histories reveal that motherhood for these women represented more a source of anxiety than of joy.

Help From the Family

Even with increased household production and a decision to limit the number of children, most of these families, especially those who lived for a number of years on the dole, could not have coped without the support of their relatives. Mutual aid within families did not of course occur simply in times of economic crisis; rather, it was a common occurrence necessitated by poverty.[36] But what stands out in the histories is the differences in the help provided depending on economic circumstances. In ordinary times, for example, services most commonly rendered would include baby-sitting during a lying-in or an illness, and the exchanging or giving of clothing, but we can also observe the very frequent practice of sharing certain implements of work, like a sewing or washing machine or the use of the telephone. The tendency of relatives to settle in the same neighbourhood or even in the same street facilitated these exchanges.

An effect of the Depression was the enlargement of the range of services rendered by relatives. Gifts of meals or foodstuffs and fuel increased, as did gifts and loans of money and of shelter for the young couple: 'Oh, they helped me a lot because they brought me lots of vegetables from the country. I had a sister who was married to a farmer and that meant she could bring me lots of vegetables. . . . We would go over to my mother's, sometimes for weeks at a time. . . . If we didn't go, she'd send someone over to us. . . . She'd say, 'Come over, I want some company. . . .' Then I'd do a lot of little things while we were there . . . like sewing, knitting. I made a lot of things when I was at my mother's. . . . We were lucky to always have my mother-in-law. . . . If we didn't have enough to eat, we would go and eat at her house, and that was that. . . . My mother-in-law would come for my little girl. . . . Sometimes she'd keep her for three or four days' (I19).

All these kinds of help obviously went beyond the framework of customary exchanges, and some of the women who benefited from them felt decidedly dependent on their families: 'It was my mother who had me under her wing. Mama would send over food to eat—we didn't have anything to eat—he was out of work' (127). Another remarked, 'I didn't like it very much. If I had been on my own, that's OK, but there was my husband and my little boy. . .' (19). Even if it came from very close relatives, these women still felt as humiliated to be on the receiving end of this sort of assistance—which exposed not merely their extreme poverty but also their husband's failure to provide for his family's needs—as they did to turn to the state for aid, something which the majority of couples viewed only as a last, and shameful, resort.[37] The ideal of financial autonomy, a measure of respectability, was a value so deeply rooted in the majority of these couples that one of them even hid the fact that they were on the dole from those closest to him.

This case is, however, exceptional. In fact, more often than not, the immediate family played an essential role in supporting those of its members who were afflicted with unemployment. In theory, the state granted aid only to those without work who absolutely lacked any resources and who could not turn to their families for help. In practice, families contributed in many ways to supply those needs that the meagre relief allowances granted to the unemployed could not provide for, especially in regard to clothing, food, and shelter. The amounts dispensed as aid were so inadequate that any hope of surviving on them, not, at least, without going seriously into debt, was an illusion. After having exhausted their own resources and every tactic for cutting down on their spending, these couples then turned to their own families. The Depression thus intensified the importance of the traditional networks of mutual aid that depended on the commitment of women relations. The contribution made by the work of female relatives, most particularly mothers and mothers-in-law, was just as essential as governmental aid to maintaining a minimum standard of living for the families who were helped. In short, it was all of these women, and not merely those wives whose husbands were out of work, who bore the brunt of the effects of the Depression.

Conclusion

Unlike their masculine counterparts, working-class women were not unemployed during the 1930s as their families counted more than ever on their labour, their dedication, their self-sacrifice, and their ingenuity in order to survive. Of course the contribution they made to supporting the family did not prevent a decline in the standard of living of their households, but the domestic labour of the wives of unemployed men, together with that of the women of the extended family and state welfare payments, meant the difference between poverty and abject destitution and made it possible to cope with material conditions of existence that would otherwise have been viewed as intolerable. In fact, women's private welfare efforts represented an essential complement to meagre public assistance. Women thus acted as an important social stabilizing factor during this troubled period in Canadian history, even though the women themselves were not considered full-fledged citizens. Montreal housewives of the 1930s held only partial political citizenship since they did not have the right to vote in provincial elections. Unlike other Canadian women, they were still deprived of their societal rights by reason of their maternal function, whereas the Bill concerning needy mothers would not be finally adopted until 1937. Both the Church and the criminal code prohibited them, at least in theory, from controlling their reproduction. According to the civil code, they were subject to the authority of the head of the house and excluded in fact, if not in law, from the job market. They were thus denied full legal competence, self-determination, and economic independence, the bases of male citizenship. Seen as dependent on a male provider, it was only thus that women had access to state support, because, except for rare exceptions, they could not claim the role of head of the family on which rested the social rights that were conferred on men at the beginning of the Depression. Established as a way of preserving the patriarchal structure of both society and the family order, the economic dependence of women, which was at the core of their non-citizenship, nevertheless camouflaged the interdependence of the family and of society on the work they did, which was unpaid and disregarded. Hidden from the eyes of their contemporaries and from history, their domestic endeavours were crucial all the same to softening the impact of the Depression on the family structure. In the end, it is probably no accident that social protest arose primarily among young single men with no family connections.

Notes

1. Terry Copp, 'The Montreal Working-class in Prosperity and Depression', *Canadian Issues* 1 (1975): 8.
2. See Andrée Lévesque, *Virage à gauche interdit. Les communistes, les socialistes et leurs ennemis au Quebec, 1929–1939* (Montreal: Boréal, 1984) for an appraisal of social conflict in Quebec and especially in Montreal.
3. Copp, 'The Montreal Working-class', 8.
4. Bettina Bradbury, *Working Families: Age, Gender and Daily Survival in Industrializing Montreal* (Toronto: McClelland & Stewart, 1993).
5. The scale of allowances fixed by the city of Montreal was set at $36.88 a month in summer and $39.48 in winter, the amounts allotted to cover the costs of food, fuel, rent, and clothing for five persons. These sums constituted barely half the minimum considered necessary by the federal Minister of Labour. See Leonard C. Marsh, *Canadians In and Out of Work: A Survey of Economic Classes and Their Relations to the Labour Market* (Toronto: Oxford University Press, 1940), 193.
6. Ruth Roach Pierson, 'Gender and the Unemployment Debate in Canada, 1930–1940', *Labour/Le Travail* 25 (1990): 77–105; Margaret Hobbs, 'Rethinking Antifeminism in the 1930s: Gender Crisis or Workplace Justice? A Response to Alice Kessler-Harris', *Gender and History* 5.1 (1993): 4–15; Cynthia R. Comacchio, *The Infinite Bonds of Family: Domesticity in Canada, 1840–1950* (Toronto: University of Toronto Press, 1999), 124.
7. This was the case except in certain narrowly defined circumstances. On the topic of aid programs adopted during the Depression, see James Struthers, *No Fault of Their Own: Unemployment and the Canadian Welfare State 1914–1941* (Toronto: University of Toronto Press, 1983).
8. In its report for 1935, the Society for the Protection of Women and Children of Montreal stated: 'During the past five years, "failure to provide" and its companion offence "desertion" by the male parent has progressively and markedly decreased.' The report attributed this decrease (of 33 per cent) to the lack of work and to the distribution of welfare that kept families together. In contrast, in 1946, the same association recorded an increase of 48 per cent in cases of desertion and failure to provide in comparison with the preceding year and concluded: 'We can look for an upswing in these figures, because it has always been our experience, proved by records, that with the return of economic prosperity, desertions, the number of which always tapers off in periods of financial depression, increase markedly.' (Archives nationales du Canada, MG28I129, Society for the Protection of Women and Children 2 Minutes and 6 Minutes, 1947–50).
9. On women as citizens and the specific mode of their integration into the state, see Carole Pateman, 'The Patriarchal Welfare State', in *Feminism: The Public and the Private,* ed. Joan B. Landes (Oxford and New York: Oxford University Press, 1998), 241–76 and Sylvia Walby, 'Is Citizenship Gendered?' *Sociology* 28 (1994): 379–95.
10. Denyse Baillargeon, *Making Do: Women, Family, and Home in Montreal During the Great Depression,* trans. Yvonne Klein (Waterloo, ON: Wilfrid Laurier University Press, 1999).
11. For summary biographies of these women, see Baillargeon, *Making Do.*
12. Thirteen married between 1919 and 1928, five in 1929, ten between 1930 and 1932, and two in 1933 and 1934. Twenty-six of the spouses were either manual or non-manual workers. One was unemployed at the time of his marriage and had rarely had a job, while the three remaining owned small businesses (a barber shop, a snack bar, two taxi cabs). We must make it very clear that the status of owner did not mean that they enjoyed a standard of living necessarily higher than that of those working for others, since the Depression forced two of them to sell up before bankruptcy. Of the other twenty-six, only four neither lost work nor suffered from salary cuts during the period. Four others had their work week shortened by one or more days, and three others, though working the same hours had their wages cut by as much as 20 per cent. Seven were without a steady job for more than three years, six for a period of between one or two years, and the remaining one for only a few months. Two other participants in the survey had to turn to the St Vincent de Paul Society for help or to home relief because their husbands refused to support them. In all, fifteen of the couples received

support of some sort and two chose to go back to the land as a way to cope.

13. The quotation is taken from interview number 23. Hereafter, references to interviews will be indicated by an upper-case I followed by the interview number.
14. Only three of them looked for a way to make money specifically because their husbands were partly or wholly out of work. Veronica Strong-Boag likewise notes that married English Canadian women often had to earn money to make up for the shortfall of the principal bread-winner in the period between the two world wars. 'The incorporation of paid work into domestic routines appeared relatively commonplace in both the 1920s and the 1930s, a good index of how tough times were not restricted to the Great Depression' in Veronica Strong-Boag, *The New Day Recalled: Lives of Girls and Women in English Canada, 1919–1939* (Toronto: Copp Clark Pitman, 1988), 125.
15. Quebec, *Annuaire statistique,* 1930 and 1934, 400 and 426; Canada, Ministére du Travail, *La Gazette du Travail,* février 1933, 249.
16. The women who did work outside the home had a maximum of two children and someone other than the husband took care of them, even when he had the free time to do it.
17. On this topic, see Hobbs, 'Rethinking Antifeminism in the 1930s'.
18. In fact, this informant had taught for a year before getting married, but she did not seem to consider this a real job.
19. On the impossibility of reversing roles during the Depression, see Mirra Komarovsky, *The Unemployed Man and His Family* (New York: Arno, 1971) and Ruth Milkman, 'Women's Work and Economic Crisis: Some Lessons of the Great Depression', *Review of Radical Political Economics* 8 (1976): 85.
20. Hobbs, 'Rethinking Antifeminism in the 1930s', 9.
21. In fact, article 23 of the Montreal Unemployment Commission regulations stipulated that 'If the husband drinks or gambles away his aid cheque, then the registrar should immediately be informed. He will see to it a new registration is made in the spouse's name or that of another responsible person or Society that can replace the head of the family. . . .' This article does not seem to have been widely circulated, and, in any event, in order to get benefits paid in her own name, this woman would have had to challenge openly her husband's prerogatives and authority, something which seemed impossible to her (Montreal, Commission du chômage, *Renseignements à l'usage des chômeurs nécessiteux et des propriétaires* [Montreal: n.p., n.d.], 6).
22. Which it was not always. During hard times, even professional dressmakers lost some of their private clientele, for example.
23. Before turning to the state for aid, or even while on the dole, six of the men tried hard to support their families by undertaking various sorts of work. Digging out a cellar with a shovel, washing walls and ceilings, shovelling snow in the fashionable districts of the city, reselling breads and cakes bought directly from a commercial bakery at the end of the day when the unsold merchandise was returned, peddling the remainders of blocks of ice, bootlegging alcohol which the man made in his shed (and hid in the baby carriage for delivery!), and opening a little restaurant at home were some of the notable stopgaps to which the men, newly unemployed, turned in order to find new sources of income.
24. Hobbs, 'Rethinking Antifeminism in the 1930s', 8.
25. Meg Luxton, *More Than a Labour of Love: Three Generations of Women's Work in the Home* (Toronto: The Women's Press, 1980), 161–99; Strong-Boag, *New Day*, 133–44, Elizabeth Roberts, *A Woman's Place: An Oral History of Working-Class Women, 1850–1940* (Oxford: Basil Blackwell, 1984), 125–68; Pat Ayers and Jan Lambertz, 'Marriage Relations, Money, and Domestic Violence in Working-Class Liverpool 1919–39', in *Labour and Love: Women's Experiences of Home and Family, 1840–1940,* Jane Lewis, ed. (Oxford: Basil Blackwell, 1986), 195–219.
26. An equipped six-room flat cost from twenty five to forty dollars a month in January 1929 and from eighteen to thirty-three dollars in January 1933. A six-room flat without modern conveniences, or only partially equipped, cost between sixteen and twenty-five dollars a month in 1929 and between fifteen and eighteen dollars in 1933 (Canada, Ministére du Travail, *La Gazette du Travail,* février 1929, 256 and février 1933, 257).
27. In this period, most shops stayed open until eleven o'clock on Saturday night.
28. White sauce was made of water and flour, also used to make wallpaper paste.
29. The number of removals in Montreal was in fact on the rise throughout the initial years of the Depression: 54,000 in 1930, 55,000 in 1931, 65,000 in 1932, and almost 82,000 in 1933, according to figures supplied by Montreal Light, Heat and Power (*La Patrie* 17 avril 1931, 3 and 17 avril 1933). Moreover, the economic situation meant that the majority of families were looking for low-cost housing. This is why the best flats remained vacant while there was overpopulation in older housing, In this connection, see Mark Choko, *Les crises du logement à Montreal* (Montreal: Editions Saint-Martin, 1980), 109. I must mention, however,

that two of the couples in the study were able to buy property thanks to the rock-bottom prices of certain houses that were being sold for back-taxes. On the other hand, a third couple, who had bought a house due to a little inheritance just before the Depression hit, were forced out of it when their unemployed tenants could not pay the rent. In fact, it appears that the Depression more often generated the sort of situation that discouraged property buying since only 11.5 per cent were homeowners in 1941 compared with 15 per cent ten years earlier (Canada, *Recensement du Canada, 1931 and 1941*, V, 989 and XI, 98, cited in Choko, *Les crises du logement à Montreal,* 114).

30. It should be recalled that Montreal Light, Heat and Power enjoyed a virtual monopoly in the Montreal region, which permitted it to maintain high rates and to disconnect with impunity clients who failed to pay their bills. According to Robert Rumilly, more than 20,000 families were cut off from electricity in the depths of the Depression, cited in Claude Lariviére, *Crise économique et contrôle social: le cas de Montreal, 1929–1937* (Montreal: Éditions Saint-Martin, 1977), 175.
31. The unequal distribution of resources in poor households has been noted on numerous occasions by feminist historians and sociologists. In this regard, see the works listed in note 25 as well as Ruth Lister, 'Women, Economic Dependency and Citizenship', *Journal of Social Policy* 19.4 (1990): 445–67.
32. There have been a number of studies of this discourse. See Andrée Lévesque, *La norme et les déviantes. Des femmes au Quebec pendant l'entre-deux-guerres* (Montreal: Éditions du Remueménage, 1989).
33. *Assistance maternelle* provided a layette, bed linen, food, fuel, and sometimes even furniture. It also paid for the costs of the delivery and for a month's supply of milk following the birth [Denyse Baillargeon, 'L'Assistance maternelle de Montreal: Un exemple de marginalisation des bénévoles dans le domaine des soins aux accouchées', *Dynamis. International Journal of History of Science and Medicine,* Special number, *Mujeres y salud. Prácticas y sabers/Women and Health* 19 (1999): 379–400].
34. That is, a little over half the fertile couples, as two of the thirty in the study had no children.
35. Three of the couples using contraception employed condoms, eight engaged in withdrawal, and four used the rhythm method ('Ogino-Knauss'). The first two methods seem to have been the most frequently employed throughout Canada. See Angus McLaren and Arlene Tigar McLaren, *The Bedroom and the State: The Changing Practices and Politics of Contraception and Abortion in Canada, 1880–1980* (Toronto: McClelland and Stewart, 1986), 22.
36. In this connection, see Andrée Fortin, *Histoires de familles et de réseaux. La sociabilité au Quebec d'hier á demain* (Montreal: Éditions Saint-Martin, 1987); Marc-Adélard Tremblay, 'La crise économique des années trente et la qualité de vie chez les Montrealais d'ascendance française', Académie des sciences morales et politiques, *Travaux et Communications* 3, *Progrés Techniques et qualité de vie* (Montreal: Bellarmin, 1977): 149–65.
37. Recent studies reveal similar attitudes. See Lister, 'Women, Economic Dependency and Citizenship'.

From 'Mothers of the Nation' to Migrant Workers: Immigration Policies and Domestic Workers in Canadian History

Sedef Arat-Koç

EDITORS' INTRODUCTION

Many mainstream feminist organizations in Canada spent a substantial part of the late 1980s and 1990s grappling with the thorny, painful, and sometimes divisive question of race.[1] The women's movement, women of colour forcefully argued, had failed to address the significance of race—not to mention class, sexuality, and ability to women's lives. This critique was not wholly new: women of Aboriginal, African, and Asian descent had long argued that an adequate feminist politics must necessarily be an anti-racist politics, and prominent Canadian activists like Rosemary Brown had worked tirelessly to link racial and gendered issues.[2] But something was different in the closing decades of the twentieth-century. The Free Trade Agreement, the North American Free Trade Agreement, the General Agreement on Tariffs and Trade, the International Monetary Fund, the World Bank, and the G7, not to mention the increasing power of media empires like those of Rupert Murdock and Conrad Black and corporations like Montsanto and the Bank of Montreal, prompted Canadian feminists to think in global terms, terms that demand an acknowledgement of differences as well as commonalities between women.[3] Not unconnected was the changing racial and ethnic constitution of Canada. The combined impact of these changes was a women's movement no longer able to, or interested in, minimizing or ignoring anti-racist critiques.

Historical scholarship inevitably reflects changing contemporary politics. Taking the question of race seriously means re-thinking our understanding of Canadian women's history in some meaningful ways. It means, as Janice Fiamengo's discussion of first-wave feminist authors in this volume demonstrates, reconsidering our evaluation of earlier generations of feminist thinkers and actors. Taking race seriously also leads us to rethink the history of women's work, as Sedef Arat-Koç does in this article. Domestic service is in many ways the archetypal woman's job and, as Maureen Elgersman Lee's analysis of women and slavery suggests, one that had racial politics from the outset of settlement. Most women who worked for wages in British North America toiled in the homes of others. Such service in the homes of neighbours, especially for younger women, was longstanding. Increasingly, however, as Magda Fahrni has illustrated, respectability was hard to assert and maintain.[4] Beginning in the mid-nineteenth-century with the industrial revolution and continuing with the feminization of teaching and the administrative revolution of the early twentieth-century, more women, not surprisingly, would opt for paid work outside of the domestic sphere. Domestic service in one form or another, nevertheless, has remained a major area of women's employment until the present.

Clearly we cannot understand the history of domestic service without paying attention to gender, to the segmentation of the labour market, to the longstanding connections among women, housework, and childcare, and to women's place within the family and household. Nor, as feminist historians of the working-class in Canada have long reminded us, can we understand it without acknowledging the importance of class. Some women worked for other women, and to treat them as part of an undifferentiated whole an ignores the chasm of class that stood between them. As Arat-Koç's analysis deftly proves, we will also fail to understand domestic work unless we pay serious attention to questions of race. Throughout its history, Canada has looked to different groups of women to perform paid domestic work: to Natives, to enslaved Africans, to working-class Britons, to southern Europeans and Scandinavians, and, in the twentieth-century, to women from the Caribbean and, increasingly, the Philippines and Eastern Europe. The working experiences, pay, respect, and, perhaps most tellingly, citizenship rights given to these different groups of women have varied in enormous and telling ways.

Arat-Koç's analysis ends in 1970, but the issues she raises do not. Sunera Thobani has recently argued that the supposed neutrality of the 'point-based' system adopted in 1962 and revised in 1976–7 masks an immigration system that perpetuates racial and gender discrimination by favouring migrants from 'developed' countries, allowing immigration officers broad discretionary powers, and channeling women into the 'family class' of immigrants.[5] It also continues to rely on the 'unfree' labour of immigrant women. Instead of addressing what Arat-Koç elsewhere has called the 'crisis of the domestic sphere,'[6] or the need for accessible, quality child care and more equitable division of household labours, the Canadian state depends on the willingness of poor, non-citizen women to take jobs as nannies and caregivers. Many of these women are denied citizenship rights under the Live-in Caregiver Program, as the Foreign Domestic Movement was re-named in 1992. It is only by examining gender, race, and class simultaneously that we can begin to understand how these women continue to be both so needed by Canada and so excluded from genuine membership within the Canadian nation.

Notes

1. On this, see Amy Gotlieb, ed., 'What About Us? Organizing Inclusivity in the National Action Committee on the Status of Women', in *And Still We Rise: Feminist Political Mobilizing in Contemporary Canada*, Linda Carty, ed. (Toronto: The Women's Press, 1993).
2. Rosemary Brown, *Being Brown: A Very Public Life* (Toronto: Random House, 1989).
3. Christina Gabriel and Laura Macdonald, 'NAFTA, Women and Organizing in Canada and Mexico: Forging a "Feminist Internationality"', *Millennium: Journal of International Studies* 23.3 (1994): 535–62.
4. Jane Errington, *Wives and Mothers, School Mistresses and Scullery Maids: Working Women in Upper Canada, 1790–1840* (Montreal and Kingston: McGill-Queen's University Press, 1995); Magda Fahrni, '"Ruffled" Mistresses and "Discontented" Maids: Respectability and the Case of Domestic Service, 1880–1914', *Labour/Le Travail* 39 (Spring 1996): 69–98.
5. Sunera Thobani, 'Closing the Nation's Doors to Immigrant Women: The Restructuring of Canadian Immigration Policy', *Atlantis* 24.2 (Spring/Summer 2000): 16–26.
6. Sedef Arat-Koç, 'Importing Housewives: Non-Citizen Domestic Workers and the Crisis of the Domestic Sphere in Canada', in *Through The Kitchen Window: The Politics of Home and Family*, 2nd ed., Meg Luxton, Harriet Rosenberg, and Sedef Arat-Koç, eds. (Toronto: Network, 1990).

Questions for Critical Reading

1. Why is the question 'who does housework?' so central to feminists? What does housework tell us about how power and resources are allocated in society?

2. How have changes in technology affected the performance of and responsibility for housework?
3. How are the child care policies discussed by Jane Jenson and the domestic servants analyzed by Arat-Koç related?
4. Why might some women choose to look after other people's children for pay? What might programmes like the Live-in Caregiver Programme offer to individual women?

In the last two decades, the legal status of domestic workers in Canada has worsened. In all countries where there are paid domestic workers, gender and class inequalities have largely structured their socio-legal status and working conditions. In Canada, however, historical variations in the status and conditions of domestic workers have more directly been linked to the histories of racism and immigration. Precisely at a time in Canadian history when citizenship rights were generally improving for women, the status and conditions of foreign domestic workers significantly deteriorated. In line with other analyses,[1] this chapter argues that changes in the racial/ethnic composition of migrant domestic workers have played an important part in this deterioration. This chapter traces the historically differential treatment domestic workers from different racial/ethnic backgrounds and different source regions have received from Canadian society and the state until 1970. It focuses in particular on the different state and societal interests, policies, and practices regulating British domestics and those foreign domestics deemed to be from 'less desirable' backgrounds.

Race, Citizenship, and Domestic Workers

Hidden in the household and considered 'women's work', domestic service has never enjoyed a favourable status. Even though subordination as women and as workers has been a universal condition of domestic workers in industrial capitalism, there is a specific relationship between the rights enjoyed by domestics and their relationship to, or membership in, the Canadian nation and the state. Most modern states are characterized by hierarchies of citizenship rights. Contrary to a model of universal citizenship whereby citizenship rights are accessible to all members of a society, some groups lack many or most such rights. Such groups can be said to exist within the boundaries of state regulation but outside the boundaries of the national collectivity, and with lesser access to state-provided citizenship rights. Women of colour, who have made up the majority of immigrant domestic workers arriving in Canada in the postwar period, are considered to be neither members of the Canadian nation nor citizen-members of the state. Yet highly regulatory immigration practices ensured that they were very much *inside* the state.[2]

Racism, Immigration, and Domestic Service

In Europe, class and gender inequalities were the main determinants of relationships in domestic service. In Canada, as well as in other settler colonies, racial and ethnic inequalities also played a very important role.[3] Immigration schemes, policies, and practices have been important mechanisms in regulating the racial/ethnic composition of society and determining the status and conditions of those who have been allowed in.

In Canada, domestic service has historically been often associated with forms of unfree labour. Contrary to popular opinion, slavery did exist in Canada until it was gradually eliminated in the late eighteenth and early nineteenth centuries. The first Canadian slaves were Native peoples, frequently Pawnee or Panis. Black slaves were also brought by their employers, who were often United Empire Loyalists. Most female slaves were employed as domestic servants.[4] Pervasive anti-black racism continued even once slavery was abolished in Canada and meant that black women had few labour market options beyond domestic service. Dionne Brand estimates that at least 80 per cent of black women in Canadian cities worked in domestic service as late as the 1940s.[5]

At different times, some groups of white immigrant women who were recruited to provide domestic service also entered as unfree labour, but this did not have the same consequences for their future status and conditions in Canada. For many white women, domestic service was only a stage of life and a bridge to a different life. In New France, domestic service was often performed by *engagés*, indentured servants from France whose passage had been paid in advance by their future employers. Given the small population of the white colony and the even smaller numbers of women, *engagés* were encouraged to marry immediately after the end of their bond. In some cases, they were even allowed to break their contract on condition of marriage.[6]

In the early nineteenth century, in the rural areas of Canada and the northern United States, local white women who were hired as domestics experienced less rigid status differences in relation to their employers. Called 'help' instead of 'servant', these were women who were hired for short periods of time to contribute to their families' income and/or to help a neighbour.[7] The conditions of help contrasted sharply with relations in bourgeois households in the cities, where the social distance between employers and employees was growing. So significant were the rural/urban differences that *The Canadian Settlers' Handbook* advised prospective immigrant domestics that they would enjoy 'social amenities' in rural Canada, but that 'no lady should dream of going as a home-help in the cities, for there class distinctions [were] as rampant as in England.'[8]

The character of domestic service changed from the middle of the nineteenth century to the 1920s. As the urban middle-class family became more privatized, its emphasis on domestic comforts and luxury increased, and therefore it became dependent on outsiders to actualize its standard of a private haven. Changes in the nature of work, and among the workers performing this type of work, precluded improvements in working and living conditions for domestic workers. The separation of the public and private sphere and the decline in the general status of the domestic sphere corresponded with a rapid feminization of domestic service. Between the early and late nineteenth century, within a period of approximately 60 years, the percentage of women among urban domestic workers grew from 50 per cent to 90 per cent.[9]

Further contributing to a decline in the status of servants, or alternatively, in certain regions, to the persistence of their low status, was the availability of groups of vulnerable workers. In American regions where there were large concentrations of people of colour, it was usually women of the oppressed racial/ethnic groups who had no choice but to accept domestic service positions.[10] In Canada and the northeastern United States, different groups of white immigrants who were perceived as socially and indeed 'racially' inferior provided a source of vulnerable labour. Irish women who were fleeing economic desperation at home found almost no alternatives to domestic work and therefore became particularly vulnerable. In the 1870s, in all urban centres in Canada except Quebec City, Irish immigrants were so highly represented among domestics that domestic service came to be identified with Irish women. Claudette Lacelle found that over the course of the nineteenth century, popular perceptions of domestics became more unfavourable, the level of discipline to which domestic workers were subjected increased, and their working conditions deteriorated.[11]

It was in the late nineteenth century that immigration began to be used systematically to recruit and control domestic workers. This was a time when the demand for domestic workers increased while the supply from among native-born women declined. The growth in demand corresponded to the higher standards of housekeeping of a rising urban middle-class at a time when household technology remained underdeveloped and housework extremely laborious. The decline in supply was due to industrialization, which opened up new labour market options for working-class women—in factories, hospitals, offices, retail outlets, and schools. The conditions of domestic work, especially live-in service, were so unfavourable that working-class women with any other choice took the latter even if the pay was lower. As Canadian-born women came to shun the isolating and menial conditions of domestic service, ever-greater efforts were made to recruit immigrant women to meet the unabating demand.

The solutions sought to this shortage by both the state and a vibrant middle-class social reform movement 'focussed more on maintaining the supply of workers through carefully supervised immigration than on reforming the conditions of household work'.[12] In the early twentieth century, more than one-third of domestic workers in Canada were foreign-born. In western Canada, the proportion was much higher. In 1991, in Winnipeg, as much as 84 per cent of domestic workers were born outside of Canada .[13]

While the demands of the labour market for domestic workers encouraged recruitment of workers from abroad, the dominant forces in Canadian society and the state were selective about where domestics would be recruited from. After Confederation, the state began to regulate immigration through legislation and to use immigration policy as the major means of actively controlling the racial composition of Canada. Immediately after the completion of the railway in 1885, which relied on the back-breaking labour of some 15,000 Chinese male workers, the government passed a Chinese Immigration Act, which imposed steep head taxes on Chinese immigrants.[14] Unique sets of regulations also severely restricted the entry of South Asians, Japanese, black Americans, and West Indians, and restricted their access to state entitlements and citizenship rights.

In the early twentieth century, British women constituted more than three-quarters of immigrant domestics coming to Canada. A number of immigration schemes introduced in the late nineteenth and early twentieth centuries were aimed specifically at attracting British women to Canada. The treatment of British domestics under these schemes reflects a complex and sometimes contradictory intersection of gender, class, race, and nationality. While the amount of planning and energy involved in immigration schemes tells us a great deal about how desirable these women were as immigrants in terms of their racial/ethnic stock and the demand for their intended occupation, their working conditions as well as their paternalistic treatment reflect a subordinate class and gender status.

British Domestic Schemes and Nation-Building in Canada

To make sense of Canada's approach to and treatment of British domestic workers in the late nineteenth and early twentieth centuries, we need to place these issues in the context of changes in Canadian society and its discourses of nation-building. White, and especially white British, women were a powerful symbol in the transition of Canada from a fur-trade to a settler society in the Canadian West. The arrival of white women decreased the prevalence of marriage between white men and Native and mixed-descent women, and underlined attempts to define Canada as a British society.[15] In their roles as mothers and culture-bearers, white British women were expected to help entrench British culture in Canada and pass it on to future generations. Through their role as 'God's police', they would also contribute to the creation of a more 'stable' and 'respectable' colonial society.[16]

The importance of women in colonies was stressed on both sides of the Atlantic. In Britain, female emigration was emphasized by some as perhaps the most important part of empire-building: 'as respects morals and manners, it is of little importance what colonial fathers are in comparison to colonial mothers.' The absence of the civilizing influence of white women could result in irresponsibility and immorality for men in a colony of all white males. In a colony with a balanced sex ratio between male and female colonizers, on the other hand, 'every pair of immigrants would have the strongest motives for industry, shrewdness, and thrift.'[17]

In the racist discourse of nation-building, class biases also shaped the perceived appropriateness of women as settlers. 'Civilization' was not thought of as a universal attribute of all women. Helen Reid, a well-known social worker in Montreal, expressed why working-class women needed to be kept out of Canada. In her view, working-class women would 'bring with them only too often, serious mental and moral disabilities. These women either glut the labour market here, reducing the wages of working men, or end up alas! too frequently in our jails, hospitals or asylums.'[18] Only women from a certain class background and of a certain moral character could embody and transmit the virtues of civilization as defined by British and British Canadian authorities and moral reform leaders.

There was often a contradiction or even a conflict between the economic dimension of colonization and its political and ideological dimension as a 'civilizing' force. The labour requirements of the colonies demanded the strenuous labour of women on farms and in domestic work. Women of the middle and upper classes, who were thought to be the ideal colonizers and civilizers, could hardly be ideal candidates for the drudgery of domestic service or the challenges of pioneer farming. The tension between the conflicting demands of colonization was partially solved in the nineteenth century with the availability in Britain of 'surplus' or 'distressed' gentlewomen. These were single women from middle-class and educated backgrounds who were impoverished by economic circumstances or the death of a spouse.[19]

The late nineteenth century was still a period when immigration was not totally formalized and bureaucratized by the state. As part of the reform movement, many middle-class women took an active part in female immigration work through women's organizations. These women were also usually the employers of domestic workers. Active in social reform work, charitable, or sometimes feminist organizations, middle-class women in late-nineteenth-century Canadian society 'were urged to delegate the household tasks which had previously occupied most of their time, in order that their civilizing influence no longer be confined to home and family'.[20] Immigration work by female reformers was directed at recruitment, 'protection' during transportation, and their placement upon arrival. While class interests were important motivations leading women reformers to this work, their interest in immigration needs to be distinguished from that of business, of transportation agents, or even sometimes of the state. Aware that British female immigrants would become the 'daughters of the Empire' and 'mothers of the race', they were concerned as much about the 'quality' of recruits as about their numbers and the potential economic benefits they would bring to Canada.[21]

The incessant concern for the 'quality' of female immigrants was not always experienced as a privilege by immigrant domestics even if they were of the 'right stock' and of a respectable class background. For women, true 'belonging' in the nation was conditional upon demonstration of Victorian morality. Poor, single women, even those from a 'gentle' background, could not be trusted to maintain high moral standards. Therefore, middle-class women who were involved with emigration and immigration societies in Britain and in Canada did not hesitate to recruit selectively and to closely monitor and curtail the freedom of the chosen ones. British emigration societies, in collaboration with Canadian organizations like the National Council of Women of Canada, required very strict recruitment and screening procedures. In addition to references and a personal interview, they introduced a compulsory medical examination, which was extended to all immigrants later.[22] Women's organizations also overtook the responsibility to 'protect' and supervise women during overseas voyages. Immigrant women usually travelled under the supervision of matrons, who were women from a middle- or upper-class background. Matrons supervising parties of women carefully watched their charges to make sure they would not waste their time or befriend unsuitable acquaintances. Once they arrived in Canada, women were taken into hostels and shelters approved by and supervised by women's groups and then accompanied to their final destination.[23] While claiming that their philanthropic immigration work was for the protection of women and their respectability, women's groups often did not hesitate to co-operate with the police and the state to help deport 'unsuitable' immigrants. In what Mariana Valverde calls 'philanthropic deportation', women reformers participated in the deportation of significant numbers of domestic workers.[24]

Compared to domestics from other racial/ethnic backgrounds who came before and after them, British domestics enjoyed a very privileged position. Unlike domestics from other backgrounds, not only were they seen as unquestioned members of Canadian society and nation, but if they lived up to 'appropriate' Victorian standards of 'true womanhood', they were also regarded as civilizers and nation-builders. Unlike other groups, British domestics at the turn of the century were brought to Canada for more than their capacity to labour as domestic workers. Like the few groups of 'desirable' immigrants, British domestics benefited from assisted passage in their arrival to Canada.[25] The sense that white British domestic workers were 'privileged' must be moderated by the knowledge of their subjection to extensive social control. Neither the demand for their work nor the desirability of their background guaranteed better working conditions. The ways in which British domestics were 'protected' and 'helped' by women reformers not only limited the freedom of domestics as women and as persons, but generally reflected the class differences between the two groups and served the needs of women reformers as employers, rather those of domestics as workers.

Between 1888 and the 1920s, when the government did not directly provide assisted passage, private agents arranged for advanced loans from employers, which would tie domestics to them for a specific length of time. The Department of Immigration sometimes evaded legislation in order to fulfill its policing function. For example, around the turn of the century, most of the provinces passed master and servant legislation, which aimed to protect domestics from an exploitative contract which they might have signed in order to immigrate. According to this legislation, contracts signed outside the province were not legally binding. The Immigration Department, however, aiming to enforce indentured status, avoided this legislation by having domestics re-sign their contract upon arrival in Canada.[26]

Being of the desirable racial/ethnic stock was also not necessarily experienced as a privilege by the 80,000 British children who were brought in as indentured farm and domestic help to Canadian farms. Between 1868 and 1925, concerns with imperial nation-building and the health of the British race led to efforts by emigrationists to remove working-class children from urban slums and rescue homes in Britain and place them in the good environment and the 'healthy family life' of colonial farms. At a period when changing conceptions of childhood and approaches to child labour were already affecting working-class children favourably in Britain, these children were not only exploited as workers but sometimes shunned for potential criminal tendencies and moral and physical degeneracies.[27]

Domestic Workers from Europe

As the Canadian state failed to fulfill its objectives to populate western Canada and meet Canada's labour needs through an exclusively British source of immigration, it looked to other sources of immigrants. In the late nineteenth century, continental Europe and the United States were considered the least objectionable alternative sources to Britain. There was a substantial increase in the numbers of non-British domestics in the 1920s. By the early 1930s, as many as one-fourth of immigrant domestic workers coming to Ontario were from continental Europe.[28]

Scandinavian Domestic Workers

In the early twentieth century, Scandinavian countries were a favoured source of domestic workers second only to Britain. Even in the midst of the Depression, in 1937 Canada started a special scheme to bring in domestics from this region. To encourage immigration of Finnish and other Scandinavian domestics, the Canadian government 'bent immigration regulations, created special categories and made easier travel arrangements'. The overwhelming majority of Finnish women who came to Canada in the early twentieth century worked as domestic servants. In Winnipeg, for example, all Finnish women, except a few who worked in restaurants, were domestic workers. When native-born women and British immigrants were starting to move to other jobs in the labour-market, Finnish women, despite the diversity of skills they brought to Canada, remained concentrated in domestic work, mainly because of language problems.[29]

Lindstrom-Best argues that Finnish domestic workers were 'proud maids' who enjoyed a high status in the Finnish community and relatively favourable conditions at work. Class, gender, and ethnocultural solidarity facilitated the emergence of a proud collective image and organizations dedicated to improving working opportunities and conditions. Because most women in the Finnish community in Canada were domestic workers, class divisions were absent among women of the same ethnocultural background. The labour and socialist organizing traditions many Finnish immigrants brought with them to Canada meant that some ethnic organizations served as virtual labour locals. The Finns built 'immigrant homes' in several cities and started employment services for domestic workers. In this climate of class and ethnic solidarity, Finnish domestics were able to share information and refuse low wages and bad working conditions. Even in their first year in Canada, many were able to change jobs frequently in order to ensure improved conditions and resist the abysmal treatment normally accorded to recent immigrant domestics.[30]

Central and Eastern European Domestics

The number of immigrants from the British Isles was insufficient to fulfill the defined objectives of populating western Canada—securing the territory from the United States and developing an agrarian economy. In response, the Canadian state began accepting immigrants from the non-preferred sources. In 1925, the government signed a Railways Agreement with the Canadian Pacific Railway and the Canadian National Railway, which authorized the two companies to recruit and place farmers and domestics. In the years following the Railways Agreement, the number of domestic workers coming to western Canada from continental Europe grew significantly. In Manitoba, in 1921, the British made up 60 per cent of immigrant domestics and Europeans accounted for 30 per cent. By 1931, the ratios were almost reversed.[31] Unlike the preferred British domestics, domestic workers coming from continental Europe were not given assisted passage. Most domestics coming from Central and Eastern Europe were considered to be 'of the peasant type' and insufficiently familiar with standards and equipment of housework in middle-class homes to work anywhere but in rural households.[32]

Among Central and Eastern Europeans, however, there was one group of domestics who were preferred for urban employment. These were the daughters of Russian Mennonites who came to Canada as refugees and were themselves from servant-employing backgrounds. The Mennonites were able to establish Maedchenheim, or Girls' Homes, in several cities including Winnipeg, Saskatoon, Vancouver, Regina, and Toronto. Similar to the hostels for British domestics run by women reformers, the Maedchenheim offered temporary shelter for new arrivals and served as social centres. Unlike the hostels but like the Finnish immigrant homes, these centres had no connections to employers and therefore worked to protect domestic workers. They would accompany the domestic to her place of employment, inspect the house with her, remove domestics from unfavourable working environments, and keep a blacklist of employers to whom they would refuse to send domestic workers.[33]

During and following the Great Depression, when many native-born women lost the few alternative sources of employment open to them, domestic work became once again the major employer of women as a whole. Despite the dire state of the economy, there was actually an increase in this period in the number of domestic workers. A generalized fall in wages and prices meant that families with fixed or steady incomes who could not previously afford domestic workers could now do so.[34] In this period, married women joined single women in returning to domestic work on a live-out, or sometimes live-in, basis while their unemployed husbands stayed home with the children. Central and Eastern European domestics who had come to Canada in the late 1920s faced special difficulties. They could only find work with very low wages and very bad working conditions.[35]

Following the trend begun in the nineteenth century, the demand for domestic workers in the postwar period again exceeded the supply. And once again, the Canadian state turned to recruiting from foreign sources, with vulnerable groups providing the obvious recruits. And as usual, racism would play an important role in determining who among the vulnerable would be recruited. In the postwar period, the first group of immigrant domestic workers came from among refugee women in the displaced persons (DP) camps in Europe. Between 1947 and 1952, Canada accepted around 165,000 displaced persons on the condition that they would work under a one-year contract in specific occupations whose wages and conditions were unacceptable for Canadians. Men were accepted as agricultural workers, miners, and loggers; women as domestic workers in institutions—as cleaners and kitchen workers in hospitals, sanatoria, orphanages, and mental institutions—or private homes. Humanitarian considerations took a back seat to economic motivations and ethnic considerations in the selection and immigration of DPs. The Canadian state not only specified the occupations in which refugees would work but also indicated ethnic and religious preferences. Racial considerations are apparent in Department of Immigration memos. They articulate a clear preference for domestic workers coming from the Baltic countries of Estonia, Latvia, and Lithuania because of their perceived similarity to Scandinavians. There was also a preference for Protestants, even though they were a minority among DPs. With the exception of an experiment placing a few Jewish women in Jewish homes, Jewish women were considered as an unsuitable source, ostensibly because very few Jews had previous experience in domestic service.[36]

The recruitment criteria reflected the gender and class assumptions that had been long applied to domestic servants but that seemed harsher given the conditions of refugees in postwar Europe. To qualify under the program, women had to be single or widowed, between 18 and 40 years of age, and of 'good average intelligence and emotional stability', and had to go through strict medical examinations which included tests for pregnancy and venereal diseases, as well as X-rays. Those who qualified signed a contract to remain in domestic service for one year. Even though prospective employers also filled out a form specifying wages and conditions of work, they did not have to show it to the domestic when she was hired.[37]

Paula Daenzer argues that the case of DP domestics constitutes a turning-point in the nature and meaning of indenture for immigrant domestic workers. In this period, the agreement to stay in domestic service for one year changed from a friendly 'gentleperson's agreement' to a mandatory imposition.[38] There were, however, no serious sanctions as yet for the non-fulfillment of contract, and domestics could easily change employers. Arthur MacNamara, the deputy minister of labour who designed the DP program, made it a policy that any DP who asked for a transfer was to be given one.[39] Despite the relative flexibility of the program, though, most DP domestics fulfilled their contract. Usually they remained with the same employer, motivated in part by gratitude to the Canadian government for the chance of a new life distant from their war-torn (and often Soviet-occupied) countries, as well as by fear of jeopardizing the chances for emigration of DPs still in camps.[40]

Southern European Domestic Workers

Refugee domestics were only a temporary solution to the problem of domestic shortage. In the early 1950s, Canada once again introduced assisted passage and made several attempts to recruit from the preferred Great Britain and Western Europe. With the exceptions of Germany and Holland, these attempts were futile. With the entrenchment of the Cold War came the end of any possibility of emigration from Eastern Europe. Only then did Canada decide to experiment with domestic schemes drawing from the least-preferred part of Europe: southern Europe.[41]

The Canadian state's approach to Italian immigration in the 1950s demonstrates how the conflicting immigration priorities of meeting labour market requirements and populating Canada with people of preferred races were played out. In the dominant racist view, Italians, especially those from the rural areas in southern Italy, were equated with hot climate, hot temperaments, dark skins, cultural backwardness, and undemocratic traditions 'better suited to the . . . "fragile" politics of Latin America'. Despite this perception, however, pressures from business in the booming economy of the postwar period compelled the government to decide that the presence of southern Italians could be tolerated provided they offered hard work and cheap labour in agriculture, mining, railway repair, and construction.[42]

A domestic scheme was also started in 1951 but ended the following year after only 357 women were recruited. The Italian scheme was similar to the one that brought in refugee women from DP camps. Prospective employers in Canada would submit 'orders' for domestic workers, and interested workers in Italy would sign a contract obliging them to stay in the designated occupation with the assigned employer for one year. Even though Canada had reintroduced the Assisted Passage Loan Scheme for domestics from Western Europe and Britain, it refused initially to extend it to Italian domestics and tried to persuade the Italian government, instead, to advance passage fares. The short life of the program had as much to do with the negative evaluation of domestics by the employers and by the state as it did with the lack of enthusiasm on the part of Italian women. Italian domestics were seen as ignorant, 'primitive villagers', whose backward cultural background had failed to prepare them for the high standards and sophisticated technology of Canadian housekeeping. They were also found to be feisty employees who complained about working conditions, demanded to change employers, or simply left domestic work before the end of their contracts to work in the factories and/or to join other family members in Canada.[43] Such demonstrations of freedom could not be tolerated in a group of women who were not considered 'mothers of the race' or carriers of culture. Like other non-British domestics, Italians were brought into Canada solely for the cheap labour they could perform in jobs that Canadians, when and if they had the choice, would not do.

Canada also organized domestic schemes with Greece and Spain in the postwar years. In a period of otherwise restricted immigration from Greece, domestic workers started to be admitted in 1956 to be placed with Greek employers. The program lasted until 1966 and brought in approximately 300 Greek women per year. A much more limited experiment involving 50 Spanish women took place in 1959–60. Placement difficulties brought an end to this program: Spanish authorities wanted Catholic homes, but most prospective employers were Protestant.[44]

Women of Colour in Domestic Work

Domestic workers from different regions of Europe experienced different levels of vulnerability in their relations with the Canadian state and society, depending on British-Canadian stereotypes, political circumstances, and their own traditions and prospects for resistance. Thus, while all foreign domestics have experienced varying degrees of coercion by the state and more powerful groups, European domestics have fallen along different points in the continuum of the treatment of immigrant domestic workers in Canada. Non-white domestic workers stand at the opposite end of this continuum. The Canadian government recruited women of colour only as a last resort. Since the 1960s, the 'liberalized' immigration policies have not expressed any explicit bias against domestics from non-European sources. Indeed, women from the Third World have predominated among immigrant domestic workers since the early 1970s. That status and conditions for domestic workers that would have been unacceptable half a century ago are currently considered acceptable suggests that racialized sexism and gendered racism are still alive and well in Canadian society and immigration policy.

Women of colour in Canada have been a source of domestic work during most of Canadian history, largely because they have historically been excluded from other possibilities in the labour market. At the turn of the century, Mi'kmaq women in Nova Scotia were excluded from industrial employment and were considered suited only for domestic work.[45] Black women did find industrial employment at a time of labour shortage during World War II but were subsequently the first group to be laid off.[46] In the postwar period, Canadian employers also utilized the cheap labour of 'Canada's own displaced persons', the Japanese Canadians.[47]

Even though employers demonstrated that they would accept domestic labour from any background providing the workers were cheap and docile, racial and ethnic considerations often dictated against an open-door policy in immigration. As long as recruits could be found from 'preferred' or 'not-so-objectionable' sources, Canada avoided non-white immigrants. The Immigration Act of 1910, in a clause which was not removed until 1978, gave the government of Canada the legal power to discriminate on the basis of race. The clause said that the government could 'prohibit for a stated period or permanently, the landing in Canada . . . of immigrants, belonging to any race unsuited to the climate or requirements of Canada'.[48]

In 1911, there was a very short-lived experiment with domestic workers from the Caribbean. With permission from the government, employers in Quebec arranged the immigration of approximately 100 French-speaking domestics from Guadeloupe. Racist assumptions about black women's sexuality played an important part in the public's perception of these domestics. The press also fabricated stories and fuelled fears of immorality. Even though the employers, in their own sexist, classist, and paternalizing way, generally responded positively, finding the women preferable to 'fussy' Canadian domestics, the government rejected most domestics in the second party on the grounds of physical and moral unsuitability.[49]

During the recession of 1913–5, when unemployed Canadians were willing to do domestic work, the government deported many Caribbean domestics already in Canada, arguing that they could become 'public charges'. More important than economic considerations was the fact that black domestic workers were, unlike their British counterparts, accepted only for their labour power, not as 'permanent assets' to contribute to the social and cultural life of Canada.[50] Department of Immigration memos suggest that Canada lost interest in Caribbean domestics even as a temporary and expedient measure when authorities calculated that the World War would result in 'better' types of immigrants.[51] Long after the end of the short-lived Guadeloupe arrangement, the alleged 'immorality' of these women was still being used to explain the restrictions on Caribbean immigration.[52] Immigration of black domestic workers did not occur again until the 1950s.

In 1955, after exhausting attempts to secure domestic workers from Europe, and with mounting pressure from Caribbean governments and Britain, Canada finally entered into a domestic scheme with Jamaica and Barbados. Because the scheme involved a breach of immigration regulations in place, the government used its Order-in-Council powers to put it into effect. Rather than acknowledging its gratitude for a much needed and qualified workforce, the Canadian government reasoned that the scheme was a favour to the countries of emigration. Caribbean domestics were not eligible to apply for the interest-free loans under the 1950 Assisted Passage Loan Scheme. Significantly different from many of

Canada's prior domestic programs, the Caribbean scheme required the sending countries to bear the responsibilities and the costs for recruiting, training, medically testing, and arranging the transportation of domestics to Canada. To qualify under the program, women had to be unmarried, between the ages of 21 and 35, and willing to do domestic work for at least a year with an assigned employer. Upon their arrival in Canada, the domestics, who had already undergone extensive medical tests, were also subjected to gynecological examinations.[53]

The gynecological tests and emphasis on the women's single status were intended to ensure that these women would be in Canada solely to fill a labour requirement and to eliminate the possibility of sponsoring spouses and children. Temporary migration, instead of permanent landed status, was contemplated for Caribbean domestics during the development of the scheme. However, the Canadian government decided against such a move on the grounds that it could be interpreted as a practice of forced labour and a blatant case of discrimination. The government also decided against temporary status on the assumption that, unlike European domestics, the Caribbean women would face discrimination in the labour market and thus most probably stay in domestic work past their one-year contract obligation. A third reason for the decision against temporary status was the possibility that the government could use 'administrative measures', instead of blatantly discriminatory policies, to prevent domestics from 'abusing' the scheme by moving on to other occupations.[54] In an unusual deal made with the governments of sending countries, Canada ruled that Caribbean domestics, if found unsuitable for domestic work, would be deported to the country of emigration at the expense of the Caribbean government concerned. No definition of 'unsuitable' was given in the agreement, which implied that Canadian immigration authorities could use unlimited discretion.[55]

At least initially, the Caribbean domestic scheme was considered to be the most successful domestic program initiated in the postwar period.[56] Canada was receiving an overly qualified workforce at no cost to itself. Many of the women recruited under the program were so highly educated that their emigration contributed to a brain drain form Barbados. Despite their qualifications, Caribbean women tended to stay in domestic service longer than European domestics arriving under similar schemes.[57]

Soon after the start of the Caribbean domestic scheme the immigration officials started raising concerns when some domestic workers made application to sponsor relatives. This perceived 'explosion' of sponsorship, with a consequent increase in numbers of undesirable immigrants, spelled an end to the usefulness of the program.[58] Immigration officials were also disappointed with the fact that despite the discrimination in the labour market, Caribbean domestics had a high mobility rate out of domestic service. Once again, measures were considered to ensure that immigrant domestics remained in domestic service. The deputy minister of immigration ruled against forceful tactics in this direction, arguing that it was 'unfair in a free market economy to try to freeze anyone in a lowly occupation'.[59] Despite the ambivalence towards the Caribbean domestic scheme, the state, fearing charges of racism from the black community in Canada and a breakdown in trade relations with Caribbean countries, continued the program until 1967, when the point-system became the basis of immigration policy.

Non-Racist Immigration or 'Justified' Discrimination? Foreign Domestic Workers Under the Point-System

Immigration criteria were 'rationalized' in the 1960s to make labour market needs the explicit basis for the recruitment of immigrants. In defining labour market needs, the point-system emphasizes Canada's need for highly educated and highly skilled immigrants, with education and skill measured in formally recognized terms. The new system has been celebrated as marking a liberalization of immigration policy. It has been declared a form of recruitment which has ended discrimination on the basis of ascribed criteria such as race and sex. Ironically, however, the use of the point-system has enabled the Canadian state to treat foreign domestic workers in the most unfavourable conditions legally possible in Canadian history since the abolition of slavery.

Because the definitions of 'skill' and 'education' in modern capitalist society approach domestic work as an unskilled and 'naturally' feminine job, domestic workers have been unable under the point-system to qualify as independent immigrants. Since the 1970s, the Canadian government initiated a temporary program to bring in domestics as migrant workers—that is, as workers lacking the freedom and rights of citizenship or landed immigrant status.[60] Indeed, immigration authorities deliberately and arbitrarily lowered the points awarded to domestic servants under the system so as to ensure that domestic workers did not qualify for entry as landed immigrants. Thus, indentured status for domestic workers, which in the 1950s was considered unacceptable in a free market economy, has become acceptable since the 1970s and remains acceptable at the beginning of the twenty-first century. Even though this practice is seemingly 'non-racist' and 'legitimate' within the sexist discourses of 'skill', 'education', and a potentially 'self-sustaining' immigrant, how this practice can be acceptable in an otherwise liberal democratic society should be subject to severe questioning.[61] It is not a coincidence that this change has taken place at a time when Third World women from previously unwanted sources constitute the major supply of foreign domestic workers in Canada for the foreseeable future.

Conclusion

Social, economic, and legal conditions of paid domestic workers are generally characterized by forms of subordination based on the gender and class status of the workers. In settler colonies like Canada, race and ethnicity have played a very important part, over and above gender and class, in shaping the status and conditions of domestic workers. This chapter has traced the differential treatment domestic workers from different racial/ethnic backgrounds have historically received from the Canadian society and the state.

While middle-class biases and paternalism were definitely a part of the schemes designed to bring British domestic workers in the late nineteenth and early twentieth centuries, these schemes also treated immigrant domestics as 'mothers of the nation' who were welcome to Canada as central participants in nation-building. Compared to British domestics, Scandinavian and Central and Eastern European domestic workers arriving in the twentieth century faced linguistic and cultural disadvantages. Even though they were not recognized as full members of a Canadian nation, they were able to improve their conditions of work to the extent that they enjoyed class and ethnocultural solidarity in their respective communities. In the postwar period, as the efforts to import domestics from the preferred source regions of Britain and Western Europe failed, Canada first tapped 'displaced labour' camps for Eastern European domestic labour and then entered into 'bulk' recruitment schemes with Italy, Greece, and Spain. Employers generally treated southern European domestics as ignorant, 'primitive villagers', who were culturally unprepared for the standards of Canadian housekeeping. Most of these schemes lasted for only a short time due to class, racial/ethnic, and religious biases against southern European women and the unwillingness of the workers to put up with unfavourable working conditions.

In immigration schemes designed to recruit domestic workers for Canada, women of colour were only considered as a last resort, when recruitment from all European sources failed. Since the late 1950s, the Caribbean and, since the mid-1970s, the Philippines have become the major source countries for foreign domestic workers. A very drastic change in immigration policies concerning domestic workers coincided with this shift in source countries from Europe to the Third World. It is ironic that the recent emergence of migrant, as opposed to immigrant, status for foreign domestic workers has come precisely at a time in Canadian history when Canada claims to have rid its immigration policies and procedures of racial and ethnic biases. Precisely at a time when Canada has started to define itself as 'multicultural', it has become easy to define some groups of immigrants as 'workers only',[62] as disposable non-members who, despite their indispensable contributions, are given no acknowledged part in the 'nation' or 'nation-building' project. The easy acceptability by many Canadians of migrant status for foreign domestic workers may have as much to do with racial/ethnic status of domestics as it does with the ever devalued status of domestic labour in modern society.

Notes

1. Abigail B. Bakan and Daiva Stasiulis, 'Foreign Domestic Worker Policy in Canada and the Social Boundaries of Modern Citizenship', in Abigail B. Bakan and Daiva Stasiulis, eds, *Not One of the Family: Foreign Domestic Workers in Canada* (Toronto: University of Toronto Press, 1997); Patricia Daenzer, *Regulating Class Privilege: Immigrant Servants in Canada, 1940–1990* (Toronto: Canadian Scholars Press, 1993); Felicita Villasin and M. Ann Phillips, 'Falling Through the Cracks: Domestic Workers and Progressive Movements', *Canadian Women's Studies* 14.2 (Spring 1994) 87–90.
2. The term 'inside the state' has been used by Beckett to characterize the overregulated lives of Aboriginal people. See J. Beckett, 'Aboriginality, Citizenship and the State', *Social Analysis*, 24 (1988).
3. See Daiva Stasiulis and Radha Jhappan, 'The Fractious Politics of a Settler Society: Canada', in Daiva Stasiulis and Nira Yuval-Davis, eds, *Unsettling Settler Societies: Articulations of Gender, Race, Ethnicity and Class* (Thousand Oaks, CA: Sage, 1995).
4. Marilyn Barber, *Immigrant Domestic Servants in Canada* (Ottawa: Canadian Historical Association, 1991) 3; Singh Bolaria and Peter Li, *Racial Oppression in Canada* (Toronto: Garamound Press, 1985) 165.
5. Dionne Brand, *'No Burden to Carry': Narratives of Black Women in Ontario, 1920–1950s* (Toronto: Women's Press, 1991).
6. Barber, *Immigrant Domestic Servants*, 3; Alison Prentice et al., *Canadian Women: A History* (Toronto: Harcourt Brace, 1988) 46.
7. Barber, *Immigrant Domestic Servants*, 4; Faye Dudden, *Serving Women: Household Service in Nineteenth-Century America* (Middleton, CN: Wesleyan University Press, 1983).
8. Cited in Helen Lenskyj, 'A "Servant Problem" or a "Servant-Mistress Problem"? Domestic Service in Canada, 1890–1930', *Atlantis* 7.1 (1981): 10.
9. Claudette Lacelle, *Urban Domestic Servants in Nineteenth-Century Canada* (Ottawa: Environment Canada, 1987).
10. Evelyn Nekano Glenn, 'From Servitude to Service Work: Historical Continuities in the Racial Division of Paid Reproductive Work', *Signs* 18.1 (1992): 1–43.
11. Lacelle, *Urban Domestic Servants*.
12. Marilyn Barber, 'The Servant Problem in Manitoba, 1896–1930', in Mary Kinnear, ed., *First Days, Fighting Days: Women in Manitoba History* (Regina: Canadian Plains Research Centre, 1987), 100.
13. Barber, *Immigrant Domestic Servants*, 7–8; Barber, 'The Servant Problem', 100.
14. Law Union of Canada, *The Immigrant's Handbook* (Montreal: Black Rose, 1981), 20–2.
15. Sylvia Van Kirk, *"Many Tender Ties": Women in Fur-Trade Society, 1670–1870* (Winnipeg: Watson and Dwyer, 1983).
16. Suzanne Buckley, 'British Female Emigration and Imperial Development: Experiments in Canada, 1885–1931', *Hecate* 3.2 (July): 26–40.
17. Cited in Barbara Roberts, 'Daughters of the Empire and Mothers of the Race: Caroline Chisholm and Female Emigration in the British Empire', *Atlantis*, 1.2 (1976): 108.
18. Cited in Mariana Valverde, *The Age of Light, Soap and Water: Moral Reform in Canada, 1885–1925* (Toronto: McClelland and Stewart, 1991), 126.
19. Susan Jackel, *A Flannel Shirt and Liberty: British Emigrant Gentlewomen in the Canadian West, 1880–1914* (Vancouver: UBC Press, 1982), xxi.
20. Lenskyj, 'Servant Problem', 4.
21. Roberts, 'A Work of Empire'; 'Ladies, Women and the State: Managing Female Immigration, 1880–1920', in Roxanne Ng, Gillian Walker, and Jacob Muller, eds, *Community Organization and the Canadian State* (Toronto: Garamond, 1990).
22. Lenskyj, 'Servant Problem', 8; Valverde, *The Age of Light, Soap, and Water*, 126.
23. Roberts, 'A Work of Empire'.
24. Valverde, *The Age of Light, Soap and Water*, 124–7.
25. See Barber, 'The Servant Problem'; Barber, *Immigrant Domestic Servants*, 9–10.
26. Genevieve Leslie, 'Domestic Service in Canada, 1880–1920', in Janice Acton, ed., *Women at Work: 1850–*

1930 (Toronto: Canadian Women's Educational Press, 1974), 122.
27. Joy Parr, *Labouring Children: British Immigrant Apprentices to Canada, 1869–1924* (Montreal-Kingston: McGill-Queens University Press, 1980).
28. Prentice et. al., *Canadian Women*, 222.
29. Varpu Lindstrom-Best, '"I Won't Be a Slave"—Finnish Domestics in Canada', in Jean Burnett, ed., *Looking into my Sister's Eyes: An Exploration in Women's History* (Toronto: Multicultural History Society of Ontario, 1986), 34–6.
30. Lindstrom-Best, 'I Won't Be a Slave'; Varpu Lindstrom-Best, *Defiant Sisters: A Social History of Finnish Immigrant Women in Canada* (Toronto: Multicultural History Society of Ontario, 1988).
31. Barber, 'The Servant Problem', 109.
32. Barber, *Immigrant Domestic Servants*, 16.
33. Barber, 'The Servant Problem', 112; Barber, *Immigrant Domestic Servants*, 16–18.
34. Prentice et. al., *Canadian Women*, 235–6.
35. Barber, *Immigrant Domestic Servants*, 18–19.
36. Ibid., 19–20; Milda Danys, *DP: Lithuanian Immigration to Canada* (Toronto: Multicultural History Society of Ontario, 1986), 76–7, 130.
37. Danys, *DP*, 133.
38. Daenzer, *Regulating Class Privilege*, 19.
39. Danys, *DP*, 157.
40. Barber, *Immigrant Domestic Servants*, 20.
41. Ibid., 21–3.
42. Franca Iacovetta, '"Primitive Villagers and Uneducated Girls": Canada Recruits Domestics from Italy, 1951–2', *Canadian Women's Studies*, 7.4 (1986): 14; Franca Iacovetta, *Such Hardworking People: Italian Immigrants in Post-War Toronto* (Montreal-Kingston: McGill-Queen's University Press, 1992).
43. Iacovetta, 'Primitive Villagers and Uneducated Girls', 13–16.
44. Barber, *Immigrant Domestic Servants*, 22–3.
45. Prentice et. al., *Canadian Women*, 121.
46. Brand, *No Burden*.
47. Beth Light and Ruth Roach Pierson, *No Easy Road: Women in Canada, 1920s–1960s* (Toronto: New Hogtown Press, 1990), 258.
48. Cited in Agnes Calliste, 'Race, Gender, and Canadian Immigration Policy: Blacks from the Caribbean, 1900–1937', *Journal of Canadian Studies* 28.4 (1993/4) 133; Vic Satzewich, 'Racism and Canadian Immigration Policy: The Government's View of Caribbean Migration, 1926–1966', *Canadian Ethnic Studies* 21.2 (1989): 77–97.
49. Agnes Calliste, 'Canada's Immigration Policy and Domestics from the Caribbean: The Second Domestic Scheme', in Jesse Vorst et al., eds, *Race, Class and Gender: Bonds and Barriers* (Toronto: Garamond Press and Society for Socialist Studies, 1989); Ian R. Mackenzie, 'Early Movements of Domestics from the Caribbean and Canadian Immigration Policy: A Research Note', *Alternate Routes*, 8 (1988): 124–43.
50. Cited in Calliste, 'Canada's Immigration Policy', 138.
51. Ibid.
52. Mackenzie, 'Early Movements', 128.
53. Ibid., 133–5.
54. Calliste, 'Canada's Immigration Policy', 143; Mackenzie, 'Early Movements', 133.
55. Daenzer, *Regulating Class Privilege*, 53–4.
56. Mackenzie, 'Early Movements', 136.
57. Calliste, 'Canada's Immigration Policy', 145.
58. Mackenzie, 'Early Movements', 138; Satzewich, 'Racism', 91.
59. Cited in Mackenzie, 139.
60. See Daenzer, 'An Affair', and Bakan and Stasiulis, 'Foreign Domestic Worker Policy'.
61. See Sedef Arat-Koç, 'Immigration Policies, Migrant Domestic Workers, and the Definition of Citizenship in Canada', in V. Satzewich, ed., *Deconstructing a Nation: Immigration, Culturalism, and Racism in the 90s Canada* (Halifax: Fernwood, 1992).
62. See Linda Carty, 'African Canadian Women and the State: "Labor Only" Please', in Peggy Bristow et. al. *'We're Rooted Here and They Can't Pull Us Up': Essays in African Canadian Women's History* (Toronto: University of Toronto Press, 1994).

Carrier Women and the Politics of Mothering

Jo-Anne Fiske

EDITORS' INTRODUCTION

Rejecting conventional sentimentalization of families, feminists in the 1960s and 1970s brought into the open some of the less savory aspects of domestic life, such as male violence against women and children, sexual abuse, alcoholism, and desertion. They questioned earlier assumptions that all members of the family benefit from the actions of its male head. By reintroducing the concept of the patriarchal family—but from a critical perspective—feminist scholars have identified the ways in which women's interests throughout much of human history have been assumed to be properly subordinated to those of male kin. This leads to a discussion of alternatives to the patriarchal family.

Certainly subordination within the family has much to do with the recurring phenomenon of male violence against women and children. This fact was acknowledged by the United Nations' adoption of the Declaration on the Elimination of Violence Against Women in 1993. It is, however, also only one part of the story. Women themselves regularly tell us of the value they attach to being daughters, sisters, wives, and mothers. The family provides them with pleasure and power as well as pain and inferiority.

Furthermore, it is not clear that women's roles in the family have relegated them in all cultures to an inferior, dependent position. Notably in Canada, the challenge has come from First Nations women who insist that family and community traditionally provided a source of strength. The Mohawk law professor, Patricia Monture, argues 'violence and abuse against women or children was not tolerated in our societies. In fact, there were strong cultural taboos against such behavior which were enforced by the woman's family members.'[1] According to such critics, the subordination of women is the legacy of European empires. White feminism is viewed as, at best, ethnocentric and, at worst, racist when it fails to acknowledge that other cultures did not always exploit women and that contact with Europeans, women and men, threatened, and even overthrew, longstanding traditions of equality within indigenous family groupings the world over.

To be true to our own demand that women be considered the experts on their own experience, feminist activists and scholars must listen to such criticisms. Anthropologists like Jo-Anne Fiske are rethinking longstanding assumptions of universal female inferiority. Her study, rooted in long hours of respectful listening in the Carrier or Yinka Dene community of central British Columbia, suggests that we revise our understanding of the roots of male supremacy and the tools women use to fight it.

Before European contact, Carrier women managed lives that were different but essentially equal to those of men. Colonialism disturbed this balance. Yet Carrier women have not been passive in the face of changes wrought by the fur trade, settler encroachment, and evangelization. They have built on the powerful role of mothers within Carrier society to construct a vision of female authority that, according to Fiske, 'makes no distinction between domestic authority and public leadership'. The welfare colonialism of the twentieth-century period ironically has given some economic substance to women's centrality to Carrier families, communities, and politics.

Carrier women have called on the resources of European as well as Aboriginal society to deal with the gendered legacies of imperialism. Fiske has elsewhere examined the figure of Rose of the Carrier, a former residential school student who local people remember as a saint. Like Kateri Tekakwitha, the seventeenth-century Mohawk Saint studied by Nancy Shoemaker, Rose of the Carrier represents the selective appropriation of patriarchal European culture for Aboriginal purposes. Rose's saintliness, argues Fiske, symbolizes the development of a Carrier women's identity that challenges the dualistic image of Aboriginal women held by European society and helps navigate the brutal and contradictory legacy of the residential school.[2]

The recovery of alternate ways of living within and viewing the family is invaluable in helping to understand women's attachment to domestic roles. Women, especially those in marginalized groups, may well experience the family as a source of protection and affirmation in face of a dominant culture that demeans them. Our analysis of the oppression and violence they might simultaneously experience within the same families must account for that.[3] We must also continue to question universals and be wary of overly sentimental portraits of pre-contact First Nations. Not all Aboriginal communities were equally respectful of women. North America's First Nations varied roughly as much as European ones, and ran the gamut from the relatively egalitarian, band-level societies to highly hierarchical slave-holding ones. Practices of polygamy or female infanticide in some of these societies alert us to the stubborn presence of female inequality. For the women in Fiske's study, however, it is the recollections of empowerment that provide the most powerful and compelling tools.

Notes

1. See 'The Roles and Responsibilities of Aboriginal Women: Reclaiming Justice', in *Thunder in My Soul: A Mohawk Woman Speaks* (Halifax: Fernwood Publishing, 1995), 237. Also see the role of the family in the novel by Aboriginal author Lee Maracle, *Sundogs* (Penticton, BC: Theytus Books, 1992).
2. Jo-Anne Fiske, 'Pocahantas's Granddaughters: Spiritual Transition and Tradition of Carrier Women of British Columbia', *Ethnohistory* 43.4 (Fall 1996): 663–81.
3. See Anne McGillivray and Brenda Comaskey, *Black Eyes all of the Time: Intimate Violence, Aboriginal Women, and the Justice System* (Toronto: University of Toronto Press, 1999). These issues are also dealt with in Sharene H. Razack, *Looking White People in the Eye: Gender, Race, and Culture in Courtrooms and Classrooms* (Toronto: University of Toronto Press, 1998).

Questions for Critical Reading

1. Many suffragists argued that women's capacity for mothering should be applied to the world at large through the mechanism of the vote. Would the vote, which Native women did not receive federally until 1960, have made a difference to Carrier women?
2. What are politics? How do Carrier women's political activities and ideas suggest that we reconsider our customary definition of what, exactly, is political?

3. How might have Fiske's status as a non-Aboriginal anthropologist influenced this study? Would it have been different if she was Carrier? Would it have been different if a historian rather than an anthropologist had carried out the study?
4. Read Lee Maracle's novel *Sundogs* (1992). How does it present the maternal power of British Columbian Native women in the urban setting of Vancouver?
5. What might distinguish the Carrier experience of gender from that of other Aboriginal societies?

Our understanding of the social status of women vis-à-vis men is commonly obscured by two assumptions that do not apply cross-culturally. One is that men are universally dominant, the other is that women's subordination is a consequence of their reproductive roles. Following Engels, a number of feminist theorists have argued that the family is the locus of women's inferior position. They argue that domestic production for use has less social significance than social production for exchange, and further, that women are confined to the domestic/private sphere and hence barred from the public, prestigious sphere open to men. Other writers, drawing on an eclectic base of structural and Weberian approaches, suggest that gender relations are defined by prestige (status) concerns: men are defined in terms of male-exclusive status and role categories that have little to do with their relations with women, whereas definitions of women's actions and responsibilities are centred around their relationships to men.[1] They go on to argue that this suggests that male social roles are granted greater social honour than female biological and reproductive roles: 'cultural construction of sex and gender tends everywhere to be stamped by the prestige considerations of socially dominant *male* actors' (emphasis in the original).[2]

These assumptions have been challenged by recent studies of gender roles in Native American communities, where fulfillment of women's domestic roles facilitates rather than retards their entry into economic and political positions.[3] In these cases traditional social values often enhance women's reproductive capabilities to the extent of equating them with human creation.[4]

Other studies, concerned with the manipulation of social power in small impoverished communities, have pointed out that the distinction between the private and the public realms is blurred in communities relying upon a domestic economy comprising subsistence food production, exchanged services, and unearned income.[5] Economic underdevelopment, coupled with contemporary state control over Aboriginal communities, has placed them in a position of economic dependency. Subordination to state control restricts the authority of elected community representatives to that of brokers for the government. Their primary role is to redistribute the resources allocated by the state: resources such as housing, chattel, and personal income that elsewhere are considered private. Under these conditions it is common for women to control the domestic provisioning within broad kin groups who rely on intensive sharing for economic survival. Because of their economic importance, it is argued, women are able to exert authority over household members and to manipulate kin networks in order to influence public decision-making.[6] This approach, however, fails to consider either the social environment that facilitates women's direct access to community authority or the interplay between women's political success and their interpretations of traditional concepts of womanhood. As we shall see, these considerations are central to explicating Carrier women's political strategies.

While it is the case that Carrier women do indirectly affect community decision-making, an analysis of their household and kin-based authority cannot provide a full description of their social influence or of their political strategies. Rather, Carrier women are involved directly in community decision-making in three ways: as elected councillors, as appointed administrators and advisers for the council, and as executive leaders of women's voluntary associations.

The purpose of this paper is to describe a situation where Aboriginal women are politically active and well known as community leaders. First, I show how economic dependency, or 'welfare colonialism',[7] has created a marginal society that enhances women's domestic functions and encourages women to unite traditional domestic responsibilities with contemporary political opportunities. Second, I demonstrate that knowing what motivates women to political action and how cultural traditions are used to justify their interventions is equally critical to our understanding of how and why women are directly involved in the political process. To this end, I examine female political action within the context of women's rights and duties as household heads, of women's self-perceptions, and of their interpretations of traditional culture. I am concerned with identifying the link women establish between the Aboriginal social organization—with its emphasis on matrilineal descent, female domestic authority, and high esteem for female reproductive roles and for older women—and contemporary political action.

This paper is organized in five sections. First, I present a brief description of traditional Carrier culture and society. Second, I describe the material conditions and changing gender roles and ideals brought about with colonialism. Third, I turn to contemporary life and the domestic and economic roles of women. Fourth, I investigate Carrier women's perceptions of the past, focusing on the ways in which women link their political actions to their understanding of a past egalitarian society marked by high esteem for women's reproductive roles. Finally, I show how mythological representations of traditional women's roles provide an ideological basis for contemporary action.

Data for this study were gathered during a 12-month period of fieldwork from 1983 to 1984, of which 9 months were spent living on one reserve. The women's statements quoted in this paper are drawn from interviews and from comments made by them at public meetings. Return visits were made in 1985, 1990, and 1991. In the eight-year span, the village has experienced few changes; a small population growth and some new houses are the most visible of these. The economic constraints described below, however, have not been alleviated. Rather, because the Carrier population is very young, economic hardships become more noticeable as adolescents leaving school confront unemployment and place a growing burden on the community's limited social and economic resources. It is important to bear in mind that while Carrier people have a common culture that values women's reproductive roles and domestic authority, the actual political participation of women varies on the 14 Carrier reserves. The data here apply to one reserve, which is smaller, less isolated, and poorer in terms of access to natural resources than several other reserves. As well, this community appears to be the best known for the active political leadership offered by women.

Carrier Traditions

The Carrier are an indigenous people of central British Columbia. Their traditional territories consist of an extensive region of high wooded plateaus with numerous large lakes, rivers, and streams, known as the Nechako Plateau. The staple of subsistence is the Pacific salmon that migrate to the region each summer. The Carrier also hunt moose, deer, and bear, trap fur-bearing mammals, and trap and net freshwater fish. Women gather berries and roots for food, medicines, and handicrafts. Despite the fact that Carrier reliance upon bush subsistence has been altered, these activities have retained cultural and economic significance over two centuries of colonization.

Prior to European contact in 1807, the Carrier lived in relatively isolated extended family settlements. Their social organization stressed sexual equality.[8] The first born, male or female, was the leader of the extended family, and in general the oldest women and men were responsible for the moral conduct and productive labour of the younger members of their sex. Interaction between settlements was mediated by the leaders of matrilineal clans, who directed intergroup trade, land and resource sharing, and the division of collective work during the fall salmon fishing. According to contemporary elders, leadership in the clans included women and men, who were often referred to as 'clan father' or 'clan mother'.

A system of ritualized interclan exchange, known among Pacific Aboriginal peoples as the potlatch, was the keystone for political action. This elaborate exchange of goods to repay debts, to compensate for transgressions, or to validate claims to leadership took place in public forums and so valorized clan leaders' actions. Today, the potlatch is said to be 'the traditional government'.

As in many Aboriginal societies, Carrier women contributed heavily to the subsistence diet and undertook the bulk of household tasks, such as childcare, cooking, and care of the elderly.[9] However, the gender division of labour was flexible; women and men became skilled in a wide range of tasks. Primarily, women were responsible for netting fish, gathering berries and other plant foods, snaring small mammals, and netting migratory waterfowl. They also helped to construct homes and canoes. Their collective labour was organized and supervised by senior women, while their surplus production was held by the eldest woman of the extended family. Men hunted large game and trapped small mammals. Under the direction of their clan leaders, men built large fishing weirs to trap the migrating salmon.

Ceremonial food distribution and trade between women proceeded independently of male exchanges of the same order; women traded food products and crafted goods within their own networks, and pooled goods with female kin for public celebrations and rituals. Women performed the same specialized ritual roles as men. Spiritual guidance and healing were achieved by the dreamers, prophets, and herbalists, the latter usually being women. However, relationships with the spiritual world were not restricted to ritual specialists. At adolescence girls and boys underwent rigorous apprenticeship in a vision quest for an animal guardian (often referred to as 'medicine power', a suprahuman capacity derived from a spiritual connection to the guardian animal).

Carrier culture affirmed women's contributions to subsistence, social regulation, and social reproduction. Ceremonial exchange of rare foods and delicacies honoured women's work. As well, the exchange of berries symbolized female fecundity and confirmed the value placed upon women. Reproductive roles were central to women's claims to social prominence. Carrier women who successfully raised their families and provided care and nurture to the needy became influential as family spokespersons. The wisdom of old women was and remains proclaimed in legend and song and institutionalized in the valued role of the grandmothers of the tribe.

Colonization and Cultural Transformation

Colonization proved to be a disruptive but contradictory and uneven process. Cultural changes came about slowly in the first decades of the nineteenth century. The fur trade, established within Carrier territory in 1807, drew women and men into trapping furs and netting and drying fish for trade. Male and female relationships to the land remained unaltered. Neither suffered exclusion from the new economic relations. They did, however, experience differences in their relationships to the traders. The Europeans preferred personal relationships with women for the purposes of extending alliances into Carrier communities, while at the same time they sought and promoted men to mediate their interactions with the community as a whole. Thus selected Carrier men were designated to act as 'chiefs', and in keeping with European traditions the sons of these men were recognized as their heirs. Even women accustomed to providing leadership were excluded from the newly established positions. Rather, they became either personal partners (rarely wives) to the traders or valued hired workers within the forts.

Expansion into the region by the Canadian state, the Catholic Church, and industrial interests in the late nineteenth and early twentieth centuries further altered the indigenous social order. Missionaries and state agents not only accepted the leadership roles introduced by the fur traders but also imposed new structures of male leadership that explicitly excluded women. To strengthen their authority, priests established local quasi-military hierarchies to uphold church law. These were composed of a chief, who acted as lay magistrate; captains, who were 'minsters of the whip'; and watchmen and soldiers, who fulfilled the functions of policemen and jailers.[10] For a time, this system of indirect theocratic control was recognized by state agents, such as the Indian Agent or other representatives of the federal government acting in a similar capacity, and officials as the village authority. Early in the twentieth century, however, the state established all-male establishments under the auspices of the Indian Act, and the two councils co-existed, sharing authority over the community and interceding on behalf of individuals with church and state officials.

Settlement and the development of railroads and highways in the 1910s drew the Carrier into wage labour at the same time as the fur trade faltered from depleted stocks and falling prices. While men were integrated directly into the labour force, receiving either individual wages or labour contracts, women were marginalized. They either were excluded entirely from wage labour or worked for male kin who held contracts to clear land or produce railway ties. Yet at the same time men relied upon women's subsistence production in fishing, farming, trapping, and berry gathering.

Had it not been for critical changes in subsistence production in the twentieth century, women might have suffered even greater socio-economic displacement. Ironically, further state intervention improved women's position. In 1911, the federal government banned the use of large salmon weirs, the traditional means of catching salmon, and forced the Carrier to adopt a net fishery. Netting fish had always been viewed as women's work; hence in conjunction with new opportunities for male employment and farming,[11] women became responsible for netting salmon. The catching and preserving of salmon was now 'women's business', and with this, women's position and prestige in the society was enhanced.[12]

By the 1930s, the consolidation of women's roles and prestige around fishing was matched by the decline of economic opportunities for men. Increased state and industrial intrusion wrenched resource territories from the Carrier and limited traditional subsistence hunting. The capitalist labour market has never been stable, so from 1914 to the present, male labour has been subject to the ups and downs of the economy. This has resulted in economic dislocation, declining wage work, and the attendant loss of traditional bush skills. Today men are not only marginalized as workers but, where their hunting and trapping has been seriously eroded, they enjoy less social prestige than women, who continue to hold status from subsistence production and other sources of domestic provisioning.

Colonization has created contradictions in women's social status. Carrier women frequently describe the period from the last quarter of the nineteenth century to the 1960s as a time when women had no say, and when Carrier men had adopted 'white man's ways'. Catholicism challenged indigenous concepts of the supernatural and female fecundity. Women's curing practices, perceptions of menstrual powers, and birth rituals were scorned by the priests. At the same time, the priests, acting through their imposed church hierarchy, arranged marriages and tried to destroy the matrilineal clan organization. Moreover, they objected to informal female political influence and banned women from community meetings. When control over Carrier communities was transferred from the church to the state early in the twentieth century, the formal position of women remained unchanged. Under the provisions of the Indian Act, the Carrier people were divided into bands (administrative units whose membership was defined by the state), each of which was eventually allowed an elected band council. Until 1952, however, women were prohibited from holding office, from electing male councillors, and from attending community meetings called by state agents.

Nevertheless, as women adjusted to Catholicism and state intervention they were able to use church-sponsored auxiliaries to influence community affairs. Women's capacity to exercise community-wide influence was augmented by the frequent absence of men. Left on their own when men were hunting, trapping, or working for wages, they established economic and social networks, effectively taking charge of community decision-making. By the mid-twentieth century, Carrier women had joined province-wide women's voluntary associations and were extending their networks across provincial boundaries.

Welfare Colonialism

Today the Carrier find themselves on the periphery of capitalist development. For the most part, they are without a stable economic base.[13] Not only are they alienated from their traditional resource territories, they also suffer from high unemployment and dependency upon welfare and state-controlled job-creation schemes. Moreover, the politics of the reserve is embedded in the 'domestic' concerns of individual households and larger kinship units; that is, office holders publicly manage resources that in other circumstances would be private property or personal concerns. Thus the elected council redistributes the few economic and social resources available to reserve residents: provision and maintenance of housing; reserve-based employment; educational and health subsidies; and social assistance. Additionally, the quest for personal goods, such as children's clothing, household furnishings, and services for elders, is a public, not a personal matter, since band members must compete for their share of social-assistance funds and engage in community-wide redistribution of goods through such activities as public auctions of handcrafted items, the sale of second-hand goods, and so forth.

Economic dependency offers few opportunities for male employment. Moreover, in this community men have limited opportunities to contribute independently to subsistence production: hunting is restricted by provincial law and trapping territories have been reduced by industrial and residential development. Apart from short-term work tied to job-creation schemes, bush labour—such as land clearing or forestry work—is also rare.

A very significant change is the increasing role that women play in provisioning their households. Not only do women supply the dietary staple, salmon, they also supplement the subsistence diet with other dried fish, wild berries, and, to a smaller extent, garden produce. Equally important is the shift towards female-centred households dependent upon female earnings. Women are employed as the administrative and support staff to the elected council and as paraprofessionals in health and welfare services. Another major source of income is social assistance provided to single mothers. In this situation of economic need, men rely upon female kin for basic necessities and, when available, for direct loans and cash gifts.

Household composition is variable and ever-changing. An insufficient number of houses in conjunction with a tendency towards female-headed households results in a preference for extended family units that place an emphasis on matrilineal ties. Nuclear family households are rarely self-sufficient. Rather, extended families of three to four generations under the direction of the eldest woman are the most stable economic unit. Matrifocal kinship units are drawn together by a common need to share cash income, subsistence production, and labour. Women are in control of household spending and the distribution of domestic provisions, including the game hunted by men.

While women with independent incomes generally enjoy personal autonomy and exercise domestic authority within their households, women who participate annually in the salmon fishery and other subsistence production enjoy a higher degree of autonomy and social prestige within the community than those who do not. Women's pre-eminence in the salmon fishery remains well established today. '[W]e teach the younger generation, our granddaughters, even if they don't live on the reserve; we teach them to fish so they can look after our people after we're gone. . . . Fishing is women's business.' Female elders of well respected families organize salmon production. They supervise the work of younger women (and the few men who assist them) and command the distribution of fish. The salmon are distributed in and sometimes beyond the community. Within the women's kin networks and the community as a whole no one is excluded, although portions may vary in quality and quantity. At public dinners and celebrations, subsistence foods are also shared throughout the community. Ultimately, food sharing is a prestige-enhancing process for women.

The growth of the economic significance of women is matched by increases in their political influence. Over the century, the state has repeatedly challenged the land and resource rights of Native peoples. In the case of the Carrier, this has jeopardized the salmon fishery, threatening their way of life and well-being and placing Carrier women squarely in conflict with the Canadian state. During this same period the state has not been forthcoming in its provision of essential community services, such as water systems, sewage disposal, health care, and the like. Consequently, women's responsibility for food production and community well-being has afforded them a political agenda in which they are at the forefront of community politics.

Women's Political Strategies

Women perceive the need to engage in explicit political actions in order to preserve the Carrier culture, to protect the environment, and to retain access to the territory of their ancestors. They provide leadership in traditional and non-traditional ways: they exert domestic influence, provide clan leadership, compete for administrative and elected office, and form voluntary associations.[14]

Although the traditional clan/potlatch system has been displaced by new political structures imposed by the state, it remains a significant social institution. As in the past, all Carrier are born into a matriclan, that is, the clan of their mother. Clan leadership is assumed by women (*ts'ekezah*) and men (*dunezah*) who claim a 'noble' status according to traditional concepts. Apart from providing a traditional frame of reference for personal and cultural identity, the clans function as exchange groups and as mechanisms for establishing personal status. Interclan exchanges take place at the death of a community member. When an individual dies, members of the other clan(s)[15] provide services to the clan of the deceased. After the funeral the bereaved clan holds a 'potlatch' or *balhats*, a public ceremony to repay services rendered and to raise money to cover the funeral expenses.

Participation in the *balhats* is important to individuals with political aspirations. Individuals who give generously at the *balhats* and who provide funeral services are held in high regard. Clan leaders are able to gain a reputation for their generosity and general concern for community well-being. Women are often more active than men in the *balhats*. It is not unusual for women to engage in personal exchanges of goods, services, and money, which they perform at the *balhats*. In so doing, they earn a solid reputation for their knowledge of and commitment to traditional ways. As well, women demonstrate their generosity at community dinners and other ceremonial occasions: they are primarily responsible for providing and preparing the food, and for bestowing traditional or modern gifts they have crafted themselves. This, too, reinforces their reputation as generous persons who honour Carrier traditions.

Women also compete for elected office. Throughout the Carrier communities women are well represented as chiefs and councillors.[16] Access to elected office is, however, limited to a few women and men whose families are held in high regard and whose ancestors attained status as *ts'ekezah* and *dunezah*. Therefore, women who wish to participate directly in community affairs also seek administrative office or become members of advisory committees to the elected council.

Finally, women who engage in community leadership in the clans, council, and administration are also found in another political role: executive members of women's voluntary associations. Women's voluntary associations were first introduced to the Carrier as auxiliaries to the church hierarchy and as community groups dedicated to maternal health and childcare. During the 1940s the Department of Indian Affairs established homemaking clubs on larger reserves, and as these organizations were emulated in smaller communities, women established interband networks. Today, local chapters of the associations are united by a provincial executive.

These associations are important to women's political aspirations in three ways. First, voluntary associations seek state funds for community services and development schemes. This generates job opportunities and enables women to establish personal networks of patronage to the women and men they employ. Clearly, such activities enhance personal and family prestige, for they meet both community and personal needs. Given the high unemployment rate, which can reach 95 per cent during the winter, it is not surprising that competition for these few jobs is severe and dependent on maintaining harmonious ties with older women.

Second, men do not organize in the same way as women do. Historically, men did not need to form auxiliaries to formal political or church offices. Today men who aspire to community leadership seek elected office. Those who choose to provide other forms of community service do so independently, as coaches for junior sports teams, for example, or as employees of the band council or the women's associations. Competitive sports teams are the only associations of men, and while these may create a basis for indirect influence, they do not directly enter into community politics. Because men do not form voluntary associations, they do not create comparable employment opportunities. This reinforces ties of dependency between women and men in the same fashion as does male reliance upon female income and domestic provisioning. It appears that men have little difficulty accepting their asymmetrical position vis-à-vis their female kin. Indeed some men expect female kin, in particular mothers and sisters, to provide them with jobs derived from voluntary associations. They accept that it will be mothers, sisters, aunts, or wives who will enter into negotiations with state agents for community services that will supply employment. Women and men view this as an extension of domestic duties. As one man explained: 'I don't have a head for all that number business. My sister and my mother do that, they're both trying to get money out of the Department. . . . My sister and I were in business and she took care of the books. . . . If I need anything I go to her.' His brother held similar views: 'I guess I'll be working on that log house all summer. If my sister gets us that money I'll be working again. . . . My mother is the one I turned to, she gets me this work.'

The absence of male associations also creates a differential level of political and organizing skills. Voluntary associations rely on large communication networks and so they create a complex structure of meetings, workshops, political lobbying, and training sessions from which women acquire essential skills and knowledge of political leadership. This affects the course of community politics. There is no effective base from which men may challenge female leadership. Speaking of her early years in a voluntary association, an elder explains: 'The men weren't organized like the women. We could stand up to the band council. We spoke for the families and they had to listen. The trouble makers [male opponents] went against us but they couldn't go nowhere. We were all pulling together and they had to listen.' Furthermore, complex multiple ties of kinship mean that male leadership, when generated (e.g., the band council), cannot take precedence over women's leadership. The band council itself is constrained by its advisory committees, whose members are mainly women engaged in parapolitical organization. While a council can show favouritism and even considerable patronage towards one association or another, it cannot subvert or exclude female leadership, since all associations rely to some degree on such leaders.

Third, voluntary associations enter into political dialogue with the state. In conjunction with provincial and/or national umbrella organizations, the associations lobby for better community conditions, for legislative changes which could improve women's status, and most significantly, for protection and/or extension of Aboriginal rights and resource territories. The latter struggle is inherently tied to the broader struggle to retain cultural identity and to re-establish economic autonomy. Women's participation is grounded in their own resource activities as well as in their commitment to transmitting their culture and history to the young.

Nevertheless, the accession of women to roles of community leadership is not without ambiguities and contradictions. The values of Catholicism and Euro-Canadian culture tell Carrier men that they should hold the power within the home and community. These same values insist that men more than women should provide for family needs. Above all, they promote the view that normal gender relationships are based on the economic and social dependency of women. Women admit that some men prefer to be treated publicly as if they were in charge of the family. Privately the same men show deference.

> He [her husband of 56 years] always defers to me. He never interferes but he's hurt if I act like a big shot everywhere. He likes to look as if he's in charge. His father was a [village chief] and his mother went second to her husband. She would never go for election [to the band council] or speak out in meetings. But at home, she was the boss.

Yet the Carrier have not embraced these values unequivocally. Rather, they have established a social order that accepts female economic autonomy and patronage and the overt political leadership of women. In the face of ambivalent male expectations of female deference, women hasten to rationalize their political involvement as inseparable from traditional expectations of domestic duty, which in turn is seen as an extension of family management. To explicate this fully, it is necessary to examine women's and men's perceptions of women's social obligations and rights to overt power.

Mothering and Political Power

Carrier women do not separate their community involvement into discrete political and social areas but integrate their diverse interventions into an ideology of 'mothering' and providing for future generations. It is their perception that cultural and social regeneration require unity of the family and community responsibility.

> You can't stop right there at home. You need to get out there and speak up for your family. Who else is going to do it? You need to go out and get those men jobs. You need to make things happen when the men don't do nothing for the water and the sewer. That's women's business, to speak up for the families.
>
> It's all the same thing, really. You have to have the respect of the people. You have to look after them if you want to be a leader. That's what I do. I've been chief. I've been president [of a voluntary association] and I'm clan leader. It's the same thing. You speak out for your people and you lead them, make things right for them. You don't sit back and say nothing.

As Carrier women constantly struggle to achieve a balance between their nurturing roles and their broader social responsibilities of communal political leadership, they look to the past for guiding ideals and role models. They say that in a true matrilineal society it is not just that 'we come from other mothers, but that we have clan mothers and community mothers who teach us and look after our people'. They are convinced that strong families rely on a woman's care and that 'unless there is a woman' involved in each aspect of community life, it will falter.

This mode of thinking makes no distinction between domestic authority and public leadership. The latter is seen to emerge from the former. Women's responsibility for the well-being of adult children, and the right to intervene in their lives, is deeply rooted in cultural traditions. In the isolated settlements of the pre-contact era, senior women were 'bosses' in their own right. Senior women managed surplus food stores, influenced children's marriage choices, and exerted considerable control over the productive activities of their daughters and sons-in-law. The maintenance of these responsibilities today requires an explicit political agenda. Carrier women see their voluntary associations as a carry-over of their foremothers' supervision of resource wealth:

> There were always two bosses, like I told you. And that woman, [s]he[17] had a cache hole. That's how everybody got looked after. And she stored up for her family. If they got hungry someplace else they came back to her. . . . That's what the [voluntary association] is all about. We put things aside and when somebody's in trouble we help out. That's why we get a little bit of money from the Department [of Indian Affairs] and make work for our people. We get jobs for our men when we can.

There is no consensus about the social status of their foremothers, but all agree that female elders had authority over their families. Some women go so far as to say that 'we were always a matriarchy', but this is not a common conception. More frequently, women's past authority is seen as complementary to that of men. As one woman phrased it, 'the two bosses [male and female] stood side by side.' The general interpretation stresses the different realms of female and male authority. In turn, this traditional division is seen as the basis for women to define and control contemporary domains of 'women's business'. Thus, the intervention of voluntary associations as lobbying groups for social improvements and community services is perceived to be the right of women.

> . . . it was women's business to get ahead with the water and housing. That's why they call me motor mouth. I spoke out when I had to. The men weren't speaking up in public, just talking to themselves. They didn't show no interest in getting to Ottawa. We sent petitions right there and our delegates to talk for us.

In fact, to refrain from social action can be construed as negligence.

> They [male state agents] try to go over our head. They want to rule us; leave us out. They say, 'Stay at home, look after your children.' How are we going to do that when our people suffer? I went to Ottawa and spoke out for housing. I put in the water system. That's for my children. That's what keeps our babies alive. We're all one big family; you can't take care of your family if everything else is no good. . . .
>
> I pity those women who don't speak out. They get pushed around. . . . Andrea, I pity her. Her mother was never strong. She didn't stand up to her husband and she has no authority in that family. Now they are all in a bad way. . . . That's what I mean, you can't stay inside. Women get involved for their families.

Women also link their traditional obligation and ability to provide food for their families to their political responsibilities. With regard to the annual salmon fishery they say, 'that's what's expected of us. That's what women do. They feed everybody they can with these fish. . . .' Within Carrier culture as a whole, notions of leadership are bound to appreciation of individuals reputed to be 'good providers'. One woman, a clan leader and an association president, has such a reputation. When young men were without work she provided salmon and other foods. 'That Isabelle, she looks after everybody. She helps them out. Last winter, them days I had nothing. She was real good to me that time. . . . When the money comes in for that log house then I work again. Isabelle gets those jobs for us to keep going all summer.' At the same time she is praised for her political leadership: 'She makes things happen. She knows what the families need. She speaks up for the community everyplace. She's been good on the council.'

This aspect of leadership is also linked to the past responsibilities of women. 'When it was just the clans, the clan mother and father, they looked after everybody. They had to give out salmon and dried meat. . . . That's what it means to be a clan leader. That's what women do all the time. Women know who needs help and what to do.' The perceived compatibility between female leadership and the general responsibilities of women hinges upon women's particular responsibility for social harmony. 'When the old timers, when they each had their own *keyoh* [settlement], women, just like the men, worked hard to make sure everything was just right. If there was any trouble, if someone acted wrong, the mother in that family would take charge. She was right beside her husband.'

Women also turn to traditional Carrier cosmology when explaining their political actions. They evoke images from mythology and popular tales that honour the wisdom of the 'old woman' or 'grandmother', who offers a steadfast role model of nurture and wisdom. The old woman figure was instrumental in transforming an inchoate world into its present form. She is credited with extending daylight from a mere five minutes to its present duration, and with converting a tiny creek into a mighty river. In other situations she is helpful to the young and vulnerable, a caring grandmother to orphaned children, and a counsellor to wilful children and young women.

Male cultural heroes who disregarded the wisdom of their grandmothers inevitably failed in their heroic endeavours. Proudly, the elders point out that even the most powerful of male cultural heroes, Stas, the creator, was dependent upon an old woman's wisdom. 'Stas, even he, that one, asked an old woman. That old woman [s]he told [Stas] how to get along with Sa [the sun].' With humour they describe how another hero, Galbaniyeh (Swift Runner) was outwitted by a woman. According to legend, Galbaniyeh could outrun everyone. An old woman had raised him and taught him the wisdom and rituals necessary for gaining his extraordinary abilities. To his displeasure, Galbaniyeh was married to a lame woman with an 'ugly face' because she excelled in women's tasks. Knowing he could outrun all men, he planned to escape his bride by quite literally running away. The lame woman, however, also possessed extraordinary powers, which enabled her to outrun her husband and to save her marriage. In the end, like Stas, Galbaniyeh 'wasn't nothing without a woman'.

The old woman of mythology becomes a metaphor for the abilities of the Carrier's real foremothers. Contemporary elders not only implicitly liken themselves to the wise grandmothers of myth but also verify their own knowledge as that of their literal grandmothers. When one leader praises the knowledge and action of another, it is often in reference to her youthful relationships with the 'old timers'. Thus one may be viewed as a knowledgeable and honourable leader because she was raised by her grandmother, who is also reputed for her wisdom. In contradistinction, the capabilities of other elders are open to question if they have been orphaned and left without a grandmother to raise them: 'she spent too much time in that residential school. Her mother died and an orphan doesn't know much without her grandmother. . . . You can't lead your people the white man way, they don't raise girls right for that.'

The older women who have demonstrated community leadership hold a special position within the community's social structure and world view. On the one hand, they represent traditional values and knowledge. But at the same time, they are recognized for skills associated with cultural change and modernization, as when they hold elected or appointed office and provide leadership to their voluntary associations. In other words, these women are esteemed for behaving as ideal nurturers and for upholding the time-honoured image of the old woman, while in reality they are successful because they have the capacity for leadership within the imposed white man's system. Despite the recognized significance of the latter, women account for their success within the image of the former.

Summary

In sum, public issues are defined largely by the immediate needs of individuals and households. Economic dependency has forced the Carrier to rely on the domestic sector of production. Women are able to provide regular support for their kin through intense sharing of cash incomes and through careful management of subsistence provisions. Additionally, they provide essential services and employment through strategic management of state funds. Not having reliable sources of income, men turn to women for assistance: domestic provisions, cash, and employment. In these circumstances of economic dependency, women's duties and contributions are not only vital to community well-being, they are part and parcel of the political process. Therefore, it is not surprising that women are central to public decision-making. Women influence public affairs directly, by holding public office, and indirectly, through voluntary associations and domestic influence.

In their struggle to maximize economic and political opportunities, women's political strategies and cultural constructions are mutually reinforcing. Women view their political involvements and capabilities as an extension of their domestic roles. Images of the female creators and female nurturers are interwoven, constituting a new political identity. The cultural meanings women ascribe to the cosmology of their foremothers unite with and become inseparable from social practice. In short, traditional domestic roles both motivate women's public interventions and justify their successful leadership.

Notes

The author wishes to thank Deborah Findlay, Rick Hadden, Evelyn Legare, and John McMullan for their comments on earlier drafts of this paper. Research was funded by a doctoral fellowship from the Social Sciences and Humanities Research Council of Canada.

1. Sherry B. Ortner and Harriet Whitehead, 'Introduction', in *Sexual Meanings: The Cultural Construction of Gender and Sexuality* (Cambridge: Cambridge University Press, 1981).
2. Ortner and Whitehead, *Sexual Meanings*, 12.
3. Patricia Albers, 'Sioux Women in Transition: A Study of Their Changing Status in a Domestic and Capitalist Sector of Production', in *The Hidden Half: Studies of Plains Indian Women*, ed. Patricia Albers and Beatrice Medicine (Lanham: University Press of America, 1983).
4. Marla Powers, *Oglala Women: Myth, Ritual, and Reality* (Chicago: University of Chicago Press, 1986); Alice Kehoe, 'Old Woman Had Great Power', *Western Canadian Journal of Anthropology* 6 (1976): 68–76; and Laura Klein, 'Tlingit Women and Town Politics' (unpublished Ph.D. dissertation, New York University, 1975).
5. See Albers, 'Sioux Women in Transition'; and Tord Larson, 'Negotiating Identity: The Micmac of Nova Scotia', in *The Politics of Indianness: Case Studies of Native Ethnopolitics in Canada*, Adrian Tanner, ed. (St John's, Nfld: Institute of Social and Economic Research, Memorial University of Newfoundland, 1983).
6. Albers, 'Sioux Women in Transition'; Powers, *Oglala Women*; and Karen Sacks, *Sisters and Wives: The Past and Future of Sexual Equality* (Westport, Conn.: Greenwood Press, 1979) are among many authors who have analyzed the significance of women's domestic production in marginal communities.
7. Robert Paine, *The White Arctic: Anthropological Essays on Tutelage and Ethnicity* (St John's, Nfld: Institute of Social and Economic Research, Memorial University of Newfoundland, 1977).
8. Irving Goldman, 'The Alkatcho Carrier of British Columbia', in *Acculturation in Seven American Indian Tribes*, Ralph Linton, ed. (New York: Appleton-Century, 1940), 333–87.
9. John McLean, *John McLean's Notes of a Twenty-Five Year's Service in the Hudson's Bay Territory* (Toronto: Champlain Society, 1932), 180.
10. Adrian Morice, *Fifty Years in Western Canada* (Toronto: Ryerson Press, 1930), 54.
11. Women and men shared farm labour, alternating farm work with seasonal activities that drew them away from home. Hayfields and animal ranges were

found adjacent to freshwater fishing sites, for example, and women maintained farms while men were at the railway-tie-cutting camps.

12. I have discussed the social and economic significance of women's economic roles more fully in an earlier paper: '"Fishing is Women's Business": Changing Economic Roles of Carrier Women and Men', in *Native People, Native Lands*, Bruce Cox, ed. (Ottawa: Carleton University Press, 1987).
13. Colonization has not treated Carrier communities uniformly. The more remote, northern bands have not been dislocated from their resources to the same extent as the smaller bands located nearer to white communities, and hence the northern bands have a more viable bush production consisting of trapping and food production. As well, one band has a large tree-farm licence and a band-owned timber company that currently is a source of secure employment. See Douglas Hudson, 'Traplines and Timber: Social and Economic Change Among the Carrier Indians of Northern British Columbia' (unpublished PhD dissertation, University of Alberta, 1983).
14. I provide a fuller discussion of the political significance of voluntary associations in an earlier article: 'Native Women in Reserve Politics: Strategies and Struggles', in *Community Organizing and the Canadian State*, Roxana Ng, Gillian Walker, and Jake Mueller, eds. (Toronto: Garamond Press, 1990).
15. The number of clans in each Carrier community varies from two to four.
16. There is considerable variation in the percentage of women in formal political office, both among Carrier communities and over time. Since 1952, however, the rate has risen steadily. In the community discussed here, women have held approximately three-fifths of elected seats during the past 15 years, yet they represent less than 50 per cent of the adult population. Records of the Department of Indian Affairs indicated that this is consistent with the average representation of women in Carrier communities during the same time period. I have discussed this issue in greater detail elsewhere. See Jo-Anne Fiske, 'And Then We Prayed Again: Carrier Women, Colonialism and Mission Schools' (unpublished MA thesis, University of British Columbia, 1981), and 'Gender and Politics in a Carrier Indian Community' (unpublished PhD dissertation, University of British Columbia, 1989).
17. In the Carrier language, the third person singular pronoun makes no gender distinction. Today, Carrier people use he or she in reference to women.

A Platform for Gender Tensions: Women Working and Riding on Canadian Urban Transit in the 1940s

Donald F. Davis and Barbara Lorenzkowski

EDITORS' INTRODUCTION

Historians are attracted to periods of upheaval since they tend to lay bare fundamental tensions in the social fabric of any given cultural or national context. In contemporary circumstances, the genocide in Rwanda, the so-called 'war on terror' and the resultant threat to civil liberties in the United States and around the world, and the disastrous response to Hurricane Katrina in New Orleans, Louisiana, serve as extreme examples of this phenomenon.[1] Social disruption tends to suspend familiar 'rules of engagement' amongst and between people and the structures and institutions thought to serve and protect them. At these moments, oppressive forces often denied or well-hidden, such as class conflict, racial and ethnic prejudices, sexism, homophobia, misogyny, and religious intolerance, are often rendered disturbingly transparent.

The Second World War serves as a major historical example of such a disruptive episode. Like previous and subsequent wars, it not only claimed the lives of millions of combatants and non-combatants alike, but it turned taken-for-granted social relations upside down and laid bare both subtle and overt sources of inequity, hatred, and oppression. Historians who have focused on the wartime experiences of Canadian women, such as Ruth Roach Pierson, have highlighted the temporary nature of 'reversals' of traditional gender norms demanded by wartime needs.[2] Women were encouraged to ignore or disavow previous social and cultural messages that had insisted a woman's place was in the home to serve a working husband and growing children. The necessity of wartime production and domestic management now carried a different message to women: patriotic wives and mothers go outside the home to work—but only for the duration of the war. After hostilities ended, Pierson contends, women were expected to retreat back to their kitchens. As Denyse Baillargeon documents for the case of women struggling with poverty in Montreal during the Great Depression, challenges to notions of feminine behaviour undertaken by women did not necessarily dismantle engrained social attitudes towards their 'proper place'. That working women could perform so-called 'male jobs' as good as, or better than, their male counterparts did not translate into equal treatment or equal pay. Jeff Keshen has revisited Pierson's work, placing the emphasis instead on the thousands of Canadian women who did not simply return to dishes and diapers after 1945.[3] He contends that the social upheaval caused by the war resulted in enduring changes for women that, while often challenged and decried, could not be denied or completely reversed in the postwar period. It is worth remembering, as Franca Iacovetta's work on Italian immigrants and their struggles over Canadian citizenship in this volume contends, that race, along with gender, needs to be added to our understanding of which Canadian women benefited most from their wartime experiences.

In this article by Donald F. Davis and Barbara Lorenzkowski, the insights of both Pierson and Keshen come together in an even more nuanced accounting of the war's effects on gender relations in Canada after the Second World War. Davis and Lorenzkowski's work breaks new interpretative ground on a number of counts. Unlike previous studies on this period, they are explicitly attentive to the importance of public space as a canvas for historical interpretation. In this way, their work has intriguing parallels with Bettina Bradbury's essay on the 'public franchise' in nineteenth century Montreal in this volume. In particular, Davis and Lorenzkowski focus on public transportation as a backdrop against which previously under-explored social changes were brought into sharp relief. For those privileged enough to have access to private transportation, it is hard to imagine contemporary struggles around 'getting around', let alone those engendered by the serious fuel and equipment shortages of the Second World War. In this essay the authors take on three interconnected themes: the gendered tensions that crowded transit fostered, the employment of women as transit workers, and the exceptional role of the Toronto Transportation Commission in explicitly fostering so-called 'feminine' contributions to that city's system during and after the war. Davis and Lorenzkowski take us onto the crowded trams and buses that moved through major Canadian cities bringing workers and shoppers, women and men, smokers and non-smokers, to their destinations. Who had a more rightful claim to a spot on a city bus, a male worker heading to the plant or a female shopper seeking food for the family dinner? When were female shoppers expected to use buses? Were they expected to ride during peak hours or when the rush hour had ended? If most women were expected to ride after peak hours, particularly in the evenings, were they entitled to increased protection from harassment and potential assault? Could women workers make similar claims to a rightful seat on public transit as their male counterparts? If women deserved equality with men, why were men still often expected to give them their seats?

Easily overlooked as the simple minutae of everyday life, such concerns were widely debated during the 1940s and reveal, with startling clarity, the beliefs and values regarding the proper role of women and men. The serious attention Davis and Lorenzkowski give these debates, and the thoroughly gendered lens they apply to their interpretations of their meanings, uncovers how high the stakes over comfortable and reliable transportation were for Canadians. More than this, their work also reveals how vitriolic the contestations over who rightfully ought to ride on, and work in, public transportation systems turned out to be.

Notes

1. On the effect of the 'war on terrorism' for feminist notions of citizenship, see Mary-Jo Nadeau's essay, 'Who is Canadian Now?: Feminism and the Politics of Nation After September 11', in this volume.
2. Ruth Roach Pierson, *'They're Still Women After All': The Second World War and Canadian Womanhood* (Toronto: McClelland and Stewart, 1986).
3. Jeffrey A. Keshen, *Saints, Sinners, and Soldiers: Canada's Second World War* (Vancouver: UBC Press, 2004).

Questions for Critical Reading

1. How is public space gendered? How is this notion demonstrated in your experience? What limits and opportunities does this process impart for women's claims to citizenship?

2. How is consumption a feminist issue? What are the gendered dynamics that shape attitudes towards women and shopping and women's experience of shopping for pleasure or for necessary goods?
3. How does the research provided by Davis and Lorenzkowski both challenge and support Jeff Keshen's argument that the wartime experience of women promoted greater equality?

Canadian use of urban public transit peaked during the 1940s. So too did Canadians' frustrations with it. With people fully employed and automobile use suppressed by tire, gasoline, and vehicle shortages, the overcrowding of buses and trams was so intense that even the 'language of the ladies' had become 'awful'. As the Toronto *Telegram* reported in 1946, one lady 'told another lady to shut her mouth', during an altercation begun by the one climbing up the other's back 'in striving to enter the street car'. The *Telegram* fretted that the 'gnawing neurosis' induced in the women passengers by excessive crowding would soon require streetcars to carry the notice: 'Ladies will kindly refrain from using abusive language.' Overcrowding was having dire implications for traditional gender roles.

As millions of riders competed for physical space, they were also redefining the meaning of public space and the appropriate behaviour within it for 'ladies and gentlemen'. Public transit in Canada had always been a socially contested terrain: in the past it had been a public forum for the debate over industrial discipline, as the burnt and overturned street cars of 1880–1920, a totem for the 'labour question', attested. On the buses and streetcars of the 1940s, by contrast, Canadians fought over such issues as sexual harassment and the rights of smokers and shoppers, as well as the employment of women drivers and conductors. In short, public transit provided a platform for negotiating and modifying Canadian gender relations.[1]

Always at issue was the place of women in a country that generally regarded women as intruders whenever they ventured into the public 'male' sphere of travel and commerce.[2] In normal times *de facto* segregation of the sexes, as they travelled at different times of day or kept to different parts of public vehicles, maintained tensions at a low level. With the coming of the Second World War, however, gender tensions in society as a whole intensified, as men left their families for the war and women took on jobs previously 'for men only'. The extraordinary overcrowding on street railway platforms intensified these pressures and produced an increase in sexual harassment.[3] How much is unknown. Then tight-lipped about sexual impropriety, Canadians only alluded to, rather than openly discussed, the violations of personal space that tight quarters permitted, however, they did openly dispute the rights of 'male smokers' and 'women shoppers', two groups who came to symbolize the larger conflict about which sex had a priority claim to seats and standing room on the crowded trams and buses of the 1940s. This discourse was, as we shall see, sometimes quite bitter in tone, its acidity a concoction of fear, hope, anguish, and resentment. The world was so global that it even had men and women forming battle lines in the middle of Canada's trams and buses.[4]

The war also created opportunities for women in an industry in which they had before then (with some exceptions during the First World War) been employed strictly to type, take dictation, and roll coins.[5] Now they became transit guides and conductors, moving into jobs that admittedly did not require much of a shift in the gender stereotype of woman as man's helpmate. The women who worked in transit garages and repair shops more obviously challenged traditional gender roles. As for female bus drivers and streetcar 'motormen', they had one of the most public platforms in 1940s Canada on which to mount their challenge to the sexual division of labour.[6]

At war's end, women transit workers were let go. By 1949, women retained only one important public role in Canada's urban transit industry that of passenger guides for the Toronto Transportation Commission (TTC), selling tickets and helping travellers to find their way into the vehicles and around the system. This occupation was so stereotypically 'feminine' that one is tempted to concur with historian Ruth Roach Pierson that, while 'the war effort necessitated minor adjustments to sexual demarcations in the world of paid work, it did not offer a fundamental challenge to the male-dominated sex/gender system'. Yet the temptation to dismiss the survival of the TTC Guide Service into the postwar era as a non-event in the history of both public transit and Canadian women should be resisted, for as historian Jeff Keshen has argued, after the war it was impossible for 'things to return to square one'.[7] Nor was the partial 'feminization' of the transit system in English Canada's national metropolis all that minor a change. This article contends that the guides helped to assure the remarkable postwar success of the TTC. As long as their role lasted, the guides made public transit a more welcoming place for women—a more 'feminine' system in effect. Some readers may baulk at the notion that 'mere' guides could have played an important role in the evolution of Canadian transit systems after the war. After all, these women were not system managers; they were hourly rated employees. Yet the work of sociologists Michel Crozier, Michel Callon, and Bruno Latour tells us that 'actors' at all levels of a bureaucracy or technological network have the capacity to shape it socially.[8]

In sum, this article discusses three main themes: first, a crisis in gender relations on public transit triggered by unprecedented wartime crowding; second, the employment of women as drivers and conductors (that is, as platform workers) as well as passenger guides; and third, the exceptional decision of the TTC to preserve those values, labelled 'feminine', that women workers *and* riders brought to its wartime system. The goal here is to shed light on Canadian gender relations and on a group of women workers hitherto in the historical shadows.

To understand the implications of increased transit crowding for women during the war, it is useful to look at the pre-war picture. Before 1939, gender relations in public spaces had been less tense. This is not to suggest that the interwar years were a 'golden age' for women on Canadian urban transit. Streetcars and buses were essentially a male domain. Climbing onto streetcars, women met the first reminder that they were entering a man's world, the steps were often too high for those short of limb, encumbered by small children, or dressed in long skirts. In 1941 the Canadian Transit Association finally recognized that 90 per cent of the passengers who had suffered injury getting on or off a streetcar were female. Its safety committee blamed the high female accident rate on improperly placed handholds, which were difficult for those holding a handbag or parcels to grasp, and on 'uneven street surfaces' at its stops, which were perilous for wearers of high heels.[9]

Once in the car, women encountered male smokers—usually to their mutual annoyance. The men were either flouting an anti-smoking bylaw or puffing away quite legally in the last three or four rows of the tram. This area was often, by custom, a male preserve, a rolling men's club. To escape its smoke and odours, non-smokers congregated in the front of street-cars, an area which in turn became a women's space. This feminine domain sometimes encompassed most of the vehicle during the off-peak, daytime hours. Nevertheless, a single lecher, drunkard, or boisterous adolescent could quickly turn the entire car into a menacingly male space. If accosted, women could turn for support to a male conductor—if there *was* one. But transit systems were gradually eliminating these positions to cut costs.[10] [. . .]

Full employment and restrictions on automobile use caused the Canadian urban transit to become overloaded during the war. Between 1939 and the end of 1945, passenger traffic rose by 124 per cent. Because it was extremely difficult to procure new equipment, Canadian companies brought back into service junked streetcars and over-age buses. By using their equipment more intensively, they were able to increase their service, expressed as vehicle mileage, by 60 per cent—just half of what was needed. These data do not, however, capture the full picture, since the war had a greater impact on some cities than on others. Between 1939 and the end of 1944, the number of revenue passengers rose by 84 per cent in Vancouver, Toronto, Montreal, and Winnipeg, 170 per cent in Ottawa, 200 to 300 per cent in Kingston, Sarnia, St Catharine's, and Halifax, 300 per cent in Windsor, and 450 per cent in Oshawa. Transit use remained abnormally high throughout the 1940s, although it began a downward trend after 1946.[11]

Canadians described urban transit in the 1940s in dehumanizing terms. They called the streetcars 'cattle cars', and the passengers who perennially blocked the entrance, a 'herd of stupid oxen'. Commuters felt like sardines. 'In the street car there's standing room only,' Gwen Lambton, a Toronto war worker, recalled; 'we're packed like sardines . . . The used smell of people who have been up all night, their sweat (and mine) is nauseating, but at least I can't fall.'[12] Canadians were urged to grin and bear this crush.

In the 1940s, Canadian women and men often resented intrusions into their physical and cultural space by people of different age, class, ethnicity, culture—and sex. With vehicles too crowded for men and women to stake out separate spheres by congregating in front or by pushing through to the rear—or even by travelling at different hours—a struggle for social space was inevitable.

Two groups found the crush loading especially vexatious in the 1940s: the 'shoppers', gender-typed as female; and the 'smokers', gender-typed as male. Both became acceptable targets for abuse as each sex vented its resentments about crowding. Attitudes towards shoppers and smokers were complex. Let us start with the female 'shoppers' who used public transit to carry home their purchases. For many, shopping by public transit was a new and unwelcome necessity, the wartime rationing of gasoline and tires having eliminated both home delivery and the family automobile as options. As 'shoppers' did their unaccustomed errands along unfamiliar routes, they found that their cultural privacy was threatened.[13] The time and space that women could call their own was greatly reduced. By 1943, the evening rush 'hour'—traditionally between 5 and 6 PM—had lengthened to three hours or more, as the major employers in a dozen or more Canadian cities joined the dominion government's plan to 'stagger' the start and end of the workday of 424,000 workers.[14]

It became difficult for shoppers to find a time when they were not competing with commuters for space. In Windsor, by December 1942, there were standing passengers 'at almost any hour'. Windsor was, to be sure, especially crowded. Elsewhere, seats were still sometimes available during the off-peak hours. Yet shoppers, especially those with jobs or children, were not always able to complete their journeys between 10 AM and 3:00 PM, because they had responsibilities that might prevent an optimal travel schedule. Wartime shortages also made shopping more inefficient and time-consuming. Working women became used to buying their groceries after work and then taking the homeward tram after 5:30 PM, by which time passenger volumes had fallen sufficiently for them to have a shot at a seat. Staggered hours made it extremely difficult for working women to find either the time or the private space for shopping. Stigmatized by their boxes and bags, they became 'shoppers', their right to ridership in clamorous dispute.[15]

Transit operators throughout the 1940s appealed to women shoppers and 'housewives' to stay off public transit during peak hours. In Edmonton, the street railway department in 1943 publicly blamed much of the crowding on 'tardy women shoppers'. As the *Journal* explained: 'Hundreds of women, despite constant appeals, still insist on heading homeward with arms full of parcels just at the peak late afternoon rush hour . . . Tram motormen say they see the same late shopping offenders day after day.' The

Journal next complained that office and store workers had to give seats to these miscreants, who showed no shame when challenged by a motorman: 'they just [gave him] the old icy stare' and reoffended the next week. Shoppers risked considerable abuse by riding after 5 PM. [. . .] The *Calgary Herald,* after admitting that '[o]ther workers frown[ed] on the strong-arm methods of disposing of shoppers', observed that 'the worker–shopper battles [had] brought about the end of chivalry.' Men were refusing to give up their seats to women shoppers.[16]

Gendered notions of politeness generally took a beating in the 1940s. As Mrs D.B. White of Ottawa remarked in 1943, 'The cars and buses are so crowded these days, that even the men have to stand!' She added that although a few men would surrender their seats, those who did were 'looked upon by their fellows as particularly odd specimens of the prehistoric animal; and by the ladies with a surprise bordering upon insult.'[17] In 1943 Ottawans could still joke about this 'standing' issue between the sexes. However, by the sultry summer of 1944 tempers had reached the boiling point. A flurry of letters in the *Ottawa Press* that August attested to the frustration and fury with which men and women observed changing gender relations on the very public, very crowded platforms of mass urban transit. Helen Scott set off Ottawa's debate over gender roles in public transit with a letter on 18 August describing boorish behaviour that included sexual harassment.

> I can stand to have men sit right in front of me and not bother to offer a seat, but what I can't stand is when they eye every girl standing within the general vicinity, up and down and back again. Besides making me so angry that I would love to slap them, this is most embarrassing. But they don't even stop there. I've seen elderly women, laden down with parcels, get on the streetcar and then have to stand and be jostled by the crowd . . . Numerous times I have been just going to get on the street-car when a man came rushing up, elbowed me aside, and rushed madly down the aisle to grab the first available seat.[18]

This letter hit a nerve, not least among those men who addressed the allegation of sexual harassment in their reply to the editor. None denied harassment. They either justified it or placed the onus on women to avoid it. Gerald Birch, though he endorsed equal rights, did so in order to argue that with rights came duties, one of which it seemed was to compete on equal terms for a streetcar seat. Birch countered: 'And so the girls are being stared at and it really peeves Miss Scott. Would she then kindly tell me why the girls spend hours beautifying their body for the apparent purpose of attraction and when they do get it, scorn it? If they want to be ignored, let them "wear something more concealing".' W.L. Farmer claimed to sympathize with Miss Scott, 'one of the few refined ladies among our very young modern generation', yet described her letter as 'pathetic to say the least'. He further accused women, who had won many rights, of taking for themselves habits that belonged exclusively to men:

> Smoking, drinking, wearing slacks and shorts (the latter so brief), a loose kind of conversation, yes and all this . . . on street-cars. And in all women have acquired more masculinity in the past twenty years than men were able to lose in a thousand years. Oh! for the days of feminine charm, when tobacco and beer dared never so much [as] to skim the sweet innocence of a maiden's lip . . . But the sparkle has been dulled by the sight of a lot of high-ball guzzling, cigar toting mamas parading everywhere in shorts with the utmost disregard for the next fellow's feelings. Women tried competing with the opposite sex and they've got the competition with all its consequences . . . Now, tell me *why* should a man give his seat to an equal?[19]

In effect, Farmer was asserting that women should count themselves fortunate to attract male attention, considering how unsexed they had become. Or was it oversexed? Those 'shorts' obviously bothered him in the hot summer of 1944. Of course, because of gender roles in the 1940s, women could not announce their sexual availability. If they did, or if they smoked, or if they insisted on sexual equality, they apparently should not expect respect.

Tellingly, men such as Farmer excused rather than denied the charge of sexual harassment. But harassment obviously occurred and certainly involved more than lecherous stares. With crowding so severe that one woman had to ride a mile on a streetcar 'on one foot as there was literally no floor space to accommodate its mate' while others had no room to lower their arms in self-defence, there was ample opportunity for lascivious contact. The fear of harassment was sufficiently menacing that 'female help' at an outlying Montreal factory refused in October 1943 to travel in buses at night.[20] There was, however, little public discussion of harassment. After all, it was not the sort of news that Canadians wanted loved ones posted overseas to hear.

People preferred, in any case, to discuss the sins of shoppers. None of the participants in Ottawa's August debate had a kind word for them. Most letters condemned them for riding at rush hour. Mildred Groh, for example had no sympathy even for 'elderly women laden with parcels', since they had all day to shop, 'so if they leave getting home with their parcels till the rush hours start . . . they deserve to stand.' J. Colucci featured shoppers in his list of misbehaving women, who also included the 'battle-axe' type of woman 'who mows her way down to a seat' as well as 'giggling young things' who make 'derogatory references to the appearances of every work-harassed male entering into the tram'.[21] His anger was palpable.

Many male commuters were angry during the 1940s—definitely about transit crowding, and probably also about feminine intrusion into their cultural privacy and social space. The bitter and defensive tone of men's remarks about women's traditional priority in seating also revealed anxiety over their own failure to meet traditional gender expectations, an anxiety that inevitably surfaced in civilian male circles in wartime. (Interestingly, none of the males who complained to the press claimed to be a soldier.) They were undoubtedly also bothered, to varying degrees, by the platform that public transit provided for growing numbers of women workers to make known both their existence and their claims to equal treatment. Nevertheless, the wartime discourse about women transit riders did not focus on the workers among them. It targeted instead the hapless shoppers, women who were being condemned for remaining faithful to pre-war gender roles. For decades women had been prized for being domestic consumers. Now their consumer role interfered with the war effort. While historians have emphasized the positive reinforcement to homemakers from government propaganda extolling their role in the war effort, one must wonder whether insults hurled their way for doing their family's shopping did not outweigh any flattery from the élites.[22]

Shoppers were not the only riders to incur the wrath of fellow passengers, for smoking had also become a flashpoint for gender tensions. In the 1940s smoking was still considered a gendered habit, even as Canadians recognized that women increasingly indulged in it. Smoking areas on trams were a man's world. Calgary males, for example, later became nostalgic about their 'smokers', as these enclaves disappeared with the trams themselves after the war. As the men gossiped about the weather, politics, exotic travel experiences, and the transit service, 'time passed quickly as well as pleasantly.'[23]

Realistically, women must have felt unwelcome anywhere the air was 'blue' with smoke. Indeed, in Ottawa they clogged the front of street cars, a newspaper editorialist remarked, rather than 'move farther down the aisle because, perhaps, by so doing they eventually land[ed] in the bay at the back which is usually occupied by men'—that is, by smokers.[24]

The male tobacco privilege, whether it existed by law or by neglect, came under attack as transit became more crowded during the Second World War. By May 1945, twenty-one of the thirty-three transit operators polled by a bus journal had banned smoking. They all reported cracking down on the practice, but men were resisting. Twenty-six of the systems reported difficulty in making their rules stick, especially in cities like Hamilton and Port Arthur (Thunder Bay) which had many manual workers and servicemen. The Sudbury-Copper Cliff Suburban Railway said that it had failed to suppress smoking because 'most of the passengers are miners who have not been able to smoke all day.' The Calgary Municipal Railway complained that it had difficulty restricting smoking to the rear vestibules of streetcars, despite periodic checks by police officers, because its 'own employees [were] offenders to some considerable degree'.[25]

The smoking debate in Edmonton had a distinctly gendered dimension: indeed, the increase in opportunity for female workers on its municipally owned tram system was explicitly linked to the decrease in opportunity for male smokers. Until the war, Edmontonians had agreed to restrict smoking to the rear compartment, but wartime crowding brought confrontation. In September 1940 the Woman's Christian Temperance Union urged city council to ban smoking on trams 'during such time as the windows have to be closed'. Their letter asked for 'a just recognition that non-smoking patrons have some rights, and that young children who use the street railway service have a right to tobacco-free air'. In October the police, in confirmation that smokers were invading the main body of the cars, promised a crackdown. Yet a city commissioner reported in January 1942 that women were still 'especially annoyed' by the large number of men puffing away well forward of the smoking compartment.[26]

Railway superintendent Thomas Ferrier believed a smoking ban would be the only solution. This was not feasible in 1942, an election year, as the council's bylaws committee still insisted that early morning smoking be permitted. Organized women, led by the Women's Missionary Society for the Free Methodist Church, rejected the compromise: they objected to cigarettes in city street cars, period. No compromise being possible, the city councilors elected to delay: they instructed the city commissioners to submit a report 'on the cost of installing smoke and dead air extractor fans in the rear of street cars'. Women lost out.[27]

However, a year later they won—not only smoke-free air, but jobs as well. Passenger traffic had risen to such a level that the street railway had to hire conductors to speed up fare collection. On 18 August 1943, it announced it would train women to be conductors and to sell tickets at busy intersections. The first twenty 'conductorettes' began work on 4 October. Superintendent Ferrier that same day praised the women's work in a statement asking city council to 'stop smoking in the rear compartments of the trams'. This step was necessary, reported the press, 'because women will be using the rear entrances to board the cars and in the winter time . . . there is no ventilation to carry off the smoke'. An 8 October news report announcing majority support on city council for prohibition pointed out that it was not only the rear entrance that doomed smoking, but also the hiring of the 'conductorettes'. They could not be expected to do their work enveloped in smoke. On 25 October 1943, Edmonton council finally prohibited smoking on urban public transit. This particular gender struggle for space had a clear victor.[28]

It might be expected that Edmonton's men would vent their anger over lost privileges at the women conductors, who were literally supplanting the smokers. Yet women *shoppers* took the brunt of male frustrations in Edmonton, as elsewhere. Women *workers* apparently bothered men less in the 1940s than is often assumed, unless of course the women in question threatened a man's *own* job.

While male and female passengers frequently defamed each other, they almost always had a kind word for women streetcar staff. As a public platform for gender conflict, Canadian mass transit displayed more a battle over gendered space than over occupational roles. This pattern becomes clearer as the experience of other cities with women conductors and drivers is examined. In the next section the narrative shifts perspective, as the nature of the sources requires the story to be told from the companies' point of view rather than, as would be ideal, from that of the women workers who 'invaded' (as the Winnipeg *Free Press* put it) 'one of the last jobs held exclusively by men in Canada'. These women workers, like the smokers and shoppers, reshaped public transit as a social space as they entered it, experienced it, and even as they left it. Glimpses into their lives appear in this essay but much of their history is yet to be learned.[29]

Canadian transit operators were as slow as one of their vintage trams to move towards hiring women platform workers. In most cases, they hired their first female conductors in the summer of 1943, by which time the number of gainfully employed women in the nation had already neared the million mark (rising from 638,000 in August 1939).[30] In January 1943, when 94 per cent of American transit companies were already employing more than 11,000 women, of whom 718 were operating vehicles, Canada still had not a single woman platform worker. Canadian transit companies explained their lack of interest in female help by pointing to the age profile of their male employees; to the fact (as a Montreal Tramways executive put it in June 1941) that 'no new transportation employees [had] been engaged or trained, in many properties, for almost ten years'. Consequently, Canadian transit was, as the TTC's general superintendent remarked later that year, 'particularly fortunate in the respect that the average age of its employees [was] relatively high and not many [were] likely to be enlisted in the armed forces or be attracted to other employment by promise of temporary advantage.' An alternative explanation would point to the sheer conservatism of Canadian transit operators, a conservatism that had made them slower than Americans to embrace the trolley coach in the 1930s.[31]

Transit companies appeared to regard the decision to hire female operators and conductors as radically innovative and inherently risky. In August 1943 Winnipeg Electric told its passengers that the original reaction to the proposal to put women on the streetcar platform had ranged from 'mild scepticism to outright scorn'. To ease such qualms, transit journals ran a series of positive articles on the performance and reception of women transit employees in the United States and, later, in Canada.[32] Meanwhile, the dominion government's manpower policies were pressuring Canadian operators to hire woman-power. By mid-1943 the men being sent to transit companies were over forty-five years old and, in the opinion of the transit association's Special Sub-Committee on Manpower, of 'very poor' calibre. It advised companies to hire women, paying them on an equal basis with the men. Union opposition had in the meantime collapsed, since the only realistic alternative to hiring women was a much longer working day for the remaining men. Consequently, systems in Victoria, Vancouver, Winnipeg, Windsor, Kitchener, Toronto, and Sydney had committed themselves by July 1943 to hiring women for platform or garage work. Before the end of the year, women were working as conductors, streetcar motormen, or bus drivers in Edmonton and St Catharines, Ontario, as well. As of March 1944, twelve Canadian transit companies were employing 263 women as streetcar operators and conductors, 70 women as bus drivers, and 154 women in maintenance work. As most of these women worked in just four cities, the numbers suggest that, in the 1940s, Canadians remained more hesitant than Americans to give women a public role in public transit.[33]

After some discussion, the principal transit operators in Montreal and Ottawa both decided against hiring women. Montreal Tramways announced that it was not considering the use of women even to sell tickets on street comers. Presumably, the company was still mindful of French-Catholic reservations about women working in as public a sphere as mass transit. It also dared not upset its unions, especially after a strike in March 1943 proved that it had backed the losing side in their jurisdictional disputes. In Ottawa the street railway, apparently fearful of being permanently saddled after the war with platforms requiring two operators, refused to hire women as conductors. As for Toronto-style passenger guides to ride the cars on an ad hoc basis and keep order as needed, the company may have shared the opinion of Ottawa's *Evening Citizen* that

'Lady Hostesses . . . would simply get in the way of squeezing one more passenger on board.' Ottawa and Montreal had plenty of company in spurning women transit workers: only a minority of Canadian transit systems hired female conductors and drivers. There must have been a generalized resistance to giving women such a public platform on which to demonstrate their ability to do 'man's work'.[34]

What resistance there was seems to have been restricted to the corporate boardroom and the union hall, for the public manifestly welcomed 'the feminine twist' in transit wherever women were employed. This positive response should have been expected, given the widespread recognition that women workers were performing an important wartime duty. Female conductors in Toronto interviewed in September 1943 said that there was 'hardly any trip' during which 'some one doesn't congratulate us'. For example, an elderly man told TTC conductor Elsie Waterford, 'I have been riding these street cars for twenty-five years and I think you girls are doing a wonderful job.' According to a Toronto transit executive, 'the people [were] taking . . . splendidly' to female bus drivers in that city. Vancouver's 'electric guides' quickly garnered 'several letters of commendation' from the public. Women conductors were praised in Edmonton for noticeably speeding up loading and unloading. There seems, then, to have been little public resentment of female platform staff.[35]

Transit companies generally gushed over the women's performance: in August 1943 the Winnipeg *Free Press* quoted the transit company's instructor, E.F. Hales, as stating that he had 'found no trainees quicker to learn than the women employees. He noted that they listened very attentively to what is said, and demonstrate themselves as very apt and quick to learn.' Hales further said that 'the advantage a man might have in his natural mechanical ability is more than made up for by the women in their quickness and ability to learn.' Women actually listened, Hales said, 'they don't just say "yes! yes!" all the time when they really don't know what I'm talking about,' as men apparently did.

The female conductors were 'doing a splendid job', Winnipeg Electric affirmed the following October. In late September 1943 the Toronto Railway Club quizzed transit executives about the performance of the new female workers. H.W. Tate, assistant manager of the TTC, responded: 'There have been no problems as far as women are concerned . . . At the present time they are very satisfactory—in fact more so than we expected.' Transit companies consistently reported that women operators had at least as good an accident record as the men—a significant virtue, given the shortage of replacement vehicles and parts. Though Winnipeg Electric stated in December 1943 that female streetcar drivers had more accidents than men, it affirmed that the 'men [had] been involved in more serious accidents than the women'. In 1945 it praised women operators for being as 'good as, and in some respects better than, male employees'. In June 1944 the Niagara and St Catharines system reported that women bus drivers were 'more courteous' than its men, and as 'accident free'.[36]

These sorts of direct, favourable comparisons obviously threatened males, and they often came with a negative qualifier. Thus, Niagara and St Catharines added that women took longer to train. It was also reported in Windsor that the work of women bus cleaners had not been 'entirely satisfactory' until the company had hired 'two older women to act as matrons'. As for those Toronto women bus drivers with the exemplary accident record, it was pointed out that they were also said to be 'on the cautious side' (which did not sound entirely complimentary); and their male rivals were depicted by TTC's superintendent of traffic as being of low calibre, not the 'type of individual' who would have been hired 'before the war'. Assistant manager Tate elaborated: 'At the present time, the men we are getting into the organization are the last selection and the women are the best of the women; so if you make a saw-off of the two, I think you are on the good end.' In other words, the 'best' woman was as good as the 'last' man. And even then, Tate said, women performed well because 'their reputation [was] at stake'—that is, the reputation of their entire sex. No wonder they were overachievers.[37]

This perception—that they had the pick of Canadian womanhood—must have influenced the attitudes of transit managers towards their female staff. They could admire the performance of exceptional individuals without having to revise their opinions about women's overall suitability to work on the public platform. Ironically, women fostered this prejudice by the high numbers in which they sought—and were rejected for—transit work. For example, 'some 200 women' responded to Winnipeg Electric's first appeal in mid-July 1943 for women streetcar and bus drivers. Of these, the company 'selected ten as suitable applicants for traffic work' and another ten as bus cleaners. Subsequent praise for the work of the first four women operators to emerge from this winnowing process did not, therefore, outweigh the company's public conclusion that 'there was a lack of first class [female] applicants for traffic work'. Similarly, the TTC, in reporting on the attrition rate among its female hirings, chose not to emphasize that 86 per cent of its streetcar staff were still working for it on 1 April 1944 (which meant that women had about the same persistence as wartime men in these jobs), but rather commented on the fact that only 70 per cent of its qualified women bus drivers had stuck with the job. They were quitting, the TTC figured, 'probably due [to] the more strenuous physical demands of that work, and partly due to the proportionately greater amount of rush hour work.'[38]

As in St Catharines, transit companies also complained, about the extra time it took to train women. While Ruth Roach Pierson and Marjorie Cohen have concluded, after looking at federal employment programs, that women were handicapped in their postwar job quest by the inadequate and superficial training they had received during the war, in the urban transit sector they actually received more training than men had at the beginning of the emergency: about three weeks instead of two. The middle-aged men being hired during wartime also generally required three weeks to qualify. Companies had to extend the qualification period because wartime traffic conditions were driving up their accident rate. Transit companies, for example, were increasing their schedule speeds in order to reduce the number of vehicles needed to assure a promised frequency of service. Moreover, although there were fewer taxicabs and automobiles in the way, bus and tram drivers had become more likely to hit them, and to be hit, as they hustled to make up time lost while loading and unloading their hordes of passengers. Inevitably, transit companies prolonged the training of novices. Yet they then blamed women for this policy change by announcing that women took longer to train. Although a woman reporter in Winnipeg tried to put a positive spin on the fact that women there were getting 'longer, tougher training than the men ever got', the opinion of he company that had to pay for this exercise (including wages for the trainees) was more negative.[39]

Managements clearly were displeased with the costs incurred in training platform workers during the war. The extra week or so must have been especially irksome, given the fact that they had not hitherto deigned to pay their trainees. Undoubtedly, the training experience reinforced the managers' prejudices against both middle-aged men and women. These two groups had, of course, the misfortune to serve their apprenticeships at a time when service conditions made it exceptionally difficult to impress their masters. While one could emphasize the positive—that women platform workers received superb training during the war, with even conductors being required in Toronto, Vancouver and Winnipeg to qualify as drivers—realism demands recognition that transit managers probably looked forward to the day when they could trim their training budgets by hiring young, male workers once again. In the meantime, they hired women. Winnipeg appears to have had fifty-three platform workers at the peak, just under half of them operating street cars, the rest conductors; as well, twenty-nine women cleaned and tidied its vehicles. Although Victoria had three such cleaners (in January 1944), Vancouver had none; it did, however, have forty 'conductorettes', with fifteen more in training. Edmonton, like Vancouver, used women primarily as conductors—there were sixty of these in April 1944—but an unknown number of women (and men) were also hired during the war to stand by the track switches, turning them manually for approaching cars. Taken together, these cities probably had fewer than 200 women working for them at anyone time. A scattered few worked on smaller systems such as those in Sydney, Kitchener, St Catharines, and Windsor.[40]

The numbers suggest that the majority of Canada's female transit workers had jobs in Toronto, inasmuch as its Transportation Commission hired 721 women during the war to do 'work usually done by men'. At the high point, the Toronto system had 340 female street railway and bus drivers, according to the press.[41]

Toronto's data indicate that transit women prized some jobs more than others, notably those that required technical skills and offered a diversity of challenges (repairwomen, handywomen, and the mechanics' helpers). They also had a preference for trams. On the other hand, women tended to leave jobs that reminded them of housework (various cleaning jobs) or involved especially heavy work, as did truck driving in the 1940s. Since many buses operated only during peak hours, driving them was exhausting work, the stop-and-go traffic requiring constant wheel and gear play; consequently, bus drivers had the second highest turnover of any of the female occupations reported by the TTC. If women themselves had arrived at a mutual conclusion with their employers that bus driving was not 'women's work', this finding would have eased the conscience of male managers as they pressured women at war's end to retire from male-gendered jobs or to transfer to 'positions more suitable for women'. Moreover, every transit company expected soon to scrap all or most of its streetcars.[42]

Transit men seem to have regarded bus driving by women as particularly invasive of their space; at least, it was the most threatening to their own masculinity. A bus driver commanded a free-wheel vehicle, alarmingly liberated from the steel and electric network that had hitherto guaranteed due subordination to the centralized, hierarchical, and male system; and unlike trams, buses could leapfrog each other. One male driver in 'a certain Canadian city' complained of a woman driver who had been running behind him: 'These dames aren't so dumb. She's been tagging behind me since 7:30 this morning so that I can pick up all her passengers and she doesn't have to risk getting tangled up. She's supposed to be 12 minutes ahead of me, but what can you expect?' A bus journal concluded that his complaints proved that 'man's feeling of security is a precious thing . . . not to be trifled with'. The most hostile remarks towards transit women typically involved buses. For example, a representative of Toronto's electric railway and motor coach union told the National War Labour Board in November 1944: 'We hear lots of sarcastic remarks about women doing our jobs, but I can tell you that women operators are not satisfactory. They are wrecking equipment . . . They haven't the strength to shift gears and handle heavy buses.'[43]

It was rare for a transit man to broadcast such views, for it was unnecessary to denigrate women to ease them out of transit jobs at the end of the war. The women themselves were supposed to realize that they had been temporary replacements in, as the Toronto *Globe and Mail* described the TTC in October 1945, a 'strictly a "for-men-only" organization'. Winnipeg Electric, having told the Canadian Transportation Association in November 1943 that it was 'not hiring women with any idea of employing them permanently', justified its 1945 decision to *stop* hiring them with the simple justification that men were now available. In Edmonton the street railway simply stopped hiring conductors in 1944, as it looked towards a return to one-man operation. Meanwhile, the TTC, having never disguised its belief that women's employment was 'of an emergency character', and that the jobs were 'for the duration' only, saw no contradiction in praising women for their 'emergency duty' and 'sacrifices', even as it claimed that women now 'were all eager and willing to step aside and let the boys have their jobs back again.'[44]

Were they indeed 'eager and willing'? Certainly, some female transit workers considered, as did Clara Clifford, their job to be 'a war measure'. Yet Clifford worked into 1946, deciding to leave (the TTC did not layoff its female employees) only after an inebriated passenger had accused her of 'taking a job now from a man'. 'This gave me food for thought,' she recalled. Yet she resented the drunk's double standard: 'He did not think . . . [of] the four years that I went through this cold to get him to where he wanted to go.' Some women also pressured female platform workers to leave; a 'middle-aged lady' in December 1945 expressed the widely held sentiment: 'It's time a lot of these girls were sent back to the farms. The war's over . . . Let the girls get themselves husbands, stay home and make room for men to get jobs.' The women workers who refused to heed this cultural message were transferred to more 'fitting' work at war's end on the TTC. Elsewhere, they were laid off.[45]

When Canadian women were asked what motivated their entry into the transit industry, they stressed the personal satisfaction they derived from their work. Streetcar operator Elsie Waterfield responded: 'They didn't want to depend on their children. They wanted to be independent.' The work also suited their interest in 'mechanical work'. Some women said that they had always wanted to drive a streetcar or that they enjoyed meeting the public. Others pointed out that work on the tram platform gave them an opportunity 'to show all the men who thought they couldn't do it that they could'; these women saw themselves as pathfinders for their sex through men's space. Personal improvement also showed up in the reminiscences: 'I was so withdrawn before I went to work,' recollected an erstwhile conductor. 'It gave me all the confidence in the world. I was able to cope with everything—including drunks.'[46]

Money also mattered, as companies advertising 'Good jobs at good wages' understood. Women platform workers emphasized the financial benefits of their jobs: 'I put in every hour I could work because I wanted to buy a home for a family,' recalled TTC conductor Clara Clifford. Urban transit was one of the few wartime occupations in which women got equal pay for equal work, thanks to the street railway unions having made their cooperation conditional on the sexes being treated equally, with respect not only to wages but also to seniority and shift work. The unions wanted to ensure that their employers had no economic reason to prefer female to male labour. Pay equity made transit work attractive to women, especially since the typical platform worker was married, and her husband in the military. These women looked to their job to supplement their dependant's allowance, and some of them undoubtedly had to be told at war's end to resign. Hints about their feminine 'duty' to cede their job to a returning veteran would not have sufficed.[47]

The TTC had been unusually open to women workers, and so its efforts at war's end to shut the door on them must have been especially unsettling to the organization. Or the TTC management may have had more opportunity than smaller systems to appreciate the contribution that female employees could make as a *social class*—rather than as *exceptional individuals*—to the well-being of their system. Whatever the motive, it was apparently only on Toronto transit that women retained a role on the public platform in the two decades after 1946. The first TTC guides had started work in April 1942 at busy spots in the downtown area, standing on the sidewalks to sell tickets, make change, and give information on routes and destinations, in order to speed up the service by reducing the number of transactions and inquiries at the fare box. In November 1945 'a new group of girls was formed, to work at points radiating from the center of the city during the . . . rush hours'. The twenty-three new 'passenger guides' (thus named to distinguish them from the more stationary 'information and ticket guides' working downtown) were not tied to a specific location; they had 'considerable latitude', as *Canadian Transportation* reported the following February, to ride the cars and buses 'within their prescribed' areas, looking for congestion and opportunities to 'be of service' to the passengers. Once on board, they continued to sell tickets and give out information while simultaneously persuading women to move to the back and men to stub out their illicit cigarettes. The guides were praised in February 1946 for having helped lost children to find their school or mother, an army nurse to carry her 'heavy suitcases', and a soldier to retrieve a typewriter forgotten on a tram.[48]

The TTC prized its guides, considering them a prime asset to be featured on ceremonial occasions. For example, in June 1947 it was a guide who held the official ribbon that Toronto's mayor cut to inaugurate the city's first modern trolley coach service. And in March 1954 two files of guides and male inspectors lined the path leading 'dignitaries', including the provincial premier, to the ceremonies that marked the opening of Canada's first subway line. Two smiling guides were at the head of the file, visually in charge not only of the women but also of the male inspectors, who were the company's most senior and respected employees in traffic operations.[49]

Despite their symbolic importance to the TTC in the decade following the war, the postwar guides are little acknowledged by historians. The health, indeed the survival, of public transit depended on women. Certainly, mothers decided whether children would ride public transit; and wives had an important say in setting family spending priorities such as whether to buy an automobile instead of a major appliance, or to move to a subdivision being built beyond the last bus stop. Moreover, the willingness of Canadians to ride during the off-peak hours was vital to the economic viability of public transit, as all transit executives recognized. They too rarely recognized that the vital but elusive off-peak passenger was more often than not female.[50]

If women abandoned it, or if they used it only during the peak hours, then transit was doomed to decline. Transit obviously could have done little to influence women's decision to work, and therefore to commute; women commuters weakened public transit as they swelled the rush-hour crowds, forcing the company to employ additional vehicles and drivers. However, those women who used transit during the off-peak period for shopping or recreation were quite another matter. They did not increase the demand for transit service, but paid the wages and amortized the vehicles that the transit company would have to operate in any case to service its peak-hour clientele. One shopper was considerably more valuable to public transit than two commuters—provided she did not ride at rush hours.[51]

Although the postwar viability of Canadian transit depended on retaining the loyalty of female riders in off-peak hours, only in Toronto did the system actively cater to their needs. The TTC guides made travel more pleasant for women—and for male non-smokers. They reduced shoving and enforced queues, to the obvious advantage of the very young, the elderly, and the small of frame. They persuaded women to move back in the cars, thereby reducing the buffeting they took from men pushing to the rear. They 'sweetly' told men to stop smoking. They patrolled the interior of vehicles, giving women a greater sense of security on the one-man trams and buses of the postwar era. They gave travel directions, to the advantage of women who, as shoppers or mothers, were more likely than their husbands to be venturing into unknown territory. Finally, it is crucial to note that most of the reported instances of special courtesy and generosity on the part of the guides involved other women. There must have been many women (as well as men) whose fidelity to the TTC was reaffirmed by experiencing or witnessing one of the passenger guides perform an act of basic human kindness such as this one, recorded by *Canadian Transportation* in February 1946:

> A very poorly dressed woman got off a car with heavy bundles on a bitterly cold evening. She seemed ill and tired. The guide took off her own rubbers and gloves and put them on the woman, and ascertaining she lived only two blocks from the main thoroughfare, she carried the parcels and took the woman home. At the door, while the woman was returning the rubbers and gloves, she burst into tears and said, 'I never had anything as nice as this done to me before.'[52]

Only the TTC provided service of this quality to urban commuters in Canada. It had 'feminized' its system the most during the Second World War, and remained easily the most feminized afterwards. The TTC's embrace of 'feminine' values, personified in the tact, cheerfulness, helpfulness, and kindness of its passenger guides, must have been an important asset in transit's postwar struggle to retain enough female patronage to remain economically viable. To be sure, the TTC was doing a lot of things right in the immediate postwar era (including its modernization program), and its regendering in the 1940s was not the sole explanation for its success. Still, the guides did constitute an outreach to women and an attempt to ease the gender tensions among its passengers that overcrowding had produced. On other Canadian systems, passengers were left to fend for themselves.

Those transit operators who believed the wartime crowds gave them hope for the future—by getting Canadians back into the 'riding habit'—had their hopes dashed by the gender and class tensions within those crowds. The 1940s 'contest over public space', as Mary P. Ryan observed for an earlier era, 'did not . . . simply pit males against females'. Conflict also broke out between smokers and non-smokers, shoppers and workers, the middle-aged and the young, the seated and the standing, the harassed and the harassers. Save possibly for the latter, these dichotomies defied neatly drawn boundaries between men's and women's spheres. For both sexes there was a range of experiences. Even so, Canadians believed that 'men' and 'women' were fundamental categories for comprehending transit's social relations; they tended to stereotype the various players on transit's public platform as either male (smokers) or female (shoppers). The complex struggle for seating, which saw both sexes defer to the elderly or the encumbered, was similarly reduced in the public discussions of the 1940s to an elaborate *pas de deux* between ladies and gentlemen.

Not surprisingly, Canadians also had difficulty getting past the idea of transit work as strictly 'men's work'. The ideology of women's and men's 'proper' sphere resurfaced in 1944–5, as a powerful 'reconstruction' discourse demanded women's postwar return to the home. The story of the women platform workers who were forced out of the paid labour force or into lower-paid, less satisfying work told a familiar tale. The individuals involved clearly paid a high price for the nation's gender bias. So too did Canada, as transit's failure to listen to the women of Canada before 1941 or to give women a working role in the system after the war (outside of Toronto) contributed to public transit's postwar slide into subsidy and senescence.[53]

Notes

1. Toronto *Telegram* editorial reprinted in Ottawa *Morning Journal,* 12 Feb. 1946. All Ottawa press items come from the City of Ottawa Archives (COA), Ottawa Electric Railway Scrapbooks. For public transit as a focus for Canada's debate over industrialization and industrial discipline see Christopher Armstrong and H.V. Nelles, *Monopoly's Moment: The Organization and Regulation of Canadian Utilities, 1830–1930* (Philadelphia: Temple University Press, 1986), 3–6. For the contested and gendered nature of public space one can usefully start with Sarah Deutsch, 'Reconceiving the City: Women, Space, and Power in Boston, 1870–1910', *Gender & History* 6 (1994): 202–3.
2. On the gendered nature of modern public transportation see, for example, Judy Wacjman, Feminism Confronts Technology (University Park: Pennsylvania State University, 1991), 126–35; and for Canada Donald F. Davis, 'North American Urban Mass Transit, 1890–1950: What If We Thought about It as a Type of Technology?' *History and Technology* 12 (1995): 318–20.
3. Sexual harassment definitely existed as a behaviour in the 1940s, though it did not yet exist as an intellectual construct. Our use of the term is admittedly ahistorical, since the phrases then used to describe unwanted sexual attention were less direct, indeed quite opaque. For a discussion of sexual harassment as an emerging social issue, see William O'Donohue, ed., *Sexual Harassment: Theory, Research and Treatment* (Boston: Allyn and Bacon, 1997). Historical discussions of this concept include, among others Penny Summerfield and Nicole Crockett, '"You Weren't Taught That with

the Welding": Lessons in Sexuality in the Second World War', *Women's History Review* 1 (1992): 435–54. For a discussion of sexual harassment in a Canadian context, see Graham Metson, *An East Coast Port: Halifax at War, 1939–1945* (Toronto: McGraw-Hill Ryerson, 1981), 113 National Archives of Canada (NA), AV, tape R8547, reminiscences of Clara Clifford.

4. Crowding intensified class, racial, and ethnic tensions as well. Class is a constant subtext of the conflicts between industrial workers, automobile owners, and shoppers that are discussed here. Moreover, subsequent interviews with Toronto conductors reveal that ethnicity and race shaped social relations on the streetcar platform. See interviews of Elsie Waterford and Clara Clifford. NA, AV, tapes R8546–8.
5. An exception to the rule were female bus entrepreneurs in North America. See Margaret Walsh, 'Not Rosie the Riveter: Women's Diverse Roles in the Making of the American Long-Distance Bus Industry', *Journal of Transport History* 17 (1996): 43–56. The most prominent female entrepreneur in the Canadian bus industry before 1950 may have been Mrs A.R. McMillan, named president of Cities Bus Service, the public transit system in Sarnia, Ontario, in 1949. *Bus and Truck Transportation in Canada (BTT)*, Sept. 1949, 103.
6. There exists a well-developed body of studies on the gendered construction of skills. See, for example, Joy Parr, *The Gender of Breadwinners: Women, Men, and Change in Two Industrial Towns, 1880–1950* (Toronto: University of Toronto Press, 1990); Ava Baron, ed., *Work Engendered: Toward a New History of American Labor* (Ithaca, NY: Cornell University Press, 1991).
7. Ruth Roach Pierson, *'They're Still Women After All': The Second World War and Canadian Womanhood* (Toronto: McClelland & Stewart, 1986), 216; Jeffrey Keshen, 'Revisiting Canada's Civilian Women during World War II', *Histoire sociale/Social History* (Nov. 1997). While revisionist studies suggested considerable continuity between women's pre- and post-war roles, recent works hold that the unprecedented employment of women during the war years did inspire subtle processes of change. See, for example, Diane Forestell, 'The Necessity of Sacrifice for the Nation at War: Women's Labour Force Participation, 1939–1946', *Histoire sociale/Social History* 22 (1989): 333–47.
8. Michel Crozier, *The Bureaucratic Phenomenon* (Chicago: University of Chicago Press, 1964); John Law, ed., *Power, Action, and Belief: A New Sociology of Knowledge?* (London: Routledge & Kegan Paul, 1986); Wiebe Bijker et al., eds., *The Social Construction of Technological Systems: New Directions in the Sociology and History of Technology* (Cambridge, Mass.: MIT Press, 1987); and Wiebe Bijker and John Law, eds., *Shaping Technology/Building Society: Studies in Sociotechnical Change* (Cambridge, Mass.: MIT Press, 1992).
9. *Proceedings of the 37th Annual Meeting of the Canadian Transit Association (CTA Proceedings), 1940–1*, Seignieury Club, Quebec, 4–6 June 1941, 42–5; *Bus Transportation,* June 1941, 298; George Harris, 'Cars of the Winnipeg Electric Railway 1904–1955', *Canadian Rail* 220 (1970): 112, City of Calgary Archives (CCA), City Clerk's Fonds, box 375, file 2454, C. Comba to J.M. Miller, 14 March 1946; Montreal *Gazette*, 19 Nov. 1948; Ottawa *Morning Citizen*, 20 June 1934.
10. Canadian systems, starting with the municipally owned systems of western Canada, began introducing one-man cars in 1917. One-man cars were blamed for a 'lady passenger being outrageously insulted with no opportunity to escape' in Edmonton. Edmonton *Bulletin*, 6 Feb. 1919.
11. *CT*, Dec. 1944, 674; July 1946, 389; COA, MG 45-1-30x box 1, Secretary of Street Railway Committee to George S. Gray, 20 Jan. 1945; NWF, vol. 61, File 11, Norman D. Wilson, *Greater Winnipeg Transit Service (Short Version),* 11 Dec 1951, 2. Canadian transit patronage fell by 3.9 per cent by 1950 after hitting its peak in 1946.
12. Montreal *Gazette*, 24 Sept. 1948; Ottawa *Morning Citizen*, 7 Dec. 1948; 12 Nov. 1942; Gwen Lambton, 'War Work in Toronto', in Ruth Latta, *The Memory of All That: Canadian Women Remember World War II* (Burnstown, Ont.: General Store Publishing House, 1992), 33.
13. Modern prejudice envisages the 1940s shopper as someone with hatbox in hand, but she was more likely to have the evening's meal or a scarce commodity like sugar or coffee in her bag. Shopping in wartime Canada was time-consuming, fatiguing work as the Kitchener *Daily Record* reported: 'It takes three hours to do half an hour's shopping . . . Mrs Shopper, who in former years drove the family car downtown now walks or rides a crowded street car . . . Aside from standing on streetcars local women are now accustomed to standing in line . . . Clerks are few'. Kitchener *Daily Record*, 12 July 1943.
14. *Chatelaine,* 22 Nov. 1942, 72, 75; CCA, City Clerk's Fonds, box 2245, City Clerk of Winnipeg to City Clerk of Calgary, 16 Aug. 1943; NA, RG 28, vol. 270, file 196-17-4, Department of Munitions and Supply, Press Release 593A, 19 Sept 1945.
15. *BTT,* Dec. 1942, 29; Feb. 1944, 40–1.
16. *BTT*, Feb. 1944, 41; *CT*, Feb. 1944, 91; Ottawa *Morning Journal*, 12 Jan. 1943; Edmonton Journal, 7 Nov. 1942, 30 Sept. 1943, and 6 Dec. 1948; Calgary *Herald*, 18 Sept. 1943.

17. Ottawa *Morning Citizen,* 17 May 1943. Edmonton at first was a strange exception to the norm of seated males. In September 1942 its Trade and Labour Council proposed 'street cars-for-men-only' at rush hour. By August 1944, Edmonton males no longer needed special protection from the constraints of their gender, according to the Edmonton *Journal*: they could now 'out-stare the most glaring woman tram rider, and remain seated without any qualm.' Edmonton *Journal,* 21 Sept. 1942 and 31 Aug. 1944. See also Vancouver *Sun,* 12 Sept. 1946.
18. Ottawa *Morning Citizen,* 18 Aug. 1944.
19. Ibid., 12 Aug. 1944. Birch was using the 'potent weapon of humiliation'. This weapon, as Karen Dubinsky has argued, 'touched all those who went public with their stories of social conflict'. Karen Dubinsky, *Improper Advances: Rape and Heterosexual Conflict in Ontario, 1880–1929* (Chicago: University of Chicago Press, 1993), 164.
20. Ibid., 8 May 1947; NA, RG 12, vol. 435, file 73-13-B-2, John Cowling to J.E. Michaud, 20 Oct. 1943.
21. Ottawa *Evening Citizen,* 22 and 26 Aug. 1944.
22. The widespread negative attitudes towards female shoppers contrasted markedly with government propaganda efforts to recognize women's traditional domestic services (i.e., thrift and price monitoring) as socially necessary. See Pierson, *They're Still Women,* 41; *Chatelaine,* Nov. 1942, 72, 75, and June 1944, 76. The wartime denigration of shoppers is an important, neglected chapter in the history of mass consumption.
23. *Saturday Night,* 30 Nov. 1912, 29, and 4 Nov. 1922, 23; Edmonton *Journal,* 31 Jan. 1942; Centre d'archives Hydro-Québec, file F6/16173, 'Rules and Regulations for the Government of Employees of the Hull Electric Company' (1913); Calgary *Herald,* 6 Dec. 1949 and 18 Feb. 1956. By 1915, Halifax, Quebec, Montreal, Toronto, Winnipeg and Vancouver had banned smoking in closed cars. However, Edmonton, Calgary, Regina, Victoria, Ottawa, and Hull, among others permitted it in the late 1930s in the rear section.
24. Ottawa *Morning Citizen,* 18 Nov. 1942.
25. *BTT,* May 1945, 72; City of Halifax Archives. City Council Minutes, 12 Nov. 1943. 338 (thanks to Kimberly Berry for this reference); CCA, City's Clerks Fonds, box 386, file 2532, 19 May 1947; CCA, Calgary Transit, Series III, box 82, file 859, Superintendent's Office Bulletin, 27 Oct. 1947. Ottawa had an acrid debate over the smoking privilege from 1942 onward, as the local press reported that male smokers, angry over the invasion of their space by non-smokers (mostly women), retaliated by smoking illegally throughout the car. See Ottawa *Evening Citizen,* 27 Oct. 1942; Ottawa *Morning Citizen,* 13 Aug. 1948; Ottawa *Morning Journal,* 11 Aug. 1943.
26. Edmonton *Journal,* 24 Sept and 10 Oct 1940, and 31 Jan. and 30 Sept. 1942.
27. Ibid., 9, 14, 26, and 27 Oct. 1942.
28. Ibid., 18 Aug. and 4 and 8 Oct. 1943; Edmonton *Bulletin,* 4 and 8 Oct. 1943; CEA, City Council Minutes, 25 Oct. 1943.
29. Winnipeg *Free Press,* 14 Aug. 1943.
30. C.P. Stacey, *Arms, Men and Governments: The War Policies of Canada, 1939–1945* (Ottawa: Queen's Printer, 1970), 416. This number did not include the 750,000 women working on family farms and the 43,000 women in the armed forces.
31. *CT,* Feb. 1942, 90; May 1943, 245; *CTA Proceedings,* 1940–1, 110.
32. Canadian transit executives apparently had forgotten or chose not to recall that twelve women had served as streetcar conductors in Halifax for a year after the explosion of 6 December 1917. They were paid off 'when the men came home'. See *Canadian Railway and Marine World,* Feb. 1933, 71. (Thanks to Kimberly Berry and Steven High for the Great War references.)
33. *BTT,* July 1943, 37; Aug. 1943, 20; Vancouver Public Library. Harold Till, *Vancouver's Traffic History, 1889–1946* (ND), 60; Public Archives of Manitoba, P608 Amalgamated Transit Union, Minutes of 13 April 1943; CT, July 1943, 378, and Aug. 1944, 441; Toronto *Globe and Mail,* 12 July 1943; Winnipeg *Free Press,*15 July 1943; Vancouver *Province,* 11 Aug. 1943; Kitchener *Daily Record,* 12 June and 7 July 1943.
34. Montreal *Gazette,* 17 May and 19 June 1943; Ottawa *Evening Citizen,* 29 Nov. 1945; NA, MG28, I103, vol. 230, file 7, A.R. Mosher, 'A Public Statement on the Montreal Tramways Strike', 5 April 1943.
35. Toronto *Daily Star,* 22 Oct. 1943; *CT,* July 1943, 378; Nov. 1943, 590; Jan. 1944. 30; Toronto *Globe and Mail,* 10 Sept. 1943; Ottawa *Morning Citizen,* 18 Oct. 1943; Ottawa *Evening Citizen,* 30 Nov. 1943 (latter two for Edmonton); Kitchener *Daily Record,* 7 July 1943; NA, AV, tape R8547, Elsie Waterford reminiscences.
36. *CT,* Oct. 1943, 542; Nov. 1943, 590; Jan. 1944, 28–30; June 1944, 330; June 1946, 328; Winnipeg *Free Press,* 14 Aug. 1943; *BTT,* June 1944, 42.
37. *BTT,* June 1944, 42; *CT,* Nov. 1943, 590; Dec. 1943. 653.
38. *CT,* Dec. 1943, 653; Jan. 1944, 27; June 1944, 330; Winnipeg *Tribune,* 15 July and 5 Aug. 1943; Winnipeg *Free Press,* 14 Aug. 1943. The male turnover was 2.3–2.5 per cent per month in 1943.
39. Pierson, *They're Still Women,* chap. 2 (written with

Marjorie Cohen); *CT*, Oct. 1943, 542; Jan. 1944, 29; Winnipeg *Free Press*, 14 Aug. 1943; *CTA Proceedings*, 1940–1, 111–12. Women got sixteen days training in Vancouver, twenty-one days in Winnipeg, and one month in Toronto; men got three weeks in Montreal.

40. Ibid., Jan. 1944, 30; Feb. 1944, 82; June 1946, 328; NWF, vol. 18, me 19, Thomas Ferrier to Edmonton City Commissioners, 19 April 1944; Colin K. Hatcher and Tom Schwarzkopf, *Edmonton's Electric Transit* (Toronto: Railfare Enterprises 1983), 116; Edmonton *Journal*, 10 Jan. and 29 March 1944.
41. *CT*, Nov. 1945, 637; Toronto *Globe and Mail*, 6 Oct. 1945. The TTC's reliance on women workers was not unusual for a Toronto company: in October 1943, more than 40 per cent of Toronto's manufacturing workers were female—the highest percentage for any Canadian city. NA, MG28 I103, vol. 362, General Part I, 1942–57, Department of Trade and Commerce, Dominion Bureau of Statistics, Employment Statistics Branch, 'Sex Distribution of the Persons in Recorded Employment at Oct. 1, 1943' (Ottawa: King's Printer, Dec. 1943).
42. *CT*, Nov. 1945. 637.
43. *BTT*, Sept. 1943, 25; Ottawa *Evening Citizen*, 1 Nov. 1944.
44. Toronto *Globe and Mail*, 6 Oct. 1945; *CT*, Oct. 1943. 542; Dec. 1943, 654; June 1946, 328, 334, Edmonton *Journal*, 10 Jan. and 7 Dec. 1944, 21 Nov. 1945.
45. NA, AV, tape R8546, reminiscences of Clara Clifford; Ottawa *Morning Citizen*, 1 Dec. 1945.
46. Winnipeg *Free Press*, 5 Aug. 1943; Toronto *Daily Star*, 22 Oct. 1943; Winnipeg *Tribune*, 5 Aug. 1943; NA, AV, tapes R8546-7, reminiscences of Elsie Waterfield and Clara Clifford.
47. NA, AV, tape R8546, reminiscences of Clara Clifford; *CT*, Jan. 1944, 27–9; Feb. 1944, 82; June 1946, 328, *Bus Transportation*, Dec. 1944, 35; Edmonton *Journal*, 10 Jan. 1944; Vancouver *Province*, 11 Aug. 1943; *BTT*, July 1943, 37. Winnipeg Electric was not particular as to whether it employed single or married women, but the other companies did give a preference to the latter. Most of the names that show up in news articles about Winnipeg electric started with 'Mrs', including three of the first four streetcar drivers to qualify. Thirty-two of the first thirty-three women in the BC Electric Railway's training program had husbands in the military, as did a majority in Edmonton and Toronto.
48. Only single women were employed as passenger guides, in keeping with the postwar trend against hiring married women. See NA, AV, tape R8546, reminiscences of Clara Clifford; *CT*, Feb. 1946, 84, 86; Jan. 1949, 30; Toronto *Globe and Mail*, 19 Jan. 1943; Ottawa *Morning Journal*, 30 Nov. 1945; *BTT*, Aug. 1949, 42. During the war, Vancouver and Victoria also employed female guides.
49. Mike Filey, *The TTC Story: The First Seventy-five Years* (Toronto & Oxford: Dundurn Press, 1996), 72, 89. The TTC guides lasted until March 1995, when the service ended for budgetary reasons. Information from Ted Wickson, the former TTC archivist.
50. For historical perspectives on the TTC's success, see Michael Doucet, 'Politics, Space and Trolleys: Mass Transit in Early Twentieth-Century Toronto' in *Shaping the Urban Landscape: Aspects of the Canadian City-Building Process*, Gilbert A. Stellar and Alan F.J. Artibise, eds. (Ottawa: Carleton University Press, 1982), 356–82.
51. The economic importance of off-peak passengers and the worsening disparity between peak and off-peak travel are discussed by John R. Meyer and José A. Gomez-Ibánez, *Autos, Transit and Cities* (Cambridge, Mass.: Harvard University Press, 1981), 58–9.
52. *CT*, Feb. 1946, 86.
53. Mary P. Ryan, *Women in Public: Between Banners and Ballots, 1825–1880* (Baltimore: John Hopkins University Press, 1990), 93. Transit's story must have been repeated in countless other industrial sectors. Yet historians have tended to assume rather than prove that the postwar departure of women from entire occupations damaged society and the economy. In effect, there has been a liberal and individualistic focus, rather than a communitarian one, to the research. Among the few studies to examine the economic damage resulting from women's return to home and hearth in North America are Lewis Humphreys, 'Women and Government Intervention in the Canadian Labour Force, 1941–1947' (MA thesis, Dalhousie University, 1986); and Sherrie A. Kossoudji and Laura J. Dresser, 'Working Class Rosies: Women Industrial Workers during World War II', *Journal of Economic History* 52 (1992): 431–46.

Passing Time, Moving Memories: Interpreting Wartime Narratives of Japanese Canadian Women

Pamela Sugiman

EDITORS' INTRODUCTION

To highlight the only recently challenged 'silences' surrounding children's experiences in the scholarship of sociologists, anthropologists, and historians, Barrie Thorne offered the poetics of Adrienne Rich's 'Cartographies of Silence':

> It is a presence
> It has a history a form
> Do not confuse it
> With any kind of absence.[1]

The simple profundity of Rich's words capture what feminist historians have also struggled with in their desire to bring the experience of women more fully into the historical record. In 1978 Veronica Strong-Boag challenged multiple sectors of the historical community in Canada to systematically and self-consciously gather, deposit, and organize material related to the history of women. To do less, she argued, was to render the historical record of the country hopelessly incomplete.[2] Out of such concern came organizations like the Canadian Women's Movement Archives which documents 'non-governmental agencies working for the political, social and economic conditions of Canadian women', particularly post-1960s grassroots organizing.[3]

Traditional historical writing simply discounted women and their perspectives as 'absent' from the documented past.[4] Such claims were, of course, circulated in a context in which women were not acknowledged as subjects capable of shaping historical change. Women were not absent from the past, however. They were rather largely invisible in much of the text-based, governmental documents thought to comprise the most 'legitimate' sources of history. For women's experiences to be reflected in studies of the past different questions needed to be asked and different historical sources had to be sought after and cultivated.

In the past twenty years, questions of diversity *within* the experiences of women from differing class, racial, religious, sexual, and regional contexts has added increasing layers of complexity into interpretations of 'women's' pasts.[5] Not surprisingly, feminist historians embraced oral history as a possible antidote to women's neglect in, and erasure from, the historical record. The longstanding oral tradition in First Nations communities, and particularly scholarly interest in listening to First Nations women, provided suitable models.[6] By listening to women of varying backgrounds, contexts, and circumstances, feminist historians not only created new historical documents but engaged in a methodology that positioned women as subjects. As such, they reinterpreted women not merely as objects of historical change but as actors in the past. That women made history in turn triggered new conceptualizations of often taken-for-granted aspects of historical interpretation, such as traditional approaches to periodization and overly simplified dichotomies between 'public' and 'private'.

A number of essays in this collection, including those offered by Epp, Chenier, and Baillargeon, bear witness to the power of memory in re-interpreting the past. As Joan Sangster argues in her classic essay on feminism and oral history, 'oral history offered a means of integrating women into historical scholarship, even contesting the reigning definitions of social, economic, and political importance that obscured women's lives.'[7] In this essay by sociologist Pamela Sugiman, we are privy to the place that oral testimony has in the self-conscious interpretive work undertaken by a scholar. Like historian Mona Oikawa,[8] Sugiman both expands how we interpret the events of the Japanese internment and explores 'the process of remembering and the ways in which the derivation of our knowledge of history may generate different types of narratives that may be used to build upon one another and to disclose the role of subjectivity, or interpretation, and of the researcher herself in constructing the past'. Sugiman's central goal, to dismantle the racist notion that Japanese Canadian women simply acquiesced to the political violence visited upon themselves and their families during the Second World War, is pursued via attention to three interrelated historical narratives: her own personal memories as a child of Japanese ancestry, the private letters written by and to second generation (*Nisei*) and first generation (*Issei*) Japanese Canadian women in the mid-1940s, and the oral testimonies of 35 *Nisei* women who endured the destruction of families—often their own—during the internment episode. As she remakes our understanding of the role of Japanese women in resisting, denouncing, and surviving the internment and repatriation, Sugiman also makes more transparent the value of seeking multiple perspectives on the past. Her work eloquently demonstrates the need for feminist historians to be comfortable with complexity and to invite different stories about the past to intermingle and converse with each other. We have become accustomed to conceptualizing history as a highly contested terrain. Sugiman reminds us that history is also constituted by voices, loud and subtle, that require and, indeed demand, respectful listening.

Notes

1. From Adrienne Rich, *The Dream of a Common Language: Poems, 1974–1977* (New York: W.W. Norton & Company, 1978) as quoted in Barrie Thorne, 'From Silence to Voice: Bringing Children More Fully Into Knowledge', *Childhood* 9.3 (2002): 251–4.
2. Veronica Strong-Boag, 'Raising Clio's Consciousness: Women's History and Archives in Canada', *Archivaria* 6 (Summer, 1978): 70–82.
3. See the Canadian Women's Movement Archives homepage at http://www.biblio.uottawa.ca/archives/cwma-acmf-e.html.
4. The classic articulation of this 'false absence' is Joan Kelly-Gadol, 'Did Women Have a Renaissance?' in *Becoming Visible: Women in European History*, Claudia Koonz and Renate Bridenthal, eds. (Boston: Princeton University Press, 1977), 137–64.
5. See, for example, the essays in *Nation, Empire, Colony: Historicizing Gender and Race*, Ruth Roach Pierson and Nurpur Chaudhuri, eds. (Indianapolis: Indiana University Press, 1998).
6. See, for example, the work of Julie Cruikshank in collaboration with Angela Sydney, *Kitty Smith and Annie Ned, Life Lived Like a Story: Life Stories of Three Yukon Native Elders* (Lincoln and London: University of Nebraska Press, 1990); Beth Brant, *I'll Sing Until the Day I Die—Conversations with Tyendinaga Elders* (Toronto: McGilligan Books, 1995).
7. Joan Sangster, 'Telling Our Stories: Feminist Debates and the Use of Oral History', in *Rethinking Canada: The Promise of Women's History*, 4th ed., Veronica Strong-Boag, Mona Gleason, and Adele Perry, eds. (Toronto: Oxford University Press, 2002), 221–34.
8. Mona Oikawa, 'Cartographies of Violence: Women, Memory, and the Subject(s) of the "Internment"', in *Race, Space, and the Law: Unmapping a White Settler Society*, Sherene H. Razack, ed. (Toronto: Between the Lines, 2002).

Questions for Critical Reading

1. View the film *Watari Dori: A Bird of Passage*. In what ways are the narratives of women used in the film similar to Sugiman's methodology? How do they differ?
2. How do the lives of the *Nisei* and *Issei* women explored by Sugiman compare to the lives of Mennonite refugee women analyzed by Epp? What historical factors account for the similarities and differences?
3. Besides oral histories which privilege the voices of often silenced women, what other historical methodologies might be considered 'feminist'? What are the characteristics of these methods that earn them this distinction?

> The wind is so sickly warm. Perhaps the same wind has blown over the bloody battlefields of the Pacific. I have so much to write to you about tonight, I mustn't waste my time by letting my imagination get the better of me—my mind wanders so easily these days—could it be what they call the 'ghost town rot'? Even with the certain amount of freedom that's allowed us in the ghost towns, we're getting so sick of the place. We're getting so dull and dry, and uninteresting. I can't help but wonder what boredom and monotony you must have to endure behind those nasty barbed-wires! It's more than three years now, *Niesan*, three long years . . . . [from sister in Bay Farm to her brother in Angler, Ontario, June 1945, written in English][1]

Acts of Political Violence[2]

The pain caused to all persons of Japanese descent by the Canadian government's actions during the years of the Second World War is etched in my memory. It has become an integral part of my existence, as well as the defining moment in my own family's history. Throughout the better part of my adult life, I have reflected on the wartime internment of my mother, father, grandparents, aunts, and uncles. As a sociologist, I have been researching these injustices for years. I do not know how familiar most Canadians are with these events in history. By now, many must know the rough contours of the story, at least the one that has entered the public discourse and been legitimated by the written word and the published record.[3]

In the years prior to the Second World War, over 95 per cent of Japanese Canadians lived in British Columbia, the first immigrant from Japan settling in this western province in 1877. Discriminatory legislation, in addition to ostracism from the Anglo-Celtic population, forced a concentration of Japanese settlements in the southwest corner of British Columbia. People of Japanese origin owned fishing boats along the coast, as well as berry farms and gardens throughout the Fraser Valley, and in Vancouver a Japanese business and residential community (known as Japan Town) flourished on and around Powell Street. Yet, in spite of their economic and cultural presence, Japanese Canadians had extremely circumscribed rights. By law, they were prohibited from holding public office, from voting in an election, and from entering institutions of higher learning and hence the professions.

Anti-Asian sentiment was strong and unabashed in British Columbia in the decades leading up to the war.[4] However, racism took on new dimensions, and its impact on the community intensified dramatically, when Japan bombed Pearl Harbor in December 1941. Days after the bombing, with claims that 'all people of Japanese racial origin' posed a threat to national security, the Canadian government closed down Japanese-language newspapers, impounded boats, and began plans to remove forcibly 21,000 persons of Japanese ancestry from their homes. Seventy-five per cent of this group were naturalized or Canadian-born citizens.[5]

Along with the uprooting, Japanese Canadians were subject to a dusk-to-dawn curfew and had their homes searched by officers of the Royal Canadian Mounted Police. Over time, thousands were herded into the stench-filled livestock buildings of Hastings Park in Vancouver, a 'clearing site' for those who would later be dispersed to isolated parts of the province. The majority of Japanese Canadians (approximately 12,000) were eventually sent to 'internment camps', where they were forced to live in hastily prepared shacks or run-down hotels.[6] These 'settlements' were situated in various parts of the British Columbia interior: Greenwood, Sandon, Kaslo, New Denver, Rosebery, Slocan City, Bay Farm, Popoff, and Lemon Creek. Tashme, another site, was set up on vacant land just outside the 100-mile 'protected area' close to Hope. A smaller number of families (approximately 1,150) were relocated to so-called 'self-supporting' camps in Lillooet, Bridge River, Minto City, McGillivray Falls, and Christina Lake. These families supposedly possessed the financial resources necessary to assume full responsibility for their own relocation and maintenance. Another small group (about 4,000) were sent to perform grueling labour in family units on the beet farms of Alberta and Manitoba.

In the first phase of the internment, many sons, brothers, and husbands were separated from their families and sent to labour in work camps in British Columbia and Ontario. Approximately 1,000 men were sent to road camps. Japanese nationals were placed in camps around the British Columbia/Alberta border, while Canadian born Nisei were sent to the Hope/Princeton highway or to Schreiber, Ontario. Men who showed even the mildest resistance were interned as prisoners of war in Petawawa and Angler, Ontario. About 700 men were incarcerated in these sites, many of whom remained there for 'the duration of the war.[7]

With the defeat of Japan in 1945, all cleared Japanese Americans were permitted to return to the coast.[8] However, Japanese Canadians, by then interned for three years, faced a 'second uprooting'. At this time, the Department of Labour announced two policies: dispersal and 'repatriation'. People of Japanese ancestry were forced to leave British Columbia by either dispersing east of the Rockies (Ontario or Quebec) or 'repatriating' to Japan. As noted by Roy Miki and Cassandra Kobayashi, the term 'repatriation' was a euphemism for what was in fact 'a forced exile'. After all, the 'patria' or country of birth for the majority of these citizens was Canada, so they could not in this sense, be 'repatriated' to Japan. Fearful, angry, and confused, approximately 10,000 Japanese Canadians signed up for expulsion. Many signed simply because they were reluctant to face the unfamiliar and racially hostile terrain of Eastern Canada, and thus a large number later changed their minds. Yet in 1946 roughly 4,000 individuals had already been deported (2,000 of these were Canadian born; one-third of the 2,000 were dependent children under the age of 16). The government did not allow Japanese Canadians to return to the 'protected zone' until 1949, roughly four years after the war's end. They were not granted the right to the federal vote until June 1948 (effective April 1949), and could not vote in the province of British Columbia until March 1949.[9]

These were acts of political violence. The government's actions resulted in dispossession, property loss (farms, fishing boats, vehicles, homes, and personal belongings of less monetary worth but great personal value), a violation of human rights, disruption of education, diminished aspirations, coerced employment (often highly exploitative in nature and typically for low pay and little recognition), the break-up of families, loss of culture (language, customs, art forms), and continued exposure to racism in its many guises. The more hidden and unquantifiable costs of these wartime injustices enter the realm of emotion and subjectivity, the most dramatic and tragic of these being suicide.[10] In short, the Second World War internment resulted in the destruction of a community and trauma to the individuals within it.

Situating the Narratives

If this story is not known to a general audience of *Hakujin* Canadians, it has no doubt been heard many times by most Canadians of Japanese descent.[11] Indeed, promoted over the last few decades as part of the community's efforts to seek redress for wartime losses, it has become part of our collective memory. The collective narrative has centred around loss of property, the indignities of Hastings Park, expulsion to ghost towns, and violation of human rights and principles of democracy. Since the Redress Settlement with the Canadian government in 1988, we have witnessed a further unearthing of personal memoirs, in a concerted effort on the part of Japanese Canadians to recover their history, consciously to remember, and to preserve memory through the literacization of experience.[12] This expanding cultural reservoir is of enormous value in enriching and extending our sense of ourselves.

Notwithstanding the political utility and empirical value of the official public history, I would caution, however, against the colonization of our thinking about Japanese Canadians and their communities by one (perhaps dominant) story. It is important to search for and listen to many different narratives, drawn from a wide array of sources. One narrative alone may conceal the diverse experiences of people—experiences shaped by age, generation, and one's location within hierarchies based on gender and social class. A uniform story, moreover, obscures the ways in which complex systems of domination come together in shaping people's lives. The dominant narrative, though always changing, remains one in which the theme of resistance (in its varied forms) is not always strongly conveyed. Indeed, one might even suggest that much of the publicized literature on the internment has promoted the idea that Japanese Canadians generally, and Japanese Canadian women especially, have been a passive and acquiescent lot.[13] These traits, assumed to be cultural, are embraced by the popular phrase *shikata ga nai*—'what can be done' or an expression of resignation to the situation.[14] The concept of *shikata ga nai* and the silent, passive Japanese woman is part of a race and gender essentialism that must be challenged. While the Redress Movement has clearly disrupted the cultural amnesia that has for so long marked Canadian history, I am not convinced that the imagery of the silent and uncritical Japanese Canadian woman has been fully contested.

Multiple stories of internment from *Nisei* (second-generation) women and, to a lesser extent, their *Issei* (first-generation) mothers indeed challenge this image. I explore the ways in which these women asserted themselves in the face of the nightmares they endured during the war. I take up this theme by describing a range of narratives of Japanese Canadian experience, derived from a different source. The first is highly personal, embedded in my own memories. The second set of stories emerges from a selection of private letters written by and to *Nisei* and *Issei* women in the mid-1940s. Finally, some images are drawn from the oral testimonies of thrity-five *Nisei* women currently living in Ontario and British Columbia.

Just as each of these narratives emerges from a distinct source, each is communicated in a different way. My personal memories were indirectly experienced, born in childhood, travelled across generations, and strongly informed by a present-day collective remembrance. The private correspondence was crafted in the context of war, intercepted and edited by government officials, and most likely not intended for a public audience. In comparison the oral testimonies were spoken to a researcher, rooted in personal memory, directly experienced. Rather than offer a direct point-by-point comparison of the narratives, I am interested in the ways in which they inform one another, bringing out the many and complex dimensions or layers of a story. At a general level, the narratives tell us something about the importance of interpretation for the construction of history and about the imposition of time and memory in the process of research and story-telling.

Personal Memory

Let me begin with a few words about my own memories of the internment.[15] For many decades, feminist academics have argued against the idea of scientific objectivity and academic distance.[16] In this project especially, I must immediately dispel any pretense of academic distance—and I make no claims of detachment. Like Annette Kuhn, while working with the materials of my research, I found that 'the distanced standpoint of the critic began to feel less and less adequate to my material, incapable of addressing such powerful responses to my critical objects.'[17]

My personal memories and the emotional essence of these memories have undeniably shaped my interpretation and construction of the two other narratives.[18] The letters and testimonies upon which I draw were never simply 'sources of data', pieces in a project of historical reconstruction. Clearly, they informed my understanding of Japanese Canadian lives, but they had also been personally experienced and are very much a part of my own 'journey through remembrance'.

My early memories of the internment were gathered largely from my parents, my aunt, and, to a lesser degree, my grandparents. Given that I could not speak Japanese and they said that they could not speak English, communication with my grandparents was largely by way of an implicit understanding based on eye and body contact, as well as their tales as told by their *Nisei* children. The grandparents whom I knew seemed stoic, displaced, and highly dependent on one another. They seemed to be passing time in Ontario, very much rooted both emotionally and materially in their past lives. My mother taught me about the internment through her caution, in addition to her fragmented stories about life in Haney, then Hastings Park, Rosebery, and ultimately the long, lonely train trip to work as a domestic for a wealthy family in Toronto. My father conveyed anger and ambivalence, and offered snapshots of a carefree pre-war existence in Vancouver, followed by incarceration in a prisoner of war camp. The most vivid of these snapshots is the white shirt with red circle that he was forced to wear in Petawawa.

My knowledge of the internment was drawn from an extremely small homogeneous group. Sheltered in my Anglo-Saxon/Eastern European neighbourhood of Toronto, my only contact with other Japanese Canadians was with people in my own family. Once in a while, I visited distant relatives, and on Sundays I saw familiar strangers at the Toronto Buddhist Church. During these years, I had curiously embraced the idea that we should not talk about the internment, that to ask too many questions would hurt my parents. This is odd because, in retrospect, my parents gave no obvious indication that they did not want to share their memories with me. I furthermore believed, albeit with an increasingly critical eye, that Japanese Canadians may be described by the phrase *shikata ga nai*. I asked my parents if they had no anger. I assumed that they had no critical feelings toward the Canadian government. I believed that Japanese Canadians then did not protest, and later wanted to forget.

Memory, of course, is fluid. As I undertook this project, my memories have changed. In encountering new information, new sources of data, voiced people beyond my own family, I have begun to remember in different ways. My memory has been transformed. I now turn to some of the sources of its transformation.

Private Letters

In the initial stages of my research, I came across a number of letters written by and to Japanese Canadians that had been intercepted and censored by government officials during the war. The extracted contents are now housed in the National Archives.[19] Among the first to catch my eye was a letter that had been written to my aunt by her brother. I later found correspondence by other members of my extended family. Many months passed before I gathered and read all of the 900 letters that I had collected, but, as I did so, another narrative began to unfold, one that contested my simple childhood memories.

The narrative that emerges from the private correspondence was produced in the context of war. Little time elapsed between the thought and the writing of that thought, the documenting and preservation of sentiments. In this sense, the letters have an immediacy and rawness. For Japanese Canadians, the time of writing was one of separation, uncertainty, and disruption. During these years, many women were living lives away from their fathers, brothers, husbands, sons, and boyfriends. Many *Issei* women were advancing to middle age, while the majority of *Nisei* were teens or relatively young. Some were children. The experiences about which they wrote were not mediated by decades of living. The letters and their authors are, in a sense, 'fixed in time'.[20]

This private correspondence seems to have served two main purposes. People used the letters to communicate information to one another about living and working conditions, finances, government policy, and family decision-making. The letters also served as a vehicle of self-expression, a means by which to convey feeling and articulate personal opinion. One theme that is clear, perhaps more directly and consistently communicated than in the oral testimonies, is that of the violence imposed upon the community and the harsh impact of this violence on individuals. Most of the letters are highly personal, thus allowing for a sense of the intimate experience of the government's wartime actions. The outright disclosure of injustice, the open airing of misery and grief, is enlightening and profound.

The Emotional Experience of Political Violence

While both *Issei* and *Nisei* women conveyed anger in their correspondence the *Issei* were more likely at the same time to declare their outright loyalty to Japan, and their criticism of the Canadian government specifically, and people generally was unqualified. While equally critical of government and politicians, letters written by *Nisei* women reveal more contradictory emotions. Their anger towards the government was tempered with disappointment and despair. Born and raised in Canada, good citizens, they were in disbelief about their treatment in this country. Because their unfair treatment based on phenotypical racial qualities, they felt that much was beyond control. Despite this, there are repeated assertions of national loyalty and national identity. In May 1945, for example, a *Nisei* woman wrote to her brother in Ontario:

> Through no fault of our own we happened to be born of Japanese parents, however, as you know, all were educated in Canadian system of governing Democracy. Right of free speech, etc. etc., no matter what race colour, or creed. Well these ignorant 'so-and'so's' think they're the only ones in this country that's entitled to live . . . . With all the raw deals and racial hatred towards us I'm still proud to say that I'm a Canadian of Japanese ancestry. I was created to be one and will live up to one. [From sister to brother?, May 1945, written in English]

A *Nisei* woman in Lemon Creek expressed similar feelings to a male friend in Angler, Ontario:

> No use going out East, when, wherever you go, the narrow minded whites (call you 'JAPS'). Might as well stay here where there are practically no white people. The nisei are sure in a tight spot. We don't know whether we're a CANADIAN or a JAPANESE. Because we were JAPANESE they forced us from the coast and now as CANADIAN they want us to evacuate EAST. Phooey a double phooey to the damn selective service guys. [From woman in Lemon Creek to male friend in Angler, Ontario, March 1944, written in English]

And in a letter to a male friend in Brantford, Ontario, a *Nisei* woman from Slocan wrote:

> It surely makes me sick—and angry . . . they may take us for enemies just cuz our parents were born in Japan but they certainly don't give us much chance to let us prove ourselves worthy of this country. . . . Oh, it made my

blood boil—'once a Jap, always a Jap' . . . . The more I think of our standing the worse it is for my poor heart so I'll stop. [From woman in Slocan to male friend in Ontario, March 1944, written in English]

My present-day political outlook and sensibilities made it difficult for me to read over and over again in these letters, the word 'Jap'. It was one thing to see this word used in official government documents or in *The Vancouver Province* newspaper, but quite another to read it in private correspondence written by and to Japanese Canadians themselves. Given its author, the language took on an even more violent and obscene quality. A *Nisei* woman in Bay Farm wrote to a female friend in Alberta:

> [I]f we are loyal we have to go east, or on the other hand back to Japan. There's work outside of this place I guess but what is the difference, wherever you go a Jap is a Jap. [Between woman friends, Bay Farm to Alberta, April 1945, written in English]

Many *Nisei* repeatedly expressed feelings of entrapment. They were marked by their own faces—trapped by physical features that identified them as Japanese. Writing about Japanese-American women, Jeanne Houston notes that slanted eyes and high cheekbones became not simply Japanese physical traits, but 'floating signifiers of difference' linked to 'negative behavioral characteristics'. The inner self may have been Canadian, but the outer self was Japanese. This separation of self is part of the violence done to Japanese Canadians.[21]

Dichotomization of the inner and outer self is evident in the following letter written by a *Nisei* woman in Toronto to her girlfriend in Alberta:

> They call us 'Japs' and think of us in the same light that they think of the native Japanese. I think there are very few people that really consider us as 'fellow Canadians' . . . even among our occidental friends. I suppose it all boils down to the fact that we have black hair and oriental features and we look so different from the other races that we can never become quite as Canadianized as the rest . . . . [Between woman friends, Toronto to Alberta, August 1944, written in English]

Imparting similar views, a *Nisei* woman in Tashme wrote her brother in British Columbia:

> I think a *Nisei* has a better chance as we know English and customs, but pretty hard for *Isseis*. Bad enough that we have black hair and slant eyes. [From sister in Tashme to brother in Sicamous, British Columbia, May 1945, written in English]

Interned in Tashme, a woman wrote to a girlfriend in Rosebery:

> Imagine we the *Nisei* have to do, what the Selective Service tells us to do when we don't even get the rights of *Canadian citizen*. Really we are treated like skunks anywhere we go—we are not wanted because of black hair and brown eyes . . . . [Between woman friends, Tashme to Rosebery, October 1943 written in English]

Reference to what had become conspicuous aspects of the physical self is made repeatedly in many of the letters. The *Nisei* were painfully aware of ways in which hair colour and the shape of one's eyes were used to homogenize a group and to deny the social factors of citizenship and cultural identity.

Daily Survival and Hardship

Much of the correspondence also concerns the women's feelings about day-to-day survival, getting by. In their letters, gendered divisions and experiences are prominent. They braved the internment as women whose oppression had been strongly shaped by both sexual and racial subordination. Some revealed a strong consciousness of this. While husbands, sons, and boyfriends wrote about exploitative working conditions in the road camps, in lumber mills, and in factories and about the inhuman treatment they endured as POWs, women wrote of their own gendered hardships: the burden of supporting a family in the absence of a male provider. This was particularly true of *Issei* women who were mothers and therefore shoulder heavy financial and familial responsibilities. To her husband in Angler, an *Issei* woman in Lemon Creek wrote:

> My worries are greater than yours. Every day with the temperature at hundred and twenty degrees I have to go to negotiate and every time I go to the Welfare I have to fight. Not receiving sufficient for our daily necessities I have had to use what I had but had saved . . . . And who has made us suffer in this way taking away my husband who is guiltless and interning him. And is it not a wilful thing to do by taking away the subsistence and then telling me to go out to work. [From wife in Lemon Creek to her husband in Angler, July 1944, written in Japanese]

Similarly, a woman in Greenwood explained to her husband in Angler:

> I took all the notes of what I had earned by working in the fields, of what I spent and bills of things I had bought . . . I had twenty-seven dollars and eighty-one cents left. . . . With that [money received from the British Columbia Security Commission] and the twenty-seven dollars and eighty-one cents I was told to maintain myself for three months. This was really too exasperating. I think one cannot be blamed for grumbling after being told a ridiculous thing like that and also after working so hard in the fields. They seem to think we can produce work for ourselves . . . . It really makes me miserable to think that we are getting no where except in years. [From wife in Greenwood to her husband in Angler, 11 July 1944, original language not specified]

Also telling are the letters that some *Nisei* women wrote about their treatment as domestic workers in private households. Many *Nisei* had been sent to work for *Hakujin* families in Ontario and Quebec, as well as in British Columbia itself. In fact, some even cared for the children of their RCMP guards. Within these homes, they sometimes faced severe racist and sexist treatment. Though women (who continued to perform paid domestic work long after the war's end) today speak warmly, uncritically, of their *Hakujin* bosses and are particularly reluctant to broach an issue such as harassment, the latter problem is raised in some of the written letters. One young woman, for example, wrote her fiancé in Ontario about her experiences in Nakusp. Apparently, her male boss had sexually harassed her when the woman of the house was away. Not only does the tone of her correspondence convey disgust, but she openly declares her intention to fight against such treatment.

She wrote:

> [T]he old lady went for her holidays so I was alone with this fat old [—] . . . he just walked right toward me and grab hold of me and he didn't let me go so I just hit [him] and scream and everything I could but he's a fat old pig so I was squashed I just told [him] I'll tell everything to your wife well I think that hurt him he sure was mad but its his fault eh . . . . I knew this will happen someday I didn't like her to go for holiday leaving 3 kids. [From woman in Nakusp to her fiancé in Ontario, January 1945, written in English]

The writer planned to leave the position immediately. However, because the British Columbia Security Commission had arranged their employment, many did not have the option of leaving such situations.

Nevertheless many Japanese Canadian women did express a defiant spirit, in spite of forced inaction. The discourse on which they drew promoted cultural constructs of womanhood, sometimes embracing a distinct racial component. A number of

Issei women, for example, asserted then resilience, their strength to persevere, as would be expected of a true Japanese woman. A wife in Lemon Creek wrote to her husband in Angler:

> Please do not worry about me . . . I'll like to do my best for the two children. I have the same intention as I had at first and even if my hair turns grey in years of waiting I will be a true Japanese woman. [From wife in Lemon Creek to her husband in Angler, November 1944, original language not specified]

Another *Issei* woman writing from New Denver expressed these sentiments to her male friend in Angler:

> It is difficult for woman alone to move but . . . I fought and fought for it and won. I worried over it so much and what with the heat I was sick in bed for 7 days . . . . If they treat me like that just because I am a woman I won't give in even one step. [From woman in New Denver to male friend in Angler, July 1944, written in Japanese]

Some women additionally drew on maternal imagery in resisting racial oppression. An *Issei* mother in Manitoba wrote to friends in British Columbia:

> We will keep our health until the day when we again tread the earth of our motherland. As a woman I may be looked upon as of the weaker sex, but as a mother I am strong. I have been able to work through the severe cold without one day of illness. I overcome all hardships as for my country and my children. [From woman in Manitoba to friends in British Columbia, March 1945, written in Japanese]

The Forced 'Repatriation' Decision

As indicated by some of the letters that I have thus far cited, a prominent subject in the private correspondence was the issue of 'repatriation' or dispersion.[22] Eager to eliminate the 'Japanese race' from the province of British Columbia, and more generally to ensure that a concentration of such people not resurface elsewhere in Canada, in 1945 the federal government forced Japanese Canadians to 'choose' either to 'repatriate' to Japan or to move east of the Rockies. The pros and cons of moving to Ontario or Quebec or relocating to Japan began to saturate Japanese Canadian communities.[23] As noted, government presented its policy as one of 'choice'. However, the *Issei* and *Nisei* alike knew that this 'choice' was illusory. Indeed, it was coercive. Repatriation decisions tore apart many families, both physically and emotionally. Faced with this so-called choice, wives, mothers, and daughters not only asserted their will against government authorities; they also had to negotiate relations of power within their own families. Contrary to the popular image of the obedient *Issei* woman, many first-generation wives firmly opposed their husbands in decisions about repatriation. An *Issei* man incarcerated in Angler warned his wife about the consequences of her resolution to remain in Canada:

> If you carry out your desire to go East you will not be able to return to (our) country [Japan]. After the war there will be great hardship and, as at present, hell on earth . . . . There is no object to be attained by going East on your own accord . . . . It is the Government's aim to separate and scatter. It is frightening . . . . Canada is a large country. Its ostracism is terrifying. [From husband in Angler to his wife in Lemon Creek, May 1944, written in Japanese]

In many cases, a wife's opposition to her husband's repatriation decision was met with the threat of desertion. For instance, an *Issei* man declared to his wife in Rosebery:

> If you disagree to go back to JAPAN with me I am afraid that I will have no more to do with you because I cannot see any other way. What is more, I will leave you behind and go back

> myself. [From husband in Angler to his wife in Rosebery, 12 April 1944, original language not specified]

A woman in Popoff wrote to her husband in Angler:

> No Sir, I won't go out of here even if you divorced me or they kill me . . . . No one in the families will move out of here so don't forget that. You think I am selfish and man but what can I do . . . . All this time I thought my husband was a man but not anymore. If you don't do or listen what I say well then, do anything you like but don't forget I'll never forgive you, never. [From wife in Popoff to her husband in Angler, May 1945, written in English]

The repatriation question resulted in even more frequent conflicts between *Nisei* children and their *Issei* parents. On the whole, the Canadian-born *Nisei* had serious reservations about moving to Japan, a country that was foreign to them. One may surmise that the majority of young *Nisei* girls and women ultimately respected their parents' decisions, contrary to their own desires. Some of these women later returned to Canada on their own. Yet a number of *Nisei* daughters did resist their parents' will. A woman in Vernon disclosed her intentions to her girlfriend in Popoff:

> [M]y parents are keen on returning to Japan after the war . . . I guess they think me unpatriotic but I do not see things their way and I firmly believe my future is in this country. I know there are families in ghost towns and elsewhere where the children and parents take the different viewpoint on this survey. The parents think they control our body, mind and soul and believe they could make us do anything they want us to. They utterly believe we would never disobey them in any way, but I think they're mistaken there. Surely our life is not theirs, surely we aren't going to suffer because we had followed them to their homeland and can't adopt ourselves to their customs . . . . I haven't as yet said any thing about my decision to my parents but when they start to survey here in Vernon they'll sure be surprised when they hear what I have to say about the whole darn nasty affair. If after all my objections I do go to Japan you'll know very well I never went because I desired to do so . . . I'll fight to my last energy to remain in Canada. [Between woman friends, Vernon, British Columbia, to Popoff, April 1945, written in English]

These letters dispel notions of a silent and accepting Japanese Canadian woman. Crafted in the immediacy of war, they impart strong emotion, notably anger, at times outrage. While historians have documented the resistance efforts of organizations such as the Nisei Mass Evacuation Group and the Japanese Canadian Committee for Democracy, we have few narratives of informal, individual protest against racial and gender oppression, often articulated by women who possessed limited structural resources.[24] These letters are especially remarkable given that the women I interviewed claimed to have then known that their correspondence might be read by government authorities. In this light, their letter writing may be viewed as a symbolic gesture of defiance.[25]

Oral Testimony

My intent in bringing these letters together with narratives generated through oral testimony does not rest on the belief that the more data sources we consult, the more valid our history become. Furthermore, I do not suggest that written documents (housed in archives) may serve as a measure of the accuracy or veracity of spoken reminiscences. In particular, there is no place in this analysis for accusations of faulty or distorted memory.[26] Rather, I wish to explore the process of remembering and the ways in which the derivation of our knowledge of history (sources of data and methods of gathering) may generate very different types of narratives that may be used to build upon one another and to disclose the role of subjectivity, of interpretation, and of the researcher herself in constructing the past.

Researcher and Narrator

My engagement with the oral testimonies forced me to confront a distinct set of concerns. Admittedly, in interpreting the written letters, I intervened, carefully selecting passages upon which to draw and comment in a formal analysis.[27] Indeed, when relying on written documents, it has been especially tempting to separate analysis on one hand from data on the other.[28] This is problematic, for, in dichotomizing data and analysis, in neatly separating the collection of data from their interpretation, we run the risk of overlooking the ways in which the data themselves are already the products of editing, reflection, and decision and are therefore not simply concrete indicators of historical objectivity. Yet, in gathering oral testimony, my role as researcher seemed even more intrusive. I was responsible for the generation of the testimony itself. Without my intervention, the testimonies would simply not exist.[29] I entered the women's lives, asked them my questions, tape-recorded and transcribed their words. In comparison, the letters rest in the archives, whether or not I examine them. Moreover, without my shaping, the spoken narratives would assume a different form. As I have noted in other writings, in gathering *Nisei* women's stories, I imposed my own agenda and sensibilities. Initially at least, I enforced a reliance on a linear historical chronology and yet, at the same time, imposed a feminist logic, highlighting the significance of the personal and its links to a wider political existence. Furthermore, my questions were guided by the collective internment narrative with which I was most familiar.

As well, over the course of the interviews, my relationship with the women evolved and itself informed the research inquiry.[30] Just as the women's narratives are the product of this unfolding relationship, so too was my standing of them and their stories. At the outset, I believed that the differences between myself and the narrators might pose a barrier, in spite of our apparent bonds. But, with each interview, I discovered that the differences in age and generation were important in helping the women to establish a sense of their value as 'informants'. My (comparatively young) age and different status (*Sansei* or third-generation) rendered me ignorant in and marginal to 'their' history. Furthermore, inequalities based on class and education proved to be far less important than I had anticipated. Though most of the women themselves lived working-class lives, their *Sansei* children have achieved remarkably high levels of education. Research projects, book manuscripts, and doctoral degrees were therefore not foreign to many of the women. More meaningful than my educational credentials was my family background. The most significant bond between us proved to be 'racial' identity and family relations and thereby an implicit understanding of the impact of internment by virtue of my place in a cross-generation 'community of memory'.[31] Before we started to talk about her life, Sue (whom I had never met before) told me that we were distant relatives.[32] She conveyed stories about my grandmother: her penchant for sweets, her sense of humour, her characteristic toothy smile. At the beginning of another interview I discovered that Yoshiye had grown up in the same small community as my mother.[33] (I never before knew that my mother had played baseball, not to mention that she was good at it.) And no one had ever told me that Yoshiye, who became a nurse after the war, was working in a Toronto hospital and happened to be on duty at my father's side when he died over 30 years after the war's end.

In the evolving relationship between researcher and narrator, secrets were exchanged. Few of the women hesitated to ask me about my own family, about my current situation, and emotional sentiments. In turn, some of them shared their secrets with me. It is paradoxical that some of these shared stories, which now dot my own narrative, are ones I cannot tell. The women's secrets, 'small and fragile', are now most vivid in my own memory of the internment.[34] Of course, some memories will never be shared with anyone. These are purely autobiographical. Others will be kept within a particular community, shared with some but not others.[35] In a hushed voice, Rose, for instance, asked me to promise never to disclose some of her sentiments to a *Hakujin* audience.[36]

Time and Memory: In Retrospect

Compared with written documents, the women's testimonies have a different relationship to time. The time at which the interview takes place, the time that passes over the course of an interview, the passage of time from the events discussed to memories conveyed are all significant in shaping the narrative. In the words of Alessandro Portelli, 'Tales go with time, grow with time, decay with time. . . . Life histories, personal tales, depend upon time, if for nothing else than because there are additions and subtractions made to them with each day 'of the narrator's life.' As Portelli states, there is only so much material that can be preserved in individual and collective memory.[37] In interpreting the spoken narratives, it is important to keep in mind that, in a way not possible with the letters, the women's thoughts have been filtered through the passage of roughly 60 years—and all that has unfolded during these years. What we are hearing, then, are the women's memories of internment.

Many of the women who participated in this project had trouble remembering events that are now prominent in the public narrative. There are silences in their narratives. Some women do not remember dates that have taken on an official importance. 'What year did the war end? When did we have to head East?' Some do not remember the sequencing of events in their lives and in the larger history. 'How could I have come to Toronto in 1947 if the war ended in 1945? That must be a mistake. Well, let's see, I got married in '45 I must have left British Columbia before then.'

Some women comment on these omissions as deliberate and willful.[38] As noted by Eviatar Zerubavel, people make choices about what to 'put behind them'.[39] As she showed me her collection of photos from the war years, Amy talked about having to leave business school because of the internment. I inquired about this.

> *Pam:* How long were you in business school?
> *Amy:* Well, from September until oh, March, I think. I don't remember. That part I can't remember. And I don't remember—if it's because I like to think of unpleasant things. I don't remember that.

Further in her testimony, she noted another gap in her memory.

> *Pam:* Did you have any communication with your father who was in the road camp?
> *Amy:* Well, I guess my mother did. But I don't remember that. It's very shattering not to remember.
> *Pam:* I think it's because of age, probably . . . .
> *Amy:* But I know that when he was moving to New Denver . . . when we arrived in New Denver, we were all sick . . . . We all vomited.[40]

Similarly, Rose stated,

> It's funny. I was twenty-two, twenty-three. Isn't it funny that I don't have too . . . maybe it's . . . like you try to block what you know. But I remember that didn't get out 'til October of that year . . . . We moved from our home . . . on Powell Street . . . across the street there was a Japanese department store.

The most distinct and graphic memories of some women seem unrelated to official facts of the internment. Yet they are very much a part of women's personal memory of the wartime suffering. In her testimony, Ruby explained that, when she was growing up in British Columbia, there was one boy who was 'really nasty' [racist].[41] To this she quickly added that there had been 'an English couple who were always being nice to us'. She maintained that, once the war was over, racial discrimination was not a problem. In her words, 'I'm sure there's always a few even up to now, you know . . . . Certain people don't like certain nationality or whatever. But on the whole, I would say it's not too bad.' However, later in her testimony, Ruby reintroduced the racist boy. She remarked, 'I don't know what he's like now. I think he still lives in Winfield . . . . [be]cause I mean, he was a real Jerk.' She continued, 'But I often think, I wonder what that guy is doing. I wonder what kind of life he has or whether he's still that way. I don't know.' She remembered him again at the end of her testimony: 'Oh, he was a real mean kid . . . I don't think he was much older than we were but he's just a mean bully. Yes, real bully. Oh, he used to be a real nasty kid. I don't think there's anybody as nasty as him.'

Since the war's end, *Nisei* women have lived in neighbourhoods and entered workplaces in which there have been few Japanese. Importantly, as their sons and daughters have married, most have acquired *Hakujin* daughters- and sons-in-law and grandchildren that are part *Hakujin*, part *Nihonjin*, and thoroughly integrated into the dominant (*Hakujin*) society.[42] Betty explained,

> I don't talk about it much to my children. We remember a few things but try not to dwell on it. We're hoping our children won't have to go through the same things we did. In those days it was all Japanese or all *Hakujin*. There was no intermarriage. Now it's different.[43]

Some no longer speak openly about 'race' and racism. Ruby concluded her commentary on the racist bully by asserting, 'But I don't think there's that mean of a kid around any more.' Neatly demarcating the war years from all those that followed, some women maintained that the experience of racism was specific to the pre-war period and the duration of the Second World War. While some women did offer powerful and damning stories of racist assault in post-war British Columbia, Ontario, and Quebec, others claimed that they seldom, if ever, heard racist remarks or encountered discrimination within employment, education, or housing. When these women spoke of racism in particular, it was almost as though the decades immediately following their internment had disappeared from memory, or at least faded in significance. Indeed, some women promoted the liberal equation of cultural/ethnic assimilation and the denial of difference with equality and the eradication of racial intolerance. Long regarded as the 'orientalist' other, they are relieved to have become culturally and economically integrated into the nation. While most no longer speak with passion about their inhuman treatment as the racialized 'other', the women did offer clear descriptions of the long, horrible train trip from one internment site to the next and from British Columbia to Ontario, the nothingness, the loss of opportunity, the ways things could have been.

Nostalgia and Critical Memory

Testimony reveals many layers of feeling. In hearing the women's memories, I was also struck by the positive sentiments, indeed the happiness, in recollections of some. Happy moments existed alongside thoughts about forced exile, the violation of rights, and losses incurred. Some described their years in the sites of internment as 'fun' and 'the best' of their lives. Hideko, for instance, explained,

> Those were very interesting years for me. That's where I met all my friends . . . . Nobody's rich or poor or educated. We were all the same. And we all helped each other. . . . In fact, the whole Tashme was . . . we were happy. Nobody sad. We all encouraged each other, you know. And helped each other so.[44]

Similarly, Sugar remarked, 'We had a lot of fun as kids, you know.'[45]

On the surface, these remarks stand in stark contrast to the narratives drawn from the letters. Yet it is not surprising that these women uphold a time in their lives, experienced in youth, free of heavy domestic burdens, in a situation of shared oppression. Though families were often separated, groups of *Nisei* women lived together in forced communities that were characterized by age, sex, and racial and ethnic homogeneity. Isolated in desolate parts of the

British Columbia interior, communities of internees established close bonds. Over time, these bonds have no doubt taken on heightened meaning. By the war's end, the government shattered these communities, severing the ties.

Moreover, thinking about years past, the women remembered what they themselves had directly experienced. They also placed the memories in the context of families, friendships, and other social relationships. Hideko commented, 'What we had to do to keep the family together it must have been horrible for my mother.' Similarly, Masako remarked, 'I myself, I guess, I've been fortunate to be born right in the middle. I didn't have to suffer. But it's my oldest brother and my mom and dad. They really suffered. And it's the person who really suffered, they didn't even get their Redress.'[46]

The same woman who recalled good times, in which she learned to sew, danced to Benny Goodman, and went ice skating with the girls, has also embraced in memory the whippings that her husband endured as a prisoner of war and the hours spent by her mother scavenging for discarded pieces of coal to heat the family's leaky shack in the cold of winter. As noted by Zerubavel, notwithstanding diverse experience and particular memories, we may speak of a common, shared memory. The common nature of memories suggests that they are not purely personal and individual.[47] Memory reveals a strong social dimension. Like the researcher herself, *Nisei* women delve into 'communities of memory'.[48]

In reading the women's stories, furthermore, it is important to consider the broader process of transmission, the ways in which people convey meaning beyond words, and the disjuncture at times between the written (transcribed) word and vocalized utterances. Much is lost or concealed in the transcribing of voices and words and in the writing of oral testimony. We do not see the tears, the visible inability to talk, the emotion welling up in a woman's eyes as her words continue to flow with calm. The women's narratives are punctuated with emotion, with throwaway phrases such as 'I don't know' and 'That's what I think, anyway.' Their recollections of both 'good' and 'bad' times were interspersed with defensive laughter that attempted to mask hurt and consequence.

Also telling is that the very women who spoke of the internment as the 'good old days' voiced strong objections to the actions taken against them, their words more subdued but nevertheless echoing sentiments articulated in the old letters. Yoshiye commented, 'It was a foolish, expensive adventure that the federal government took . . . . At least [with the Redress Settlement] it came out in public that it was a horrible thing.' Similarly, after providing decades of faithful domestic service to the same *Hakujin* woman, Ritsuko recollected with exasperation her former employer's remarks about the internment.

> Like [Mrs Whitton] said, 'Well, that was a great mistake.' She used to say that Mackenzie King, he made a big mistake. Well, I don't think that was a mistake! . . . How can she ever say that was a mistake! . . . To evacuate is different. But the thing what the Japanese went through, leaving their things behind, leaving their business . . . behind. Just like that in twenty-four hours? You lose everything? And [Mrs Whitton] calls that a mistake of Prime Minister? It was so crazy for her to tell me that! I think there was a better way . . . I know. I guess they were so afraid of Japanese after the war . . . . That's why it happened you know. I guess they weren't afraid of the Germans.[49]

In many women, nostalgia co-exists with a critical eye toward the injustices that they and their families endured. Leo Spitzer's concept of 'critical nostalgia' is useful in understanding this juxtaposition of happiness and suffering.[50] While critics of nostalgia have regarded it as 'inauthentic, reactionary, and offering a falsification of the past', Spitzer argues that, although nostalgic memory may be viewed as 'the selective emphasis on what was positive in the past', it is not by any means antithetical to a critical awareness of the negative aspects of one's past.[51]

Roughly six decades after the war's end, the women also offered explanations as to why, back then, they did not and could not collectively (effectively) resist the government's actions. Having witnessed the emergence of a human rights framework, a discourse of liberalism, and most immediately the successful campaign of the Redress activists, they were prompted to explain. Indeed, an explanation of their apparent lack of resistance becomes part of the narrative. However, these explanations do not rest on ideas about essential cultural traits. Rather, the women highlighted their position of structural powerlessness. During the war, they were young, propertyless, uneducated—and female. Pauli remarked,

> There was some young men that resisted, naturally, back at the Coast. But the men at the RCMP got word of it. They were pilfered out and taken right away. They were the ones that were sent to the internment camps [POW camps]. An of course, all the younger men, able men, were all sent out to the road camp. So only the older, and the women and children. So there couldn't have been much resistance. There just was no way.[52]

She continued, '[M]any people just sort of gave up, you know, if we were here so what else can we do . . . . There's no way you could write a letter or anything and have somebody come out and help you and say, well, we'll send you here or there, you know. There was nothing like that.' Sachi likewise commented,

> But there was nothing we could do. We're too young to fight. . . . 'Why didn't you fight? Why didn't you stand up against the Government? They were taking your legal rights.' Well, heck, we're only teenagers. We weren't old enough to think. Well some did, but the fighting only meant they were incarcerated and sent to a prison camp. So, there was no way we could stop that racial prejudice that was so great in Vancouver days. And I know, you might think we were dumb not to fight but we couldn't. We couldn't do anything.[53]

The passing of time is important in shaping these responses. Though we can never accurately predict the pieces that will appear in unfolding narratives, one wonders whether, 20 years earlier, these women would have freely volunteered an analysis of their powerlessness.

Just as the women told a story of the past, they also presented an image of themselves in the present.[54] In doing so, they remained keenly aware of the audience to whom they were speaking. The women in this study presented their past suffering partially, selectively. While they wanted their pain to be acknowledged, they also did not wish to reduce themselves to the status of victims.[55] They told their stories in such a way that highlighted their endurance, as well as their agency. Judy Giles's concept of 'composing subjectivities of dignity and self-respect' aptly describes this manner of presentation. Giles notes that women sometimes create stories as expressions of their attempts to compose subjectivities that offer dignity and self-respect m a world characterized by their own powerlessness.[56]

In asserting dignity, the women gave me many happy endings. The conviction of a happy ending indeed was resonant at the conclusion of most of the testimonies. In their narratives, one could detect an ideology of positive thinking and the theme of 'triumphant social mobility'.[57] Echoing the words of many others, Hannah said,

> Well if this hadn't happened and we were still living at the coast, we'd probably be discriminated. And people have been able to further their education and they wouldn't be what they are today, a lot of people. So in a way, maybe it was, it was terrible to go through that, but I guess in the end, you look at it now. People are scattered all over. . . . And maybe it was a good thing *[softly spoken]*.[58]

According to Michiko, 'Everybody has done well because of the suffering. They achieved.'[59]

There is a corrective sense to these reminiscences. *Nisei* women frequently voiced the view that the suffering of the past has been 'a blessing in disguise', but this statement contains many layers of meaning and therefore should not necessarily be taken at face value. It is not a statement of forgiveness. It is not redemptive. Nor is it spoken by women who have neatly put the past behind them. Rather, it is part of an attempt at healing, though, in hearing their memories, we see that this process of healing will never be complete. Nonetheless, the women attest: we have not only survived; we have succeeded. The past is remembered but will not be relived. Though they experienced violation at the hands of the state, their children did not endure such suffering, and they are resolved in the belief that their grandchildren never will. They have not been defeated.

Conclusion: A Multiplicity of Stories

Writing about her edited collection on memory and working-class consciousness, Janet Zandy notes that the essays 'do not dissolve into one blended working-class essence'.[60] Like the collection that Zandy describes, the narratives that I present here do not simply merge into one single story. Rather, they suggest a multiplicity of stories. When we consider them together, when we think about the ways in which the different narratives weave in and out of one another, we begin to see the complexity of internment experience. The conditions of their creation—the different sources from which they stem and the social process of their communication—lead us to reflect on the significance of time and memory in the construction of these narratives.

If we turn to documents written in the midst of war, we read one set of stories. When we ask women to remember the past in the present time, we hear different tales. To all of this, the researcher brings her own past as well as her current concerns, sensibilities, and political agenda. These narratives inform one another. They present history itself as a social and political construct, and the process of historical/sociological research as one that must be self-conscious and multi-layered. According to Walter Benjamin, 'it is the task of those who deal not only with chronicles, but with history, to study not just the mechanics of the material event, but the events of the remembering and of the telling—the patterns of the remembering, the forms of the telling'—the conditions under which our 'historical materials' have been created. In this sense, though the event may be over, the telling of that event is 'boundless'.[61]

In what ways has this study contributed to a reconfiguring of the historical narrative and the telling of history? Much of the early literature points to a silent and uncritical Japanese Canadian woman. This portrayal, once so familiar as to be at times compelling, is much too narrow. Growing up with fragments of memory, imparted by the close members of my small family, I long viewed the internment of Japanese Canadians as a shameful episode in our nation's past, a blatant act of injustice but one far removed from our present existence. My own exposure to racism as a child growing up in an Anglo/European neighbourhood of Toronto, along with my parents' unspoken warnings about the safety of staying at the social margins of my world, suggested however that the wartime violations still touched our lives. As a teenager, I was burdened with many questions about my family's history in this country: Why didn't my parents and their generation fight back? Why hadn't they stood up for their rights and resisted? Over the years, why had they chosen to remain silent about such a blatantly unfair and tragic experience?

Prompted by the Redress campaign in the 1980s, I took these questions beyond my family and began to read the early published accounts of the internment.[62] I participated in a growing 'community of memory'. As this community broadened, encompassing both those who had lived through the war and those born afterward, it seemed to offer new space and thereby legitimated my presence. My active intervention as a researcher revealed many dimensions to the story that I had heard years ago. The multiple stories, voiced and written, uncovered detail where before there seemed only to be silence. The contents of old letters housed in archives revealed intense emotion, notably anger and despair. Upon reading them, I learned that many *Nisei* women had indeed displayed a strong spirit of resistance, contained by a structural powerlessness. In the narratives, I detected a range of emotions and forms of defiance—inside the individual, if not presented to an external, public audience. These feelings may or may not have been seen or noticed.

Alongside the emotion, the different narrative sources unfolded layers of injustice. Beyond property loss and the stench of Hastings Park, I heard and read about diminished aspirations, lost opportunities, troubled relationships, generational conflict, a yearning for privacy, boredom to tears, deportation, work-related injuries, attempted rape, suicide, and death due to inadequate medical care. All of this produced in me a heightened sense of loss. In their oral accounts, women carefully selected memories for sharing with an unfamiliar audience. They conveyed some thoughts as secrets, experiences that had no clear fit with the collective history. These secrets told of episodes that had caused their holders memorable grief. When I asked them to sum up their stories as a way of concluding their narratives, most women tempered personal pain and critical thought with the passage of time. They minimized the suffering of the past with the successes, comforts, and the contentment of the present. The voices of the present offered forgiveness, perhaps for the preservation of dignity.

In *The Battle of Valle Giulia*, Alessandro Portelli writes about presenting a paper to an academic audience and afterward receiving comments such as 'Yes, nice, very interesting—but what difference does it make?' Portelli writes in reply, '[F]ieldwork is always a form of political intervention because it encourages an effort at self-awareness, growth and change in all those involved.'[63] Hearing the women's testimonies, reading their letters, has inspired me to nuance my own narrative and to reconsider the ways in which I study women's lives. More importantly, I regard the women themselves as active participants in the creation or promotion of the narratives, and thereby of images of themselves. In short, I see both the act of putting pen to paper and articulating thought, as well as sharing memories in the oral tradition, telling personal stories and disclosing thoughts to a researcher and her community of listeners, to be a deliberate and interpretive act—an act of agency. The women's narratives are 'a mixture of the telling of their lives' and a statement of their minds.[64]

Notes

1. This and all subsequent censored letters are located in the National Archives of Canada [hereafter NAC], Record Group [hereafter RG] 27, Department of Labour, Japanese Division, 'Intercepted Letters', vols. 655, 661, 662,1527,1528. To respect the privacy of the individuals named in these letters, I specify relationships only and do not disclose names.
2. I employ the term political violence to describe the uprooting, dispossession, and incarceration of various groups of Japanese Canadians by the federal government, in an effort to convey the devastating and long-term impact of these acts on individuals and the community as a whole. I do not 'compare' this form of violence to historical acts of genocide, massacre, lynching, and bodily rape. I see the need to consider, however, the government's treatment of Japanese Canadians as part of a continuum of political violence that takes into account emotional and physical pain and suffering, as well as material losses.
3. See Kirsten Emiko McAllister, 'Captivating Debris: Unearthing a World War Two Internment Camp', *Cultural Values* 5.1 (2001): 98.
4. In a thoughtful analysis, Mona Oikawa argues that the violations committed against Japanese Canadians should be more generally viewed as 'reflective of the war for white bourgeois supremacy being waged against people of Japanese origin (and against Aboriginal people and other marginalized communities) living *in* Canada.' Pointing to exclusionary laws against Asians in British Columbia from the time of their immigration to Canada, Oikawa is critical of the representation of the internment 'wartime event'. See Mona

Oikawa, 'Cartographies of Violence: Women, Memory, and the Subject(s) of the "Internment"' (PhD dissertation, OISE/University of Toronto, 1999), 13.

5. On 16 January 1942, the federal government passed Order-in-Council PC 365, calling for the removal of male Japanese nationals, 18 to 45 years of age, from a designated 'Protected Area' 100 miles from the British Columbia coast. Three weeks later, the government passed Order-in-Council PC 1486, expanding the power of the Minister of Justice to remove all persons of Japanese origin from the 'protected zone'. As military officers responsible for defence of the Pacific coast did not regard the Japanese in Canada as a security threat, the government established the British Columbia Security Commission. This civilian body carried out the expulsion of Japanese from the area. For a comprehensive discussion of these events, Adachi, *The Enemy That Never Was: A History of the Japanese Canadians* (Toronto: McClelland & Stewart, 1991); Ann Gomer Sunahara, *The Politics of Racism: The Uprooting of Japanese Canadians During the Second World War* (Toronto: James Lorimer, 1980).
6. I use the term internment to describe a wide range of experiences, including forced relocation to ghost towns, 'self-supporting camps', and sugar-beet farms; incarceration in prisoner of war camps; movement to labour camps; compulsory resettlement from British Columbia to Ontario or Quebec; and deportation to Japan. In some government documents, in comparison, the term refers only and specifically to the incarceration of Japanese and Japanese Canadian men in prisoner of war camps. Ann Sunahara notes that, legally, the *Nisei* could not be interned, as they were Canadian citizens. Under the Geneva Convention, internment is a legal act that applies only to 'aliens'. As a result, the federal government referred to the 'detainment' of Japanese Canadians. Sunahara, *The Politics of Racism*, 66.
7. Roy Miki and Cassandra Kobayashi, *Justice in Our Time: The Canadian Redress Settlement* (Vancouver and Winnipeg: Talonbooks and National Association of Japanese Canadians, 1991), 4.
8. For a comparison of American and Canadian wartime policies toward persons of Japanese origin, see Daniel J. O'Neil, 'American vs. Canadian Policies Toward their Japanese Minorities During the Second World War', *Comparative Social Research* 4 (1981): 111–34.
9. Adachi, *The Enemy That Never Was*; Miki and Kobayashi, *Justice in Our Time*; Sunahara, *The Politics of Racism*.
10. Mentions of cases of suicide within the Japanese Canadian community were found in NAC, RG 27, 'Intercepted Letters'. In at least one of these cases, the suicide was directly linked to the experience of extreme racism in Canada. Out of respect for surviving family members, I do not discuss these cases in detail.
11. *Hakujin* is a Japanese term translated as 'white person' or Caucasian.
12. The Redress Agreement was signed by the National Association of Japanese Canadians and the Canadian government on 22 September 1988. For a discussion of the Redress Movement and Agreement, see Audrey Kobayashi, 'The Japanese Canadian Redress Settlement and its Implications for Race Relations', *Canadian Ethnic Studies* 24 (1992): 1–19.
13. It is interesting that some of the earlier wartime literature on Japanese Canadians highlights the protests of Japanese Canadians against the Canadian government. For example, after interviewing Japanese Canadians interned in British Columbia during the war, sociologist Forrest E. La Violette wrote at length about their complaints and demands to the British Columbia Security Commission, federal government representatives, and the Spanish Consulate. Forrest E. La Violette, *The Canadian Japanese and World War II* (Toronto: University of Toronto Press, 1948). Mona Oikawa notes that La Violette's analysis stands in contrast to that presented by Ken Adachi. Adachi's post-war account presents an image of Japanese Canadians as 'relatively docile' and 'co-operative'.
14. In conducting interviews with aging *Issei* in Canada in the contemporary period, sociologist Atsuko Matsuoka has observed that the Western interpretation of *shikata ga nai* may differ from the meaning given by the *Issei*. In the context of her interviews, Matsuoka discerned *shikata ga nai* to mean 'we do/did the best we can/could' rather than resignation or 'giving up'. She further found that the *Issei* revealed a remarkable resiliency. (Atsuko Matsuoka, personal correspondence, November 2003).
15. For a more detailed story of my own family's experience of see 'These Feelings that Fill My Heart: Exploring Japanese Canadian Women' s Lives Through Oral Testimony' (Paper presented to the 'Feminism and the Making of Canada' Conference, McGill University, 7–9 May 2004).
16. See, for example, Susan Geiger, 'What's so Feminist About Women's Oral History?', *Journal of Women's History* 2.1 (Spring 1990): 169–82; Sherna Berger Gluck and Daphne Patai, eds., *Women's Words: The Feminist Practice of Oral History* (New York: Routledge, 1991); Joan Sangster, 'Telling Our Stories: Feminist Debates and the Use of Oral History', in Robert Perks and Alistair Thomson, eds., *The Oral History Reader* (London: Routledge, 1998), 87–100.

17. Kuhn, 'A Journey Through Memory', 185.
18. For a discussion of the researcher's emotional engagement with the research, see Ruth Behar, *The Vulnerable Observer: Anthropology that Breaks Your Heart* (Boston, Mass.: Beacon Press, 1996); Antoinette Errante, 'But Sometimes You're Not Part of the Story: Oral Histories and Ways of Remembering and Telling', in Sharlene Nagy Hese-Biber and Michelle L. Yaiser, eds., *Feminist Perspectives on Social Research* (Oxford: Oxford University Press, 2004), 411–34; Suzanne Fleishman, 'Gender, the Personal, and the Voice of Scholarship: A Viewpoint', *Signs: Journal of Women in Culture and Society* 23.4 (Summer 1998).
19. In correspondence with the office of Arthur MacNamara, Deputy Minister, Department of Labour, T.B. Pickersgill, Commission of Japanese Placement for the Department of Labour, stated that most of the private letters intercepted by the federal government were written by individuals who had family members either interned in prisoner of war camps or relocated outside British Columbia (NAC, RG 27), Department of Labour. vol. 1528, Japanese Division, Intercepted Letters, Pickersgill to MacNamara, 2 March 1946). Most of the letters cited here were originally written in English. Those letters that had been composed in Japanese had been translated during the war by employees of the federal government. I have read only the translated versions of these letters, retyped by the Directorate of Censorship, Department of National War Services. The majority of the intercepted letters that can be found in the collections at the National Archives appear in translated form only. As a result, some of the nuance and meaning in the original letters may be lost. The Censor also indicated whether or not correspondence was to be 'held', 'released', or 'condemned'. Most of the letters cited here were released, some with passages deleted.
20. See Alessandro Portelli, 'The Peculiarities of Oral History', *History Workshop Journal* 12 (1981): 96–107.
21. Jeanne Houston (1973) cited in Traise Yamamoto, '"The Other, Private Self": Masking in Nisei Women's Autobiography', in *Masking Selves, Making Subjects: Japanese American Women, Identity, and the Body*, Traise Yamamoto, ed. (Berkeley: University of California Press, 1999), 116.
22. The 'repatriation survey' as well as the general dispersal of Japanese Canadians were administered by T.B. Pickersgill, Commissioner of Japanese Placement. Before asking people to sign the repatriation forms, RCMP officers posted two notices in each internment site. The first notice stated that anyone who sought repatriation, received free passage to Japan and were expected to declare a desire to relinquish their 'British nationality and to assume the status of a national of Japan'. The second notice offered (limited) financial support to people who agreed to move east of the Rockies. This support, however, was contingent on one's willingness to accept ever employment the government deemed appropriate. Failure to do so would be regarded as evidence of disloyalty to the nation. Adachi, *The Enemy That Never Was,* 298. For a full discussion of gender relations, and repatriation policy, see Pamela Sugiman, 'Home and Family: Acts of Intimacy in the Transnational Politics of Wartime Canada', in *Transnational Communities in Canada: Emergent Identities. Practices, and Issues*, Lloyd Wong and Victor Satzewich, eds. (Vancouver: UBC Press, forthcoming).
23. Miki and Kobayashi, *Justice in Our Time,* pp. 46–55.
24. On the Japanese Canadian Committee for Democracy and the Nisei Mass Evacuation Group see Miki and Kobayashi, *Justice in Our Time,* 36, 56.
25. All of the women narrators said assuredly that everyone in the ghost towns knew that government authorities were reading letters. Whether or not they believed that their own correspondence had been intercepted, however, is not clear. It is significant, though, that the authors of a small number of the letters in the Department of Labour collection did make direct reference to the Censors, claiming that they did not care what the Censor thought of their feelings of anger and violation.
26. See Iwona Irwin-Zareck, *Frames of Remembrance: The Dynamics of Collective Memory* (New Brunswick, NJ: Trasaction Publishers, 1994); Portelli, 'The Peculiarities of Oral History'.
27. In part, these letters have also been authored by government censors. Surely, there were hundreds, perhaps thousands, of other letters that moved directly from sender to receiver, read in full by friends and family. Just as the women's testimonies are products of our culture, the letters too have been constructed in time.
28. See Alessandro Portelli, *The Battle of Valle Giulia: Oral History and the Art of Dialogue* (Madison, WI: University of Wisconsin Press, 1997).
29. Among many others, this issue has been discussed by Michael Frisch and Dorothy L. Walls, 'Oral History and the Presentation of Class Consciousness: The *New York Times* versus the Buffalo Unemployed', *International Journal of Oral History* 1.2 (June 1980): 88–110; Ronald J. Grele, *Envelopes of Sound* (Chicago: Precedent Publishing, 1985).
30. The oral testimonies on which this discussion draws were gathered by myself, in addition to research assistants, both young women. One research assistant was a *Yonsei* (fourth-generation) Japanese Canadian.

A *Hakujin* graduate student conducted some of the early interviews. I decided to employ this student because of her strong interview skills, maturity, and intelligence. As well, she was given the task of interviewing only those women (a minority) who have been active leaders in the Japanese Canadian community. I recently communicated with some of these women about the interview experience. They said that they felt more obliged to provide details about the internment because the researcher was a *Hakujin.* Recognizing the importance of race and subjectivity in shaping the researcher/narrator relationship, I have arranged to conduct a second and, in cases, a third interview myself with some of these women. In doing so, I hope to understand more fully the interaction between researcher and narrator, as well as the role of time in shaping narratives.

31. The concept of 'community of memory' is introduced by Iwona Irwin-Zarecka. A community memory, she writes, in its most direct meaning, 'is one created by that very memory'. A shifting of the boundaries of the community is ongoing as, over time, the trauma functions as a 'key orienting force' in the lives and public actions of those who did not themselves live through that trauma. *(Frames of Remembrance,* 47–9).
32. Sumi (Sue) Kai, Toronto, Ontario, 7 February 2003.
33. Yoshiye Kosaka, Toronto, Ontario, 10 July 2001.
34. Irwin-Zarecka, *Frames of Remembrance*, 55.
35. Eviator Zerubavel, 'Social Memories: Steps to a Sociology of the Past', *Qualitative Sociology* 19.3 (1996): 284.
36. Rose Kutsukake, Toronto, Ontario, 7 April 2003.
37. Portelli 'The Peculiarities of Oral History', 163.
38. In addition, though we have witnessed a recent proliferation of writing on the internment, the women in this study were still reticent about some topics and spoke with greater ease and energy about others. It was extremely difficult, if not impossible, to broach with most women issues pertaining to sexuality. This matter seemed to be off-limits. To put it on the agenda would be to risk violating the understanding that existed between researcher and participant. In the rare case that a woman did raise the issue on her own initiative, it seemed to generate such discomfort, embarrassment, and unease that I decided not to communicate this part of her testimony to other listeners, perhaps less known and trusted. In making this decision, I myself have participated in a selective remembrance.
39. Zerubavel, 'Social Memories', 286.
40. Amy Miyamoto, Montreal, Quebec, 1 March 2003.
41. Ruby Hanako Ohashi, Vernon, British Columbia, 29 July 2002.
42. As noted by Audrey Kobayashi, marriages between Japanese Canadians and individuals of other ethnic backgrounds currently make up over 90 per cent of all marriages. Audrey Kobayashi, *A Demographic Profile of Japanese Canadians and Social Implications for the Future* (Ottawa: Department of the Secretary of State, 1989), 40.
43. Betty (a pseudonym), Steveston, British Columbia, 24 August 2002.
44. Hideko (a pseudonym), Kamloops, British Columbia, 20 July 2002.
45. Sugar Sato, Toronto, Ontario, 26 March 2003.
46. Masako Yakura, Vernon, British Columbia, 17 July 2002.
47. Zerubavel, 'Social Memories', 284.
48. Irwin-Zarecka, *Frames of Remembrance*, 47–65.
49. Mrs Whitton is a pseudonym. Ritsuko Sugiman, Toronto, Ontario, 16 July 2003.
50. Leo Spitzer, '"Back Through the Future": Nostalgic Memory and Critical Memory in a Refuge from Nazism', in *Acts of Memory: Cultural Recall in the Present*, Meike Bal, Jonathan Crewe, and Leo Spitzer, eds., (Hanover, NH: University Press of New England, 1999), 87–104.
51. See for example, Herbert J. Gans, 'Symbolic Ethnicity', in *On the Making of Americans: Essays in Honor of David Riesman*, Herbart Gans, et al, eds. (Philadelphia: University of Philadelphia Press, 1979), 193–220; Christopher Lasch, 'The Politics of Nostalgia', *Harper's* (November 1984): 65–70.
52. Pauline (Pauli) Inose, New Denver, British Columbia, 28 July 2002.
53. Sachi Oue, Toronto, Ontario, 24 May 2001.
54. This point is elaborated upon by Portelli. He notes that, while '[t]he historian is mainly interested in reconstructing the past; the speaker seeks to project an image . . . .' ('The Peculiarities of Oral History', 166).
55. See Mary M. Childers, '"The Parrot or the Pit Bull": Trying to Explain Working Class Life', *Signs: Journal of Women in Culture and Society* 28.1 (special issue on 'Gender and Cultural Memory', Autumn 2002): 214.
56. Judy Giles, 'Narratives of Gender, Class and Modernity in Women's Memories of Mid-Twentieth Century Britain', *Signs* 28.1 (Autumn 2002): 36. I present a more comprehensive discussion of these points in Sugiman, 'Memories of Internment: Narrating Japanese Canadian Women's Life Stories', *Canadian Journal of Sociology* (forthcoming).
57. Childers, '"The Parrot or the Pit Bull"', 204.
58. Hannah Tabata, Kamloops, British Columbia, 21 July 2002.
59. Michiko [a pseudonym], Vernon, British Columbia, 14 August 2002.
60. Janet Zandy, *Liberating Memory: Our Work and Our*

Working Class Consciousness (New Brunswick, NJ: Rutgers University Press, 1995), xi.

61. Walter Benjamin cited in Portelli, 'The Peculiarities of Oral History', 175.
62. Most importantly, Adachi, *The Enemy That Never Was*; Sunahara, *The Politics of Racism*.
63. Portelli, *The Battle of Valle Giulia*, 51–2.
64. Ibid., 80.

Recipes for Democracy? Gender, Family, and Making Female Citizens in Cold War Canada

Franca Iacovetta

EDITORS' INTRODUCTION

Who can legitimately claim to be a citizen of Canada? How are these claims made? Who decides whether such claims are successful or desirable? Canadians often assume that immigrants are, and were in the past, unproblematically welcomed into the nation's fold. The American image of the 'melting pot', in which newcomers were made to conform to the dominant culture, is judged less favourably than our homegrown 'salad bowl' approach. Each unique ingredient or 'citizen' is visible, autonomous, and yet critical to the success of the whole. Such national myth-making was bolstered by the policy of multiculturalism adopted by Prime Minister Pierre Elliott Trudeau in 1971. Recent scholarship suggests that these images serve present ideological needs rather than accurately reflect the past. As the essays by Marlene Epp, Mary-Jo Nadeau, and others in this volume demonstrate, racism and exclusion have shaped the country since contact and continue to do so. Franca Iacovetta and Tania Das Gupta have recently concluded, 'nation-building, the privilege of a few, is a process of inclusion and exclusion, of distinguishing between "us" and "them", of conferring rights of citizenship to some but not "others".'[1]

Denyse Baillargeon's study of poor working class women's exclusion from citizenship in Depression-era Montreal makes clear the notion that 'citizenship' is a relative, historically contingent term. This was certainly the case following the Second World War. With the traditional source of 'preferred' migrants, Britain, no longer supplying sufficient numbers, Canada had to look farther afield for new citizens. In the 1950s, they would increasingly come from southern Europe, especially Italy and Portugal. After the removal of the explicit 'colour bar' in Canadian immigration policy in the 1960s, they would more often come from East and South Asia and the Caribbean. The women who joined the migrations at this time would not be subject to the same racist and nativist policies as the women described by Sugiman and Arat-Koç. But, as Iacovetta shows here, they would find themselves under subtle yet clear pressure to adopt what were promulgated as 'Canadian' customs. That their domestic habits, including cooking, were targeted in these campaigns for 'Canadianization' suggests something about the intimate connections among women, national identity, and the state.

In this contribution, Franca Iacovetta focuses on some of the official efforts to remake immigrant women, particularly Italian working-class immigrants, into 'acceptable' citizens in postwar Canada. She analyzes the efforts of various experts, including government officials, social workers, and settlement house workers, to 'Canadianize' women through the potent politics of 'domestic containment'. Campaigns aimed at changing the ways immigrant women fed their families were one expression of the war against the non-Anglophone way of life, against 'godless communism' and its potential inroads among those considered more ignorant and less modern. In examining the complicated interaction between social workers and immigrant women, Iacovetta illustrates one of the strengths of recent works on Canadian gender history, namely a nuanced view of the process of moral regulation.

To make her argument, Iacovetta, like Valerie Korinek, explores a 'rereading' of ideological subtexts in *Chatelaine* magazine, an enduringly important source of information on women's history in Canada.[2] Within the magazine's food features, Iacovetta argues, images and texts confirmed a white middle-class ideal as the only sanctioned model of family life. Under the guise of health and welfare concerns regarding well-balanced diets, efficient households, economical meal planning, and shopping, 'experts' pathologized the food customs and preferences, as well as preparation methods, of immigrant women. In particular, Iacovetta points out, the large influx of Italian immigrants after 1945 and their reluctance to abandon food traditions for Canadianized substitutes brought them considerable scrutiny.

Italian women responded to their Cold War culinary surveillance in a number of different ways. Some were adamantly opposed to adopting 'Canadian' ways of cooking, citing, for example, the habit of throwing out leftovers as particularly wasteful and sinful. Others simply ignored efforts at change. Others experimented with Canadian recipes, inventing a kind of hybrid cookery that combined Italian and Canadian styles and tastes. Debates about the appropriateness of traditional versus unfamiliar food terrain, Iacovetta found, divided wives from husbands and children from parents. At the end of the day, the food women brought to the kitchen table reflected a great deal about the personal and public politics of belonging in Cold War-era Canada.

Notes

1. Tania Das Gupta and Franca Iacovetta, 'Introduction—Whose Canada Is It? Immigrant Women, Women of Colour and Feminist Critiques of "Multiculturalism"', *Atlantis* 24.2 (2000): 1–4.
2. Valerie Korinek, '"Don't Let Your Girlfriends Ruin Your Marriage": Lesbian Imagery in Chatelaine Magazine, 1950–1969', in *Rethinking Canada: The Promise of Women's History*, 4th ed., Veronica Strong-Boag, Mona Gleason, Adele Perry, eds. (Toronto: Oxford University Press, 2002).

Questions for Critical Reading

1. What are the criteria for determining a 'good citizen'? What role do race, age, class, gender, and sexuality play in this process?
2. In what ways do the 'politics of food' shape the status of women? Do they play the same role for men?
3. What are the limitations associated with using magazine imagery to reflect women's lived experience? What are the strengths?

During the past several decades, feminist and left scholars of immigrant and refugee women and women of colour have exposed—through both empirical documentation and careful rethinking of conventional categories of nation, immigrants, and citizen—the material and ideological processes central to the 'making' of nation-states and national identities. Many now acknowledge that nation-building is premised on the political and social organization of 'difference', and that it creates both citizens (or potential citizens) and non-citizens denied rights. That First World nations in the EU and NAFTA champion globalization and free trade zones while at the same time 'policing' their borders against 'others' (especially Third World migrant workers) speaks volumes on the topic.[1]

Studies of contemporary migration note the growing female presence among migrant workers around the world, while those focused on Canada show how racist, class-based, and heterosexist paradigms continue to define mainstream notions of Canada and Canadian. This situation prevails despite the long history and enduring impact of immigration to Canada and its increasingly multi-racial profile—especially since the 1970s. Immigrant women of colour from the Caribbean, Asia, Africa, and other 'Third World' nations—who are exploited as temporary workers but discouraged from settling permanently and stereotyped as sexually promiscuous single mothers undeserving of citizenship—experience most directly the cruel hypocrisy of liberal capitalist countries that promise opportunity and freedom to all while simultaneously creating pools of unfree labour and perpetuating damaging race and gender stereotypes. Immigration and citizenship policies are also sexualized and shaped by bourgeois and heterosexual norms regarding reproduction and motherhood. Lesbian women face particular challenges in the face of hetero-normative discourses, and women of colour are eroticized in ways that affect adversely their claims to citizenship.

Specialists of migrant, immigrant, and refugee women workers in Canada have sought to disrupt the dominant liberal construction of Canada as 'an immigrant nation' that has always opened its doors to the world's peoples. As their work documents, liberal histories of Canada erroneously depict state-sanctioned racist policies, such as the infamous Chinese head taxes and other laws prohibiting the entry of wives and children of Chinese male workers, as blips in an otherwise smooth and linear development towards mature nationhood. Similarly, nationalist boosters, past and present, see the presence of 'successful' white ethnic and 'non-white' Canadians as proof of even greater national progress. We must remain aware of the critical distinctions between, on the one hand, an official liberal and highly flawed policy of multiculturalism, and, on the other, Canada's historical and continuing transformation into a multiracial society and the reality of many Canadians who in daily practice live multicultural, multiracial lives.

As a historian of post-World War II Canada, I wish here to tackle the dominant liberal framework of Canada as a land of genuine opportunity, where all hardworking newcomers can prosper, contribute to the country's rich cultural mosaic, and eventually join the Canadian 'family'. Such portraits of Canada as a place where everyone can be both 'different' and 'equal' ignore the fact that, as Tania Das Gupta and I observed elsewhere, Canadian immigration and refugee policy have long been exclusionary and discriminatory with regard to so-called 'undesirables'. But I want also to take the point further. The liberal 'we are an immigrant nation' discourse (which perhaps only the US has more aggressively promoted) also ignores or downplays the more invidious aspects of gatekeeping efforts to remake into something else even those newcomers ostensibly 'welcomed' into the nation.

In addressing this theme, my article shifts the focus from the present to the recent past, and from the exclusionary practices described above to the immigrant and refugee reception and citizenship campaigns of the early postwar and Cold War decades before 1965. More specifically, it examines the gendered nature of reception activity and nation-making after 1945. And rather than addressing forms of outright exclusion—such as screening for Communists or deporting newcomers deemed politically or morally suspect, or deemed potential burdens on the state—I adopt an analytical framework central to the emerging social and gender histories of Cold War capitalist societies—domestic containment. By focusing on women, nutrition, food, and gender and family ideals, I explore how the dominant gender ideologies of liberal democracies in the early Cold War—including a bourgeois model of homemaking and food customs and family life—informed reception work and social service activities among immigrant and refugee women. By 'domestic containment' I mean, of course, both state-sanctioned and volunteer efforts within Western countries to police not only the political but also the social, personal, moral, and sexual lives of its citizens—a process that, ironically, involved the repression in liberal Western democracies of individual rights and freedoms in the name of demographic rights and freedoms. The Cold War, as US scholars such as Elaine Tyler May and Canadian historians such as Gary Kinsman have documented, witnessed the resurgence of a conservative and hegemonic family ideology that 'normalized' an idealized bourgeois Anglo-Celtic nuclear family, and that in turn served as an (unrealistic and oppressive) standard against which 'non-conformists' were harshly judged, harassed, and punished.

I have documented elsewhere that even as Canada's social welfare elite boldly declared the birth of the brave new world, they also debated at length the fragility of postwar democratic society and swore to attack all threats—from within and without—to democratic 'decency'. The threat of the atomic bomb, the Soviet Empire, and homosexual spies were marked features of the Cold War, as were working mothers, juvenile delinquents (especially, but not exclusively, gang girls), women deemed sexually promiscuous, and male 'sex perverts', and they legitimated a 'corrupted democracy' in which the state, and its civilian accomplices, was obliged to censor its citizenry. Historian Geoffrey Smith has effectively used the metaphor of disease to describe how the US state waged a dirty war against all those considered sources of contamination—godless communists, gay civil servants, marginal African-American welfare mothers, and others. Similar patterns obtained in Canada; indeed, recent research on the domestic side of the Cold War, made possible in part because of recent access to security intelligence materials (such as RCMP case files), has begun to challenge the conventional wisdom that Canada's Cold War was essentially, or comparatively, benign.

Mariana Valverde's *The Age of Light, Soap and Water: Moral Reform in English Canada 1885–1925* showed how Canadian nation-building in an earlier era required more than protective tariffs, backroom political deals, and a transcontinental railway. It also involved various moral campaigns aimed both to encourage middle-class white Canadian women to procreate (or face 'race suicide') and to ensure the moral 'uplift' of working-class immigrants and racialized Canadians deemed inferior on both moral and mental health grounds. The desire for a healthy body politic, both literally and figuratively, also fuelled nationalist boosters and social and psychological experts committed to national reconstruction after the Second World War. While hardly the sole cause of these post-1945 agendas, the arrival of the Cold War did impart a particular kind of political and moral urgency to campaigns meant to ensure the long-term physical, mental, and moral health of Canada's current and future citizens. Both men and women were targeted by such campaigns, but women, as in the past, were more vulnerable to moral assessment and branding.

My research on immigrant and refugee women and families offers another lens through which we can explore some of these key issues. Here, I take one thematic slice—nutrition and food campaigns and what front-line health and welfare workers called 'family life' projects intended to improve poor and immigrant children's lives and remake their mothers. In tackling this topic, I have considered a wide range of players and activities. They include, on the one hand, a variety of gatekeepers, from front-line settlement house workers, citizenship activists, adult literacy workers, and women's organizations to professional social workers, psychologists, and government bureaucrats; and, on the other, the more than two million women, men, and child immigrants and refugees, especially, but not exclusively, from Europe. Taken together, the activities under scrutiny were many and varied: from the more explicitly ideological work of the Citizenship Branch and the RCMP, both of whom engaged in the political surveillance of the left ethnic press and organizations, to the numerous English classes, social agency services, and neighbourhood 'projects for newcomers' undertaken in these years, particularly those aimed at low-income immigrant mothers and children in inner-city neighbourhoods in Toronto.

'Selling' Canadian Abundance and Modernity to Europe's 'Backward' Women

As the Second World War ended, the media alerted Canadians to the widespread hunger, starvation, and health disasters affecting people from around the world. Canadian newspapers, for instance, contained graphic and heartbreaking images and tales of emaciated Holocaust survivors, flood and disaster victims in Europe and beyond, and malnourished mothers and children from towns ravished by war. Indeed, a central theme emerging in these early years stressed the great gap between Canada as a land of modest affluence and a devastated Europe.

With the coming of the Cold War, this theme also served ideological ends. Among the most popular texts of the day were what I call 'iron-curtain escape narratives'[1] published in newspapers and magazines. Highly dramatic, these stories featured the trials and tribulations of those who had escaped 'Red' countries, risked health and death to trek across frontier border towns, and eventually reached the western zone in Europe, finally settling in countries like Canada. A *Toronto Star* front-page story (23 September 1950) that told about the escape of a 'pretty little Czech girl' who 'outwitted' Soviet Police' and 'waded mountain snows' to reach Canada is emblematic. A PhD student from Prague, 23-year-old Irene Konkova had been arrested 'for not conforming to Communist dictates'. After escaping jail, she gave the Soviet police the slip at a remote inn and finally reached safety in West Germany. There, she worked in the US zone as a physical education director with the YWCA-YMCA until taking a YWCA job in Winnipeg. Though worried about her parents, Konkova told reporters she was 'looking forward to the Canadian way of life', which she associated with Western modernity and affluence. When asked what most impressed her about Canada, she noted the 'smart clothes and immaculate appearance' of Canadian women and the abundance of food. She loved it all: 'hot dogs and potato chips impressed her as much as steaks, cakes and candy.'

Both US and Canadian propaganda material contrasted the good fortunes of mothers of North America, where liberal capitalism permitted them to raise and nurture well-fed and moral children, with those mothers working far away from their children and in other ways struggling under the exploitation and scarcity prevailing in 'Iron Curtain' countries. From stoves to one-stop grocery stores, boosters sang the praises of Canadian modernity. In the Displaced Persons and refugee camps, on ships sailing overseas, and in locales across Canada, women newcomers confronted these messages of Canadian affluence and modernity everywhere: in films, pamphlets, and newspapers, in English and citizenship classes, and in settlement house mothers' clubs and YWCA meetings. Cooking lessons, sermons, and health 'interventions' sought to reform both Canadian and New Canadian women's cooking regimes and food customs, household management, and child welfare. Indeed, health and welfare experts offered their version of the postwar bourgeois homemaker ideal, with their middle-class and sexist denunciations of married women and wives who worked for pay—among them, huge numbers of refugee and immigrant women.[2] Canadians were encouraged to embrace the newcomers but also teach them the superior values of democracy, 'freedom', and, not least of all, the well balanced Canadian meal.

After 1945, Canadian nutritionists, food writers, and health and welfare 'experts' focused much of their attention on the hundreds of thousands of Europeans who figured prominently among the more than 2.5 million newcomers who had entered the country by 1965. Food and health campaigns aimed at immigrant women and their families were varied and numerous. They were part of the larger campaigns intended to 'improve' the homemaking skills of all women—resident or soon-to-be resident—in Canada. When, for example, British war brides were offered health lectures and cooking classes, both in England and in Canada, they were not only taught to measure ingredients the Canadian way (i.e., the British measured liquids by weight, North Americans by volume), but were deliberately being 'trained' for their new role as wives and mothers of Canadian husbands and children. Media coverage of the war brides' resettlement in Canada—a major government undertaking, in which the military and Canadian Red Cross played important roles—garnered enormous public attention, and was everywhere punctuated by the image of the fresh faces of young, white British women and their ruby-cheeked children. By contrast, the non-British war brides, including Dutch and Italian women, and their children never attracted as much attention.

Central to these health and welfare campaigns were certain overriding concerns: preaching the value of a well-balanced diet, efficient shopping and household regimes, planned menus, and budget-conscious shopping. Much of the food advice prioritized middle-class ideals regarding preparation and consumption—clean and uncluttered homes, formal dining rooms or kitchen 'dinettes', and a stay-at-home wife and mother. This was a far cry from the crowded and substandard flats, low and vulnerable incomes, and harried and tired working mothers that were the hallmarks of many newly arrived immigrants and refugees in Toronto and other urban locales.

Canadian Culinary Ways

As Valerie Korinek's important new book, *Roughing It in the Suburbs: Reading Chatelaine in the Fifties and Sixties,* well illustrates, Canada's top selling women's magazine offers us an indirect but excellent source about postwar food and health campaigns. In saying this, I am not suggesting a direct causation between immigrant women, *Chatelaine* magazine, and changed habits. Rather, the magazine's food features and recipes provide valuable glimpses into the images, assumptions, messages, recipes, profes-

School Days are Soup Days
by Anne Marshall
SCHOOLDAY LUNCH EATEN AT HOME
SCHOOLDAY LUNCH CARRIED TO SCHOOL
CAMPBELL'S ARE CANADA'S FAVORITE SOUPS

sional advice, and other features of postwar health and homemaking campaigns. Korinek persuasively argues that the magazine, despite its image as a conventional women's magazine, was not composed exclusively of 'happy homemaker' images. She also cautions against simple and reductionist theories that assume women readers are passively duped by bourgeois women's magazines. Still, as she adds, the food advertisements and features did provide many conventional images of traditional middle-class femininity—including images of mothers who showed their love in part by baking bread, shopping well, and producing a grand variety of cheap but well-balanced meals, nicely presented on table-clothed tables. The ads that delivered such messages also reflected the interests of food corporations whose much-needed funds kept *Chatelaine* afloat. Central images emerged in these food features. For example, the 'Canadian way' (as Korinek and I detail elsewhere) was usually portrayed by attractive, white, middle-class Canadian women pushing overflowing grocery carts down aisles with well-stocked shelves, or cooking meals in modern and well-appointed kitchens using canned, frozen, and other ingredients from their well-stocked pantry shelves, freezers, and refrigerators. Recipes featured affordable meals using cheap cuts of meat—hamburger, for example, in the ever ubiquitous casserole (though by the 1960s curry chicken casseroles actually hit the pages!) and, on occasion, fancy hors d'oeuvres and brunches.

By the early 1960s, the magazine began to feature more 'ethnic' recipes and even discuss the plight of working wives and mothers, but these were very modest concessions. A case in point is Italian food. US food historians such as Harvey Levenstein and immigration historians such as Italian specialist Donna Gabaccia have documented both that Italians were among the most resistant of the immigrants in the US when it came to pressures to change their food customs and that Italian foods, including pasta, were among the most successfully 'mainstreamed' ethnic foods in the US diet. For the US, the conflicts and accommodations involving immigrant and particularly Italian foods occurred in particularly dramatic

ways during the interwar decades, following the mass migration of Southern and Eastern Europeans to the US during the period from the 1880s to the 1920s. Levenstein and Gabaccia trace the promotion of Italian and other ethnic foods that were inexpensive, nutritious, and filling—in food magazines, food corporation ads, and also the military, where large numbers of young American men were first introduced to Italian foods. That process invariably involved modifying 'foreign' or 'exotic' foods for the more timid palates of North American consumers by removing pungent cheeses, or other offensive ingredients, and perhaps including more recognizable ones (cheddar cheese instead of parmesan, for instance). Similar developments occurred in Canada especially, though not exclusively, during the post-1945 era, when the country witnessed its mass migration of incoming newcomers. Yet, it's also clear that Canadian women did experiment with ethnic recipes, particularly by the 1960s. By then, *Chatelaine* also began featuring (white) 'ethnic' women, including working mothers, and their recipes, although this did not preclude a reliance on 'cute' and patronizing racial-ethnic and sexual stereotypes.

Nursing Inner-City Kids, Pathologizing Immigrant Mothers

In contrast to media depictions of ethnic foods, the records of Canadian health and welfare experts from the 1950s and 1960s are less ambiguous with respect to the 'problems' posed by the huge influx of immigrant and refugee mothers and their families. Indeed, they are replete with examples of the ways in which Canadian experts singled out immigrant women for special attention or blame, particularly those from more impoverished and 'peripheral' rural regions of southern Europe. Invariably the 'experts' stereotyped these humble immigrants and low-income mothers (and fathers) as too ignorant, isolated, backwards, stubborn, and/or suspicious to access 'modern' health care, secure their children's health needs, and otherwise raise their children appropriately as future Canadians.

Such themes emerge in a popular postwar food guide, *Food Customs of New Canadians*, that was prepared by professional home economists and nutritionists for use by health and welfare personnel working with newcomers. Although presented as a scientific and objective assessment of the food customs of racial-ethnic groups, the guide sought to equip front-line activists with ways of encouraging immigrants to adapt their food patterns to Canadian foods, recipes, equipment, and eating regimes. Some recommendations—drink more milk, for instance—were intended for everyone. Overall, however, the guide reflected middle-class, pro-capitalist, North American assumptions, such as the wisdom of a three-meals-a-day pattern because it was well suited to Canadian school and work hours. It also reflected the superiority of Canadian utensils, equipment, and modern appliances.

The guide isolated particular problems for each group under review and assigned teaching suggestions for eliminating them. No group received an entirely negative (or positive) evaluation. For example, while the Chinese scored poorly in hygiene on what the experts considered insufficient cleaning of pots and shared use of chopsticks, they scored well overall on their use of fresh foods, including vegetables. Overall, North-Western Europeans generally fared much better, though there was room for improvement here too. The guide referred to the propensity of 'Czechs' to be overweight because of their love of dumplings, and Austrians were cited for consuming too many sweets, and so on.

More problematic were the Italians and Portuguese. Italian immigrant women emerged in the guide as uneducated and primitive peasants who were forced to cook on outdoor clay or brick ovens and whose homes lacked the necessary equipment of a modern household: a gas or electric stove, a refrigerator, and storage space. Although praised for their ability to 'stretch' meats through use of pastas and other starches, Italian women in Toronto were chastised for spending too much of their modest family income on purchasing specialty foods from Italy, such as fine-grade olive oil, when cheaper Canadian substitutes were available! (Curiously, only the Italian entry refers explicitly to the possibility that the high rate of female labour participation meant that, after migration, Italian women had less time to produce food.) Similarly, Portuguese women were criticized for buying fresh fish from the market because it was more expensive than the frozen variety. Professional nutrition experts appear to have prioritized their professional repertoire over the values and cultural preferences of their clients. Italian mothers, I should add, were also singled out for their 'bad' habit of serving their children a bit of wine with dinner. Their advice, of course, ran counter to that of today when we are told to more closely emulate various features of the continental European diet.

Many of the recommendations contained in the guide reflected the concern of nutrition experts to determine the capacity of immigrant women in low-income families to produce well-balanced meals. Since family economic need pushed many of them into the paid force, these women had even less time for 'improving' homemaking skills. Thus, even while public and professional campaigns intended to raise homemaking standards were aimed at the entire female population, class distinctions, which overlapped with racial-ethnic ones, accounted for some differing remedies. Regrettably, home economists have long assumed that poor people's diets were more the result of their ignorance of nutrition and food preparation than material scarcity. Proposed solutions usually meant imposing austere diet and meal plans on the poor, while the approved diets and advertised meal plans for middle-class families permitted various frills and luxuries. In postwar Toronto, experts serving immigrant neighbourhoods were routinely asked whether people in the area seemed aware of general health guidelines such as The Canada Food Rules, cod liver oil for children, what constitutes adequate hours of sleep, and so on. School nurses and child welfare workers held differing expectations for the mother and children of bourgeois and poor families. On one level, this was a reasonable response: as Cynthia Comacchio observed for an earlier period, it was insulting to teach the finer points about child personality training, or food fussiness and toy fetishes, to poor immigrant mothers who could not even afford 'decent' housing. Yet, rather than attack class inequities, the experts focused on teaching mothers the fundamentals of health—cleanliness, nutrition, fresh air—as though mothers alone could prevent ill health.

Toronto provides a valuable case study for considering how low-income immigrant and refuge women were both given some critical assistance by front-line social workers and health and welfare personnel keen to improve health care among struggling working-class immigrants—and also pathologized by the experts. Front-line social and welfare personnel identified several major problems. They worried about the ill effects of crowded and substandard housing on low-income immigrant families and the special burdens that inadequate wages imposed on women who, whether housewives or working mothers, had to stretch inadequate paycheques to cover rent, food, drugs, clothing, furniture, and other necessities. If the family had purchased bigger-ticket items like furniture on credit (which became more accessible to low-income people in these years) there was the burden of additional bills and collection agencies that would demand payment. The lack of proper cooking facilities in many substandard rental flats encouraged unhealthy eating. Furthermore, the budget item that invariably appeared most flexible was food. To pay the bills, women, it was feared, turned to cheap, usually starch-heavy foods while cutting out comparatively more expensive and healthy alternatives. The result, claimed nutrition experts, was malnutrition, which might not be detected for years but would nonetheless take its toll on the mental, emotional, and physical health of immigrant adults and children. An additional concern was that as more middle-class Canadians abandoned the urban core for the suburbs, cities like Toronto would become host to 'decaying' inner-city neighbourhoods. In response, experts basically applied old remedies to the current context—home visits, family budgets, meal plans—and tried to attract particularly stay-at-home immigrant mothers into their cooking and nutrition programs. Some modest successes were scored, but the main response recorded is continuing frustration with absenteeism.

A related problem earmarked by health and welfare experts was that immigrants' seeming ignorance of Canada's social services, combined with their needless suspicion or distrust of outsiders, meant that many immigrant parents, especially mothers, were unwittingly neglecting their children's health. When both parents worked, mothers were unavailable or too exhausted to tend to their children's needs. Social workers referred to the 'tremendous job' required to educate the newcomers about the value of nursery school, summer camps, parent education, and other valuable services 'new' and 'strange' to them.

Once again, rural non-English-speaking immigrants transplanted to major urban centres were considered most pathetic. In the heavily Portuguese neighbourhood of Parkdale, the International Institute of Metropolitan Toronto (IIMT), the city's largest immigrant aid society, opened up an extension office in 1961 to reach these women. The project supervisor, veteran social worker Edith Ferguson, collected field work notes and produced case histories meant to illustrate the value of social work interventions. One such case involved a mother who told the visiting caseworker that her daughter had infected tonsils but could not afford to have them removed. Although the family had been registered with the Ontario hospital plan, the mother, who had recently undergone an operation, erroneously assumed that time had to elapse before they could return to hospital. They could not afford a private surgeon's fee because they held a heavy mortgage on a recently purchased house and the husband was sidelined by a workplace injury. Their 17-year-old daughter was the family's only income earner.

In response, the IIMT caseworker contacted the girl's school nurse, who, wrote Ferguson, saw the child immediately, determined her tonsils were badly infected, and referred her to Toronto Hospital for Children. Having secured the parents' trust, they could assist with other things—completing the husband's workman's compensation application, enrolling him in a training course, and checking out job possibilities for a nephew wishing to come to Canada. They also found the daughter, who had been earning a dismal factory wage, a better-paying clerical job in a new pharmacy interested in a Portuguese-speaking employee.

Like the *Food Customs* manual, front-line workers also stressed the lack of prenatal instruction for immigrant and refugee women. While the guide focused on the absence or inadequate prenatal education in the women's homelands, front-line caseworkers dwelt on a continuing widespread ignorance about modern child-feeding and child-rearing methods among immigrant women. Immigrant women, they argued, suffered needless 'complicated pregnancies' for lack of doctor appointments. Those convinced to go to out-patient clinics or prenatal courses learned very little as the lectures and mimeographed diet and instruction handouts were in English. When 'costly vitamins or medicines' were prescribed, women 'seldom' took them 'because of a lack of understanding of their worth'. Too often, community social workers had to convince parents to rush a sick child to hospital.

In response, experts searched for better ways to reach immigrant women, including translating information pamphlets and more systematic home visiting. Public health workers also began enrolling in Italian and Portuguese language classes, while others lobbied for more local prenatal and child nutrition clinics. However, the initiatives of professional nutrition and health experts determined to reshape immigrant behaviour were not always effective. For example, city settlement records in the early 1960s commented on the high rates of absenteeism to courses organized for recently arrived newcomers.

Health and welfare personnel also frowned on what they dubbed the inadequate, makeshift daycare arrangements of immigrant working mothers who reportedly left babies and toddlers in the care of grandparents, siblings, and other sitters incapable of providing proper supervision, nutritious meals, healthy recreation, or moral guidance. While all working mothers were vulnerable to such criticism, non-English-speaking immigrants and refugee women were considered particularly prone to bypassing modern daycare centres for informal, often kin-based arrangements. The result in downtown areas was a so-called 'epidemic of inadequate child care arrangements'. Home visitors reported on a range of inappropriate sitters: an old-age pensioner who lived next-door, a six-year-old child in charge of a two-year-old, and harried mothers with their own children.

Determined to raise the standard of child care in the community, St Christopher House (SCH), along with the neighbouring Protestant Children's Home and the Victoria Day Nursery, began experimenting in 1962 with small daycare programs 'in specially selected family settings'. Like other social welfare programs, including progressive ones intended to support low-income working mothers, a carrot-and-stick approach characterized this scheme: all participating mothers had to attend SCH sessions on child care and homemaking.

By the early 1960s, efforts aimed at inner-city immigrant mothers included downtown experiments intended to 'strengthen family life' by addressing 'part of a complex of problems of family living', namely, meal planning, food purchasing on limited funds, and child and adult eating habits. In 1961, SCH (whose neighbourhood was bounded by Queen Street, Bathurst Street, College Street, and Spadina Avenue) participated in a hot lunch program with the Toronto Board of Education and the Metro Toronto Social Planning Council at Ryerson Public School. An important program that deserves praise for addressing the needs of low-income children, the hot lunch project nevertheless came with conditions: a dozen 'undernourished' children from the neighbourhood were given money subsidies (donated by the Rotary Club) to purchase nutritious hot lunches at school provided that their mothers agreed to attend fortnightly classes at St Christopher House for 'help in nutrition and meal planning'. The children were selected in consultation with school and St Christopher House staff, who could supply 'knowledge of family conditions', while a family life worker hired by St Christopher House conducted follow-up visits. The hot meals were not described but likely consisted of conventional cafeteria fare of this era, such as hot roast beef sandwiches with peas and carrots, or cooked ham with (canned) pineapple and (canned) vegetables, and, of course, milk.

According to St Christopher House staff, the hot school lunch produced positive results for both children and mothers. Within a year, they reported a general increase in the number of students buying hot lunches at Ryerson Public School. Meanwhile, the mothers of the subsidized children had shown much 'enthusiasm' for their meetings and their 'excellent' instructor, a nutritionist from the Visiting Homemakers Association, who used a good mix of films, kitchen demonstrations, and lectures. Two years later, a report claimed that teachers had 'observed improvement in the health of the children and in the quality of their work in school', while their mothers had 'gained practical knowledge through their contact with a nutritionist and a social worker'. Furthermore, the classes had provided the women with 'their only social experience in an otherwise drab existence' and had given them 'the feeling that somebody cared'. On a more negative note, nutritionists expressed 'some concerns about finding methods to ensure that the families are taking full advantage of the subsidy to purchase the lunches at school'—suggesting that some immigrant mothers, by choice or circumstance, were spending the money on other items

The Hot Lunch campaign quickly became incorporated into a more intrusive two-year Family Life project, launched at SCH in 1962. With funds from the Laidlaw Foundation, this project, too, aimed to 'reach' rural immigrant women now transplanted to an urban centre and provide them with 'a very basic type of adult education e.g., consumer buying, citizenship etc.'. The primary target was the growing number of Portuguese newcomers in the Kensington market area, though Italian, Chinese, Caribbean, and other newcomers were also contacted. A full-time Family Life worker and a Portuguese-speaking nutritionist with experience in Home Economics education in Angola were hired. The IIMT also collaborated on the project.

Like other community experiments with inner-city immigrants, the Family Life project produced mixed results. Also, like other front-line work with newcomers, it reflected and perpetuated the marginal status of women from rural, impoverished, and formally uneducated Old World backgrounds.

Immigrant and Refugee Women's Recipes for 'Canadian' Living

Although anecdotal, the available evidence suggests that refugee and immigrant women also responded selectively to postwar health and homemaking campaigns, even if they could not control the terms of their encounter with social welfare personnel. Like surviving written sources, oral testimonies[3] attest to the critical importance of food to immigrants and refugees and to women's efforts to negotiate a complex culinary terrain. Immigrant and refugee women had their own versions of European scarcity and Canadian abundance; their recollections contain horrific tales of starvation in Nazi camps and heroic ones of gentiles and partisans who risked their lives to get food to hungry prisoners across Europe. Some testimonies offer us humorous recollections of the joys of eating Canadian bread and fruit upon arrival in Halifax, while others record the serious complaints and protests of refugees clearly disgusted by what they saw as overindulgence and the (sinful) throwing out of leftovers. In addition, immigrant women's cooking and their families' food-eating patterns varied greatly during these years and thus defy easy categorization: some immigrant mothers steadfastly stuck to 'traditional' meals in the home, while others were keen to experiment with Canadian recipes or convenience foods. The example of Polish Jewish survivors who responded differently to Canadian food customs and the availability of many commercial products suggest, too, the importance of individual choice. One woman explained her insistence on cooking traditional 'Jewish food' in part as a concrete way of continuing to defy Hitler's final solution; the other embraced Betty Crocker and other US as well as Canadian products because these newfangled things offered her one of several ways of putting behind the past and moving forward.

While these briefly summarized testimonies are highly suggestive, the gender and generational dynamics involved still require more research and closer scrutiny. Here again, my research sheds some light on various intriguing patterns. For example, some immigrant and refugee husbands pressured their wives to stick to familiar meals and insisted that their children eat their homeland foods at home. In some cases, this gender dynamic overlapped with political as well as ethnic or cultural tones. During the early Cold War years, for instance, left-wing Ukrainian Canadians who belonged to the Farm-labour Temple in Winnipeg evidently insisted on eating Ukrainian as a sign of their continuing resistance to a repressive Canadian state—but they also left it to women to do the time-consuming labours involved to prepare the food. By the same token, certain immigrant or ethnic Canadian men deliberately encouraged their wives to incorporate some Canadian foods because they wished to 'embrace' Canada; other times, the opposite pattern emerged. Children also played a role, usually by pressuring their mothers to 'try' or 'buy' Canadian goods—with hot dogs, hamburgers, and pop being favourites. In short, the evidence, though fragmentary, points to a seemingly endless number of permutations of hybrid diets in the households of working-class and middle-class immigrants who increasingly combined familiar foods with Canadian foods and 'ethnic' foods from other homeland origins.

Particularly for cities like Toronto, immigrant foods (and ethnic restaurants) have clearly changed the city's culinary landscape even as the immigrants' own food customs have themselves been modified. But we still need to trace more closely and to develop a sharper analysis of what some have called the 'yuppification' of ethnic foods. I find it especially ironic that the foods that had caused me much embarrassment as a child—spicy and pungent salami, prosciutto, strong and smelly cheeses, dense and crusty bread—have become markers of middle-class taste. But they have also been embraced by people from diverse racial-ethnic and class backgrounds, many of whom, in my view, are not merely using food to affect a certain sophisticated, worldly, or snobbish big-city style. Rather, they (we) clearly value the sensuality involved in eating a range of foods, of experimenting with new smells and tastes, of embracing food practices that see eating as a social and cultural practice, not merely a biological function, during which people talk, laugh, argue, debate, and in this and other ways spend hours making and re-making community.

Equally important, we cannot deny the power politics embedded in food wars and customs—to make only brief mention of the so-called 'wok wars' that recently received media attention in Toronto, when a WASP Canadian couple complained bitterly and publicly against their Chinese neighbour's cooking habits and 'smells'. Nor can we omit the role that food corporations, saturation-advertising, and capitalist imperialism have played in shaping women's cooking and shopping habits and family eating customs—how else can we explain what I have called the postwar Dole Pineapple conspiracy? As suggested by the New Left scholars of the late 1960s and the 1970s, who exposed the insidious links between US imperialist ambitions in Latin America, the creation of so-called banana republics, and multinational food corporations' aggressive promotion of their various tinned and packaged citrus fruits to (North) Americans, the political economy of food must inform our analysis of the social and gender practices surrounding the purchase, production, and consumption of food.

So, too, do people matter; their curiosity, willingness to experiment—in short, their agency—should also figure in our efforts to discern key changes in food customs, including the recent rise of 'multicultural' eating in Canada. Nevertheless, when we focus on the immigrant and refugee women and families who encountered Canadian nutrition and food experts on their doorsteps or in their children's schools, health and welfare offices, hospitals, or settlement houses during the early post-1945 decades, a particularly strong theme looms large: working-class immigrant women residing in inner-city neighbourhoods bore the brunt of professional discourses that attributed women's failure to conquer the kitchen and ensure 'quality' food and family life to ignorance and distrust of modern standards and distrust of social service interventions.

Notes

I am indebted to Valerie Korinek for sharing her research materials and ideas with me. We have co-authored a lengthy article on related themes, entitled, 'Jello Salads, One-Stop Shopping, and Maria the Homemaker: The Gender Politics of Food', *Sisters or Strangers: Immigrant Women, Minority Women, and the 'Racialized Other' in Canadian History*, Marlene Epp, Franca Iacovetta, and Frances Swyripa, eds. (Toronto: University of Toronto Press, 2004). The photographs in this article originally appeared in the following editions of *Chatelaine*: Oct. 1956 (© Paul Rockett); Sept. 1951; Jan. 1948; Aug. 1981.

1. See, for example, *The Toronto Star* from 1945 to 1965.
2. Sources listed in order of appearance in the text: Toronto City Archives: Social Planning Council (SC) 40, Box 53 File 3 A-International Institute Parkdale Branch (IIPB) 1961–3, Report on School Principals at Grace, Alexander Muir, Old Orchard, Charles E. Fraser, and Lansdowne Public Schools; SC 24 D Box 1 University Settlement House, Executive Director's Reports, 1939–1975, Head Resident's House Report, 14 February 1952; Executive Director's Monthly Report, 28 May 1956 on Housing and Suburbs: National Federation of Settlements Conference; St Christopher House, SC 484 IA1, Box 1, Folder 5, Minutes 1951–2: Annual Report 8 February 1951; SC 484 IA1 Box 2 St Christopher House Folder 1 Minutes 1959, dated 23 April 1959; Box 1 Folder 7 Minutes 1955; Folder 8 Minutes 23 May 1956; SC 40, Box 53, File 3 A-IIPB 1961–3, Report from Parkdale Branch, International Institute (Edith Ferguson) to School Principals at Grace, Alexander Muir, Old Orchard, Charles E. Fraser, and Lansdowne Public Schools; SC 484 IB2 Box 1 Folder 6 'Briefs and Reports 1962–1970' St Christopher House to the Select Committee on Youth. October 1964; Box 2 folder 4 Minutes 1962; Folder 6 'Briefs and Reports 1962–1970' Draft Presentation of the St Christopher House to the Select Committee on Youth. October 1964 (description of School Lunch Committee, Child and Family Section, Social Planning Council of Metropolitan Toronto, May 1964; Box 2 Folder 5 Minutes 1963, 24 January 1963; Report filed by Family Life worker Miss

Spadafore regarding Visiting Homemakers Nutritionist.

3. The oral testimonies were selected from a larger database of more than 100 interviews with post-1945 immigrants culled from the Oral History Collection, Multicultural History Society of Ontario. My sample here is of 28 interviews, most of them conducted in the 1970s, with immigrant women and couples asked about food customs, with the following breakdown: European (18), including European Jewry (4), Asian (2), Caribbean (1), and South Asian (India) (3). I also drew on a few anecdotes collected from numerous colleagues and members of audiences who have heard me speak about this research. I thank them for sharing their stories with me.

References

Adams, Mary Louise, *The Trouble With Normal: Postwar Youth and the Making of Heterosexuality*. Toronto: University of Toronto Press, 1997.

Belmonte, Laura A. 'Mr and Mrs America: Images of Gender and the Family in Cold War Propaganda', Paper presented at Berkshire Conference on the History of Women, Chapel Hill, North Carolina, June 1996.

Brienes, Wini. *Young, White, and Miserable: Growing Up Female in the Fifties*. Boston: Beacon, 1992.

Comacchio, Cynthia. *Nations Are Built of Babies*. Montreal: McGill-Queen's University Press, 1993.

Gabaccia, Donna. *We Are What We Eat: Ethnic Food and the Making of Americans*. Cambridge: Harvard University Press, 1998.

Gleason, Mona. *Normalizing the Ideal: Psychology, the School and the Family in Postwar Canada*. Toronto: University of Toronto Press, 1999.

Iacovetta, Franca. 'Gossip, Contest and Power in the Making of Suburban Bad Girls, Toronto 1956–60'. *Canadian Historical Review* 80.4 (Dec 1999).

———. 'Making Model Citizens: Gender, Corrupted Democracy, and Immigrant Reception World in Cold War Canada'. *Whose National Security? Canadian State Surveillance and the Creation of Enemies*. Eds Gary Kinsman, Dieter K. Buse, and Mercedes Steedman. Toronto: 2000.

——— and Tania Das Gupta, eds, 'Whose Canada Is It?' *Atlantis* 24.2 (Spring 2000).

Kingston, Anne. *The Edible Man: Dave Nichol, President's Choice and the Making of Popular Taste*. Toronto: McFarlane, Walter, & Ross, 1994.

Kinsman, Gary. *The Regulation of Desire: Homo and Hetero Sexualities*. Montreal: Black Rose Books, 1987. Revised edition 1996.

———, Patrizia Gentile, et al. '"In the Interests of the State": The Anti-gay, Anti-lesbian National Security Campaign in Canada'. A Preliminary Research Report. Laurentian University, April 1998.

Korinek, Valerie. *Roughing It in the Suburbs: Reading Chatelaine in the Fifties and Sixties*. Toronto: University of Toronto Press, 2000.

Levenstein, Harvey. *Revolution at the Table: The Transformation of the American Diet*. New York: Oxford University Press, 1988.

———. *Paradox of Plenty: A Social History of Eating in Modern America*. New York: Oxford University Press, 1993.

May, Elaine Tyler. 'Gender, Sexuality, and Cold War. For the U.S.' *Homeward Bound: American Families in the Cold War Era*. New York: Basic Books, 1988.

Meyerowitz, Joanne. 'Beyond the Feminine Mystique: A Reassessment of Postwar Mass Culture, 1946–58'. *Journal of American History* 79 (March 1993).

———, ed. *Not June Cleaver: Women and Gender in Postwar America, 1945–1960*. Philadelphia: Temple University Press 1994.

Parr, Joy, ed. *A Diversity of Women: Ontario, 1945–1980*. Toronto: University of Toronto Press, 1995.

Smith, Geoffrey S. 'National Security and Personal Isolation. Sex, Gender, and Disease in the Cold-War United States'. *The International History Review* 54.2 (May 1992).

Toronto Nutrition Committee, *Food Customs of New Canadians*, 2nd ed. Archives of Ontario, International Institute of Metropolitan Toronto Collection, MU6410, File: Cookbook Project, Booklet. Published with funds from Ontario Dietic Association. 1959, 1967.

Valverde, Mariana. *The Age of Light, Soap and Water: Moral Reform in English Canada, 1885–1925*. Toronto: McClelland & Stewart, 1991.

Visser, Margaret. *Much Depends on Dinner: The Extraordinary History and Mythology, Allure and Obsessions, Perils and Taboos, of An Ordinary Meal*. Toronto: McClelland & Stewart, 1986.

Whitaker, Reginald and Gary Marcuse. *Cold War Canada: The Making of a National Insecurity State: 1945–1957*. Toronto: University of Toronto Press, 1994.

The Heterosexualization of the Ontario Woman Teacher in the Postwar Period

Sheila L. Cavanagh

EDITORS' INTRODUCTION

The history of education in Canada has, for decades, provided feminist historians with unique opportunities to explore public and private aspects of women's pasts. Early work on women and girls as students, teachers, and administrators concentrated primarily on attitudes towards 'women's place' vis-à-vis formal education on the part of educational leaders, primarily white, middle-class men. The role of institutionalized education in shoring up patriarchal values, particularly in the nineteenth century, was not difficult to establish. As Paul Axelrod notes, 'careers were highly unusual for female graduates, but their education was considered useful in the promulgation of middle-class virtues such as civility, sociability, and service to the church.'[1] Schooling—whether it took place in the parlour, the one-room schoolhouse, the religious academy, or the urban public school—prepared girls and boys for their supposedly divergent, yet complementary, futures as devoted wives and mothers or righteous, hardworking men. The inculcation of acceptable gender roles (and, as scholars would subsequently explore, racialized and classed identities) was positioned as the bedrock of formal education in the Canadian context.[2]

Despite the fact that formal education reified and hierarchized gendered, classed, and racialized differences between, and among, women and men, scholars also point out that many educated women also used their schooling to their own benefit. Girls and women were hardly simple 'dupes' of a rigid, patriarchal system.[3] Fighting initially merely to be allowed access to higher education in the late nineteenth and early twentieth centuries, for example, women as students, faculty, and staff came to demand equality in all aspects of university life.[4] Similarly, while the advent of compulsory schooling increased the dissemination of patriarchal, white, middle-class values, it also afforded women the opportunity to engage in work for pay as classroom teachers. The teaching life—the 'professional' aspect of teaching would be developed later in the twentieth century—appealed to young unmarried women who sought to expand their horizons beyond their front yard, and to older more seasoned women who intended to stay in their teaching position for the long duration. Many female teachers pursued this occupation with no formal training and only the minimum of academic qualifications. These 'ungraded' teachers would spur many educational jurisdictions around the country to push teaching toward more formalized and stringent qualification procedures.[5]

The history of the teaching profession in Canada has been thoroughly saturated in gender politics. The commonly held misconception that women dominated teaching is far from accurate. Once the reserve of young men in the late nineteenth-century looking for temporary work until something better paying and more stable came along, teaching became 'femininized' over the course of the twentieth century as young unmarried women took up positions vacated by their male peers.[6] Despite the low wages and often appalling working conditions, particularly in isolated rural communities around the country, the profession of teaching still offered women a degree of independence and self-sufficiency that few avenues allowed.[7] The fact of teaching as a profession for women has, not surprisingly, cultivated a rich historical literature produced by feminist historians of women and education, such as Alison Prentice, Susan Houston, Rebecca Coulter, Ruby Heap, Elizabeth Smyth, and Sharon Anne Cook.[8] The gendered dimensions of teaching have been an on-going theme in this work and continues to spawn increasingly sophisticated studies from scholars interested in the lived experiences of women teachers. Kristina Llewellyn has recently offered feminist readings of women teachers' experiences in postwar Toronto high schools, a context in which the ramped up rhetoric of democratic citizenship sat uneasily with the continuing prevalence of women's subordinate position in Canadian society.[9] In a new collection exploring the history of women teachers Rebecca Coulter and Helen Harper present findings from oral histories of women regarding their union experiences and the 'pleasures of their profession'. Coulter's work reminds us that many women who taught found a niche for themselves that was not only professionally rewarding, but provided a haven from constricting gender norms.[10]

It is in the context of a deepening subfield on the history of women teachers that the following essay by Sheila L. Cavanagh takes its place. Here Cavanagh revisits and re-visions the fact that married women in Ontario, initially barred from teaching in 1925, were allowed, and indeed encouraged, to remain in the profession by 1946, the year the marriage bar for teachers ended in Canada. Cavanagh asks us to think differently about what the lifting of the marriage bar meant for women teachers in the context of postwar Ontario. She suggests that while the lifting of the bar may indeed be seen as a triumph for working women who married but who wanted to remain in paid jobs, it put those women who sought a life outside the heterosexual ideal in a precarious position. Much of the research on the marriage bar, Cavanagh argues, fails to consider this dimension of sexual regulation evidenced by the lifting of the marriage bar: the spectre of female homosexuality represented by the 'spinister teacher'.

Placing the bar in the context of heightened postwar anxieties over homosexuality, fuelled by psychological theories linking it with abnormality, neurosis, and 'emotional maladjustment', Cavanagh succinctly explores the 'double-meanings' present in the public discussions about the 'natural suitability' of married women to the task of teaching whilst bemoaning and demonizing the single woman as abnormal. Importantly, Cavanagh explores why single women went from being the preferred candidate for teaching to objects of derision and scorn by the end of the war. Her essay, like that of Elise Chenier's in this volume, reminds us that sexuality is a powerful category of critical analysis with the ability to trouble conventional and comfortable assumptions about women's 'sameness'.

Notes

1. Paul Axelrod, *The Promise of Schooling: Education in Canada, 1800–1914* (Toronto: University of Toronto Press 1997), 16.
2. See, for example, Marion V. Royce, 'Arguments over the Education of Girls: Their Admission to Grammar Schools in this Province', *Ontario History* 47 (March 1975): 1–13; Alison Prentice, 'Towards a Feminist History of Women and Education', in *Monograms in Education*, D.C. Jones, ed. (Winnipeg: University of Manitoba Press, 1981); Jane S. Gaskell and Arlene Tigar McLaren, *Women and Education: A Canadian Perspective* (Calgary: Detselig Enterprises, 1987); Ian Davey, 'Capitalism, Patriarchy and the Origins of Mass Schooling', *History of Education Review* 16.2 (1987): 135–46; Jean Barman, 'Knowledge is Essential for Universal Progress but Fatal to Class Privilege: Working People and the Schools in Vancouver during the 1920s', *Labour/Le Travail* 22 (Fall, 1988): 9–66; David Chuenyan Lai, 'The

Issue of Discrimination in Education in Victoria, 1901–1923', *Canadian Ethnic Studies/Etudes Ethniques au Canada* 19.3 (1987): 47–67; Celia Haig-Brown, *Resistance and Renewal: Surviving the Indian Residential School* (Vancouver: Tillicum Library, 1988).

3. As Marta Danylewycz explored in her groundbreaking book, *Taking the Veil: An Alternative to Marriage, Motherhood, and Spinsterhood in Quebec, 1840–1920* (Toronto: McClelland and Stewart, 1987) in the ultra-conservative context of mid-nineteenth century Quebec, becoming an educated nun allowed some women to 'opt out' of the reproductive heteronormative marriage system that dominated the province and the country. See also Rebecca Priegert Coulter, 'Between School and Marriage: A Case Study Approach to Young Women's Work in Early Twentieth-Century Canada', *History of Education Review* 18.2 (1989): 21–31; Terry Crowley, 'Adelaide Hoodless: Women's Education and Guelph', *Historic Guelph* 25 (1985–6): 26–49; Lee Stewart, *'It's Up to You!': Women at the University of British Columbia in the Early Years* (Vancouver: UBC Press, 1990).
4. See, for example, Anne Rochon Ford, *A Path Not Strewn With Roses: A Hundred Years of Women at the University of Toronto, 1884–1984* (Toronto: University of Toronto Press, 1985), Margaret Gillett, *We Walked Very Warily: A History of Women at McGill* (Montreal: Eden Press Women's Publications, 1981); Margaret Gillett and Anne Beers, eds., *Our Own Agendas: Autobiographical Essays Written by Women Associated with McGill University* (Montreal and Buffalo: McGill-Queen's University Press, 1995); Margaret Gillett, 'The Four Phrases of Academe: Women and the University', in *The Illusion of Inclusion: Women in Post-Secondary Education*, Jacqueline Stalker and Susan Prentice, eds. (Halifax: Fernwood Press, 1998), 36–47; Sara Z. Burke, 'New Women and Old Romans: Co-education at the University of Toronto, 1884–1895', *Canadian Historical Review* 80.2 (June 1999): 219–41.
5. Such was the case for some of the four Grandy sisters who taught in Newfoundland in the 1920s and 1930s as 'ungraded' teachers. Kay Whitehead and Judith Peppard, 'Placing the Grandy Sisters as Teachers in Pre-Confederation Newfoundland', *Historical Studies in Education/Revue d'histoire de l'éducation* 17.1 (2005): 81–105.
6. John Calam, 'Becoming a Teacher: Some Historical Perspectives', *The Alberta Journal of Educational Research* 27.3 (September 1981): 272–84; Cecilia Reynolds, 'Hegemony and Hierarchy: Becoming a Teacher in Toronto, 1930–1980', *Historical Studies in Education/Revue d'histoire de l'éducation* 2: 1 (Spring 1990): 95–118; Marta Danylewycz and Alison Prentice, 'Teachers, Gender, and Bureaucratizing School Systems in Nineteenth Century Montreal and Toronto', *History of Education Quarterly* 24 (Spring 1984): 75–100.
7. See, for example, the tragic story of young Vancouver Island teacher, Mabel Jones, who committed suicide in 1928. Alastair Glegg, 'Anatomy of a Tragedy: The Assisted Schools of British Columbia and the Death of Mabel Jones', *Historical Studies in Education/Revue d'histoire de l'éducation* 17.1 (2005): 145–64.
8. This is only a partial list of contributors to the field. Important works include: Alison Prentice and Marjorie R. Theobald, eds., *Women Who Taught: Perspectives on the History of Women and Teaching* (Toronto: University of Toronto Press, 1991); Alison Prentice and Ruby Heap, eds., *Gender and Education in Ontario* (Toronto: Canadian Scholars' Press, 1991); Susan Houston and Alison Prentice, *Schooling and Scholars in Nineteenth Century Ontario* (Toronto: University of Toronto Press, 1988); Rebecca Priegert Coulter and Ivor F. Goodson, *Rethinking Vocationalism: whose work/life is it?* (Toronto: Our Schools/Our Selves Education Foundation, 1993); Elizabeth Smyth, *Challenging Professions: Historical and Contemporary Perspectives on Women's Professional Work* (Toronto, University of Toronto Press, 1999); Sharon Anne Cook, *'Through Sunshine and Shadow': The Women's Christian Temperance Union, Evangelicalism, and Reform in Ontario, 1874–1930* (Montreal: McGill-Queen's University Press, 1995).
9. Kristina Llewellyn, 'Gendered Democracy: Women Teachers in Postwar Toronto', *Historical Studies in Education/Revue d'histoire de l'éducation* 17.2 (Fall 2005). See also Kristina Llewellyn, 'When Oral Historians Listen to Women Teachers: Using Feminists' Findings', *The Oral History Forum* 23 (December 2003): 89–112.
10. Rebecca Priegert Coulter and Helen Harper, eds. *History is Hers: Women Teachers and Their Worlds* (Calgary: Detselig Enterprises, 2005).

Questions for Critical Reading

1. Why has teaching been an attractive profession for women in the past? Is this still the case today? Are social attitudes towards gender roles a factor in its popularity? Why or why not?

2. What kinds of stereotypes and assumptions about women teachers continue to be propagated in popular film and media? Why?
3. What role did psychology's interest in 'normalcy' and 'maladjustment' after the war play in shifting attitudes towards unmarried and married female teachers?

> Once upon a time, seven or eight years ago, in a respectable boarding-house, there dwelt a beautiful, unhappy maiden, named Minerva Wellington. Many of the fairies had attended her christening, and some of them had given her quite nice gifts—beauty, long life, and things like that. But one malicious old fairy had spat out before anyone could silence her, 'Let her be clever', and no one had thought to add, 'Let her have the wit to conceal it.'
>
> . . . and so Minerva grew up, beautiful but intelligent. Naturally, few wished to marry her, and as she was too intelligent to marry those who did, she had been forced to earn her bread and become a teacher. (Miller, 1932: 32)

This passage comes from a story printed in 1932 by the *Educational Courier*, a joint publication of the Federation of Women Teachers' Associations of Ontario (FWTAO) and the Ontario Public School Men's Teachers' Federations. The story of Minerva Wellington is of particular interest with regard to the changing production of the woman teacher in the first half of the twentieth century. It is important to note that a formal 'marriage bar' was put into place in early-twentieth century Canada and the United States. In many Canadian school districts the ban was not lifted until the early 1960s when attitudes toward women, work, and motherhood began to shift. The bar worked to prohibit a married woman from attaining or retaining a teaching post in a large number of Ontario schools. It was most rigorously enforced during the interwar period (Peters, 1934). In the 40-year span between 1931 and 1971, however, there was a significant demographic shift in the marital status of women teachers.[1] Prior to 1931 married women had difficulty attaining or retaining a teaching post in Ontario schools. By 1971, the majority of women employed in these schools were married.

Feminist historians of women's work have drawn attention to the marriage bar in the teaching profession (see Reynolds, 1983; Gaskell, 1989). Most explain the bar in terms of the economic climate of the interwar period and in terms of postwar feminism. Married woman teachers were understood to be a 'reserve army of labour' (Oram, 1983: 134–48), expendable during periods of teacher surplus and a valuable resource during periods of teacher shortage. Feminist historians tend to regard the eradication of the marriage bar as a progressive step toward the equal employment of men and woman in the public sphere and a tribute to the success of liberal feminism. While I do not wish to suggest that the eradication of the marriage bar is *not* a necessary step forward, I want to raise questions about the meaning of the marriage bar to women who wished to live independent of men. I situate the lines of argument taken against the bar in relation to the social climate leading up to the postwar period.

To date, feminist historians have rarely placed the change in attitude toward the married woman teacher in the context of increasing concern about female homosexuality in the postwar period.[2] Teaching and the accompanying marriage bar afforded white, middle-class, educated, Canadian women a socially acceptable means to opt out of heterosexual family structures, up until the late 1930s and early 1940s. If a woman was unmarried, she was assumed to be celibate. Canadian historians, Rooke and Schnell (1987), argue that

> celibacy provided women with personal power in their own lives, opened choice and opportunities for mobility otherwise denied them, and fuelled ambitions which would have been constrained by marriage. (190)

'Celibacy' is, in some sense, a dubious term. It refers both to women who opt out of sexual relationships altogether, *and* to women who opt out of sexual relationships only with men. The latter option, of course, does not preclude the possibility of sex with other women. So, in speaking about celibate women, we are, also, speaking about women who may be defined, by contemporary standards, as lesbian.[3]

During the Second World War, professional women often lived together in what was called a 'Boston marriage'. As Lillian Faderman suggests, some of these relationships were sexual while others were not (1991: 15). The important point being that, prior to the postwar period, it was possible for economically independent women to opt out of heterosexual and marital relationships with men. Following the Second World War, however, there was a concerted effort on the part of government officials to impose 'traditional' family values upon unmarried women employed in semi-professional occupations. With this return to heterosexual and nuclear family values came what scholars of lesbian history identify as a concerted attempt to denigrate and punish women who refuse to organize their private lives and sexuality around a man (see Faderman, 1991; Kennedy and Davis, 1994).

In this article, I argue that the eradication of the marriage bar and the subsequent esteem and regard for the married woman teacher, together, can be read as an example of a postwar moral panic about female homosexuality. Thus, the married woman teacher became a preferable candidate to her single counterpart on moral grounds. The latter came to be understood as 'emotionally maladjusted', sexually inverted, celibate and/or queer.

Like the fictional character of Minerva Wellington, the woman teacher of the 1920s and 1930s was expected to board in approved lodgings and to remain single. Until the late 1930s, the FWTAO regarded the *single* woman teacher with a high degree of esteem while the married woman teacher was a subject of ridicule and contempt. The Federation executive held the official position that married women should not retain teaching posts. In fact, the 'Federation urged boards to give preference to the unmarried woman except in cases where the married teacher [was] the sole support of the family' (Graham, 1974: 196). Elizabeth Graham, historian of women teachers, explains that only during wartime and periods of teacher shortage did the Federation support the entry of married women into the teaching force. She argues that the will to eradicate the marriage bar

> did not originate with the organization which had set itself up ostensibly to protect the welfare of its members; the eventual support of married women teachers by the FWTAO came only as a response to pressure by its membership. (196)

Doris French, author of *High Button Bootstraps* (1968), a formal history of the FWTAO, also acknowledges the Federation's reluctance to support the needs of married women in the Ontario public school system. She explains that

> while protesting discrimination against themselves, the FWTAO has not always been above reproach. It is not to their credit that they accepted married women reluctantly, sharing the view of most boards that teaching and marriage don't mix. (133)

According to French, the Federation did not take an active stand against the dismissal of married women teachers until the late 1950s. Mary Labatt, author of *Always a Journey*, a fairly recent formal history of the FWTAO, does not comment on the Federation's position on the marriage bar but concludes that 'married women lived a separate existence and since the focus of FWTAO was women who were teaching, married women were generally not part of it' (1993: 31).

As Lillian Faderman notes,

> education may be said to have been responsible for the spread among middle-class women of what eventually came to be called lesbianism . . . and [as a result women could now] create all-female societies around those professions, (13)

for which education was a prerequisite. It was highly unlikely that members of the Federation executive (who were predominantly unmarried) would easily abandon their commitment to the single woman teacher and the 'marriage bar' that secured their special place in the teaching profession.[4]

Because the marriage bar was only selectively enforced by district school boards, women did, at times, attain and retain employment in Ontario schools upon marriage. In the late 1930s and early 1940s, French says that

> there were 12,000 women teachers in the public schools, of Ontario, but not quite half of them had joined their Federation. [One reason for this was the] continual flow into and out of the rural schools of marriage-minded girls who had enjoyed only a slight brush with professional pedagogy. (105)

The 'marriage-minded girl' was assumed to accept a low salary and was often accused of underbidding—a practice that would deter the implementation of fixed salary schedules and professional practices. She was not concerned with working conditions and pay schedules because she was a 'temporary' worker.

The temporary status of women teachers appears to have been a long-standing concern, not only with executive members of the Federation, but with ratepayers and school board officials. For example, in 1894 the *Port Arthur Herald*, a regional Ontario newspaper, printed the following report:

> One of the Rainy River school boards passed a resolution asking the Ontario government to pass an act to forbid the granting of a marriage licence to a school 'marm' while under contract to teach. They did this because of not being able to keep any schoolmarm for six months—they all got married before. (4)

It was not only members of Ontario school boards, but Federation officials who concerned themselves with the private lives of women teachers. It is interesting to note that at this historical juncture concern with the private lives of women teachers was not about homosexuality, but with *heterosexuality* and its marital trappings. The predominant concern was with the woman identified to be of the 'marrying mind'. Not committed to her profession for life, she was designated temporary, transient, uninterested in improved working conditions. As French explains she is likely to 'forget the harrowing experiences of the classroom and the county school' (31) once she enters marriage.

It was not until the 1950s that the Federation executive began to change its position in regard to the married woman teacher. This change in perspective, however, came only after it became apparent than an overwhelming number of women employed in Ontario's schools, already, were married. The shift can be understood in relation to what scholars of lesbian history have identified as a period of heightened intolerance toward independent women living outside of heterosexual and marital relationships with men (Faderman, 1991).

Persons demanding access to higher education for women and access to paid work in the public sphere in the late 1940s and through to the 1950s were, also, responding to what they correctly identified to be new opportunities for women to opt out of heterosexual and marital relationships with men.

> Since it was generally agreed that marriage and career were incompatible for a woman, those who found marriage distasteful and preferred to live with another female realized that they would be granted a social license to arrange their lives as they pleased if they pursued an education and a profession. (Faderman, 1991: 17)

It is within this social climate, leading up to the postwar period, that persons protesting the entry of women into the public sphere began to position the single woman teacher as emotionally maladjusted and deviant. The single woman teacher came to be endemic of a greater moral panic about female homosexuality. I argue that this concern about female homosexuality exerted an unparalleled impact upon the debate about the marriage bar and the subsequent production of the single woman teacher as spinster. The single woman teacher came to be defined not in terms of Minerva Wellington; saintly and angelic, but as sexually inverted, deviant, and queer.

The first article, published in the *Educational Courier*, written in support of the married woman, was published in 1949. The article begins with the following warning: 'Violation of a teacher's right to a life of her own frightens young women away from teaching' (Ellison, 1949: 13). This concern about frightening young women away from the profession of teaching comes with an insistence that the married woman teacher is better equipped to work with young children 'than those [single women] who do not have so normal an emotional life' (14).

Not only is the married woman teacher now positioned as better equipped and more emotionally stable than her single counterpart, but she is thought to be of superior human stock. The legislation prohibiting married woman from attaining and retaining employment as teachers is, now, thought to be responsible for the 'decline' in the quality of teachers populating North American schools. In the *Education Digest* it is suggested that the requirement of celibacy 'excludes from marriage and motherhood many of the country's most superior young women' (Popenoe, n.d.: 4). It is also argued that 'if a woman is not inferior, she should be a wife and mother. If she is inferior, she should not be teaching' (Popenoe, n.d.: 5).

The side of the debate in support of the eradication of the marriage bar was fought, in part, along the lines of eugenics. A good example of this debate can be traced to the report prepared by the National Education Association of the United States, entitled 'status of the Married Woman Teacher'. The report quotes a number of passages from several prominent American journals of education to be discussed below. The first reference utilized in the report, to be discussed here, is from the *Education Digest*, which makes claims about heterosexual superiority.

> Just as the married are, on the whole, biologically superior to the unmarried (as shown by a long series of statistics on such things as health, longevity, keeping out of jail, and freedom from mental disease) so are the fertile superior to the sterile. It is desirable not merely that teachers should marry, but also that they should have children. (Popenoe, n.d.: 5)

This statement is consistent with the pronatalism leading up to and following the postwar period. The pronatalist movement touches on the problem of homosexuality because it is understood to be detrimental to the reproduction of the population. Further to this, young, eligible, white women who refuse marriage were thought to be in danger of negating their role as mothers.

In the American context, concern about the 'emotional adjustment' of the single woman teacher became a matter of public debate in the 1930s. Pieces of this debate can be found in a number of American education journals, which are also cited in the above-mentioned report. Consider the following quotation taken from the California Journal of Secondary Education:

> And we must further bear in mind that many women consider school teaching a calling worth sacrificing for. They take many years and spend tens of thousands of dollars educating themselves for the teaching profession, and we now force them in most cases either to abandon this chosen career or to live an emotionally poverty-stricken life, admittedly unnatural and injurious

to them and to the profession. (Schwankovsky, 1937: 167)

In the same article, it is suggested that the woman teacher who remains celibate is, in some sense, not fully adult. It is argued that the single woman teacher needs assistance in becoming fully adult.

> Even the tyro in modern science and physiology and psychology knows that men and women do not mature properly as a rule if they do not live the normal adult life, involving marriage and parenthood. . . . Is there not as much education applicable to school teaching—in becoming a parent as there is in a one term course in the growth and development of the child, taught by a celibate and childless woman instructor? (Schwankovsky, 1937: 167)

Another dimension of the debate touches upon questions about the dangers of single women educating young, impressionable children. Consider the following statement taken from the *Clearing House*, again utilized in the report on the status of the married woman teacher:

> The removal of marriage restrictions will protect the pupils of America's public schools from the effects of daily contact with the enervating negativism of abnormality. Many have wondered at the increasing neuroticism of America, and the steadily mounting toll of mental illness. Undoubtedly many factors contribute to that state of affairs, but the influence of a system of secularized nunneries is unmistakable. (McColley, n.d.: 195–200)

It is assumed that the 'celibate' or sexually deviant women teacher can, in fact, induce a similar state of being upon her students. What is of added interest is the conflation of celibacy with sexually deviant behaviour. While it was increasingly apparent that single women teachers thought to be 'celibate' may have engaged in sexual relations with a member of the same sex, it is important to note that a shift in public sentiment has occurred. Historian Jackie Blount points out that

> the public recognition that some spinster teachers may have experienced same-sex sexual desire and relationships transformed older visions of single women educators as virtuous, selfless, asexual pillars of morality into those of sexual and mannish deviants. (1996: 325)

In the postwar period, the *Educational Courier* began to print articles depicting the married woman as a 'natural' teacher with a predisposition to love and care for children. A good example of this trend can be found in an article entitled 'The Married Woman Career Teacher is Here to Stay', printed in 1963. The author says that married women teach for the 'love of children and a desire to help them, force of habit, or [because] they just couldn't be happy without teaching' (14). It is also suggested that married women teachers 'come from happy, well-run homes and are teaching to enrich their own lives, the lives of others, and to raise their family's standard of living'. The married woman attains employment as teacher not 'to enhance selfish desires or [to] escape an unpleasant situation'. Instead, married women express 'a desire to improve conditions for others, not themselves' (Dwyer, 1963: 14). It is concluded that teaching is truly a labour of love and who better to provide this love than the married woman?

The article shields the married woman teacher from postwar anxieties about working women. She is positioned as a loving mother. Her work is an extension of the mother role and consistent with nuclear family and heterosexual values. It is the single woman who is left to fight her own battles against postwar advocates of nuclear family values and pronatalism. Her sexuality is rendered deviant, strange, aberrant. The eradication of the official marriage bar in 1946 is, as I have argued, not so much about the emancipation of the working woman, but about a concerted attack on the single woman teacher characterized as spinster. The story of the Ontario woman teacher—from the fairy tale of Minerva Wellington to the married woman teacher depicted as loving mother, is, about the heterosexualization of the woman teacher.

Notes

The author would like to thank Patti Phillips who read a much earlier draft of this paper and offered valuable feedback, and Susanne Luhmann for especially thoughtful criticism with respect to the heterosexualization of the woman teacher.

1. See Reynolds or Francis for a brief discussion of how white, middle-class, professional women (teachers included) in the United States were predominantly 'single' in the 30-year period between 1900–30.
2. The one exception of which I am aware is an article published by Julie Blount; see also Kennedy and Davis for a discussion of a growing intolerance of lesbian sexuality in the postwar period.
3. It is important to note that the term 'lesbian' is a product of twentieth-century studies of female sexuality conducted by sexologists and was, therefore, not a term used prior to this period.
4. It is important to note that up until the late 1940s and early 1950s the Federation executive was, for the most part, composed of single (and not married) women.

References

Blount, Julie. 'Manly Men and Womanly Women: Deviance, Gender Role Polarization, and the Shift in Women's School Employment, 1900–1976', *Harvard Educational Review* 66.2 (1996): 318–37.

Dwyer, Kay. 'The Married Woman Career Teacher is Here to Stay', *Educational Courier* 24.2 (November–December 1963): 13–15.

Ellison, Lucille. 'When a Teacher Weds: Are Marriage and Teaching Incompatible?', *Kansas Teacher* (1937), Rpt. in *Educational Courier* (June 1949): 13.

Faderman, Lillian. 1991. *Odd Girls and Twilight Lovers: A History of Lesbian Life in Twentieth-Century America.* New York: Penguin.

Francis, M. '"For This Girl Was My Grand Passion . . .": Re-interpreting the First Large Scale Survey of Women's Sexuality in America (1929)', *Canadian Woman Studies/Les cahiers de la femme* 16.2 (1996): 36–41.

French, D. 1968. *High Button Bootstraps.* Toronto: Federation of Women Teachers' Associations of Ontario.

Gaskell, S. 1989. 'The Problems and Professionalism of Women Elementary Public School Teachers in Ontario, 1944–1954', PhD diss. Ontario Institute for Studies in Education: University of Toronto.

Graham, E. 1974. 'Schoolmarms and Early Teaching in Ontario', pp. 165–209 in *Women at Work, Ontario, 1850–1930*, Janice Acton et al., eds. Toronto: Canadian Women's Educational Press.

Kennedy, Elizabeth Lapovsky, and Madeleine D. Davis. 1994. *Boots of Leather, Slippers of Gold: The History of a Lesbian Community.* New York: Penguin Books.

Labatt, Mary. 1993. *Always a Journey: A History of the Federation of Women Teachers' Association of Ontario, 1918–1993.* Toronto: FWTAO.

McColley, Walter S. 'The Vestal Virgins of Education' *Clearing House* 11: 195–200.

Miller, Sadie G. 'Little Fairy Stories for Adults', *Educational Courier* 2.4 (April 1932): 32.

National Education Association of the United States. 1938. *Status of the Married Woman Teacher.* Washington.

Oram, Alison M. 1983. 'The Introduction of a Marriage Bar in Teaching in the 1920s', pp. 134–48 in *The Sexual Dynamics of History: Men's Power, Women's Resistance*, London Feminist History Group, eds. London: Pluto Press.

Peters, David Wilbur. 1934. *The Status of the Married Woman Teacher.* New York Teachers College: Columbia University Press.

Popenoe, Paul. n.d. 'Better Teachers, Biologically Speaking', *Education Digest* 2.4.

Port Arthur Herald (Port Arthur, ON). 2 March 1894.

Reynolds, Cecilia. 1983. 'Ontario Schoolteachers 1911–1971: A Portrait of Demographic Change', PhD diss. Ontario Institute for Studies in Education: University of Toronto.

Rooke, P.T., and R.L. Schnell. 1987. *No Bleeding Heart: Charlotte Whitton, A Feminist on the Right.* Vancouver: UBC Press.

Schwankovsky, Frederick J. 'Permitting School Teachers To Be Parents', *California Journal of Secondary Education* 12 (March 1937).

Victims of the Times, Heroes of Their Lives: Five Mennonite Refugee Women

Marlene Epp

EDITORS' INTRODUCTION

Marlene Epp's article on Mennonite women who immigrated to Canada after the Second World War demonstrates two types of contributions that women's history makes to the historical record. First, she places the spotlight on a population that is too often invisible: non-English-speaking refugees. This group, like many Canadians, beginning with the United Empire Loyalists in the eighteenth century and continuing to the present with refugees from various conflict zones around the world reminds us of the recurring brutality of non-voluntary migrations and the frequency of sexual harassment and rape.[1] Second, Epp encourages us to reconsider our interpretation of Canadian history in the light of the women she interviewed. Their stories remind us that women experience war and postwar years in many different ways.

Political and economic refugees—these categories are far from hard and fast—have regularly fled to Canada. After the Loyalists came Irish escaping famine, highlanders forced out by the enclosure movement, Blacks on the run from American slavery, Doukhobors in flight from Cossacks, and a few—a very few—Jews escaping fascism. More recently, Vietnamese rejecting Communist reunification and Chileans fleeing military dictatorship have arrived in the country. Newcomers lacking English or French, like the Mennonites Epp discusses, faced special problems in adapting.[2] As feminist scholars and activists are increasingly telling us, the life of refugees, like that of immigrants generally, is highly gendered. Women in flight are only too likely to encounter violence, ranging from relatively minor acts of harassment to gang rape and death. Their particular vulnerability was acknowledged in 1993 when Canada's Immigrant and Refugee Board led the world in recognizing gender persecution as one basis for claims of refugee status.[3] Nor do refugees always find safe haven. The title of one study, *Isolated, Afraid and Forgotten*, sums up a continuing pattern of domestic abuse.[4] As Patrick J. Connor reminds us elsewhere in this volume, women deal with sexual violence in a variety of ways. Here Katie, Justina, Lena, Gertrude, and Anna resisted and compromised in the course of their desperate efforts to guarantee survival for themselves and those they loved. Scars, whether left by stranger rapists or battering husbands, cannot be forgotten by survivors. Yet in deference to the feelings, and sometimes the condemnation, of others, women have often had to edit and hide personal histories of violence and pain.

As Epp's account suggests, the history of Canada can often be better understood in the context of developments elsewhere in the world. The 'Dirty Thirties' offered more than their share of bitter experiences to Canadian residents, but the desperate lot of other peoples, whether in Ukraine, Ethiopia, Spain, or China, facing civil wars and totalitarian regimes, was regularly brought to the attention of Canadians. International networks like the Mennonite Central Committee kept many citizens in touch with the sorrows of co-religionists and ethnic compatriots. During wartime, the lines between friends and foes were ultimately shifting and uncertain. Canadians would not only fight German and Italian enemies, they would sometimes marry them, or Allied nationals, and the newcomers would join an evolving multicultural community in the Dominion. When we consider the meaning of the Second World War, we need to look beyond the experiences of Canadian servicemen and servicewomen to include those, too, of foreign and enemy military personnel and civilians. In Canada, former enemies—as would be seen later on with the Albanian, Serb, and Muslim refugees from the Balkans in the 1990s—would have to find ways to share a new common homeland.

The presence of newcomers such as the Mennonites described here prompts us to question commonplace images of the 1950s with their stress on complacency and homogeneity.[5] Even the suburbs, the heart of the imagined good life, were complicated by a diversity of representation and opportunity. Migrants such as Katie and the others who turned up in the prairie west without much English, and as members of suspect minorities, found the transition worsened by discrimination and prejudice. In their various encounters with a new world, described in greater detail by Epp in *Women without Men: Mennonite Refugees of the Second World War* (2000), these women helped change the face of Canada. Like the Italians studied by Franca Iacovetta,[6] they affirmed the nation's connection to the broader world as they cobbled together lives in their new land.

Notes

1. See Janice Potter-McKinnon, *While the Women Only Wept: Loyalist Refugee Women in Eastern Ontario* (Montreal and Kingston: McGill-Queen's University Press, 1993); Vesna Nikolic-Ristanovic, 'Victimization by War Rape: The International Criminal Tribunal for the Former Yugoslavia', *Canadian Woman Studies/Les cahiers de la femme* 119.4 (1999–2000): 28–35.
2. See Jo-Anne Lee, '"Living in Dreams": Oral Narratives of Three Recent Immigrant Women', in *'Other' Voices: Historical Essays on Saskatchewan Women*, ed. David De Brou and Aileen Moffatt (Regina: Canadian Plains Research Center, 1995), 148–9, for her discussion of the language barrier.
3. See, inter alia, *Gender Analysis of Immigration and Refugee Protection Legislation and Policy* (Ottawa: Citizenship and Immigration Canada, 1999); and Wenona M. Giles, Penny Van Esterik, and Helene Mossa, *Development and Diaspora: Gender and the Refugee Experience* (Dundas, ON: Artemis Publishers, 1996).
4. Linda MacLeod and Maria Shin, *Isolated, Afraid and Forgotten: The Service Delivery Needs and Realities of Immigrant and Refugee Women Who Are Battered* (Ottawa: Public Health Agency of Canada, 1990).
5. See Douglas Owram, *Born at the Right Time: A History of the Baby Boom Generation* (Toronto: University of Toronto Press, 1996).
6. Franca Iacovetta, 'From Contadina to Worker: Southern Italian Immigrant Working Women in Toronto, 1947–1962', in *Looking into My Sister's Eyes: An Exploration in Women's History*, ed. Jean Burnet (Toronto: Multicultural History Society of Canada, 1986), 195–222.

Questions for Critical Reading

1. Compare the impact of the Second World War on the women studied by Epp and those described by Donald Davis and Barbara Lorenzkowski in this volume.
2. View the film *The Vienna Tribunal: Women's Rights Are Human Rights* (National Film Board, 1994) and compare the experiences described by its subjects with those of the Mennonite women in Epp's essay.

3. Compare Epp's subjects with another group of refugees in Canada. Does it make a difference whether they come from Asia, Africa, Latin America, or Europe?

Observers and analysts of contemporary world events, such as social scientists and newsmakers, frequently cite the statistic that 80 per cent of the world's refugees are women and children.[1] Given this fact, anthropologist Doreen Indra has called for the study of gender as central to the refugee experience, pointing out that most research concerning refugees is primarily a 'male paradigm'.[2] Historical writing on immigration to Canada has also, until recently, been dominated by interpretation that has 'assumed (heterosexual) male behaviour and male-dominated public activity to define the immigrant experience'.[3] While research into the female experience of migration is increasing, the stories of refugee women in the Canadian past remain largely unexplored.[4]

Unlike other immigrant women, who may have their eyes turned to future opportunities in their new chosen homeland, refugee women are frequently looking back over their shoulders, reluctantly leaving their homes and, often, family members behind. Since the refugee identity usually arises in a context of war or persecution, these women will have been victims of violence, deprivation, and untold other physical and emotional hardships. While swept along by the merciless forces of history, refugee women nevertheless devise strategies of survival that see them through impossible situations and bring them to new lives and sometimes prosperity in a new land. As one analyst of contemporary displaced women has observed: 'The women refugees who have endured the horrors of war, dislocation, loss of loved ones, hunger, humiliation, and still opted for life and safety of their children are not weak women.'[5]

The five women whose stories are told here are part of a larger narrative recounting the migration to Canada of approximately 8,000 Mennonites in the decade following the Second World War. These five refugee women were victims of social and political events that caused tragedy and loss in their lives. Their families were torn apart, they experienced violence and hunger, and they lost opportunities for education and professional development. However, in a context in which they had limited choices, all of the women developed strategies for survival and accomplishment. Interpreting their lives within frameworks of either victimization or agency does not suffice to explain the complexities of the decisions they made and actions they took within equally complex situations.

As women living within family units that had no adult males, they took on roles that were traditionally allocated to the opposite sex—from driving a team of horses and fixing broken wagon wheels, to negotiating with or bribing border guards and immigration officials, to working for wages to provide for themselves and their children. Although they exhibited a pride of accomplishment in successfully filling male shoes, like the 'gold rush widows' of the American Midwest described by Linda Peavy and Ursula Smith, they interpreted their roles as head of the household as 'something to be endured, not relished'.[6] For Mennonite refugee women, conclusions that ascribe to widowhood either liberating or debilitating outcomes are too simplistic. Women without husbands or fathers had to negotiate through a community terrain, in which roles were strictly stratified by gender, and a personal terrain of independence and self-sufficiency that derived from their experience of being women without men.

The stories of these five 'great dames' is constructed from conversations that I had with each of them in the early 1990s. In gathering their stories for the purposes of a larger research project, I promised anonymity to all the women, and therefore I have chosen pseudonyms in writing this collective biography. Other identifying information has also been changed.[7] The life stories of the women are simultaneously unique and representative. While each of their individual stories as well as their combined story offers insight into the history of other groups of which they were part—such as postwar refugees in Canada or the Soviet Mennonites—and thus they are representative of a wider experience, at the same time each of the women's lives demonstrates singular responses to events and circumstances.

Their stories are both individual life histories and also microcosms of the communal story of which they were part. As Betty Bergland has argued, the 'I' of each woman's oral autobiography reveals the culture and ideology within which she lived at a given time.[8] At times certain events and choices in their lives diverge from the master immigrant narrative, and these incongruities are revealed in patterns ranging from defiance to repression. The lives of the five women have marked similarities in terms of events and chronology, but differ on the basis of personality, choices made, and outcomes. Their life stories are also mediated by their identification with a small, ethno-religious community—the Mennonites—and by their experience of being female in a patriarchal social and religious order.

Lena, Justina, Katie, Gertrude, and Anna were all born in the Mennonite colonies of Chortitza and Molotschna in southern Ukraine in the former Soviet Union. The Mennonites are an ethno-religious group with origins in the sixteenth-century Reformation in Germany, Switzerland, and the Netherlands, who established autonomous settlements near the banks of the Dnieper River in Ukraine beginning in the late eighteenth century. Their distinctive religious beliefs included voluntary adult baptism into the church, pacifism and non-participation in military service, mutual aid as an expression of Christian love, and the exercise of discipline towards members within their communities as a way of maintaining a pure church. Many of their cultural forms have their origins in a Dutch ancestry, yet Mennonites in Russia were identified as ethnic German colonists within the Russian empire. A small minority in a large empire, Mennonites nevertheless carved out a thriving economic and cultural niche for themselves in imperial Russia. Following the Bolshevik revolution in 1917, however, Mennonite institutions and customs began to erode under a political program that was diametrically opposed to the Christian values, German culture, and capitalist economy of the Mennonite 'commonwealth'.[9]

The five women grew up during what was probably the most difficult era of history for Mennonites living in Russia. Revolution, civil war, famine, collectivization, the repression of minorities, and the terror of the Stalin era all were forces that shaped their lives as children and young women. Beginning in the late 1920s and throughout the next decade, Mennonites and others considered subversive by the Soviet state were subject to arrest, imprisonment, and exile to labour camps in the northern and eastern regions of the country. The fate of those who were taken—a minority were released—was often death due to execution, starvation, or exposure; however most families never received any word from members who were taken. The majority of the disappeared were men, so by the end of the 1930s, estimates suggest that about 50 per cent of Mennonite families were without a father.[10] The male population was further depleted during the early years of the war, as the Soviet army evacuated German colonists eastward, and later in the war, as men, young and old, were conscripted into the German army.

Katie, who was born in Ukraine in 1932, correlates the onset of unhappiness in her life with the arrest of her father in 1937. He was falsely accused of poisoning the horses in his care on the collective farm. The night before his arrest, Katie's nine-year-old sister had died of scarlet fever. Her mother, left with Katie and her infant brother, then went out to work in the vineyards of the collective. Katie recalled that after her father left, there was nothing but 'eating, and working, and crying' in her home.

Like Katie and other women whose fathers were taken when they were children, Anna also held her father in high regard, expressing almost reverence for his abilities as a talented engineer and accomplished flautist. He also was taken in 1937, and so

Anna's mother went to work cooking for the tractor operators of the collective in order to support her three young daughters. Anna said: 'How my mother managed I don't know. She sold my father's clothes, she sold his drafting tools, she sold them and she somehow managed to get us a little house.' To supplement wages earned on the collective farm Anna's mother obtained a knitting machine, on which she learned to make stockings, and also constructed house slippers from fabric and glue made of flour and water. Justina, born in 1926, was the middle of three daughters, when both parents were drafted for the Soviet labour army in 1941 and sent to the war front to dig trenches to stall advancing German tanks. Although their family was fortunate in that both parents returned after several months, for that period of time the population of Justina's village was a curious mix of seniors and children.

Lena and Gertrude both became young widows during the same time period. Gertrude's husband was spared during the widespread arrests and disappearances of the 1930s but was deported to the East in 1941 as Germany declared war on the Soviet Union. Gertrude was left with three children under the age of five, her first-born having died in infancy in 1936. Lena, whose husband was the son of a Christian preacher, spent the first years of her married life as a fugitive, moving frequently and occasionally living in hiding in order to avoid arrest and exile. In 1938, when officials came and searched their home, Lena fully expected that her husband would be taken. However, her father was taken instead, while her husband and two brothers remained at home until they were sent east with the village's machinery and livestock in August 1941. Lena was left with the care of two small children, her mother, and her teenaged sister.

The German occupation of the Ukraine brought a sense of stability to the Mennonite colonies for a two-year period (1941–3). Although one historian's assessment that the occupation represented 'years of grace for the Mennonite church in the fullest sense of that word'[11] is probably an exaggerated idealization of what was still a wartime environment, nevertheless under the administration of German authorities, some things did improve from the perspective of Soviet Mennonites. Public religious practice was resumed, German educational institutions were opened, and a move was made towards privatizing agriculture. The positive aspects of German occupation were offset for some Mennonites by knowledge of Nazi atrocities towards Ukrainian Jews. Yet Mennonite memories of Hitler's final solution are strangely mixed and include denial of any such knowledge, as well as recollections of individual Mennonites interceding on behalf of Jewish neighbours as best they could. Nevertheless, amongst German colonists, there were strong hopes that Germany would win the war and that exiled family members might return home.

For Mennonite women, the German occupation presented a variety of new job opportunities, especially as translators and interpreters. Lena became a translator for the German army, housing several German officers at the same time. Anna's mother moved with her three daughters to the city of Dnjepropetrovsk to take advantage of such work, and Anna was able to attend school while her two older sisters worked for occupation authorities. In Justina's case, the German occupation coincided with severe illness that put her in the hospital for several weeks; the Romanian soldiers accommodated in their home had brought with them lice, which resulted in typhus for Justina and many others in her village. For Katie, the German occupation meant a new family formation. Her mother, now a young 'widow'—although her first husband was not officially known to be dead—was courted by a German officer at the agricultural training station where she had obtained work as a cook. Despite condemnation from many of her Mennonite relatives and neighbours, Katie's mother married the officer and had a child with him. The happiness in having a father once again was, for Katie, short-lived, when her stepfather was killed in action towards the end of the war.

The hopes that a German occupation might mean the reunification of families declined along with Germany's diminishing fortune on the war front. When German forces began their westward retreat from Ukraine in the fall of 1943, they took with them approximately 350,000 Soviet Germans, of which about 10 per cent were Mennonites. The 1943 trek from the Ukraine has been mythologized through depictions in film, painting, photography, and numerous autobiographical narratives.[12] The images that arise from these portrayals liken the trek to the biblical exodus of the Israelites. Wagon caravans several miles long, with thousands of people burdened both materially and psychologically, wended their way westward as winter approached. Deep mud and bone-chilling cold are recurring images in the narratives of all five women. After several days of travel, the continuous rain and overburdened wagons made travel treacherous, and most families had to dispose of their heavier belongings, thus leaving sewing machines, butter churns, chests, and even sacks of dried fruit by the roadside. Many deaths occurred along the way, most from illness, but there were also violent deaths after attacks by partisan groups in the Ukrainian countryside. There were also births in and under wagons, often prematurely induced by the hardships of travel. Food was increasingly scarce as the trek progressed, and many families sent their children to beg in nearby villages, or furtively stole leftover produce from farmers' fields. Gertrude's daughter asked at one point why the corpses lying by the roadside were so fat (they were bloated) when she was so hungry. After a westward trek by horse and wagon and train, the refugees were resettled in that part of Poland that was now under German control.

Soviet Mennonites who had remained in Poland or the eastern territories of Germany were faced with another westward flight as the Soviet army advanced rapidly towards Berlin in the winter of 1944–5. Those who were overcome by Soviet forces or remained in the Russian occupied zone at war's end were faced with some of the most tragic and difficult experiences of the war. As persons who were born in the Soviet Union, the Mennonite refugees faced repatriation according to a postwar agreement between the Allied nations. As ethnic Germans, they faced retribution from Soviet soldiers as wartime enemies. What German women feared most was rape by individual or groups of Soviet soldiers. One estimate states that as many as two million women were raped in the aftermath of the war, 12 per cent of whom died as a result.[13]

Many Mennonite women were also raped, although rarely are such experiences spoken of directly or with any detail in autobiographical accounts, oral or written.[14] Katie, at the age of thirteen, escaped rape only because her mother hid her under a pile of coal when their house was taken over by Soviet troops. Both her mother and grandmother were raped, as were two schoolfriends, who both died as a result of infections following the rapes. She recalled that day vividly:

> We were all hiding in the basement. The tanks drove over everything, the orchards, everything. The worst thing was molesting women and girls. My mother hid me under coal and she herself had to suffer. The grandparents had a very big house right beside a freshwater lake. Very beautiful area. How women and girls ran into the lake, drowning themselves. Yes. Bodies were just coming to the shore. I saw all that. It was . . . I could almost think hell.

It was this experience that made Katie's mother resolve to flee to the Allied zone. The family, which at this point included an invalid aunt and an uncle together with Katie, her mother, and two younger brothers, made a dangerous night-time escape across the border. When they were first stopped by a Soviet patrol, they were given leeway to pass if they left Katie with the soldiers. The offer of a watch and a wedding band from Katie's mother assuaged them, while a bribe of several whisky bottles was enough to get them past the next group of soldiers who threatened them. With that they were able to cross a muddy river through the fog to arrive in the American zone. Katie recalled, 'I had my first slice of baloney that night.'

Those who fled ahead of the advancing Soviet army in the winter of 1944–5 found themselves in the midst of total chaos. Attempting to board a westbound train in Poland, Anna was overwhelmed by the hordes of panicked people also trying to find a place. 'There was no way that three of us—my shy mama, my sister Mary who had been quite ill, and I just a schoolgirl—had a chance to get on that train. We must have looked like chickens in the rain.' They were eventually assisted by an unknown soldier who lifted and pushed each one of them through a train window. Having lost their own protector in the form of husband and father, they looked to another man to take that role. Like other German women caught in the war, they displayed a psychological ambiguity between their need to be 'strong, brave and tough' and take on unconventional leadership and management roles, and their need for warmth and security, often epitomized in a 'male saviour figure'.[15]

Justina became separated from her family for two-and-a-half years towards the end of the war. Justina had just returned to school in Poland after saying good-bye to her father, who had been drafted into the German army, when the rapid Soviet advance forced the evacuation of the school. Justina began the flight west with two other schoolgirls and two of their teachers, but the girls were quickly abandoned by their Polish wagon driver and the teachers. The three teenaged girls attempted to continue on through the January cold in hopes of reaching the city of Pozen, where their families lived. Their horses soon collapsed and with sounds of bombing coming ever closer, they simply started to run, leaving all their possessions on the wagon. Justina arrived in Pozen only two hours after her mother and two sisters had also fled, and so, with one of her schoolmates, she caught the last train to leave the city, after which the tracks were to be bombed. The train was severely overcrowded with refugees and soldiers, and the two girls had to hang onto the outside of the train, almost freezing as a result. Ironically, and miraculously, Justina discovered later that her mother had been on the same train.

Upon arriving in Berlin, Justina and her friend Hilda, who was an ethnic German from Volhynia, were placed as labourers on a German farm, where they were treated well and had plenty to eat. When the Soviets came in she recalled that many girls were raped and molested, including the farmer's daughter where she worked as well as another twelve-year-old labourer there, although Justina denies being raped herself. At night, she and the farmer's daughter hid in a concealed closet in the horse barn. During the day, the young girls and women put on kerchiefs and attempted to disguise themselves as boys or old women while working in the fields. On one occasion, Justina hid under a pile of hay while Soviet soldiers poked around with their bayonets. Even after they left, she remained hidden for hours, fearful that perhaps her employers had been bribed and would give her up. Eventually, she came out but was so shaken up that she remained in bed and couldn't eat for several days.

Although she was initially inclined to join those refugees who were not resistant to repatriation, and who held hopes of being reunited with family members in the Soviet Union, Justina decided instead to escape to the West. She considers her border crossing a miraculous event, with her Soviet passport stashed in her shoe, and herself so tongue-tied that the border officials grew impatient with her and waved her across. The next miracle was her reunification with her mother and sisters and their later discovery of her father, who was a prisoner of war in France.

Gertrude also found herself living under Soviet occupation at war's end, a situation that for her meant difficult choices and even more difficult consequences. Gertrude, together with a friend and their seven children, joined the westward flight from Poland, her only destination being the train's last stop. This happened to be a town near Berlin, where they found refuge in a horse stable at a racetrack. Later Gertrude and her friend Elizabeth were both assigned work cooking and housecleaning for Soviet officers and were given the basement of a house as accommodation for themselves and their children. Although they had work, the women struggled to bring home adequate food and, like many German families, were severely malnourished, if not on the brink of starvation.[16]

Smuggling or stealing food was common, particularly for refugees in the Soviet zone, where food shortages were severe immediately after the war. Gertrude and Elizabeth received their noon meal free, while their seven children survived on the watery soup made of ground-up grain, potato peels, or any other scraps that their mothers could smuggle home past the guards. In one instance, Gertrude hid a small roast in a pail full of water that had been used for washing the floor. When relating this story, she laughed when recalling how, to her horror, the roast floated to the top as she was exiting past the guard, and she quickly threw a dirty rag over the meat to conceal it. For Gertrude's family, the meal that resulted was an unheard-of treat. In the same manner, the two women smuggled out pieces of coal, potato peelings, and anything else that would supplement their meagre existence. In recalling her family's strategies of survival, Gertrude's daughter said: 'Some people would likely say, "you were stealing". . . . sure it's stealing, [but] we would never do it under ordinary circumstances. Mom didn't become a thief because of it.'

Stealing food wasn't the only strategy that Gertrude adopted in order to sustain herself and her children. Like some other German women, Gertrude entered into a sexual relationship with a Soviet officer, in part to avoid becoming vulnerable to rapes by many different soldiers. She said, 'if you had a friend, then the others would leave you alone.' Historian Annemarie Tröger has analyzed the postwar situation for German women, caught between 'rape and prostitution', pointing to the difficult ethical choices that women made in a context where options were limited.[17] Recognizing that her willingness to enter into such a liaison represented a moral problem, given her upbringing in a Mennonite home, Gertrude nevertheless pointed to the protection that she and her children received from the officer, arguing that 'it was better that way.' Her rationale for committing what was, in her mind, sin was simple. Motivated by a desire to keep her children alive, she recalled that she would have submitted to almost any sin to prevent them from starving. The outcome for Gertrude was a daughter, born in 1949. Gertrude and her three older children loved the new baby in their family and considered her a gift of hope in a time of tragedy. The circumstances of the child's conception followed Gertrude to Canada, where she was compelled to seek forgiveness from a Mennonite minister there, and where on at least one occasion the daughter's own sexual innocence was challenged in light of her history.

Gertrude made choices that favoured life, while many other refugees and Germans chose suicide to avoid rape or abortion in the aftermath of rape. Gertrude's friend Elizabeth almost bled to death after receiving an abortion from a back-alley butcher. In addition to rape, hunger, and other forms of mistreatment by Soviet soldiers, Gertrude feared discovery as a Soviet citizen. Much of her energy went into hiding the fact that she understood the Russian language.

Although fortuitous circumstance had saved the family from repatriation on earlier occasions, Gertrude began to make plans to escape to the West. Numerous times she had crossed into the American zone of Berlin, where she obtained food and clothing from a refugee depot there. When she realized she was being watched, she made one last trip with her two daughters, sending her two sons on an earlier train carrying only small bundles each. From Berlin the family was airlifted to Hamburg, after signing a declaration that they would not return.

Of the 35,000 Mennonites who left Ukraine in 1943, approximately 23,000 went missing in the war or were repatriated to the Soviet Union in accordance with the terms of the Yalta agreement. In the five years following war's end, the remaining 12,000 Mennonite refugees scattered throughout Europe found their way to Displaced Persons camps or otherwise connected with relief and immigration agencies operating in the Allied zones. Most of the Mennonite refugees that succeeded in reaching the West made contact with Mennonite Central Committee (MCC), a North American agency that was providing relief and immigration assistance to refugees in Europe. Through MCC, the refugees investigated possibilities of emigration from Europe. Canada was the preferred country, but in the years immediately after the war, Canadian immigration policy was restrictive, and in an effort to expedite the migration of Mennonites who were faced with repatriation, MCC arranged the settlement of approximately 5,000 Mennonite refugees in Paraguay.[18]

Medical criteria was one aspect of Canadian immigration regulations that posed problems for refugees, many of whom suffered health problems related to starvation, exposure, and exhaustion. Katie's mother, who had bad varicose veins and lower labour potential as a result, decided to have surgery to increase the family's chances for migration to Canada. Her act of hope turned into a tragedy when she died from infection after surgery on her legs, leaving her three children orphans. Katie, at 16 years old, had already lost her father and stepfather, and now became a mother of sorts to her two younger brothers. Lena's mother continued to have 'problems with her nerves' after suffering a nervous breakdown when her husband was arrested in 1938, while Lena herself developed stomach problems which she attributed to poor diet, stress, and overwork. In Germany, Lena had undergone a folk treatment in which hot glasses were placed on one's back to draw out illness. The glasses had burned marks on her back, which proved awkward when she went before Canadian immigration doctors. In Canada, her stomach continued to be 'loose in the body', and so she had several operations to sew it up.

The first priority for all the women on arrival in Canada was to find a home and secure employment in order to pay off travel debts owed to relatives or sponsors. When Katie arrived in Manitoba, she resisted attempts on the part of individuals in the Mennonite community to adopt her two younger brothers, then aged 13 and 6. She did agree for them to be temporary boarders when she found a live-in position working in the laundry at a hospital in north Winnipeg. Her wages were $50 per month, all but $2 of which she sent promptly to her grandmother's cousin in British Columbia, who had advanced money for their transportation. After repaying all but $100 of their $440 debt, the cousin waived the remainder. Much of her $2 in spending money was used to buy streetcar tickets that took her to night school, where she was learning English.

Justina was similarly single-minded and notably upwardly mobile, as she was always seeking a new position that would bring her wages up. During her first year in Canada, Justina held various positions as domestic help in rural Manitoba and experienced one of the main dangers of being live-in help. At one placement where she helped out before and after the arrival of a new baby, Justina was repeatedly molested by her male employer.

> . . . with my milk pails full of milk he pressed me to the wall and squeezed me and even gave me a kiss. I was so very ashamed. He always did that. [His wife] was so good to me. I felt so guilty . . . I couldn't look her in the eyes. . . . I didn't like it when his body came to mine always in such a corner. I was very uncomfortable. But I had to stay there. They gave me $45 a month.

Like many immigrant domestics, Justina was caught between a distasteful situation—more so because her employers were distant relatives—and her need to earn money to repay her debts and send money to family members left behind for health reasons in a refugee camp in Germany. When released from this position, she spurned further domestic work and moved to Winnipeg, sharing an apartment with other immigrant women and pursuing higher earning power from one factory job to the next.

After stopping in Ontario to meet some of her relatives, Gertrude and her four children continued on to southern Alberta, where they lived in a small house on the farm of other relatives, hoeing sugar beets and helping with the chores. Their living costs were minimal, since rent was free, and milk, eggs, and garden produce were plentiful on the farm. Gertrude's daughter recalls that they had sardines for lunch every day because they were cheap.

Many Mennonite refugees were sponsored and employed by near or distant relatives in Canada. While this relationship often meant an immediate sense of being at home for new immigrants and created community bonds that were absent for newcomers with no connections in Canada, the existence of blood ties between employer and employee could also make a bad situation that much worse. This was evident in Justina's encounter with sexual misconduct on the part of her employer. Some refugee immigrants were exploited by their employers, whether they were relatives or not, and many were demeaned or otherwise made to feel inferior. Justina recalled that the cousin sponsoring her and her sister was 'very mean,' and feared that her sons would become interested in the 'Russian girls'. The cousin also refused to buy the young women sanitary napkins, forcing them to revert to the old practise of using rags during their menstrual periods.

When Lena arrived in Canada in 1948 with her two young children and sickly mother, she was given a job at her cousin's café in Saskatoon, where she worked from 6:30 a.m. until one o'clock in the night. 'There was not much time to think,' she said. 'I did not expect it to be so hard.' After six months they moved to British Columbia, where they lived in an unheated cabin on her uncle's farm and picked raspberries, strawberries, and hops. Eventually, Lena was able to purchase her own house with two acres of berries that generated a small amount of income. She found it difficult to obtain a well-paying steady job because she also had to care for her mother, who was at home and unwell, and so she was limited to part-time and flexible work cleaning houses. Later she moved to Vancouver, where wages for housework were even better.

Like many other female-headed refugee families of this era, these women established themselves economically with minimal outside help. Rather, the labour resources of themselves and their children, combined with well-practised strategies of frugal living, allowed them to pay their debts, buy or build houses, and feed and clothe their families. Although all of the five women associated themselves with Mennonite churches in Canada, material help was less forthcoming than spiritual nurture and rehabilitation, which was viewed by the church as a priority in addressing the needs of the refugees. Lena, caring for two young children and her elderly mother, said they received assistance from neither the church nor the government. 'I didn't want any welfare. We managed,' she said. She did accept the newly instituted Family Allowance cheque from the government, which some Mennonite churches in Canada cautioned their members against.

Besides making a living, integrating themselves into Mennonite communities, and making a recovery from years of tragedy, refugee women also had to accommodate to Canadian society. Although the term 'displaced person' was an official United Nations designation for certain categories of war refugees, the label 'DP' was frequently used in a derisive manner to refer to postwar immigrants. Anna viewed language as one of the greatest barriers facing her as a new immigrant to Canada in 1948. Mainly, it prevented her from taking what she considered to be 'important jobs'. While her mother and sister sewed men's shirts in a factory, Anna worked in an industrial laundry, where language wasn't as important. Even within Mennonite communities, where all of the women had near or distant relatives, refugees were often set apart and looked down upon because of their limited religious training, lack of formal education, and initial poverty. Justina felt that she and her sister were always thought of as 'the Russian girls'. Katie felt inferior because she was an orphan and was particularly jealous of other families that had fathers.

For women whose families had been torn apart by the Soviet purges of the 1930s and by death and disappearance during the war, the re-creation of family life that was 'normal' by Canadian Mennonite standards was a main goal. The 'grab bag' family that characterized many refugee families was in stark contrast to the patriarchal nuclear family exalted by Mennonite religious discourse and also the 'happy united family' that was normative for postwar Canadian society generally.[19] For refugee widows in Canada, restoring 'normalcy' to their families might mean remarrying, with or without confirmation of their first spouse's death, or struggling against all odds to be reunited with family members far away. Young single women usually married shortly after settling in Canada, and often at a relatively young age, perhaps to begin creating for themselves a certain kind of family life that they had never experienced.

Katie married in 1951, at the age of 19, partly to recover a father-figure in her life, a motive she readily admitted. 'I got married so young partly I think out of security. I felt vulnerable all my life since I was five [the year her father was arrested]. And here was a gentleman very much like what I used to know, my Dad. Who I could trust.' Justina also married young, to a man she had met in a refugee camp in Germany, two years after arriving with her sister in Canada. She proudly described her wedding, which she had financed completely on her own. Her wedding dress of lace and pearls cost a week's wages at $15.50, while the cake alone cost $3.50. She also purchased bridesmaid dresses for three of her friends. The bouquet was store bought and was couriered by bus to the southern Manitoba town where the wedding was held. In Justina's words:

> I did the whole wedding. I invited the whole church. I think there were 250 people. We had cookies, cheese, buns. I arranged everything. I even gave the ladies in the kitchen some money for all they did. They were very impressed with how far an orphan had come.

Happily married for over 40 years, with seven children born in 9 years, Justina's memories of marriage are positively correlated with the end of her refugee identity. Anna's memories of marriage, by contrast, are so negative that they are almost completely repressed in her personal narrative.

Anna was married already in Germany and in fact arrived in Canada with her husband, separately from her mother and sisters. However, her account of travel and arrival in Canada contains anecdotes that include her mother and sisters, with no reference to her husband at all. Further conversation revealed that she divorced her husband after an abusive and unhappy marriage, and thus her oral life history, while highly personal on many other topics, initially eliminated what was for her the most painful part of her life. Although she moved with him to western Canada and had a daughter there, she began to fear for her life and returned to the community where her family had settled.

> It didn't work out. I was too unhappy. I couldn't manage. I tried my best. There was no way out. After he tried to kill me one night . . . there was no way out. . . . for me to save my child and me, we had to leave.

In leaving her former husband out of the main text of her narrative, Anna was not only repressing that which was especially painful for her, but she was also removing an episode in her life that did not fit the culture of her community. In the 1950s, domestic violence was unspoken of in Mennonite communities, while divorce was proscribed by the Church altogether. Although Anna was quietly allowed to remain in the Mennonite Church despite her divorce, her experience marginalized her within that group. As theorists of memory and personal narrative have argued, individuals frequently eliminate from their life story elements that are at variance with the 'social memory' of their communities.[20]

Anna's life was problematized even further when her widowed mother, who had remarried in Canada, experienced a similar pattern of abuse. Anna's mother, whose first husband had disappeared in 1938, at age 70 married a man who came from the same village in the Soviet Union. According to Anna, 'It turned out very sad. He was everything we girls had feared. He didn't look after her. . . . All he wanted was a housekeeper.' When it became apparent that their mother's health was in danger, Anna and her sisters retrieved their mother from British Columbia and took legal action to prevent her second husband from trying to take her back.

Like Anna's mother, Gertrude also remarried after she received a letter confirming her first husband's death in the Soviet Union. The man was also a postwar immigrant, although a bachelor, and people in their community discouraged him from marrying Gertrude, saying, 'What do you want with her and all her four children? He should find someone younger who could bear his children.' As historians of widowhood have demonstrated, and as the experience of Gertrude and others like her revealed, the widow with children was viewed as a financial and emotional burden and in fact a threat to the patriarchal social order.[21]

Lena's restoration of her fragmented family came about in a very different manner. As a young woman, Lena had many opportunities to remarry in Canada but chose not to, given that she never received confirmation whether her first husband was dead or alive. Although Canadian legal stipulations, as well as guidelines established within the Mennonite Church, allowed for remarriage after 7 years of hearing no word from one's spouse, Lena felt she simply could not take this step. After 15 years of hearing no word from her husband, Jacob, one Easter morning Lena received news that he was still living in the Soviet Union. Fortunately Jacob had not remarried either, and so the two began corresponding, and Lena began a 16-year campaign lobbying the Canadian government and writing endless appeals to have him emigrate. After several occasions on which Jacob's permit to leave the Soviet Union was denied at the last minute, Lena refused to place any more trust in promises. Ironically, the final telegram of confirmation never reached Lena, and so one night in the early 1970s she was awoken with a telephone call that announced Jacob's arrival at the Vancouver airport. They were reunited after a separation of over 30 years.

Although some couples reunited in this manner found that after such a long separation they were no longer compatible, Lena insists that she and Jacob simply resumed what had been a very happy marriage. Undoubtedly there were adjustments to make, especially in the area of gender roles that had been altered when Lena became head of the family in Jacob's absence. Lena continued to do all the business because her husband spoke no English and she was 30 years ahead of him in assimilating to Canadian society. Within the household, she frequently found herself doing 'male' tasks such as hammering a nail when he would step in and say, 'what am I here for?'

Life in Canada, despite its hardships and obstacles, represented stability and prosperity in sharp contrast to the years of war. Even though the prewar years in Ukraine and the decade following as war refugees represented a much smaller portion of their lives than their residence in Canada, the era of the war took a central place in the memories of these five women as told in their oral narratives. Pamela Klassen, who has chronicled the life histories of two Mennonite refugee women, noted that the autobiography of one woman ended before her immigration to Canada at the age of 24, indicating the 'overwhelming importance' of the war and prewar years to her self-identity.[22] Katie became closely involved in the Canadian Mennonite community but always felt that her war experiences created a vast gap in understanding. Her 'horrible' memories had a debilitating affect for the remainder of her life:

> I would probably not have wanted to talk about [the horrible experiences] much because I cried a lot more than I ate. My hands are not steady. The doctor saw it and asked, what is the matter with you. I said that's a long story. I can't help this. I have very bad handwriting.

All of the five women periodically referred to themselves as *Flüchtlinge* (refugees) in their narratives, thus maintaining a strong identification with the dramatic early decades of their lives. Even in the midst of their hesitancy to talk about horrible experiences, the detail in chronicling the years surrounding the war are in sharp contrast to the lesser time and space devoted to their lives as immigrant women in Canada. This allocation of narrative space may be due to the greater societal merit attributed to their heroic deeds in the public arena of war than to their lives as househelp, factory workers, and mothers, wives, or widows in the new land.

Even while describing in lesser detail their lives as Canadians, the five women nevertheless exuded an understated pride over their success in coming through the refugee sojourn. While their anonymity here reduces their visibility as heroic women, it also allowed their voices to speak more candidly at a personal level and perhaps allowed their stories to depart at times from the master immigrant narrative that is common in published life histories. The collective biography of these five women thus becomes at the same time a possible glimpse into the lives of refugee women around the world, past and present.

Notes

1. Susan Forbes Martin, *Refugee Women* (London: Zed Books, 1992), 5. Also, Ellen Cole, et al., *Refugee Women and Their Mental Health: Shattered Societies, Shattered Lives* (Binghamton, NY: Haworth Press, 1992), p. xii. Several authors have noted the predominance of women and children in refugee movements from Cuba, Cambodia, and Vietnam, for instance. See Silvia Pedraza, 'Women and Migration: The Social Consequences of Gender', *Annual Review of Sociology* 17 (1991): 303–25.
2. Doreen Indra, 'Gender: A Key Dimension of the Refugee Experience', *Refuge* 6 (February 1987): 3–4.
3. Franca Iacovetta, 'Manly Militants, Cohesive Communities, and Defiant Domestics: Writing about Immigrants in Canadian Historical Scholarship', *Labour / Le Travail* 36 (Fall 1995): 217–52.
4. Historical literature on refugee women in the Canadian context includes the following: Janice Potter-MacKinnon, *While the Women Only Wept: Loyalist Refugee Women in Eastern Ontario* (Montreal & Kingston: McGill-Queen's University Press, 1993); Isabel Kaprielian, 'Creating and Sustaining an Ethnocultural Heritage in Ontario: the Case of Armenian Women Refugees', in *Looking into My Sister's Eyes: An Exploration in Women's History,* Jean Burnet, ed. (Toronto: Multicultural History Society of Ontario, 1986), 139–53; Milda Danys, *DP: Lithuanian Immigration to Canada After the Second World War* (Toronto: Multicultural History Society of Ontario, 1986); Franca Iacovetta, 'Remaking Their Lives: Women Immigrants, Survivors, and Refugees', in *A Diversity of Women: Ontario, 1945–1980,* Joy Parr, ed. (Toronto: University of Toronto Press, 1995), 135–67.
5. Sultana Parvanta, 'The Balancing Act: Plight of Afghan Women Refugees', in *Refugee Women and Their Mental Health: Shattered Societies, Shattered Lives,* Ellen Cole, et al., eds. (Binghamton, NY: Haworth Press, 1992), 127.
6. Linda Peavy and Ursula Smith, *The Gold Rush Widows of Little Falls: A story drawn from the letters of Pamela and James Fergus* (St Paul: Minnesota Historical Society, 1990), 55.
7. During the early 1990s, I conducted interviews with Mennonites who had immigrated to Canada as refugees after the Second World War. This research was part of a larger study: *Women without Men: Mennonite Refugees of the Second World War* (Toronto: University of Toronto Press, 2000). All references to the stories of the five women are from these interviews.
8. Betty Bergland, 'Ideology, Ethnicity, and the Gendered Subject: Reading Immigrant Women's Autobiographies', in *Seeking Common Ground: Multidisciplinary Studies of Immigrant Women in the United States*, Donna Gabaccia, ed. (Westport, CT: Praeger, 1992): 101–21.
9. Studies which examine developments within the Mennonite colonies under the Soviet regime include: John B. Toews, *Czars, Soviets & Mennonites* (Newton, KS: Faith and Life Press, 1982), chapters 11–12; John B. Toews, 'Early Communism and Russian Mennonite Peoplehood', 265–87 and Victor G. Doerksen, 'Survival and Identity in the Soviet Era', 289–98, in *Mennonites in Russia, 1788–1988: Essays in Honour of Gerhard Lohrenz,* John Friesen, ed. (Winnipeg: CMBC Publications, 1989); 'Mennonites and the Soviet Inferno', special issue of the *Journal of Mennonite Studies* 16 (1998).
10. The 1930 population of Soviet Mennonites was about 100,000. 'World War II', *Mennonite Encyclopedia*, Volume 5, 941–2, George K. Epp, 'Mennonite Immigration to Canada After World War II', *Journal of Mennonite Studies* 5 (1987), 110. For more detail on the loss of men, see Epp, *Women without Men*, Chapter 1.
11. George K. Epp, 'Mennonite Immigration to Canada', 112.
12. The film, *The Great Trek* (1992), was produced by Otto Klassen, a former refugee who obtained film footage from German government archives that provide graphic visual images of the hardships of the trek. (Sponsored by Faith and Life Communications of the Conference of Mennonites in Manitoba.) Kitchener artist Agatha Schmidt, also a postwar immigrant, has produced a number of oil paintings portraying the departure of men and the trek. Autobiographies include: Katie Friesen, *Into the Unknown* (1986, Author); Susanna Toews, *Trek to Freedom: The escape of two sisters from South Russia during World War II*, Helen Megli, trans.

(Winkler, MB: Heritage Valley Publications, 1976); Jacob A. Neufeld, *Tiefenwege: Erfahrungen und Erlebnisse von Russland-Mennoniten in zwei Jahrezehnten bis 1949* (Virgil, Ont.: Niagara Press, n.d.).

13. Barbara Johr, 'Die Ereignisse in Zahlen', in *BeFreier und Befreite: Krieg, Vergewaltigungen, Kinder*, Helke Sander and Barbara Johr, eds. (Munich: Verlag Antje Kunstmann, 1992), 59.
14. For a discussion of memories of wartime rape, see Marlene Epp, 'The Memory of Violence: Soviet and East European Mennonite Refugees and Rape in the Second World War', *Journal of Women's History* 9.1 (Spring 1997): 58–87.
15. Annemarie Tröger, 'German Women's Memories of World War II', in *Behind the Lines: Gender and the Two World Wars,* Margaret Randolph Higonnet, et al., eds. (New Haven: Yale University Press, 1987), 293–4.
16. All sectors of postwar Germany were characterized by what Eve Kolinsky has called a 'culture of physical survival'. Shortages of food, heating materials, clothing, and household goods meant that most Germans had to develop pre-industrial methods for meeting daily needs. Poor health and malnutrition were common, and some individuals in fact 'lived close to starvation levels'. See *Women in Contemporary Germany: Life, Work and Politics* (Providence, RI: Berg, 1993 revised edition), pp. 26–8.
17. Annemarie Tröger, 'Between Rape and Prostitution: Survival Strategies and Chances of Emancipation for Berlin Women after World War II', in *Women in Culture and Politics: A Century of Change*, Judith Friedlander, et al., eds. (Bloomington: Indiana University Press, 1986).
18. Detailed discussions of the policy and negotiations surrounding the postwar Mennonite migration can be found in: Frank H. Epp, *Mennonite Exodus: The Rescue and Resettlement of the Russian Mennonites Since the Communist Revolution* (Altona, MB: D.W. Friesen & Sons, 1962), chapters 24–6; T.D. Regehr, *Mennonites in Canada, 1939–1970: A People Transformed* (Toronto: University of Toronto Press, 1996), chapter 4. A personal memoir from the perspective of two MCC relief workers is: Peter and Elfrieda Dyck, *Up from the Rubble: the epic rescue of thousands of war-ravaged Mennonite refugees* (Scottdale, PA: Herald Press, 1991).
19. The term 'grab bag' is applied by Sheila Fitzpatrick to families in which individuals with or without a blood relationship come together to share housing, food, and other resources for the purpose of survival under wartime conditions. See *Stalin's Peasants: Resistance and Survival in the Russian Village after Collectivization* (New York: Oxford University Press, 1994), 221. The phrase 'happy united family' is borrowed from Annalee Golz, 'The Canadian Family and the State in the Postwar Period', *left history*, 1 (Fall 1993), 9–49.
20. For discussion of the way in which personal narratives are shaped to fit the communal or social memory of a group, see James Fentress and Chris Wickham, *Social Memory* (Cambridge, Mass: Blackwell, 1992); Raphael Samuel and Paul Thompson, eds, *The Myths We Live By* (London and New York: Routledge, 1990).
21. See for instance, Barbara J. Todd, 'The remarrying widow: a stereotype reconsidered', in *Women in English Society, 1500–1800,* Mary Prior, ed. (London & New York: Methuen, 1985), 54–92. Also, Ida Blom, 'The History of Widowhood: A Bibliographic Overview', *Journal of Family History*, 16, 2 (1991), 191–210.
22. Pamela E. Klassen, *Going By the Moon and the Stars: Stories of Two Russian Mennonite Women* (Waterloo: Wilfrid Laurier University Press, 1994), 66–7.

Rethinking Class in Lesbian Bar Culture: Living 'The Gay Life' in Toronto, 1955–1965

Elise Chenier

EDITORS' INTRODUCTION

The history of lesbian experience presents an unparalleled opportunity for students to not only 'rethink' Canada, but also to 'rethink' the experience of Canadian women. Feminist scholars from a range of disciplinary backgrounds have long rallied for more critical attention to notions of difference as they impinge on the category of 'woman'. As bell hooks remembered of her own experiences in university courses, 'I was disturbed that the white female professors and students were ignorant of gender differences in black life—that they talked about the status and experiences of "women" when they were only referring to white women. . .that surprise turned to anger.'[1] hooks's anger emanated, at least in part, from assumptions regarding the unitary nature of the experience of women. Race, scholars such as hooks underlined, matters. In an effort to redress this monolithic attitude, Janice Fiamengo's essay in this volume explores the complex racism of white feminist 'foremothers' in Canada. What also matters in accounting for the historical experience of women is sexuality and sexual orientation. As Sheila L. Cavanagh demonstrates in her essay, the presumption of heterosexual identity, like the presumption of white identity, clouds our understanding of the past and blinds us to the subtle and explicit differences accenting women's pasts.

To date, scholars have made important progress in reclaiming the experiences of lesbians and gays in Canada. This has not been an easily uncovered history. Like the challenges faced by other scholars who focus on topic areas seemingly hidden from history, information about sexual minorities in the past is challenging to recognize and uncover. Where do we go to document the lives of lesbians in Canada's past? Groundbreaking work by historians and sociologists has, in recent years, significantly enriched our understanding of the importance of sexuality as a mainstream category of historical analysis. Historian Line Chamberlain relies on oral histories to examine a group of lesbians in Montreal between 1955 and 1975. Much like Elise Chenier's article, Chamberlain's work focuses on the working-class bar culture as one of the few public homosocial settings available to lesbian women. Making use of queer theory, Valerie Korinek has analyzed *Chatelaine,* the most popular mainstream women's magazine in Canada, in the postwar period and discovered that lesbians would have found their interests reflected within its pages.[2] Along with important studies by Becki Ross, Gary Kinsman, Mary Louise Adams, Paul Jackson, Steven Maynard, and David Churchill,[3] this work has challenged the presumption of a unitary past characterized by a heterosexual orientation. Once the assumption of heterosexuality amongst all women is challenged, other seemingly fixed markers of identity are also opened to closer scrutiny.

In Chenier's article living 'the gay life' in downtown Toronto in the late fifties and early sixties impinged on sexual orientation as it was intimately shaped by class differences. Building on the work of Chamberlain, Chenier pursues the world of lesbians by revisiting settings in which they were visible: public bars. While Davis and Lorenzkowski's essay in this volume draws our attention to the neglected role of public transit for understanding women's experiences, the import of public space in recovering lesbian history is heightened here. Bar culture was not the domain of all lesbians in the past, it is important to consider, but it does present the historian with critical and accessible sources on a topic hidden and silenced in the past.[4] Chenier is able to marshal oral history testimonies from bar owners and patrons, accounts of surveillance and regulation on the part of law enforcement, and popular and pulp media accounts of this important aspect of living 'the gay life' in the midst of a largely intolerant society. Chenier is particularly attentive to the role that significant class differences played in shaping the lesbian subculture of urban Toronto's bar scene, evident in the experience of so-called 'uptowners' and 'downtowners' who frequented bars such as the Continental and the Rideau. Linking the classed experience of bar-going lesbians in Toronto to a wider literature in the North American context, Chenier's goal in this piece is to deepen our understanding of subtle and overt differences between and *within* working- and middle-class experience in Toronto after the Second World War.

Chenier's work also significantly develops the Canadian historiography on the postwar years. Feminist historians have worked hard to debunk the simplistic notion of this period as a 'golden era' of family, prosperity, and contentedness.[5] Just as Franca Iacovetta's piece testifies, markers of 'difference' from the mainstream white, middle-class Canadian society, based on race, gender, class, and sexuality had a profound impact on the lived experience of women and their families in this decade. Far from simply contented and prosperous, those outside the sanctioned mainstream often struggled for survival, never mind comfort. Here Chenier, like Cavanagh, underscores the fact that intolerance for homosexuality reached an increasingly shrill peak throughout the era, fueled by the social uncertainty following the war. In a most ironic twist, the era in which concern over the well-being of liberal democracy and democratic citizenship caused much hand-wringing, homosexuals were denied many of the most basic human rights. That many of the women Chenier tells us about lived 'the gay life' full time testifies to their tenacity and commitment to remain true to themselves, regardless of the high price such pride exacted.

Notes

1. bell hooks, *Teaching to Transgress: Education as the Practice of Freedom* (New York and London: Routledge, 1994), 120. For a comprehensive account of the debate regarding 'difference' in feminist theorizing, see V. Olsen, 'Feminisms and Qualitative Research At and Into the Millenium', in *The Landscape of Qualitative Research: Theories and Issues*, 2nd ed., N.K. Denzin and Y. S. Lincoln, eds. (California: Sage Publications, 2003), 332–97.
2. Line Chamberlain, 'Remembering Lesbian Bars: Montreal, 1955–1975', in *Rethinking Canada: The Promise of Women's History*, 3rd ed., Veronica Strong-Boag and Anita Clair Fellman, eds. (Toronto: Oxford University Press, 1997); Valerie Korinek, *Roughing It in the Suburbs: Reading 'Chatelaine' in the 1950s and 1960s* (Toronto: University of Toronto Press 2000).
3. Becki Ross, *The House that Jill Built: A Lesbian Nation in Formation* (Toronto: University of Toronto Press, 1995); Gary Kinsman, *The Regulation of Desire: Homo and Hetero Sexualities* (Montreal: Black Rose Books, 1996); Mary Louise Adams, *The Trouble with Normal: Postwar Youth and the Making of Heterosexuality* (Toronto: University of Toronto Press, 1997); Steven Maynard, '"Hell's Witches in Toronto": Notes on Lesbian Visibility in Early Twentieth-Century Canada', *Left History* 85 (Spring/Summer 2004): 191–205; Steven Maynard, 'The Maple Leaf (Gardens) Forever: Sex, Canadian Historians and National History', *Journal of Canadian Studies* 36.2 (Summer 2001): 70–106; Steven Maynard, 'Respect Your Elders, Know Your Past: Historians and the Queer Theorists', *Radical History Review* 75 (1999): 56–78; Paul Jackson, *One*

of the Boys: Homosexuality in the Military during World War II* (Montreal and Kingston: McGill-Queen's University Press, 2004); David Churchill, 'Mother Goose's Map: Tabloid Geographies and Gay Male Experience in 1950s Toronto', *Journal of Urban History* 30.6 (September 2004): 826–52.

4. See for example Katherine Arnup, ed., *Lesbian Parenting: Living with Pride and Prejudice* (Charlottetown: Gynergy Books, 1995).
5. See, for example, Veronica Strong-Boag, 'Home Dreams: Women and the Suburban Experiment in Canada, 1945–1960', in *Rethinking Canada: The Promise of Women's History*, 4th ed., Veronica Strong-Boag, Mona Gleason, and Adele Perry, eds. (Toronto: Oxford University Press, 2002), 313–34; Mona Gleason, *Normalizing the Ideal: Psychology, Schooling, and the Family in Postwar Canada* (Toronto: University of Toronto Press, 1999); Joy Parr, ed., *Diversity of Women: Women in Canada, 1945–1980* (Toronto: University of Toronto Press, 1995).

Questions for Critical Reading

1. What does an understanding of lesbian experience tell us about women's history as a whole? How might this enrich our understanding of the ways in which traditional thinking regarding gender influences all women's lives?
2. Compare the tenor of the film *Forbidden Love: The Unashamed Stories of Lesbian Lives* (NFB, 1992) with the experiences Chenier highlights in her essay. How do these sources complement and contradict each other?
3. What are the strengths and limitations of Chenier's historical sources? What are the implications of these for our understanding of the variety of lesbian experience in Canada's past?

When Joji Hazel came to Toronto in the early 1960s, her search for a gay women's bar landed her at the Continental Hotel, a public house long considered home to local bar-going lesbians.[1] Hazel lived in a small town one hundred miles outside the city, and what she knew of lesbian bars was gleaned from pulp fiction novels and *The Ladder*, a magazine published by the Daughters of Bilitis, a San Francisco-based lesbian organization, where the evils and merits of lesbian bars and butch and fem 'roles' were the subject of regular debate.[2] Hazel claims that she felt well prepared for what she would find, but as she stood before the 'dingy building' located in 'a seedy section of Chinatown, noted for prostitution and narcotics', she almost lost her nerve.

Had Hazel never read about lesbian bars, she probably would have been struck by the tough masculine demeanour of many of the women inside. She might have been put off by the constant stream of sex trade workers and johns moving in and out of the ladies' and escorts' room. But after three hours of careful observation, what took her by surprise was how the gay women inside were segregated into two distinct groups. They are 'stalwarts from two different worlds', she explained in a short article published in *The Ladder* in 1963. 'One . . . was condescending and at times a little jeering; the other was brash, defiant, puzzlingly defensive . . . . A line might have been drawn on the floor, so divisible were the players'.[3] Significantly, Hazel knew exactly where she stood, or more precisely, sat. Her description of 'brash' butches at the Continental was unequivocally critical; presumably why some women might jeer at them needed no explanation.

Butch and fem 'roles' have long been regarded as a definitive feature of post-Second World War working-class lesbian culture, but as Hazel discovered, sociability within Toronto's lesbian subculture was tied to a much more complex set of friendship networks that divided women as much as they united them.[4] In Toronto, women whose lives centred on the Continental Hotel called themselves downtowners, and referred to other gay women in the bar—women like Hazel—as uptowners. Uptowners typically lived outside the downtown core, usually in the rapidly expanding suburbs. Some still lived at home, others with friends and lovers. Most held down pink and, to a lesser extent, white-collar jobs, and were careful to separate their 'gay lives' from their familial and working lives. Limiting their time in the Continental and the surrounding neighbourhood to weekends has been described as an important strategy to minimize the perceived risk of being discovered in a 'homosexual haunt', but it also reflected typical patterns of socializing among the gay urban employed. Lesbians and gay men referred to the process of separating, negotiating, and living out two distinct lives as 'the double life'.[5]

In contrast, downtowners lived 'the gay life'. They were a constant presence in the back room of the Continental Hotel's public house, and their daily activities were deeply enmeshed with most every aspect of the social and economic activities of the beer parlour and its surrounding neighbourhood. From the early 1950s until the mid-1960s, to live the 'gay life' was to live in tandem and in tension with the sex and drug trades, local Chinese residents, the police, the courts, and the prison system. Those who did so gave clear expression to their particular location within the community through their rough and ready style. Butch *and* fem downtowners were identifiable to insiders and outsiders alike: more assertive in staking their claim on physical and social spaces, more willing to challenge conventions concerning sex and gender comportment, and more sexually explicit in their verbal and physical interactions, they comprised a distinct social group of sexual outsiders. Of course, the line that divided the two groups was not immutable. Most downtowners arrived as uptowners, and some women dated and socialized across the 'line'. However, as 'kiki' was to butch and fem, lesbians who sought out and enjoyed the friendship and trust of both groups were the exception to the rule.[6] For the purposes of this article, downtowners can be distinguished as a unique and relatively stable social category.

In this essay I show that the working class character of Toronto's tough bar lesbians derived not simply from the rough and tumble nature of working-class culture but from the concrete survival strategies lesbians carved out from the street and underground economy, strategies that were shared by a number of different marginalized groups, including prostitutes. Like other gay women, downtowners' identities took shape in the context of homosexual repression and considerable sexual, social, and economic restraint imposed on women. What distinguished downtowners from other working class gay women, however, was the result of their direct and indirect involvement in a variety of criminalized socio-economic activities, all of which occurred in and around the public spaces they themselves secured. Downtowners' economic relationships were also social relationships, and they shaped female sexual subjectivity in ways that cannot be explained by lesbian identity or class difference. Instead, I argue that class and sexuality were mutually constitutive.[7] By examining the social and economic consequences of living 'the gay life' full time, we can begin to think more carefully about how we use 'working class' as an explanatory tool in the shaping of sexual cultures and gender identities.

This article is part of a larger study of lesbian bar culture in post-war Toronto that I began in the early 1990s. Primary source material includes interviews conducted in the mid-1980s by the Lesbians Making History collective; in 1992 and 1993 I added seven interviews of my own. These are supplemented with gossip columns and news stories in Toronto's weekly tabloids *Justice Weekly, Confidential Flash*, and *Hush Free Press* where local lesbians' engagements with the police and the courts were occasionally covered, and by the records of the Liquor Licensing Board of Ontario. No sources provide us with a transparent view of the past, and oral histories and the yellow press come with their own peculiar limitations.[8] However, historians of queer cultures have skilfully demonstrated that when approached with an eye and ear sensitive to language and narrative these rich resources can be mined to great effect, and offer critical insights into class, culture, and processes of identity formation.

In his 1983 study of American homosexual communities, John D'Emilio argues that the Second World War was a turning point in lesbian and gay history. Wartime mobilization disrupted traditional family and community relationships, placing millions of women and men in homosocial environments that contributed to same-sex sexual exploration and discovery. After the Allied victory, large numbers of women and men mobilized by the war effort stayed on in America's port cities and urban centres, where they formed visible public communities in bars and other commercial social spaces.[9] Subsequent studies, including Kennedy and Davis's massive ethnography of Buffalo's lesbian bar cultures, support his thesis.[10] Despite similar preconditions, the emergence of a postwar lesbian bar culture in Toronto did not follow the same trajectory. Paralleling the wartime developments described by Kennedy and Davis, women from all over Ontario flocked to Toronto, the centre of Canadian wartime production where the demand for female labour was high and paycheques were handsome. Inglis, a Toronto-based manufacturer of appliances, converted to wartime production and, by 1944, employed over nine thousand female workers, making it Canada's largest private employer of women.[11] One of those women was Margaret, a middle-class Anglo-Ontarian who met her life partner at the plant. Bud was the plant's calisthenics instructor, and she and Margaret pursued a sexually intimate relationship that evolved into a celibate, life-long domestic partnership.[12] According to Margaret, for decades neither she nor Bud understood herself as homosexual, lesbian, or queer. Until the 1990s they remained unaware of any public or private lesbian or gay social networks despite the fact that they lived together for most of their adult lives and Margaret worked in a variety of professional and journalistic positions at the Canadian Broadcasting Corporation which was known for its homosexual cliques.[13]

Margaret and Bud's experience illustrates the great care with which many lesbians and gay men guarded their homosocial interests and homosexual relationships. Still, other lesbians and gay men were able to use public spaces to make themselves more visible, and provide opportunities to socialize with one another. During and after the war, gay women established a discrete but discernable presence on both the Inglis and other organized women's softball teams, and some participated in the predominantly gay male social activities, including dances, sunbathing, and private parties on Toronto's Ward and Centre Islands.[14] The Wheat Sheaf, a private, unlicensed dance club located at Yonge and College Streets, was frequented by gay men and women and survived into the 1950s.

However, for many women these conditions were quickly eroding. Toronto's industrial economy peaked with 160,000 labourers in 1950, but over the next decade, factory jobs dried up as heavy industry moved their operations out of the downtown core.[15] Female workers maintained a strong presence in small manufacturing outfits that clung to the city's economy, but inside the few large-scale operations that remained men were once again the preferred employees. By 1961, for example, only fifty women were employed at Inglis's downtown factory. Moreover, wartime labour gains were unevenly distributed. For example, few Asian Canadian women were able to break into the mainstream labour market, and African Canadian women were quickly pushed off the shop floor and into the service sector at war's end.[16]

Economic change was accompanied by seismic shifts in popular culture; particularly with respect to expectations about female behaviour.[17] Plentiful opportunities in retail, restaurant, and administrative sectors meant that single Toronto women would have little trouble finding work, but each of these types of positions demanded feminine deportment. Butch women determined to live the gay life full time were less able to access these jobs. In 1950s and 60s Toronto, butch lesbians found employment driving cabs, and a small group of gay women held down jobs as pieceworkers at McFarlane-Gendron, a Toronto manufacturer of baby carriages.[18] A few trained as auto mechanics (the 1961 census reports a total of fourteen female mechanics in the city); some picked up work at local car washes, or as bowling pin setters, handbill distributors, or couriers; and by the late 1960s Tilden, Avis, and other car rental companies employed a sizable contingent of butch lesbians as car jockeys.[19] Overall however, employment options for young masculine women were becoming increasingly scarce. When women landed jobs that allowed them to wear pants, shirts, and hair fashioned after contemporary icons of youthful masculinity, they hung onto them as long as they could. Job vacancies were quickly filled by word-of-mouth.[20] According to Arlene, it was not that butch downtowners refused to work in traditional female sectors, only that they refused to style themselves according to contemporary female fashions. When they applied for work, they were usually turned away at the door. '[A] person could be hiring one hundred people and [a butch] walk[s] in and: "Sorry, we're not hiring." Which is why a lot of criminal activity went on: people had to live, they had to eat.'[21] Despite the greater availability of full time work for young single women, butch lesbians, who chose to live the gay life full time found they had depressingly limited options. The street economy provided an alternative that many were willing to take.

A 1966 sociological study of Toronto's female homosexual subculture supports Arlene's claim. Jo Ann Pratt, a master's student in the School of Social Work at the University of Toronto, interviewed thirteen lesbians most of whom had a criminal record; among the most frequently laid charges were drinking (ten), theft (six), prostitution (five), drugs (five), and robbery with violence (three).[22] These and other criminal charges were often the result of a combination of poverty and what we would now call homophobia. For example, a charge of breaking and entering might be laid against a woman who broke into a car so she could sleep for the night; a charge of disturbing the peace could be laid against two women having a lover's quarrel on the street, and women breached their probation when they refused to stay out of the Tenderloin and Chinatown areas.[23]

Of course, Pratt's methodology determined the outcome of her research. She relied on a middle class lesbian to escort her to the Continental and other commercial establishments with a lesbian clientele, but most of the women who filled out her questionnaire were contacted through the Mercer Reformatory, the Don Jail, and Probation Services.[24] Pratt's goal was to understand the lesbian and her relationship to the social world around her, but rather than provide readers with a snapshot of 'the lesbian', by relying on the criminal justice system to gain access to informants, her sources offered her a snap-shot of the downtowner. Indeed, in the 1950s and 60s prisons, jails, and probation services were a sure bet for finding lesbian subjects. When jobs were impossible to find, or paid too little, or were simply too hard to hang on to, the local sex and drug trade provided a variety of ready economic opportunities that some were willing to exploit. These women's social location within the bar and their allegiances to the women and men in it was largely determined by just that decision.

The cultural changes evinced by women's war work may have helped create the conditions necessary for greater female autonomy, but if a public community accessible to outsiders emerged during the war, gay women in Toronto were unable to sustain it. Instead, the 1950s evolution of Toronto's lesbian bar culture followed pre-war urban patterns when public homosocial cultures emerged in vice districts where female prostitutes were a stable and visible presence. Sex trade workers were scattered throughout the downtown core, but in the early 1950s Toronto had two particularly well-known red light districts. The 'Tenderloin' ran along a section of Jarvis Street near Carleton in Cabbagetown, an east end Anglo-Celtic working-class neighbourhood. The other was to the west, at the corner of Elizabeth and Dundas Streets, the heart of Chinatown. In the first half of the 1950s, gay women were a constant and visible presence in the Tenderloin, but after 1955,

Chinatown was widely known as the centre of public lesbian life.

Up until the mid-1950s, lesbians were most likely to be found in public houses along Jarvis Street. The Rideau Hotel was one of the more popular, perhaps because it had one of the few remaining 'ladies only' rooms.[25] In an effort to prevent sexual immorality (and appease temperance advocates), Ontario liquor licensing laws required that public houses thwart heterosexual contact between strangers by providing at least two physically separate rooms: one for men only, and the other for women. Up until the early 1970s when feminists launched a successful campaign against such forms of segregation, men could gain access to what were called 'ladies and escorts rooms' only by entering with a woman.[26] The Rideau's 'women only' room made it particularly well suited to gay women's social needs. Not only did it allow them space to socialize with each other, but it also shielded them from heterosexual advances and male antagonism. As Davis and Kennedy have argued, bars frequented by straight men were hostile environments for butch and fem lesbians. The combination of excessive alcohol consumption and the greater tendency for arguments to escalate into physical violence in and around working-class bars meant that the likelihood of assault was much greater in 'street bars' than in other, more upscale places.[27] Indeed, liquor authority complaints regarding drunkenness, rowdiness, and fights among patrons preceded the arrival of gay women.[28]

Given these circumstances, it seems logical to assume that butch and fem lesbians were eager to maintain a distance from heterosexual men. This was not, however, the case among Toronto downtowners. Rather than avoid male patrons, these women worked to take advantage of straight men's heterosexual interests. For example, butches frequently solicited drinks from male patrons, and men often responded positively to their requests. For women with little or no cash, inviting men to buy them drinks meant a cheap night out, even though it also increased opportunities for friction. Such was the case in 1954 when, according to a story in *Justice Weekly*, a group of five 'husky young women' ranging in age from twenty-three to thirty-two sat drinking together at the Westminster Hotel, just down the street from the Rideau.[29] One of the women asked a lone male patron named Ethier to buy her a drink. When he refused, she called him a pimp. He replied by calling her and her friends 'queers'. She retaliated by throwing a beer glass at him, and he responded in kind. When Ethier left the hotel a short time later, the women followed him out onto the street. An officer called to the scene reported only that the group was 'swearing, shouting and incommoding passersby', but Ethier later testified that the five women threatened to kill him and threw punches and kicked him. All six were charged with causing a disturbance, but charges against Ethier were dropped.

Each of the five women pleaded guilty and was ordered to pay a five-dollar fine or serve five days in prison. Two of the five women were unable to cover the cost of the fine, indicating that the attempt to have their drinks bought for them—public houses were licensed to sell only beer, which then cost ten cents a glass—was born of economic necessity. But the fact that three in the group each had at least five dollars suggests that soliciting drinks from men was an acceptable, not a desperate, practice.

Inviting men to buy you a drink and join your table could also be highly lucrative. Downtowners like Jerry and Joan supported themselves for almost a decade through a variety of illegal activities, but 'rolling' men was by far their most profitable. Once seated together at a table inside the bar, one would hold his attention while the other would steal his wallet. The method was not terribly original: pick-pocketing was a ubiquitous form of petty theft, and women have long used the sexual interest of men to their advantage. In the 1950s, pickpocketing was known among its practitioners as 'rolling', and local sex trade workers employed similar tactics before, during, or after sexual contact with johns. Downtowners likely learned these skills from them.[30]

Rolling men in bars other than those frequented by gay women would have better enabled women to escape before the theft was discovered and would also have decreased the likelihood of the victim being able to find and identify them. It would have substantially reduced the risk of disrupting other types of activity within the bar and would have made the bar less dangerous for other women. Yet narrators and newspaper reports indicate that theft was common in and around bars popular with gay women. In 1956, four women 'in the habit of wearing male attire' reportedly offered a lift to a Japanese man waiting for a streetcar outside the Continental (we might guess that the offer was for something altogether different). He accepted, and they subsequently assaulted him and stole his wallet containing a disappointing $27. When the accused appeared in court, 'close to a dozen teenaged girls . . . wearing male attire and masculine hair-dos' came to cheer the defendants on.[31] Whether or not their friends participated in similar activities is unknown, but those who did clearly enjoyed the support of other downtowners, at least in the face of criminal prosecution.

Inside the bar, women were more likely to befriend a potential victim than assault him, but once theft was discovered, some type of altercation between the victim and his female drinking companions could be expected. However, the danger was greatly minimized by the willingness of other downtowners and the male staff to defend those under attack. Whenever a male patron threatened a woman, including fems and prostitutes, butch downtowners were expected to rise to her defence. And whenever violent conflict erupted, bar staff were quick to intercede and remove the troublemaker. Oftentimes it was the male victim and not the women who stole from him who was forced to leave.[32] Bar staff could have discouraged the practice by assisting victims in retrieving their stolen goods and laying formal charges, but according to narrators, theft victims who threatened retaliation were promptly removed from the premises. When women were banned from the bar, it was usually because they became too violent themselves, not because they were stealing from male patrons.[33]

Women who sought out interaction with male patrons were motivated by financial gain, but what inspired men to respond positively to their overtures? Men looking to make a 'date' with a sex trade worker needed to gain access to the ladies and escorts room. The requirement that men could enter only with a female patron was not always strictly enforced, particularly in public houses with an active sex trade, but 'johns' were often too timid to attempt it, and 'even less certain about how to proposition a sex trade worker'. As a result, butch women often agreed to take men inside in exchange for beer. Lynn, who relied on panhandling for much of her income during the early 1960s, figured 'we had it made because we could get all these tricks that wanted to go in there because they wanted to be able to sit and get the women that were hooking. So we'd say, "Okay, you sit with me but you've got to buy my booze for me and my friends".'[34] On a good night, Lynn could treat her mates to an entire evening drinking and socializing without spending any money at all.

Johns were also motivated by sexual interest in butch women. 'You'd have a feminine person sitting beside a dyke,' Lynn explains, 'and the femme going crazy trying to grab a trick and [she's] really pretty and everything, and the guy's looking at the dyke.' Lynn thinks that men were attracted to butch women because they believed lesbians hated men, and having sex with one would be an accomplishment of sorts. Hooking among butches was strongly disapproved of in Buffalo, but in Toronto, it was common and accepted practice among downtowners. Narrators recall different circumstances under which butches hooked. Since street prostitution was especially fraught with danger, some butch downtowners dating fem prostitutes would rather hook themselves than allow their lovers to go out on the streets.[35] Lynn recalls butches might hook for their fem lovers when they were not able to work during menses, and Jerry, a butch who had never had sex with men, turned a trick one night when she was stranded in Montreal with no means to return to Toronto. Normally Jerry worked as part of a team with her best friend and roommate Joan. Joan was also butch, and she actively pursued johns in and around the downtown core. Once a date was arranged, Jerry would follow the pair to a hotel or rooming house and enter the room while they were having sex to steal the john's wallet. 'To make sure the door wasn't locked, she'd always leave gum [or] ... matches stuck in between the door so it wouldn't lock properly.' Jerry and Joan were not the only women to master this method, but no matter how proficient they became it was always an extremely risky venture.[36] Jerry felt that if they were discovered, she was the one who would either be beaten up or turned in to the police, but Joan was persistent and good at talking people into and out of all sorts of things: 'She'd pick up these guys and she'd say to me, "well, we've got one." [I'd say] "Oh no, not again." And like it wouldn't be just one or two guys. Fuck, she'd have two or three a night.' When Jerry balked, Joan's charm and persuasiveness usually helped convince her to participate. It also helped get them out of a number of difficult situations. On the few occasions men discovered the theft in progress, Joan was able to convince the male victim not to get angry or lay charges.[37]

For women with no resources, few skills, or little desire or ability to commit to a regular job, hooking provided fast, but not easy, money. Since gay women congregated in public houses with an established sex trade, the opportunity to turn a trick was always at hand, and if sex trade workers did not actively mentor women, learning how to 'crack a trick' (to approach a potential john and negotiate sex for money) could be learned simply by observation. Less obvious was the personal toll it took on women's daily lives. In Pratt's 1966 conversations with gay women about their criminal records, she found that 'prostitution evoked more by way of response than any of the other offences.'[38] Women were unanimous in their dislike of the trade, and explained that they did it only for the money. More experienced prostitutes sometimes developed amiable relationships with regular tricks, or 'marks', but sex trade work was a source of tremendous emotional and physical stress. Many women used excessive amounts of alcohol or drugs to gird themselves against the danger and discomfort it caused them.[39]

Besides sexually transmitted diseases, one of the trade's major occupational hazards was pregnancy. Narrators claim that butch women were more likely to get pregnant than fems. This suggests that while butch women were known to turn tricks, they did not socialize with fems as sex trade workers, but as friends and lovers, and therefore were less likely to discuss methods of birth control.[40] However, it also seems likely that the incongruity of pregnant women in full masculine attire left a more lasting impression. Since fem sex trade workers relied on the bar for work and pleasure, those who were pregnant were likely to continue coming to the bar, but straight sex trade workers were less reliant on the bar as a source of social contact. Consequently, any pregnant woman was rather conspicuous. Pregnant butches who continued going to the bar did nothing to alter their appearance, although some wore female clothing to the hospital when they gave birth in order to avoid harassment from nursing and medical staff.[41] Clearly downtowners accepted both sex trade work and pregnancy as part of the gay life for both butches and fems. Both of these activities set downtowners apart from other gay women who visited the bar.

Further evidence of the important link between the sex trade and Toronto's postwar lesbian bar culture is provided by the mid-decade shift from the Tenderloin to Chinatown as the centre of lesbian public bar culture. In 1949 Montreal's revitalized Morality Squad began a five-year crackdown on gambling and prostitution that culminated in the 1954 electoral victory of Jean Drapeau, an outspoken supporter of anti-vice campaigns, as city mayor.[42] As a result, a significant number of Montreal prostitutes and pimps migrated to Toronto. As the earlier account of the conflict between 'five husky women' and Ethier suggests, downtowners took a dim view of pimps and competed with them for the right to use Tenderloin public houses. According to Toronto police inspector Jack Webster, many of the Montreal pimps were weightlifters, and there were 'some hell of fights' between the two groups.[43] Tabloid reports if 'he-shes' getting picked up on the streets reveal that downtown butches were arming themselves with knives and other sharp objects.[44] They also began staking out a new neighbourhood.

It is not clear why or how women migrated to the Continental Hotel in Chinatown, but conditions there proved particularly favourable to downtowners. Notable for its social and economic isolation from the rest of the city; Toronto's Chinatown provided shelter from the rest of the city's inhabitants. It also had a well-established sex trade.[45] Decades of racist immigration laws that at first discouraged the migration of Chinese women and eventually prohibited entry to any person of Chinese origin created what historians have called a married-bachelor society.[46] In the city of Toronto, for example, there were 1,758 Chinese men and only 194 Chinese women in 1951.[47] The demand for commercial sex continued well into the early 1960s, despite postwar changes to immigration laws.

There was tremendous poverty in the Toronto Chinese community, but there was also a great deal of wealth, and those who had it were willing to pay for more than just sex. Chinese men sought long-term companionship and were not averse to propositioning lesbians. In 1954, Albert Lee approached two gay women in the Nanking Tavern and offered to take them home for drinks. Once there, he proposed to set one of them up 'in her own business and buy her a coat if she agreed to stay with him'. Unfortunately for Lee, she declined his offer and, after he had one too many drinks, his guests left the apartment with some of his personal belongings.[48] Others proved much more receptive to such arrangements. In 1959, a young Marilyn Johnson left Louis Luke, her much older Chinese lover, for another woman, but when her new lover assaulted her she promptly returned to Luke.[49]

Where the typical john offered women the possibility of free drinks and a small amount of cash, Chinese men offered women stable housing, spending money, and more. Jerry lived with a Chinese man, but only as his tenant. In 1959 a *Hush Free Press* reporter claimed, 'numerous notorious "Butch Broads" . . . are "common-law" mates of Chinatown merchants, chefs, etc'.[50] How many were just renters and how many had more complicated arrangements is impossible to know, but gay women affirm that women and Chinese men formed a variety of personal relationships to one another.[51] Lois Stewart, for example was a good friend to a lesbian 'nurse and go-go dancer' who wanted children and a secure relationship that presumably she felt unable to find with another woman. The nurse/dancer married a Chinese man who accepted her relationships with other women in exchange for her commitment to their family.[52]

Plenty of Chinese men were charged with running bawdy houses and living off the avails of prostitution, but none apparently were male pimps, or at least not in the Continental. The absence of organized crime and male pimps made Chinatown safer for downtowners by reducing the likelihood of conflict with straight men, but it also created opportunities for exploitation. Men with particular sexual interests paid butches to arrange dates with women who met their particular requirements. For example, Jerry was well remunerated by an older white male who was interested exclusively in virgins. On one occasion, Jerry took advantage of one newcomer's attraction to her by convincing her to have sex with Jerry's contact. She finally acquiesced, though on the condition that Jerry remain in the room with her during the sex act.[53] According to Jerry, this was not the only date she arranged for this particular john, but it was the only one in which his 'date' was a virgin.

For many (but certainly not all) sex trade workers and downtowners exploiting johns was fair game, but women who exploited other women were regarded with contempt. Two downtowners in particular were well known for their abusive behaviour that included pimping.[54] Lynn, a young butch who maintained good relationships with prostitutes, explains that Jan and 'Father Murphy' were 'rough sons of bitches' who 'pretend[ed] they were going with [dating] them and they'd only meet them every day long enough to collect their god damn money'. It was nothing for them to grab a woman, throw her up the alley (behind the Continental) and say, "You're fucking around. You're spending all your money on dope and booze. I need money for my car", for this and that.'[55] They were also known to steal money out of the bras of prostitutes who were either drunk on beer or high on drugs.

Most downtowners rejected this kind of behaviour but were unable to prevent it from happening. Many were terrified to stand up to Jan's clique, who aggressively intimidated other, younger butches and expected other butches to join them. On one occasion Lynn was called upon to participate in the assault of a new young butch, but she refused. 'I was sitting and I remember this real cute little dyke came in and they started their shit and one of them grabbed her and threw her on the floor and just like vultures they were there. Mitch turned right around and looked at me and said "Come on". I looked right at her and I said, "You don't fuckin' need me, Mitch, there's four of you on her now. Why the fuck don't you just leave her alone?" I was shocked myself [for having said that] and she looked like she just wanted to grab me and eat me up. But I didn't care anymore, I was fed up seeing it because there was no excuse for it as far as I was concerned.'[56] Lynn expected she was next in line for a beating, but instead Mitch bought her a beer the following evening. There was no discussion about what had happened, and while it did not discourage Mitch from meting out the same treatment to other new butches, she never again called on Lynn to join in.

The expectation that butch downtowners be able to fend for themselves may have contributed to their reluctance to intervene in these situations, but this was not the case for fems.[57] There was no expectation that fems be willing and able to fight (though some did), and in fact, butches were expected to shield their fem partners from outside threats. However, as we saw, Jan made no effort to hide her willingness to exploit and steal from fem sex trade workers. Ivy, a fem and sex trade worker who was well respected by many downtowners affirms that 'nobody would disapprove of Jan', that the typical reaction was 'it's none of our business', and that she was 'the only one down there who had any balls to speak up'. It's not clear how Ivy communicated her disapproval, but Jan was aware of Ivy's views, and 'never took any money off [hookers] if I was there'.[58]

Individual expressions of disapproval were important, but had only a limited impact. Why didn't more women act to oppose violence and exploitation? The positions of downtowners as sexual outsiders living on the city's economic margins spawned unwritten rules of conduct that militated against collective action directed at other women in the community. All women who went to the bars were expected to keep out of the affairs of others, a fact well understood by downtowners and uptowners alike. Denise, an uptowner who went to the Continental with women she met in her parents' neighbourhood fruit and vegetable store, explains that downtowners 'either liked you or they didn't like you', that people were judged on their ability to accept without judgment everyone in the bar, and to take everything and everyone in stride. She thinks she was accepted because 'I minded my own business. I was quiet. I didn't cause any problems . . . . There could be some very bad fights and knives and all, that stuff . . . . I did walk out one night through the back door and there was somebody being pulverized in the parking lot. Well, you just kept going. You didn't interfere. It had nothing to do with you so you made a point of not getting involved.'[59] Unless an incident involved you or a close friend, women (and men) were expected to keep their thoughts and hands to themselves.

Downtowners had cause to remain careful about how involved they became with other gay women, including other downtowners, and it showed in the various ways they guarded personal information. For example, most women were known to each other only by their nicknames, some adopted an alias, and only a very few revealed their last name to anyone but their closest friends.[60] The reasons varied: some feared another downtowner might spitefully call the place of work and inform their boss that they were seen at the Continental, a call that would surely result in an immediate dismissal. Others had family actively looking for them, and did not want to be found. But women's participation in criminal activities made minding your own business imperative. Downtowners' involvement with petty theft and the sex trade united them in their vulnerability to police interference and arrest, but maintaining a careful distance from all but one's closest friends was an effective way to guard against the potential threat posed by other women in the bar who could prove unwilling or unable to withhold information from the police. The less others knew about you, the less they could reveal. While an effective way to manage the various risks downtowners faced, it undermined their ability to develop stronger and wider friendship networks that would likely have greater success (in opposing or preventing violence and abuse within the group.

Added to the mix was the lack of physical, economic, and political resources available to most downtowners. Whereas other Torontonians might call on the police in cases of violent assault, for downtowners this was out of the question (for reasons that will become much clearer below). Additionally, up until the early 1960s there were few other social spaces where women could enjoy the same kind of freedom to be openly butch and fem, and many women did not want to endanger these spaces by calling in the authorities. The Continental was one of the few places where women felt relatively free from harassment; it was the outside world that was dangerous, especially when women traversed it alone. As Lynn's testimony vividly illustrates, women who challenged the behaviour of a few known troublemakers put their own physical safety at risk. If their efforts failed, they might find themselves unable to access the community of people who made them feel most safe. Undoubtedly some women expressed their disapproval by simply retreating from the bar altogether, but for women committed to living the gay life there was nowhere to retreat. The more women came to rely on the social networks that centred on the Continental, the more they risked censure by their peers. Despite the damaging effect violence and abuse had on all women who participated in Toronto's lesbian bar culture, disagreements over how some women conducted their lives and treated their partners were rarely openly expressed.[61]

Jan, Father Murphy, Mitch, and their clique stand out in the memories of most narrators because their behaviour was the exception, not the rule. Still, most women agree that arguments among women in the bar were frequent and sometimes escalated into physical conflict. Yet remarkably, neither the Liquor Licensing Board of Ontario nor local police forces made any effort to close the bar down. As we now know, the postwar era was a period of widespread social anxiety about the threat of sex deviants, but it was men, not women, who were the primary targets. Up until the end of the 1950s, the police did not raid the Continental, and there are no records to suggest that any effort was made to force the owner or management to ban their lesbian customers even though liquor licensing laws contained provisions that allowed them to do so.[62]

Local authorities were keeping an eye on the Continental, but it was mixed heterosexual couples that were of concern, not the 'mannish', 'husky', he-shes' beginning to make it their home. Up until 1954, the LLBO enforced racial segregation in licensed establishments by treating 'race-mixing' as a signifier for disorderly conduct.[63] When Syrian-born Lenia Chamandy bought the Continental in 1948, she knew the previous owners were reprimanded for allowing non-white men to mingle with white women.[64] Eager to reassure the Liquor Board that she intended to run a respectable business, her lawyer informed them 'in order to improve the operation of the . . . beverage rooms, we have decided to eliminate mixed-race drinking . . . [by which] we mean Chinese entering with white women, Negros with white women, etc'. The LLBO continued to monitor the situation. In a 1952 spot check, it was noted that, 'lately with increasing numbers Negro men have been congregating in front of this establishment and are picking up white girls.' The LLBO inspector promptly informed the local police inspector, who reported that his officers were 'trying to clear it up.'[65] In the fall of 1955, an African Canadian man attempted to enter the Ladies and Escorts room with 'an old white woman' but the staff refused them entry. There was nothing new in denying service to black Canadians, except that after 1954 it, was a violation of the Fair Accommodations Act, and proprietors who refused service on the basis of race, creed, colour, nationality, ancestry, or place of origin could be fined.[66] With the law now ostensibly on his side, the aggrieved male patron alerted a journalist at the *Toronto Telegram*, a daily newspaper that offered supportive coverage of the Fair Accommodations Act the previous year.[67] Although the LLBO file does not indicate how the Board responded to the incident, there were no further reports concerning mixed-race patronage.

It was around the same time that gay women moved from the Tenderloin on Jarvis Street to a public house at Elizabeth and Dundas Streets in Chinatown, but curiously, local liquor authorities made no formal complaints or even benign observations about the growing presence of the 'sapphic set', even though some members of the set were African Canadian, and all mixed openly with Chinese sex trade workers inside the public house.[68] When the police focused their attention on gay women, it was usually a result of their involvement with the sex trade, theft, or public brawls such as the one that occurred near the Westminster Hotel. The police and the courts also made liberal use of established vagrancy laws to try to keep Continental regulars off the streets and away from the Tenderloin and Chinatown, but in the 1950s the police rarely entered the bar, and they never conducted the sort of 'paddy wagon' raids and mass arrests commonly associated with gay bars in this period. Moreover, unlike gay men whose public cruising made them vulnerable to charges of gross indecency, downtowners were rarely caught having or pursuing sex with one another. When the police discovered two women necking in Riverdale Park in 1954, the same year the Criminal Code of Canada was revised to allow for women to be charged with gross indecency, the police charged 'mannish' Patricia Hendrick under section C of the vagrancy laws, having no visible means of support.[69] According to her testimony in court, she had not held a regular job for a year and supported herself as a prostitute. Hendrick was hauled off to prison, but her lover was never charged. Instead Salvation Army Major Mabel Woollcott, who promised to provide housing and help her find a job, escorted her out of the court.

Even as other forms of sexual deviation (a modernized and medicalized term) became the subject of intense media, medical, and social concern in the 1950s lesbianism remained a lesser threat.[70] With the exception of the scandal sheets, Canada's print media focused almost exclusively on pedophilia and male homosexuals.[71] As late as 1962 the Associate Editor of *Chatelaine*, Canada's leading national women's magazine, rejected an article about lesbians of the 'nasty practicing kind . . .' After all,' she wrote, 'sex with men is what worries moms because it often ends up showing.'[72] Pregnancy remained the real sexual peril for young women. Despite warnings by American experts like Frank Caprio who insisted homosexuality was as dangerous in women as it was in men, Canadian experts were surprisingly blasé.[73] During the 1954–7 hearings of the Royal Commission on the Criminal Law Relating to the Criminal Sexual Psychopath, medical experts from across the country were called upon to give testimony on the problem of sexual deviancy. Only one witness bothered to comment on lesbianism. As far as Dr J.N. Senn of Hamilton, Ontario knew, 'The female homosexual conducts herself in such a way that she never comes to public attention', and he did not seem to think that there was any reason to 'alter this situation'.[74]

Senn may not have been aware of the growing visibility of butch and fem lesbians and lesbian prostitutes in Canada's major urban centres, but Toronto's Chief of Police John Chisholm certainly was. Yet Chisholm was surprisingly circumspect about the sex panic that was driving anti-homosexual campaigns, throughout Canada and the United States. Asked to testify on the problem of sex deviants in his city, Chisholm told the same commission that in his opinion motor vehicles were a greater threat to the safety of children than were sex perverts. Although his officers conducted sweeps on male homosexual haunts, he did not demonstrate the same kind of zeal as many of his contemporaries in other urban centres.[75] Indeed, in the 1950s gay women seemed to enjoy somewhat congenial relations with local officers. Ivy, whose work in the sex trade brought her into regular contact with the police, claims they never hassled her. In fact, she remembers a time when off-duty officers worked security at a wedding ceremony for two gay women.[76] Ivy is the only narrator who offers such a positive assessment of gay women's relations with local police forces. However, downtowners who were regulars in the 1950s say surprisingly little about their relationship to the police.

Political corruption also contributed to the peace in the 1950s. Public houses and other licensed establishments generally received their permits in exchange for financial donations to the reigning Conservative Party. Fred Gardiner, a high profile criminal lawyer known for representing local gambling interests, managed these transactions. This explains why private unlicensed clubs like the Wheat Sheaf were very likely to be raided by the police, whereas public houses rarely had their licenses revoked, and were little bothered by local authorities. In the 1950s, women encountered the police on the streets not in the bar.[77]

At the end of the 1950s, however, relations between downtowners, prostitutes, and the police changed dramatically. In 1958 Chisholm committed suicide, and his replacement had a much different attitude toward urban vice in general, and homosexuals in particular.[78] Chief James P. Mackey promoted long-time friend Herbert Thurston to the position of Inspector, who launched a sustained campaign against prostitutes and homosexuals.[79] In 1959, *Hush* reported that two officers were assigned to the Tenderloin to 'haul in all girls found loitering'. The formal charge was causing a disturbance. Unlike Section C of the vagrancy laws, the law against causing a disturbance allowed the police to arrest and detain any woman simply for being out on the street at night. 'This gives the police a wide margin to work on,' wrote the *Hush* journalist. 'The babes are being swatted like flies.'[80] Police efforts to put down urban vice are often prompted by public calls for a crackdown on sexual immorality, but in the early 1960s, it was the police that were trying to rouse public ire. In a 1963 interview with the *Globe and Mail*, Thurston complained that Torontonians 'lack disgust' for homosexuals, and their indifference was contributing to the growth of the city's sex deviant population.[81] This contrasted sharply with the sentiment among his officers who, according to a *Maclean's* report, 'might beat deviates in disgust'.[82]

Thurston was also determined to prove that lesbians were as much of a threat as gay men. He described them as part of a community of deviants that included men and that in total numbered around 40,000. Lest citizens think that mannish looking women posed no danger, he ominously told the reporter that a female officer who 'ventured into' the Jukebox, an unlicensed Yonge Street club that catered to a lesbian clientele, was informed that if she used the washroom, she would be raped. His squad 'harassed the club out of existence'.[83]

Thurston was not exaggerating about the increasing visibility of homosexuals in certain parts of the city. In the early 1960s gay women suddenly had a greater variety of social spaces available to them and were more likely to be congregating beyond the invisible boundaries that marked off Chinatown from the rest of the city. The Jukebox was run by a straight male ex-con, but gay women and men were starting to open up their own clubs. Heather and Georgie, a mixed-race lesbian couple, opened The New Orient on Queen and Spadina where women could come for soft drinks and dancing. British-born musician Robin York and her partner opened the upscale Regency Club on Prince Arthur Avenue.[84] Customers there enjoyed a piano bar, a pool table room and television room, a dance floor, and a cafe and patio. Perhaps the most important development was Sara Dunlop's persistent efforts, despite police harassment, to maintain an after-hours club. The Music Room, later renamed the Penthouse, drew lesbians to Yonge Street where they began to frequent restaurants and cafes nearby. Adult gay women quickly developed a following of younger women and together they made themselves at home in the front room of the Parkside Tavern, a bar that already had an established gay male clientele. However, while the Jukebox, Music Room, and Parkside provided an escape from the problems associated with the Continental, it also brought gay women physically closer to gay men. Male homosexuals were subject to greater police scrutiny, and drinking in bars and clubs where gay men congregated automatically increased the amount of contact, and the potential for conflict, between gay women and the police.[85]

Finally and most fatally, around the same time that Mackey was promoted to Chief of Police, heroin (and soon thereafter speed and pharmaceuticals) became as much a part of 'the gay life' as prostitution. Downtowners and sex trade workers were some of the city's earliest users and dealers, and the Continental and surrounding neighbourhood quickly earned a reputation as a drug haven. The impact was profound. It changed the way women socialized; rather than become rowdy and boisterous from consuming alcohol, they became lethargic, lost their appetite, and began to show signs of physical deterioration. The cost of a single cap of heroin was six dollars, significantly more than a glass of beer, and women's participation in the sex trade and other illegal activities increased in order to support their addiction.[86] By the end of the decade, countless women died as a direct or indirect result of drug use.[87]

Heroin also led to a dramatic increase in the level of police attention downtowners attracted. All levels of Canadian law enforcement, including the local Metropolitan Toronto police division, the Ontario Provincial Police, and the Royal Canadian Mounted Police (RCMP) actively participated in the effort to stop the traffic in illegal drugs, and in the 1960s gay women were more likely to encounter law enforcement officials than they had at any other time. In the late 1950s, four Toronto officers were assigned to the drug squad, and they made it their business to become intimately familiar with downtowners' comings and goings.[88] They also worked in cooperation with other police organizations.[89] Unconcerned with the system of political payoffs that kept the police out of public houses, the RCMP planted female informants in the Continental and other bars and restaurants.[90] This was not the first time the RCMP assigned undercover agents to homosexual bars. During the 1950s, investigations of 'subversion' in the civil service prompted the same force to use similar tactics to identify homosexuals.[91]

The intensity of police efforts and their willingness to use a wide range of methods of intimidation, including physical violence, made the gay life significantly more dangerous. Even women who were not involved in the drug trade were affected. Neither Jerry nor Lynn used heroin or speed, but both were questioned about the drug trade. Lynn remembers one time when she was picked up by the RCMP and taken into the station:

> The cops knew enough about everybody, they knew fuckin' well that I did not use, but they knew that my girlfriend did. So they figured that I must know who the pushers are and where this shit is coming from. I said, 'I don't fucking know nothing. I don't want to know nothing, I hate drugs. If you fuckin know so much, then you know I am only a drunk and I start drinking at 12 and by 12:30 I don't know my ass from a hole in the ground.' This one guy got his knuckles and he hit me right on the bone in the top of my skull here, bang! The tears came flying out of my eyes. And he took his big shoe, they wear steel toes . . . [and kicked me] right in the shin. I still have a mark to this day on my shin. He was saying 'you know where she gets it you fucking little dyke'. And he'd smack me. And then he got his hand and he had my whole throat. I swear I could feel my eyes start to bug right out of my head and I started to panic inside. I got to where I really couldn't breathe, my tongue was coming out and I really thought I was going to die.

Eventually they released her, but not before warning her to stay away from the corners. Lynn ignored the warning.

Jerry confirms that if the police 'thought that you were dealing in heroin; they didn't give a shit . . . especially the horsemen [RCMP] . . . if they got an address, they'd bust it.' Like Lynn, she too was picked up off the street.

> The cops knew who I was . . . and this little bastard picked me up, told me to get into the car, so I did. And he was asking questions about somebody who was dealing heroin and I said, 'I don't fucking know who you're talking about.' He said, 'You don't eh?' Rack! . . . This bastard hit me in the left arm and he broke it, broke it with a fuckin' billy club.

The police may have been vicious in their methods, but they were not wrong in their assessment. Lynn and Jerry both knew who was doing and who was dealing drugs, but refused to provide this information. Regardless of how much Lynn despised the drug trade, there was a general expectation that 'you don't cop out somebody.'[92] We might guess that some women succumbed to the pressure tactics the police employed. The RCMP searched Ivy's home on at least two separate occasions, possibly because they were acting on tips from other women.[93]

Arlene, who did deal in drugs, was also victimized by local police forces, although she never was charged with a drug-related crime. 'Many [police officers] used to pick you up and kick your head in. It was a fun time; take you down to Cherry Beach and beat the shit out of you.' Cherry Beach was a stretch of undeveloped land along Lake Ontario. Surrounded by heavy industry, it was deserted most nights. Its remote location made it popular among sex trade workers who sometimes took tricks there, but it was also used by local police officers to beat and rape prostitutes and downtowners. Lynn and Jerry were each taken there twice by the police and physically assaulted, and Arlene was raped and left to make her way back into the city without the benefit of either clothes or shoes. No wonder Lynn felt that 'all [the police] needed was the excuse that you were queer . . . and that gave them the license to beat the living supreme shit out of you.' Women's relationship to the sex trade and their involvement in petty theft and physical assault increased the likelihood that they would attract the attention of local police forces, but at the end of the 50s, the introduction of street drugs and the new Toronto police chief's more aggressive anti-homosexual stance made those interactions more frequent and more violent.

These accounts confirm our worst fears about the way lesbians and gay men were treated by the police in the postwar period, but they also reveal that some women were much more likely to be targeted by the police than others. As downtowners grew increasingly fearful of the police, uptowners remained astonishingly confident that they would have no trouble with the law. They also understood that the police did not target gay women indiscriminately, but directed their attention toward downtowners. So long as they did not participate in illegal activities or carry weapons, uptowners were certain that they would never be harassed. Instead, they were more likely to fear being identified by 'tourists', men and women who came to the Continental to gawk at the lesbians.[94] But not even that troubled Denise and Lois Stewart. The daughter of Italian immigrants who ran a neighbourhood fruit market in the west end, Denise was very careful about her family's reputation, and placed a high value on sexual discretion and privacy. Yet she had no misgivings about going to the Continental in the 1960s because she was certain no one she knew would ever come to such a dive. As a middle class schoolteacher, Lois understood that being seen in a bar with a lesbian crowd would bring her career to an abrupt end, but since she worked in another city, she decided the risk was small. For her the Continental posed little danger at all. 'Most of the people knew about [us] and we didn't get much flack,' she explains. 'Not in that place . . . . We could spot a tourist a mile off, they'd watch us, but the rest of the people in the bar were used to us. That's why we went there. You could go there reasonably safely.'[95] The same applied to the police, who she said, would 'often arrest everyone in the place except me and a couple others. Because they all knew who we were. Everyone knew . . . I didn't deal drugs and they knew it. . . 'Indeed, not one of the four uptowners that inform this study were ever bothered by the police.[96]

Participating in Toronto's lesbian bar culture demanded that uptowners (and downtowners) accept or at the very least turn a blind eye to a variety of activities that they might otherwise find objectionable.[97] They had to sit alongside prostitutes, johns, and rounders without passing judgment, and they had to learn the rules of discretion that governed a street economy subject to police and state regulation. Most women accomplished this by keeping a distance from downtowners. Beth claims, 'As long as you didn't interfere with other people you didn't know or didn't want to know, you were fine.' Even those keen to cultivate friendships with downtowners developed social strategies to shield them from trouble. Lois Stewart prided herself on her ability to cross the 'invisible line' that separated the two groups but refused to give downtowners a ride in her car for fear that they might stash drugs in it.[98] On the whole, most downtowners maintained cordial, but not intimate, relations with uptowners.[99] Downtowners kept them at a distance, and when they took offence to uptowners' conduct, were willing to use physical force and intimidation to drive them out.[100] Mutual distrust and sometimes disdain marked the uneasy relationship between uptowners and downtowners. However great their shared experience of social isolation and their common interest in sexual relations with other women, there were other forces at work that precluded the creation of a unified community bound together by their status as sexual outsiders. At the Continental Hotel, some were much further outside than others.

Two years after Joji Hazel visited the Continental, an anonymous writer offered a playfully affectionate description of the downtown butch:

> When a female baby doesn't outgrow dirty denims, scuffed shoes, chain smoking and picking fights and acquires so much brashness that her family doesn't dare introduce her to their friends, she becomes a butch . . . . She is a piece of skin stretched over a rebellion. A war on two legs . . . . She is a confused situation to be cuddled, fed, liquored, and loved at all times: a boy forever, a policeman's nemesis, the offspring of our times, the scourge of a nation. Every one molded is a taunt that woman can equal man . . . . If not worked too often and if praised at regular intervals will survive fights, thirty days for vagrancy, starvation, hangovers and a hard night of love.[101]

Ironically, at the same time 'What is a Downtown Butch' was published, the conditions that created downtowners as a distinct social group were unravelling. Chinese married bachelors were aging; those still living were moving out of the neighbourhood entirely, and Chinatown's sex trade workers gradually returned to the Tenderloin.[102] After the mid-1960s, lesbians were more likely to congregate in the bars, clubs, and restaurants around the Music Room and Parkside on Yonge Street, or in even newer bars on Church Street and in the city's east end.[103] The Continental developed a reputation as a place where the older crowd hung out. When its doors finally closed in 1975, a new generation of lesbians offered an entirely different 'taunt that woman can equal man'.[104] Though gay women's involvement in the sex and drug trades did not end in the 1960s, the maintenance of a public lesbian bar culture would no longer depend on the illegal economy to sustain it. And with the rise of lesbian-feminism in the 1970s, new social divisions emerged to displace uptowners and downtowners as one of the primary categories of difference.

According to one of sociologist Jo Anne Pratt's informants, living openly as a butch lesbian was 'an indication of pride in the homosexual way of life.'[105] It also meant exposing oneself to economic and social peril. Limited job options drove women to pursue opportunities available to them in some of the city's rougher bars, and time spent in rough bars guaranteed exposure to verbal conflict and physical danger. So long as women remained dependant on the street economy, they remained wedded to street bars. Tough bar lesbians did not congregate in street bars because they wanted to expand the number of spaces available to women, as Davis and Kennedy argue. Nor were they attracted to them because they were necessarily familiar environments. Existing sex trade cultures provided the conditions necessary for gay women to establish themselves as a regular and stable presence, but tough bar lesbians preferred street bars because the sex trade also provided opportunities to combine remunerative labour with pleasure. Downtowners were homosexual, but expressions of gender and sexual identity were informed by the economic consequences of living the gay life full time. As a result, downtowners were much more aggressively policed by law enforcement officials, and much more likely to come into conflict with the law. Their intimate familiarity with prostitution, drugs, and local Chinese men established firm boundaries between themselves and other gay women whose sexual identities bore no apparent relationship to other local, marginalized groups. In the 1950s and 60s being gay 'at all times' generated strategies of survival, rules of discretion, and forms of social discourse that set downtowners apart from other working-class lesbians.

Notes

This author would like to thank the editors of *Left History* and the anonymous reviewers for their thoughtful critical commentaries and suggestions on an earlier and much different version of this article. I am especially indebted to Marc Stein, Steven Maynard, and Suzanne Morton for their helpful comments at a critical stage in the preparation of this paper. I would also like to thank the Lesbians Making History collective for granting me permission to use their interview collection, the women who generously granted interviews, and 'Jerry' for tolerating more than a decade of prying questions. Lois Stewart, Ivy, and Lynn are all the real names of narrators. All others are pseudonyms, either at the request of the interviewee or because permission was not obtained at the time the interview was conducted. The Lesbians Making History collection, to which I have added my own interviews, is currently being prepared for donation to the Canadian Lesbian and Gay Archives in Toronto, Ontario. Anyone interested in contributing their own history to this collection should contact the author at the Department of History, Simon Fraser University.

1. Joji Hazel, 'Main St- Lesbianville', *The Ladder,* May 1963, 22.
2. On lesbian images in pulp fiction see Kate Adams, 'Making the World Safe for the Missionary Position: Images of the Lesbian in Post-World War II America' in *Lesbian Texts and Contexts: Radical Revisions,* Karla Jay and Joanne Glasgow, eds. (New York: New York University Press, 1990), 255–74; see also *Forbidden Love: The Unashamed Stories of Lesbian Lives,* dirs. Lynne Fernie and Aerlyn Weissman, 84 mins., National Film Board, 1992, videocassette; Donna Penn, 'The Meanings of Lesbianism in PostWar America' *Gender and History* 3.2 (Summer 1991): 191.
3. Hazel, 'Main St- Lesbianville', 22.
4. Historians typically describe participants in lesbian bar cultures as members of a bar 'community', but the homogeneity this term implies is misleading. For useful suggestions about how historians might rethink community as a category of analysis, see John C. Walsh and Steven High, 'Rethinking the Concept of Community', *Historie sociale/Social History* 32.64 (1999): 255–73. The meanings of butch and fem roles have been the subject of much debate, and the sources are too many to list here. For a brief summary of some of the key arguments, readers should consult Elizabeth Lapovsky Kennedy and Madeline Davis, *Boots of Leather. Slippers of Gold: A History of a Lesbian Community* (New York: Routledge, 1993), 152–4.
5. Gay men used the term 'the double life' to refer to the same practice decades earlier. See George Chauncey, *Gay New York: Gender, Urban Culture, and the Making of the Gay Male World, 1890–1940* (New York: Basic Books, 1994), 273–80.
6. On the use of 'kiki', see Kennedy and Davis, *Boots of Leather, Slippers of Gold*; 212, 213; Lillian Faderman, *Odd Girls 'and Twilight Lovers: A History of Lesbian Life in Twentieth Century America* (New York: Columbia University Press, 1991),175–84.
7. For a similar examination from the perspective of middle class lesbians, see Gilmartin, 'We Weren't Bar People'.
8. Among the most significant American studies to use oral history are Davis and Kennedy, *Boots of Leather, Slippers of Gold*; Chauncey, *Gay New York*; and Marc Stein, *The City of Sisterly and Brotherly Loves: The Making of Lesbian and Gay Communities in Greater Philadelphia, 1945–1976* (Chicago and London:

University of Chicago Press, 2000). For an assessment of the tabloids as a resource for historians see Ross Higgins and Line Chamberland, 'Mixed Messages: Gays and Lesbians in Montreal Yellow Papers in the 1950s', in *The Challenge of Modernity: A Reader on Post-Confederation Canada*, Ian MacKay, ed. (Toronto: McGraw-Hill Ryerson, 1992), 421–38, and Stephen Maynard, '"Hell Witches in Toronto": Notes on Lesbian Visibility in Early Twentieth-Century Canada', *left history* 9.2 (Spring/Summer 2004): 191–205.

9. John D'Emilio, *Sexual Politics, Sexual Communities: The Making of a Homosexual Minority in the United States, 1940–1970* (Chicago: University of Chicago Press, 1983), 31–2. See also Allan Berube, *Coming Out Under Fire: The History of Gay Men and Women in World War Two* (New York: Free Press, 1990). Paul Norman Jackson details a similar effect in Canada in 'Courting homosexuals in the military: The management of homosexuality in the Canadian military, 1939–1945' (PhD diss., Queen's University at Kingston, 2002).
10. Nan Alamilla Boyd, *Wide Open Town: A History of Queer San Francisco* (Berkeley: University of California Press, 2003).
11. David Sobel and Susan Meurer, *Working at Inglis: The Lift and Death of a Canadian Factory* (Toronto: James Lorimer and Company, 1994), 66–8.
12. Margaret, interviewed by author, Toronto, Ontario, 1995.
13. Ibid. Remarkably, Margaret claims that it was not until 1993 when she saw the Canadian documentary *Forbidden Love* that she first understood herself as a lesbian. Karen Duder describes similarly isolated lesbian couples in 'The spreading depths: Lesbian and bisexual women in English Canada, 1910–1965', (PhD diss., University of Victoria, 2001), 362. On friendship networks among professional women in Ontario see Kato Perdue, 'Dear Lamb, I Am At Your Feet', unpublished paper presented at 'Passion in Prose: Love Letters from the Queer Past', University of Toronto, June 2001.
14. On industrial baseball leagues see Sobel and Meurer, *Working at Inglis*, 69; on lesbians and organized ball teams in Toronto see Trisha, interviewed by Lesbians Making History (LMH), [Toronto], 1986; on ball teams and lesbians in Kingston, Ontario see Marney Elizabeth McDiarmid, 'From Mouth to Mouth: An Oral History of Lesbians and Gays in Kingston from World War II to 1980', (MA thesis, Queen's University at Kingston, 1999); on the gay beach on the Toronto Island see *Forbidden Love*. On Hanlan's Point, see Becki Ross, 'Dance to "Tie a Yellow Ribbon", Get Churched, and Buy the Little Lady a Drink: Gay Women's Bar Culture in Toronto, 1965–1975', in *Weaving Alliances: Selected Papers Presented for the Canadian Women's Studies Association at the 1991 and 1992 Learned Societies Conferences*, Debra Martens, ed. (Ottawa: Canadian Women's Studies Association, 1993), 272.
15. Donald Kerr and Jacob Spelt, *The changing face of Toronto: a study in urban geography* (Ottawa: Geographical Branch, Mines and Technical Surveys, 1965), 130; 'Women Workers in Canada, 1954–1964', *Labour Gazette* 65 (April 1965), 65.
16. Tamara Adilman, 'A Preliminary Sketch of Chinese Women and Work in British Columbia, 1858–1950', in *British Columbia Reconsidered: Essays on Women*, Gillian Creese and Veronica Strong-Boag, eds. (Vancouver: Press Gang Publishers 1992), 309–39; Dionne Brand, '"We Weren't Allowed to Go Into Factory Work Until Hitler Started the War': The 1920s to the 1940s', in *'We're Rooted Here and They Can't Pull Us Up': Essays in African Canadian Women s History*, Peggy Bristow, et al, eds. (Toronto: University of Toronto Press, 1994), 171–92.
17. See Elaine Tyler May *Homeward Bound: American Families in the Cold War Era* (New York: Basic Books, 1988); Mary Louise Adams, *The Trouble with Normal: Postwar Youth and the Making of Heterosexuality* (Toronto: University of Toronto Press, 1997), and Annalee Golz, 'Family Matters: The Canadian Family and the State in the Postwar Period', *Left History* 1.2 (1994): 9–49, On post-Second World War labour trends among women see Veronica Strong-Boag, 'Canada's Wage Earning Wives and the Construction of the Middle Class, 1945–1960', *Journal of Canadian Studies* 29: 3 (1994): 5–25.
18. Jerry, interview by author, Toronto, 1992.
19. Lynn, interview by author, Toronto, 1993; Jerry, interview (1992); Jan, interview by LMH, [Toronto?], 1985; Arlene, interview by LMH, [Toronto?], 1987. See also Becki Ross, 'Destaining the (Tattooed) Delinquent Body: The Practices of Moral Regulation at Toronto's Street Haven, 1965–1969', *Journal of the History of Sexuality* 7.4 (April, 1997): 591.
20. Arlene, interview.
21. Ibid.
22. Two charges were for crimes committed against themselves, one for attempted suicide and the other for overdosing on sleeping pills. Jo Anne Pratt, 'A Study of the Female Homosexual Subculture', (MA thesis, School of Social Work, University of Toronto, 1964), 42.
23. Arlene broke into cars to sleep, Jerry was arrested outside the New Orient during a lover's quarrel, and Lynn was told not to return to the corners after being interrogated by the RCMP. See Arlene, interview; Jerry, interview; Lynn, interview,

24. Pratt, 'A Study of the Female Homosexual Subculture', 8–9.
25. Jan, interview; see also Jean in *Forbidden Love* (NFB, 1992).
26. On similar practices of gender segregation in Vancouver, see Robert A. Campbell, 'Managing the Marginal: Regulating and Negotiating Decency in Vancouver's Beer Parlours, 1925–1954', *Labour/Le Travail* 44 (1999): 109–27.
27. In the 1930s Toronto police constables working the night shift were required to check in on the city's downtown hotels at closing time when fights were most likely to occur. James P. Mackey, *'I Policed Toronto': An autobiography by James P. Mackey, Chief of Police. Metropolitan Toronto. 1958–1970* (1985), 18.
28. Ontario Archives, RG 36–8 Establishment Files, 'Lamb's Star Hotel', report by Inspector W.H. Cool, 28 July 1947. In 1948 The Lamb's Star was renamed the Continental Hotel.
29. 'Five Women Assault Man', *Justice Weekly* (2 August 1952): 2, 13.
30. For a brief description of the practice, see Pratt, 'A Study of the Female Homosexual Subculture', 43. See also Jerry, interview (1992).
31. 'Jap Says Four White Young Girls Picked Him Up In Car And Robbed Him of $27 After Assaulting Him', *Justice Weekly* (22 September 1956), 2, 16.
32. Jerry, interview (1992); Denise, interview.
33. Jerry, interview (1992, 2004).
34. Lynn, interview.
35. Arlene, interview.
36. For another account of the team approach to rolling tricks, see 'Bargain Chippy Had Sour Taste', *Confidential Flash* (9 July 1955), 5.
37. Jerry, interview (1992).
38. Pratt, 'A Study of the Female Homosexual Subculture', 43.
39. Ibid. See also Ivy, interview by author, Toronto, 1993.
40. On the regulation of condoms and other forms of birth control in this period, see Angus McLaren and Arlene Tigar McLaren, *The Bedroom and the State: The Changing Practices and Politics of Contraception and Abortion in Canada, 1880–1997*, 2nd ed. (Toronto: Oxford University Press Canada, 1997).
41. Jerry became pregnant with twins and like many other downtowners, gave her children up for adoption. Jerry, interview (1992).
42. William Weintraub, *City Unique: Montreal Days and Nights in the 1940s and 50s* (Toronto: McClelland and Stewart, 1996), 59–87. See also Higgins and Chamberland 'Mixed Messages', 422.
43. Jack Webster, interview by author, Toronto, 1994.
44. See 'Lesbian Beat Murder Trial Now Stabs Man', *Flash* (7 January 1956), 1, 8; 'Lesbian Quintet Dream Up Attempted Rape Story to Cover Up Knife Wound', *Justice Weekly* (28 July 1956), 3, 16; 'Toronto Breeze Around', *Hush Free Press* (23 August 1958), 5.
45. Valerie A. Mah, 'The 'Bachelor' Society: A look at Toronto's early Chinese Community from 1878–1924', Part II Student paper, 'Independent Research', Multicultural History Society of Ontario (April 1978), 18. On prostitution in Vancouver's Chinatown in the early twentieth century, see Adilman, 'A Preliminary Sketch of Chinese Women and Work in British Columbia, 1858–1950', 309–39.
46. Peter S. Li, *The Chinese in Canada* (Toronto: Oxford University Press, 1998).
47. Ibid., 97.
48. *Justice Weekly* (3 July 1954), 5.
49. 'Aged Chinese Wins Marilyn', *Hush Free Press* (12 September 1959), 6.
50. 'Lesbians Overflow Chinatown', *Hush Free Press* (28 November 1959), 12.
51. See also Ross, 'Destaining the (Tattooed) Delinquent Body'.
52. Lois, interview by LMH, [Toronto?], 1985.
53. Jerry, interview (1992).
54. Lois, interview.
55. Ivy, interview; Lynn, interview. Buffalo women also pimped. See Davis and Kennedy, *Boots of Leather, Slippers of Gold*, 119.
56. Lynn, interview.
57. Arlene explains that when a friend first offered to bring her to the Continental, she insisted that Arlene first learn how to fight. Not all women had the benefit of anticipating violence, however, but neither were all women similarly attacked. Arlene, interview.
58. Ivy, interview.
59. Denise, interview.
60. Arlene, interview; Jerry, interview (2004).
61. Of course, the same was true for heterosexuals. The issue of abuse among women stands out largely because we are more likely to imagine women as victims, not as perpetrators of violence. Women like Eve also made that assumption. After leaving an abusive marriage, she responded positively to a butch's advances because she assumed that a woman would not assault her. Unfortunately she was wrong; her partner physically abused her on many occasions, though always behind closed doors. Eve, interview by author, Toronto, 1993.
62. Kennedy and Davis report that police raids of lesbian bars in Buffalo were rare and that after-hours clubs were more likely to be raided. Kennedy and Davis, *Boots of Leather, Slippers of Gold*, 41–2. On police raids of lesbian bars in other American cities in the

1950s and 1960s, see Faderman, *Odd Girls and Twilight Lovers*, 164–6; Stein, *City of Sisterly and Brotherly Loves*, 274–7; Boyd, *Wide Open Town.*

63. For more on this practice see James W. St G. Walker, *'Race', Rights and the Law in the Supreme Court of Canada* (Toronto: The Osgoode Society for Canadian Legal History and Wilfred Laurier University Press, 1997).
64. Lenia Chamandy was born in 1887, and appears to have had little involvement in the management of the Hotel. All of the correspondence in the LLBO file is from her lawyer, usually written on behalf of a male relative. Narrators identify Johnny Roussy as the manager, though his title was head waiter. Whether or not he had a financial interest in the hotel is unknown. See Archive of Ontario, RG 36 Series 8, Establishment Files 1927–1961, 'Continental Public House'.
65. (AO) RG 36 Series 8, Establishment Files 1927–1961, Box 92, 'Continental Public House' Spot Check, 6 September 1952.
66. Backhouse, *Colour-Coded,* esp. chapter 7. On the Fair Accommodations Act see Ross Lambertson, '"The Dresden Story": Racism, Human Rights, and the Jewish Labour Committee of Canada', *Labour/Le Travail* 47 (Spring 2001): 43–82.
67. (AO) RG 36 Series 8, Establishment Files 1927–1961, Box 92, 'Continental Public House' Letter from Edward Chamandy to LLBO, 6 October 1955.
68. *Hush Free Press* and *Justice Weekly* include descriptions of black butch and fem women among the predominantly white downtowner crowd and narrators also recall their presence, but the collection of interviews this study draws provides testimony from women of white heritage, with the exception of Jan, who was part French and part First Nations. We need to learn more about the way race and racism influenced and organized women's lives, but I believe we can safely assume that women of colour, especially African-Canadian women, were more likely to be picked up on the street by the police and either harassed or formally charged with vagrancy. In the mid-1960s a black woman opened The New Orient, an unlicensed lesbian dance club, with her white girl friend, and most of the patrons were the white Continental regulars. This suggests that city streets were more dangerous for women of colour than the bar was hostile to their presence. See Davis and Kennedy who found that 'street bars' were much more racial mixed than other types of bars, and that black women were much more likely to be harassed by the police than were white women, *Boots of Leather, Slippers of Gold*, 116, 2, 127. On Chinese sex trade workers, see Ivy, interview.
69. 'Two Girls Necking in Park', *Justice Weekly* (3 July 1954), 2, 15. Eight years later the police raided a west end home where the female resident offered paying customers card games and alcohol. The police found two women engaging in sex together in one of the bedrooms. They laid charges of gross indecency, not vagrancy. The women were fined 500 each. 'CADI Who Freed Socialite Madam "Tosses Book" At Female Lovers', *Hush Free Press* (17 February 1962), 11.
70. See also Del Martin and Phyllis Lyon, *Lesbian/Woman,* 6th ed. (San Francisco: Bantam Books, 1983), 204.
71. On media coverage of sex crimes and perversion in 1950s Toronto see Elise Chenier, 'Seeing Red: Immigrant Women and Sexual Danger in Cold War Canada', *Atlantis: A Women's Studies Journal* 24.2 (Spring 2000): 51–60; Kathryn Campbell, '"Deviance, Inversion and Unnatural Love": Lesbians in Canadian Media, 1950–1970', *Atlantis: A Women's Studies Journal* 23.1 (Fall/Winter 1998): 128–36.
72. Cited in Valerie J. Korinek, 'Don't Let Your Girlfriends Ruin Your Marriage: Lesbian Imagery in *Chatelaine* Magazine, 1950–1969', *Journal of Canadian Studies* 33.3 (Fall 1998): 88.
73. Although lesbianism was not directly addressed, there was a tremendous emphasis on the importance of raising 'normal' children, which ultimately influenced social perceptions of gender transgression. See Mona Gleason, *Normalizing the Ideal: Psychology, Schooling, and the Family in Postwar Canada* (Toronto: University of Toronto Press, 1999); Frank S. Caprio, *Female Homosexuality: A Psychodynamic Study of Lesbianism* (New York: Citadel Press, 1954).
74. National Archives of Canada, Dr J.N. Senn, reporting to the Royal Commission on 'the Criminal Law Relating to the Criminal Sexual Psychopath. RG 333/131 Acc. 8384/253 v. 2.
75. This is not to suggest that the police did not target homosexuals as a group under Chisholm's watch. For a more critical assessment of Chisholm's testimony to the Commission, see Gary Kinsman, *The Regulation of Desire, Homo and Hetero Sexualities*, 2nd ed, 190–1, (Montreal: Black Rose Books, 1996).
76. Ivy, interview.
77. Sometimes the police simply parked their car outside the bar and waited for women to leave. Women tried to avoid getting harassed by either leaving through the back door, or leaving in large groups. See Arlene, interview.
78. Jocko Thomas, *From Police Headquarters: True Tales from the Big City Crime Beat* (Toronto: Stoddart, 1990), 164–73.
79. Kinsman, *The Regulation of Desire,* 228.
80. 'Tenderloin Overflow', *Hush Free Press* (20 June 1959), 7.

81. *Globe and Mail* (14 November 1963), 13.
82. F. Russell, 'Clinic to Curb Sex Crimes Before they Happen', *Maclean's* (23 September 1961): 47.
83. On other clubs similarly 'harassed out of existence' in this period, see Donald W. McLeod, *Lesbian and Gay Liberation in Canada: A Selected Annotated Chronology, 1964–1975* (Toronto: ECW Books/Homewood Press, 1996), 9.
84. *Lesbian and Gay Heritage of Toronto,* Canadian Gay Archives Publication No.5: 1982; 'The Regency Club', *Two* 1 (1964): 15.
85. Davis and Kennedy also make this argument. See Davis and Kennedy, *Boots of Leather, Slippers of Gold,* 147; Stein explores the complexity of the relationship between gay men and lesbians in chapters two and ten of *City of Sisterly and Brotherly Loves.*
86. *Hush Free Press* (29 March 1958), 5
87. Ivy thinks she was one of the very first women at the Continental to become addicted to heroin—she says it helped her deal with turning tricks, and attributes her survival 'to an early decision to kick the habit'. Lynn remembers a night when she and some friends decided to draw up a list of all the women they knew who died from drug-related causes. By the time they were done, the list included more than fifty names. Toronto's Street Haven actively outreached to this community. For a critical assessment of Street Haven's work with gay women, see Ross, 'Destaining the (Tattooed) Delinquent Body', 561–95. Ross's review of the Haven's case files confirms both the prevalence and deadly impact of heroin use (591).
88. Hanley, 'Functions of Argot Among Heroin Addicts', 294–307.
89. Webster, interview.
90. Denise, interview.
91. Many years later Arlene discovered that the RCMP had placed her name on a list of subversives without her knowledge. Perhaps the RCMP used the intelligence they gathered in their drug investigations to supplement their work on subversion. Arlene, interview. On RCMP investigations of homosexuals, see Gary Kinsman and Patrizia Gentile, '"In the Interests of the State": The Anti-gay, Anti-lesbian National Security Campaign in Canada: A Preliminary Research Report', Laurentian University, 1998.
92. Jerry, interview (1992).
93. Ivy, interview.
94. This was a concern for Betty. See Betty, interview by LMH, [Toronto?], 1987.
95. Lois Stewart, interview.
96. Betty and Sandy, interview by LMH, [Toronto?], 1987; Lois Stewart, interview; Denise, interview.
97. Lynn was encouraged to assault and steal money from male patrons, but refused. Theft violated her personal moral code, but 'I wasn't about to admit to them that I thought it was wrong.' Lynn, interview. One of Pratt's informants also described acceptance within the community as contingent upon one's willingness to 'support and/or participate in some of their activities'. Pratt, 'A Study of the Female Homosexual Subculture', 44.
98. Lois Stewart, interview.
99. I do not want to suggest that these groups were immutable. Indeed, many women who arrived as an uptowner became a downtowner, and many downtowners left the gay life for the suburbs.
100. In the late 1950s Betty, Sandy, and a gay male friend were chased out of the Continental and down the street by two butch downtowners. Betty and Sandy, interview.
101. Anonymous, 'What is a Downtowner Butch', *Two* 5 (1965): II.
102. On demographic changes among the Chinese in the 1960s, see Thompson, *Toronto's Chinatown*, 138.
103. On lesbian bars in Toronto after 1965 see Ross, 'Dance to "Tie a Yellow Ribbon"'.
104. On lesbian feminism in Toronto, see Becki Ross, *The House that Jill Built: A Lesbian Nation in Formation* (Toronto: University of Toronto Press, 1995).
105. Pratt, 'A Study of the Female Homosexual Subculture', 48.

Race, Culture, and the Colonization of Childbirth in Northern Canada

Patricia Jasen

EDITORS' INTRODUCTION

To varying degrees, all bodies are socially constructed. As Patrick J. Connor's essay on the meaning of rape in Upper Canada testifies, social categories label bodies, social conditions affect their health and welfare, and social institutions empower or constrain them.[1] The body is, nevertheless, also lived. The manufacturing of particular bodies as acceptable or not, good or bad, weak or strong, has real consequences for human beings. In this essay, Patricia Jasen explores the consequences for Aboriginal women in the North of particular constructions of their bodies by agents of the colonial state. Conceptions of Aboriginal women and childbirth among Europeans and Canadians, Jasen demonstrates, effectively inscribed upon bodies unequal relations of power.

Since ancient times, male medical experts represented and treated female bodies as problematic. The womb, characterized as a source of disease that could affect different parts of the body, wreaked havoc on women's health. As Wendy Mitchinson's important work has shown, Victorian Canadians subscribed to a modified version of this belief, understanding women as more vulnerable to disease than men precisely because of the nature of their physiology.[2] Women's central purpose, experts reasoned, was reproduction. Consequently, their health was associated primarily with the system that distinguished them from men: the reproductive/sexual system.

Race mattered in this process. European images of Aboriginal women as primitive and 'natural' helped reinforce nineteenth-century theories of evolution and racial difference. As both Anne McClintock and Anne Fausto-Sterling explain in related colonial contexts, differentiating the 'savage woman from civilized females of Europe' was an important preoccupation of imperial science. Missionaries to Canada, both male and female, as described by Myra Rutherdale, also contributed in particular ways to this process.[3] Shifting representations of Native women informed by notions of 'race' featured prominently in the influential writings of Susanna Moodie and her sister Catharine Parr Traill, as Carole Gerson has explored.[4] While those settlers succeeded to a considerable degree in speaking of Native women as friends, mentors, and partners—the 'nobler savage'—they could not escape the colonial frame of reference that informed their work.

The 'myth of painless childbirth' that grew out of the connection between Native women and nature ignored the complex culture of Aboriginal childbirth and the important role of midwives. As Mary Ellen Kelm argues in *Colonizing Bodies: Aboriginal Health and Healing in British Columbia, 1900 to 1950* (1998), ignorance of pre-existing ways of healing among Native people was a common feature of North American colonization.[5] The widely held belief that Aboriginal women suffered little in labour and delivery confirmed their association with animal nature and vindicated Eurocentric theories of racial hierarchy. The new science of craniometry, the measurement of skull size to determine intelligence, held that since the 'lower races' had smaller heads (and thus supposedly lower intelligence), ease of childbirth for Aboriginal women was to be expected. In contrast, experts reasoned, European women, burdened with bearing children of higher intelligence, sophistication, and civility, were destined to suffer.

Committed to a dual agenda of civilizing and Christianizing Native peoples, government agents and missionaries easily justified intervention into Aboriginal childbirth practices in the twentieth century. This was particularly true as high rates of infant morality among the Inuit population necessitated some attention from governments, while presenting a convenient excuse to blame women. Thus, as Jasen skilfully maps out, earlier neglect of Aboriginal mothers quickly metamorphosed into heavy-handed intervention. Evacuated (sometimes against their will) to hospitals hundreds of miles from home, pregnant women left their families for weeks at a time. If racism distinguished the treatment of Aboriginal women, governmental neglect and professional prejudice recalled the experience of white women in the Canadian West in the late nineteenth century. Nanci Langford shows that childbirth on the prairies was a perilous event, made more so by the absence of affordable and accessible heath care services. Lack of support for a vital network of midwives made a bad situation still more intolerable. Until about 1924, provincial maternal and infant mortality rates were highest on the prairies.[6]

Women resisted their mistreatment. Jasen is careful to point out that Aboriginal women in the North have continually questioned efforts to deny their unique approach to childbirth, often rejecting removal from their homes. Signposts of their continuing commitment to community are evident today. The establishment in 1984 of Pauktuutit, a national non-profit association representing Inuit women in Canada, epitomizes this resistance. It aims to 'foster a greater awareness of the needs of Inuit women and to encourage their participation in community, regional and national concerns in relation to social, cultural and economic development'. Central to its mandate are efforts to 'promote the rights of Inuit women and children' and to 'familiarize our children with Inuit values, heritage, culture and language'.[7]

Notes

1. Chris Shilling, *The Body and Social Theory* (London: Sage Publications, 1993); Bryan Turner, *Regulating Bodies: Essays in Medical Sociology* (New York: Routledge, 1992); Patricia Vertinsky, 'The "Racial" Body and the Anatomy of Difference: Anti-Semitism, Physical Culture, and the Jew's Foot', *Social Science Review* 4.1 (1995): 42.
2. Wendy Mitchinson, *The Nature of Their Bodies: Women and Their Doctors in Victorian Canada* (Toronto: University of Toronto Press, 1991). See also, Wendy Mitchinson, *Giving Birth in Canada, 1900–1950* (Toronto: University of Toronto Press, 2002).
3. Anne Fausto-Sterling, 'Gender, Race, and Nation: The Comparative Anatomy of "Hottentot" Women in Europe, 1815–1817', in *Deviant Bodies: Critical Perspectives on Difference in Science and Popular Culture*, Jennifer Terry and Jacqueline Urla, eds. (Bloomington: Indiana University Press, 1996), 19–48; Anne McClintock, *Imperial Leather: Race, Gender, and Sexuality in the Colonial Conquest* (New York: Routledge, 1995); Myra Rutherdale, '"I Wish the Men Were Half as Good": Gender Constructions in the Canadian Northwestern Mission Field, 1860–1940', in *Telling Tales: Essays in Western Women's History*, Catherine Cavanaugh and Randi R. Warne, eds. (Vancouver: UBC Press, 2000), 32–59.
4. Carole Gerson, 'Nobler Savages: Representations of Native Women in the Writings of Susanna Moodie and Catharine Parr Traill', in *Rethinking Canada: The Promise of Women's History*, 4th ed., Veronica Strong-Boag, Mona Gleason, and Adele Perry, eds. (Toronto: Oxford University Press, 2002).
5. Nor was this a uniquely North American phenomenon. In the later context of Communist China, Joshua Goldstein traces 'how the government attempted to dislodge women's reproductive practices from local networks and institutions in order to restructure them within a

new state system'. Joshua Goldstein, 'Scissors, Surveys, and Psycho-Prophylactics: Prenatal Health Care Campaigns and State Building in China, 1949–1954', *Journal of Historical Sociology* 11.2 (1998): 153–84.

6. Nanci Langford, 'Childbirth on the Canadian Prairies', *Journal of Historical Sociology* 8: 3 (1995): 278–302.
7. Pauktuutit Inuit Women's Association, www.pauktuutit.ca.

Questions for Critical Reading

1. What does it mean to say that women and their bodies are measured against male standards and physiology?
2. How are bodies 'racialized', 'classed', and 'gendered'?
3. Have women in contemporary society been 'liberated' from their bodies? Is this a desirable goal?

The process of childbearing among Aboriginal women has been the subject of diverse interpretations by agents of colonization in Canada's northern regions.[1] In the first section of this essay, I argue that, during the exploration period, European impressions of Aboriginal women were dominated by associations with animal nature and the myth of painless childbirth, while traditional practices surrounding childbearing, including the role of the midwife, were overlooked. In the second section, I show how the emphasis upon racial differences was reinforced by evolutionary theory during the nineteenth century, and how the myth of the 'savage' woman's 'parturition without pain' was widely employed as a model for the 'civilized' woman to emulate. Meanwhile, the realities surrounding childbirth in Aboriginal communities received little attention from colonial authorities until high infant and maternal death rates began to arouse official concern in the early twentieth century, as the third section of the essay demonstrates. Instead of recognizing the impact of colonization on Aboriginal health, authorities attributed these problems to women's ignorance of healthy childbearing practices. As part of its 'civilizing mission', the Canadian government adopted an interventionist policy that eventually led to the practice of evacuating pregnant women to distant hospitals—a form of intervention that has had adverse social consequences. Resistance on the part of Aboriginal women has included the attempt to legitimize a traditional culture of childbirth disregarded throughout the colonization process.

I

Theories of racial difference are one of the oldest and most enduring features of European imperialism. They were inspired and perpetuated, in good part, by the desire to measure the level of European civilization and racial progress in comparison with more 'primitive' peoples, and the history of ideas regarding Aboriginal women and childbirth needs to be examined with this context in mind. During the exploration period, the notion that women in 'savage lands' were fundamentally different from European women gained a wide following through the myth of painless childbirth. Expressing this common view, Quebec intendant Jacques Raudot declared in 1709 that 'savage women are never sick at confinement. . . . when they have just given birth they go to wash their child in the water and do not discontinue doing the housework as usual.'[2]

There was some disagreement, however, over whether this distinction suggested a biological difference between Aboriginal and European women or was simply the product of a different way of life. Seventeenth-century Jesuit missionaries, for example, agreed that Aboriginal women were delivered easily and often without assistance, but unlike many later observers, they tended to emphasize cultural rather than natural differences by way of explanation. Some argued that the drudgery of their lives caused these women to produce smaller offspring, often born prematurely, thus accounting for their short labours while at the same time providing evidence of the poor treatment they allegedly endured compared to women in Christian lands.[3] Any evidence of inferior moral and social conditions was useful to the missionaries, as conversion would promote civilization, it was said, and the improvement of women's lot. Unlike the accounts of many explorers, those of the missionaries seldom portrayed such people as truly wild or animal-like, as proselytization could only take place among beings who were clearly human and had souls to save.

The focus on innate biological differences in childbearing became much more pronounced in the eighteenth century. One influence was the rise of natural history and the growing passion for classifying species and 'races'.[4] Early scientists wrote volumes on the sexual characteristics of women around the world, their reproductive capabilities, and the apparent differences in pelvis and fetal head size. Although these theories were hardly consistent, the idea that European intellectual supremacy must be reflected in the larger head size of white, male babies proved a popular explanation for white women's apparent difficulty in giving birth.[5] But it was not just the work of scientists which helped to foster myths of racial difference. With the growth of exploration, trade, and empire came the extraordinary popularity of the travel narrative as a literary genre, which satisfied the desire of many Europeans to compare themselves to other races and draw moral and social lessons from this exercise. What was at issue, in good part, was how close other races might be to a state of nature, and whether the condition of the 'wild man' or the 'noble savage' was an enviable one or not. While these were primarily masculine images, there were female versions of them as well.[6] The image of the Aboriginal mother with her baby at her breast was offered as an ideal of the 'natural' woman, and it was not uncommon to portray her as entirely governed by instinct, like the animals with whom she shared the wilderness.[7]

Hudson's Bay explorer Andrew Graham authored a typical description of painless childbirth and proposed that Aboriginal mothers might even be exempt from the curse that Eve had brought upon womankind. He affirmed that, in his presence, 'women have been taken in travail while on a journey; and they only drop behind the company, bring forth the little stranger, tie it up in a cradle, and carrying it on their backs, proceed to overtake their companions as if nothing had happened.' In their case, he mused, 'the malediction denounced on our general mother seems here to be repealed, or at least greatly mitigated.'[8] What is significant in such accounts is the insistence upon the Aboriginal woman's bodily strength and self-sufficiency, and the suggestion that she, like other mammals, simply relied upon natural forces and her own natural instincts to carry her and her infant through birth. Graham, among others, associated painful childbirth with a higher level of human development, a belief that would become more pronounced under the influence of evolutionary theory.

Nevertheless, all explorers, as evidenced by those few who challenged the prevailing view, did not accept the idea of painless childbirth. John Long, who spent time among the Ojibwa in the late eighteenth century, remarked that 'It is said that the Indian women bring forth children with very little pain, but I believe that it is only an opinion.' And Samuel Hearne, travelling from Hudson's Bay to the Arctic Ocean, told how his party was delayed by one of the women who was in labour for 52 agonizing hours, and was then required to resume travelling again, with her heavy pack on her back, knee-deep in water and wet snow.[9]

Taken together, and despite their differences, these accounts illustrate how gendered images of wildness informed early descriptions of Aboriginal women and childbirth. Strength was associated with savagery, natural or animal instincts were emphasized, and the possibility that childbirth had a culture and a history in North America was seldom considered. Little mention is made of midwives or helpers, and, on the subject of preparation for birth and the ways in which women may have supported one another, the record is largely silent.

How did Aboriginal women experience childbirth? Did they suffer less than European women and, if so, why? That question must surely be unanswerable; even if the subjective experience of pain could be measured in such a fashion, contemporary accounts are few, as most European observers were male and without access to the private world of childbearing. But the reminiscences of elders recorded over the past century do suggest that women in northern Canada traditionally sought to minimize the pain and peril of childbirth through attention to diet and ritual observances, and that they were often assisted during labour and delivery by female helpers, though solitary births were not uncommon.[10] There were similarities between their practices and those of European midwives, including the use of herbs to treat various conditions before, during, and after childbirth.[11] Even though customs varied according to region and circumstance, the culture of childbirth among Aboriginal women embodied both an ethic of self-sufficiency and a recognition of the midwife or helper's vital role.

Not only was the culture of childbirth ignored during the exploration period, but so, too, were the changes caused by contact with Europeans which transformed women's experience of giving birth. The fate of the woman in Samuel Hearne's party, for example, was in all likelihood affected by his very presence. Fur traders may have marvelled at the heavy burdens women carried even before and after bearing a child, but their weight owed much to the packs of furs intended for the trade, and although Aboriginal people were often willing participants in the fur trade, historians have convincingly argued that women's status deteriorated as a result of its demands.[12] It is probable, therefore, that the experience of childbirth and the status of women's health were also deteriorating throughout this period, at the same time as Europeans still toyed with images of wild women and the myth of painless childbirth.

II

Even though the bodily strength and powers of instinct possessed by Aboriginal people had been idealized by newcomers, advancing colonization would bring a transformation in the way Europeans and Euro-Canadians constructed their notions of racial difference. The reasons were very practical. After the War of 1812, Aboriginal people were no longer required as military allies, and, with the decline of the fur trade during the same period, the old economic alliance became less important, as well. Rather than being seen as a robust and youthful race, they were increasingly cast as a weak and declining one. In turn, the westward and northward expansion of settlement in British North America was supported, ideologically, by theories of race which eventually found their most powerful expression in Social Darwinism. The ideas are familiar: weak races give way to stronger ones; wild races cannot survive contact with civilized ones; weak races display signs of degeneracy which confirm that they are indeed weak; racial degeneracy is hastened by miscegenation which brings out the worst in both races, or, alternatively, racial extinction may be prevented through the assimilation of the weaker race by the stronger.[13]

Evidence to support most of these notions could be found, or so it was often thought, in the deteriorating conditions that developed in many Aboriginal communities during the nineteenth century. Economic and social malaise was a side effect of the closure of fur trade posts, the shortage of big game animals, and the loss of lands to European settlement. Poverty and hunger undermined health and increased susceptibility to epidemic disease—smallpox, influenza, measles, and, most menacing of all, tuberculosis.[14] Populations were dramatically reduced throughout much of the Northwest, which seemed to give credence to a self-fulfilling prophecy of racial extinction.

In most regions, Aboriginal people were left to deal with these problems largely on their own. The Canadian government took almost no responsibility during the nineteenth century for Aboriginal health, despite the fact that its decline was a direct outcome of the colonial process. Missionaries, who tended to believe most strongly in the possibility of assimilation, provided medical care as part of their larger Christianizing mission and attempted, with only limited success, to supplant traditional medicine men or shamans as community healers and spiritual leaders. Control over childbirth, however, was generally not contested territory, for male healers avoided assisting in births except in extreme emergencies, and neither shaman nor missionary coveted the spiritual role of the midwives.[15]

Oral histories show that women continued to manage pregnancy and childbirth in their traditional fashion, though often under worsening circumstances. There is evidence that among the Métis population, childbearing became more frequent and arduous as old taboos and customs passed away.[16] During the latter half of the nineteenth century, the poverty and ill health that accompanied confinement on newly created reserves throughout the West must also have affected childbirth. These communities received the occasional services of travelling medical personnel (at least yearly when treaty payments were made), but such a schedule did not generally involve physicians in the delivery of babies. Professional discussion of women's circumstances was therefore scant, though Dr Robert Bell, who travelled with the Geological Survey of Canada and addressed the Medical Association in Ottawa in 1886, provided one example of official naïveté. He testified to the continued self-sufficiency among 'Indian and Eskimo' women, but added that a 'profound knowledge of obstetrics is seldom called for, as parturition is generally extremely easy, owing, principally, to the comparatively small size of the infant's head'.[17] In an era when head size was taken as a prime indicator of the intelligence of a race, Bell's comment associated easy delivery not with racial vitality but with lower intelligence as a racial characteristic.[18] Furthermore, the belief that knowledge of obstetrics was unnecessary obscured, once again, the midwife's role.

Quite distinct from the realities of Aboriginal life, the myth of painless childbirth took on new cultural meanings around the middle of the nineteenth century. The growing preoccupation with racial hierarchy and degeneracy did not preclude a belief that primitivism and health were somehow linked, and many Europeans and white North Americans sought to internalize the qualities of 'wildness'—to adopt certain aspects of Aboriginal culture, in other words—which would counter the ill effects of civilized life.[19] Outdoor sport would help to preserve the qualities of 'natural man', but even more urgent was the quest for the 'natural woman'. There was a common fear that through some accident (or logic) of evolution, women of superior breeding experienced the most pain and debility in childbearing—that civilization, or over-civilization, made them less fit for reproduction.[20] The survival of the race seemed to depend on alleviating this suffering and countering the growing reluctance, on the part of middle- and upper-class women, to undertake the maternal role.

As historians have shown, the rise of gynecology, or 'the science of woman', occurred within this Social Darwinian context, and the taxonomies of both racial and sexual difference served as primary analytical tools in the debate over women's health. Many specialists embraced an evolutionary model and looked to anthropology or ethnography in their search for woman's essential nature. Defining the feminine also involved emphasizing profound biological differences between women and men which, in turn, associated childbearing with social dependency and reinforced a belief in the inevitable inequality of the sexes. The notion that women should submit to their physicians' care during childbirth was part of this developing ideology, and Mary Poovey has shown how the controversy over the 'naturalness' of women's pain and the use of anaesthetics was part of the process by which childbirth was claimed for the medical profession.[21] Did God really require that women bring forth children 'in sorrow', as the Bible maintained? A negative answer was often supported in medical literature through reference to the 'accounts given by travellers of the marvelous ease, quietness, painlessness, and freedom from disablement, with which many savage women bring forth children', to quote the American author of *Parturition without Pain, A Code of Instruction for Escaping from the Primal Curse*.[22] If such examples proved that the relief of pain was not an affront to God, then the physician was free to 'read' the woman's body and relieve her pain as he saw fit.

But the myth of painless childbirth was useful on a variety of rhetorical fronts. If regular physicians were anxious to establish that, under their care, the terrors of childbirth could be overcome, there were many alternative practitioners, health reformers, and feminists who argued that the process was by nature painless, and that cultural, not innate anatomical differences, were responsible for women's plight. They argued that if women learned the laws governing their own bodies, adopted sensible dress, and returned in their habits and diet to a more 'Aboriginal condition' or 'state of nature', the danger would be removed.[23] Such writers often resorted to the image of the 'Indian woman' who, 'when she feels the signs of coming labour, repairs to the nearest brook, gives birth to her child, it may be amid the snows of winter, washes it and herself in cold water, and is ready to resume her journey', as one water cure advocate wrote.[24] Feminist Elizabeth Cady Stanton believed that women, if properly informed, would cease to fear the trials of childbirth. 'We must educate our daughters to think that motherhood is grand and that God never cursed it,' wrote Stanton. 'We know that among Indians the squaws do not suffer in childbirth. They will step aside from the ranks, even on the march, and return in a short time bearing with them the new-born child. What an absurdity, then, to suppose that only Enlightened Christian women are cursed.'[25] Clearly, none of this discussion of 'women in savage life' had much to do with the actual conditions or experiences of Aboriginal women in colonized North America in the nineteenth century, but worked instead to accentuate divisions between the worlds of the colonizers and the colonized.

III

By the turn of the century, a different reform impulse was beginning to affect attitudes and policies regarding childbirth—one based on the notion that giving birth was no mere matter of nature and instinct. In good part, this change was inspired by the Social Darwinian fear that the 'civilized races' were failing to reproduce in sufficient numbers to ensure survival, and by a growing conviction that high rates of maternal and infant mortality would only be alleviated if women fully surrendered to their physicians' authority before, during, and after childbirth. As David Armstrong has pointed out, infant death rates were in themselves used to measure a society's level of civilization, and Canada's response to the problem was to initiate a campaign for 'scientific motherhood', whereby not only childbirth but child care underwent a process of medicalization.[26] Although reformers, physicians, and government officials (who were sometimes the same individuals, as in the case of Dr Helen McMurchy) believed that national 'regeneration' depended especially upon the reproductive capacities of white, middle-class women, they also turned their critical eye upon the childbearing practices of the nation's poor and immigrant populations and their untenable preference for home births and the assistance of midwives.[27]

Aboriginal health remained a marginal concern during the early decades of the twentieth century, but there were many Canadians, including those in government, who were convinced that the 'Indian race' was too degenerate to survive, that a concerted policy of cultural assimilation was the only practical and humane response, and that the retention of cultural traditions, especially those associated with religion and medicine, was the primary obstacle to the success of such a policy.[28] The Department of Indian Affairs appointed its first chief medical officer in 1904, and his reports reflected such an attitude coupled, however, with a determination to persuade a parsimonious government to provide health care. Dr Peter Bryce collected data on the disastrous impact of tuberculosis and the relatively high incidence of other maladies on Indian reserves, and he included what were likely the first statistics, unreliable as they must be, on problems relating to childbirth. He found the incidence of serious complications such as puerperal septicemia and chronic uterine disorders to be high, a situation 'not to be wondered at', he wrote, 'remembering how frequently "native customs" prevail at childbirth'.[29] For the most part, outside involvement in childbirth and other aspects of health care proceeded slowly in Aboriginal communities, although, on some prairie reserves, church-run hospitals took on this mission with enthusiasm. Bryce opened the first government-run nursing station on a Manitoba reserve in 1930.[30]

The medicalization of more northerly communities did not begin in earnest until the mid-twentieth century. This was a complex process which involved, in its early stages, a variety of government agencies, religious institutions, and the Royal Canadian Mounted Police. The nature and rate of change varied greatly from place to place, for the territories affected extend into the high Arctic. There was some unity to this history, however, because of the way that patterns of ill health were reproduced in one region after another, as outside intrusion disrupted traditional economies, created new settlement patterns, and introduced new diseases.[31] By 1955, the federal Department of Health and Welfare extended its responsibility to include both 'status Indian' and Inuit health care, and its goal was frankly assimilationist.[32] Services were offered within the colonial context; status Indians were wards of the state, and Inuit lived in territories directly subject to federal control. The government's aggressive policy of evacuating tuberculosis patients to southern hospitals provided a model of what this could mean in practice, as well as a prototype for future policy regarding childbirth.[33]

It was during the 1950s that the federal government started to give serious attention to the problem of infant mortality in Aboriginal communities. It began, moreover, to use this information as a prime indicator of its own success or failure as a civilizing agency, not only in its own eyes but in those of the world, which had learned in 1958 that no other ethnic group had as high an infant death rate as the Inuit.[34] But the gravity of the situation had long been suspected, even if it was not acknowledged or addressed. Statistics compiled from the 1930s onwards indicated that both maternal and infant deaths were higher than the national average among 'status Indians', and considerably higher again among the Inuit.[35] Equally arresting was the fact that birth rates among Aboriginal people were also much higher than average; their numbers were increasing despite their precarious health and unfortunate allegiance to 'native customs' in pregnancy, birth, and infant care. Now regarded as members of a sickly and misguided race destined to proliferate rather than become extinct, Aboriginal women became the subject of statistical surveys and the development of a far-reaching assimilationist policy aimed at transforming the culture of childbirth.

A turning point came in 1962, when the Medical Services Branch of Health and Welfare conducted a major (if unsophisticated) survey aimed at monitoring the health of 'all Indian and Eskimo' infants born that year in Canada. Its rationale was the high incidence of infant mortality, which it anticipated would be closely related to where babies were born and by whom they were delivered. The results were interpreted in a way that confirmed these expectations. The authors of the reports were particularly concerned that a considerable percentage of births were not 'adequately supervised', having been 'handled by native midwives untrained in the usual meaning of the term'. They were also frustrated by what they called the 'hard core' of mothers who managed to escape almost any contact with the nursing services now provided in some regions by the federal government, and they held these women responsible for maintaining the high infant death rate.[36] An underlying assumption was that maternal and infant ill health was directly related to lack of contact with outside agencies, which left no room for the possibility that an alternative culture of childbirth might have existed and been viable. Although there was tacit recognition that a changed way of life (including the move to permanent settlements which were without sanitary provisions) had created a more hazardous environment for giving birth, the preoccupation with infant mortality, rather than with the well-being of the family and community, focused attention on the alleged inadequacies of Aboriginal birth and child care.[37] They became problems to be solved through outside management of women's reproductive lives.

The results of the survey were used to support the policy of intervention that gained momentum during the years that followed, and which transformed the experience of childbearing throughout the Arctic and much of the sub-Arctic from Labrador to British Columbia. This policy developed in stages and, as mentioned earlier, was part of a broader process of medicalization which affected the Far North most dramatically because it took place with such speed and thoroughness there. Nursing stations were established in all centres of 100 people and more, and many were originally staffed by nurses from Britain chosen partly because of their midwifery skills, as the practice of midwifery was still not legally recognized at that time in Canada.[38] It was their job to implement policies determined in Ottawa, and some brought their own 'off to the colonies' attitudes and treated their patients as children in need of perpetual monitoring. Some of their autobiographies reveal a tendency to devalue the knowledge and coping skills of Aboriginal women or to assume that such women knew little about their own bodies. Part of their mandate was gradually to supplant traditional midwives, and, at the nursing stations, they themselves delivered women defined by government policy as 'low risk'.[39]

During the 1980s, however, policy shifted—particularly in the Far North—to entail the evacuation of most women to give birth in distant centres, where every technological advantage was available but where they might spend several weeks or even months separated from their families. The speed of change was such that it was not unusual for a woman to have had her first-born child delivered in camp by a traditional midwife, her last in an urban hospital a thousand miles away.[40] Dissent was soon voiced, however, both by sympathetic professionals and by the women themselves. The effect of the evacuation policy on women and their families has been well documented during the past couple of decades, and communities have organized to promote the integration of traditional midwifery with modern obstetric practices in centres closer to home.[41]

Medical anthropologists have highlighted connections between the ideology underlying this policy and the consequences that followed. They have shown how, even though evacuation has been justified through the language of risk, the very notion of 'risk' was itself constructed, for it was based upon information recorded on obstetrical forms created by individuals with their own, culturally specific understanding of childbirth.[42] As a result, a considerable gulf separated—and still separates—Aboriginal women's notions of risk and the biomedical models used to determine where they should give birth. For many women, the concept of risk is not focused solely on the unborn child but encompasses the risk posed to the family when the mother is absent for several weeks. They worry about who will care for their other children, they fear their husbands' resentment of their absence, and they believe that family violence is related to the exclusion of partners and siblings from the entire process of birth.[43] Researchers who have analyzed the impact of this policy in the Keewatin District of the Northwest Territories conclude that declining infant death rates have become 'a metaphor for the success and moral virtue of Canadian colonial penetration' in the Arctic. By isolating infant mortality in this fashion and by seeking a clinical solution in the separation of birthing women from their communities, the authorities have transferred the impact of resettlement, poverty, and disease 'to the body of the Inuit woman'.[44]

In any region where evacuation is an issue, women have described what this loss of control has meant to them as individuals. Whereas in the past they had learned about birth by assisting relatives and friends, many women of the current generation have never seen a baby born and will travel out of their communities alone when their time comes to give birth. 'In a real sense, Native women have become alienated from their own bodies,' writes one activist. 'This general lack of awareness and education, coupled with difficult social and economic conditions in the communities, sets Native women up to be high risk.'[45] Although women have acknowledged the benefits of hospital delivery in difficult cases (and some prefer it as a matter of course), there are many who feel that childbirth has been made more difficult under the hospital regime, and that fear itself plays a part in creating complications. The determination to avoid evacuation even leads some women to deny their pregnancies, to lie about their due dates, and to involve others in the community—including nursing staff—in deceiving the medical authorities. Stories of subterfuge and escape highlight this sense of desperation, such as that of a woman 'in her ninth month of pregnancy who had been brought down to Sioux Lookout from Pikangikum [in northwestern Ontario] and who wanted so badly to be back home to have her baby that she managed to get part way back on a skidoo.'[46] Older women have felt loss of self-sufficiency and competency, as well, for those who acted as midwives in the past believe their own knowledge has been discredited, wasted, and ignored.

In recent years, oral histories and interviews conducted by community members, health professionals, academics, and Aboriginal women's groups such as the Native Women's Association of the Northwest Territories and Equay-wuk Women's Group in Sioux Lookout, Ontario, have recorded some of these women's recollections. Despite differences among communities and regions,[47] what emerges most clearly is that even though childbirth is regarded as a 'natural' process, what has always mattered—as it does in any culture—is how pregnancy and birth have been managed. Traditional prenatal care included frequent monitoring and counselling by older women or midwives, an appropriate diet, and the insistence that women remain active: 'We were taught to be fit to have an easier delivery.'[48] Modern problems in childbirth are often attributed to a loss of bodily strength resulting from the decline of traditional occupations, a reliance on 'white' food, and a general lack of prenatal care. Midwives also prided themselves on their knowledge of herbal medicines used in combination with other techniques to calm women, ease their delivery, and manage complications as they arose.[49] Some women say that childbirth was much easier when they were physically and spiritually prepared for it, but seldom is the pain itself denied. A high value was placed upon endurance, but one Inuit woman said simply that it was best not to cry out because it would frighten 'the woman who was helping with the delivery'.[50] Despite the tendency of some women to idealize the past, most speak their own language of risk and remember, as mothers or midwives, deliveries that did not go well—hence their willingness to combine traditional practices with modern technology and techniques according to the needs of their communities, as has occurred at the Innulitsivik Maternity at Povungnituk on Hudson's Bay. Some former midwives also emphasize that their role went beyond the period of delivery itself, and involved a lifelong bond of kinship and mutual responsibility between midwife and child.[51]

IV

In the experience of many Aboriginal women, a traditional sense of community and self-sufficiency in childbearing has been eroded by a process of colonization that introduced new health risks, and by a civilizing mission that undermined old knowledge. As this paper has shown, the ideas of racial difference dominant during the early contact period worked against an understanding that there were practices and forms of expertise that helped women manage childbirth under demanding physical circumstances. Whether the 'savage' woman's reputation for 'parturition without pain' was attributed to culture or to race, the assumption that she could rely upon instinct to see her through reinforced the myth of difference. In any case, the primary function of such rhetoric was to construct an image of 'natural' woman that was useful in the developing discourse on women's health on both sides of the Atlantic—at least until fears of racial degeneration became so extreme that the notion of leaving such matters to 'nature' lost much of its appeal. By the early twentieth century, the medicalization of childbirth in Canada, as elsewhere in the industrializing world, was well under way. As authorities became preoccupied with alleviating infant mortality and as overall health among Aboriginal people deteriorated, an assimilationist policy was directed towards bringing childbirth among these women under direct government control. Subjected, simultaneously, to ideologies of both gender and race, Aboriginal women in the North underwent a particularly stark and sudden transformation in their reproductive lives. Only within the last generation, because of organized resistance to that process, is the culture of childbirth in northern Canada finally being recognized, by outsiders, as having a history of its own.

Notes

1. The word 'northern' takes on different meanings over time. In this paper it includes the areas north of the St Lawrence River and the Great Lakes, but refers especially to the vast regions north and west of Lake Superior.
2. Jacques Raudot, Letter 25, in W. Vernon Kinietz, *The Indians of the Western Great Lakes, 1715–1760* (Ann Arbor: University of Michigan Press, 1940), 345.
3. Rueben Gold Thwaites, ed., *Jesuit Relations and Allied Documents* (New York: Pageant Book Company, 1959), Vol. XXXII (1647–8), 277; Vol. XXXVIII (1653), 259; Vol. I (1610–13), 257; Vol. III (1611–16), 103; Vol. IV (1616–29), 205; Vol. XVI (1639), 107.
4. Throughout this paper, the term 'race' is used to refer to a socially constructed concept.
5. Londa Schiebinger, *The Mind Has No Sex? Women in the Origins of Modern Science* (Cambridge, MA: Harvard University Press, 1989), 189–213; Schiebinger, *Nature's Body: Gender in the Making of Modern Science* (Boston: Beacon Press, 1993), 142–83. And see Sylvana Tomaselli, 'Reflections on the History of the Science of Woman', *History of Science* 29 (1991): 185–205.
6. See Edward Dudley and Maximillian Novak (eds), *The Wild Man Within: An Image in Western Thought from the Renaissance to Romanticism* (Pittsburgh: University of Pittsburgh Press, 1972); Hayden White, 'The Forms of Wildness: The Archaeology of an Idea', in *Tropics of Discourse: Essays in Cultural Criticism*, White, ed. (Baltimore: Johns Hopkins University Press, 1978); Olive Patricia Dickason, *The Myth of the Savage and the Beginnings of French Colonialism in the Americas* (Edmonton: University of Alberta Press, 1984).
7. For example, see J.A. Stewart, M.D., 'An Obstetrician Adventurer in the Hudson's Bay in 1812—Dr Thomas McKeevor', *Canadian Medical Association Journal* 28 (1928): 738–40. On Europeans' idealization of the lactating mother, see Schiebinger, *The Mind Has No Sex?*, 219–20.
8. Glyndwr Williams, ed., *Andrew Graham's Observations on Hudson's Bay 1767–91* (London: Hudson's Bay Record Society, 1969), 176–7.
9. 'John Long's Voyages and Travels in the Years 1768–88', excerpt printed in James Axtell, ed., *The Indian Peoples of Eastern America: A Documentary History of the Sexes* (New York: Oxford University Press, 1981), 18; Richard Glover, ed., *Samuel Hearne: A Journey from Prince of Wales Fort in Hudson's Bay to the Northern Ocean, 1769, 1770, 1771, 1772* (Toronto, Macmillan Press, 1958), 58.
10. Letitia Hargrave, resident at York Factory for 10 years in the mid-nineteenth century, provided a rare account by a British woman. See Margaret A. MacLeod, ed., *The Letters of Letitia Hargrave* (Toronto: Champlain Society, 1947), 60–1. References to childbirth by Aboriginal women are found in such works as Regina Flannery, *Ellen Smallboy: Glimpses of a Cree Woman's Life* (Montreal and Kingston: McGill-Queen's Press, 1995) and Julie Cruikshank, with Angela Sidney, Kitty Smith, and Annie Ned, *Life Lived Like a Story: Life Stories of Three Native Elders* (Vancouver: UBC Press, 1990).
11. A comparison of ethnobotanists' accounts and European herbals reveals comparable uses of certain plants, such as raspberry leaves to hasten labour.
12. Carol Devens, *Countering Colonization: Native American Women and Great Lakes Missions, 1630–1900* (Berkeley: University of California Press, 1992), 124; Richard J. Perry, 'The Fur Trade and the Status of Women in the Western Subarctic', *Ethnohistory* 26 (1979): 363–75.
13. See Robert E. Bieder, *Science Encounters the Indian, 1820–1880: The Early Years of American Ethnology* (Norman, OK: University of Oklahoma Press, 1986) for the use of race theory in North America.

14. T. Kue Young, *Health Care and Cultural Change: The Indian Experience in the Central Subarctic* (Toronto: University of Toronto Press, 1988), 32–47; James B. Waldram, D. Ann Herring, and T. Kue Young, *Aboriginal Health in Canada: Historical, Cultural, Epidemiological Perspectives* (Toronto: University of Toronto Press, 1995), 60–2.
15. See Devens, *Countering Colonization*, 24. Medicine men or shamans usually avoided contact with menstruating and parturient women because of the effect they might have on their own healing powers.
16. On women in Métis society, see Jennifer Brown, *Strangers in Blood: Fur Trade Companies Families in Indian Country* (Vancouver: UBC Press, 1980); Sylvia Van Kirk, *Many Tender Ties: Women in Fur-Trade Society in Western Canada* (Winnipeg: Watson and Dwyer Pub, 1980).
17. Robert Bell, 'The "Medicine-Man": Indian and Eskimo Notions of Medicine', *Canada Medical and Surgical Journal* (March–April 1886).
18. Stephen Jay Gould, *The Mismeasure of Man* (New York: Norton, 1981).
19. White, 'Forms of Wildness', 176–8.
20. For example, see Judith Walzer Leavitt, *Brought to Bed: Childbearing in America, 1750–1950* (New York: Oxford University Press, 1986), 64–86; Wendy Mitchinson, *The Nature of Their Bodies: Women and Their Doctors in Victorian Canada* (Toronto: University of Toronto Press, 1991), 48–76.
21. See Ornella Moscucci, *The Science of Woman: Gynaecology and Gender in England, 1800–1929* (Cambridge: Cambridge University Press, 1990), 7–41; Mary Poovey, *Uneven Development: The Ideological Work of Gender in Mid-Victorian England* (Chicago: University of Chicago Press, 1988), 24–50.
22. M.L. Holbrook, *Parturition Without Pain* (Toronto: Maclear, 1875), 317. This work was appended to George Henry Naphey's well-known work, *The Physical Life of Woman* (Toronto: Maclear, 1875).
23. Thomas Leadam, *Homeopathy as Applied to the Diseases of Females and the Most Important Diseases of Childhood* (London: James Leith, 1851), 76. And see George Julius Engelmann, *Labor Among the Primitive Peoples: Showing the Development of the Obstetric Science Today, from the Natural and Instinctive Customs of All Races, Civilized and Savage, Past and Present* (St Louis: J.H. Chambers & Co., 1883), 4–9.
24. T.L. Nichols, 'The Curse Removed: A Statement of Facts Respecting the Efficacy of Water Cure on the Treatment of Uterine Disease and the Removal of the Pains and Perils of Pregnancy and Childbirth', *Water-Cure Journal* 10 (1850), 168.
25. Prudence Saur, *Womanhood: or Helps for Wives and Mothers* (London, Ontario: McDermid and Logan, 1895), 199–200.
26. David Armstrong, 'The Invention of Infant Mortality', *Sociology of Health and Illness* 8 (1986), 211–32; Cynthia Comacchio, *'Nations are Built of Babies': Saving Ontario's Mothers and Children, 1900–1940* (Montreal and Kingston: McGill-Queen's University Press, 1993), 3–63.
27. Angus McLaren, *Our Own Master Race: Eugenics in Canada, 1885–1945* (Toronto: McClelland and Stewart, 1990), 28–67.
28. See Brian Titley, *A Narrow Vision: Duncan Campbell Scott and the Administration of Indian Affairs in Canada* (Vancouver: UBC Press, 1986).
29. Canada, Sessional Papers 27–8, XLIV no. 17 (1910), 268.
30. Laurie Meijer Drees, 'Reserve Hospitals and Medical Officers: Health Care and Indian Peoples in Southern Alberta, 1890s–1930s', paper presented at a conference on Race, Gender, and the Construction of Canada, University of British Columbia, October, 1995; Waldram, Herring, and Young, *Aboriginal Health in Canada,* 157.
31. Ibid., 65–176. And see Canada, Department of Indian Affairs, *The Government of Canada and the Inuit, 1900–1967* (Ottawa: Indian and Northern Affairs, 1985); R.Q. Duffy, *The Road to Nunavut: The Progress of the Eastern Arctic Inuit Since the Second World War* (Montreal: McGill-Queen's University Press, 1988).
32. Previously, the Department of Indian Affairs and then the Department of Mines and Resources has assumed responsibility for health care. When Health and Welfare took on this role, jurisdiction for 'Indian affairs' was divided between government departments, and health care was treated separately from other socio-economic concerns. For some years, even the Indian agents, later called superintendents, remained the legally designated Health Officers on reserves, not the medical personnel of Health and Welfare. See G. Graham-Cumming, 'Health of the Original Canadians, 1867–1967' *Medical Services Journal* (1967): 125–8.
33. Pat Sandiford Brygier, *A Long Way from Home: The Tuberculosis Epidemic among the Inuit* (Montreal and Kingston: McGill-Queen's University Press, 1994).
34. Duffy, *The Road to Nunavut*, 78.
35. National Archives of Canada, RG29 Vol.2870, File 851-1-6, pt 1, typescript, 'Draft—Child and Maternal Health'.
36. NAC RG29 Vol.2870, File 862-1-5-M22, 21 July 1966; File 851-1-6 pt 2A, progress reports.
37. For example, see John S. Willis, M.D., 'Disease and Health in Canada's North', *Medical Services Journal Canada* 19 (1963): 748–9.

38. On the history of midwifery, see C. Lesley Biggs, '"The Case of the Missing Midwives": A History of Midwifery in Ontario from 1795–1900', and Helene Laforce, 'The Different Stages of the Elimination of Midwives in Quebec', in *Delivering Motherhood: Maternal Ideologies and Practices in the 19th and 20th Centuries,* Katherine Arnup, Andrée Levesque, and Ruth Roach Pierson, eds. (London: Routledge, 1990), 20–50; Brian Burtch, *Trials of Labour: The Re-emergence of Midwifery* (Montreal and Kingston: McGill-Queen's University Press, 1994).
39. John O'Neil, 'The Politics of Health in the Fourth World: A Northern Canadian Example', in *Interpreting Canada's North: Selected Readings,* Kenneth S. Coates and William B. Morrison, eds. (Toronto: Copp, Clark, Pitman, 1989); John O'Neil and Patricia A. Kaufert, 'The Politics of Obstetric Care: The Inuit Experience', in *Births and Power: Social Change and the Politics of Reproduction,* W. Penn Handwerker, ed. (Boulder: Westview Press, 1990), 53–68. For an autobiographical account, see Donalda M. Copeland and Eugenie Louise Myles, *Nurse Among the Eskimos* (London: Adventurers' Club, 1965). Otto Schaefer recalled his own arrogance when he arrived in the North in 'Luttamiut (Doctor's People) and "Old Wives' Tales": Their Unrecognized Value in Medicine', in *Circumpolar Health,* Brian D. Postl et al., eds. (Winnipeg: University of Manitoba, 1990).
40. O'Neil and Kaufert, 'The Politics of Obstetric Care', 55–6; Kaufert and O'Neil, 'Cooptation and Control: The Reconstruction of Inuit Birth', *Medical Anthropology Quarterly* 4 (1990): 432.
41. On the Arctic, see John D. O'Neil and Penny Gilbert, eds., *Childbirth in the Canadian North: Epidemiological, Clinical, and Cultural Perspectives* (Winnipeg: Northern Health Research Unit, University of Manitoba, 1990); 'Ikajurti (The Helper): Midwifery in the Canadian Arctic', produced by Pauktuutit (The Inuit Women's Association) and the Inuit Broadcasting Corporation. On developments in northwestern Ontario, see Scott-McKay Bain Health Panel, *From Here to There: Steps Along the Way* (Sioux Lookout: Scott McKay Bain Health Panel, 1989); Laura Calm Wind and Carol Terry, *Nishnawbe-Aski Nation Traditional Midwifery Practices* (Sioux Lookout: Equy-Wuk Women's Group, 1993).
42. Kaufert and O'Neil, 'Cooptation and Control', 435; and see 'Analysis of a Dialogue on Risks in Childbirth: Clinicians, Epidemiologists, and Inuit Women', in *Knowledge, Power and Practice: The Anthropology of Everyday Life,* Shirley Lindenbaum and Margaret Lock, eds. (Berkeley: University of California Press, 1993).
43. For example, see Peter Ernerk and Nellie Kusugak, 'CBC Phone-in Show, December 16, 1988', and Lesley Paulette, 'The Changing Experience of Childbirth in the Western N.W.T.', in *Childbirth in the Canadian North,* O'Neil and Gilbert, eds. Similar concerns are voiced in other regions.
44. Kaufert and O'Neil, 'Cooptation and Control', 438–9.
45. Paulette, 'The Changing Experience', 46–7.
46. Royal Commission on Aboriginal Peoples, Hearings, Presentation by the Interim Regulatory Council on Midwifery. Toronto, 92-11-02 87, Vicki Van Wagner, 100.
47. The Royal Commission on Aboriginal Peoples heard statements on this subject across Canada and, as one commissioner said, 'midwifery has a different definition to different people. For example, when the Keewatin women talk about midwifery, it is not necessarily the same as the midwifery being talked about by the Ontario women, or by the Nunavut women.' Hearings, Ottawa, 93-11-15 174 Commissioner Betty Sillett, 207.
48. Annie Napayok, 'Cultural Perspectives on Pregnancy and Childbirth', in *Childbirth in the Canadian North,* O'Neil and Gilbert, eds., 40.
49. Calm Wind and Terry, *Nishnawbe Aski Nation,* 2–3.
50. 'Ikajurti (The Helper)'.
51. Carol Terry, 'Traditional Aboriginal Midwife: Holistic, harmonious, sacred', *Bmaadiziwin: A Magazine about People and Health* 1 (1994); Carol Terry and Laura Calm Wind, 'Do-Dis-Seem', *Canadian Woman Studies* 14 (1993): 77–81.

Violence and Poverty on the 'Rock': Can Feminists Make a Difference?

Glynis George

EDITORS' INTRODUCTION

As Rusty Bitterman's essay in this volume clearly shows, women in Canada are no strangers to social activism. Like the nineteenth century protesters he highlights, twenty-first century women often take to streets in protest against a range of forces that endanger their interests, their lives, and their families. Angela Miles argues that '(f)eminism is necessarily an internationalist politics, for the systems of exploitation and control we resist are global.'[1] The 'globalization' of protest, seen most poignantly in the recent vigorous protests against the World Trade Organization (WTO) meetings in Seattle and Quebec City, is one response to the globalization of economic exploitation and its various oppressive offshoots.[2] As Vandana Shiva writes, '(t)he project of corporate Globalization is a project for polarising and dividing people—along axis of class and economic inequality, axis of religion and culture, axis of gender, axis of geographies and regions.'[3] Women have responded to, and resisted, these polarizing forces by forging connections throughout history. While much of women's organizing has been spontaneous, it can also be quite formal and institutionalized. At international levels, the General Assembly of the United Nations designated 1975 International Women's Year, organizing World Conferences on women held in Mexico, followed by meetings in Copenhagen in 1980, and Nairobi in 1985.[4] The Fourth World Conference on Women was held in Beijing, China in 1995. At the national level, the National Action Committee on the Status of Women, representing approximately seven hundred member groups, has existed since the 1970s and is the largest feminist organization in Canada.[5] As this essay by Glynis George makes clear, however, local conditions of poverty and violence require 'made in the community' solutions if they are to have any kind of impact locally, or indeed, in wider contexts.

George clearly demonstrates that grassroots feminist organizing has been critical to developing government policy that addresses the particular interconnections between poverty and violence in the context of Newfoundland and Labrador. The discourse of economic crisis as it relates to Newfoundland and Labrador is familiar to many Canadians. Throughout the history of the province, a heavy reliance on non-renewable resource extraction has meant that economic crisis is a familiar leitmotif of the region's past. Barbara Neis and Susan Williams have refined this discourse by drawing attention to the impact of the fishery collapse on marginalized women who were often invisible in state offered solutions.[6] The discourse around violence, as it is connected to economic hardship and poverty, particularly in domestic situations, has only recently entered onto the policy radar in the province. This, according to George, belies the stereotypical image of the region as folksy and affable. The work of grassroots organizations led by activist feminists, she relates, challenged the silence that traditionally surrounded domestic violence against women and children and bought it to the forefront of public discussion.

Grassroots feminist groups in the province worked effectively to impart a systemic gendered analysis to two government initiatives of the late 1990s: the Provincial Strategy Against Violence (PSAV) and the Social Policy Committee. This was forged at a particular confluence of difficult contextual forces: fiscal restraint, welfare restructuring, and the dismantling of the social services department and the denominational school systems. The turmoil caused by this disruption and re-construction of services offered an opportunity for community-based activists to insert themselves into the process. Feminist organizations, as George argues, not only seized the opportunity but had a significant impact on ways in which implementation of new social services was structured and achieved. Not only was the PSAV implemented through a consultation process, feminist organizations insisted that such initial input from community stakeholders be monitored and efforts made to coordinate needs and responses from the government.

George reminds us that the particular historical circumstances of the province that have helped label it 'chronically underfunded' now complicates feminist struggles for an end to poverty and violence. Of the most intractable reasons for lack of government initiative in social policy, cries of fiscal poverty are perhaps the most difficult to counter. Using grassroots organizations, feminist critics have exposed the often invisible and silenced consequences of lack of political will for change. By opening space for community-based input, grassroots feminist organizations in Newfoundland and Labrador bring the lived reality of violence and poverty to its rightful place at the policy table.

Notes

1. Angela Miles, 'Local Activisms, Global Feminisms and the Struggle Against Globalization', *Canadian Woman Studies/Les cahiers de la femme* 20.3 (Fall 2000): 6–10.
2. On the Seattle protests against the World Trade Organization in 1999, see the WTO History Project website http://depts.washington.edu/wtohist/index.htm.
3. Vandana Shiva, 'The Polarized World of Globalization', *Z-net Daily Commentaries* (27 May 2005), http://www.zmag.org/sustainers/content/2005-05/27shiva.cfm.
4. A useful website highlighting United Nations World Conferences on Women is http://www.earthsummit2002.org/toolkits/women/intro/intro.htm.
5. http://www.nac-cca.ca.
6. Barbara Neis and Susan Williams, '"Women and Children First": Fishery Collapse and Women in Newfoundland and Labrador', in *Rethinking Canada: The Promise of Women's History*, Veronica Strong-Boag, Mona Gleason, and Adele Perry, eds. (Toronto: Oxford University Press, 2002), 367–74.

Questions for Critical Reading

1. Extrapolating from the Newfoundland and Labrador example, suggest some basic principles of feminist activism that might be applied across national and international contexts to foster change. What difference might a feminist perspective make and why?
2. How might critical attention to the role of gender help expose other factors that play a part in social inequality in Canada such as race, ethnicity, and status as a recent immigrant? How are these connected and how do they differ from each other?

The 1990s were a cultural watershed in Newfoundland and Labrador. While the decline of the fisheries threatened the livelihood which had sustained settlement for centuries, the public discourse regarding violence against women, children, and dependent adults broadened, provoking a significant re-thinking of the way people live in this province, fondly referred to as 'The Rock'. As someone who has worked with activists in women's councils on the West coast, and in St John's, I was impressed by the coordinated efforts of women who were differently positioned within government and community to address violence and poverty through lobbying, protest and advocacy in their paid work and in community-based initiatives.

This was particularly difficult in the 1990s when government restructuring and fiscal restraint generated immense changes to government services. At the same time, issues raised by women, poverty groups, and labour organizations in this politically conservative climate were marginalized as the 'narrow' claims of special interests which were somehow distinct from the concerns of 'ordinary' citizens (Bashevkin, 1998; George, 2000). Hence, this period presented feminists with a formidable task. How could they address violence and poverty and its impact on women and children, given this chilly climate of change?

This paper focuses on the involvement of activists in government initiatives that have taken place in the 1990s, specifically, the Provincial Strategy Against Violence, a government initiative undertaken in 1993. I suggest that it is the multi-dimensional character of their activism that permits the expression of a critical, grounded, and substantive feminist politics. This is crucial in light of the apparent contradictory behaviour of the provincial government and its dependence on federal decision-making. On the one hand it has expanded its attention to violence and the experiences of vulnerable populations, in its plan to create 'safe, caring' communities. On the other, the structural changes it has developed and the fiscal restraint it exercises has made these initiatives difficult to realize in a meaningful way.

While violence and poverty have been on the feminist agenda since the early 1970s, the 1990s mark a significant shift in feminist organizing. By this time, women were better positioned to participate in this process as a result of their paid work in government, as 'femocrats' (Rankin and Vickers, 1998: 352–60), and because they had developed a strong political and social network to make issues politically and locally meaningful (George, 2000). In this context, grassroots organizing is central to ensuring that the complex connections between poverty and violence in the lives of Newfoundlanders are addressed in government policy and provide a basis for critical reflection on the substantive changes that underlie government rhetoric. Moreover, because these concerns are hardly peculiar to the province, this examination illustrates the centrality of grass roots organizing for sustaining feminism during times of political conservatism and structural transformation, and supports Brodie's call for an attention to the grassroots (Brodie, 1998).

Violence, Poverty, Activism and Government in Newfoundland and Labrador

When a recent Statistics Canada report cited Newfoundland and Labrador as having the lowest rate of violence (five and four per cent), against both women and men (Government of Canada, 2000: 14), Joyce Hancock, the President of the Provincial Advisory Council on the Status of Women was concerned about the effect of this statistic, or rather that its report would belie more than it revealed. It certainly resonated with the depiction of Newfoundlanders as egalitarian, friendly, and resilient folks more accustomed to being violated (at last economically) than engaging in such actions themselves. Yet, it didn't speak to the experiences of front-line workers who observe the impact of uneven or inaccessible direct services on women's experiences of violence. Moreover, it had little bearing on the interests of Aboriginal women in their efforts to document the number of violent crimes that go unreported in their communities, or in their concern for the paucity of community policing in Labrador (see Pauktuutit, 1995). Indeed, the problem of violence is one that was taken on and legitimated in the 1980s and 1990s across the province.

There was a significant increase in reports of violence and sexual abuse against women and children from the 1980s to the present. Cases of child sexual abuse for example, rose throughout the 1980s, by 5,000 per cent (Community Response Team, 1993). Moreover, while Newfoundland reported lower rates of violence for women in national surveys, a more effective documentation process was indicating that the incidence of violence against women was much higher than criminal justice statistics had reported (Government of Newfoundland and Labrador, 2000: 2–3). Prominent cases, such as the sexual abuse of boys by Christian brothers at Mount Cashel orphanage galvanized public opinion. Perhaps more so than elsewhere in Canada, this latter issue brought into sharp focus the way power over dependent persons had been historically exercised in families, the church, and communities.

While the concern for these forms of violence is relatively new in public discourse, economic crisis in the province is not. Periods of financial crisis have characterized Newfoundland's history, both before and after Confederation. But the moratorium on cod fishing has intensified related social and economic problems. Although out migration has stabilized somewhat recently, more than 20,000 persons have left the province since 1993, the year the moratorium was imposed. There has been a 75 per cent increase in those who have sought short-term government assistance between 1989 and 1996. This represents 100,000 men, women, and children in a province of 500,000 people who receive only 50 per cent of the recommended annual incomes for families in official Statistics Canada assessments. Unemployment rates are twice the national average at 19 per cent, and 29 per cent amongst youth (Social Policy Advisory Committee, 1997). This has contributed to a loss in government revenue, which was already reduced by federal changes including reduced transfer payments, and funds for social assistance and unemployment insurance. Families are equally affected by the loss of local and regional government revenue.

The provincial government responded to these conditions through dramatic restructuring throughout the 1990s and a vow to create 'safe, caring' communities. The dismantling of the department of social services and the denominational school system was accompanied by the creation of regional economic and regional health boards. It is in this context of restructuring, fiscal restraint, and economic crisis that activists lobbied for community input in how changes would be implemented. This resulted in two government initiatives that permitted consultation from a variety of residents and community-based organizations: a Provincial Strategy Against Violence and a Social Policy Committee.

The creation of these kinds of committees is, however, no guarantee that substantive consultation will occur. Nor does the call for 'safe, healthy communities', a gender-neutral discourse, necessarily attend to the experiences of women and vulnerable persons.

Rather, this context of change necessitates activists to participate in many ways. As advocates, watchdogs, lobbyists, and agents of government change, they seek to address the impact of changes on women with diverse problems and backgrounds.

Feminists working within and outside government have long pointed to the differential impact of the economy, labour market, and training on women and men (see Provincial Advisory Council on the Status of Women, 1994; Porter, 1990; George, 2000). Moreover, violence against women and poverty had been important issues for feminists and activists in the anti-poverty and shelter movements since the early 1970s (Pope and Burnham, 1993; Hebert and Foley, 1997). Prominent cases such as Mount Cashel, as well as a few cases of women convicted of physically abusing children, drew media attention that sometimes implicated men and women as equal participants in the problem of violence. By contrast, feminists acknowledge that women can be abusive; yet, they consider the cultural context in which such women are historically located as mothers, foster mothers and caregivers. This means situating the family as an institution within the larger context of Newfoundland history: poverty, large families, and powerful churches.

By the early 1990s women were positioned to develop multi-pronged, province-wide strategies to address these problems. They lobbied to participate in the way these changes were implemented, through their participation in community-based organizations, and the Provincial Strategy Against Violence. The networks between grassroots activists and feminists working within institutions has been important in developing a feminist, inclusive process within the strategy, and for centering and communicating the experiences of women. And yet, the context of economic restructuring and restraint have impinged upon the implementation of the strategy and curtailed the input of less powerful residents.

Feminist Activism and the Provincial Strategy Against Violence

The Provincial Strategy Against Violence (PSAV) began as a consultation process in 1993, and developed into the first coordinated and provincial-wide initiative in the province. The Strategy sought to create 'safe caring communities' through enhanced prevention and service delivery. Its mandate was informed by the assumption that 'solutions to the problem of violence against women, children and elderly and dependent adults' must be achieved through coordinated efforts of community and government (Government of Newfoundland and Labrador, 1995). The Strategy targeted specific aspects of legislation, policy, direct services, community, education, research, and evaluation.

The Strategy is a plan to address violence in all areas of government in a way that incorporates community. Hence, its efficacy is directly connected to the way government departments operate and are restructured and the extent to which the diverse experiences of less powerful residents are represented. Five years later, an independent evaluation report summarized the limitations and achievements of the plan and confirmed what activists had themselves observed. Some successes had been made in the area of legislation and justice, and in the establishment of regional and community links. However, there was still a limited role for community-based players in areas of decision-making, and the strategy was unfulfilled due to a pre-occupation with government restructuring in other areas, and 'government-wide restraint'. Successes and limitations were significantly related to pre-existing networks and initiatives in regions as well as the larger historical context of regional disparity within the province.

For regions which had little community-based networks of persons working on these issues, the strategies appeared to be 'top-down' and hence, did not always reach a wide range of residents. These problems were exacerbated by the large size of Newfoundland and Labrador, which made meeting and networking difficult and expensive. Also, the cultural and racialized divisions (between whites and Aboriginals for example) contributed to feelings of distrust, and inequity. Moreover, even in those regions that were considered very well coordinated, such as Bay St George on the West coast, government restructuring posed numerous roadblocks. Firstly, government representatives did not always give time to the 'Strategy' and were often pre-occupied with implementing immense changes in their own departments. As Sharon Whalen, the coordinator of the Bay St George Women's Council put it,

> There were so many changes and directives coming from St John's, that we didn't have time to absorb or interpret them never mind to consider their impact on women lives, or on our attempts to address violence.

How then were feminists able to make an impact? Feminists had some impact through their incorporation of a gender analysis in the creation of an inclusive process within the strategy. Also, pre-existing links at the grassroots with community-based organizations, allowed a greater range of residents to make more substantive contributions in certain regions, and to critically assess the changes that were being implemented.

The incorporation of a systemic gender analysis in all areas of the strategy would ideally inform new policies in areas of justice, policing, and education. This included the training of those who work with victims, offenders, and clients. Also, the broad and systemic nature of the analysis was used to offset tensions and conflicts, such as the finger-pointing and the narrow outlook that can preoccupy those who work in criminal justice, health, and human resources on issues of child protection or the treatment of offenders. The incorporation of such an analysis however, is dependent on the ability of activists to be heard, to exchange information, and to reach those who actually implement specific projects.

Hence, feminists also attended to creating *an inclusive feminist process* through which the strategy was implemented. For example, the strategy included regional coordinating committees (along with government representatives) in its structure. Two of these, representing St John's and the Western region, were considered to have made strong substantive contributions to the 'Strategy'. It is noteworthy that both regions had developed community-based models *prior* to the strategy, the Interagency Committee on Violence Against Women in St John's, and the Sexual Abuse Counseling Service in Bay St George, which had laid the groundwork for an inclusive process (see George, 2000). Moreover, activists in Bay St George for example, had already learned to utilize government initiatives where possible and had developed strong networks to do so effectively. For example, although council members recognized the problems regarding the 1993 Royal Commission on Violence Against Women (see also Gotell, 1998) they were nonetheless, able to use the resources and information gathering process provided by the Commission, to increase awareness in the community through their media activism, and to expand their informal group for survivors of violence.

Grassroots links such as this were also important for critically monitoring the strategy and advocating for substantial community input, particularly in the context of fiscal restraint and restructuring. Activists are concerned that the mandate of the strategy will be undermined by some of the changes being implemented. For example, services previously provided by a social services department, are now accessed by two separate departments: Human Resources and Health. This change can make it more difficult for service workers to apprehend connections between financial need and the social problems women may experience with partners, in cases of separation and in terms of child welfare, or disabilities. In this case, community-based organizations and networks are increasingly important contexts for these connections to be made, in others words, for a woman's social and economic experience to be considered in her attempts to get training, or child care.

Ultimately, the Provincial Strategy has not yet produced significant increases in direct services although its mandate has been extended. To paraphrase one activist: how can you call for prevention by educating people on violence and then provide few resources for them to address the problem in their lives in a meaningful way? The Newfoundland government has invoked its 'have not' status and the effect of globalization in response to the criticism that changes within government departments or failure to develop services, are fiscally driven.

This kind of response exemplifies the dilemma that activists who work within government face. Their complex and ambiguous relationship with the state, a problem that is familiar to feminist elsewhere (Brodie, 1998: 24), allows for some negotiation and influence. But in the context of government restraint activists need to ask broader and more critical questions. In this context, the diversity of activism at play in anti-poverty and violence networks in the province is evermore important. Aside from 'femocrats' who work within the Women's Policy Office for example, there are eight women's councils that are community based and critical, yet provide services for, and are funded by government. There are also community-based organizations, such as the Provincial Association Against Family Violence, which receive ad hoc funding; and more autonomous, well-resourced groups, such as those linked to the labour movement.

Grassroots activists such as Helen Murphy, a representative of the Provincial Association Against Family Violence, who have been involved in these issues for years, are well positioned to consider the impact of changes, or the absence of resources on women's lives over time.

> Women (who experience transition houses) have illusions of what people can do for them; women come with enthusiasm, determination to change their living circumstances and are then faced with the full extent of the problem that may underlie their particular abusive situation.

This includes their place of residence (rural or urban), their lack of training and access to education, the difficulty of getting adequate legal representation, or the larger changes in their sub-regional economy. Because her organization is 'community-based' and has limited government funding, Helen considers that she often acts as a critic of government policies. She is also well-placed to 'ask the really hard questions', including, for example, whether moves toward mediation and alternate dispute resolution will reduce costs without negatively impacting on women's access to fair treatment in legal matters.

At the same time, grassroots initiatives are hardly a panacea to making change particularly when the government points to its own impoverishment or powerlessness. This makes it crucial to maintain strong links between violence and anti-poverty activists and more autonomous feminist organizations, which can provide a critical public space for organized protest, and the expression of alternate ways of making change. This is exemplified by the strong networks linking a very active provincial advisory council to annual provincial conferences, and representation on the National Action Committee (NAC). The 2001 annual Provincial Conference, for example, incorporated the 'World March', an international series of meetings involving over 6,000 organizations, into its program. Their 'March in Gander', like its predecessor in Quebec in 1995, Bread and Roses March against Poverty, focused on the violence, poverty, and structures that keep women poor, excluded, and violated. Having completed more than 40 visits to communities across the province in 1999, activists at the Provincial Advisory Council for the Status of Women hoped to achieve widespread support for this event.

Activists recognize that their work within government and at the grassroots requires them to draw upon the gender-neutral discourse of 'safe' communities, or to underplay their analysis as 'feminist'. This poses several problems, including the 'watering-down' of feminist insights, and the difficulty of actually documenting the impact of feminism itself. By focusing on activist links I do not mean to suggest that there is consensus among women who consider themselves to be feminist activists, or that all women who support these initiatives would be comfortable with the label. At the same time, it is important to draw attention to the way women work on a daily basis to make and influence changes in the province to counter the impression that feminist activists represent the interests of a narrow few.

References

Bashevkin, Sylvia. 1998. *Women on the Defensive: Living Through Conservative Times.* Toronto: University of Toronto Press.

Brodie, Janine. 1998. 'Restructuring and the Politics of Marginalization', in *Women and Political Representation in Canada*, Manon Tremblay and Caroline Andrew, eds. Ottawa: University of Ottawa Press.

Community Response Team. 1993. 'Proposal for Bay St George Sex Abuse Counselling Service'. Bay St George, Newfoundland.

George, Glynis. 2000. *The Rock Where We Stand: An Ethnography of Women's Activism in Newfoundland.* Toronto: University of Toronto Press.

Gotell, Lisa. 1998. 'A Critical Look at State Discourses on "Violence against Women": Some Implications for Feminist Politics and Women's Citizenship', in *Women and Political Representation in Canada*, Manon Tremblay and Caroline Andrew, eds. Ottawa: University of Ottawa Press.

Government of Canada. 2000. *Family Violence in Canada: A Statistical Profile.* Statistics Canada, Catalogue no. 85-224-XIE, 14.

Government of Newfoundland and Labrador. 1995. 'Towards the Year 2000: The Provincial Strategy Against Violence, An Action Plan'. St John's: Women's Policy Office.

Hancock, Joyce. 2000. Personal interview, August.

Hebert, Cheryl, and Jan Foley. 1997. 'Building Shelter . . . Taking Down Walls', in *Ties That Bind: An Anthology of Social Work and Social Welfare in Newfoundland and Labrador*, Gale Burford, ed. St John's: Jesperson Publishing.

Murphy, Helen. 1999. Personal interview, Summer.

Pauktuutit Inuit Women's Association. 1995. 'More Than They Say: Unreported Crime in Labrador'. Unpublished report submitted to the Solicitor General, Canada.

Pope, Sharon, and Jane Burnham. 1993. 'Change Within and Without: The Modern Women's Movement in Newfoundland and Labrador', in *Pursuing Equality*, Linda Kealey, ed. St John's: Institute of Social and Economic Research.

Porter, Marilyn. 1990. *Women and Economic Life in Newfoundland: Three Case Studies*. Report on Project 482-870005. St John's: Institute of Social and Economic Research.

Provincial Advisory Council on the Status of Women. 1994. 'Women of the Fishery'. Educational St John's: Planning and Design Associates Ltd.

Rankin, L. Pauline, and Jill Vickers. 1998. 'Locating Women's Politics', in *Women and Political Representation in Canada*, Manon Tremblay and Caroline Andrew, eds. Ottawa: University of Ottawa Press.

Social Policy Advisory Committee. 1997. *Investing in People and Communities: A Framework for Social Development*. St John's: Report of the Social Policy Advisory Committee.

Against the Current: Child Care and Family Policy in Quebec

Jane Jenson

EDITORS' INTRODUCTION

How is the provision of accessible, quality child care outside the home a feminist issue? Debates surrounding this question are informed by ideological understandings of traditional gender roles, attitudes towards women as workers, the needs and capacity of children, and the connections between family, economy, and state. Since the turn of the nineteenth century day nurseries established by philanthropic and religious organizations have existed in cities throughout Canada. The impetus for many day nurseries was ostensibly linked to poor school attendance in the late nineteenth century. Trusted with the duties of looking after younger children while parents worked, significant numbers of older children, especially girls, in major urban centers remained home as primary caregivers. These early day nurseries were not intended, however, to support women's right to paid employment outside the home and children's rights to education. Rather, as Donna Varga has argued, day nurseries were instituted 'to provide charitable social aid to relieve family poverty'.[1] During the Second World War, the federal government grudgingly supported child care services for working mothers but only as a temporary measure to maximize wartime production.[2] The critical work of Susan Prentice, Sonya Michel, and Rianne Mahon has shown us that the liberal roots of child care provision, conceptualized primarily as a service to the poor, has had critical effects on the ability of many women to choose their futures.[3] The notion that only the impoverished both desire and need child care further assumes that the majority of citizens are 'able to rely on market income and family, especially the unpaid household labour of women, to provide the requisite care'.[4] Not surprisingly, the 1970 *Report* of the Royal Commission on the Status of Women sought to reframe debates over the state's responsibility for universal child care from a measure to ameliorate poverty to a step towards social and economic equality for all women and men.[5]

Scholars in Canada are increasingly sensitive not only to the political machinations that surround child care policy, but also to variations in the way local, national, and international jurisdictions both conceive and implement this policy.[6] In this essay by Jane Jenson, Quebec is singled out as forging a distinct path towards universally affordable and accessible child care, particularly in the context of its own past. Her approach to this 'distinctiveness' is grounded firmly in the history of family policy in the province. Historians who focus on women in Quebec, including Denyse Baillargeon and Bettina Bradbury in this volume, have drawn our attention to the family's constant and central role in the province's political fortunes. Micheline

Dumont surmises that the role of women in the fight over Quebec nationalism, for example, has been a feature of the province since the nineteenth century.[7] With the Quiet Revolution in Quebec in the 1960s and the turn away from the Catholic Church as arbitrator of the province's social agenda, women's movements gained strength. And, as Chantal Maille as argued, 'since the end of the 1960s, the number of women's groups have grown; this growth has played an important role in social reforms affecting women.'[8] Child care is centrally implicated in reforms that shape many women's experiences. Jenson demonstrates that important features of Quebec's family policy, particularly early childhood education and care, mark a significant break with its own past and from that of many other liberal democracies. Most recently, Manitoba's New Democratic Party government has, like Quebec, developed an approach to child care that signals social solidarity rather than liberal individualism as a goal.[9] Jenson argues that Quebec nonetheless stands as a case study in how reform can serve and protect the interests of vulnerable society members, particularly children and the economically disadvantaged, while resisting the worst offences of neoliberal welfare restructuring.

Quebec's family policy mix introduced by Lucien Bouchard's Parti Québécois in the late 1990s was, as Jenson shows, characterized by three innovative programs: a public system of early childhood education and care, a new family allowance, and an insurance program covering parental and maternity leave more generously than the provisions outlined by the federal government. In particular, the provisions for universal, affordable, and educative child care has garnered the lion's share of attention. The goals of the model were to establish universal, non-profit child care available to all children regardless of whether or not mothers were employed outside or inside the home. As Jenson points out, this universal aspect of the model runs counter to trends in other liberal welfare states. The Parti Québécois Family Policy was phased in starting in 1997 and was aimed at four-year-olds. Subsequent years would see funding provided for children aged three, then two, and lastly for those aged one year. In 2002–3, the number of regulated child care spaces in Quebec doubled to 164,410 to accommodate 50 per cent of the demand for care. Elsewhere in the country, 12 per cent of the need for child care is accommodated.[10] A fee of $5.00 per day for the new child care arrangements, paid by all parents regardless of income, was introduced. This fee rose to $7.00 per day in 2004.

As Jenson's careful analysis makes clear, this new family policy approach was not intended to deemphasize parental employment. On the contrary, the intention was to support parents' capacity to find employment while reducing the burden of inadequate or inaccessible child care. By supporting both working parents and children's need for developmentally appropriate education and care, across both gender and class lines, the government was, as Jenson points out 'going against the grain' of its own history, of that of other Canadian provinces, and of many other liberal democratic countries. While the Quebec model is far from perfect (only 1 in 5 Quebec children still have access to a regulated child care spot[11]), it has surpassed the rest of Canada. Whether the move to greater government funding and regulation of organized child care will meaningfully improve the lot of child care workers—who are overwhelmingly women—remains to be seen.

In June 2004 the federal government promised to put five million dollars into creating 250,000 child care spaces by 2009. How will this alter the lives of women both as mothers and as child care workers? Jenson encourages students interested the history of social policy to adopt a gendered lens for critical analysis. Despite its flaws and shortcomings, Quebec's Family Policy placed at the centre what other jurisdictions in the country, with the exception of Manitoba, have yet to acknowledge: affordable and regulated daycare is deeply gendered and imbricated with any claim to social equity.

Notes

1. Donna Varga, *Constructing the Child: A History of Canadian Day Care* (Toronto: Lorimer, 1997).
2. See Susan Prentice, 'Militant Mothers in Domestic Times: Toronto's Postwar Childcare Struggle', PhD dissertation, York University, 1993; Alvin Finkel, '"Even the Little Children Cooperated": Family Strategies, Child Care Discourse, and Social Welfare Debates, 1945–1975', *Labour/Le Travail* 36 (1995): 91–118.
3. See, for example, Susan Prentice, ed. *Changing Child Care: Five Decades of Child Care Advocacy and Policy in Canada* (Halifax: Fernwood Publishing, 2001); Sonya Michel and Rianne Mahon, eds. *Child Care Policy at the Crossroads: Gender and Welfare State Restructuring* (New York: Routledge, 2002).
4. Rianne Mahon, 'The Never-Ending Story: The Struggle for Universal Child Care Policy in the 1970s', *Canadian Historical Review* 81.4 (December 2000): 582–615.
5. Royal Commission on the Status of Women, *Report* (Ottawa, 1970).
6. On the precariousness of state-supported child care in times of welfare restructuring see Susan Prentice, 'Less, Worse and More Expensive: Child Care in an Era of Deficient Reduction', *Journal of Canadian Studies* 34.2 (Summer 1999): 137–59.
7. Micheline Dumont, 'Women of Quebec and the Contemporary Constitutional Issue', *Gender and Politics in Contemporary Canada*, Francois-Pierre Gingras, ed. (Toronto: Oxford University Press, 1995), 153–74.
8. Chantel Maille, 'Quebec Women and the Constitutional Issue: A Scattered Group', *Journal of Canadian Studies* 35.2 (Summer 2000): 98.
9. Susan Prentice, 'Manitoba's Childcare Regime: Social Liberalism in Flux', *Canadian Journal of Sociology* 29.2 (2004): 193–207.
10. Canadian Labour Congress, 'Lobby Fact Sheet #5, Child Care: The Time is Now', 27 July 2004, 1–4. Available at http://www.clc-ctc.ca.
11. See, for example, Institute for Research on Public Policy/Institut de Recherche en Politiques Publiques, 'Shortcomings of "Quebec Model" of Family Policy: A Warning to Governments Across Canada', News Release, 12 January 2000, 29–30. Available at http://www.irpp.org.

Questions for Critical Reading

1. In 2004 the influential Organization for Economic Co-operation and Development (OECD) reported that Canada's child care system was chronically under-funded and lacked direction and coordination, particularly in a global context of increasing economic competition. Is universal child care in Canada best supported by arguments of economic competitiveness? What are the possible advantages and disadvantages of this argument for mothers and families?
2. Should quality child care be understood and debated primarily as a 'woman's issue'? What are the alternatives and how might these help foster or discourage social equity?
3. Are issues of social class and racial identity equally prevalent in debates over child care and the state's involvement than those involving gender? What separates these issues and what braids them together?
4. As mothers, women are the primary users of child care while as day-care providers and child-care workers they are the primary providers. Do workers and mothers have the same interests in child-care or are they different? Why?

In 1997 the government of Quebec legislated a new family policy. It provided, among other things, three innovative programs. First is a family allowance targeted to low-income families and set at a level sufficiently high to recognize the basic needs of a child. The second is universal educational child care at a very low cost, with parents paying full fees at only five dollars per day. The third is the promise of a paid parental leave, including a portion reserved to fathers, which would be longer, more comprehensive, and at a higher replacement rate than the limited leaves already in place in Canada.

These three innovative steps identify Quebec's strategy as being very different from that of many European countries and certainly its neighbours in North America, whether other Canadian provinces or the United States. Where many European countries have been moving in the direction of encouraging a diversification of services and expanding the range of choice, in part by encouraging and even financing informal care (Jenson and Sineau, 1998, 2001), Quebec is rowing against that current. It simply eliminated the tax deductions for informal care and non-educational care, which had been in place for two decades, and poured the savings into the creation of regulated spaces providing developmentally focused professional child care. It was moving, in other words, if not toward a one-size-fits-all model, certainly in the direction of inducing parents to use either centre-based care or family child care linked to the new Early Childhood Centres. At the same time, by eliminating the universal Family Allowance, the government was signaling that it did not consider such benefits were meant to compensate parents who chose to provide their own child care. Moreover, while the parental leaves would be extended, they were by no means the 'long leaves' of several years that some European jurisdictions have been instituting in order to reduce demand for services for those under three years of age.

Even more dramatic was Quebec's divergence from the liberal welfare-state model of North America. The first difference was the dramatic recommitment to universality. This engagement with a value that is rapidly losing what little legitimacy it ever had in liberal welfare states has been strengthened in Quebec. Recently, the highest-ranking civil servant responsible for Quebec's family policy listed as his first goal 'to ensure fairness by offering universal support to families'.[1] The low-cost child care services, as well as a range of universal tax credits and the implementation of full-day kindergarten for five-year-olds, all express this commitment to maintaining solidarity via universality. By promising that middle-class families could, at a reasonable price, gain access to quality services, the province was rejecting the liberal welfare state's long-standing form of targeting, which subsidizes licensed care for poor families, while in the name of 'choice' sending middle-income families into a market in which they confront hard decisions about trading off quality and dependability against affordability.[2]

Second, although since 1997 family allowances have been targeted to low income recipients, no strings are attached. As with a similar benefit paid by Ottawa, the only condition is the presence of a dependent child under eighteen. But in addition in Quebec, the level of benefits depends on the number of adults living with the child; single-parent families receive more generous benefits, as well as particular tax advantages.[3] The design decisions, in other words, reflect nothing of the 'moral panic' about lone mothers characterizing some liberal welfare states in the years of welfare reform. Nor do they reproduce the neutrality of programs that do not take into account the particular difficulties faced by lone parents.

In these ways, then, we can see that Quebec is moving against the current. Is this simply because Quebec is continuing down a path that has always been 'distinct', it being the only North American jurisdiction that has had an explicit 'family policy' for two decades? Here the answer is negative. While Quebec has been distinct, the policies and programs put into place since 1997 do not support a story of path dependency.

The new policy marked a break with past practices in at least two ways. It banished an increase in the birth rate from the list of goals of family policy, despite the fact that previous governments, both Liberal Party and Parti Québécois, had made natalism a principal axis of concern, as we will see below. Second, while this family policy, like previous ones, arises from a concern with fostering social solidarity, the ways selected to do so have been quite simply reversed. In the past universal family allowances and income redistribution were the preferred instrument for expressing solidarity, and child care as a program essentially targeted to working parents, with subsidies going to those 'in need'. After 1997, rapidly rising government investments in educational child care have become the symbol of societal cohesion, while family allowances serve as the instrument for assuring cross-class equity.[4]

Given this flip-flop with respect to Quebec's own history and the 'lone ranger' quality of several of its actions, we need to seek an explanation in factors other than the path dependency of liberal welfare regimes, the category into which Quebec has been slotted in the past. This example is a fascinating case study, because these different policy choices were instituted explicitly in order to confront the same challenges as those in other liberal welfare regimes: globalization, the transformation of women's economic activity and family forms, and especially the poverty trap in which so many lone parent families find themselves. The policy recognizes that labour markets have been restructured and—most important for the comparison to other liberal welfare regimes—it is also seen as part of a strategy to promote employability.

As the civil servant quoted above told his audience, 'We decided that we had to increase our support to families . . . . As a result we put in place a number of structural measures for the society of the year 2000, the harmonious functioning of which centres on employment' (Boisvert, 2000). And, as the Ministry of Child and Family Welfare puts it bluntly,[5] 'Poverty is less present in families with full-time jobs. This is why the government has chosen to fight against it not only through providing financial support to the poorest families but also in the field of employment by offering parents conditions making it easier to balance family and job responsibilities.'[6] Even the educational emphasis in child care and the extension of school to younger children is justified as much in terms of avoiding costly school failures by promoting school readiness, as it is in terms of the development of the child.

The Quebec story is not, it should be clear from the start, one of social democratic progressivism forging ahead in the face of neoliberalism found everywhere else. Its reform of social assistance, begun in the mid-1980s, has been widely criticized for being coercive, instituting 'workfare' even before the word was well known in English (Bouchard, Labrie, and Noël, 1996: 94). Coupled with this coercion have been, however, what Gérard Boychuk (1998) terms market-performance features. These programs reward efforts to enter and stay in the labour force (88). The combination has generated a social assistance regime that includes both sticks and carrots. The reformed family policy fits into this mixed regime, albeit falling more on the market-performance side, as we will see.

Already however, it should be clear that Quebec is not following some 'golden age' welfare regime tradition; its eye is clearly on the twenty-first century and the needs of this small society in which many actors harbour hopes of becoming independent and being able to go it alone in the era of globalization. Thus, as this chapter will argue, we need to seek the explanation for the specifics of this program in the balance of political forces that created it, the goals the various actors sought to achieve, the compromises they worked out among themselves, both for family policy and the broader economy, and always with an eye on the effects for the political future of Quebec in Canada.

The Roots of the System—Ideas, Institutions, and Actors

Quebec's Summit on the Economy and Employment in October 1996 brought together employers, unions, and a broad selection of popular sector groups to reflect upon plans for the medium-term future of the province. At the end of the summit, Premier Lucien Bouchard announced a fundamental revision of family policy that eventually culminated in the three programs described above. Maligned by students because he refused to freeze tuition fees, under pressure from antipoverty activists to embrace the goal of *appauvrissement zéro* (zero poverty) rather than striving to achieve a 'zero deficit', Bouchard might be accused of searching for a theme that would unite rather than divide.[7] But the decision to announce a major reform of family policy, with universal and affordable child care at its centre, was much more than an effort to get out of a sticky political situation. It represented the victory of a coalition of activists and officials seeking to address the needs of families and children within Quebec's societal strategy (*projet de société*).

Indeed, the summit was only one moment, albeit a crucial one, in a decades long controversy about family policy. By the mid-1990s positions were aligned, in part, with reference to the government's Third Family Action Plan (1995–7). Elaborated after broad public consultations in the 1995 International Year of the Family, the plan focused on prevention (including measures to prevent spousal abuse and encourage greater participation of fathers in child rearing), balancing work and family (including more child care and teaching adolescents about the importance of both parents sharing family responsibilities), financial support for parents, and improving the environment of families (including housing, valuing solidarity across families, and emphasizing the family dimension in all services).[8] This list represents the compromise arrived at among feminists, the family movement, antipoverty activists, social workers, and experts on development and early childhood education, as well as municipal government and the provincial public sector.

Family policy has never been a policy domain apart from the great issues agitating Quebec politics. By 1996 it had become a part of a broader process of welfare-state redesign, touching on social assistance and labour market policy. The multidimensional reform, laid out at the summit, sought to (1) improve parents' capacity to balance work and family life; (2) provide child care services which were both financially accessible and developmentally sound, in particular for facilitating school readiness; and (3) induce parents with low incomes or on social assistance to find employment or better jobs.[9] Given this strategic location in the process of modernizing social policy, it is not surprising that the announcement of the new family policy garnered a huge amount of attention. Nor did this abate over the next months. In January 1997 the government published a white paper, *Les enfants au Coeur de nos choix* (Children at the Heart of Our Choices), and legislated the following July.

Family policies can set a number of priorities. They might seek, for example, to promote children's development, to maximize equality of opportunity and condition among all types of families, or to advance gender equality (Jenson and Stroick, 1999, provides one such list). Quebec's family policy over the last decades has always had a range of goals, as the Third Action Plan described above well indicates. Nonetheless, promoting parental employment has recently risen to the top. But this is not surprising. The institution responsible for family policy, the Ministère de la Famille et de l'Enfance (Ministry of Child and Family Welfare) was created in 1997 by amalgamating the Family Secretariat, the Office des Services de Garde à l'Enfance (Office of Child Care Services, or OSGE) responsible for regulating and licensing child care, and the Ministère de la Securité du Revenu (Ministry of Income Security).

This has not always been the case. The use of the state to encourage parental labour-force participation, as well as the provision of public services, is a relatively new phenomenon. As Yves Vaillancourt (1988, 144) says, 'Quebec is the Canadian province that had the most privatized social services (before 1970) and the most public ones (after 1970).' Quebec's social services were altered fundamentally by the wave of reforms initiated after 1960. Services had been provided either by the Catholic Church (to Catholic Quebecers) or via a network of charitable and non-profit agencies (to the non-Catholic communities). This changed dramatically as a new team of reformers, based in both the Quebec Liberal Party and the Parti Québécois, took the reins of power in the next decades. Modernizing politicians, bureaucrats, and other experts have had a major influence over the shape of policy since 1960, but they have also had to contend with a mobilized civil society that has sometimes had different assessments of the best direction for change. The 1960s thrust to reform also intersected with initiatives from Ottawa that were setting all the provinces down some new paths.

In Quebec, the combination of internal and external forces for change was dramatic. The Social Assistance Act of 1969 was Quebec's response to the 1965 Canada Assistance Plan (CAP), while the Health and Social Services Act (1971) established Quebec's universal health care system. Both pieces of legislation followed in the tracks of the Castonguay-Nepveu Commission, a major investigatory body that framed the terms of debate about health and social services for several decades. Its work had involved most of the thinkers about social policy in the province, both conservative and reformist, and it had heard from almost every sector of Quebec society (Lesemann, 1981).

Despite a new social assistance regime that adopted an individualized approach to social security and was non categorical (Boychuk, 1998), there was a concomitant concern about families. One result was a provincial family allowance regime, put in place in 1969, that did not share with Ottawa the distrust of large families that had shaped federal family allowances since 1946 (Bergeron, 1997: 261–8). These Family Allowances, altered at each moment of reform over the last decades remain a key pillar of Quebec's family policy.

The Castonguay-Nepveu Commission was very critical of private services whether non-profit or commercial; it clearly put the accent on public services (Vaillancourt, 1988). Nonetheless, opposition to non-profit provision was somewhat tempered because, in the 1960s and continuing today, Quebec civil society was traversed by a dense network of community groups, agencies, projects, and popular initiatives whose political project was and remains to provide services 'differently'. From the early 1960s, citizens' committees were actively intervening in the social policy domain. They were critical of the individualistic 'case work' approach of social workers as much as the charity-based religious orientations. They sought instead to provide collective solutions and services that would build local leadership and develop community capacity. While they turned to local governments, as well as to Quebec and Ottawa, for funding and support, their take on social services was never statist. By the late 1960s these popular sector groups' (*groupes populaires*) political project was quite explicit. Rather than lobbying for public services they mobilized self-help groups and community action through legal aid, literacy training, help with family budgeting, child care centres, and people's clinics (Belanger and Levesque, 1992: 715–24). Unions were also active participants, for example by backing local self-help groups intended to promote financial independence among low-income groups, including by setting up food, child care, or other cooperatives.

This mobilization, both in cities and rural areas, might have gone the way of comparable collective action throughout North America at the time—that is, toward obscurity—if it had not been institutionalized in important locales, two of which are of central importance to this chapter. A central action of the popular sector movement involved establishment of child care centres (*garderies*), the first of the two institutions. These were incorporated as non-profit organizations run by councils of parents and staff which embraced both democratic and child development goals.

Such services had also been a major goal of the second wave of the women's movement since its appearance in the mid-1960s. The Fédération des femmes du Québec (Federation of Quebec Women, or FFQ) had state-provided child care on its list of six demands at its founding in 1965, and continued to agitate for child care, for example, in its brief to the Royal Commission on the Status of Women, or RCSW (Collectif Clio, 1992: 464). The Confédération des Syndicats Nationaux (Confederation of National Unions, or CSN) also presented a brief to the RCSW centreed on child care. Taking things in their own hands, women's and other popular sector groups accessed the funds of the federal Local Initiative Program (LIP) to set up non-profit, democratically and parent-managed centres in disadvantaged and other neighbourhoods (Desjardins, 1991: chap. 3; Lamoureux, 1992: 699). These first politicized child care centres have been reclaimed as the model for today's central institution for child care and development: the early childhood centres (ECCs) created by the 1997 reform.[10]

A second important institution created at this time was the *centre local de services communautaires* (local community service centre, or CLSC). Modeled on the people's clinics, the CLSC serves as a point of entry to the healthcare system-providing home care (including postpartum services for multiple births), perinatal care, parenting support, and so forth—and is supposed to be a pivotal actor in community development projects.[11] The CLSC was in many ways an institutionalized expression of a community-based progressive approach to health and social services, one that was suspicious of 'medical' solutions, professionals, centralization, and commercialization. Employing social animators as well as social workers and health care professionals, the CLSC has official responsibility for liaison with the voluntary sector and the community (Roy, 1987). The CLSC remains a key partner in virtually all programs for children and families. The local CLSCs have become a crucial link in the family policy chain, working closely with early childhood centres in their catchment areas.

For its part, the government of Quebec did not move very quickly onto the child care field (Baillargeon, 1996). Its first formal involvement was in 1974, when the temptation of the shared-cost CAP program led the government to institute (as did all other provinces) subsidies for low-income parents using licensed child care.[12] New legislation in 1979 continued subsidies to low-income parents, established direct subsidies to centres, and created an allowance for the care of children with disabilities. The regulatory and licensing body, the OSGE, was created at the same time.

Over these same years, despite the philosophy and rhetoric privileging non-profit and community groups, the commercial private sector was not at a standstill, in part because of governmental foot-dragging. It, too, expanded when the supply of services could not keep up with demand (Vaillancourt, 1988). The mix was always an uneasy one, however, with ministers frequently expressing an aversion to commercial expansion and even seeking to halt it.

By the end of the 1970s, a child care system was in place that looked very much like those of the other Canadian provinces. Just as elsewhere, child care services were a mixed bag, including regulated day care centres and family day care, as well as unregulated 'nursery schools' and drop-in centres, and school-based child care under the jurisdiction of the Ministry of Education (Childcare Resource and Research Unit, 1997: 25). Non-profit groups delivered most of the licensed services, but a commercial sector also existed. This system had been built by a variety of actors involved in the family policy network. Alongside bureaucrats there were activists and 'femocrats' from the women's movements, and community development activists who sought to change society from the bottom up. They sought to facilitate the balancing of work and family responsibilities, but also to use democratically governed child care centres as a locus for community empowerment.

In this mix, the one factor that did distinguish Quebec from the rest of Canada was the active presence of a mobilized family movement. As the next section will make clear, this actor became more important in the next decade as a family policy was redesigned to meet a set of new challenges. The sharp drop in the birth rate that coincided with the Quiet Revolution increased the fragility of the French language and culture in North America, at the same time as the governments were going through the first of their neoliberal 'cures'.

Juggling Purposes and Multiple Instruments: Family Policy in the 1980s

There has never been full consensus on family policy in Quebec. Debates range over the types of services, to be sure. Some vaunt non-profit groups while others argue for a level playing field for commercial services. Some claim public financing is sufficient while others believe services must also be publicly delivered. Beyond these controversies, there is always the issue of the birth rate, and whether public policy should be pronatalist in its goals. The continued predominance of concerns about the birth rate is hardly surprising, given the fact that in the single decade from 1961 to 1971, the average size of a Quebec family fell from four to two children, while in the mid-1980s the birth rate dropped to 1.4 (Dandurand, 1992: 368).

The new economic and cultural concerns of the 1980s, which had a significant demographic content, meant that while the actors remained the same, the balance of forces was different. Thus, the women's movement—by the 1970s supported by femocrats within several ministries as well as the Conseil du Statut de la Femme (Council on the Status of Women)—was there. But demographers and the family movement also were influential actors, as were bureaucrats in a range of social and economic ministries and outside experts.

In 1979, three years into its first term in office, the Parti Québécois (PQ) government launched what would become a long and vibrant debate about family policy, one that continued through the terms of the succeeding Liberal government, to culminate in 1987–8 in a new family policy and two new institutions, the Conseil de la Famille (Council of the Family, a parapublic body responsible for advising the minister) and the Secrétariat à la Famille (Family Secretariat).[13] It started as a discussion of economic growth, including the population size needed to sustain a growth model. This was prompted by the PQ government's economic strategy statement *Bâtir le Québec* (*Building Quebec*, 1979), a document that reasoned from a heavy dose of demographic fears and was natalist in its prescriptions. Soon there was a wholesale public debate about families, equality and social equity.

The next step was a policy document explicitly addressing family policy. Nonetheless, it is important to understand the context surrounding the Green Paper, *Pour les familles québécoises* (For Quebec Families), issued by the government in 1984, because it framed the debate and positions adopted by the major actors. In 1984 the PQ government was already actively considering tax reform and strategies for protecting the French language and Quebec culture in the face of a declining birth rate. The tax reform process was tending in the direction of favouring two-parent and working families, while an important parliamentary commission, headed by Richard French and reporting in 1985, had a mandate to analyze the demographic situation in the context of cultural policy. It proposed a dualistic approach of increased immigration and fostering a higher birth rate.[14]

Seeing both these policy developments emerging, women's groups were anxious. Despite Quebec's 1975 Charter of Rights and Liberties guaranteeing gender equality, and a progressive policy to advance equality between the sexes put into place in 1978, the province appeared to be moving back toward traditionalism, via the tax treatment of families and in order to deal with cultural challenges (Dandurand, 1987: 353). Therefore feminists, coming from both the FFQ and the more traditionalist Association Féminine d'Éducation et d' Action Sociale (Women's Association for Education and Social Action, or AFEAS) actively intervened in the consultations organized by the consultative committee on the green paper that toured Quebec throughout 1985–6. Women were optimistic that their voices would be heard, because one member of the consultative committee, Nicole Boily, was a feminist who had worked with the FFQ, and another, Christiane Berube, had just ended her term as President of AFEAS.

In addition to tax reformers, natalists, and feminists, debate was engaged with professionals who had a stake in establishing clear new norms and gaining additional resources for social work, psychology, health, and so on (Dandurand, 1987: 355). And last but never least, the family movement was actively involved. This movement of individuals or groups promoting healthy families and family life has been an important actor for decades. Renée Dandurand (1987: 355–6) describes its two wings.

There is a conservative and Catholic one, very close to the Church. But there is also a liberal wing, which looks to the state to support families in their diverse needs and their diverse situations. The third member of the consultative committee, the author Maurice Champagne-Gilbert, was associated with this second branch of the family movement, as well as being a well-known human rights advocate.

The consultative committee's reports came down strongly in favour of the principle of shared responsibility between parents and the community;[15] they recognized the variety of situations in which families live, and they downplayed natalism. More generally, the committee argued that there was no 'crisis of the family'. The real challenge was to institute new forms of solidarity between the sexes. In its recommendations, the committee sought to avoid supporting natalist policy, proposing higher levels of spending and more coherent support for families, as well as improved parental leaves, conditions of part-time employment and family allowances. It was strangely silent on the matter of child care, making only the recommendation that the current regime be better organized and that everyone, including employers, do their part. However, it did recommend retaining the existing subsidy for low-income families using services.

With the Quebec Liberal Party in government by the time the second report was issued, some adjustments to expectations were inevitable. However, the change from one party to another did not mark a major policy reorientation. The statement on family policy issued by the Ministry of Health and Social Services in 1987 stood on four principles, most of which reflected the general thinking of the consultative committee. The fourth was, of course, the exception to that generalization. The four principles were: providing public support for the costs of child rearing, fighting poverty, encouraging parents to seek employment, and supporting a higher birthrate (Lefebvre, 1998: 221).

The second and third principles provided the rationale for needs-based subsidies for child care, tax credits, recurring funding to child care centres, and generous maternity and parental leave packages, as well as allowances for young children and income support for working parents. Thus, 1988 saw the creation of the Parental Wage Assistance Program, known as APPORT in French. This provides a wage supplement to families with even a tiny amount (now $100 per month) of earned income and extra support for child care expenses, in order to draw them into the labour force (Beauvais and Jenson, 2001: appendix A, table 11).

Principles one and four generated four types of family allowances. One was universal. Others addressed the particular needs of young children and the disabled. Perhaps the best known was the birth allowance (*prime à la naissance*), whose amount increased to very generous levels for third and higher children.[16] The birth allowances favouring 'the third child' never had unanimous support, and controversy over them touched on all the central issues of Quebec politics. As had occurred throughout the 1980s, the issues ranged from economic development to the role of the state, immigration, and linguistic assimilation. Demographers debated feminist demographers, proponents of social spending confronted neoliberals, and natalists verbally sparred with familialists and feminists. The controversy shook the National Assembly, government agencies such as the Secrétariat à la Famille, parapublic bodies (for example, the Conseil du Statut de la Femme, as well as the Conseil de la Famille), the press, and intellectuals.

The post-1987 system was coherent in the sense that it stood on the four principles listed above, but it was complicated, with a wide variety of different programmes. Moreover, while other governmental goals were coherent in themselves, as an expression of the goals of family policy, the design did not always mesh well with them. Despite targeting low-income families and paying wage supplements, there were still problems linking family policy to employability measures; there was mounting concern about the 'poverty trap' and intergenerational reliance on social assistance.

After its election in 1995, the PQ government, like its Liberal predecessor, undertook to reform social assistance programs. In a decade, Quebec had transformed its social assistance regime into one based on both income support and 'employability' (Noël, 1996). But because of the limited results obtained by training and other programs and because of rising rates of unemployment and welfare, a large debate on the subject opened. From the beginning, child benefits were part of this discussion, as was expanding child care, because of the place single mothers and other poor families occupied in policy-makers' concerns.[17]

In preparation for reforming social assistance, the government asked a group of experts to make proposals for redesigning the system. Eventually, the majority (headed by psychologist Camil Bouchard, and therefore called the *Bouchard Report*) and the minority (headed by economist Pierre Fournier) reports were written, because the experts could not agree (Noël, 1996). Nonetheless, despite their disagreements on a range of other matters, both groups did agree that 'children should be removed from social assistance' and both recommended the creation of an integrated family allowance (Lefevbre, 1998: 215–16).

The Estates-General of Education, which reported in 1996 after months of touring the province for consultations, also recommended increased, more accessible child care for the youngest children and extended preschool education services, in order to combat high drop-out rates and school failure in general. The Conseil Supérieur de l'Éducation (Higher Council of Education) did the same, as did the majority report of the expert group on social reform mentioned above. The experts reminded Quebecers that years ago the *Parent Report*, which had been the blueprint in the 1960s Quiet Revolution for secularizing and modernizing education, had recommended kindergarten for four- and five-year-olds.

The claims and proposals of these expert studies, consultations, and other groups addressing poverty and promoting gender equality all fed into the announcement at the Summit on the Economy and Employment in 1996 and especially into the white paper released the next January.

Toward a Family Policy with 'Children at the Heart of Our Choices'

As we have seen throughout this chapter, changes to child care programs in Quebec have always been located in a broader set of family policies. The 1997 reform known perhaps best for the five-dollars-per-day spaces, is no exception here. This shift in funding arrangements as well as the emphasis on universality and a developmentally appropriate curriculum, were all part of a much broader effort to reform social assistance, develop broad-based support for the PQ's political vision, promote gender equality, and demonstrate Ottawa's recalcitrance with respect to the federal principle. With such an all-encompassing agenda, it is not surprising that a number of actors considered the reform to be crucially important for them.

First into the lists were the fiscal conservatives, who wanted to achieve a zero deficit and saw in the universal family allowances and generous birth allowances a 'waste' of state spending. Going as they did to families whether they 'needed' them or not, those who shared with the minister of finance, Bernard Landry, an overwhelming fear of deficit spending (at least on social programs) were looking for a change. But because this was a PQ and not a Liberal government, certain intragovernmental compromises were necessary. Feminists and social democrats, such as Pauline Marois and Louise Harel, had risen to high cabinet responsibility, and femocrats were scattered throughout the bureaucracy. The women's movement was mobilized after the 1995 March for Bread and Roses and the President of the FFQ, Françoise David, was an important player at the Summit on the Economy and Employment. Movement women had ties to women within the state, but if perhaps equal relevance was the desire of the PQ to assure that no gender gap would interfere with its support in the next referendum on independence for Quebec.

Other crucial actors in this policy network, often providing the 'glue' that held all the parts together, were child development experts. Camil Bouchard, for example, had published a formative document in 1991, *Un Québec fou de ses enfants* (*Quebec, Mad about its Children*) (MSSS, 1991). It made the case that early childhood education was crucial to proper development and that poverty and disadvantage were the factors most likely to place children at risk for negative developmental outcomes. In the preparations of the 1997 white paper he helped to make the links across domains such as social assistance (recall he had signed the majority report coming out of the 1996 consultation of experts on reform of social assistance), early childhood education, and social solidarity.

The white paper was not preceded by any formal public consultation. It was written by the secretariat of the Committee of Priorities of the Executive Council and signed by one of its members, Marois, the minister of education.[18] The government deemed it was important to keep the process well under control for a number of reasons. First, the major lines of the reform had already been announced at the summit; the government knew what it wanted to do. Second, the direction of reform was not universally popular. The natalist wing of the family movement was not happy about the threat to the birth allowances. Commercial child care operators were also opposed to the reform. Indeed, part of the impetus for reform had come from Marois's concern about the rising importance of commercial providers of child care in the system and her decision immediately after the 1995 election to place a moratorium on new licenses. Therefore, the commercial sector knew its future was on the line. Third, the government was meeting resistance to its parallel reform of social assistance and it did not want to open up another line of attack. And fourth, the government as well as the bureaucrats and experts who supported the reform understood that it made sense *only as a package*. None of the pieces in and of itself was a compelling reform, but together they created a momentum for positive change. Therefore, it had to hold together, and be held together.

The white paper made this argument for coherence, presenting a strong case for 'integration' across domains, including social, educational, and employment.[19] Family policy is now described as having four main objectives:

- to ensure fairness by offering universal support to families;
- to give more assistance to low income families;
- to facilitate the balancing of parental and work responsibilities;
- to foster children's development and equal opportunity.[20]

In the white paper the emphasis was somewhat more on promoting employment and equal opportunity. Despite such differences, however, the policy has a number of clear principles, some of which continue past practices, and others that break with the past:[21]

- An integrated family allowance, targeted to low-income parents, covering the estimated costs of raising a child from birth to age eighteen;
- universality in the tax regime, including a tax exemption for dependent children's basic needs and a nonrefundable tax credit for dependent children;
- insurance providing paid parental leaves to virtually all employed new parents;
- educational and developmental child care services organized by early childhood centres;
- accessible child care services, at fees of five dollars per day; reduced-cost child care for low-income working parents and 23.5 hours per week free child care for social assistance recipients, in order to ensure that children at risk use the developmental service;
- full-day kindergarten for five-year-olds; half-day kindergarten coupled with child care for four-year-olds in disadvantaged neighborhoods in Montreal.

The focus on equal opportunity, equity and solidarity across classes is expressed in the integrated family allowance, available to all low-income families with dependent children under eighteen. It replaces three family allowances,[22] and those parts of the social assistance regime that had been paid with respect to children. The amount varies according to the birth order of the child and whether two parents live with the child or not, as well as according to family income. The family allowance supplements the Canada Child Tax Benefit (CCTB), which Revenue Canada pays to Quebec families (Jenson, 2001); in other words, it tops it up if necessary to arrive at Quebec's preferred level. [23]

The overall assessment of the effects of this unification of programs is that they keep low-income parents more or less where they were in terms of benefits, as long as they stay on social assistance (Rose, 1998). However, because the benefits are neutral as to employment, there is a gain made by those who are working in a low-paying job. Therefore, reflecting the tie back to employability goals, there is an incentive to seek employment.

The major losers in this shift to a single, targeted family allowance were better-off families with more than two children. They no longer could count, for example, on a birth allowance injecting up to $8,000 into the family treasury. While middle-income parents lost the previously universal family allowance, they acquired less costly child care. This was a gain for those who used the places, but not for families who cared for their own children or used informal care. Therefore, there has been some dispute about the fairness of the new system, and about whether it recognizes the diversity of family needs (IRRP, 2000; Vérificateur Général, 1999).

In contrast to the targeted family allowance, the emphasis on universality is evident in the fact that the 1997 reform maintained the tax exemption for dependent children, the nonrefundable credit for the first child of single parent families and the nonrefundable tax credit to all families.[24] This third credit is the only universal tax credit for families with children in the country (Clarke, 1998) and it is worth $598 for the first child ($897 for a single-parent family) and $552 for subsequent children. These tax advantages are a key expression of solidarity in the form of universality; the same principle underpins the child care programs, presented in more detail below.

The white paper also announced that the government would institute a program of parental insurance. This idea of redesigning parental leave, to extend coverage and unlink it from eligibility to unemployment insurance, had been promoted by the PQ for almost a decade. It was part of the 1981 election campaign. In addition, the Conseil du Statut de la Femme had also been pushing for such a change since 1988, when it published a detailed analysis of the gaps in coverage. Between 1997 and 2000 this became much more than a gender-equity measure. For the *indépendantiste* PQ government, promoting parental insurance became a way to reveal the intransigence of Ottawa vis-à-vis what the Quebec government described as its rightful area of constitutional competence. It was also presented as yet another piece of evidence of the greater generosity and progressiveness of Quebec governments toward the population.

The announcement of parental insurance continued the established tradition of Quebec having the most generous programs of paid maternity and unpaid parental leave in Canada.[25] The only paid leave available to Canadian parents (outside that provided privately through collective agreements) comes from the unemployment insurance (UI, but now called Employment Insurance) regime. That insurance program has never covered all workers. For example, it excludes the self-employed, and until 1997, it also excluded part-time workers. Second, in order to claim benefits, workers have to meet strict eligibility requirements based on the number of hours worked. Third, it does not replace lost wages, but only 55 per cent of them up to a fixed limit. Therefore, it is a very partial program, covering at best about one of every two new mothers (Beauvais and Jenson, 2001: 9).

Despite these limits, the federal government has recently accumulated much political capital by extending parental leaves, for those eligible, to fifty-two weeks. This is a formula competing with that proposed by Quebec's white paper, which hoped to break the link to employment completely. A new regime, based on earned income rather than weeks or hours of work, would make leaves available to any parent who earned at least $2,000 during the year prior to the birth. Management of the program would be transferred to the *Régie des Rentes* (government control of allowances) and the rate would be 75 per cent of the previous year's income.[26] It also proposed a paternity leave of five weeks, with the rate calculated on the father's income. There would also be an adoption leave of twelve weeks (Lepage and Moisan, 1998).

Parental insurance has not been implemented in Quebec, but it is on its way, the product of a go-it-alone strategy built on appeals to Quebec's 'distinctiveness'. The PQ promised to create a new regime both in the 1998 election campaign and at the March 1999 opening of the National Assembly. In May 1999 consultations with employers, unions, and family organizations on a go-it-alone strategy began, and in fall 1999 consultations with employers led by the ministry brought agreement, in principle—although with some change to the details (Quebec, 2000). The February 2000 Youth Summit endorsed a 'made in Quebec' plan; included in the consensus were not only youth groups but also employers, unions, women's groups and so on. In the face of continued rejection by Ottawa, and a growing mobilization in Quebec, the minister of state, Pauline Marois, tabled Bill 140 on June 6, 2000, doing so in the name of the 'historic demand of "women's groups"' and other socioeconomic groups, as well as the consensus expressed in the two summits, of 1996 and 2000.[27]

The history of this program illustrates well the capacity of the government to break with past practice and innovate, by using a strategy critical of constitutional arrangements and appealing to the 'differences' of Quebec society, as well as to the need for adaptation in the face of new global realities and in the name of gender equality. In this context employers and unions were willing to pay the extra costs that the reform would bring.

Of course a major dimension of family policy reform in 1997 was the redesign of child care delivery. In 1995, the licensing body, the OSGE, imposed a moratorium on new licenses because officials and the minister responsible were concerned that the commercial sector was taking too much of a place in the overall system. The 1997 reform ended that moratorium but, more importantly, it created a new institution, the early childhood centre (*Centre de la petite enfance*).[28]

Once up and running as intended throughout the province, such centres will mark a major shift in thinking about young children, work and family, and the transition to school. They are governed by a non-profit corporation, with a majority of parents on the governing council, and offer different kinds of child care, either centre based or through family day care. In other words, incorporated under a single roof are both the traditional *garderies* (for at least seven children) and the supervisory responsibility for family day care.[29] The family day care option tends to be selected for infants (almost half of children under twelve months are in a family day care) and older children who are in kindergarten part of the day. Centre-based care predominates among two- to four-year-olds (Quebec, 1999). Centres may also take school-age children who do not have access to an after-school facility.

There are twenty centres operating in Aboriginal communities, and an agreement is being developed to transfer administrative responsibility for governing and oversight to the Kativik Regional Government. Services are also available as far north as Inuktitut (Boisvert, 2000).

Family day care providers have access to the resources and educational programs of the centres, which provide a variety of programs open to the community in collaboration with other agencies—particularly that other important local institution in Quebec, the CLSC.

Probably the best known part of the child care reform is the promise to phase in truly affordable child care by setting a standard rate, paid by all parents no matter their income, of five dollars per day, or twenty-five per week, for full-time day care, up to ten hours a day. The province fills the gap between fees and operating costs with direct grants to the centres. The money for financing the program was found, among other places, in the decision to cancel the tax deduction for child care expenses. As sufficient low cost spaces become available, parents can no longer deduct child care expenses from their provincial income taxes. Nor can they claim the federal CCED because providers do not issue receipts.

Beginning in 1997, four-year olds were offered low-cost spaces, with three year-olds and after-school care covered in September 1998. The aim was to reach newborns by the year 2001, but the calendar was actually sped up so that as of September 2000 the rate parents of any child in centre care, family day care, or after-school care, pay is five dollars per day (Quebec, 2000: vol. III, 132).

Parents on social assistance, with preschool children over two or children with a medical certificate prescribing attendance, have access to free child care for 23.5 hours a week in a centre or in family day care. The goal here is clearly not to allow parents' exclusion from the labour force to hinder their child's development. The Ministry of Social Solidarity will pay for hours in excess of 23.5 for parents on social assistance participating in employability programs. Finally, parents who are eligible for the income supplement program, the Parental Wage Assistance Program, receive a three-dollars-per-day subsidy, so they only pay ten dollars per week.

The encouragement, by means of free or very low cost care, illustrates how child care policy is directly and unabashedly based on the principles of enabling even parents with low earning capacity to enter the labour force. All parents on social assistance with children older than two are now classified as 'employable'. Simultaneously, however, it provides strong inducements for such parents to use child care that is not only regulated but also has strong educational content.

Early childhood education and development is a clear focus of this reform, promoting school readiness for all children and seeking to overcome the learning disadvantages often associated with low income and poverty. Early childhood education is defined as the key program for successful integration of children into society, for school readiness, and for preventing problems later in life. Thus, early childhood centres have a strong educational mandate, based on a new and province-wide program. Tailored to different age groups, it is a play-based learning program.

Developmental priorities also underpin the extension of kindergarten to a full day for five-year-olds (schools extended their kindergarten services in September 1997). Compulsory schooling still begins at age six, and full-day kindergarten attendance is optional, but over 98 per cent of children in the age category do attend. In addition, four-year-olds living in areas designated as 'disadvantaged' on the island of Montreal have access to half-day junior kindergarten and educational child care.

The educational emphasis demanded some serious attention toward improving the credentials of child care workers and also raising their wages. The former was long overdue; Quebec's regulations for training and staff ratios are among the least demanding in the country. Moreover, in 1999, 23 per cent of the early childhood centres did not meet the licensing requirements for trained workers (Vérificateur Général, 1999). New training programs are being developed. For example, managers of child care facilities can take a program developed by the Université de Québec à Montreal, while family day care providers can now be trained in the province-wide educational program, via distance learning through Quebec's Télé-Université.

Wages have been raised, under pressure from workers who threatened to strike in the spring of 1999. Seeking to avoid the disruption such a strike would provoke, the government settled with the union, which was affiliated to the CSN, after a series of short stoppages and well-publicized threats. Wages have been improved by an average of 38 per cent, and the ministry has allowed the early childhood centres to increase the income of family day care providers (Quebec, 2000). Despite the hoopla, the starting salary of a child care worker with a CEGEP (junior college) diploma will only be $25,000 (currently it is $20,293). Nevertheless, the ministry reports an increase of 56 per cent in enrollments in such programs.[30]

Problems and Pressure Points

The new family policy, along with the child care component, has many supporters, not least of whom are its designers and promoters inside the state. However there is also a good deal of popular support for it. During the 1998 election campaign, the leader of the Quebec Liberal Party, Jean Charest, floated a critique of the five-dollars-per-day program as 'not meeting the needs of all parents'. In less than thirty-six hours the item had disappeared from the campaign agenda, as negative reactions and objections swamped the Liberal leader.

This said, there are still critics. First, as everywhere else, are those parents who cannot get a space for their children. While any parent may use child care, centres still ration access, via waiting lists and the like, because there are not enough spaces to meet demand. In 1998–9, for example, the number of spaces increased by 17 per cent overall. There were major differences across regions, however, with rural and peripheral regions benefiting particularly. Spaces in Montreal increased 6 per cent, while those in the region Nord du Québec rose from 356 in 1996–7 to 712 in 1998–9, and fully 68 per cent in the latter year. The same year, spaces in the Côte Nord increased by 35 per cent.

Often parents with 'atypical needs' still do not feel their needs are met, and they must resort to all the usual strategies of using unregulated care, including drop-in centres or unlicensed kindergartens. However, several pilot projects were announced in 2000 to provide services twenty-four hours a day for shift workers, a promise that had earlier been included in the white paper but was left aside until recently.

There is constant pressure to create new spaces. Waiting lists continue despite the increase of spaces. Indeed, the Auditor-General reported a shortfall of 135,213 places in March 1999. Of the 229,323 children needing a space, only 94,110 had one (Vérificateur Général, 1999). The government claimed in June 2000 to have added 34,000 spaces over the previous two years, or 300 a week in 1999–2000.[31] An additional target is 12,000 new jobs by 2005.

This juggling of numbers and targets represents, in part, the difficulty of predicting demand. The initial calculations that informed the white paper were based on a survey done under the old regime in 1993–4 (Vérificateur Général, 1999); many more parents than anticipated appeared at the door of the early childhood centres, seeking to place their children in the educationally focused programs rather than the informal care or other arrangements they had been using.

Among the critical parents are those who are losers under this new program. They have not hesitated to make their voices heard. One group is those who saw their tax deductions disappear: parents employing nannies and in-home babysitters or using unregulated but receipted care could no longer deduct those expenses from their Quebec taxes (of course they retained the federal deduction). Parents also complain that, in this competitive market for spaces, centres are charging additional fees—for registration, for example—or hiding higher costs in 'program fees'. Therefore, the promise of fixed costs may in some cases be illusory.

A second important critic has been the Auditor General, who issued a damning report in 1999 that criticized the ministry for mismanagement as well as a lack of evaluation criteria of the central goals—that is, child development and school readiness. Beyond these somewhat accountant-like criticisms were others going to the heart of the matter. The Auditor General found an increased use of family day care from 26 per cent of spaces in 1996 to 34 per cent in 1999, with an oversight by the ECC that is minimal, at best (Vérificateur Général, 1999). The report also pointed out that Quebec still lacked the administrative capacity to license drop-in centres and private kindergartens, although this type of service is still providing a goodly amount of child care in order to fill the gap between supply and demand described above.

The ministry has responded to the criticisms about training, as described above, and has established a task force to investigate the 'contribution' of drop-in centres (Ministry Press Release, 22 June 2000). Nonetheless, there are still gaps in the capacity to regulate and to manage the system.

The third group of vociferous and long-standing critics is the other segment of major losers under the new regime: commercial operators. They have difficulty making ends meet with the limited grants to which they are entitled, and the minister made no bones about preferring to see them play a more diminished role. The original white paper had suggested that commercial providers would be phased out, but after a major mobilization and a rising recognition that without them there would not be enough spaces available, a compromise was eventually struck. Existing licensed operators receive public funds, but at a lower rate, via an 'agreement' in which the government 'rents' spaces. Since 1997 there has been a five-year moratorium on new licenses. Owners have also been offered the possibility of being transformed into centres, by selling their businesses to non-profit associations of parents that would become the governing bodies. The Auditor-General was also critical of the ministry's mishandling of these transformations. The process is cumbersome and slow, and in the meantime the ministry is even closing its eyes to illegal operators because it cannot afford to lose the spaces (Vérificateur Général, 1999).

A fourth set of critics comes from within the family movement. These opponents of the 1997 design support state spending on children and families, but they would prefer to see the generosity that Quebec directs toward child care diverted to a universal family allowance recognizing the contributions of *all parents* to society. For example, in 2000 the Institute for Research on Public Policy reissued a report written by researchers close to the family movement documenting that three-fourths of families received less money under the new regime than the previous one. The authors were critical of the retreat from universal family allowances in favour of targeting low-income parents. They recommended, as in the traditional French system, generous and universal family allowances for all parents, in the name of horizontal redistribution across families, rather than vertical redistribution from better-off to low-income families. However, their recommendation with respect to child care was exactly the reverse. The authors claimed that it should *not* be universal but more market driven, allowing parents to chose whether to pay for care or provide it themselves, as well as to select the type they preferred.

These two positions are exactly opposite those adopted by the government in 1996–7, which seeks to build solidarity via universality and invest in children's development in the realm of child care while expressing a commitment to equity with its targeted family allowances. In part the divergence comes from differing assessments of two elements of the family policy mix. One is clearly the educational component of child care. The authors of the IRPP study insist that 'parents know best' about the quality of care, and that governments should not be in the business of establishing standards for credentials or programs.[32] The editor's note, signed by Carole Vincent of the IRPP, makes a plea not only for greater choice, but for revaluing parental care. She also writes, 'Indeed it is difficult to argue that the benefits generated by daycare services exceed those generated by parental care' (IRPP, 2000: 3). The government, in contrast, inspired by the literature on child psychology and early childhood development, has opted for another position: it seeks to overcome the threat to children that may come from their parents' circumstances, such as living in poverty, or from the failure to act quickly on a diagnosis—often begun by childhood educators—of developmental problems that children of any socioeconomic background may experience.

A second difference is in the attention to matters of equality, especially gender equality. Even if there has been a discernible decline in the rhetoric of gender equality in the post-1997 Family Policy as compared to its predecessors, it is still present.

Therefore, the design of parental insurance, child care, and family allowances reflects, among other things, attention to gender inequalities in the labour market for all women, whether low-income lone mothers or professionals living in two-parent families. The IRPP report, in contrast, is virtually silent on matters of gender equality—never the strong suit of the family movement. In other words, this debate takes us back to the fundamental issues raised by women's movements and experts in child development for decades. While the issues are familiar, the responses of familialists and the current government of Quebec to the challenges are not the same. They have alternative models.

There are lessons to be drawn from this 'mini comparison' as well as from the longer history recounted in this paper. Even in a liberal welfare state, there is space to develop more progressive programs. Quebec shares with other liberal welfare states a concern with employability and fostering parents' labour-force participation; indeed, it was something of an 'innovator' in the 1980s in implementing coercive forms of employability policies (Boychuk, 1998). Yet at the same time, it has developed universal social programs and avoided putting children at risk of poor quality child care. Therefore, rather than a story of path dependency, this is a story of how a determined reform coalition sensitive to children's developmental needs as well as to gender and class equality can row against the neoliberal tide, saving some values in the general process of welfare-state design.

Notes

This research is supported by the Social Science and Humanities Research Council of Canada and Founds pour la Formation de Chercheurs et l'Aide á la Récherche.

1. See the 26 June 2000 speech by the highest-ranking civil servant of the Ministry of Family and Child Welfare, which lists four goals, of which this is the first (Boisvert, 2000). This list is not idiosyncratic by any means; see the ministry's presentation of family policy online at http://www.famille-enfance.gouv.qc.ca.
2. This is the Head Start model used in the United States. It is also used in Canadian Aboriginal communities by the federal government, as well being the practice in all Canadian provinces as a legacy of the Canada Assistance Plan (CAP) since 1965 (Beauvais and Jenson, 2001).
3. Quebec is not the only province to do so. A number of other provinces—including Manitoba, Saskatchewan, and recently Ontario—provide some additional benefits to lone parent families (Beauvais and Jenson, 2001: Appendix A).
4. This inversion of priorities has not gone unnoticed or without criticism. For a well-argued defense of universal family allowances and targeted subsidies for child care see IRPP (2000).
5. The Ministère de la Famille et de l'Enfance chooses to translate its name this way. Therefore, out of respect for self-naming, we will do the same.
6. This is a quote from 'Family Policy-Financial Support', available online at http://www.famille.enfance.gouv.qc.ca.
7. The press at the time made such arguments. See, for example, Mario Cloutier, 'Le sommet sur l'economic et l'emploi' (Summit on Jobs and the Economy), *Le Devoir*, 1 November 1996 and Donald Charette, 'Les jeunes claquent la porte' (Young People Banging at the Door), *Le Soleil*, 1 November 1996.
8. For a description of this Action Plan see 'Family Policy History', online at http://www.famille.enfance.gouv.qc.ca.
9. See the press at the time for a recent review of the summit declarations; see the Auditor General's 1999 report (para 4.16), available online at http://www.vgq.gouv.qc.ca.
10. See Boisvert (2000), who says of the new ECC, 'I would be remiss if I failed to mention the beginnings of these child care centres. The current network was created out of parent-run day care centres and home day care providers who formed agencies responsible for their management. The collaborative spirit between educators and parents has been maintained, protected—I would even say made a priority. . .' (5).
11. The CLSCs resemble the 'people's clinics' in many ways, especially in the emphasis on empowerment of communities through mobilization and action. Nonetheless, several of the groups running people's clinics (which were staffed by a mix of medically-trained personnel, social animators and volunteers) opposed Bill 65, which established the CLSCs because they saw them as excessively statist (Belanger and Levesque, 1992: 721–2).
12. For the current situation across Canada, putting

Quebec in comparative perspective, see Beauvais and Jenson (2001: Appendix a, tables 5 and 6).

13. A Secrétariat à la Politique Familiale (Secretariat for Family Policy) was set up in 1984, but reorganized and renamed in 1988.
14. Academic demographers, always important actors in this policy network in Quebec, had been writing of demographic crisis for years. The parliamentary commission, reporting in September 1985, had a mandate to 'study the cultural, social, and economic impact of current demographic tendencies for the future of Quebec as a distinct society' (Dandurand, 1987: 354).
15. These were *Le soutien collectif réclamé pour les familles québécoises : Rapport de la consultation sur la politique familiale* (Collective Support Demanded for Quebec Families: Report of the Consultative Committee on Family Policy), 1985, and *Le soutien collectif recommande pour les parents québécois : Rapport de la consultation sur la politi que familiale* (Collective Support Recommended for Quebec Parents: Report of the Consultative Committee on Family Policy), 1986. The move from 'families' to 'parents' signals the shift in perspective that the committee was trying to provoke.
16. The *prime á la naissance* was profoundly natalist in design: $500 for the first and second births (which in 1989 became $1,000 for the second birth). In 1988, third births brought $3,000, in 1989, $4,500 and, until 1997, $8,000 spread over five years. Prior to the 1997 reform, the basic family allowances and young child allowance also rose with birth order.
17. Quebec was not alone in framing the debate about reforming social assistance and developing employability measures via policies directed toward families and children (Beauvais and Jenson, 2001: 15–23).
18. Her executive assistant and the chief negotiator throughout this process was Nicole Boily, who had been a member of the 1984–6 consultative committee and who would subsequently be named president of the Conseil de la Famille.
19. For a description of the movement across Canada toward 'integration' and the development of new machinery for breaking out of the traditional silos of policy categories, see Mahon (2001).
20. These three goals are constantly reiterated in a range of documents. This English version is from Boisvert (2000). Sometimes, however, the first and second are merged, to generate three main objectives (see, for example, 'Family Policy: Main Measures and Objectives' available online at http://www.famille-enfance.gouv.qc.ca.
21. Current information about the programs can be obtained online at http://www.famille-enfance.gouv.qc.ca.
22. A separate allowance for children with disabilities is still available.
23. Quebec was among the eight provinces taxing back the CCTB going to families on social assistance, at least until 2000. When the federal government increased the amount paid out in the CCTB and its supplement in the 2000 Budget, Quebec decided not to tax back all the increase, as some said because it would remove their involvement with too many families.
24. There is also a range of other tax benefits for families with children. For details and comparisons to other provinces, see Appendix 1, Table 6 in Beauvais and Jenson.
25. In 1978 Quebec created a maternity allowance that provided coverage for the first two weeks of maternity leave *not* covered by federal unemployment insurance (now employment insurance, or EI). Quebec also had the most generous unpaid parental leave in Canada until 2000. In 1990, new parents, both by birth and through adopting, could access thirty-four weeks of unpaid parental leave; the unpaid leave was extended to fifty-two weeks in 1997. Ottawa decided to extend paid parental leave for those eligible under EI to a full year. The provinces have had to adjust their labour codes accordingly in order to give the right to leave.
26. The PQ had been promoting this idea of a separate *caisse* (fund) for parental leave, as well as extended coverage, for a number of years. See 'La cause des femmes selon Louise Harel' (The Women's Cause According to Louise Harel), *La Gazette des femmes,* July–August 1996: 16.
27. In addition to a paternity leave of five weeks, the draft bill sets out two options for parents: forty weeks at 75 per cent replacement of the previous year's earnings or fifty weeks at 70 per cent for the first eighteen and 55 per cent for the rest. See the *Communiqués de Presse* of the Ministère de la Famille et de l'Enfance, 6 June 2000, and 9 June 2000, available online at http://www.famille-enfance.gouv.qc.ca.
28. The Ministry's documentation in English calls these 'child care centres', but I believe 'early childhood centre' is a better translation, because it both marks a distinction from what has become the term in many places for *any* day care centre, and makes the link to 'early childhood development', which is a major part of their mission.
29. Family day care providers can care for up to six children, or nine if they have an adult assistant. For details about the early childhood centres, see *Les centres de la petite enfance* or the overview in 'Family Policy—

Educational and Child Care Services', both available online at http://www.famille-enfance.gouv.qc.ca.
30. See the *Communiqué de Presse* of the Ministere de la Famille et de l'Enfance, 22 June 2000, available online at http://www.famille-enfance.gouv.qc.ca.
31. The first figure is from page seven of Boisvert (2000) and the second is from the ministry's 22 June 2000 press release.
32. They do, however, concede a role for regulation of health and safety.

References

Baillargeon, Denyse. 1996. 'Les politiques familiales au Québec' (Family Policies in Quebec), *Lien social et Politiques-RIAC* 36: 21–32.

Beauvais, Caroline, and Jane Jenson. 2001. *Two Policy Paradigms: Family Responsibility and Investing in Children.* Ottawa: CPRN F-12. Available online at http://www.cprn.org/publications.

Belanger, Paul R., and Benoit Levesque. 1992. 'Le mouvement populaire et communautaire: de la revendication au partenariat (1963–1992)' (The Popular and Community Sector Movement: From Demands to Partnerships), in *Le Québec en jeu* (Quebec at Stake), Gerard Daigle, ed. Montreal: Presses de l'Université de Montréal.

Boisvert, Maurice. 2000. Speech to the World Summit on Social Development, Geneva, 26 June 2000. Available online at http://www.famille-enfance.gouv.qc.ca.

Bergeron, Josée. 1997. 'Les frontiéres imaginaires et imaginées de d'l'État-Providence' (The Imaginary and Imagined Borders of the Welfare State). PhD dissertation, Carlton University, Ottawa, Canada.

Bouchard, Camil, Vivienne Labrie, and Alain Noel. 1996. *Chacun sa part: Rapport de trois membres du comité externe de réforme de la sécurité du revenu* (To Each His Share: Report by Three Members of the External Reform Committee of Income Security). Montreal: Ministére de la Securité du Revenu.

Boychuk, Gerard William. 1998. *Patchworks of Purpose: The Development of Provincial Social Assistance Regimes in Canada.* Montreal: McGill-Queen's University Press.

Childcare Resource and Research Unit. 1997. *Child Care in Canada: Provinces and Territories 1995.* Toronto: Childcare Resource and Research Unit.

Clarke, Christopher. 1998. *Canada's Income Security Programs.* Ottawa: Canadian Council on Social Development.

Collectif Clio. 1992. *L'Histoire des femmes au Québec depuis quatre siecles* (The History of Women in Quebec for the Last Four Centuries). Montreal: Le Jour.

Daigle, Gerard. 1992. *Le Québec en Jeu* (Quebec in Play). Montreal: Presses de l'Université de Montreal.

Dandurand, René B-. 1987. 'Une politique familiale: Enjeux et débats' (Family Policy: Stakes and Debates) *Récherches sociographiques* 28: 2–3.

———.1992. 'La famille n'est pas une île' (The Family Is Not an Island), in *Le Québec en Jeu*, Gerard Daigle, ed. Montreal: Presses de l'Université de Montreal.

Desjardins, Ghislaine. 1991. *Faire garder ses enfants au Québec. . . une histoire toujours en marche* (*Getting Child Care in Quebec ... an Ever-Unfolding History*). Quebec: Office des services de garde à l'enfance.

IRPP. 2000. 'Quebec Family Policy: Impact and Options' *Choices* 6: 1.

Jenson, Jane. 2001. 'Canada's Shifting Citizenship Regime: The Child as Model Citizen' in *The Dynamics of Decentralization: Canadian Federalism and British Devolution,*Trevor C. Salmon and Michael Keating, eds. Montreal: McGill-Queen's University Press.

Jenson, Jane, and Mariette Sineau. 1998. *Qui doit garder les jeune enfant? Le travail des mères dans l'Europe en crise* (Who Should Care for Young Children? Mothers' Work in a Europe in Crisis). Paris: LGDJ.

———. 2001. *Who Cares? Women's Work, Childcare and Welfare State Redesign.* Toronto: University of Toronto Press.

Jenson, Jane, and Sharon M. Stroick. 1999. *What Is the Best Policy Mix for Canada's Young Children?* Ottawa: CRPN F-09. Available online at http://www.cprn.org.

Lamoureux, Diane. 1992. 'Nos luttes ont changé nos vies: L'impact du mouvement féministe' (Our Struggles Have Changed Our Lives: The Impact of the Feminist Movement), in *Le Québec en Jeu*, Gerard Daigle, ed. Montreal: Presses de l'Université de Montreal.

Lefebvre, Pierre. 1998. 'Les nouvelles orientations de la politique familiale du Québec: une critique de l'allocation unifiée' (New Trends in Family Policy in Quebec: A Critique of Unified Benefits), in *Quelle politique familiale à l'aube de l'an 2000?* (What Family Policy at the Dawn of the Year 2000?), R.B- Dandurand, Pierre Lefebvre, and Jean-Pierre Lamoureux, eds. Paris and Montreal: Éditions l'Harmattan.

Lepage, Francine, and Marie Moisan. 1998. 'L'assurance parentale: la nouvelle politique québécoise et les prestations réservées aux pères' (Parental Insurance: The New Quebec Policy and Benefits Reserved for Fathers), in *Quelle politique familiale à l'aube de l'an 2000?* (What Family Policy at the Dawn of the Year 2000?), R.B- Dandurand, Pierre Lefebvre, and Jean-

Pierre Lamoureux, eds. Paris and Montreal: Éditions l'Harmattan.

Lesemann, Frédéric. 1981. *Du pain et des services: la réforme de la santé et des services sociaux au Québec* (Bread and Services: Health and Social Service Reform in Quebec). Laval: Eds. Saint-Martin.

Mahon, Rianne. 2001. *School-Aged Children Across Canada: A Patchwork of Public Policies.* Ottawa: CRPN, F-II. Available online at http://www.cprn.org.

MSSS (Ministère de la Santé et des Services Sociaux). 1991. *Un Québec fou de ses enfants. Rapport du Groupe de travail pour les jeunes* (Quebec, Mad about Its Children. Report of the Working Party for Young People). Quebec: MSSS.

Noël, Alain. 'La contrepartie dans l'aide sociale au Québec' (Social Security Compensation in Quebec). *Revue française des affaires sociales* 50.4 (1996): 387–99.

Québec. 1999. *Un portrait statistique des familles et des enfants au Québec* (A Statistical Portrait of Families and Children in Quebec). Quebec: Gouvernement du Québec.

———. 2000. *Budget de dépenses 2000–2001,* vol. 3, *Plans ministériels de aestion des dépenses* (Expenditure Budget 2000–2001, vol. 3, Ministerial Expenditure Management Plans). Quebec: Gouvernement du Quebec.

Rose, Ruth. 1998. 'Politiques pour les families pauvres: supplément au rcvenu gagne et revenus minimums garantis' (Policies for Poor Families: Supplement to Earned Income and Guaranteed Minimum Incomes), in *Quelle politique familiale à l'aube de l'an 2000?* (What Family Policy at the Dawn of the Year 2000?), Dandurand et al., eds. Paris and Montreal: Éditions l'Harmattan.

Roy, Maurice. 1987. *Les CLSC. Ce qu'il faut savoir* (CLSCs: What You Need to Know). Montreal: Éds. Saint-Martin.

Vaillancourt, Yves. 1988. 'Quebec', in *Privatisation and Provincial Social Services in Canada,* J.S. Ismael and Yves Vaillancourt, eds. Edmonton: University of Alberta Press.

Vérificateur Général du Québec. 1999. *Rapport à l'Assemblee nationale pour l'annee* 1998–1999 (Report to the National Assembly for 1998–1999). Quebec: Gouvernement du Québec.

On the Same Wavelength? Feminist Attitudes Across Generations of Canadian Women

Brenda O'Neill

EDITORS' INTRODUCTION

Feminism has a history. The word itself was not widely used until the 1910s, and what we might now dub feminism has variously been referred to as the women's movement or women's liberation. Some have argued that the term should be rejected in favour of 'womanist', while others opt to hyphenate their feminism into, among other things, socialist-feminism, anti-racist-feminism, or lesbian-feminism. Throughout history and across cultures and societies we can find examples of people who argued and acted in favour of increased rights, opportunities, and resources for women. How do we distinguish this ongoing, intermittent activity from the organized and visible social movements that have emerged in different times and places? How do we acknowledge that feminism has taken radically different guises—that, in other words, we are speaking of the history of feminism*s* in the plural rather than a monolithic, singular *feminism* in the singular? Within this volume alone, we can see that the feminism of the first-wave writers analyzed by J. Fiamengo and the contemporary activists examined by Mary-Jo Nadeau are different, to say the least. And where might we fit the activism of the Carrier women analyzed by Jo-Anne Fiske, who may or may not identify themselves as feminist?

The metaphor of the wave has provided many scholars, including Brenda O'Neill, with a way of navigating the tricky business of feminism's variable and multiple history. The idea that feminism flows in 'waves' allows us to acknowledge that feminist ideas, activities, and organizations exist in most times, but discernibly crest in particular ways at particular times. Some historians object to the metaphor of the wave, arguing instead for imagining feminism as skirmishes and battles in an ongoing war, or, to keep the metaphors geomorphological in nature, as an iceberg that is both partially and variably visible above the water, or as a series of eruptions. Numbering and naming the waves is another problem. Like O'Neill, most scholars see three major waves, while others point out that sorting feminist activity into first, second, or third wave is based on an American experience that is not easily applicable to other societies, or that, within the American context, it fails to account for a major wave associated with the anti-slavery or abolitionist movement of the early nineteenth-century.

In Canada, historians have also found the metaphor of waves useful but not always supported by the available evidence. Mary Kinnear's biography of internationalist Mary McGeachy and Ruth Compton Brouwer's study of three Canadian missionary women working overseas in the interwar period echo a point made in earlier studies, that feminism did not die after the First World War—it rather changed its most visible forms and shifted its concerns. The politics of the private sphere and internationalism increasingly focused women's attention.[2] Valerie Korniek has pointed out that the ideas we generally associate with the 'second wave' of feminism, beginning in the late 1960s—reproductive rights and workplace equity—were in fact being articulated in the pages of *Chatelaine* magazine in the 1950s. Julie Gaurd's research into women communists active for consumer rights in the 1950s similarly reminds us that different kinds of feminism thrived outside of the so-called 'waves'.[3] Beyond Becki Ross's fine work on lesbian-feminist organizing in Toronto in the 1970s and Meg Luxton's insightful work on the relationship between working-class feminism and the women's movement in Canada, the second wave of feminism in Canada awaits its historian.[4] Former National Council of Women chair and journalist Judy Rebick has recently published a book about second-wave feminism based on interviews with Canadian activists. Rebick's work suggests some of the ways that historians might begin to uncover the history of second-wave feminism.[5]

In this article O'Neill borrows the metaphor of 'waves' to analyze polling data from 1997. O'Neill is part of a new group of feminist political scientists doing empirical work that moves beyond questions of whether women are simply present or absent from political spaces. They ask 'a new order of questions about women and representation' which address 'the articulation of citizen concerns, issues, and goals' and the 'decision-making, or "outcome" stage of representation'.[6] Here, O'Neill discusses generational differences in feminist beliefs amongst Canadian women. In doing so, she directly addresses a question that haunts contemporary discussions of feminism's present and future, namely whether young women are rejecting or embracing the label of feminist and the politics that go with it. What she finds is that women of the 'third wave', or those born between 1958 and 1979, are likely to hold feminist beliefs about key issues, including women's rights to freely choose abortion. In keeping with the politics we tend to associate with the 'third-wave' of feminism, many of these younger women wanted to see a society where gays, lesbians, and racial minorities had more influence, though they were notably less enthusiastic about extending that welcome to Indigenous peoples. Older women, in contrast, were less supportive of sexual diversity, racial minorities, and reproductive rights, but more willing to see the workplace as haunted by discrimination against women. As O'Neill suggests, this tells us a great deal about how generations of Canadian women have experienced gender in different ways.

Yet for all their support for various feminist goals, the young women polled remain, like their older counterparts, ambivalent about feminists as a group. O'Neill suggests some of the ways that feminists and the organized women's movement Canada might address the implications of the 'I'm not a feminist but. . .' perspective. Does this ambivalence reflect a wider, anti-feminist backlash that helped produce the extreme reaction to Thobani's 2004 speech analyzed by Nadeau in this volume? Anti-feminism also has long roots in Canada.[7] Perhaps we should not be surprised that feminism will inspire backlash and opposition as long as it does what it must: call attention to, and demand redress for, the fundamental inequalities of our changing society.

Notes

1. See the posts made to the 'H-women' discussion network on 'feminism in waves' in 1996 and 1998, and especially the short essay by Jo Freeman available at http://www.h-net.org/~women.
2. Mary Kinnear, *Woman of the World: Mary McGeachy and International Cooperation* (Toronto: University of Toronto Press, 2004); Ruth Compton Brouwer, *Modern Women Modernizing Men: The Changing Missions of Three Professional Women in Asia and Africa, 1902–69* (Vancouver: UBC Press, 2002).
3. Valerie Korniek, *Roughing it in the Suburbs: Reading Chatelaine in the 1950s and 1960s* (Toronto: University of Toronto Press, 2000); Julie Guard, 'Canadian Citizens or Dangerous Foreign Women? Canada's Radical Consumer Movement, 1847–1950', in *Sisters of Strangers: Immigrant, Ethnic, and Racialized Women*

in *Canadian History*, Marlene Epp, Franca Iacovetta, Frances Swyripa, eds. (Toronto: University of Toronto Press, 2004).

4. Becki L. Ross, 'How Lavender Jane Loved Women: Re-figuring Identity-based Life/Stylism in 1970s Lesbian Feminism', *Journal of Canadian Studies* 30.4 (Winter 1995–6): 110–128; Meg Luxton, 'Feminism as a Class Act: Working-Class Feminism and the Women's Movement in Canada', *Labour/Le Travail* 48 (Fall 2001): 63–88.
5. Judy Rebick, ed., *Ten Thousand Roses: The Making of a Feminist Revolution* (Toronto: Penguin, 2005).
6. Jane Arscott and Linda Trimble, 'Introduction', *In The Presence of Women: Representation in Canadian Governments*, Jane Arscott and Linda Trimble, eds. (Toronto: Harcourt Brace and Company, 1997): 3.
7. Karen Dubinsky, *Lament for a Patriarchy Lost? Anti-Feminism, Anti-Abortion, and REAL Women in Canada* (Ottawa: Canadian Research Institute on the Advancement of Women, 1985); Veronica Strong-Boag, 'Independent Women, Problematic Men: First and Second Wave Anti-Feminism in Canada from Goldwin Smith to Betty Steele', *Histoire Sociale/Social History* 57 (May 1996): 1–22.

Questions for Critical Reading

1. Why might the young women interviewed in 1997 have been supportive of feminist goals but ambivalent about 'feminists' as a group? Does this reflect a negative image of feminists circulating in popular culture? Where does this image come from? How might feminists address it?
2. How do the goals and values of the 'second-wave' and 'third-wave' feminists discussed by O'Neill reflect their different social and historical experiences?
3. How many different kinds of 'feminism' can be found in this volume? What accounts for the different definition of what is feminist or not?

Introduction[1]

Feminist thought has changed over time. So too has feminist activism. Most researchers and historians now accept a certain set of labels to differentiate periods in feminist thought and activism. The *first wave* of the feminist movement refers to activist women in the early twentieth century who fought for basic rights for women, such as the right to own property, to vote, and to sit in the Senate. The *second wave* refers to a later generation of feminists that emerged in the 1960s and 1970s, and that was dominated by the quest for women's substantive equality with men, a fight often predicated on minimizing gender differences; this was in direct contrast to feminists in the previous wave who more often extolled women's virtues as a means of justifying their inclusion in male-dominated political processes. The *third wave* refers to the youngest feminist activists, who came into their consciousness in the 1980s and 1990s, and whose beliefs, values, and activism distinguish them from earlier feminist activists and earlier feminist thought. This most recent wave is identified in part by its unwillingness to limit women to a defined set of gender roles, by its acceptance of gender as only one of women's many identities, and by its use of technology for disseminating feminist material.

This chapter explores generational differences in Canadian women's attitudes toward feminism in Canada and the importance of these differences for electoral politics. The commonly held view is that younger women are less willing to adopt the feminist label than women who came of age in the second wave, in spite of their general support for women's equality. This has been identified as the 'but I'm not a feminist' phenomenon, as in 'I believe in equality for women and in the right of access to abortion services, but I'm not a feminist.'[2] This unwillingness stems in part from the backlash against feminists in mainstream culture and media that creates a number of myths and falsehoods surrounding the feminist movement and its goals (Baumgardner and Richards, 2000; Faludi, 1991).

Feminism has been particularly successful in selling its message to young Canadian women; the feminist movement has been less successful, however, in getting younger women to identify with the movement itself. The 'but I am not a feminist' phenomenon appears to be alive and well in Canada. While women do not reveal particularly positive attitudes toward feminist spokespersons, they are nevertheless supportive of the movement's goals and of particular policy positions associated with feminist thought.

The level of public support for feminism, feminists, and feminist policy prescriptions shapes electoral politics in Canada. The literature on the gender gap makes clear that the feminist opinion is associated with more liberal attitudes overall (Conover, 1984; Gidengil, 1995; O'Neill, 2001). Thus the level of support for feminism among the general public determines the likelihood of electing parties into office that will be sympathetic to, if not also directly supportive of, feminist objectives and feminist policy goals. Moreover, such support is directly relevant to the likelihood of Canadian parties' endorsing alliances with feminist organizations and adopting more feminist policy stances (Young, 2000). And perhaps on a somewhat more ambitious note, support for feminists and feminism would seem to be a necessary condition for the electoral success of a decidedly feminist party.

The Waves of Feminism

The idea that there are distinct waves of feminism provides the foundation for this study. The existence of distinct waves should not be taken to mean that Canadian feminists within each wave have spoken in a unified voice (Adamson, Briskin, and McPhail, 1988). Moreover, there are varying interpretations of the transition points in and focuses of each wave. Barbara Arneil's *Politics and Feminism* (1999) provides an account of the transitions feminism has undergone that is comprehensive in its inclusion of an academic treatment of the most recent third wave.

Feminists of the first wave included among their goals the acquisition of liberal rights for women within a public/private framework that presumed the existence of gender difference. In contrast, second-wave feminism, despite its many manifestations,[3] adopted an acceptance of universality, that is, of the duality of gender with its emphasis on the differences between women as a group and men as a group. This claim rested uneasily with the often-employed argument of the 'sameness' of the genders, adopted in part to allow for a basis on which to demand equal treatment and the challenging of the public/private and culture/nature dichotomies. The difficulty, as identified by Naomi Black, was that 'women wanted to stay different without being disadvantaged' (1993: 153). In the 1960s women were very much socialized to assume domestic responsibilities, but this socialization came in direct contrast with the fact that many of these same women entered the workforce, in part to escape the 'feminine mystique', as it was identified by Betty Friedan (Baumgardner and Richards, 2000).

Canadian feminists of this period fought to remove the many formal and informal barriers that existed, such as 'glass ceilings' in employment (Baumgardner and Richards, 2000). The Royal Commission on the Status of Women served as a lightning rod for Canadian feminists in the late 1960s and 1970s, documenting many of these barriers and generating public awareness of such issues as access to abortion, equal pay, pension discrimination, and violence against women (Baumgardner and Richards, 2000). Finally, the second wave accorded a higher value to the public than to the private sphere, in part to counter the dominant culture, which assigned women to the domestic sphere; this, however, provided a target for criticisms launched by a subsequent generation of feminists.

Third-wave feminism is distinct from the previous waves of feminist thought in both thought and action (see Arneil, 1999). The focus on the 'universal' woman by a previous generation of feminists provided a jumping-off point for the third wave. Many women, particularly lesbians and women of colour, failed to see themselves reflected in the second wave's discourses. Third-wave feminists differ as well in that they 'grew up with feminism as their birthright', and many are 'reaping the benefits . . . of the second wave women's movement's labour' (Steenbergen, 2001: 9). These benefits have provided young feminists with the freedom to question second-wave feminist theory and prescriptions. The result is that they are 'pushing the boundaries of who and what constitutes feminist community and defines feminist theorizing' (Pinterics, 2001: 15).

As a result, third-wave feminism can be differentiated from its predecessor in several respects. First, the newest feminist wave uses personal narratives as a basis of knowledge development to a greater extent than in the past, in part because such accounts are considered more political (as in 'the personal is political'), accessible to a wider audience, and more respectful of women's diversity than are the more traditional or academic feminist treatments. Second, third-wave feminism adopts a belief in the multiplicity of identity, reflecting the difficulty many women feel in categorizing themselves with unique and singular identities based on gender, race, sexuality, or ability. Women, it is argued, are more than simply women; they also possess a sexual identity, a racial identity, and many others. Third-wavers are less likely to see gender as transcending any of these multiple identities, a belief that very often sets them at odds with the previous generation of feminists. Third, this wave of feminism expresses a desire to openly address the contradictions within feminism while simultaneously challenging the 'perceived rigidities in the ideals of second-wave feminist politics' (Arneil, 1999: 153), resulting in a re-embracing of femininity, motherhood, and women's sexuality in an attempt to straddle the contradictory desires of embracing women's similarities (and hence difference from men) and their differences from one another.[4] According to Candis Steenbergen,

> the desire to analyze body image, self esteem, desire, sexuality and sexual pleasure has been strong in third-wave writings to date. To many, those pursuits have revolved around continual self-analysis and personal negotiation, an attempt to reconcile the desire to create their own version of 'femininity' and the fear of betraying their allegiance to feminism and the struggle for female empowerment. (2001: 11)

Finally, the third wave has adopted a new strategy for the accumulation and dissemination of knowledge, characterized by the grassroots distribution of 'zines' (photocopied and stapled articles distributed through feminist networks) and through the medium of cyberspace, especially e-mail, web sites, and chat groups.[5]

Feminist thought among feminist activists is, however, distinct from feminist thinking in the broader public, although the two are related. Given feminists' commitment to the cause, their opinions on a number of issues are likely to be more strongly held, more consistent with feminism's core values, and more stable over time. Yet Joanna Everitt's research (1998) reveals that the movement's efforts have coincided with an increased liberalization of Canadian attitudes on a small set of issues, including the election of women as political leaders and women in the workplace. Moreover, Everitt shows that younger Canadians, both women and men, have been especially open to the feminist movement's arguments, and as such have attitudes that are more in line with those of the feminist movement than do older Canadians. As Everitt notes, 'young adults, who have weaker attachments to traditional ideas, may adopt the policy positions of a movement without adopting a movement identification' (1998: 749). The movement has had a particularly powerful impact on young, well-educated, employed women, given their greater ability to identify personally with the movement's goals and exposure to the movement's messages during their formative years (Everitt, 1998).

Data and Methods

The data employed in this investigation come from the 1997 Canadian Election Study (CES),[6] which provides a recent survey of Canadian political attitudes that is comprehensive both in the types of questions asked and in the number of Canadians sampled. For the purposes of this investigation, only women respondents were selected for examination (*N* = 2008)[7] and these respondents were grouped into four cohorts:

- Pre-Second Wave: born before 1943
- Second Wave: born between 1943 and 1957
- Third Wave I: born between 1958 and 1968
- Third Wave II: born between 1969 and 1979

The Pre-Second Wave cohort identifies women who entered their young adult years prior to the advent of second-wave feminism. As such, they likely exhibit attitudes that are rather traditional with respect to women's roles. The Second Wave cohort identifies women who came into adult consciousness at the height of the second wave of the feminist movement during the 1960s and 1970s. Their attitudes regarding women's roles are likely to most resemble those of second-wave feminists and activists. The next two cohorts identify women who came of age in the 1980s and 1990s, a period normally identified with third-wave activism and feminist thought. Women in these two groups were anticipated to hold attitudes that more closely resemble the attitudes exhibited by this most recent generation of feminists.

This breakdown provides a significant sample of respondents in each group. The Pre-Second Wave group constitutes 24 per cent of the sample (*N* = 477), the Second Wave group 32 per cent (*N* = 641), the Third Wave I group 24 per cent (*N* = 488), and the Third Wave II group 20 per cent (*N* = 402).[9]

The objective of the analysis was to examine differences in feminist attitudes and beliefs across these four groups in an effort to assess whether attitudes in the general population reflect differences across the waves of feminism as discussed in academic literature and by feminist activists themselves. The first consideration was Canadian women's attitudes toward feminists and the feminist movement; that is, do Canadian women generally identify with feminists? The second was to assess Canadian women's attitudes toward the various policy positions associated with feminist thought; that is, are Canadian women feminist, given the values and opinions they hold? In each case these investigations break down the sample of women down by cohort in order to compare results across women coming of age during each of the three feminist waves. In most instances the examination employs contingency tables to evaluate attitudes across these feminist cohorts.[10]

Results

Attitudes to Feminists and the Feminist Movement

The survey question in the 1997 CES that comes closest to assessing subjective identification with feminists is a thermometer scale asking respondents to rank how they feel about feminists, using a scale from 0 (really dislike them) to 100 (really like them). This is not, it must be pointed out, a measure of subjective identification as a feminist but rather a measure of affect for feminists. The measure can nevertheless be argued to be highly correlated with such a subjective measure; women who identify themselves as feminist would, it is argued, respond positively toward feminists as a group. The measure provides a valid and reliable correlate of subjective feminist identification rather than a measure of that concept itself.[11] Respondents were also asked to rank several additional groups (big business, unions, people on welfare, Aboriginal peoples, the police, racial minorities, the baby-boom generation, and gays and lesbians). Table 1.1 provides the results of several of these questions as well as the average score accorded all groups by cohort.

Table 1.1: Thermometer Ratings for Groups by Feminist Cohort

	Third Wave II	Third Wave I	Second Wave	Pre-Second Wave
Feminists*	48.4	45.5	44.1	42.2
Gays and lesbians*	61.2	55.3	51.9	40.6
Racial minorities*	66.1	61.7	59.7	58.9
Aboriginal peoples	58.8	58.8	59.5	59.6
Big business*	60.5	56.8	56.2	56.1
Average*	57.9	55.6	55.7	53.8
N[a]	317	363	463	313

[a] Minimum sample size recorded across all variables.
* $p < .01$

The results reveal significant differences across the cohorts in the rankings that women assigned to various groups. Every cohort ranked feminists below the midpoint on the 0–100 thermometer scale; there was, however, significant variation in this absolute ranking, with younger women appearing to have ranked feminists more highly than did older Canadian women. But when compared to the average ranking accorded to all groups, women in each cohort ranked feminists roughly 10 percentage points below the average ranking that they assigned to all groups. The difference in the ranking of feminists across the cohorts comes, then, from the differences in the average score each cohort assigns to groups; since younger Canadians provided higher rankings to all groups, feminists only appear to have come out ahead.

The fact that feminists were ranked significantly below average for all groups by all cohorts underscores the effect of the backlash and the negative baggage that accompanies the label. As shown below, despite support for many of the key planks in the feminist movement's platform, feminists as a group were not ranked very highly by women in any cohort. Indeed they ranked well below several of the other groups asked about in the survey and, in particular, significantly below big business, which was ranked above the overall average by each cohort.

When the question turned to gays and lesbians, a significantly different result emerged (see Table 1.1). An acceptance of diversity, particularly with regard to gays and lesbians, is one of the key defining characteristics of third-wave feminism. The results suggest that the ranking provided to gays and lesbians by Canadian women varies significantly by cohort: 20 percentage points separated the youngest and oldest cohorts on this question. And the difference is not simply because of the higher overall average ranking that younger women assigned to groups. While the two cohorts of third-wave women ranked the group 3 points above and roughly at the average, respectively, the two oldest cohorts ranked gays and lesbians at 4 and 13 points below average, respectively. In terms of affect, the difference between old and young women is unquestionable.

A similar, but far less striking, result appears in feelings toward racial minorities. The youngest cohort gave the group a positive evaluation of 66, but this fell somewhat across the cohorts and reached a low of 59 among the oldest cohort. An examination of the relative ranking accorded the group suggests that this difference is not simply because of the higher overall ranking that young women accorded to groups in society. Women in the Third Wave II cohort ranked racial minorities 8 points above the average for the listed groups; among the two oldest

Table 1.2: Desired Change in Influence for Various Groups by Feminist Cohort[a]

	Third Wave II	Third Wave I	Second Wave	Pre-Second Wave
Feminists*	48.4	45.5	44.1	42.2
For feminists	−.19	−.17	−.30	−.30
For gays and esbians*	.25	−.13	−.50	−.91
For racial minorities**	.06	−.15	−.47	−.52
For Aboriginal peoples	.05	−.12	−.08	.42
N[b]	168	206	284	184

[a] Average difference between how much influence a group should possess and how much influence they currently possess, ranging from –6 to 6. Negative values suggest the group has too much influence; positive values suggest the group should have more. The midpoint (0) identifies respondents who desire no change in the group's influence level.

[b] Minimum sample size for each cohort across the questions.

* $p < .01$

** $p < .05$

cohorts, this ranking is closer to the average, at 4 and 5 points above it. Thus an acceptance of diversity, at least as it extends to feelings toward racial minorities, exists across women of all ages but is somewhat higher among third-wave women.

A slightly different pattern emerges when the group in question is Aboriginal peoples. There is no apparent difference in the rank accorded the group across the cohorts. But given the overall difference in the average rank each cohort assigns to all the groups, a difference emerges in the relative ranking assigned to Aboriginal peoples across the cohorts: older women provide a higher relative rank to the group than do younger women. Thus, if younger women are more open to diversity, this diversity is limited to particular groups, especially gays and lesbians; and most interestingly, this openness to diversity appears to exclude feminists themselves.

Respondents were asked to assess the influence that they believed various groups possessed as well as the influence they believed these same groups should possess. Positive affect for feminists and the movement can be argued to include a desire to see the group accorded greater political influence. Several of these groups are the same ones that appeared in the closeness thermometer question (see Table 1.1). Respondents were asked to judge possessed influence and desired influence on a scale of 1 (very little influence) to 7 (very influential). A measure of desired influence change was created by subtracting the influence believed to be possessed by each group from the influence desired for each group. The results for this 'desired influence change' measure for each cohort appear in Table 1.2.

The results appear, on first glance, to suggest relatively little difference between the cohorts in their attitudes to feminist influence. Respondents seem to agree on the desired change in the level of influence possessed by feminists: each cohort believes that feminists should have *less* influence than they currently possess. The feminist movement has not, then, been very successful in justifying its continued importance to Canadian women.

The cohorts do not, however, agree on the level of desired influence change for gays and lesbians: while the Third Wave II cohort believes the group should possess more influence than is currently the case, the other cohorts, particularly the Pre-Second Wave cohort, believe the group should have less. And the differences are significantly different across the

Table 1.3: Attitudes by Feminist Cohort[a]

	Third Wave II	Third Wave I	Second Wave	Pre-Second Wave
Feminist Movement				
Tries to get equal treatment for women	68.1	71.3	62.9	70.1
	(144)	(181)	(251)	(184)
Encourages women to be independent	78.3	79.8	80.9	81.3
	(152)	(203)	(277)	(198)
Abortion (π^2)[b]				
Should never be permitted*	7.4	7.1	7.2	15.6
Should be permitted only after need established by a doctor*	23.8	26.7	32.1	37.3
Should be a matter of the woman's personal choice*	68.7	66.2	60.7	47.1
N (all responses)	323	382	499	359
Women and the Workplace				
Lay off women whose husbands have jobs first*	7.4	4.6	9.0	28.1
	(177)	(221)	(300)	(221)
Discrimination makes it hard for women to get jobs*	58.7	68.9	63.7	71.9
	(172)	(209)	(300)	(213)
Use quotas in job hiring*	18.4	10.5	9.4	8.7
	(163)	(209)	(286)	(218)
Gender Differences				
Gender equality can exist even with different responsibilities	76.9	79.0	75.7	78.1
	(169)	(214)	(301)	(219)
Men by nature are less caring and giving towards babies and children*	21.9	37.4	38.5	49.0
	(173)	(217)	(304)	(212)
Better off if women stayed home with children*	26.4	43.3	46.8	67.8
	(394)	(480)	(620)	(456)
Feminist Thought				
Gone too far pushing equal rights*	31.7	36.4	48.5	60.8
	(164)	(198)	(284)	(209)
Need greater tolerance for others**	70.7	69.0	67.6	63.5
	(171)	(213)	(293)	(211)
Newer lifestyles contributing to society's breakdown*	42.1	41.7	59.2	68.9
	(166)	(187)	(282)	(196)

Table 1.3: Attitudes by Feminist Cohort[a] *cont.*

	Third Wave II	Third Wave I	Second Wave	Pre-Second Wave
Fewer problems if more emphasis on family values[*]	63.4	66.8	77.1	84.9
	(164)	(208)	(297)	(218)
Only married couples should have children[*]	22.9	25.6	37.1	56.9
	(397)	(477)	(620)	(444)
Homosexual couples should be allowed to marry[*]	74.4	52.0	44.1	22.5
	(164)	(196)	(288)	(196)

[a] Percentages of respondents selecting or agreeing with a particular statement. See Appendix for question wording

[b] $\pi^2 = 50.04$, $p < .01$

[*] $p < .01$

[**] $p < .10$

cohorts on this question. On this second measure, then, the youngest cohort of Canadian women is significantly different from other Canadian women in their attitudes to the influence desired for gays and lesbians.

A similar but somewhat weaker result appears in the set of questions tapping the desired influence change for racial minorities. The youngest cohort is willing to accord a slightly higher level of influence to the group overall, but the other cohorts believe the group's level of influence should decrease. Women in the youngest cohort not only 'feel' more positive toward racial minorities and gays and lesbians, they also believe that each group deserves a greater measure of influence in Canadian society. The final rows in Table 1.2 suggest that when the group in question is Aboriginal, it is the Pre-Second Wave cohort that is most willing to accord greater influence to the group. And interestingly, this group is the only one among the four whose influence the oldest cohort is willing to see increased.

Although differences appear in this set of questions across the cohorts, they should not be inflated in importance. A slightly greater acceptance of diversity does appear among the youngest of the Third Wave groups: this cohort would accord a greater level of influence to gays and lesbians and, to a lesser degree, racial minorities and Aboriginal peoples than each group currently possesses, but all would still fall below the overall average level of influence desired for all of the groups included in the set of questions.[12] And it is clear that this desire is not extended to feminists as a group.

Respondents were also asked to render an opinion on the goals of the feminist movement; these two survey questions are an attempt to assess popular perceptions and support of the movement's objectives rather than affect toward the group's members. Results by cohort for these questions appear in Table 1.3. The breakdown of responses, however, reveals little in the way of differentiation across the cohorts: a majority in each cohort believes that the feminist movement tries to get equal treatment for women and that the movement encourages women to be independent and to speak up for themselves.

Interestingly, however, there is a significant degree of uncertainty regarding the feminist movement's objectives, an uncertainty that occasionally varies by cohort. For instance, on the first question, between 18 per cent and 19 per cent of respondents in each of the cohorts responded that they were not certain whether the feminist movement just tries to get equal treatment for women or whether it puts men down. On the second question, a smaller but equally large share of women gave the same response to the choice of whether 'the feminist movement encourages women to be independent and speak up for themselves or to be selfish and think only of themselves'. On this second question, however, variation is evident across the cohorts: while 15 per cent of respondents in the youngest cohort answered 'not sure', only between 9 per cent and 12 per cent of the other cohorts answered similarly. One could conclude, then, that there exists a significant degree of uncertainty among women in the general public over the goals and objectives of the feminist movement and that, in some cases, this uncertainty is greater for younger rather than older women.

Attitudes to Feminist Positions and Beliefs

Women in the 1997 CES were asked for their beliefs regarding access to abortion. Abortion has been, and continues to be, one of the key political lighting rods for the feminist movement: equal rights for women, it is maintained, must at the very least ensure that women have the right to determine their reproductive choices. The 1997 CES included a question wording experiment to assess the importance of answer order to responses.[13] For our purposes, responses to these three questions have been merged; results, broken down by cohort, appear in Table 1.3.

Table 1.3 confirms that younger women, particularly in the Third Wave cohorts, are very much on side with this one element of the feminist movement's agenda. For women who came of age before the second wave, however, opinion is more divided: fewer than half believe that abortion is a matter of personal choice, and more women in this cohort than in any other believe that abortion should never be permitted. Attitudes on this issue reveal a decidedly linear pattern across the cohorts: subsequent generations of women are more likely to believe that women should be provided access to abortion services whenever desired. The majority of second- and third-wave women are 'feminist' given their opinion on abortion.

Table 1.3 also breaks down results from the 1997 CES tapping attitudes toward gender and the workplace. There appears to be a significant association between cohort and these attitudes—although not always in the anticipated direction. The vast majority of women in each of the cohorts disagreed with the statement that women whose husbands have jobs should be laid off first. Nevertheless, some differences in attitudes do exist: the three youngest cohorts were far less in agreement with the statement than women in the Pre-Second Wave Cohort.

On the second question, dealing with discrimination, the pattern is reversed. Although a majority of women in each cohort agreed that 'discrimination makes it extremely difficult for women to get jobs equal to their abilities', this share was highest among the three oldest cohorts. This pattern may reflect the fact that the youngest cohort has yet to experience such discrimination at first hand and as such is less willing to acknowledge its existence.

On the last question, addressing the use of job quotas to increase the number of women in good jobs, the cohort least accepting of the existence of discrimination appears to be the most willing to adopt quotas for job hiring. Equally puzzling is the unwillingness of the Pre-Second Wave cohort to adopt quotas in spite of their overall agreement that there is discrimination in job hiring. Correlation analysis of these two questions reveals that for only the two middle cohorts is a connection, although modest, made between the questions at the individual level.[14]

Table 1.3 next presents the cohort breakdown for a set of questions dealing with core differences between the sexes. The results suggest that Canadian women in the youngest cohort are the least accepting of essentialist arguments. On the first question, dealing with gender equality in spite of different responsibilities, women across the cohorts appear to be in agreement. On the next two questions, however, differences in attitude are more apparent.

When read the statement 'When it comes to caring for babies and small children, men by nature are less patient and giving than women', younger women are much less likely than older women to agree. The same pattern appears in responses to the following statement: 'Society would be better off if women stayed home with their children'. Younger women, it appears, are far less willing to accept gender-defined roles, especially those directed at caring for children and that suggest that a successful society requires women to remain at home to care for their children.

Finally, Table 1.3 reports cohort attitudes on several questions included in the 1997 CES that are related to feminism thought but not directly concerned with women or gender equality. Breaking opinion down by cohort reinforces the distance separating younger and older women in their attitudes on various issues. The first statement, 'We have gone too far in pushing equal rights in this country', reveals a significant degree of attitudinal difference between the cohorts: almost 30 percentage points separates Third Wave II women from Pre-Second Wave women with the latter group far more likely to agree that an equal rights agenda has been too forcefully promoted. The question does not specifically mention equal rights for women but nevertheless taps into opinion on the extension of equality to all Canadians.

The second question reveals far less distance between the cohorts but nevertheless reinforces the conclusion that younger women are more tolerant of diversity. Agreement with the statement 'We should be more tolerant of people who choose to live according to their own standards, even if they are very different from our own' decreased with each cohort from 71 per cent of Third Wave II women to 64 per cent of Pre-Second Wave women. The difference was greater on the related statement, 'Newer lifestyles are contributing to the breakdown of our society'. Young women are far less willing to attribute societal problems to the appearance of 'newer lifestyles' than are older women.

The final three questions in Table 1.3 relate to 'family values' and the belief that the moral fibre of Canadian society is dependent in part of the maintenance of the traditional family structure: mother, father, and children. There is very little agreement across cohorts on the need for protecting this traditional institution. A majority of respondents in each cohort does believe that fewer problems might exist if there was a greater emphasis on 'traditional family values'. This majority is at its weakest, however, among the Third Wave cohorts and increases steadily with the Second Wave and Pre-Second Wave cohorts. Thus, while tolerance for diversity might be highest among the youngest cohort of Canadian women, this in no way means that they have completely dismissed a role for the traditional family unit.

When the question shifts to restricting access to legally accessible marriage or to who ought to care for and raise children, the distance separating the cohorts increases dramatically. When presented with the statement 'Only people who are married should be having children', only roughly one in four women in the Third Wave cohorts agrees compared with more than half of the women in the Pre-Second Wave cohort. And when the question is one of extending legally recognized marriage to homosexual couples, the difference becomes larger still: from almost three out of four in the Third Wave II cohort to less than one out of four in the Pre-Second Wave cohort. Thus, while the youngest cohort agrees in the importance of 'family values', these women's definition of a family appears to differ significantly from that of previous cohorts.

On many questions, then, Canadian women who came of age at the time of the third wave possess opinions and values very much in line with those of the most recent period of feminist thought and activism. These young women are more likely to support access to abortion and the use of quotas for job hiring. They are also more inclined to believe that different gender responsibilities need not translate into inequality and to dismiss arguments that women are better at caring for children and that children are better off if women stay home to care for them. Yet they are also more likely to believe that some things are much better than they were in the past, including workplace equity.

More broadly, young Canadian women are more tolerant, more supportive of past efforts at securing equal rights, and more supportive of newer lifestyles. Yet, interestingly, a majority of younger Canadian women also believes that 'family values' deserve greater emphasis, although this share is lower than in each of the remaining cohorts. In many respects, feminism has found a home among the values and attitudes of the youngest of Canadian women if not in their affect toward feminists themselves.

Discussion and Conclusion

Canadian women do not appear on the surface to be particularly open to feminists and the feminist movement. They respond that they 'like' feminists less than they do many other groups, and they believe that feminists deserve less influence than they currently possess. Feminists, and the feminist movement, appear on the surface to have not been particularly successful at winning women over.

There is a hint, however, that this rejection may reflect the effects of a backlash against the movement as much as a rejection of feminists and their objectives. The first clue is the significant degree of uncertainty among women of all ages as to the objectives of the movement. This uncertainty may stem form the many mixed messages that women receive about feminists and the feminist movement in the popular press and in popular culture.

The second hint is that many women, particularly young women, have nevertheless wholeheartedly endorsed many feminist beliefs and policy prescriptions. This unwillingness to 'identify' with feminists belies, then, a significant degree of feminist thinking among many Canadian women: the vast majority of third-wave women would be labelled 'feminist' given the set of beliefs that they hold about women's roles and gender equality. Despite such thinking, however, the cohort is no more likely to 'like' feminists than are women who came of age earlier in the twentieth century. The 'but I'm not a feminist' phenomenon appears to be alive and well among the youngest cohort of Canadian women.

In other ways, however, the differences that appear in the waves of feminist thought are reflected in the corresponding generations of Canadian women. In particular, the third wave of Canadian women, those born after 1957, is distinctive for its adoption of feminist beliefs and values and also for its greater acceptance of diversity, one of the defining characteristics of the youngest wave of feminist thought. This greater acceptance of diversity is striking and undoubtedly reflects in some measure the Charter of Rights and Freedom's impact on ideals of equality and tolerance. But the Charter is broader than the feminist movement, and the shift in attitudes may also reflect broader changes in the beliefs and opinions of Canadian women. Women of succeeding generations differ on many counts, including their weaker religious commitment, their higher educational attainment, and the fewer number of children they bear (O'Neill, 2002). The changes have been many, and our ability to disentangle the causes of attitude shifts based on one cross-sectional survey is limited.

Furthermore, the electoral consequences of this particularly liberal set of attitudes among younger Canadian women may not be as large as one might immediately suppose. Feminist values and attitudes generally fall on the liberal end of the ideological spectrum: for example, advocating a governmental role in promoting and protecting equal rights for women in the private and public spheres, and promoting a more tolerant attitude toward gays and lesbians and supporting efforts to ensure equality for them. One could suggest that the adoption of these more liberal attitudes by young Canadian women might translate into the election of more liberal governments in the future.

A number of conditions would have to be met, however, before the election of an overtly feminist-friendly government were to occur. First, these young women would have to get out and vote in significant numbers. Not all women are particularly liberal in their opinions; women of previous generations are more conservative on a number of the attitudes measured here. Unfortunately, research suggests that today's young Canadians are unlikely to vote in numbers similar to previous generations (O'Neill, 2001). Second, the adoption of a particular set of attitudes need not translate directly into support for a political party whose platform includes a related set of policy prescriptions. Voting decisions are tremendously complex and reflect more than support for or opposition to particular party platforms. Although young women voters may support a particularly liberal party platform, the party leader, its performance during the campaign, and the salience of feminist and other policies could all translate into a vote against a feminist-friendly party. Additionally, an examination of women's attitudes and values in the end provides only half of the picture: men make up almost half of the voting population. The ability to elect feminist-friendly governments requires more than the votes of young Canadian women—it also requires the votes of young Canadian men. Finally, the ability to cue these particular attitudes and values at the ballot box requires that political parties include such policy recommendations in their campaign platforms. Past practice among Canadian political parties, their brokerage style, and the recent shift of the party system to the ideological right suggest that this is unlikely to occur any time soon (Young, 2000). In the end it may take the reform of the electoral system to allow for the election of a feminist party: until vote shares are more closely reflected in seat shares, there seems to be little chance of overcoming the dominance of centrist political parties in Canada.

Appendix: Question Wording, Table 1.3

Attitudes to the Feminist Movement

- The feminist movement just tries to get equal treatment for women OR puts men down.
- The feminist movement encourages women to be independent and speak up for themselves OR to be selfish and think only of themselves.

Attitudes Related to Abortion

Of the following three positions, which is closest to your own opinion:

1. Abortion should never be permitted.
2. Abortion should be permitted only after need has been established by a doctor.
3. Abortion should be a matter of the woman's personal choice.

Attitudes to Women and the Workplace

- If a company has to lay off some of its employees, the first workers to be laid off should be women whose husbands have jobs.
- Discrimination makes it extremely difficult for women to get jobs equal to their abilities.
- When it comes to job hiring, quotas should be used to increase the number of women in good jobs OR hiring should be based strictly on merit.

Attitudes to Gender Difference

- Which comes closest to your own view: Men and women can only be equal when they have the same responsibilities in government, business, and the family OR Equality can exist even when men and women have very different responsibilities.
- When it comes to caring for babies and small children, men by nature are less patient and giving than women.
- Society would be better off if women stayed home with their children.

Attitudes Related to Feminism

- We have gone too far in pushing equal rights in this country.
- We should be more tolerant of people who choose to live according to their own standards, even if they are very different from our own.
- Newer lifestyles are contributing to the breakdown of our society.
- This country would have many fewer problems if there were more emphasis on traditional family values.
- Only people who are married should be having children.
- Homosexual couples should be allowed to be legally married.

Notes

1. The author wishes to thank Tyler Jivan for his research assistance.
2. Much of the literature identifying this phenomenon comes from the United States. See, for example, Baumgardner and Richards (2000).
3. As Arneil points out, the second wave of feminism is identified in part by its many hybrids: liberal feminism, socialist feminism, psychoanalytic feminism, and radical feminism, among others. Despite the diversity of thinking across the approaches Arneil nevertheless

provides an account of the commonality among them (Arneil, 1999).

4. As one young feminist declared in explaining her decision to launch a web site (GirlCrush) for girls between the ages of 13 and 18,

   > GirlCrush is feminist, yet girly (we have fashion and makeup sections) . . . because 'feminist' and 'girly' are NOT opposites. I want girls to know that you don't have to be one or the other; that there are stereotypes they don't need to conform to, and that there are definitely more than one or two or a hundred ways to be a feminist and to be a girl. (Anna Humphrey, PAR-L discussion list, 22 December 2000)

5. The first such Web site, http://www.cybergrrl.com, launched in 1995 by Aliza Sherman, has since mushroomed into a globally linked network of chapters, with some, such as the Toronto chapter, providing technical training and advice, community work, social events, and job and housing help to members (Cameron, 2001). For Canadian examples, see http://www.goodgirl.ca, http://www.girlcrushzine.com, and http://www.marigoldzine.com.
6. Data from the 1997 CES were provided by the Institute for Social Research, York University. The survey was funded by the Social Sciences and Humanities Research Council of Canada, grant number 412-96-0007, and was completed for the 1997 CES Team of André Blais (Université de Montréal), Elisabeth Gidengil (McGill University), Richard Nadeau (Université de Montréal), and Neil Nevitte (University of Toronto). Neither the Institute for Social Research, SSHRC, nor the CES Team are responsible for the analyses and interpretations presented here.
7. The data have been weighted to accurately reflect a Canadian national sample. See 1997 CES, *Technical Documentation*, at the CES Web site: http://www.fas.umontreal.ca/pol/ces-eec/ces.html.
8. This breakdown roughly approximates that adopted by Everitt in her study of the relevance of the feminist movement to public opinion in Canada. The dates in her study are selected to correspond to the changes taking place in feminist activism and thought. Where Everitt adopts a single post-1958 cohort to identify those who came of age 'after the initial mobilization of the second-wave women's movement' (1998b: 750), however, this paper breaks this cohort into two distinct groups to allow for a more detailed examination of differences across the youngest Canadian women given the more recent data set employed.
9. Sample sizes for each group varied from these numbers depending on which of the three waves of the survey the question appeared in (campaign period, post-election period, and mail-back). The reported samples are from the campaign-period group. Group sample size is reported in all tables.
10. The strength of association is assessed with a Chi-square measure of association. Although the age groups and many of the dependent variables examined are ordinal measures that would allow for the use of stronger statistical tests, such tests very often do not allow for the existence of non-linear relationships in the data, and there is little theoretical justification for assuming linearity in the relationship between age and feminism.
11. Others have employed similarly worded survey questions in their research on feminist opinion (Conover, 1988; Cook, 1989; Gurin, 1985). Additionally, Rhodebeck has shown that the feeling thermometer for the women's liberation movement (using slightly different wording than that employed here) 'serves as a more reliable indicator of feminist identity than does the index of closeness to women' (1996: 391–3).
12. The groups that scored above average on the level of influence the groups should possess are in descending order, consumers, small business, farmers, environmentalists, seniors, and big business.
13. The order in which the three responses were given to respondents was altered in order to evaluate whether order mattered for responses.
14. For the Third Wave I cohort, $r = .19$; for the Second Wave Cohort, $r = .29$. Both were significant at the $p < .01$ level.

References

Adamson, Nancy, Linda Briskin, and Margaret McPhail. 1988. *Feminist Organizing for Change: The Contemporary Women's Movement in Canada*. Toronto: Oxford University Press.

Arneil, Barbara. 1999. *Politics and Feminism*. Malden, MA: Blackwell.

Baumgardner, Jennifer, and Amy Richards. 2000. *Manifesta: Young Women, Feminism, and the Future*. New York: Farrar, Strauss and Giroux.

Black, Naomi. 1993. 'The Canadian Women's Movement: The Second Wave', in *Changing Patterns: Women in Canada*, Sandra Burt, Lorraine Code, and Lindsay Dorney, eds. Toronto: McClelland & Stewart.

Conover, Pamela. 1988. 'Feminists and the Gender Gap', 50 *Journal of Politics:* 985–1010.

Everitt, Joanna. 1998. 'Public Opinion and Social Movements: The Women's Movement and the Gender Gap in Canada', 31 *Canadian Journal of Political Science*: 743–65.

Faludi, Susan. 1991. *Backlash: The Undeclared War Against American Women*. Toronto: Doubleday.

Gidengil, Elisabeth. 1995. 'Economic Man—Social Woman? The Case of the Gender Gap in Support of the Canada–US Free Trade Agreement', 28 *Comparative Political Studies*: 384–408.

O'Neill Brenda. 2001. 'A Simple Difference of Opinion? Religious Beliefs and Gender Gaps in Public Opinion in Canada', 34 *Canadian Journal of Political Science*: 275–98.

———. 2002. 'Sugar and Spice? Political Culture and the Political Behaviour of Canadian Women', in *Citizen Politics: Research Theory in Canada Political Behaviour*, Joanna Everitt and Brenda O'Neill, eds. Toronto: Oxford University Press.

Pinterics, Natasha. 2001. 'Riding the Feminist Waves: In with the Third?', 20/21 *Canadian Woman Studies*: 15–21.

Steenbergen, Candis. 2001. 'Feminism and Young Women: Alive and Well and Still Kicking', 4.1 *Canadian Woman Studies*: 6–14.

Young, Lisa. 2000. *Feminists and Party Politics*. Vancouver: UBC Press.

Who is Canadian Now?: Feminism and the Politics of Nation After September 11

Mary-Jo Nadeau

EDITORS' INTRODUCTION

In the early years of the twentieth century the atrocities of the South African and the First World War pointed some Canadian feminists toward a pacific politics, one that wedded first-wave feminist beliefs in women's inherently peace-seeking nature to critiques of militarism and the imperialism that so often justified it.[1] Flora MacDonald Denison, discussed by Fiamengo, was a pacifist, as was Francis Marion Beynon—editor of the populist and progressive *Grain Grower's Guide*'s 'women's page' from 1912–17. Theirs were brave and often lonely positions to take in wartime English Canada, and Benyon, for one, would pay dearly for her opposition to what was called the Great War. Her job and her life were both threatened, and in 1917 she left Winnipeg for New York, an experience she retold in her novel *Aleta Day*.[2]

War and militarism have marked the lives of Canadian women in no uncertain terms. Davis and Lorenzkowski's analysis of gender and public transit in Canada during the Second World War makes this point, as does Pamela Sugiman's examination of Japanese Canadian women's memories of internment. From the women loyalists of the 1780s to the Mennonite refugee women of the Second World War discussed in Epp's essay, to women currently fleeing Sudan's civil war, repeated generations of women have arrived in Canada as war refugees.[3] Others have participated directly in war. Métis women played significant roles in the Battle of Batoche, the final military showdown that saw the federal government put down the Northwest Rebellion of 1885.[4] It is not an accident that the 'heroines' of English and French Canada, Madeline de Verchères and Laura Secord respectively, both entered the public record for the actions in war—de Verchères for defending a seigneurie against Iroquois attack in 1692, Secord for aiding the British in the War of 1812.[5] Canadian women served as nursing sisters during the First World War and the Second World War saw the creation of female sections of the armed forces, the Canadian Women's Army Corps (CWACS), the Women's Royal Canadian Naval Service (WRENS), and the Royal Canadian Airforce Women's Division. Some 45,000 women signed up for overseas duty, but the prevailing ideas of appropriate activities for men and women ensured that no women directly participated in combat roles.[6] This would only change in the 1991 Gulf War, which was the first military conflict in which Canadian women took active combat roles. In 2005 a little over 10 per cent of the Canadian Armed Forces and about 18 per cent of the reserves were female.[7]

The mixed response of organized English-Canadian feminism to war and militarism reflects this history. In 1915 the Women's International League for Peace and Freedom was founded, and it served as a forum for left-leaning pacifist women, including prominent activists like Violet

McNaughton and Laura Jamieson.[8] Other feminists, like Nellie McClung and ultimately Denison, wrested with divided loyalties and ultimately opted to support Canada's participation in the First World War. Pro-war and pro-empire organizations like the Imperial Order of the Daughters of the Empire, formed in the midst of the South African War, would not only be significant in numbers and profile, but would help to chart the political course taken by more mainstream women's organizations like the National Council of Women, Canada's 'parliament of women'.[9]

The Second World War would again make peace-seeking activities dangerous, or at best difficult, but pacifist-feminist activity would resurface in the postwar, especially with the 1960 formation of Voice of Women [VOW]. The VOW voiced opposition to the cold war, the American-led but Canadian supported war in Vietnam, and the nuclear arms race. While the IODE knit socks for soldiers overseas, the Ontario VOW sent knitting to women in Vietnam.[10] In 1986–7, the first chapter of the 'Raging Grannies' was formed in Victoria, British Columbia. The Grannies exploit stereotypes of older women to make feminism and pacifism non-threatening, and even fun. They dress in over-the-top granny get-ups culled from thrift stores and sing, loudly and intentionally off-key, old songs with their lyrics re-written to protest war, corporate greed, environmental destruction, violence against women, poverty, and the erosion of public services. The ongoing American-led war in Iraq has given new impetus to the Raging Grannies' cause. At last count there thirty-five chapters of the Raging Grannies or Les Mémés déchaînées throughout the world.[11] Women in Black is a more sombre and though-provoking international network of women motivated by 'a feminist understanding that male violence against women in domestic life and in war are related'. Wearing black to symbolize mourning, the WiB stand silently on street corners across the globe, including Regina, Edmonton, Montreal, Halifax, and other Canadian cities, to bear public witness to the destruction of war.[12]

In this essay, sociologist and activist Mary-Jo Nadeau analyzes the furor that erupted across Canada in response to an October 2001 speech made by Sunera Thobani to an Ottawa conference on violence against women. Thobani, a Women's Studies professor and former president of the National Action Committee on the Status of Women drew links between American foreign policy, the ongoing colonization of Indigenous and Third World peoples, and violence against women. The response, as Nadeau explains, was swift and extreme: Thobani was denounced as anti-American and dangerous in newspapers, on television, and on radio by a range of Canadians, including then Prime Minister Jean Chrétien. Nadeau argues that the response to Thobani's speech reflected the ongoing process of race and nation-making in Canada, much the same one that informed the exclusionary immigration policies discussed by Sedef Arat-Koç in her essay. The 'third-wave' feminist values discussed by O'Neill in this volume remain contested ones, and pointing out the relationship between violence 'at home' and at war can still be a dangerous thing for Canadian women.

Notes

1. Barbara Roberts, *'Why Do Women Do nothing to End the War?' Canadian Feminist-Pacifists and the Great War* (Ottawa: Canadian Research Institute on the Advancement of Women, 1985).
2. Frances M. Beynon, 'Loyalty and Political Corruption', *Grain Growers' Guide* 3 June 1914; Kurt Korneski, 'Liberalism in Winnipeg, 1890s–1920s: Charles W. Gordon, John W. Dafoe, Minnie J. B. Campbell, and Francis M. Benyon' (PhD thesis: Memorial University of Newfoundland, 2004).
3. Janice Potter-MacKinnon, *While Women Only Wept: Loyalist Refugee Women in Eastern Ontario* (Montreal and Kingston: McGill-Queen's University Press, 1993).
4. Diane P. Payment, '"La vie en rose"? Metis Women at Batoche, 1870–1920', in *Women of the First Nations: Power, Wisdom, and Strength*, Christine Miller and Patricia Churchryk, eds. (Winnipeg: University of Manitoba Press, 1996).

5. Colin M. Coates and Cecilia Morgan, *Heroines and History: Representations of Madeleine de Verchères and Laura Secord* (Toronto: University of Toronto Press, 2001).
6. The best treatment of women in World War Two remains Ruth Roach Pierson, *'They're Still Women After All': The Second World War and Canadian Womanhood* (Toronto: McClelland & Stewart, 1986).
7. http://www.swc-cfc.gc.ca/dates/whm/factsheet_e.html.
8. Veronica Strong-Boag, 'Peace-making Women: Canada 1919–1939', in *Women and Education for Peace*, Ruth Roach Pierson, ed. (London: Croom-Helm, 1987).
9. Katie Pickles, *Female Imperialism and National Identity: Imperial Order Daughters of the Empire* (Manchester and New York: Manchester University Press, 2002).
10. Kay Macpherson and Sara Good, 'Canadian Voice of Women for Peace', *Peace Magazine*, (Oct–Nov 1987): http://www.peacemagazine.org/archive/v03n5p26.htm.
11. http://www.vcn.bc.ca/ragigran/; http://www.geocities.com/raginggrannies/.
12. www.womeninblack.org. For an insightful discussion of WiB, see Joan Scott, 'feminist reverberations', *Differences* 13.3 (Fall 2002): 1–24.

Questions for Critical Reading

1. Why have some women been attracted to the military and to war? What might supporting or directly participating in war offer to women?
2. What does the furor that greeted Thobani's speech tell us about the challenges that lay before the Canadian women's movement at the dawn of the twenty-first century? How might groups like the National Action Committee on the Status of Women meet these challenges?
3. Is there a relationship between the domestic and sexual violence discussed in the George and Connor articles and war? How is violence against women related to or different from the violence men and, increasingly, women do during war?
4. Is the idea that women are more peaceful than men a limiting, outdated stereotype or a realistic recognition of women's particular social role and perspective?

Herizons, one of Canada's most popular feminist magazines, called it 'The Speech That Shook the Country' (2002). On 1 October 2001, Sunera Thobani, well-known Canadian feminist, former President of the National Action Committee on the Status of Women (NAC), and a professor of Women's Studies, presented a keynote address to the 'Women's Resistance Conference' in Ottawa. In the post-September 11 'race toward war', Thobani's speech cogently outlined, and unequivocally challenged, some of the well-established and brutalizing intentions and outcomes of US foreign policy (Black Radical Congress, 2001). Drawing attention to the 'patriarchal, racist violence' fuelling the current 'war against terrorism', Thobani's address was also framed around an urgent call for activism. In her words: 'The women's movement has to stand up to this. There is no option for us. We have to fight back against this militarization. We have to break the support that is being built in our countries for this kind of attack.'[1]

Thobani's speech, presented to an audience of five hundred feminists at an historical women's conference, 'brought delegates to their feet in applause no less than five times' (Croft, 2002: 6). This is hardly surprising. In addition to being timely and relevant, the speech presented a well-contextualized and multi-layered analysis of several pressing concerns. Thobani drew incisive connections among globalization, colonization, anti-racist organizing, racial profiling, peace coalitions, the role of US foreign policy in installing the Taliban regime, and the current scapegoating of immigrants and refugees in Canada and the US after September 11. Despite this complexity, the media coverage produced a highly selective and decontextualized account that attacked both the speech and Thobani herself. Most of the coverage was a mix of racist, anti-feminist, and anti-immigrant epithets from editorial boards, columnists, cartoonists, letter-writers, a premier, a Liberal senator, and some academics. Targeted as a particularly extreme and irrational feminist, Thobani was thoroughly chastised for a number of apparent transgressions. To name a few, she 'ranted' and 'raved' throughout her speech, was 'simply outrageous', she propagated hate, was historically inaccurate, and was 'manipulative', 'fanatic', 'terrorist', and 'anti-American'.[2]

In this paper, I analyze the media coverage that constructed Thobani's speech as an event of national concern. I argue that the media reaction was more than just an attack on Thobani and her speech. It also generated a moral-political discourse of 'national security'[3] which uncritically backed the growing support for war, in the process calling for a narrowing of the definition of who is considered 'Canadian'. In particular, immigrants of colour (perceived to be) non-Western, especially 'Arabs' and 'Muslims', were targeted.[4] But as the attacks on Thobani reveal, such attacks had serious and particular implications for immigrant women and women of colour in Canada.

I next examine a popular critical discourse which was already circulating as a critique of post-September 11 abuses of civil liberties, but which developed a specific critique of the media attack on Thobani. I argue that this critique, which circulated in various public sites (such as e-mail, petitions, press releases and a few articles in mainstream media), was important but limited. It identified the media attack as part of a generalized crackdown on freedom of expression and argued, in opposition, for Thobani's right to express her opinions. I argue instead that it is crucial to understand this attack more comprehensively through anti-racist feminist analyses which foreground the dynamics of gendered and racially-organized national exclusions and inclusions. As Nandita Sharma has argued, in such nationalist moments, women conventionally 'rendered as the Other are seen as embodying the very differences between nations' (2000: 11). The attack on Sunera Thobani is a specific example of this nationalist Othering process, part of a long history of nationalist discourses, which operate at the nexus of intersecting and exclusionary racist, anti-immigrant and sexist 'ideological and material processes that make some people and not others—"Canadian"' (Sharma, 2000: 6). The central argument of this paper is that in their attack on Thobani and her speech, the media were key participants in widespread post-September 11 calls for a further narrowing, and intensified regulation, of the racialized and exclusionary insider/outsider relations of belonging that have historically constructed Canada (Bannerji, 2000; Das Gupta and Iacovetta, 2000; Sharma, 2000; Thobani, 2000). I further demonstrate that 'white backlash', evident in current constructions of national belonging, is continuous with historical forms of racist and gendered nationalist forms of exclusion, regulation and belonging.

The paper ends with a brief commentary on the range of feminist perspectives that emerged in response to the attack on Thobani, and offers some reflections on the challenges and possibilities these responses imply for strategies of resistance in the current climate.

Anatomy of an Attack

Over a period of six days, in six newspapers, a total of 119 items focused on Sunera Thobani and her speech. Judging by sheer volume alone, 'excessive' seems an apt descriptor for this outpouring of commentary. A 'national security' discourse, coupled with a Eurocentric sense of national pride over Canada's perceived esteemed place in 'Western Democracy', overwhelmingly dominated the coverage. The authority of this 'national security' discourse hinged on the selective repetition of the 'soaked in blood' phrase from Thobani's speech, which was meant to convey her 'extreme anti-Americanism'. Naming Thobani 'anti-American' positioned her simultaneously as an enemy of (and outsider to) both 'Western democracy' and 'Canadian values'. Indeed, the incessantly repeated claim that Thobani's speech was 'anti-American' operated as a code that evoked a broader terrain of gendered, racialized, and national meanings, all intended to undermine her authority as a speaker.

This discursive terrain was well-represented in editorials, regular columns, guest columns, headlines and letters to the editor. For example, all four Editorials published that week reduced the content of her speech to 'virulent anti-Americanism', which became their basis for a complete condemnation of the speech and the speaker. A selectivity process was also evident in the practices employed around the publication of the transcript. Despite the fact that the full text of the speech was available from the Cable Public Affairs Channel (CPAC) almost immediately, both the *Ottawa Citizen* and the *National Post* chose to publish only small and distorted portions of it (each amounting to less than one-quarter of the entire transcript). The *Toronto Sun*, which was arguably the most unrelenting in its attack, chose not to publish any portion of the transcript. While the *Vancouver Sun* might be praised for publishing the entire transcript, it nevertheless provocatively framed the speech within the highly decontextualized and vilifying phrase 'It's bloodthirsty vengeance'. Ultimately, the hyper-selective editorializing that week produced a representation of the speech that reduced Thobani's argument to a '[vicious, poisonous] diatribe' against the United States and Western democracy.

At one level, these homogenizing practices functioned to delegitimatize her arguments by representing Thobani as extremely irrational and inflammatory. Of the eighteen regular and guest columns that appeared in those six days, for example, all but two used their allotted space as a forum for discrediting Thobani. One regular columnist called her an 'idiot', some characterized her speech as 'hate-filled', one called her the 'Nutty Professor', several charged her with 'ranting' and 'raving'. Over thirty letters expressed profound moral indignation, variously claiming that Thobani's speech rendered them 'outraged', 'dismayed', 'horrified', 'appalled and ashamed', and 'disgusted'.

Anti-feminism and anti-immigrant racism were also central sustaining discourses as many commentators connected Thobani's so-called 'anti-Americanism' to her feminist affiliations (especially her long-past term as elected President of NAC and her current post as a professor in a Canadian Women's Studies department) and to her history as an immigrant to Canada. Prominent in both letters and columns, for instance, was a taxpayer discourse that drew on both anti-immigrant and racist nationalist sentiments. Those employing this discourse secured their own sense of belonging in the nation by referencing the misuse of 'our' taxes by Others/outsiders to the nation. A letter printed in the *Ottawa Citizen*, for example, argues that '[o]nly in Canada, it seems, could such an ill-informed and hateful person as Ms. Thobani get so much public-funding to put forward her awful agenda.' A *Toronto Sun* columnist extended the discourse to include an anti-feminist agenda that also situates NAC as an outsider to the nation. In her words, '[t]his hatred for our free world comes from a lady, who didn't mind Western world taxpayers paying her salary . . . while NAC took millions of our hard-earned tax dollars.'

Interspersed throughout this dominant media framing were some occasional, but rare, challenging voices. Most took the form of letters to the editor expressing support for Thobani's right to speak. A number praised her for providing a 'refreshing' feminist political analysis, for raising 'serious questions' about US foreign policy, and for having the courage 'to tell the truth after September 11'. Some even rebuked the mainstream media for its 'hysterical coverage' of the event. Such items provided a welcome and much-needed counter-framing to what one reader called the media's 'cowardly spectacle'. In reinterpreting the speech as a defense of freedom (not an attack on it), this reader was one of the few published who actually acknowledged Thobani as 'an accomplished scholar' having 'extensive expertise' on the subject. However sparse, such representations were an important reminder that there was actually more than one interpretation of this event circulating in the public sphere.

Making Sense of the Crackdown on Dissent

While not well-represented in the media, a common critical response to the attack on Thobani and her speech did emerge in broader public discussions. This response explained the attack primarily as an example of the generally intensified crackdown on political dissent and/or freedom of speech. *Globe and Mail* columnist Michael Valpy, for example, was one of only two renegade columnists that week who chose not to contribute to what he called the 'political and media bile dumped this week on feminist academic Sunera Thobani'. Instead, he employed this critical discourse to focus on how it is currently '[r]isky for whoever speaks out'.

This critical discourse was necessary for highlighting and explaining the underlying implications of the broader, more generalized, post-September 11 policing of popular dissent or opposition. The seriousness of this crackdown on dissent has been abundantly evident. In Thobani's case, there were calls for her to be fired as well as a 'hate-crime' complaint filed against her with the RCMP. With its broadly inclusive framework and its incisive focus on acts of censorship, the mainstream 'freedom of speech' discourse is needed to make connections between seemingly isolated events. In the US context, for example, this critique has highlighted the silencing of prominent public critics and celebrities (e.g., writer Susan Sontag, talk-show host Bill Maher, documentarian Michael Moore). And, across North America, this critical framework has been useful for highlighting post-September 11 attacks on academic critics and for organizing in their defence. For example, the president of University of British Columbia, and a number of Thobani's colleagues there, defended her by using this discourse. Politically effective for building broad-based coalitions of support and resistance, this critical discourse has facilitated calls in support of academic freedom, freedom of expression, and the right to dissent. Without a doubt, this critical framework has been vital for acknowledging current power imbalances (national and international) in which a decisive shift to the right has allowed conservative forces to exert real influence over academics, governments and the media.

Given its obvious relevance as a framework for critical analysis and political mobilization, a critique of the limits of the discourse is important as a means for strengthening it. In this regard, my main concern is that it was not effectively mobilized to incorporate and sustain a critique of the politics of difference, especially those inherent in nationalist invocations, underlying the generalized crackdown on dissent. It does not adequately acknowledge how the terrain of dissent and representational legitimacy is not (and has never been) equal for all in Canada, nor has it actively addressed how the consequences for speaking against the nation in the aftermath of September 11 is highly contingent upon one's historical location in the Canadian national imaginary.

Most broadly, the 'freedom of speech' framework typically fails to interrogate the specificity and multiplicity of subjects' (often contradictory) material and discursive locations, thereby often failing to highlight that not all speakers are equally at risk of censorship. In the attack on Thobani, for instance, it did not adequately account for why some, and not others, were disproportionately subjected to a massive and sustained attack on the front pages of the nation's major dailies. It did not explain why many who spoke out have mostly been ignored by the media (as in the case of former NAC President Judy Rebick) or, when covered by the media, were not vilified (as in the case of former Governor General Adrienne Clarkson). Both of these prominent national figures also spoke out in opposition to the post-September 11 war-mongering and other atrocities, but neither was subject to the kind of attack experienced by Sunera Thobani. As a generalized focus on the crackdown on dissent, this mainstream critical discourse did not adequately account for these different responses to, and treatments of, dissent.

Another limit is its failure to highlight how certain freedoms of speech are systematically permitted and particular discourses (re)produced. For example, there was no discussion of the fact that those who contributed to the attack on Thobani were themselves allowed a great deal of freedom to produce extensive anti-feminist, anti-immigrant, and racist rants about such topics as the apparently destructive 'forces of feminism and political correctness' and 'the feminist war against western society'. And, as a generalized critique, it failed to highlight how many enjoyed the freedom to volley a vitriolic barrage of well-worn racist/sexist tropes at Thobani and (implicitly or explicitly) feminists/women of colour. All week, commentators projected onto Thobani a range of classic Orientalist tropes, invoking and revealing the racist and imperialist imagination that fuelled this representational terrain. Most notably, Thobani was variously described as 'poisonous' and 'venom[ous]'; other-worldly (i.e., she was discussed as 'a profoundly, mysteriously, angry woman', 'a strange woman', and 'bereft of human decency'); inherently and dangerously emotional (i.e., 'anger-driven', 'irrational', 'hateful', 'excitable', 'intemperate', 'extreme', and 'delusional'). Many were also accorded the freedom to deploy the currently prevalent racist discourse whereby all (perceived) Arabs and Muslims are targeted as suspected terrorists and religious fundamentalists. Thobani, for example, was described as using 'extremist rhetoric' and 'rhetoric of terrorism', was frequently likened to 'terrorists' and 'fanatics', and was accused of 'hijacking' the women's movement. Critics focusing on the fact of a generalized crackdown on dissent failed to make visible, or to explain the significance of, the gendered and racialized content of the representational terrain being constructed on these terms.

Finally, while a critique of nationalism is certainly implied in this critical mainstream discourse, it nevertheless generally failed to foreground and examine the invocations to nation and national belonging that loomed large in this sustained public/media attack on Thobani. Primarily focusing attention on a critique of organized state and media-based right-wing suppression, a specific analysis of nationalist invocations remained largely implicit. This silence is evident in its general failure to highlight parallels between similar (but not identical) nationally—or racially—motivated sites of exclusionary meaning-making. For example, it did not produce analyses of earlier related attacks on Thobani because these were not motivated by an attempt to explicitly silence her. In 1993, two months prior to her actual acceptance as the President of NAC, Sunera Thobani was subjected to a similar series of attacks by the media and some politicians. At that time, she was labelled an 'illegal immigrant' by a federal Tory MP. While the nuances of the press coverage differed from the current attack, the broad focus and content was strikingly similar. That is, both events invoked the terrain of her contested belonging in the nation as an immigrant, a woman of colour, and a feminist. In both moments, the media became a key site for a broad interrogation of whether Thobani is 'fit' to represent 'Canadian women' and a national feminist organization. The parallels between the two events clearly suggest the importance of bringing the earlier attack into the current analysis. The narrow parameters of this 'freedom of expression' discourse, however, did not require (and usually did not produce) an elaboration of these nationalist expressions.

On the whole then, paying attention to the generalized attack on dissent and/or freedom of speech could have, but generally did not, illuminate the politics of difference at work in this moment, and it has not emphasized important continuities with relevant nationalist moments across space and time. Towards a strengthening of this mainstream critical discourse, the following section outlines how to produce an integral and sustained analysis of the hierarchies and dynamics of difference that were (and are) operating in this broader crackdown on dissent.

Who Is Canadian Now?: An Anti-Racist Feminist Reading of a National Event

In Canada, as in the United States, '[r]ace has become a touchstone.' As David Theo Goldberg argues in

Racial Subjects, 'the idea of race . . . furnishes the terms around and through which a complex of social hopes, fears, anxieties, resentments, aspirations, self-evaluations, and identities gets to be articulated' (1997: 8). For this reason, a complex and critical grammar is required to adequately comprehend how racial and national subjects are invoked in specific historical instances. It must be able to interpret, for example, the strikingly large number of calls to 'we Canadians' and 'our country' that infused the attack on Thobani. A *Toronto Sun* editorial, for example, represented her as outside the nation—a foreigner attacking 'Canada . . . our allies . . . our way of life'. Several letter-writers also chimed in on this note: 'Ms Thobani does not know how good she has it here in this wonderful country of ours, and yet we, as passive Canadians, sit back and say, oh well. . . .' Who (or what) national presence was being invoked (or imagined) in these words of belonging and ownership?

Anti-racist feminism is arguably the best author of the kind of critical language currently available to address these questions. In a recent collection of essays, for example, Himani Bannerji conceptualizes these politics and paradoxes of nation from an anti-racist feminist position. Her work integrally acknowledges how Canada's history of racial-colonial formation (including the policies and ideals of official multiculturalism) is constructed through a deep association between national belonging and whiteness. As she puts it: 'The category "Canadian" clearly applied to people who had two things in common: their white skin and their European North American (not Mexican) background' (2000: 64). Those who do not share these 'things in common', (or who are identified as not being able to lay legitimate claim to them), are located through an 'insider/outsider' status in the nation, an individual and collective experience characterized by 'both belonging and non-belonging simultaneously' (Bannerji, 2000: 65). Anti-racist feminists have consistently revealed that, in Canada (and 'the West'), citizenship is no guarantee of becoming an 'insider' and that immigrant/women of colour, even legal citizens, have been rendered 'permanent outsiders within the Canadian nation' (Gajardo and Macias, 2000: 27; Dua and Robertson, 1999; Sharma, 2000).

This kind of critical language and analysis, which seeks to understand the interrelated border politics of gendered, racial, colonial, and national belonging, is necessary to comprehend the complex of situated meanings operating in this current attack. It helps to reveal that the speech and Thobani's individual and historical presence (as an immigrant-citizen, feminist/woman of colour) on the conference/national stage were clearly marked out by Thobani's critics as transgressing gendered and racialized national boundaries. The aftermath of the event exposed the emerging and intensified political pressure towards narrowing the boundaries of what is currently considered a permissible and legitimate space for both feminist and national politics after September 11. This is evident in the fact that most commentators were quick to contain and stabilize Thobani's personal and political history around significant markers of national and racial belonging. An article in the *National Post*, for example, used the occasion to suggest that there was something particularly suspect about the fact that Thobani 'obtained landed immigrant status in 1993, the same week she was elected president of the [NAC]'. Such statements made visible the historically persistent 'insider/outsider' construction in the national imaginary that can be, and was in this instance, powerfully invoked to displace Thobani's actual 'insider/citizen' location. It also raises questions about the place of feminism in current imaginings of the nation. Despite the lengthy and effective history of an organized anti-racist feminist movement in Canada, does the position of NAC's President continue to draw authority from a particular claim to Canadian identity (i.e., as originating from within the imagined nation and/or 'the West')? Is NAC's founding category, 'Canadian women', still predominantly equated with whiteness? Clearly at stake here was the gendered politics of national-racial exclusion and belonging made visible by reiterations of Thobani's ever-contingent position in the nation, her conditional place of belonging in the Canadian imaginary, and the fragility of her claim to represent

Canada and Canadian women. An anti-racist feminist reading of the attack is needed, then, to reveal and challenge the operations of the long historical gender and racial exclusions in this call for a current narrowing of borders around 'insider/outsider' status in the nation.

Towards such an analysis, the remainder of this section delves into an interrogation of what Eva Mackey calls the 'unmarked, yet dominant, Anglo Canadian core' that inhabits the centre of national invocations, and which is certainly circulating in this entire event (1999: 2). This focus draws attention to the naturalized subject of the insider/outsider presence within the nation: specifically, the historical presence of those white Canadians who secure this position through identifying with dominant constructions of an imagined national community, commonly invoking 'our' and 'we' to claim an otherwise unmarked insider place in Canada's 'racial geography' (Walcott, 1997: 36). In perhaps the most explicit comment of this kind, one columnist went so far as to claim that Thobani's presence made her 'feel a stranger in my own land'. It is difficult to know whether she was expressing fear, resentment, anxiety or all-of-the-above. Regardless, such an utterance reveals her comfort, her sense of entitlement, in claiming uncontested ownership rights to Canada as 'my own land'. This persistent (but always contested) historical pairing of national and racial codes of identity (e.g., Canadian = white, immigrant = non-white) continues to allow whiteness to operate as a marker for securely claiming insider belongingness and identity in the national imaginary. Given the prevalence of such invocations displayed in the media attack, it seems crucial to consider this event as a specific enactment of what Eva Mackey has called a 'broader trend of white backlash against the gains made by minorities in Western nations' (1999: 141). While Mackey's book examines a slightly different national 'crisis' of almost a decade ago, her analysis of white backlash remains instructive for comprehending this current round of national reckoning.

First, as her interviews with some white Canadians revealed, white backlash is 'not framed as an overt defence of *whiteness*, but rather . . . as a defence of national identity and unity' (Mackey 1999, 142—italics in original). The parallels to the current attack on Thobani are striking and disturbing. I have already highlighted some of the ways that racist and Orientalist discourses have constructed Thobani as a threat to 'Canadian values'. The frequently-invoked national 'we' was used to position Thobani as a foreigner and outsider. Moreover, the racist construction of Thobani as a 'terrorist' that underlies the national security discourse renders her a distinct threat to Canada. As discussed above, these kinds of invocations simultaneously reference and index a racialized construction of the nation in which a defence of whiteness is always at the (unmarked) centre. This current episode of hysteria over national security, principally targeting racialized citizens, is a telling reminder that whiteness need not speak its name to be effective.

Second, Mackey has noted that, in periods of such backlash, 'liberal discourses of equality, rationality, tolerance, and progress are used to make intolerance and hierarchy *logical and rational*' (1999: 142—italics in original). After September 11, intolerance, and a backlash against insider/outsiders, is becoming explicitly permissible if it is invoked in defence of 'western democracy' (a construct which is often made interchangeable with 'American values'). Indeed, the attack on Thobani was entirely premised on, and justified through, the idea that 'western democracy', and therefore freedom and equality, are under attack by outsiders. As such, it is not surprising that some of these invocations carried an explicit threat (desire?) for Thobani's expulsion from 'the West', as in the following excerpts from letters:

> 'Canada is a democracy . . . maybe she would prefer to live elsewhere in a nondemocratic state such as Afghanistan.' (*National Post*)

> 'If she did not live in a country blessed with the values and morals championed by the US, she would be imprisoned, tortured and perhaps killed for saying such things.' (*Globe and Mail*)

> 'Women and men the world over should be thankful for Western civilization, . . . It is also Western Civilization that gave Ms Thobani a new home and the right to criticize.' (*National Post*)

Such comments demonstrate Mackey's point while also revealing the operation of Eurocentric discourse, a terrain of fantasy and mythology of 'the West' which (re)produces a 'fictitious sense of the innate superiority of European-derived cultures and peoples' (Shohat and Stam, 1994: 1). The comments themselves demonstrate the absurdly contradictory, irrational, and perverse logic of exclusion at work. Each of these expressions hails Canada as the height of 'Western civilization' and 'democracy' and 'freedom' at the same time that it carries within it an utterly anti-democratic and brutal call for the suppression of a citizen's right to express a fully rational critique of the nation-state in a public forum.

On this point, it is also useful to pay attention to the attack on Hedy Fry, the state official in attendance at the conference. She was severely chastised by both opposition leaders and in the press (and eventually lost her ministerial post). Many called for her resignation for the (apparently criminal) act of 'sitting silent' on the national stage during Thobani's speech. One letter-writer reprimanded Fry through an appeal to liberal values, making calls for Fry's dismissal seem rational on the basis that she 'didn't even bother to stand up and defend this wonderful nation with our rights and freedoms'. Despite Fry's deplorable attempt to distance herself publicly from Thobani immediately after the speech, it is important to recognize that she was nevertheless disciplined for failing to do her job according to the post-September 11 consensus of 'national security'. As one letter-writer put it, she 'did nothing to protest Ms Thobani's hateful slurs on our American neighbours,' and, post-September 11, this seems to be justification enough to replace her in cabinet.

The different attacks on Thobani and Fry illustrate Mackey's third point that white backlash is 'used to rationalize the desire for a more overtly exclusionary national identity' (1999: 142). Perhaps the most disturbing manifestation of this desire emerged in letters and editorials suggesting that Thobani be expelled from the nation. One writer, for example, suggested that '. . . perhaps Sunera Thobani would like a tour of Afghanistan, led by a pro-Taliban ambassador'. And two other letter-writers suggested that she 'return to whence she emigrated' and that she 'go back'. One even suggested that 'Canadian taxpayers' would be happy to provide 'some additional funding to get her to the country of her choice'. It is difficult to read such utterances as innocent suggestions, and they appear much more as either a thinly disguised threat, or a punishment for stepping outside her place as silent other of the national/western democracy. At the same time, Hedy Fry was reprimanded for failing to adequately cater to this desire for exclusion. While I certainly do not see Fry as a victim of the backlash, I think it is crucial to note how the white backlash exerted its influence even on agents of the state. Clearly, Fry was being disciplined, as Canada's 'Multiculturalism Minister', for failing to contain and control the unruly multicultural 'Others' on the national stage, for failing to secure the national borders from the insider/outsiders. A *Vancouver Sun* Editorial succinctly illustrates this sentiment in the following way: 'If this woman [i.e., Hedy Fry] can't speak up in a forceful and timely way for her government and her country, then it's time for her to go.' Clearly, both the cases of Thobani and Fry reveal that a desire for a more exclusionary national identity is at work in this current context.

In this moment, when the national security discourse is taking on a disproportionate and alarming significance, anti-racist feminist analysis of nation and nationalism is urgently needed to make sense of these media and political attacks and the hierarchies of difference that sustain them. While it is clear that there was no singular 'Canadian feminist' response to the attack on Thobani, the strongest responses did nevertheless come from within the organized women's movement and feminist communities.

The following section examines several different feminist responses as a means to highlight, and reflect strategically upon, how multiple feminisms concretely struggle to define the broad and multi-faceted women's movement.

Feminism in Canada After September 11

Feminists across the country responded quickly in the immediate aftermath, many expressing support for Thobani and bearing witness to the attack. As is appropriate for 'the largest feminist organization in the country', NAC promptly issued a press release denouncing 'recent media reports unfairly targeting women and racialized people following comments by Sunera Thobani'. Although feminist responses contributed to ongoing public analysis through the circulation of press releases and statements on e-mail and the web, most were denied access to the mainstream media (Croft, 2002: 8). Broadly speaking, three (sometimes overlapping) streams of critical response emerged from a diverse range of feminist supporters.[5]

First, the most complex critical analysis came from within feminist communities articulating an anti-racist analysis. The Battered Women's Support Services in Vancouver, for example, questioned 'whether Sunera Thobani's speech would be making headlines . . . was she not a feminist immigrant of colour', and called particular attention to the media's pronounced racist 'anti-immigrant sentiment'. 'Women's Studies professors, staff, and racialized feminist academics' in the Department of Women's Studies at the University of Victoria wrote a joint public letter stating their absolute support for Thobani while also providing a thorough analysis of 'how racism, sexism and hegemonic nationalism work to shape "reality"' in moments like this one. Feminist *Toronto Star* columnist Michele Landsberg's article focused on 'Unmasking Bigotry Behind the Hysteria' (Landsberg, 2001). These kinds of interpretations emerged from, and remain a testament to, the substantial (albeit increasingly fragmented) presence of organized political communities in Canada whose analyses are grounded in feminist and anti-racist politics of difference.

A second broad-based strand of feminist support emerged around the call to protect freedoms of speech (including academic freedom) and the right to dissent freely. This was a prominent theme on PAR-L, an extensive and active Canadian-based feminist e-mail discussion list that encompasses a range of feminist perspectives. For almost three weeks following the attack, this issue was addressed on the list by individual feminists, national organizations (e.g., NAC and Canadian Federation of Students), local or regional feminist organizations/groups, and feminist journalists. This stream characteristically (and importantly) highlighted the vilification and demonization of Thobani. It also provided a useful site for activism through the circulation of petitions. However, as feminists at University of Victoria rightly noted, and as I have elaborated in this paper, it tended not to emphasize and integrate the gendered, racialized, and national foundations at work in the vilifying impetus. Certainly, given the support this position enjoys amongst many feminists, there is room here for further strategic discussion of how to build a stronger feminist position around the very important issue of intensified curtailments on freedom of speech/dissent. Thobani herself, in her first public speaking appearance after the initial speech, suggests the potency of a position that understands the recent media events as an attack on *both* 'the anti-racist women's movement' *and* the 'freedom of dissent'. My analysis in this paper supports this strategy and suggests some avenues for elaboration.

A third critical strand emerged in the context of, and was articulated through, the burgeoning post-September 11 anti-war movement. In fact, Thobani's initial speech, and her subsequent public response to the attack articulated in an essay titled 'War Frenzy', clearly advanced a strong feminist anti-war position. As some have noted, however, much of the post-September 11 activism within the broader left anti-war movement (in which feminists were active) has not adequately addressed or integrated questions of gender or the specificity of the current 'war on terrorism' for women (Wright, 2002). Given these fissures and gaps in organizing across broad-based movements, it seems important to reflect on strategies for combining these activist efforts more thoroughly and for building links between overlapping movements. And finally, as a recent essay on the topic so clearly indicates, it is always necessary to develop critical anti-racist analyses for debating the distinct, and sometimes conflicting, feminist positions articulated and being advanced in anti-war activism and peace coalitions (Arat-Koç, 2002).

The broader tenor of this critical response from within feminist communities also produced some notable silences and fractures. If Judy Rebick is correct in her assessment that the attack on Thobani was possible partly because of 'the isolation of an already seriously weakened women's movement', then it is crucial to acknowledge and seek to grasp the complicated dynamics contributing to this isolation. Much of this isolation, of course, is attributable to the past several years backlash against feminism and social movements generally, including severe cuts to social spending and funding for women's organizations over the past decade. Nevertheless, the following discussion suggests points for further reflection upon weaknesses currently apparent in feminist political organizing in Canada.

It seems useful, and necessary, to begin with a deeper analysis of NAC's response to the attack on Thobani. NAC is to be credited for taking the lead in articulating and circulating a quick response, and for representing the organization through a definitive anti-racist position. Nevertheless, it also needs to be recognized that NAC staked out a decidedly moderate position, allowing it to respond to the criticism of Thobani without mobilizing around a strong position on the substance of Thobani's speech. Instead, NAC focused primarily on defending 'her democratic right to free speech' and identifying the 'suppression of dissent' as a particular problem. NAC's decision to remove itself from the debate on the substance of Thobani's speech is reflected in both the content of its statement, and in its choice of activism: i.e., to launch a website campaign against 'media targeting of NAC this past week' (NAC, 2001). On the whole, the statement was organized primarily as a defense of NAC itself (from media attacks), and it is on this basis that it enjoined women to engage the issue. In terms of content, the actual Press Release sidestepped a specific analysis of the substantive issues raised by Sunera Thobani in her speech. How might NAC have taken a stronger political lead to act in coalition to define and sustain a formidable feminist public discourse in this moment? What questions does its response raise about its current (and future) effectiveness and ability to carry on the legacy of anti-racist struggles at redefining NAC? What does it suggest about internal conflicts within the umbrella organization? NAC's response indicates the need for broadening the discussion, amongst feminist communities, about the political direction of the movement's largest national organization.

And finally, it is important to note also that there was not unanimous support for Thobani within feminist communities. While most felt it was legitimate to rally in defence of her right to dissent, some also focused blame on the content of the speech itself (or, in Thobani's style of presentation). An extensive discussion on this nature ensued on the PAR-L e-mail list, and some of the invocations warrant further critical discussion. Particularly, this line of discussion often failed to attend to the relevance of the political and social climate that cultivated the attack, focusing instead on a singular and decontextualized analysis of the meaning of her words. In a context where new lines of legitimacy are being drawn in terms of national, racial and gendered belonging, such arguments must always be contextualized within an examination of how the attack is one example of how space of legitimate claims to represent Canada and women in Canada is being further disciplined and narrowed.

Notes

A very special thanks to Cynthia Wright, Kasia Rukszto, and Amanda Glasbeek for critical intellectual contributions and encouragements when I needed it most. Thanks also to Steven Tufts for much support and technical assistance. I also want to acknowledge funding from CUPE Local 3908 at Trent University, without which I could not have presented an earlier draft of this paper for discussion at the fabulous Open the Borders! Conference in Vancouver in March 2002.

1. See *Fuse Magazine's Special Issue: War?* (February 2001). This excellent collection forcefully records the post-September 11 content of racial-national and political profiling as it happened in Canadian contexts for 'citizens, immigrants, visitors of colour and any people who dared to differ or publicly dissent' (Mootoo, 2002: 14–15). It also documents some aspects of the emergent anti-war movements within which Thobani's speech/activism is located.
2. All of the media remarks cited throughout this paper were published between 2 October and 7 October 2001 in six English-language newspapers, including three national daily newspapers (*Globe and Mail, National Post, Toronto Star*) and three major dailies (*Ottawa Citizen, Toronto Sun, Vancouver Sun*). I am not French-speaking, so was not able to include any francophone coverage in my analysis.
3. 'National security' is a hearty nationalist trope. It has long-standing resonance in the Canadian national imaginary, and is a recurring theme in the ongoing construction and regulation of 'proper Canadian subjects' (see Kinsman et al., 2003: 3).
4. Bill C-36, the Canadian government's post-September 11 Anti-Terrorism Act (indeed, its 'national security' legislation) is the most obvious act of state violence that marks this current rise of nationalist exclusion. As cultural critic Nuzhat Abbas notes, the bill was initiated specifically as a mechanism for 'obsessive surveillance', a device legitimating racial profiling which targets 'those who look Arab, bear Muslim names, those whose citizenship might be suspect' (2002: 20). To place this recent construction in the broader context of the rise of anti-immigrant discourses and legislation in the 1990s see Thobani (2000) and Wright (2000).
5. Most of the statements and responses discussed in this section are available in the PAR-L online archive.

References

Abbas, Nuzhat. '21st Ramadhan, 1422–8th December 2001', *Fuse Magazine* 25.1 (2002): 17–21.

Arat-Koç, Sedef. 'Imperial Wars or Benevolent Interventions? Reflections on "Global Feminism" Post September 11', *Atlantis* 26.2 (2002): 53–65.

Bannerji, Himani. 2000. *The Dark Side of the Nation: Essays on Multiculturalism, Nationalism and Gender.* Toronto: Canadian Scholars' Press.

Black Radical Congress. 2001. 'Letter to Representative Barbara Lee', on BRC-NEWS, 28 September.

Croft, Stephanie. 'Thobani Speech Prompts Outpouring of Support', *Herizons* 15.3 (2002): 6–7.

Das Gupta, Tania, and Franca Iacovetta. 'Whose Canada Is It? Immigrant Women, Women of Colour and Feminist Critiques of "Multiculturalism"', *Atlantis* 24.2 (2000): 1–4.

Dua, Enakshi, and Angela Robertson, eds. 1999. *Scratching the Surface: Canadian Anti-Racist Feminist Thought.* Toronto: Women's Press.

Gajardo, Lorena M., and Teresa Macias. 'From Terrorists to Outlaws: Transnational and Peripheral Articulations in the Making of Nation and Empire', *Atlantis* 24.2 (2000): 27–37.

Goldberg, David Theo. 1997. *Racial Subjects: Writing on Race in America.* New York: Routledge.

Herizons, 15: 3 (2002): Front cover (headline).

Kinsman, Gary, Dieter K. Buse, and Mercedes Steedman, eds. 2000. *Whose National Security? Canadian State Surveillance and the Creation of Enemies.* Toronto: Between the Lines.

Landsberg, Michele. 'Unmasking the Bigotry Behind the Hysteria', *Toronto Star*, 14 October 2001: www.thestar.com/columnists/landsberg.

Mackey, Eva. 1999. *The House of Difference: Cultural Politics and National Identity in Canada.* New York: Routledge.

Mootoo, Shani. 'Initial impact . . . an immediate response', *Fuse Magazine* 25.1 (2002): 14–16.

NAC Press Release. 2001. 'NAC Upholds Peaceful Solutions to All Forms of Violence', October 2: http://www.nac-cca.ca.

Sharma, Nandita Rani. 'Race, Class, Gender and the Making of Difference: The Social Organization of "Migrant Workers" in Canada', *Atlantis* 24.2 (2000): 5–15.

Shohat, Ella, and Robert Stam. 1994. *Unthinking Eurocentrism: Multiculturalism and the Media.* London: Routledge.

Thobani, Sunera. 'Closing the Nation's Doors to Immigrant Women: The Restructuring of Canadian Immigration Policy', *Atlantis* 24.2 (2000): 16–26.

Walcott, Rinaldo. 1997. *Black Like Who? Writing Black Canada.* Toronto: Insomniac Press.

Wright, Cynthia 'Nowhere at Home: Gender, Race and the Making of Anti-Immigrant Discourse in Canada', *Atlantis* 24.2 (2000): 38–48.

———. Interview with Tariq Ali, 'The Wars: Tariq Ali on building anti-war movements, debating the "civilization mongers" and narrating the history of Islam', *Fuse Magazine* 25.1 (2002): 28–40.

Contributors

Sedef Arat-Koç has taught in the Women's Studies Program at Trent University in Peterborough, Ontario and is currently a member of the department of Politics and Public Administration at Ryerson University in Toronto. Her writing has mostly focused on women, immigration, and citizenship. Her latest book, *Caregivers Break the Silence* (2001) explores the impact of policy on the live-in caregiver program in Canada. Arat-Koç's recent research is on racism in Canada in the post 9/11 context, and 'whiteness' in Turkey, in relation to globalization, neoliberalism, and imperialism.

Denyse Baillargeon is a professor of History at the Université de Montréal. She has published numerous articles on women's and family history and is the author of *Ménagères au temps de la crise* (Remue-ménage, 1991 and 1993), translated as *Making Do: Women, Family and Home in Montreal during the Great Depression* (Wilfrid Laurier University Press, 1999) and of *Un Québec en mal d'enfants: La médicalisation de la maternité, 1910–1970* (Remue-ménage, 2004). She is currently working on a history of the Sainte-Justine Hospital for Children, and on the dissemination of new psychological theories in Quebec after the Second World War.

Rusty Bitterman is a member of the History Department at St Thomas University in Fredericton, New Brunswick. His research interests concern land struggles, social movements, and environmental history.

Bettina Bradbury is a member of History and Women's Studies departments at York University. She is a feminist family historian and her past work was on working-class families. She is currently researching issues of marriage, widowhood, and inheritance in the law and politics of nineteenth century white settler societies. This article draws from her manuscript entitled 'Wife to Widow—Lives, Laws and Politics in Nineteenth Century Montreal.'

Josette Brun is an assistant professor at the département d'Information et de Communication of the Université Laval, where she teaches media history and a seminar on gender and the media. Her forthcoming book, *Vie et mort du couple en Nouvelle-France: Québec et Louisbourg au 18e siècle* (McGill-Queen's University Press) is based on her doctoral thesis 'Le veuvage en Nouvelle-France: dynamique familiale et stratégies de survie dans deux villes coloniales du 18e siècle, Québec et Louisbourg' (Université de Montréal, 2000).

Sheila L. Cavanagh, an assistant professor in the School of Social Sciences at York University, specializes in gender and sexuality studies. She has a book in progress tentatively titled: *Sexing the Teacher: School Sex Scandals and Queer Pedagogies of Female Desire*.

Patrick J. Connor teaches in the departments of History and Criminology at York University in Toronto. His current work focuses on crime and the royal pardon in Upper Canada, 1790–1840.

Elise Chenier is an assistant professor in the department of History at Simon Fraser University where she teaches courses on gender, sexuality, and the family. She has published work on the history of postwar lesbian bar culture and the medicalization and treatment of sexual deviancy. Currently she is researching the history of the debutante ball in Canada.

Donald F. Davis, a professor of History at the University of Ottawa and author of *Conspicuous Production: Automobiles and Elites in Detroit*, is currently researching the privatization of the car culture in Canada.

Maureen Elgersman Lee is an associate professor of History and the faculty scholar for the African American Collection of Maine at the University of Southern Maine. Her research interests are Black women's history and Black community history. She is the author of *Unyielding Spirits: Black Women and Slavery in Early Canada and Jamaica* (1999) and *Black Bangor: African Americans in a Maine Community, 1880–1950* (2005).

Marlene Epp is an associate professor of History and Peace & Conflict Studies at Conrad Grebel University College, University of Waterloo, Ontario. She is the author of *Women without Men: Mennonite Refugees of the Second World War* (2000) and the co-editor of *Sisters or Strangers? Immigrant, Ethnic, and Racialized Women in Canadian History* (2004).

Janice Fiamengo teaches Canadian literature at the University of Ottawa. She is currently writing a monograph on the strategies of rhetoric and self-presentation of early Canadian woman journalists, essayists, reformers, and activists.

Jo-Anne Fiske is currently a professor and coordinator of Women's Studies at the University of Lethbridge, where she also holds an associate membership in anthropology. She has conducted extensive research with First Nations women of Central British Columbia and is the author of *Dideen Kat: When the Plumes Rise, the Way of the Lake Babine Nation*. Her current work addresses the social and political ramifications of federal Indian policies on education, health, and community membership for First Nations women.

Glynis George is an assistant professor in the department of Sociology and Anthropology at the University of Windsor. Her work has included research in India on gender, feminism, and community-based activism. Most recently, she has returned to her interest in the impact of neo-liberal governing on activism in the province of Newfoundland and in the national context.

Mona Gleason is an associate professor in the department of Educational Studies at the University of British Columbia and the author of *Normalizing the Ideal: Psychology, Schooling and Family in Postwar Canada* (1999). She teaches and researches in the history of children and childhood, education, gender, and the body. She is currently working on a manuscript tentatively titled *Small Matters: Children in Sickness and Health in English Canada, 1900–1960*.

Margaret Hillyard Little is an anti-poverty activist and academic who works in the area of single mothers on welfare, welfare/workfare reform, and retraining for women on welfare. She teaches in the departments of Women's Studies and Political Studies at Queen's University and is the author of *No Car, No Radio, No Liquor Permit: The Moral Regulation of Single Mothers in Ontario, 1920–1997* (1998) which won the 1998 Chalmers Book Award.

Franca Iacovetta is a professor of history at the University of Toronto and co-editor of *Studies in Gender and History* at University of Toronto Press. Her recent books include *Sisters or Strangers? Immigrant, Ethnic and Racialized Women in Canadian History*, co-edited with Marlene Epp and Frances Swyripa, 2004 (University of Toronto Press) and *Gatekeepers: Reshaping Refugee and Immigrant Lives in Cold War Canada* (Between the Lines, forthcoming).

Patricia Jasen teaches history at Lakehead University in Thunder Bay, Ontario. Her publications include the award-winning book *Wild Things: Nature, Culture and Tourism in Ontario, 1790–1914* (1995). Her current research in medical history focuses on women, cancer, and historical perspectives on the concept of risk.

Jane Jenson was named a member of the Successful Societies programme of the Canadian Institute for Advanced Research in 2004 and a Fellow of the Trudeau Foundation in 2005. A Fellow of the Royal Society of Canada, she was awarded the Canada Research Chair in Citizenship and Governance in 2001 at the Université de Montréal, where she is now a professor of Political Science. Her current research interests and publications include social policy, social movements, the relationship between Quebec and the rest of Canada, citizenship, diversity, and gender studies.

Barbara Lorenzkowski, a research assistant professor at Concordia University in Montreal, Quebec, has published several articles on the history of ethnicity and modernity, community and nation. Her new research project explores the cultural exchanges on the public platforms of Canadian and Newfoundland railways during the years of the Second World War.

Lynne Marks teaches Canadian history at the University of Victoria. She has published *Revivals and Roller Rinks: Religion, Leisure and Identity in Late Nineteenth-Century-Small-Town Ontario* (University of Toronto Press, 1996), as well as various articles on gender/women's history and the social history of religion. She is currently working on a project on irreligion in late nineteenth and early twentieth century British Columbia.

Mary Jo Nadeau works as a contract lecturer in Sociology, Women's Studies, and Labour Studies at several Ontario universities, including York, Trent, Wilfrid Laurier, and McMaster. Her research interests include the history of social movements organizations, whiteness and national identity, racism and anti-racism in the Canadian women's movement, and the politics of nationalism in Canada. She has recently completed her dissertation, 'The Making and Unmaking of a New Parliament of Women: Nation, Race and the Politics of the National Action Committee on the Status of Women, 1972–1992' in Sociology at York University.

Brenda O'Neill is an associate professor of Political Science at the University of Calgary. Dr O'Neill's research focuses on Canadian political behaviour, specifically the political opinions and voting behaviour of Canadian women and youth.

Adele Perry teaches and is Canada Research Chair in Western Canadian History at the University of Manitoba. Her new research examines the relationship between gender, kin, migration, and colonialism over the nineteenth-century.

Nancy Shoemaker, a professor of History at the University of Connecticut, is the author of *American Indian Population Recovery in the Twentieth Century* (1999) and *A Strange Likeness: Becoming Red and White in Eighteenth-Century North America* (2004). Her current research focuses on New England Indians and the American whaling industry.

Pamela Sugiman is an associate professor of Sociology at McMaster University. She has an ongoing research interest in the social history of working-class women in Canada, with a focus on Japanese Canadian women during the Second World War. She is currently writing about the relationship between official history and personal memory, the inter-generational transmission of memory, and memory as a gendered and racialized concept.

Sylvia Van Kirk has retired from the University of Toronto. She is continuing work on the history of fur trade families in Victoria, British Columbia.

Index

Aboriginal peoples: attitudes to, 372; Carrier, 210–22; childbirth and, 323–33; child care and, 357; Christianity and, 10–25; domestic workers, 205; gender roles among, 212–17; health of, 327–8, 329–31; Huron, 10, 12, 117; infant mortality and, 330–1; Iroquois, 10–25; marriage to non-Aboriginals and, 115–23; Mi'kmaq, 205; Mohawk, 14; Montagnais, 12–13; slavery and, 198; social organization and political action by, 213; Tsimshian, 11; violence and, 338; white feminists and, 148–52, 153–4; women, 2, 3, 4–5; women's leadership among, 210–22
Aboriginal Women's Action Network, 116
abortion, 375
abuse, sexual, 338–9; *see also* violence
activism: in Newfoundland and Labrador, 336–42
Act of 1790, 51–2
Alberta: mothers' pensions in, 172
Anderson, Elias, 108
Anderson, Karen, 10, 12
Anderson, Kay, 147
Anderson, Lauren, 3
Angélique, Marie Joseph, 45, 52
anti-Americanism, 384–5
anti-feminism, 366, 385, 387
anti-war movement, 391–2
Appiah, Kwame Anthony, 147
Armstrong, David, 329
Arneil, Barbara, 368
Arnold, Marybeth, 101, 105
assault, sexual, 3; *see also* violence
assistance, mutual: in New France, 29–37
Assisted Passage Loan Scheme, 204
Association Féminine d'Éducation et d'Action Sociale (AFEAS), 352
atheism, 133
Auditor General, 359–60
Axelrod, Paul, 278

Bacchi, Carol Lee, 144–5
Backhouse, Constance, 100, 104, 159
backlash: anti-feminist, 368, 377; white, 389–90
Bagg, Stanley, 76, 78, 80–1, 87
Bagot Commission, 120
balhats, 217
Bancroft, Hubert Howe, 122
Bannerji, Himani, 388
Baptist Religious Intelligencer, 135
Bâtir le Quebec, 352
Battered Women's Support Services, 391
Beattie, John, 100
Begas, Marie-Anne, 34
Beijing Conference, 336
Beijing Declaration, 1
Bell, Robert, 328
Bell, Rudolph, 21
Benjamin, Walter, 259
Bergland, Betty, 290
Berube, Christiane, 352
Beynon, Francis Marion, 381
Bhabha, Homi, 147
Bills, Ann, 100
birth rate: in Quebec, 352
Black, Naomi, 368
black people: slavery and, 198; as domestic workers, 205
Blanchard, David, 22
Blount, Jackie, 285
body, soul, power: Aboriginal and Christian view of, 18, 20, 21–2
Bohstedt, John, 70
Boily, Nicole, 352
Boisselle, Jeanne, 32
Bouchard, Camil, 354–5
Bouchard, Lucien, 348
Boucherville, Charles, 36
Boychuk, Gérard, 348
Brand, Dionne, 198
Brant, Joseph, 52, 149–50
Britain: domestic workers from, 199–201; slavery in, 50
British Columbia: church periodicals in, 127, 132–3, 137; intermarriage in, 121; Japanese Canadians in, 245–6; mothers' pensions in, 163–75; women in, 2
Brouwer, Ruth Compton, 124, 365
Brown, Euphemia, 104, 105, 106–7
Brown, Jennifer S.H., 115
Brown, Rosemary, 46, 195
Bryce, Peter, 169, 330
budgets, family, 185–8
Bullock, Mary Ann, 98, 109
Bultan, Margaret Ann, 101
Burgess, Frances, 103
Burns, George, 110
Bynum, Caroline Walker, 21

Cable Public Affairs Channel (CPAC), 385
Campbell, Sara, 83, 91
Canada Assistance Plan, 350
Canadian Churchman, 127, 134, 135
Canadian Committee on Women's History (CCWH), 4
Canadian Election Study (CES), 370–8
Canadian Epworth Era, 132
Canadian Forces: women in, 381
Canadian Suffrage Association, 158
Caprio, Frank, 313
Card, Ethan, 108
Caribbean Domestic Scheme, 46
Caribbean: domestic workers from, 205–6
Carrier people, 210–23; cosmology of, 221; men's view of women's leadership, 218–19; mothering and political power, 219–22; traditions of, 213–14; women's leadership among, 210–22
Carter, Sarah, 121
Cartier, Jeanne Elisabeth, 33–4
Cary, Mary Ann Shadd, 46
Castonguay-Nepveu Commission, 350
Catholic Church: Carrier people and, 215; family and, 126–37; Great Depression and, 188–90; in New France, 12, 29–37; in Quebec, 349; *see also* Christianity; religion
Catholic Register, 128–9, 130, 131, 134, 136
celibacy: women teachers and, 281, 285
centre local des services communautaires (CLSC), 351
Chamberlain, Line, 301, 302
Champagne-Gilbert, Maurice, 353
Champlain, Samuel de, 118
Charest, Jean, 359
Charter of Rights and Freedoms, 116, 377
Chatelaine, 265, 269–70
Chauchetière, Claude, 14–17, 19–20
Child and Family Tax Benefit, 164
childbirth: Aboriginal women and, 323–33; 'painless', 323–4, 325, 328, 329
child care: equity issue, 344; immigrants and, 274; poverty issue, 344; private, 350, 360; public, 349; Quebec, 344–61; spaces, 359; universal, 346–7; workers in, 358–9
children: immigrant, 271–5; as indentured workers, 201; Indian status and, 116, 120; orphaned in New France, 29–37; rape of, 101–2, 105; violence against, 3, 337–8, 339, 340–2
Chinese Immigration Act, 199
Chisholm, John, 313–14
Cholenec, Pierre, 14–15
Christianity: Aboriginal peoples and, 10–25; early feminism and, 148, 150–3; family and, 126–37; 'manly', 134; race and, 147; *see also* Catholic Church; religion
Christie, Nancy, 164
church: attendance at, 130
citizenship: domestic workers and, 196, 197, 206, 207–8; 'masculine', 83; women in Great Depression and, 182, 191
Civilian Mothers' Pension Association, 174
clan leadership, 217–19

Clark, Anna, 101, 102, 105, 107, 111
Clarkson, Adrienne, 386
class: domestic workers and, 196, 200; lesbian bar culture and, 301–18; mothers' pensions and, 164, 168
Cleverdon, Catherine, 144
Cold War: immigration during, 264–76
Cole, Henry, 108, 109
colonialism: Carrier people and, 210–11, 214–16; childbirth and, 327–9, 332–3; welfare, 213, 216–17
Comaroff, John, 147
Conat, Abel, 103
Confédération des Syndicats Nationaux, 350
Congress of Black Women, 46
Connolly, William, 119
Conrad, Margaret, 74
Conseil de la Famille, 352
Conseil du Statut de la Femme, 352, 356
Conseil Supérieur de l'Éducation, 354
contraception, 189–90
Cooley, Chloe, 45, 51–2
Cooper, Carol, 11
Cooper, William, 63
Copp, Terry, 179, 181
corruption, political: in Toronto, 314
Cotton, Michel, 35
Coulter, Rebecca, 279
court cases: intermarriage and, 119, 121–2
critical race theory, 147
Custom of Paris (*coutume de Paris*), 73, 77
Cuvillier, Austin, 84–5, 88
cyberspace, 369

Daenzer, Patricia, 203
Dandurand, Renée, 352–3
Darwinism: race and, 147
David, François, 354
Davies, Megan, 166
day nurseries, 344
death: rates of, 27–8
Debonville, Mathurin Palin, 36
Delancy v. Wooden, 55
Delauney, Madeleine, 32
D'Emilio, John, 305
Denison, Flora MacDonald, 145, 158, 381, 382
dependent people: violence against, 337–8, 339, 340–2
Depression; *see* Great Depression
Desmond, Viola, 46
Devens, Carol, 10, 12
Dick, Nancy, 109, 111
discrimination: attitudes to, 375
'dispersal', 246, 251–3
displaced persons (DP), 203, 296
dissent: crackdown on, 386–7
diversity: attitudes to, 376, 377
dogiques, 18–19, 20
'domestic containment', 266–7
domestic workers: assisted passage and, 201, 204; Barbados, 205, 206; British, 199–201; Caribbean, 205–6; central and eastern European, 202–3; Finnish, 202; Greek, 204; Guadeloupe, 205; Irish, 198; Italian, 204; Jamaican, 205; Japanese Canadian, 251; Philippines, 207; race/ethnicity and, 195–208; Russian Mennonite, 202; Scandinavian, 201–2; southern European, 203–4; Spanish, 204; status of, 206, 207–8; white women as, 199–204; women of colour as, 204–6
Dominion Women's Enfranchisement League, 144
'double life, the', 304
Douville, Francoise, 36
drugs, illegal, 314–15
Dubinsky, Karen, 95, 102
Dumont, Micheline, 26, 344–5
Duncan, Sara Jeanette, 145, 147–50

early childhood centres (ECEs), 351, 357, 358
Edmonton: urban transit in, 228–9, 231
education, 1, 2; history of, 278–9
Educational Courier, 281, 284, 285
Education Digest, 284
employment: butch women and, 305–6; child care and, 344–5; as domestic workers, 195–208; in urban transit, 226–7, 232–8
engagés, 198
Epworth League, 132
equal rights: attitudes to, 376
Equay-wuk Women's Group, 332
escheat movement, 61–70
Estates-General of Education, 354
ethnicity: domestic workers and, 195–208; *see also* race
eugenics, 168
evacuation, medical: childbirth and, 331–2
Everitt, Joanna, 369–70
exile, 'forced', 246

Faderman, Elizabeth, 282, 283
Fahrni, Magda, 195
Fair Accommodations Act, 313
family allowance, 345, 355–6; targeted, 346–7; types of, 353
family: 'Christian', 124–37; 'ideal Christian', 127–31; nuclear, 127; patriarchal, 210; prayer and, 130, 135–6; widows, widowers, orphans and, 29–37
Family Life project, 274–5
family movement, 351, 360–1
family policy, Quebec, 344–61; critics of, 359–60
'family values', 376
fasting, 21
fathers, Christian, 129–30
Fausto-Sterling, Anne, 323
Fédération des femmes du Québec (FFQ), 350, 352, 354
Federation of Women Teachers' Associations of Ontario (FWTAO), 281, 282–3
feminism: anti-racist, 387–91; attitudes to, 370–8; 'death of', 3; first wave, 144–59, 367, 368; generational differences in, 366–78; grassroots, 336–7, 338, 340–2; history of, 365–78; identity with, 368, 377; Newfoundland and Labrador, 336–42; Quebec, 352; second wave, 367, 368–77; after September 11, 391–2; third wave, 367, 368–77; waves of, 365–6, 367–70
'femocrats', 338, 341
Ferguson, Edith, 273
Field, Eliza, 120–1
Fitzpatrick, Patrick, 98, 103, 109
Flynn, Karen, 46
food: Canadian, 269–70, 275–6; immigrants and, 264–76; Italian, 270, 271; Portuguese, 271
Foster, Anna, 81–1, 83
Fournier, Pierre, 354
freedom of speech, 386–7
free thought, 133
French, Doris, 282, 283
French, Richard, 352
Friedan, Betty, 368
Friendly Aid Society, 167
Fruella, Liza, 1
Fry, Hedy, 390
fur trade: Carrier people and, 214–15; intermarriage and, 115–16, 117–18, 119–20, 122

Gabaccia, Dona, 270
Gandeacteua, Catherine, 13–14, 15–16
garderies, 350, 357
Gardiner, Fred, 314
Gaurd, Julie, 366
Gautier, Catherine, 36
gays: attitudes to, 371, 372, 374; 'gay life, the', 304
Gérin Lajoie, Marie, 115
Gerson, Carole, 323
Giles, Judy, 258
globalization, 336, 347
Globe and Mail, 386
Goldberg, David Theo, 147, 387–8
Gorham, Deborah, 158
Gosselin, Louis, 35
government: restructuring and, 338; women in, 1–2; *see also* state; specific jurisdictions
Graham, Andrew, 326
Grant, Maria, 170
Great Depression: domestic workers and, 202–3; government aid programs in, 182, 191; Montreal housewives and, 179–91
Greaves, Ida C., 53, 55
Greenlee, James, and, Charles Johnston, 150
Greer, Allan, 10–11, 62, 73, 85, 89, 90
Greig, Alexander, 105
guardian spirits, 20–1
Gulf War, 381
Gunn, Marcus, 106
Gutteridge, Helena, 169
gynecology, 328

Haberman, Jurgen, 88
Haight, Canniff, 66
Hallett, Mary, and Marilyn Davis, 157
Hallman, Dianne, 150
Hamilton, Sylvia, 47
Hancock, Joyce, 338
Harel, Louise, 354
Harper, Helen, 279
Harrison, Sarah, 91
Hazel, Joji, 303
health: Aboriginal peoples, 327–8, 329–31
Health and Social Services Act, 350

Health and Welfare, Department of, 330
health care, in Quebec, 351
Hearne, Samuel, 326
Henry, Landon, 107
heterosexualization: women teachers and, 278–85
history: method and theory of, 6–7; oral, 242–3, 253–8, 290; women's, 3–8, 242–3, 253–8
Hobbs, Margaret, 184
homosexuality: female, 281, 284; visibility of, 314–15; *see also* gays; lesbians
hooks, bell, 48, 301
household production: Great Depression and, 185–8
housework: Great Depression and, 184–8
Houston, Jeanne, 249
Howells, Emily, 121
Hudon, Christine, 134
Hudson's Bay Company, 119, 122
Huppe, Marie-Françoise, 34

Immigrant and Refugee Board, 287
immigrants: Asian, 167–8; 'Canadianization' of, 264–76; domestic workers, 195–208; food and, 264–76, 273; independent, 207; Italian, 270, 271; media and, 384; medical criteria for, 295; mothers' pensions and, 167–8; point-system for, 206–7; Portuguese, 271, 274; white feminists and, 154–8
Immigration Act (1910), 205
Immigration Department, 201, 203
imperialism, 148
Imperial Order of the Daughters of the Empire, 382
income, women's, 2
Indian Act, 116, 120, 215, 215
Indian Affairs, Department of, 329–30
Indra, Doreen, 289
Innulitsivik Maternity , 332
Institute for Research on Public Policy, 360–1
Interagency Committee on Violence Against Women, 341
intermarriage: Aboriginal view of, 117; Aboriginal/non-Aboriginal, 115–23; as problematic, 117; religious, 135–6
International Institute of Metropolitan Toronto, 273
International Women's Year, 336
intervention: medical, 331
Inuit: infant mortality and, 330–1
Issei, 243, 247, 252–3

Jamieson, Laura, 382
Japanese Canadian Committee for Democracy, 253
Japanese Canadian women: domestic workers, 205; McClung and, 156–7; memory and, 247–8, 254–8; narratives of, 242–60; oral testimony of, 253–8
Jean, Michaëlle, 46
Jesuits, 12–23; intermarriage and, 117
job quotas, 375
Johnson, E. Pauline, 122, 149
Johnson, George, 121
Johnstone, Walter, 67
Jones, Jonas, 104
Jones, Peter, 120–1
Jones, Robert Leslie, 66

Kahnawake, 13, 14, 17, 18, 22
Kativik Regional Government, 357
Kearney, Margaret, 103, 108
Keele, W.C., 98, 99, 104, 108
Kelm, Mary Ellen, 323
Kennedy, Elizabeth Lapovsky, and Madeline Davis, 305, 306
Keough, Willeen, 62
Keshen, Jeff, 224, 226
kindergarten, full-day, 355
Kinnear, Mary, 365
Kinsman, Gary, 267
Klassen, Pamela, 298
Korinek, Valerie, 269–70, 301, 366
Kuhn, Annette, 247

Labatt, Mary, 282
labour market: immigration and, 200, 204, 206–7
labour movement: mothers' pensions and, 169
Lacelle, Claudette, 198
Lacombe, Michèle, 159
Ladder, The, 303
Lambert, Jane, 100–1
Lamberville, Jacques de, 14
Lamoureux, Diane, 82
Landry, Bernard, 354
Landsberg, Michelle, 392
Langford, Nanci, 324
Larcher, Jacques, 35–6
Lee, Mary, 105
LeLecheur, John, 70
Lemire, Madeleine, 33
lesbians: attitudes to, 371, 372, 374; bar culture of, 301–18; crime, and, 306, 307–9; 'downtowners', 304–18; police and, 312, 313–16; 'uptowners', 304, 316–17; working class characteristics of, 304
Lesbians Making History, 304
Levenstein, Harvey, 270
Lewsey, Marjorie, 46
Liberal Party (Quebec), 353
Liquor Licensing Board of Ontario (LLBO), 307, 312–13
literature, first-wave feminist, 144–59
Live-in Caregiver Program, 196
Llewellyn, Kristina, 279
Local Council of Women, 169, 170
Long, John, 326
Louis XIV, 40, 50
Loyalists: slavery and, 50
Luxton, Meg, 366

McClintock, Anne, 323
McClung, Nellie, 145, 147, 149, 153–8
McDannell, Colleen, 130
MacDonald, Isabella, 61, 63, 68, 69
McGeachy, Mary, 365
MacGill, Helen, 169, 170
MacGregor, John, 67
Machar, Agnes Maule, 145, 147, 149, 150–3
McInnis, Allan, 104, 106–7
McIntyre, Robert, 109, 111
McKay, Ian, 62
Mackey, Eva, 389–90
Mackey, James P., 314, 316
McLaren, Angus, 156, 167
MacNamara, Arthur, 203
McNaughton, Violet, 381–2
McVarish, Donald, 63–4
Maille, Chantal, 345
Manitoba: child care in, 345; mothers' pensions in, 164, 172
Marandeau, Jacqueline, 33
March for Bread and Roses, 354
Marois, Pauline, 354, 355, 357
marriage: Aboriginal and Christian, 13, 14–15; Aboriginal/non-Aboriginal, 115–23; 'after the custom of the country', 119, 121–2; attitudes to, 376; 'Boston', 282; definition of, 117–18; slavery and, 49
Marshall, T.H., 166
masculinity: 'crisis of', 182, 184
maternal leave, 345; *see also* parental leave
matriarchy, 220
matriclan, 217
May, Elaine Tyler, 267
media: Thobani and, 384–6
medical care: childbirth and, 328–33
medicalization: childbirth and, 330–3
memory, 'critical', 256–8
men: Aboriginal, 120–1; Christian family and, 129–30; church periodicals and, 125, 131–7; Great Depression and, 182–5, 189–90, 191; as 'normal', 163; Jesuits and, 18–19; urban transit and, 226, 228–31
Mennonite Central Committee, 288, 294–5
Mennonites: female refugee, 287–99; male, 290–1
Messager Canadien, Le, 127, 129, 130, 133, 134, 135, 136
Messenger and Visitor, 130
Métis, 115, 122; childbirth and, 328
Michel, Sonya, and Rianne Mahon, 344
midwives, 323–4, 325, 327, 331, 332
Miki, Roy, and Cassandra Kobayashi, 246
Miles, Angela, 336
Minerve, La, 76, 79, 84, 85, 87
Ministry of Child and Family Welfare, 348, 349
minorities, visible, 2, 4–5, 371–2, 374
miscegenation, 121–2
missionization, 12–23
Mitchinson, Wendy, 323
'Mohawk Saint', 10–11
Monk, Coram, 119
Montreal: Great Depression and, 179–91; lesbians from, 309–10; urban transit in, 231; voting in, 73–94
Montreal Gazette, 76, 79, 83, 87
Monture, Patricia, 210
Morgan, Cecilia, 62, 83
mortality: infant, 329, 330–1; maternal, 329, 330
Morton, Suzanne, and Janet Guilford, 124
Mossion, Anne, 34
motherhood: Great Depression and, 188–90; 'scientific', 329
mothering: Carrier people and, 219–222

mothers: divorced, 171; ideal, 127, 137; 'of the race/nation', 200, 207; sons and, 131–2; suitable/unfit, 170; unwed, 170, 171
mothers' pensions, 163–75; BC lobby for, 166–71; development and administration of, 171–5; discretionary clause and, 171, 174; hearings on, 170–1; Pension Act, 171; rates of, 173–4; rights–based, 172–3
Mount Cashel, 339
Mukherjee, Arun, 154, 155
multiculturalism, 264, 266
Murphy, Emily, 145
Murphy, Helen, 341–2
Murray, James, 48–9
Myers, Tamara, 95; and Joan Sangster, 95

names: black women and, 48
natalism, 346, 353
National Action Committee on the Status of Women (NAC), 336, 342, 382, 383, 388, 391–2
National Council of Women of Canada, 200
nationalism, 384; race and, 387–91
National Post, 385, 388
Native Women's Association of Canada, 3
Native Women's Association of the Northwest Territories, 332
Neis, Barbara, and Susan Williams, 336
Nelson, Barbara, 166, 173
New Brunswick: slavery in, 56–7
Newfoundland and Labrador: violence and poverty in, 336–42
New France: domestic workers and, 198; widows, widowers, orphans and, 26–37; *see also* Quebec
newspapers: gender and election coverage in, 83–5; reporting of rape and, 98, 101
Nielson, John, 89
Nisei, 243, 247, 252–3
Nisei Mass Evacuation Group, 253
Noel, Jan, 26, 73
Normandin, Pierre, 35
North West Company, 119
North-West Rebellion, 115, 122, 151, 154
nostalgia, 'critical', 257
Nova Scotia: blacks in, 52, 55–6
nuns, 127–8
nursing stations, 331
nutritionists: immigrants and, 271–6

O'Meara, Sarah, 103
O'Neil, Brenda, 3
Ontario: mothers' pensions in, 169, 170, 172
Othering, nationalist, 384
Ottawa Citizen, 385
Ottawa: urban transit in, 229, 232–3
Ouellet, Fernand, 81, 85

pacifism, 381–2
'Panis', 45, 48
Papineau, Louis-Joseph, 85, 89
parental leave, 345, 346–7, 355, 356–7
Parental Wage Assistance Program, 353
Paris, Marguerite, 74, 76–6, 77–9, 83, 90, 91
PAR-L, 391, 392
Parti Québécois (PQ), 74, 345, 352, 353–4, 356, 357
passenger guides: women as, 227, 236–7
patriarchy: Aboriginal Christians and, 10–23; church periodicals and, 135
Patterson, George, 67
Pauktuutit, 324
pay equity, 236
Payment, Diane, 115
penance, 21–2
periodicals, church, 124–37
Perrault, Agathe, 90
Perrault, Marie-Claire, 84–5, 88
Perry, Adele, 121
'persons', 77, 145
Perthius, Charles, 32
Picard, Nathalie, 76, 77, 81, 90
Pickles, Katie, and Myra Rutherdale, 10
Pierson, Ruth Roach, 224, 226
politics: Carrier women and, 213, 217–22; women and, 61–70, 73–94
polygamy, 119
Pooley, Sophia, 52–3
Poovey, Mary, 328
Portelli, Alessandro, 259
Porter, Ann, 164
postcolonial theory, 147
potlatch, 214, 217
Pour les familles québécoises, 352
poverty, 2; Aboriginal peoples, 327–8; employment and, 348; in Newfoundland and Labrador, 336–42
Powell, William Dummer, 100, 106, 109
Pratt, Jo Ann, 306, 309
Prentice, Susan, 344
Presbyterian, 132
Prince Edward Island: escheat movement in, 61–70; slavery in, 56
pronatalism, 284
Protestants: family and, 126–37
Provincial Strategy Against Violence (PSAV), 336, 338, 339, 340–2

Quebec: 18th c. slavery in, 45, 50, 53–5; 18th c. widows, widowers, orphans and, 26–37; family policy in, 344–61; Great Depression and, 179–90
Québec fou de ses enfants, Un, 355–9

race: childbirth and, 323–33; domestic workers and, 195–208; first-wave feminism and, 144–59; income and, 2; mothers' pensions and, 164, 166, 167–8, 170–1, 173, 174; nationalism and, 387–91
racialism, 147
Racine, Joseph, 35
racism, 45–6, 121–2, 384, 385, 387; anti-Asian, 245–6, 255–6; definition of, 147; domestic workers and, 203–6; immigration and, 197–9; white feminists and, 146–7
radicalism, agrarian, 63
Raging Grannies, 382
Railways Agreement, 202
rape: accounts of, 102, 104–5; accused and, 105–7; conviction rate for, 100; defence for, 108; financial settlement and, 111; in Upper Canada, 95–114; medical professionals and, 105; men's attitudes towards, 107–8; pardon and, 108–10; punishment for, 100, 108–10; refugees and, 292; reporting of, 97–8; Upper Canada definition of, 98–9; victim's behaviour/character and, 103–4
Rascak, Sherene, 45
Rastin, Audrey, 3
Raudot, Jacques, 325
Rebick, Judy, 366, 386, 392
Redress Settlement, 244, 246
Red River Resistance, 115
refugees: children as, 289; as domestic workers, 203; female, 287–99; gender persecution and, 287; Mennonite, 287–99; sponsorship of, 295–6
region: religion and family and, 125, 127, 131–7
Reid, Helen, 200
religion: gender and family and, 124–37; Iroquois and Christian, 13, 17–23; mothers' pensions and, 169; obedience to, 129–30; syncretic, 17–23
Religious Intelligencer, 128, 130–1
remarriage: in New France, 30–1, 37
Rendall, Jane, 77
'repatriation', 246, 251–3
reproduction: Great Depression and, 188–90
Requickening ceremony, 18, 19
Rich, Adrienne, 242
Richie, Mary, 104
Richter, Daniel, 18
Richter, Molly G., 27
Riddell, William Renwick, 55
Riel, Louis, 151
rights: civil, 166; political, 166; social, 166, 172–3
Roberge, Madeleine, 32
Robert, Jean-Claude, 86
Robertson, John, 65, 69
Robinson, John Beverly, 105
Robitaille, Therese and Madeleine, 33
Rooke, P.T., and R.L. Schnell, 281–2
Rose of the Carrier, 211
Rose, Marie Marguerite, 45
Ross, Becki, 366
Rousset, Nicolas, 35
Royal Canadian Mounted Police (RCMP), 315–16
Royal Commission on the Criminal Law Relating to the Criminal Sexual Psychopath, 313
Royal Commission on the Status of Women, 344, 350, 368
Royal Commission on Violence Against Women, 342
Russell, Dennis, 109
Ryan, Mary P., 238

Sagerman, Emma, 99
St Christopher House, 274
St Jean, Idola, 145

Sandwell, Ruth, 62
Sangster, Joan, 243
Saskatchewan: mothers' pensions in, 172
Scott, Joan, 4
Second World War: child care and, 344; Japanese internment during, 242–60; lesbian/gay history and, 305; urban transit during, 224–38; women and, 382
Secord, Laura, 381
Secrétariat à la Famille, 352
segregation: occupational, 45–6; racial, 312–13; school, 45
Senn, J.N., 313
'separate spheres', 124–5, 182–5
sexes: core differences between, 375–6
Sexual Abuse Counseling Service, 341
'sexual deviancy', 313
sexual harassment, 251; urban transit and, 226, 229–30
sexuality, 7; teachers and, 279–85
shamans, 17
Sharma, Nandita, 384
Shiva, Vandana, 336
'shoppers', female, 226, 228–31, 232
silencing, 386
Simcoe, John Graves, 45, 50–1, 97
Skarichions, Marie, 15
Skinner, Chauncey, 104, 109
slavery, 45–60, 197–8; Aborignal, 45; British transition and, 48–51
smallpox, 13
Smith, Geoffrey, 267
Smith, Hannah, 100
Smith, Mary Ellen, 164, 170, 171
'smokers', male, 226, 228–31
Social Darwinism, 327
Social Policy Committee, 336, 339
social reform, 171; immigration and, 200; suffrage and, 167
social services: immigrants and, 266–7, 271–6
Sorell, Thomas, 65
space: men's/women's, 227, 228; public, 225, 226, 302
Spitzer, Leo, 256
Spofford, Cecilia, 170
sponsorship, family, 206
Spray, William, 56–7
Standish, John, 102, 110
Stanton, Elizabeth Cady, 329
state: women and, 165–75
status, Indian, 116, 117, 120
Statute of 1793, 50–1
Steenbergen, Candis, 369
Still, Susan Ann, 99
Strong-Boag, Veronica, 146, 166, 242
suffrage: social reform and, 167; *see also* voting
Summit on the Economy and Employment, 348–9, 354
Switzer, Mary, 108

Talbot, Margaret, 99
Tavernier, Emilie, 77, 80–1, 90, 91
taverns: in Upper Canada, 102–3
taxes: parents and, 346, 355, 356, 359
teachers: feminization and, 279; marriage bar and, 279–85; married, 279, 281–5; single, 279, 281–5; temporary workers, 283; women, 278–85
Tekakwitha, Kateri, 10–25
theosophy, 158
Thobani, Sunera, 106, 382, 383–92
Thurston, Herbert, 314
Tilly, Charles, 70
toleration, religious, 152–3
Tonsahoten, François Xavier, 13
Toronto: lesbian bar culture in, 301–18; social services to immigrants in, 272–5; urban transit in, 226, 232, 235–8
Toronto Star, 392
Toronto Sun, 385, 388
Toronto Transportation Commission (TTC), 225, 226, 236–8
Townshend, Flora, 61, 62
Tracey, Daniel, 75, 78, 81, 87
transportation, public, 224–38
Travise, Courtland, 98
Tröger, Annemarie, 294
Trudeau, Pierre, 264
Turnbull, John, 109

unemployment, 2; *see also* employment; work
unions: family policy and, 350
United Nations, 336
United Nations Convention on the Elimination of All Forms of Discrimination Against Women (CEDAW), 2
United States: slavery in, 51
University of Victoria, 391
University Women's Club, 169
Upper Canada: rape in, 95–114; slavery in, 50–3
urban transit: female employment in, 231–8; female lay-offs in, 235–6; 'feminization' of, 227, 238; pre-war conditions of, 227; wartime crowding of, 227–32; women and, 224–38

Vaillancourt, Yves, 349
Valpy, Michael, 386
Valverde, Marianna, 154, 201, 267
Van Kirk, Sylvia, 115
Vancouver Sun, 385, 390
Varga, Donna, 344
Verchères, Madeleine de, 26, 381
Vergeat, Joseph, 32
Vermette, Marie-Anne, 34
Veterans' Allowances, 174
Viger, Jacques, 77, 78, 85–9, 91
Vincent, Carole, 360
violence, 3; domestic, 297; in Newfoundland and Labrador, 336–42; political, 245–6, 248–50; rape and, 105
virginity, 21
Vivier, Claude, 35
Voice of Women, 382
voluntary societies, Aboriginal, 18, 19–20
voting: 73–94, 377–8; bill to remove women's right to, 91
Voyageur, Cora, 74

wages: Great Depression and, 183
wage supplement, 353
Walker, Barrington, 96
war: 'against terrorism', 383; women and, 381–2
war brides, 269
Waterhouse, Vashty, 102
welfare colonialism, 213, 216–17
welfare, private/public, 167
welfare state: citizenship rights and, 166; women and men and, 163–4, 166, 173
Welsh, Elizabeth, 109
Welter, Barbara, 62
Western Methodist Recorder, 127–8, 132, 134, 135
Westminster, 132
Whalen, Sharon, 340
Wheat, Hannah, 107
'Whig view of history', 73
white supremacy, 147
widowers: in New France, 28–31, 34–7
widows: in New France, 27–37; voting and, 77–83
Windsor: urban transit in, 228
Winnipeg: urban transit in, 232
women: Aboriginal, 115–23, 127, 200; black, 45–60; Carrier, 210–22; colour, 204–6, 384; country, 66–8; demographics of, 1; Great Depression and, 179–91; Japanese Canadian, 242–60; middle-class, 127, 200; 'missing', 3; single/married and voting, 79–80; supplementary income and, 183; teachers, 278–86; urban transit and, 224–38; violence against, 336–42; voting and, 73–94, 377–8; welfare state and, 163–75; widowed, 77–83; working-class, 125, 170–91
Women in Black, 382
Women's International League for Peace and Freedom, 381
Women's Resistance Conference, 383
work, 1, 2; gendered division of, 182–5; *see also* employment
Workers Compensation, 166, 172
workers: indentured, 207; migrant, 206, 207–8
workplace: attitudes to, 375
World Conference on Women, 336
'World March', 342
Wright, Donald, 4
Wright, Julia Ann, 99, 102

Yee, Shirley, 46

Zandy, Janet, 258
Zerubavel, Eviatar, 254
zines, 369